Housing Law – Residential Security and Enfranchisement

Housing Law – Residential Security and Enfranchisement

Christopher P Rodgers LLM (Cantab), FRSA
Solicitor
Professor of Law, University of Wales, Aberystwyth

Butterworths
London, Edinburgh, Dublin
2002

Members of the LexisNexis Group worldwide

United Kingdom	LexisNexis Butterworths Tolley, a Division of Reed Elsevier (UK) Ltd, Halsbury House, 35 Chancery Lane, LONDON, WC2A 1EL, and 4 Hill Street, EDINBURGH EH2 3JZ
Argentina	LexisNexis Argentina, BUENOS AIRES
Australia	LexisNexis Butterworths, CHATSWOOD, New South Wales
Austria	LexisNexis Verlag ARD Orac GmbH & Co KG, VIENNA
Canada	LexisNexis Butterworths, MARKHAM, Ontario
Chile	LexisNexis Chile Ltda, SANTIAGO DE CHILE
Czech Republic	Nakladatelství Orac sro, PRAGUE
France	Editions du Juris-Classeur SA, PARIS
Hong Kong	LexisNexis Butterworths, HONG KONG
Hungary	HVG-Orac, BUDAPEST
India	LexisNexis Butterworths, NEW DELHI
Ireland	Butterworths (Ireland) Ltd, DUBLIN
Italy	Giuffrè Editore, MILAN
Malaysia	Malayan Law Journal Sdn Bhd, KUALA LUMPUR
New Zealand	LexisNexis Butterworths, WELLINGTON
Poland	Wydawnictwo Prawnicze LexisNexis, WARSAW
Singapore	LexisNexis Butterworths, SINGAPORE
South Africa	Butterworths SA, DURBAN
Switzerland	Stämpfli Verlag AG, BERNE
USA	LexisNexis, DAYTON, Ohio

A CIP Catalogue record for this book is available from the British Library.

ISBN 0 406 91103 7

Typeset by Phoenix Photosetting, Chatham, Kent
Printed and bound in Great Britain by Hobbs the Printers Ltd, Totton, Hampshire

Preface

Housing law, like many other branches of modern law, has been subject to massive change since the first edition of this work appeared in 1995 under the title 'Private Sector Housing Law'. The text has been enlarged to take account of these changes, and new chapters have been added dealing with public sector residential tenancies. The expanded text now seeks to cover the whole of the law of residential landlord and tenant, rather than simply private sector tenancies, and the title has been changed to reflect this wider coverage. The focus remains, however, firmly on security of tenure and the legislative regulation of residential lettings. Hence the subtitle to the new text – 'residential security and enfranchisement'.

Of the many changes in this area of the law since 1994, two in paticular merit a brief mention. The Human Rights Act 1998 is already beginning to make an impact in this area of law, as on so many others. The application of human rights principles is a major challenge for property lawyers, requiring a sea change in attitudes to dispute resolution and statutory construction. A number of important decisions have been reported very recently, most notably *McClellan v Bracknell Forest DC* [2002] 1 All ER 899 on the termination of introductory tenancies in the public sector, and *Donoghue v Poplar Housing and Regeneration Community Association* [2001] 3 WLR 183 on the provisions for terminating assured shorthold tenancies. While the text was in press the Law Commission published their long-awaited review of residential tenancy law (*Renting Homes 1: Status and Security*, Law Commission consultation paper 162, 2002). I am grateful to Butterworths for their forbearance in allowing me to make (often substantial) changes to the text to reflect these important recent developments. Finally, and after a long gestation period, the Commonhold and Leasehold Reform Act 2002 has at last made it onto the statute book. The 2002 Act introduces major changes to the law governing leasehold enfranchisement and leasehold management. This has required the substantial rewriting and expansion of chapters 12 and 13 to cover the new law in detail, although at the time of going to press, the statutory instruments implementing many of the detailed requirements of the new legislative framework were not available. Discussion of these will have to await a further edition of this work. The provisions on Leasehold Reform in Part II of the 2002 Act are to be brought into force by order (2002 Act, s 181). The Commonhold and Leasehold Reform Act 2002 (Commencement No 1 etc) (England) Order 2002 (SI 2002/1912) brought the following into force on 26 July 2002 in England: (i) the reforms to collective enfranchisement for tenants of flats, and on the acquisition of new tenancies by tenants of flats, (ii) the extension to the enfranchisement provisions for tenants of houses, (iii) reform of the provisions applicable to the appointment of managers by the Leasehold Valuation Tribunal and (iv) the changes made by the 2002 Act to the grounds for varying a lease. At the time of going to press, commencement orders had not been laid for the introduction of the new law on the tenants 'right to manage', and the reform of the law regulating service charges, the two other principal areas of the new law covered in Chapters 12 and 13 of this book. These are expected to be brought into force shortly.

A number of colleagues have assisted in the preparation of this work, and to all I owe a debt of gratitude. Peter Williams and Michael Johnstone very kindly offered comments on Chapters 1–8. Several colleagues who read material for the first edition are owed thanks, inasmuch as this new edition builds upon the existing text, including Jill Martin and Nic Madge. I am, in particular, grateful to my colleague Anne Barlow who provided the material on the Leasehold Reform Housing and Urban Development Act 1993 in the first edition, and the original chapter on the Rent Act 1977. Although much of this material has been substantially rewritten for the new edition, my job would have been incomparably more difficult without Anne's initial contribution to the work. Finally, I am grateful to the staff at Butterworths for their patience and fortitude in dealing with my script and the numerous amendments and additions made, often at a late stage and very messily, to the script.

My aim throughout has been to provide a readable guide through what is, by common consent, a highly complex area of law. If it provides some modest assistance to those whose misfortune it is to have to study the rent legislation (be they practitioners or students) then it will have achieved its purpose. The text endeavors to state the law at 31st May 2002.

Christopher Rodgers
Aberystwyth
June 2002

Contents

Table of Statutes

Paragraph numbers in **bold** indicate where the section is set out in part or in full

Table of Statutory Instruments

Table of Cases

PARA

A

PARA

B

D

N

O

T

CHAPTER 1

Introduction

A Historical introduction

PROTECTIVE LEGISLATION IN THE PRIVATE SECTOR

[1.1] Successive Rent Acts – starting with a temporary measure: the Rent and Mortgage Interest (Restrictions) Act 1920 (RMIA 1920) – have imposed restrictions on the operating of the market for private rented housing, both by limiting the rent lawfully recoverable for lettings, and inhibiting the landlord's ability to repossess by conferring security of tenure upon tenants. The RMIA 1920 consolidated the Rent and Mortgage Interest (Restrictions) Act 1915, a measure introduced to deal with the shortage of housing occasioned by the 1914–18 war, and imposed security of tenure and control of rent rises on unfurnished lettings. Although some de-control was pursued in legislation between the wars, rent control was re-imposed by the Rent and Mortgage Interest (Restrictions) Act 1939. Unfurnished lettings covered by the RMIAs 1920 and 1939 were known as 'controlled' tenancies – as yet, there was no regulation of furnished lettings.

[1.2] A short-lived attempt at limited de-control was attempted by the Housing Act 1957 (HA 1957), but this was replaced in 1965 by a new system of 'regulated' tenancies for which fair rents could be registered by a rent officer. The Rent Act 1965 represented a major extension of statutory protection for tenants, but as yet full protection still only applied to unfurnished lettings. Fully furnished lettings were covered by a separate code of more limited protection, introduced by the Furnished Houses (Rent Control) Act of 1946. This provided for rent tribunals to be established to adjudicate on rents, and gave them limited power to suspend possession orders. The furnished tenancy provisions were consolidated, along with the 1965 legislation, in the Rent Act 1968 (RA 1968) – the first of the modern consolidations, and the first to bring the law on furnished and unfurnished lettings into one legislative framework. The rent tribunal jurisdiction on furnished lettings was consolidated into the Rent Act 1968, Pt VI, and lettings to which this protection applied were renamed 'restricted contracts'[1].

1 They are still often referred to as 'Pt VI contracts' due to their origin in the RA 1968, Pt VI.

[1.3] Full protection was extended to all furnished lettings by the Rent Act 1974 (RA 1974), under which restricted contracts were limited to specific categories of letting – principally those with resident landlords. The legislation was consolidated in the Rent Act 1977 (RA 1977), which remains in force today and governs tenancies granted before 15 January 1989, when the Housing Act 1988 (HA 1988) came into force.

RENT LEGISLATION AND THE DECLINE OF THE PRIVATE SECTOR

[1.4] The successive Rent Acts, culminating in the RA 1977, imposed restrictions on the operation of the market for rented housing, by both limiting the rent lawfully recoverable for lettings, and inhibiting the landlord's ability to repossess by conferring security of tenure upon tenants[1]. Under the 'fair rent' system, which still governs tenancies within the RA 1977[2], a tenant with a regulated Rent Act tenancy can register a 'fair' rent – in practice considerably below market levels, as scarcity value is to be ignored by the rent officer in fixing the rent[3]. The statutory tenancy – a concept to which the Rent Acts gave rise – effectively created a 'status of irremoveability' vested in the tenant as long as he occupies the dwelling as his home[4]. Under the RA 1977, moreover, it can be transmitted to successors (a spouse or other family members)[5], thus extending the landlord's inability to repossess beyond the lifetime of the tenant to whom the tenancy was initially granted.

1 Rent Control was extended to furnished lettings by the RA 1974, the legislation being consolidated in the RA 1977 – the complexity of which is notorious. For a detailed account of the development of the legislation prior to 1974 see Megarry's *Rent Acts* (11th edn, 1988) p 9 ff.
2 RA 1977, Pt III.
3 Ibid, s 70(2).
4 Ibid, s 2(2). And see *Jessamine Investment Co v Schwartz* [1978] QB 264, CA.
5 See RA 1977, Sch 1.

[1.5] The legislation has been subject to two fundamental criticisms:

(1) It was arguably responsible for the steady decline in the private rented sector of the housing market, in that the security of tenure provisions are an obvious disincentive to potential landlords.
(2) Calculating a fair rent involves an unrealistic and artificial exercise – an assumption that the number of tenants seeking accommodation in similar dwelling houses is not substantially greater than the number of such dwellings available.

[1.6] The 'fair rent' system meant, also, that there was an insufficient return for landlords to invest in improvement, repair and enhancement of rented property. Critics of the rent legislation therefore argued for a re-introduction of free market principles into rented housing – for instance, by adopting the scheme applicable to business tenancies under the Landlord and Tenant Act 1954 (LTA 1954), Pt II[1].

1 Eg *The Road to Reform* (Society of Conservative Lawyers, 1987) esp pp 11–23; Michael Barnes QC, *The Rent Acts: The Way Ahead.*

[1.7] Under this model there would be no control of rent levels, but the tenant would be entitled to security of tenure during the currency of the (freely negotiated) contractual tenancy, and have a statutory right to a new tenancy on similar terms – unless the landlord could prove breach of tenancy or wished to redevelop the property (eg, for re-letting). This concept was introduced on a limited basis by the Housing Act 1980 (HA 1980)[1], which enabled landlords of newly built or altered property to grant 'assured' tenancies with security of tenure modelled on the LTA 1954.

1 HA 1980, ss 56–8.

REFORM AND DEREGULATION OF THE PRIVATE RENTED SECTOR

[1.8] The HA 1988 abolished Rent Act protection for all new tenancies granted after its commencement, and replacing it with the 'assured' tenancy (based on the HA 1980 concept) under which there would be no rent control, and security of tenure based on a mixture of Rent Act safeguards and the grounds for possession under the LTA 1954. In so doing, it represented the most radical deregulation of the market in private rented housing since 1957, when a limited de-control was attempted by the HA 1957[1].

1 For criticism see, inter alia, articles at (1987) 137 NLJ 75 and 111 (M Partington) and (1988) 138 NLJ 436 (N Madge).

Public policy for the private sector

[1.9] According to the White Paper which preceded the HA 1988[1], one of its principal aims was to put new life into the private rented sector and encourage the growth of the 'independent' rented sector (ie the housing association movement). This would be achieved by removing rent controls so that letting private property would again become an economic proposition, while restructuring the housing association grant system to encourage the use of private sector finance[2]. Housing benefit would continue to be available for those on low incomes. In the public sector, it was envisaged that local authorities should be encouraged to change their role; the provision of housing by local authorities as landlords should diminish, and alternative forms of tenure be increased[3]. This aim was reflected in the Tenants' Choice Scheme established by the HA 1988, Pt IV, which enabled tenants to take the initiative in choosing a new landlord, and (thereby) gave them the means to improve their housing conditions. As a corollary to this approach, the White Paper also promised the creation of central government agencies, to be known as 'housing action trusts', which would take over local authority housing stock in problem areas and concentrate the provision of public money on its improvement and renovation[4]. As an overall objective for the legislation, the White Paper proposed the encouragement of the introduction of private sector finance into public sector housing. Pressure on public funds should be eased by encouraging disposal (compulsory or voluntary) of public sector stock to private landlords and housing associations, and local authorities should be encouraged to adopt a more 'strategic' role. Purchase and management of property by the private sector would, it was hoped, broaden the choice available to tenants and give them better housing options[5]. These objectives were enshrined in the HA 1988, arguably the most radical measure in the area of housing law for many years, which came into force on 15 January 1989.

1 Housing – The Government's Proposals (Cm 214, 1987). For criticism see (1988) November *Legal Action* 8 (Campbell).
2 Ibid, para 1.15.
3 Ibid, para 1.16.
4 Ibid, para 1.17. These proposals are enacted by the HA 1988, Pt III.
5 Ibid, para 1.18.

Two models for private residential tenancies

[1.10] The policy underlying the HA 1988, Pt I was ostensibly an extension of the philosophy of the HA 1980, which liberalised the private market by introducing two new forms of tenure – the assured tenancy and the protected shorthold tenancy. The HA 1988 made provision for all lettings after its commencement to be on one out of two new forms of tenancy – the assured tenancy and the assured shorthold. The policy underlying these provisions is for landlords to choose to let either:

(a) on the assured tenancy basis, with rents freely negotiated but security of tenure protected; or
(b) on the shorthold basis, with no security of tenure beyond the period of the tenancy but the right for either party to seek registration of an 'appropriate' (note, not a 'fair') rent[1].

1 See Cm 214, para 3.11.

[1.11] These proposals are enshrined in the HA 1988, Pt I, Ch I (assured tenancies) and Ch II (shortholds). Although presented as extensions of existing tenancy structures, they are on closer examination in many respects different, and altogether more radical[1]. As a corollary to deregulation of the private sector the HA 1988 removed of most of the remaining restrictions on repossession by resident landlords, aiming thereby to encourage increased lettings by this category of landlord[2]. The HA 1988 also amended the protection from eviction legislation to strengthen the law on criminal harassment of tenants, and to give the latter a more effective statutory damages claim for unlawful eviction[3]. It was hoped, however, that the lifting of rent control and a return to market rents would remove the financial incentive for unlawful evictions. Another consequence of the lifting of rent controls would, naturally, be a greater return on investment by landlords. The HA 1988 also increased landlords' statutory repairing obligations to encompass the common parts and exterior of buildings comprising multiple dwellings[4], in an attempt to ensure that a proportion of increased returns is used to enhance the quality and repair of housing stock.

1 See Chapters 3 and 4 below.
2 Cm 214, para 3.14.
3 Ibid, para 3.27, and the HA 1988, ss 27–29. Below Chapter 2, para 2.17 ff.
4 Ibid, s 116.

Impact of deregulation

[1.12] The deregulation implemented in the HA 1988 led to an increase in private sector letting, and a significant decline in the number of tenancies still covered by the RA 1977. The number of regulated Rent Act tenancies with registered rents fell from 322,000 (18 per cent of all private sector tenancies) in 1990 to 128000 in 1996/97 – just 6 per cent of all private sector tenancies. There were a further 114,000 regulated tenancies without registered rents in 1996/97[1]. In total, therefore, by 1996/97 there were a little over 240,000 regulated tenancies within the RA 1977, representing approximately 11 per cent of all private sector tenancies. In the same period (1990–1997) the number of assured and assured shorthold lettings rose considerably. Assured shorthold tenancies have, in particular, proved very popular with landlords. In 1990 there were 143,000 assured shortholds, representing 8 per cent of all private sector lettings. By 1996/97 this figure had risen dramatically. By 1997 there were 1,074,000 assured shorthold tenancies, representing no less than 47 per cent of all private sector tenancies. Assured tenancies have proved less popular, owing to the security of tenure conferred on 'fully' assured tenants under the HA 1988. In 1990 there were 357,000 assured tenancies (20 per cent of all private lettings). In 1997 this figure had shrunk slightly to 331,000 (15 per cent)[2].

1 See Housing and Construction Statistics 1986–96 (HMSO 1997) Table 11.4.at p 179. Also DETR Press Release 1101/98.
2 See Housing and Construction Statistics 1986–96 (HMSO 1997) ibid at Table 11.4.

Further reform: The Housing Act 1996

[1.13] The success of the deregulation attempted by the HA 1988 prompted the introduction of further liberalising reforms in the Housing Act 1996 (HA 1996). Although the primary focus of the HA 1996 was on reform of the homelessness legislation and public sector tenancies, the HA 1996, Pt V introduced important changes in the assured tenancy regime for private sector tenancies. Principally, all assured tenancies granted on or after 28 February 1997 will automatically be assured shorthold tenancies unless the landlord gives notice that the tenancy is to be a 'fully' assured tenancy, or one of a number of special circumstances apply[1]. Prior to the reforms introduced in the HA 1996 , in order to grant a shorthold the landlord had to give a shorthold notice on grant, and enter into a written tenancy for a fixed period of at least six months. These formalities gave some security to the tenant, although no statutory security applies once the initial shorthold tenancy has expired. The need for a written agreement and shorthold notice was removed by the HA 1996 for all new tenancies after it came into force, and the shorthold regime now applies to periodic as well as fixed-term tenancies. The tenant is afforded residual protection, in that the landlord cannot obtain possession during the first six months of the tenancy, and (if the agreement is oral) the landlord is obliged to provide a written statement of its terms. These provisions are considered more fully in Chapter 5. The HA 1996 also amended the regime for 'fully' assured tenancies by strengthening the landlord's right to repossess for arrears of rent, and providing a new ground for possession where tenants are involved in anti-social behaviour.

1 HA 1996, s 96 and Sch 9, adding a new s 19A to HA 1988.

PUBLIC SECTOR TENANCIES: THE 'TENANTS' CHARTER'

Secure tenancies

[1.14] As we have seen, many private sector tenancies have enjoyed statutory protection and security of tenure since the 1960s, and in the case of 'controlled tenancies' for considerably longer than that. It was not until 1980 that security of tenure was introduced for tenants of public sector landlords. The most well known aspect of the Tenants' Charter introduced by the HA 1980 was the right to buy, which afforded council tenants the right to purchase the freehold of their home, often at considerable discounts[1]. The HA 1980 also introduced the concept of the 'secure' tenancy, with statutory security of tenure for public sector tenants[2]. Secure tenants also enjoy the right to exchange tenancies, to have repairs carried out, and to be consulted in matters of housing management[3]. These rights are now consolidated in the Housing Act 1995, Pts IV and V.

1 HA 1985, s 118, Pt V et seq. See further Chapter 10, para 10.69 ff below.
2 Ibid, s 79. The security of tenure provisions are set out in the HA 1985, ss 82–86. See further Chapter 10, para 10.14 et seq below.
3 These rights are set out in the HA 1985, Pt IV. They are considered below in Chapter 9, para 9.38 et seq.

[1.15] The secure tenancy regime applies primarily to tenants of local housing authorities, and of certain other public sector landlords, such as new town corporations[1]. Before the passage of the HA 1988, all tenancies granted by registered social landlords were also 'secure' tenancies for the purposes of the security of tenure provisions in the Housing Act 1985 (HA 1985). The RA 1977, Pt VI also applied the fair rent system to many housing association tenancies. However, the HA 1988 fundamentally changed the legal status of all tenancies granted by registered social landlords on or after 15 January 1989. All tenancies granted by registered social landlords after the commencement of Part I HA 1988 would be assured tenancies. Any tenancy granted by a Housing Association or other registered social landlord on or after 15 January 1989 cannot be a 'Housing Association tenancy' within the RA 1977, Pt VI[2], neither can it be a secure tenancy[3]. The secure tenancy status of tenancies granted by registered social landlords prior to 15 January 1989 is preserved, and saving provisions apply eg where there is a re-grant of the same or alternative accommodation, by the same landlord, or where the court gives possession using the suitable alternative accommodation grounds for possession under the HA 1985[4].

1 The HA 1988, s 35(4) limits public sector 'secure' tenancies, to which the HA 1985 applies, to situations where the landlord's interest belongs to a local authority new town corporation, urban development corporation or housing action trust set up under the HA 1988, Pt III.
2 HA 1988, s 35 (2).
3 HA 1988, s 35(4).
4 HA 1988, s 34(4).

[1.16] In general, then, tenancies granted on or after 15 January 1989 by a registered social landlord will be assured tenancies and not 'secure'. Tenancies granted by a registered social landlord before 15 January 1989 will be 'secure' tenancies within the HA 1985. Tenancies of a non-registered social landlord will, similarly, be assured tenancies within the HA 1988, Pt I if granted on or after this date. If granted before 15 January 1989, they will normally be private sector protected tenancies within the RA 1977.

The Housing Act 1996

[1.17] The HA 1985 has been successively amended, by the Housing and Planning Act 1986, HA 1988, Local Government and Housing Act 1989 (LGHA 1989), the Leasehold Reform Housing and Urban Development Act 1993 (LRHUDA 1993) and – most recently – by the HA 1996. The HA 1996, Pt V introduced several measures giving public landlords stronger powers to deal with anti-social behaviour. Local authorities and housing action trusts can introduce Introductory Tenancy Schemes under which new tenants do not acquire a secure tenancy for a period of 12 months from grant. During the 12-month 'trial' period the new tenant has no security of tenure and the other statutory rights of secure tenants (such as the right to exchange, carry out improvements and take lodgers) do not apply. The landlord can recover possession under a special procedure laid down in the HA 1996 if the new tenant proves unsatisfactory. The HA 1996 also introduced a new ground for possession for domestic violence, and broadened the existing grounds for possession for anti-social behaviour and nuisance to cover misbehaviour in the locality of the tenant's home and nuisance occasioned by visitors to the tenant's property. Public sector landlords were also given a new power to apply for an injunction to restrain breaches of the tenancy agreement and to prevent anti-social behaviour by public sector tenants[1].

1 These provisions are considered in Chapter 10, para 10.34 ff below.

B Legal techniques of protection

RENT ACT PROTECTION v FREEDOM OF CONTRACT

[1.18] The assured tenancy, as provided for in the HA 1988, Pt I is firmly based on principles of freedom of contract. The parties are free to agree a rent and period of tenancy, the 'assurance' guaranteed by the HA 1988 being security of tenure during the agreed term, and continuation of the tenancy on its expiry as a 'statutory periodic tenancy'. This is a reversal of legislative policy, for the protection previously afforded by successive Rent Acts[1] was based on the status of the tenant as a residential occupier. Protection (in the form of the statutory Rent Act tenancy) accrued after termination of a contractual tenancy if the tenant then occupied the dwelling as a residence, and subsisted as long as he did so. It is characteristic of protective legislation that – paradoxically perhaps – protection based on notions of contract is less extensive than that based on the status of the occupier, even though a contract-based approach will normally vest in the occupier a legal interest (and not a merely personal right of 'irremoveability'). Maine's famous dictum[2] that 'the movement of the progressive societies has hitherto been a movement from status to contract' has, to this extent, proved suspect. Certainly, the re-introduction of free market principles in the HA 1988 reinforced the landlord's strict property rights, and it is no longer be possible to see the right to live in a house for life, immune to market forces, as an emerging species of property interest vested by statute in the tenant[3]. This approach is also open, of course, to the criticism that it ignores the relative inequality in the bargaining position of landlord and prospective tenant, and that there is in reality no 'free' market in rented housing. Many tenants will need to rely on housing benefit to meet rents based on market rents, and the market will itself inevitably be heavily subsidised by public sector finance.

1 Culminating in the RA 1977, s 2.
2 See *Ancient Law* (Everyman edn, 1972) p 100; see also Honore, The Quest for Security: Employees, Tenants, Wives (1982) Chapter 2.
3 Cf C Hand (1980) Conv 351.

[1.19] Further consequences of the change to principles of freedom of contract derive from the nature of the protected interest vested by statute in the tenant. The fact that the statutory Rent Act tenancy conferred a merely personal right of possession, and not an interest in rem, had a variety of consequences. It could not be disposed of by will, nor would it vest on intestacy in personal representatives, or on bankruptcy in a trustee. Nor could a statutory tenant sublet the whole, as he had no legal estate out of which to create such an interest[1]. A statutory tenancy, being a right in personam, is also not capable of assignment[2]. By contrast, the statutory periodic tenancy which vests in the tenant under the HA 1988, on expiry of a fixed-term assured tenancy, is expressly stated to be an interest taking effect in possession[3]. It therefore creates an estate in rem vested in the tenant, unlike the statutory Rent Act tenancy, and one which in principle would not only be assignable but also capable of devise by will or transmission on intestacy. As a consequence, it was necessary to provide rules in the HA 1988 intended to regulate (and in some instances nullify) the legal consequences that this change in the technique of legal protection would otherwise occasion.

1 *Solomon v Orwell* [1954] 1 WLR 629, CA.
2 Because its existence depends upon continued occupation by the statutory tenant himself. See, on the nature of his interest, inter alia, *Jessamine Investment Co v Schwartz* [1978] QB 264 at 277; *Lloyd v Sadler* [1978] 2 All ER 529 at 537, per Lawton LJ. Also *Skinner v Geary* [1931] 2 KB 546; *Ellis & Sons Amalgamated Properties Ltd v Sisman* [1948] 1 KB 653; *Hemns v Wheeler* [1948] 2 KB 61; *East End Dwellings Co Ltd v Finsbury BC* [1952] AC 109, HL.
3 HA 1988, s 5(3)(a). This has now been judicially confirmed as the correct interpretation of the effect of the HA 1988 provisions: *N & D (London) Ltd v Gadsdon* [1992] 02 EG 176 (see esp at 180 per Auld J).

[1.20] The difference in legislative technique has the following consequences:

(1) Although at common law it would be freely alienable the HA 1988, s 15 implies into every assured periodic tenancy an absolute covenant against assignment. The tenant's common law right of alienation remains intact, however, if the tenancy is a fixed-term, or if it is a periodic tenancy ab initio with an agreed alienation clause which varies the statutory model, or if a premium was paid on grant. As protection under the Rent Act attached only to the tenant's status as a residential occupier, the former statutory tenancy was by its nature incapable of assignment and the need for such rules did not arise[1].

(2) Since it is a right in rem, an assured tenancy can pass on death by intestacy or be devised by will. Transmission in this way would, however, effectually perpetuate security of tenure beyond the lifetime of the original tenant[2], and sidestep the statutory succession provisions of the HA 1988 itself[3]. The HA 1988, Sch 2 therefore gives the landlord a mandatory ground for possession (Ground 7) where the tenant has died and action is commenced within 12 months of death. This problem could not arise under the Rent Act, as the statutory tenant had no estate in law that was capable of transmission on death by devise or on intestacy.

(3) Under the RA 1977, once the initial contractual tenancy had expired, the statutory tenancy would itself only subsist as long as the tenant occupied the dwelling. If he ceased to do so, his protected interest also ceased. The nature of the statutory periodic tenancy is altogether different, although the HA 1988 achieves a similar result by different means. The tenancy, being a right in rem, continues to subsist in law irrespective of whether the tenant occupies the dwelling as his home. It is expressly provided, however, that the tenancy (although subsisting) will cease to be 'assured' if the tenant ceases to occupy the dwelling as his 'principal' home[4]. This means that the restrictions on possession provided for in s 5, and the need to establish one of the grounds for possession in Sch 2, will automatically cease to apply, thus facilitating repossession by notice to quit[5].

(4) By virtue of the HA 1988, s 5(3)(e), the terms of the statutory periodic tenancy are deemed to be the same as those of the fixed-term tenancy 'immediately before it came to an end', with the exception that any provision for determination by the landlord shall not have effect while it remains an assured tenancy[6]. The HA 1988 lays down procedures for variation of the rent and other terms by the Rent Assessment Committee once the tenancy has become statutory[7]. Note, however, that the nature of the statutory periodic tenancy as an estate taking effect in possession has implications for the operation of the rent review provisions. By virtue of s 14(2)(c) the committee must disregard any reduction

in the value of the dwelling attributable to the failure of the tenant to comply with any terms of the tenancy. Consequently, the committee will not, when adjudicating on the rent under a statutory periodic tenancy, be entitled to disregard disrepair by the tenant during a *previous* fixed-term; the onus is thus on the landlord to enforce the terms of the tenancy as to repair and fitness. The interpretation section makes no reference to predecessors when defining 'tenant' and 'tenancy'. The committee is therefore limited to looking at the conduct of the parties' obligations during the statutory periodic tenancy itself – for it is only that over which they have jurisdiction under s 14(2). This can lead to incongruous results where the tenant has taken an assured tenancy by way of succession from a previous Rent Act tenant[8]. Under the RA 1977, disrepair by previous tenants was discounted when assessing a fair rent for a dwelling. In *N & D (London) Ltd v Gadsdon*[9], however, it was held that previous disrepair by a statutory Rent Act tenant could not be disregarded where an *assured* tenancy has vested by way of succession in a member of the tenant's family. Being a 'new' tenancy the statutory disregard under the RA 1977 did not apply, and a nominal market rent was appropriate due to the unlettable state of the property. Note, however, that had the successor here been the tenant's *spouse*, she would have received a statutory Rent Act tenancy, and the Rent Act disregard of disrepair would have applied, leading to the award of a fair rent based on the state of the premises in habitable condition.

1 It was constituted a criminal offence to assign the contractual tenancy in contravention of the RA 1977, however; see RA 1977, Sch 2, para 12.
2 One of the central criticisms (and alleged disincentives) of the previous Rent Acts themselves.
3 HA 1988, s 17 provides for one succession, but only by a spouse. See Chapter 3, para 3.138 ff below.
4 See HA 1988, s 1(1).
5 Subject, of course, to the requirements of the Protection from Eviction Act 1977 as to due process and minimum notice.
6 This includes a break clause, but not a proviso for forfeiture or re-entry; s 45(4) ibid. If the tenancy ceases to be assured at any time, a break clause would again become operable at that point in time, subject to its terms.
7 See ss 13 and 14 ibid, discussed further below, Chapter 3, para 3.102 ff.
8 Under the HA 1988, s 17 the spouse of a Rent Act protected tenant will receive a statutory Rent Act tenancy by succession, even after the coming into force of the HA 1988, but other members of the deceased tenant's family who succeed to the tenancy can receive only an assured tenancy by way of succession.
9 [1992] 02 EG 176. For the Rent Act disregard when assessing the 'fair' rent see the RA 1977, s 70(3)(a).

RESIDENTIAL SECURITY AND PUBLIC POLICY

[1.21] The central thrust of the private sector provisions of the HA 1988 is twofold: first, as we have seen, to separate the concepts of rent control and security of tenure (the former applying to shortholds only and the latter to 'assured' tenancies); and second, as a close study of the grounds for possession will show, to subject the tenant's security of tenure to more stringent financial requirements. The latter is signaled by an increased emphasis on rent arrears and other financial matters in the grounds for possession in Sch 2[1]. Separating rent control and security of tenure in this way arguably ignores the basic principle that the two concepts are mutually interdependent. There is little point in having rent control if a tenant can be evicted for seeking to register a rent; likewise, there seems little point in conferring security of tenure if the landlord can increase the rent to a level beyond the tenant's means, in order to remove the latter without recourse to possession proceedings. The declared aim of the legislation – to offer a choice to landlords of letting with security and no rent control, and vice versa – may in practice mean that those statutory rights enjoyed by tenants under the HA 1988 prove to be more illusory than real.

1 There are now three grounds for possession in HA 1988 based on rent arrears (Grounds 8, 10 and 11), whereas previously only one applied (RA 1977, Sch 15, Case 1).

[1.22] The principle that rent control and security of tenure are inextricably linked has been maintained by successive Rent Acts. The first breach in the principle was made by the introduction in the HA 1980 of the protected shorthold tenancy. This policy has now been made explicit and extended to the whole field of private rented housing. Its critics will argue that this is a fundamental weakness in the philosophy underlying the HA 1988. Certainly, it could affect the effectiveness of not only the rent control and security of tenure provisions, but also of the other rights introduced by the HA 1988. The extended repairing obligations introduced by s 116[1] may prove unenforceable in practice by tenants without security of tenure (for instance, assured shortholders). Similarly, the rules against unlawful eviction may prove of most utility to pre-existing tenants with Rent Act tenancies; there will be little incentive to unlawfully evict an assured tenant who is paying a market rent, and possession can be obtained anyway; eg if redevelopment is in prospect[2]. Their utility to assured tenants may, in practice, be open to doubt.

1 Amending the LTA 1985, s 11.
2 Under HA 1988, Sch 2, (new) Ground 6.

C Residential tenancies: proliferation of categories

A CASE FOR REFORM

[1.23] The Law Commission has, on several occasions, strongly criticised the current state of the tenant protection legislation, which has spawned a variety of different categories of tenancy and license – each with different qualifying conditions, different security of tenure provision and varying levels of rent control[1]. This has led to an unacceptable degree of complexity, and rationalisation and simplification have been strongly urged – possibly by concentrating protection on a single tenancy structure with appropriate variation for special groups of residential tenant[2]. The HA 1988 made some limited moves in this direction, by abolishing housing association tenancies and concentrating all housing provision in the private and housing association sectors on the assured tenancy regime laid down in the HA 1988, Pt I. The legislation is also arguably less complex than previous Rent Acts. It must also be said, however, that the HA 1988 increased the proliferation of categories rather than the reverse. Protection under the Rent Acts was preserved for existing tenancies, to which it added three new categories of tenancy: the assured tenancy, assured shorthold and assured agricultural occupancy.

1 See Landlord and Tenant: Reform of the Law (Cm 162, 1987) esp para 4.12 et seq. Also now Reform of Housing Law: a Scoping Paper (Law Commission March 2001) at para 25 et seq.
2 The Law Commission's review of the existing legislation was damning: 'The complication and confusion produced by this proliferation of categories of protection is highly undesirable. Only relatively few experts can claim to understand all the detailed rules. Most landlords and tenants cannot find their way through this tangled maze, and their professional advisers may well experience similar difficulty. This must be an unacceptable state for any part of the law. It is all the more deplorable when it relates to

rules which are intended to protect the vital interests of individuals who include some of the most vulnerable in our society. The danger is that the complexity of the law has the effect of depriving tenants of their rights' (ibid, para 4.14).

CATEGORIES OF RESIDENTIAL TENANCY

[1.24] The current legislation provides for a formidably complex list of tenancy structures[1]. The principal categories of tenancy, each with different regimes for security of tenure and rent control, are the following:

(1) Protected and statutory Rent Act tenancies created prior to the commencement of the HA 1988.
(2) Secure tenancies granted by public sector landlords[2].
(3) Long tenancies (21 years or more) at a low rent[3].
(4) Assured tenancies under the HA 1988. 'Old style' assured tenancies were converted to come within the HA 1988[4].
(5) Housing association tenancies granted before the HA 1988 came into force[5]. All housing association lettings on or after 15 January 1989 will be assured tenancies.
(6) Secure tenancies granted by housing associations before the HA 1988 came into force. Housing association tenancies granted before 15 January 1989 were treated as secure tenancies for the purposes of security of tenure.
(7) Protected agricultural occupancies of tied accommodation, granted before 15 January 1989, come within the Rent (Agricultural) Act 1976 (R(A)A 1976)[6].
(8) Assured agricultural occupancies granted on or after 15 January 1989 are within the HA 1988[7].
(9) Restricted contracts granted before 15 January 1989; eg by a resident landlord[8]. No new restricted contracts can be created under the HA 1988.
(10) Protected shorthold tenancies granted under the HA 1980[9]. These were not 'converted' into assured tenancies by the HA 1988, and following termination continue as protected Rent Act tenancies subject to the availability of Case 19 (protected shortholds) if the landlord wishes to terminate the agreement (cf old style assured tenancies under the Housing Act 1989, which were converted into fully assured tenancies within the HA 1988).
(11) Assured shorthold tenancies granted under the HA 1988, Pt I, Ch II.

1 See also the Law Commission's analysis (now superseded by the HA 1988) at ibid, para 4.12.
2 Defined by HA 1985, s 79 and confined to lettings by specified public bodies, eg local authorities (see s 80).
3 That is less than two-thirds rateable value on 23 March 1965 (or specified other dates). These are given assured tenancy protection by the Local Government and Housing Act 1989, Sched 10.
4 See HA 1988, s 1(3) below.
5 These are defined by RA 1977, s 86. They are also 'secure' tenancies for the purposes of security of tenure.
6 See Chapter 8 below, para 8.3 ff for the R(A)A 1976.
7 Under HA 1988, Pt I, Ch III. The main import is to deny rent control once the employee's employment has ceased, whereas formerly it was available on a 'fair rent' basis under the R(A)A 1976. See Chapter 8 below.
8 RA 1977, s 19, ie where there is a resident landlord or the rent includes payment for furniture or services. Rent tribunal jurisdiction applies, but the tribunal's power to suspend possession orders depends on whether the interest was granted before or after 8 November 1980.
9 See HA 1980, s 52 ff and Chapter 11 below.

[1.25] The legislation is clearly in need of rationalisation. The opportunity to simplify and reform the tenancy structures has been eschewed in successive Housing

Acts. Indeed, rather than attempt reform, the position has arguably been made worse in that the principal measures (such as the HA 1988) have borrowed heavily from the RA 1977 and previous legislation, thus importing previous case law, often of a complex nature, when simplification and reform might have been attempted.

AN AGENDA FOR REFORM

[1.26] The Law Commission has recently revisited the need for reform, and has put forward a reform programme based upon the premise that simplification of the law would be served if the number of housing statuses could be reduced[1]. Some moves in this direction have already been signaled. For example, the government has accepted that there is a case for introducing a single type of tenancy structure for the provision of social housing by registered social landlords[2]. As we have seen, the tenancy status of tenants of social landlords is currently complex. Some hold secure tenancies granted before the HA 1988 came into force, while others have assured tenancies under the HA 1988. These would be merged under the Department of the Environment, Transport and the Regions (DETR) proposals.

1 Renting Homes 1: Status and Security (Law Commission Consultation Paper No 162, 2002) at 3.78–3.81. See also Reform of Housing Law: a Scoping Paper (Law Commission 2001), para 26.
2 Quality and Choice: A Decent Home for All – The Way Forward for Housing (DETR 2001), Chapter 8.

[1.27] The Law Commission's reform project is more ambitious. This envisages the establishment of two tenancy models for all residential lettings: a 'long-term tenancy' and a 'short-term residential tenancy'[1]. The long-term tenancy would be for use primarily by social landlords and local authorities wishing to give tenants security of tenure when renting on a long-term basis[2]. The short-term tenancy, on the other hand, would be modelled on the existing assured shorthold tenancy, and would be primarily for use by private sector landlords[3]. Social landlords would be able to use the short-term tenancy in defined circumstances, and introductory tenancies of council accommodation could also be brought within its framework. One question for the reform project is whether existing Rent Act tenancies could be brought within the long-term tenancy model, without losing established rights to long-term security and rent control. This will involve careful consideration of the extent of security of tenure afforded to long-term tenancies under the reform proposals, and the degree to which rents are to be regulated (and the basis on which this is to be done). If brought to fruition, these proposals would undoubtedly simplify a notoriously complex area of law.

1 Renting Homes 1: Status and Security (Law Commission 2002) para 3.78. See also Reform of Housing Law: a Scoping Paper (Law Commission 2001) paras 28–32.
2 See Law Commission Consultation Paper 162, ibid, Part VII for detailed consideration of the security regime proposed for long term tenancies (referred to as 'Type 1' Agreements for this purpose).
3 See ibid Part VIII ('Type 2 Agreements').

[1.28] The reform project is to be conducted in two phases. The first phase will deal with housing status, and examine several technical issues arising from the possible move to a dual tenancy arrangement based on short-term and long-term tenancies. For example, formalities for the creation of the tenancy, information about its terms, the grounds for possession available to the landlord, and the position of minors[1]. The second phase will focus on substantive reform of housing rights in two areas where the potential for simplification has been clearly identified: the law relating to harassment and unlawful eviction, and succession rights for relatives of deceased tenants[2]. As will be seen in Chapter 2 below, the range of remedies for unlawful eviction requires simplification, and there are overlaps in the measures under which, for instance, evicted tenants can claim damages, with different tests to establish liability and different measures of damages at common law and under statute[3]. Similarly, the succession rights of relatives of a deceased tenant vary, depending upon whether the tenancy is a Rent Act protected or statutory tenancy, an assured tenancy or a public sector 'secure' tenancy. There are also anomalies in the way in which the law treats certain classes of potential successor; eg same sex partners[4]. The Law Commission's reform programme will, clearly, be a long-term project, but if brought to fruition will be of major benefit in rationalising this area of law for the future.

1 Reform of Housing Law: a Scoping Paper (Law Commission 2001) para 105 et seq.
2 Reform of Housing Law: a Scoping Paper (Law Commission 2001) para 111 et seq.
3 Consider for example the different civil remedies available under HA 1988, ss 27 and 28, and at common law for breach of the covenant for quiet enjoyment implied into the tenancy agreement. See below Chapter 2, paras 2.20 and 2.47 et seq.
4 See *Fitzpatrick v Sterling Housing Association Ltd* [2001] 1 AC 27.

D Long residential tenancies

PROTECTION ON TERMINATION OF LONG LEASES

[1.29] Long leaseholders occupying residential property at a low rent are outside the full protection of the RA 1977 or the HA 1988. Indeed, until the passing of the Landlord and Tenant Act 1954, Pt I (LTA 1954), long leaseholders were excluded from statutory protection altogether. The LTA 1954, Pt I conferred Rent Act-style security of tenure on long leaseholders occupying residential property under leases for a fixed-term exceeding 21 years, at a low rent, by providing that at the end of the contractual tenancy, it would statutorily continue unless or until the landlord offered a statutory tenancy under the LTA 1954. The statutory tenancy could only be terminated by the landlord making out one of the grounds provided for in the LTA 1954, Sch 3. These are similar in most respects to the Rent Act grounds for possession. The LTA 1954 gave Rent Act protection to long residential tenants occupying both houses and long leasehold flats.

[1.30] Following the introduction of assured tenancies in the HA 1988, this regime was replaced by protection based instead on the assured tenancy model, and governed by provisions to be found in the Local Goverment and Housing Act 1989, Sch 10 (LGHA 1989). Schedule 10 makes provision for protection based on an assured tenancy arising post-expiry, and introduced a modified assured tenancy scheme for long residential tenancies. The change to protection based on the assured tenancy model was phased in. By virtue of the LGHA 1989, s 186 and Sch 10 the assured tenancy regime applies to a long tenancy at a low rent which is entered into on or after 1 April 1990 *and* on the termination of *all* long residential tenancies (including those to which the LTA 1954, Pt I formerly applied) which *terminate* on or after 15 January 1999. It will also apply to all long residential tenancies *granted* on or after 1 April 1990. After the transitional phase ended on 15 January 1999, therefore, the assured tenancy regime applies to all existing long leases that terminate on or after that date, whenever initially granted.

LEASEHOLD ENFRANCHISEMENT

The Leasehold Reform Act

[1.31] Historically, houses in some parts of the UK (eg South Wales) have been sold on long leases of up to 99 years, rather than freehold. By the 1960s it had become apparent that many long leaseholders had a wasting asset, as the investment value of the house reduced substantially towards the end of the leasehold term. This was perceived as unfair to the occupying leaseholder, who in the majority of cases had either built the house at his own expense, or made substantial improvements to it over the period of the lease. The Leasehold Reform Act 1967 (LRA 1967) gave tenants of houses with a long lease (ie of at least 21 years) at a low rent two important new rights: the right to compulsorily purchase the landlord's freehold interest (ie to enfranchise), or to obtain a 50-year extension of the tenancy. These measures were based on the philosophy that the land belongs in equity to the landowner, and the house to the leaseholder[1]. The price to be paid by the leaseholder was based on the market price of the property, with certain statutory assumptions set out in the LRA 1967[2]. High value properties with rateable values exceeding £500 or (in London) £1000 were initially excluded from the right to enfranchise. The Leasehold Reform Housing and Urban Development Act 1993 (LRHUDA 1993) extended enfranchisement rights of long leaseholders to all houses irrespective of their high value, although in this case purchasers had to pay not only a market price but also an element of marriage value. A number of further reforms were made by the HA 1996; eg to the low rent test.

1 Leasehold Reform in England and Wales (Cmnd 2916, 1966), para 4.
2 See LRA 1967, s 9, discussed below Chapter 12, para 12.32 ff.

Collective enfranchisement of leasehold flats

[1.32] The LRHUDA 1993 implemented the next major reform, by extending a right of collective enfranchisement to long leaseholders of residential flats. The proposals for collective enfranchisement were closely related to the proposals to introduce commonhold tenure for occupants of interdependent buildings such as blocks of flats, and in part may be seen as a compromise between the existing leasehold system and the commonhold proposals. Despite the publicity surrounding the proposals to introduce commonhold as a new form of tenure in the early 1990s, it was instead decided to enact legislation conferring a right of collective enfranchisement and a right of lease renewal on tenants of flats. The aim was not only to meet some of the criticisms of the current law relating to residential long leases but also, perhaps, to provide a first stage of enfranchisement which would speed up the phasing out of leasehold tenure and eventually make the conversion to an altogether new form of commonhold tenure easier to achieve.

[1.33] The LRHUDA 1993 introduced three sets of reforms:

(1) It provided for a collective right for long lessees to acquire the freehold of the premises in which their flat is situated, paying a market value to be determined in accordance with the provisions of the LRHUDA 1993.
(2) It provided a separate right for long lessees to purchase a lease extension.
(3) It strengthened a number of the statutory rights of lessees contained in the Landlord and Tenant Acts 1985 and 1987 (LTAs 1985 and 1987).

[1.34] The provisions contained in the LRHUDA 1993, Pt I owe a great deal not only to the LRA 1967, but also to the LTA 1987, Pt I of which had given tenants with long leases a collective right of first refusal when the landlord proposed to sell the reversion on the block in which their flats are situate. The LRHUDA 1993 subsequently attracted criticism similar to that of the LTA 1987. In particular, the procedural requirements for a successful enfranchisement were thought to be too complex, and too reliant on the timely service of notices and the taking of other procedural steps. The procedure and time limits which must be adhered to for enfranchisement place a heavy burden on those seeking to organise a collective purchase.

The Commonhold and Leasehold Reform Act 2002

[1.35] The criticisms of the collective enfranchisement regime in the LRHUDA 1993 led to calls for its substantial extension, and for the reform of the procedures and qualifying conditions for the purchase of leasehold flats. The Commonhold and Leasehold Reform Act 2002 (CLRA 2002), Pt II has now made substantial reforms. These are controversial, and were preceded by two public consultation exercises before the draft Bill was finalised[1]. The CLRA 2002 removes a number of procedural obstacles to successful enfranchisement; eg by abolishing the requirement that at least two-thirds of the long leaseholders affected must take part in the enfranchisement process and abolishing the former 'residence' test which required at least half the participating leaseholders to have lived in the flats for the previous 12 months. It also extends the scope of enfranchisement by increasing the proportion of a building that can be occupied for non-residential purposes from 10 per cent to 25 per cent, a change which will enable more people living in flats above business premises to qualify. In future, enfranchisement will require the use of a qualifying company as the 'nominee purchaser' to acquire the freehold, and this will have to be a company limited by guarantee with a prescribed memorandum and articles of association. These will be similar to those of limited companies used for managing Commonhold Schemes, established under the CLRA 2002, Pt I.

1 See 'Residential Leasehold Reform in England and Wales – A Consultation Paper' (DETR 1998), 'An Analysis of Responses to Residential Leasehold Reform in England and Wales – a Consultation Paper' Final Report (DETR 1999), and finally 'Commonhold and Leasehold Reform: Draft Bill and Consultation Paper (Cm 4843, DETR 2000), Pt II, p 107ff.

MANAGEMENT AND REPAIR

[1.36] The enfranchisement legislation leaves the existing legislation dealing with the repair and maintenance of leasehold flats unaffected. Private blocks of residential flats present considerable problems in ensuring efficient management, and in providing a comprehensive legal framework in which the reciprocal maintenance and repairing obligations of landlord and tenant can be enforced. Problems in enforcing satisfactory standards of repair and maintenance will commonly be most severe where blocks contain flats of mixed tenure, ie some held on long leases and others on rack-rented tenancies. Some problems will be present whatever the form of tenure, however. The James Committee (set up under the auspices of the Royal Institution of Chartered Surveyors) reported in 1982 that the most persistent complaints by tenants focused on their difficulty in identifying their landlords, lack of consultation relating to the insurance arrangements of their properties, and the level of service charges and their administration by landlord-appointed managing agents[1]. They recommended the introduction of legislation to improve tenants' rights to details of their landlords' identity and address, increased standardisation of leases, and an extension of legal controls on service charges to control the *cost* of services levied on tenants[2]. The LTA 1985 subsequently introduced legal controls on service charges.

1 See the 'Report of the Working Party on the Management of Blocks of Flats' (Chairman J James) (RICS 1982) (the 'James Report'). The James Report was published as Annex 1 to the 'Report of the Committee of Inquiry on the Management of Privately Owned Blocks of Flats' (Department of the Environment 1985) (the 'Nugee Report').
2 James Report (ibid) para 14.6.

[1.37] A thorough survey of long leasehold tenure was subsequently undertaken by the Committee of Inquiry on the Management of Privately Owned Blocks of Flats (the Nugee Committee) in 1985[1]. The Nugee Report singled out five recurring problems for particular criticism. The majority of tenants complained of excessive delay by landlords in acting on requests to carry out maintenance or repairs, and in acting on requests to provide information. A large proportion of tenants complained of excessive service charges, and of the poor quality of services provided, and only a third of the tenants questioned had a sinking fund into which regular service charge payments could be paid[2]. The worst problems were found to exist in ageing mixed tenure blocks, and especially those with foreign landlords or owned by property companies – a fact already noted by the James Committee[3].

1 'Report of the Committee of Inquiry on the Management of Privately Owned Blocks of Flats' (1985) paras 5 and 6, Table A. See generally (1986) Conv 12 (A J Hawkins).
2 Ibid, para 5.13.
3 Ibid, para 5.8. See also James Report para 1.6. The Nugee Report, Chapter 3, Table 1 gives a detailed breakdown of ownership, region by region.

The Landlord and Tenant Act 1987

[1.38] The Nugee Committee made specific proposals, aimed chiefly at improving communication and promoting a better understanding of the legal regime governing the relations of landlord and tenant. If a landlord failed to carry out his obligations as to repair and maintenance of a block comprising leasehold flats, then the tenants should have the right to remove him and seek the appointment of a manager by the court. Money collected by managing agents should be set aside in a trust fund and used solely for the purpose for which they were collected, and there should be a legal mechanism for varying deficient leases; eg those which failed to deal with repairing obligations. Perhaps most controversially of all, it suggested that a landlord, when selling his reversion in a block of flats, should be legally obliged to give his tenants the right of first refusal[1].

1 Ibid, para 6.3 and 6.25. More radical solutions, such as the adoption of strata titles on the Australian model, were beyond the committee's remit.

[1.39] Most, but not all, of the Nugee Report's suggestions were incorporated in the LTA 1987. Although the LTA 1987 in some respects went further than the Nugee proposals (for instance by providing for compulsory acquisition by tenants of the landlord's interest in cases of persistently bad management), it was essentially a conservative measure[1]. It was aimed chiefly at improving communication, and control of repair issues within the landlord/tenant relationship, rather than providing for compulsory expropriation of the landlord's interest in leasehold property. The tenants' right of first refusal on the sale of a block (introduced by the LTA 1987, Pt I), the power to apply for the appointment of a manager by the court, and the powers of compulsory acquisition conferred by Pt III ibid have in practice proved of limited utility. Indeed, a comprehensive survey undertaken for the DETR concluded that there was a marked lack of awareness (especially among tenants) of the provisions and implications of the LTA 1987[2]. A limited reform was made by the HA 1996 to meet these criticisms. Jurisdiction over service charge disputes, and over the appointment of a manager, were transferred from the county court to the leasehold valuation tribunal from 1 September 1997, and the procedures for the tenants pre-emption rights on a freehold sale were also strengthened.

1 See generally Percival (1988) 51 MLR 97, Rodgers (1988) Conv 122 and Smith (1992) 12 LS 42.
2 The Landlord and Tenant Act 1987: Awareness, Experience and Impact (Department of the Environment 1991), p 32.

Commonhold and Leasehold Reform Act 2002

[1.40] The consultation process preceding the CLRA 2002 revealed continuing dissatisfaction, especially among long leaseholder groups, with the effectiveness of the existing law in preventing abuses of service charge accounts by unscrupulous landlords, and in securing appropriate standards of management by managing agents. The law was therefore considerably strengthened in the CLRA 2002, Pt II.

Right to manage

[1.41] The CLRA 2002 gives leaseholders of flats a new right to compulsorily take over the management of the building without having to prove negligence or malpractice against the landlord or his managing agent. Under the LTA 1987, the power to compulsorily appoint an agent was dependent upon proof of fault on the part of the latter. The new remedy is seen as an alternative route to collective enfranchisement where leaseholders either cannot afford to enfranchise or do not want to. Where leaseholders exercise the new right to take control, management will be exercised by a managing company, established on the same model as that for management after a collective enfranchisement ie a company limited by guarantee with a prescribed memorandum and articles of association. The rules for eligibility for 'right to manage' are the same as for collective enfranchisement.

Service charges

[1.42] The LTA 1985 introduced measures to control abuses of service charge funds and to introduce a requirement to consult leaseholders before entering into major works contracts. However, the protective regime of the LTA 1985 only applied to 'service charges' and the definition was limited to charges payable for services, repairs, and maintenance or insurance, or the landlord's management costs. Long leases commonly provide for payments to the landlord for other matters; eg in respect of improvements, or management fees for the giving of landlord's consent for a variety of matters under the terms of the lease. The consultation preceding the CLRA 2002 revealed considerable disquiet at abuses in this area, especially regarding high charges for processing consents and charges for improvement work[1].

1 See Commonhold and Leasehold Reform: Draft Bill and Consultation Paper (DETR 2000), Pt II, Chapter V pp 162–163.

[1.43] The CLRA 2002 widens the definition of 'service charges' to cover improvements and gives leaseholders similar rights in respect of administration charges; eg penalties for late payment or for processing applications for landlords consent. It also strengthens and simplifies the arrangements for consulting leaseholders about major works and imposes a requirement to consult before entering into contracts for the provision of works or services lasting 12 months or more. The CLRA 2002 also imposes a new accounting regime in an effort to improve transparency and accountability in the way landlords spend and account for service charge money held for tenants. Landlords will in future have to give leaseholders a service charge statement giving the balance in the account at the beginning of each year, and details of costs incurred and income during the year, as well as the balance at the end of the year. Previously this information was only available on request, and the landlord's reporting obligation was not laid down in detail. Together these changes represent a major extension of legal control over the administration of, and accounting requirements for, expenditure of leaseholders' money by landlords and their agents[1].

1 See further Chapter 13, below, where the new law is considered in detail.

E Statutory interpretation and protective legislation

INTRODUCTION

[1.44] It will be appreciated that the law of residential landlord and tenant is a subject of considerable complexity, and that statutory rules have a very prominent role to play in this area. Much of the law is contained in a plethora of Acts of Parliament, and the principal statutes (such as the HAs 1985 and 1988) have been successively amended by later statutes. This makes for 'hard' law, and for technical law. Nevertheless, many of the statutes employ basic concepts which are shared, and the interpretation of which can be aided by considering the interpretation given to the same term or concept in earlier legislation; eg concepts such as 'dwelling' and 'dwelling house' are critical to the protection given by the RA 1977, the HA 1988, and to qualification for enfranchisement rights under the LRA 1967. There is, however, no common interpretative code applicable to these basic concepts, whose meaning may change depending on the statutory context in which they appear. The canons of statutory interpretation must therefore be borne in mind when using cases decided under one Act to aid the interpretation of other landlord and tenant statutes.

[1.45] Although tenancies under the RA 1977 are being phased out, and replaced by assured tenancies, much of the jurisprudence developed by the courts under the RA 1977 will remain relevant to the operation of the HA 1988. For example, in defining assured tenancies the HA 1988 employs many of the qualifying conditions contained in the RA 1977 – so under the HA 1988, as under the 1977 legislation, protection only accrues if a 'dwelling house' is 'let as a separate dwelling'. Similarly, protection will not be available if the letting is by a 'resident' landlord. These are fundamental concepts in housing law, on which a considerable body of case law was developed under the previous rent legislation[1]. When construing the modern legislation, however, one fundamental point must be borne in mind. The RA 1977 was, as we have seen[2], primarily a consolidating statute which brought together the then extant legislation (principally the RAs 1968 and 1974) into one statute, without introducing substantive changes or additions to the law. The HA 1988, however, is not a consolidating statute. Different canons of statutory interpretation apply, therefore, when construing the two statutes.

1 Likewise, many of the grounds for possession available to the landlord under the HA 1988, Sch 2, pursue similar objectives – and employ similar terminology – to those available under the RA 1977, Sch 15, eg the grounds for out of season holiday lets, lettings to students and ministers of religion, and where suitable alternative accommodation is available etc (HA 1988, Sch 2, Grounds 3–5 and 9).

2 Above para 1.3 ff.

THE RENT ACT 1977

[1.46] Notwithstanding that the RA 1977 is primarily a consolidating measure, the court should in the first instance interpret the provisions in the RA 1977 if reasonably possible *without* recourse to decisions on the previous legislation, now consolidated.

[1.47]

> 'Self-contained statutes, whether consolidating previous law or doing so with amendments, should be interpreted if reasonably possible without recourse to antecedents, and . . . recourse should only be had where there is a real and substantial difficulty or ambiguity that classical methods of construction cannot resolve. This is particularly true of Acts such as the [RA 1968] which have to be applied by the county courts and which have to be understood or at least explained to great numbers of citizens[1]'.

1 *Farrell v Alexander* [1977] AC 59 at 72, HL (Lord Wilberforce).

[1.48] Being a consolidating statute, however, the court can legitimately depart from the normal rules of construction and, in rare cases, can construe the RA 1977 by reference to the decisions on a consolidated enactment. For example, this will be the case where the purpose of a word or phrase can be established only by examination of the social context in which it was first used in the (now consolidated and repealed) earlier legislation[1]. But this is permissible only where the primary canons of construction fail to establish the meaning of the provision under consideration. The fact that the RA 1977 is a consolidating measure simply provides an additional, secondary, canon of construction, ie the presumption that a consolidating statute does not change the law[2]. Therefore, if the primary approach to construction discloses an ambiguity in a consolidation Act it may sometimes be resolved by examination of the superseded legislation[3]. Subject to this caveat, the courts have indicated that in the first instance the RA 1977, although complex (indeed, perhaps because of its notorious technicality), should be construed in a manner which brings 'common sense' and a 'reasonable interpretation' wherever possible[4], and construe the statutory language employed 'in the primary and most natural sense which it bears in the context'[5].

1 Ibid [1977] AC 59 at 83 (Lord Simon). See also *Maunsell v Olins* [1975] AC 373, HL; *EWP Ltd v Moore* [1992] QB 460, CA (a decision on the Agricultural Holdings Act 1986).

2 The RA 1977 was enacted under the terms of the Consolidation of Enactments (Procedure) Act 1949, by virtue of which it is to be presumed that its provisions have the same effect as those provisions of the earlier statutes that it replaced.

3 *Farrell v Alexander* [1977] AC 59 at 84 (Lord Simon). And see ibid at 97 (Lord Edmund Davies). For an authoritative discussion of the interpretative techniques to be applied to construction of the RA 1977 see Megarry's *Rent Acts* (11th edn), Vol 1 at pp 12–18. And see Pettit, *Private Sector Tenancies* (2nd edn), pp 1–3.
4 For example, see *Curl v Angelo* [1948] 2 All ER 189, CA; *Remon v City of London Real Property Co Ltd* [1921] 1 KB 49 at 55 (Bankes LJ).
5 *Farrell v Alexander* [1977] AC 59 at 83 (Lord Simon).

THE HOUSING ACT 1988

[1.49] The HA 1988 is not a consolidating measure. It follows that, although it extensively employs terminology derived from previous Rent Acts, the presumption that its provisions are not intended to change the law does not apply. Although not strictly of authority, however, it remains the case that decisions on similar terminology in earlier Acts will retain considerable persuasive force when construing the HA 1988 – especially on basic principles such as the distinction between tenancies and licenses, and the qualifying conditions for protection. It should also be appreciated that, freed from the constraints of the interpretative rules applicable to consolidating statutes, the court may take into account the different social and housing background against which previous landlord and tenant legislation was passed when interpreting the HA 1988. For example, in *Hammersmith and Fulham LBC v Harrison*[1] the Court of Appeal refused to apply the rent legislation – dating back to 1920 – when interpreting provisions in the HA 1980 conferring security of tenure on public sector tenants. The Rent Acts were introduced to deal with shortages caused by demobilisation after the 1914–1918 war, whereas the HA 1980 was not passed to deal with any acute housing shortage per se; it seeks, rather, to equate the protection for public sector tenants with those in the private sector. The objectives, if not the terminology, of the two statutes were therefore dissimilar and Rent Act jurisprudence of doubtful interpretative use.

1 [1981] 2 All ER 588, CA.

[1.50] Although Rent Act decisions may be of utility as an aid to interpretation, two particular points should be noted when construing the HA 1988.

[1.51] First, the HA 1988 adopts an altogether different method of conferring security of tenure to that employed in the RA 1977[1]. The latter did not interfere with the landlord's common law right to bring a periodic residential tenancy to an end by notice to quit. Instead it conferred security by creating a new relationship (the statutory tenancy) after contractual termination had taken place – a relationship giving the tenant a personal right of occupation, not a tenancy in the traditional sense. The HA 1988, as we have seen, operates quite differently by removing the contractual principles by which periodic and fixed-term assured tenancies would otherwise be terminated, and substituting a statutory mode of termination which applies while the tenancy remains 'assured'[2]. Moreover, the statutory periodic tenancy which arises following termination of a fixed-term assured tenancy is an interest which vests in possession, *not* a mere personal right of occupancy. It follows that jurisprudence on the Rent Act statutory tenancy may be of limited utility in interpreting the parallel provisions in the HA 1988. So, in *N & D (London) Ltd v Gadsdon*[3] the court, when construing the statutory succession provisions in the HA 1988, refused to extend the meaning of s 14 ibid, by analogy with the RA 1977, s 70(3), to include a disregard of disrepair caused by previous tenants when valuing the rent payable by a successor. Because the succession provisions operate differently under the HA 1988 the latter must be construed on its own terms, and without reference to the succession provisions in the Rent Act. The omission of any reference to dilapidations by previous tenants in HA 1988 was a deliberate omission which the court would not rectify – albeit the position is different under the RA 1977.

1 See above, para 1.18 ff.
2 HA 1988, s 5(1), (2) and Sch 2. Above, paras 1.18 and 1.19.
3 [1992] 02 EG 176.

[1.52] It might be added that the method of protection adopted by the HA 1988 is similar to that employed by the HA 1985 in relation to public sector 'secure' tenants. The basic difference in legislative technique was a principal reason motivating the Court of Appeal's refusal in *Hammersmith and Fulham LBC v Harrison*[1] to interpret the public sector provisions by reference to the RA 1977, and particularly by reference to the jurisprudence on statutory tenancies under the latter. It follows that similar considerations should apply, in principle, to the interpretation of the relevant provisions of the HA 1988[2].

1 [1981] 2 All ER 588.
2 Especially the HA 1988, ss 5–7, 13 and 14.

[1.53] Second, some of the security provisions in the HA 1988 are drawn not from the RA 1977, but from the LTA 1954, Pt II, which regulates business lettings. For example, Sch 2, Ground 6 gives the landlord a right to possession to carry out improvements and work of reconstruction, and is modelled on the LTA 1954, 30(1)(f). Although decisions on the latter may be of assistance in construing the HA 1988, and are cited in the text below, the principle that the court can have recourse to the different social and housing background of its antecedents when construing the HA 1988 may carry additional weight in this context[1]. The LTA 1954 – although employing similar terminology – was introduced to deal with altogether different social and economic problems from those addressed by the HA 1988, namely, guaranteeing continuity of business occupancy for commercial tenants and protecting goodwill.

1 The principle in *Hammersmith and Fulham LBC v Harrison*, above.

[1.54] Subject to these caveats, decisions on the RA 1977 and (where appropriate) the LTA 1954, will be of assistance in interpreting the HA 1988, and are extensively cited in the text below. Additionally, the House of Lords have now held in *Pepper v Hart*[1] that reference to parliamentary material (such as Hansard) is permissible as an aid to statutory construction where the legislation under consideration is ambiguous or obscure. The relaxation in the traditional canon of construction (which formerly excluded travaux preparatoires as an interpretative aid) is limited, however, to permitting the court to consider clear ministerial statements made in promoting a Bill, and associated parliamentary papers necessary to explain or simplify such statements[2]. Given the notorious complexity of the rent legislation, this relaxation in the canons of construction may prove useful.

1 [1993] AC 593.
2 [1993] AC 593 at 634 per Lord Browne-Wilkinson. Parliamentary proceedings on (especially) the HA 1988 are noted at various points in the text below, where the purport of the legislation is unclear.

CHAPTER 2

Protection from eviction and harassment

A Introduction

[2.1] The Protection from Eviction Act 1977 (PEA 1977) confers protection against unlawful eviction and harassment on residential tenants and some categories of licensee. This is achieved by creating criminal offences of eviction and harassment, and by conferring on the aggrieved residential occupier a civil right of action for damages. Further, the PEA 1977 restricts a landlord's right to effect forfeiture without a court order, and prohibits the recovery of possession without a court order where any person is lawfully residing in a dwelling. It also imposes minimum requirements for a valid notice to quit which go beyond the common law requirements otherwise applicable. The Housing Act 1988 (HA 1988) strengthened the law by widening the scope of the criminal offence of unlawful eviction, and creating a new statutory damages claim in tort. The tenant's common law rights remain unaffected by either the PEA 1977 or the HA 1988, however, and potential civil claims, for instance, for breach of the landlord's implied covenant for quiet enjoyment and/or trespass must also be considered. The tenant can, like any other, also rely upon the Protection from Harassment Act 1997 in appropriate circumstances. This makes it both an actionable civil wrong, and a criminal offence, for any person knowingly or unreasonably to pursue a course of conduct which amounts to harassment of another[1]. Harassment is widely defined to include 'alarming the person or causing the person distress'[2]. This remedy is not specific to the law of landlord and tenant, however, and this chapter will focus primarily on the protection from eviction legislation and remedies specific to landlord and tenant.

1 Protection from Harassment Act 1997, ss 1, 2(1) and 3(1).
2 Ibid, s 7(2).

B Criminal liability for harassment and eviction

UNLAWFUL EVICTION AND HARASSMENT

[2.2] PEA 1977, s 1 creates two offences that may be committed by a landlord interfering with the quiet enjoyment of a tenant's residential accommodation:

(1) *Unlawful eviction.* It is an offence under s 1(2) for any person unlawfully to deprive the residential occupier of premises of his occupation of the whole or part of the latter, or to attempt to do so. The landlord has a defence if he proves

that 'he believed, and had reasonable cause to believe, that the residential occupier had ceased to reside in the premises'.

(2) *Unlawful harassment.* By virtue of s 1(3), it is illegal to do acts calculated to interfere with the peace or comfort of a residential occupier or members of his household, or persistently to withdraw or withhold services reasonably required for the occupation of the premises as a residence. Furthermore, these acts must be committed with intent to cause the occupier to give up occupation of the whole or part of the premises, or to refrain from exercising some right and/or remedy in respect of the premises.

[2.3] Both offences carry liability to a fine not exceeding £5,000 (summary conviction) or (on indictment) an unlimited fine, and/or imprisonment for a term not exceeding six months or two years, respectively. It might also be noted that, by virtue of s 1(1), these offences cover harassment not only of protected and assured tenants, but of any 'residential occupier', namely any person occupying premises as a residence, whether under a contract or by virtue of any enactment or rule of law restricting the owner's right to recover possession. It clearly applies to a tenant with a contractual assured tenancy, or a statutory periodic tenancy, to a statutory Rent Act tenant, and also to licensees and service occupiers.

SOME PROBLEMS DEFINED

[2.4] The offences created by the PEA 1977 have given rise to a number of problems, some of which were addressed by the HA 1988, Pt I, Ch IV.

[2.5] As substantial penal consequences are involved, the courts have interpreted these offences strictly, requiring for conviction proof of a specific intent to harass someone who was known or believed by the defendant to be a residential occupier[1]. Acts of harassment covered by s 1(3) vary greatly, from interrupting supplies of gas and electricity to threats of violence and the physical removal of clothes and furniture from the premises. However, proving the necessary intent to ground a prosecution is not always easy. If the defendant genuinely believes the occupants to be other than lawful occupiers; eg squatters and not lawful subtenants, the necessary mens rea is missing – the PEA 1977, s 1(3) requires acts done with intent to harass someone known or believed by the defendant to be a residential occupier[2].

1 *R v Phekoo* [1981] 1 WLR 1117 at 1127, per Hollings J; *McCall v Abelesz* [1976] QB 585 at 597, per Ormerod LJ.
2 Ibid.

[2.6] Similarly, the landlord may have an ulterior motive for his actions, other than a specific intent to cause an occupier to quit. Thus, failure to provide services such as gas and electricity will come within s 1(3) only if the services concerned are contracted for, and even then, the reason for non-supply may be the existence of a pre-existing debt on the account[1]. The burden is on the prosecution to prove beyond reasonable doubt that the landlord's acts were motivated primarily by an intent to harass, not to achieve some other bona fide purpose. Thus, in *Schon v Camden LBC*[2], it was not illegal harassment under s 1(3)(a) to lift a tenant's roof in order to effect repairs, as an intent to encourage the tenant to leave permanently was absent. A further complication is added by the requirement that actus reus and mens rea coincide in point of time. If the landlord lacks an intent to cause an occupier to give up possession at the time of committing the acts complained of, but forms that intent later, no offence is (it seems) committed[3]. It is, therefore, no offence to remove fixtures and fittings in order to carry out repairs, and then, having formed an intent to harass the occupier into vacating, to refuse to replace them so as to render the property uninhabitable. The offences require the commission of 'acts' of harassment with intent: non-feasance will not suffice, although one act in isolation probably will. Refusing to replace a lost key will, it seems, suffice (*R v Yuthi-Wattana*)[4].

1 *McCall v Abelesz* [1976] QB 585.
2 [1986] 2 EGLR 37.
3 *R v Ahmad* (1986) 52 P&CR 346, CA.
4 (1984) 16 HLR 49, CA.

[2.7] Finally, it might be noted that the nature of the specific intent required differs under s 1(2) and (3). Under s 1(2), unlawful eviction, the defendant must intend unlawfully to deprive the occupier of 'occupation', meaning in this context not permanent occupation but, rather, occupation as the occupier's home. Something less than permanent deprivation will suffice if the occupier effectively has to leave the premises and find other accommodation[1]. In the context of s 1(3), however, it seems that for the offence of harassment the landlord must intend an occupier to leave the premises permanently. A mere intention to cause the latter to leave temporarily will therefore not, it seems, suffice[2], although it may ground a prosecution under s 1(3)(b)[3].

1 *R v Yuthi-Wattana* (1984) 16 HLR 49, CA.
2 *Costelloe v London Borough of Camden* [1986] Crim LR 249; *Schon v Camden LBC* [1986] 2 EGLR 37.
3 For criticism of decisions on the PEA 1977, see (1986) Legal Action 125–6; Hill (1987) Conv 26572. See generally O'Dwyer (1985) Legal Action 159.

THE FURTHER OFFENCE OF HARASSMENT

[2.8] The HA 1988, s 29 created a new, much broader, offence, for the establishment of which proof of specific intent is not required. The wider offence is intended to avoid the difficulties of proving an intention to harass (in the sense outlined above) by providing that it will be sufficient to show that a landlord harassed the occupier knowing, or having reasonable cause to believe, that his conduct would lead that occupier to leave and he then does so[1]. This was achieved by adding a new s 1(3A)–(3C) to the PEA 1977. The pre-existing offences remain unaffected, and are merely supplemented by the additional wider remedy. The only amendment to existing offences was to that of unlawful harassment (s 1(3)), which will now be committed by acts likely to interfere with the tenant's peace and comfort, and not merely by acts 'calculated' to do so.

1 See HC Deb, Standing Committee G, 13th Sitting, 28 January 1988, col 530.

[2.9] By virtue of s 1(3A), it will be an offence for a landlord, or his agent, to:

(a) do acts likely to interfere with the peace or comfort of the residential occupier or members of his household; or
(b) persistently withdraw or withhold services reasonably required for the occupation of the premises as a residence.

[2.10] In both cases the offence will be committed only if, additionally, the landlord 'knows', or has reasonable cause to believe, that that conduct is likely to cause 'the residential occupier to give up the occupation of the whole or part of the premises or to refrain from exercising any right or pursuing any remedy in respect of the whole or part of the premises'.

[2.11] The constructive harassment offence will prove easier to establish than the pre-existing offences requiring intent to evict or harass. The essence of the offence is constructive knowledge – there must be facts that would lead the reasonable man, having at his disposal the facts known to the landlord, to believe that the occupier is likely to give up occupation if the course of conduct complained of is pursued. The intended test is clearly objective. It should be noted, however, that the landlord must commit acts that he knows are likely to cause *the residential occupier* to give up possession. If the landlord did not believe the occupier to be a lawful 'residential occupier' (as defined by the PEA 1977, s 1(1)), but merely a trespasser, it seems the new offence will not be made out. It seems that the principle in *R v Phekoo*[1] and *McCall v Abelesz*[2] will still hold good. It should also be noted that the intended effect must be on 'the' (not 'a') residential occupier, which suggests that knowledge of the identity and residential status of the occupier is a necessary prerequisite to the commission of the offence. The constructive harassment offence will clearly cover situations where the landlord, with knowledge of the occupier's identity, is merely completely indifferent to the effect of his conduct on the latter[3]. It will also, it seems, apply where the occupier can show that he has warned the landlord of the likely consequences of his conduct, but the latter persists in his conduct with indifference to whether the occupier leaves or stays[4].

1 [1981] 1 WLR 1117.
2 [1976] QB 585.
3 Cf *McCall v Abelesz* [1976] QB 585 at 587, per Ormerod LJ.
4 See HC Deb, Standing Committee G, 13th Sitting, 28 January 1988, col 530.

[2.12] The landlord is given a defence, if charged with withholding or withdrawing services (s 1(3A)(b) above), if he can prove that he had 'reasonable grounds' for withholding or withdrawing the services in question, or doing the acts complained of. What constitutes 'reasonable grounds' in this context is not defined, but this will be a question of fact for the court. Non-payment of rent or service charges would presumably suffice in the case of withdrawal of services.

[2.13] It should be noted that only the landlord or his agent can commit the offence. A 'landlord' to whom liability can attach is strictly defined by s 1(3C) to mean the person who would, but for the occupier's right to remain in possession, be entitled to occupation of the premises, namely the person with the immediate reversion expectant. 'Agent' is not defined – it is suggested that a factual definition, encompassing persons acting under the landlord's control and direction, would be more apposite in this context than a technical definition based on notions of the law of agency.

C Civil remedies for harassment and eviction

INTRODUCTION

[2.14] The PEA 1977, s 1(5) provides that any available criminal penalty shall not prejudice civil remedies to which an occupier may be entitled. The courts have consistently refused to interpret the PEA 1977, s 1(3), however, as creating a civil remedy for unlawful harassment, reasoning that existing civil remedies provide adequate recompense[1]. Harassment, and especially forcible eviction, may give rise to a miscellany of causes of action in tort and/or contract – trespass, nuisance, breach of covenant for quiet enjoyment, non-derogation from grant, and possibly even torts of assault and battery.

1 See *McCall v Abelesz* [1976] QB 585 at 594, per Lord Denning MR, and at 597, per Ormerod LJ.

[2.15] Although extensive, the common law remedies have not always proved a potent disincentive, and have certain shortcomings – exemplary damages are available only in tort claims (eg, trespass) and not for breach of covenant, and amounts awarded by way of damages are often small. If civil liability is established, the tenant may be entitled to damages under one or more of several heads. The court can award *general damages*, aimed at putting the tenant back in the position he would have been in had there been no tort or breach of contract by the landlord. General damages may include compensation for loss of protected occupancy rights, and damages for any pain and/or inconvenience suffered as a consequence of the unlawful eviction. *Special damages* represent any specific or quantifiable loss suffered by the tenant as a consequence of the landlords unlawful acts; eg the costs of renting alternative accommodation or loss of earnings. *Aggravated damages* can, in appropriate cases, be awarded to reflect extreme suffering and the courts' disapproval of the landlord's actions. Finally, in cases where the landlord's actions were calculated to make a profit, the court can award *exemplary damages*[1]. Additionally, the tenant may seek an interim injunction, restoring him to occupation of the premises. Interim injunctions are a discretionary remedy, and the tenant must show that damages are not a sufficient remedy, that there is a serious issue to be tried, and that the balance of convenience favours the grant of an injunction to maintain the status quo ante pending a trial of the issues[2].

1 *Rookes v Barnard* [1964] AC 1127, 1227.
2 The principles in *American Cyanamid Co v Ethicon* [1975] AC 396, HL.

[2.16] The HA 1988 introduced a new statutory tort of illegal eviction, intended to provide a more realistic deterrent to unlawful eviction by depriving landlords of any financial gain achieved by such activity[1]. The measure of damages for commission of the statutory tort is therefore fixed as the difference in the value of the premises concerned, with and without a sitting tenant. By virtue of the HA 1988, s 27(4), the statutory tort remedy is in addition to any civil liability arising apart from the HA 1988. Other potential civil remedies are therefore preserved, and due to the narrow scope of the statutory tort, continue to be of considerable significance. They are considered in more detail below[2].

1 See, inter alia, Parl Debs (HC) vol 134, col 1061 ff.
2 See para 2.47 et seq, below.

UNLAWFUL EVICTION: THE STATUTORY TORT

[2.17] The HA 1988, s 27 creates a statutory tort based on the existing criminal offences under the PEA 1977, s 1(2) and (3).

Basis of liability

[2.18] Liability accrues in *either* of two situations:

(1) If, at any time after 9 June 1988[1], a landlord or any person acting on his behalf unlawfully deprives the residential occupier of premises of his occupation of the whole or any part of the premises (s 27(1)).

(2) If, at any time after 9 June 1988, a landlord or any person acting on his behalf either attempts to deprive the residential occupier of premises of his occupation of the whole or part of those premises, or does acts likely to interfere with the peace and comfort of the occupier, or withholds services, with actual or constructive knowledge that that conduct is likely to cause the occupier to give up occupation of the whole or part of the premises, or to refrain from exercising any right or remedy in respect of the premises (s 27(2)).

1 The provisions in ss 27 and 28 are retrospective, in that a claim may arise from acts done on or after 10 June 1988, but the Act was not brought into force until 15 January 1989. This does not constitute a breach of the European Convention for the Protection of Human Rights and Fundamental Freedoms 1950, Art 7, the claim in ss 27 and 28 being civil in nature, and not penal; *Jones v Miah* (1992) 24 HLR 578, CA. Note also that the new criminal offence created by s 29 (ibid) is not retrospective in operation, and is therefore consistent with Art 7. See also *Waddington v Miah* [1974] 1 WLR 683 at 694, HL, and (generally) *R v Secretary of State for the Home Department, ex p Brind* [1991] 1 AC 696, HL.

[2.19] The tort, however, is committed only if, as a result, the residential occupier gives up his occupation of the premises as a residence.

[2.20] Although the statutory tort undoubtedly provides an additional disincentive to illegal eviction, the new remedy is, on closer examination, of more limited scope than initially might be thought. Several features of the statutory tort should be noted. First, the liability is based squarely on the existing tests for the imposition of criminal liability under the PEA 1977, s 1(2) and (3). It has proved difficult to establish the necessary mens rea in the latter context, and the problems of definition are now also transposed into the sphere of civil liability. To obviate the likelihood of this occurring, the definition of civil harassment leading to loss of occupation rights – (2) above – was widened to require merely the commission of acts 'likely' to lead to an occupier giving up occupation (not 'calculated' to make an occupier do so, as formerly). Constructive knowledge of its likely effect is also all that is required[1]. In *Tagro v Cafane*[2] Lord Donaldson characterised the ground of liability under s 27(2) as 'constructive eviction', as opposed to 'actual eviction' – 'namely conduct which is such that the occupier cannot reasonably be expected to remain, although physically he or she could remain, and the occupier accordingly gives up his occupation'. This would clearly encompass threats of violent eviction or physical violence by the landlord or his agents. It will also include the re-letting of the premises in the tenant's temporary absence, in circumstances where (on his return) the tenant is forced to share his accommodation and any shared facilities with the new 'tenants'[3]. In both cases, liability will be established only if the occupier actually vacates the premises. The court will not put a gloss on the section, requiring it to investigate the landlord's behaviour and assess its culpability. All that is required is conduct such that it is unreasonable for the tenant to remain. The concept of constructive eviction itself gives adequate protection[4].

1 See HL Deb, vol 500, cols 1414 ff ('calculated' was felt to carry too strong a subjective element of intent).
2 [1991] 1 WLR 378,382.

3 *Abbott v Bayley* (2000) 32 HLR 72.
4 *Abbott v Bayley* ibid (Wilson J).

[2.21] For the tort of unlawful eviction, the landlord has to intend to deprive the occupier of the use of the residence as his 'home', and an intention to permanently deprive is not necessary[1]. The tort under s 27(2), however, differs from its criminal counterpart (the PEA 1977, s 1(3)) in that it is committed when there is an intent to cause the residential occupier to give up his occupation of the premises as a residence, a requirement omitted from the definition of the parallel criminal offence. *Query*, therefore, whether something less than an intent permanently to deprive the occupier of possession may suffice here, whereas it will not under of the PEA 1977, s 1(3) (a)[2]. An occupier can clearly be deprived of the use of premises as a residence, even if such deprivation is less than permanent. The statutory tort is also committed only where eviction has occurred, or where the occupier has voluntarily vacated following harassment. To ground liability, the required intent (actual or constructive) on the part of the landlord must also be established.

1 See *R v Yuthi-Wattana* (1984) 16 HLR 49, CA, above.
2 Cf *Schon v Camden LBC* [1986] 2 EGLR 37 and see para 2.7, above.

[2.22] The statutory remedy does not apply where the landlord is guilty merely of the offence of harassment created by the HA 1988, s 29, possession not having been given up. There is, therefore, an inconsistency in the scope of the criminal and civil law. It should be noted, also, that some of the problems associated with proof of intent may well be encountered in establishing the statutory tort. For example, the tort will presumably be committed only if the landlord believed the occupier to be a 'residential occupier', and will not be committed if the necessary intent is formed after the acts complained of, for instance, by deliberately failing to replace fittings which were originally removed with consent[1].

1 Cf *R v Phekoo* [1981] 1 WLR 1117; *R v Ahmad* (1986) 52 P&CR 346.

Reinstatement as residential occupier

[2.23] The HA 1988, s 27(6) provides that no liability in damages arises if, before proceedings are finally disposed of, the former residential occupier is reinstated in the premises 'in such circumstances that he again becomes the residential occupier of them'. Similarly, no liability arises if the occupier is reinstated as a result of a court order (eg, an injunction). An interim injunction, which allows the occupier to regain entry to the premises, does not constitute 'reinstatement', however, as it gives him no more than temporary occupation until the injunction is discharged[1]. The scenario envisaged by s 27(6) is where proceedings for damages are begun, following which an offer of reinstatement is made. In this situation the tenant has a choice whether to accept reinstatement or not. If he accepts, the defence becomes available to the landlord, and no liability accrues, whereas if he refuses then his right to claim damages under the HA 1988 is unaffected. The occupier can obtain either statutory damages or reinstatement in the property, but is not entitled to both. He has a right to elect between these remedies, and the election may be exercised at trial, if not before[2]. Whatever 'reinstatement' requires (see below) it clearly has to be voluntary; if actual reinstatement is to afford a defence, as envisaged by s 27(6), then it clearly has to be effected with the voluntary cooperation of the tenant. Although this is undoubtedly the effect of the statutory provisions, there is some merit in the view that the tenant is thereby enabled to obtain an enormous financial reward that is only available if he does not accept the offer of reinstatement[3].

1 *Mehta v Royal Bank of Scotland* (2000) 32 HLR 45.
2 *Wandsworth LBC v Osei-Bonsu* (1998) 31 HLR 515.
3 *Tagro v Cafane* [1991] 2 All ER 235 at 239–40.

Offer of reinstatement

[2.24] The HA 1988, s 27(7) also affords grounds for reducing damages where the landlord has offered to reinstate the tenant before the proceedings are begun, but the latter has unreasonably refused reinstatement. If the occupier has found alternative accommodation before the offer is made, damages can still be reduced if it would have been unreasonable for him to refuse the offer if he had not obtained alternative accommodation. This is, of course, open to the objection that harassment has occurred which should be compensated for irrespective of an offer of reinstatement, especially if the tenant has, as a result, been forced to find alternative accommodation.

[2.25] The HA 1988, s 27(7) affords a partial defence, in that damages can be reduced if an offer is made before proceedings are begun. It should be compared with s 27(6), which provides a complete defence where reinstatement has taken place before termination of the proceedings. For the wider defence in s 27(7) to apply, an offer of reinstatement must be made *before* proceedings are begun. It was established in *Tagro v Cafane*[1] that the offer must be made before a claim for damages is made in proceedings under the HA 1988, ss 27 and 28. It will not suffice to bar this defence if proceedings are issued under the general law, eg for damages for breach of the landlord's covenant for quiet enjoyment. Where, as in *Tagro* itself, proceedings are issued under the general law, the defence in s 27(7) is available to the landlord until the pleadings are amended to include a claim for damages under s 27(3) of the HA 1988. This is a technical point of some importance; a claim for damages under s 27 should always be made at the outset of proceedings, thus shutting off any possibility of the landlord tendering reinstatement and securing thereby a reduction in damages.

1 [1991] 2 All ER 235, CA.

Reinstatement defined

[2.26] No definition of 'reinstatement' is offered by the HA 1988. It clearly connotes, however, the re-establishment of the occupier in his former position with its attendant privileges. This involves a consideration both of the nature and quality of accommodation offered, compared to that originally enjoyed by the tenant, and of the terms on which the landlord proposes to reinstate the former occupier. A degree of latitude is allowed to the landlord, however, in that it is clear that a restoration of possession to an evicted tenant can amount in law to 'reinstatement' even if the physical quality of the accommodation offered, and the terms on which it is offered, are not exactly equivalent with that previously enjoyed. A relatively broad measure of equivalence will, it seems, suffice. Two facets of the concept of 'reinstatement' should be considered separately.

Equivalence of legal status

[2.27] First, there is no requirement that the reinstated occupier enjoy the same legal status as previously. If, as a consequence of illegal harassment, the occupier has ceased to occupy the premises as his 'principal home', then his tenancy will cease to be assured[1]. If reinstated as a licensee with no legal protection, it would seem no claim for damages would accrue, for 'residential occupier' (reinstatement in which capacity is required) is widely defined by the PEA 1977, s 1(1) to include licensees, lodgers, service occupiers and many others with a merely contractual right of occupation. The same problem would arise if a hitherto Rent Act statutory tenant were evicted and later reinstated under an assured or shorthold tenancy. The occupier, it seems, should be wary of resuming possession on terms less favourable than those previously enjoyed, and may be better advised to refuse and protect his right to claim damages.

1 See the HA 1988, s 1(1)(b).

Equivalence of accommodation offered

[2.28] Second, there is the matter of equivalence of accommodation offered. In the absence of statutory guidance, the Court of Appeal gave some useful (if somewhat tentative) guidance as to the factual basis on which reinstatement must be offered in the leading case of *Tagro v Cafane*[1]. Having been unlawfully evicted from her bedsit, the tenant here obtained an ex parte injunction to re-admit her to the premises. The landlord then relented and returned her keys. On seeking readmittance to the flat, however, she found that its front door had been smashed, that it had been ransacked, and that many of her clothes and personal effects had been stolen. In this situation the tenant (not surprisingly) gave evidence that she was too frightened to sleep at the premises, and had not subsequently done so. The landlord appealed against an award of £31,000 damages, both on the issue of quantum of damages and the alleged reinstatement of the tenant. It was held in the Court of Appeal that merely giving the tenant the keys and readmitting her to the premises will not suffice as 'reinstatement'. There was, according to Lord Donaldson MR, 'no suggestion that the room was put in proper order, the locks repaired or any offer made to Miss Tagro to allow her to resume occupation in any realistic sense of the word'[2]. The court rejected outright the contention that reinstatement can consist in giving the tenant the key to a lock that does not work, and inviting her to occupy a room that has been completely wrecked.

1 [1991] 2 All ER 235.
2 Ibid at 241 per Lord Donaldson MR.

[2.29] The facts in *Tagro* were admittedly extreme, allowing the court to dismiss such a suggestion with little difficulty. Although the Court of Appeal gave useful guidance as to what will *not* amount to reinstatement, however, it gave little indication as to what *will* suffice for this purpose. Clearly, two views are tenable. One is that the premises must be put back in exactly the same condition as previously, in order that the tenant may resume possession as if the unlawful eviction had never occurred. The other would suggest that reinstatement is a wider concept, and connotes putting the premises back into reasonable order, sufficient to enable them to be occupied as a residence. The latter view receives some support from the PEA 1977 itself[1], which (as we have seen) defines the residential occupier, to whom the statutory remedies accrue, as 'a person occupying the premises as a residence'. The HA 1988 itself requires merely that the evicted tenant be reinstated as 'the residential occupier', which can involve occupation under a licence, service tenancy or some other tenurial arrangement, and not necessarily subject to the same tenancy terms and protected status as hitherto enjoyed. This being the case, one would expect the courts to afford a degree of latitude when considering the physical attributes of the dwelling, and the facts necessary to constitute 'reinstatement' in this context. The precise ambit of the concept – and consequently the defences under s 27(6) and (7) – awaits further judicial consideration, however, in the absence of positive guidance in *Tagro v Cafane*.

1 See the PEA 1977, s 1(1).

Defences

Prior cesser of residence

[2.30] A defence is provided by s 27(8), which provides that no liability in damages accrues if the landlord proves he believed, and had reasonable cause to believe, that the residential occupier had ceased to reside in the premises at the time when he was deprived of occupation or, as the case may be, when the attempt was made or the acts done, as a result of which he gave up occupation of the premises. This will prove difficult to establish in most cases, and places a heavy burden of proof on the landlord[1]. A mistaken belief as to the legal status of the occupier is capable of founding a defence under this provision eg a genuine belief that a valid notice to quit had been given and that the tenant was accordingly no longer a 'residential occupier' for the purposes of the HA 1988. However, the landlord must still go on to prove that his belief was, on the facts, a reasonable one[2].

1 For an example of its being unsuccessfully pleaded see *Jones v Miah* (1992) 24 HLR 578, CA.
2 *Wandsworth LBC v Osei-Bonsu* (1998) 31 HLR 515.

[2.31] This defence will, in practice, probably chiefly apply to s 27(1) and (2)(b). It is difficult to see how a landlord can *attempt* to deprive someone of occupation if he does not believe him to be residing in the premises concerned. It is more appropriate to the position where services (such as gas and electricity) are withheld or withdrawn from the premises.

Unreasonable behaviour

[2.32] A further defence is provided by s 27(7), by virtue of which a reduced liability in damages will accrue if it appears to the court that the tenant's conduct prior to the acts of harassment was such that it is reasonable to mitigate the damages awarded. The courts have interpreted this provision widely. In *Regalgrand Ltd v Dickerson*[1] the Court of Appeal held that it is not limited to serious misconduct, but is equivalent to 'behaviour' and can include omissions as well as positive acts. Here, the fact that there were arrears of rent, that the tenant had decided to leave and that he had started to remove his belongings and furniture were all circumstances which could be taken into account when mitigating damages. Similarly, in *Wandsworth LBC v*

Osei-Bonsu[2] domestic violence by one of two joint tenants, leading to an ouster injunction, was relevant conduct justifying the application of s 27(7) to mitigate the award of damages.

1 (1997) 29 HLR 620,625.
2 (1999) 1 EGLR 26

Scope of liability

Residential occupier

[2.33] A claim for damages can be made by any 'former residential occupier'[1], namely 'the person who was the residential occupier until he was deprived of or gave up possession' as a consequence of the harassment or eviction complained of[2]. 'Residential occupier' is defined by reference to the PEA 1977, s 1, and includes not only a tenant, but any person 'occupying the premises as a residence, whether under a contract or by virtue of an enactment or rule of law giving him the right to remain in possession'. Protection is thus extended to licensees, service occupiers, statutory Rent Act tenants and tenants with a statutory periodic 'assured' tenancy, etc.

1 See the HA 1988, s 27(3).
2 HA 1988, s 27(9)(d).

Landlord in default

[2.34] The primary liability falls to the 'landlord' (note, not his agent; see s 27(3)), defined by s 27(9)(c) to mean 'the person who, but for the occupier's right to occupy, would be entitled to occupation of the premises', namely the person with the immediate reversion expectant, including an intermediate or head lessee, and not necessarily just the freeholder. It also includes any superior landlord from whom the person with the immediate reversion expectant derives title. In *Jones v Miah*[1] it was held that this provision would also include a purchaser of the landlord's reversion following exchange of contracts. Following exchange a purchaser will have an equitable interest in the property, and thus is 'entitled to occupation'[2] in the required sense, and the fact that, as between vendor and purchaser, any entry into occupation prior to completion would be as a licensee only, is immaterial[3]. In *Jones* the purchasers were liable in damages under s 27 where they had been given the keys by the owner after exchange of contracts in order to evict the tenants prior to completion, in a situation where the owner had contracted to sell with vacant possession. It is now clear, however, that where a prospective purchaser evicts a sitting tenant before exchange of contracts, no liability will arise, at least under s 27, there being no equitable interest or licence from which a right of occupation can be implied. A prospective purchaser who evicts a sitting tenant is therefore not a 'landlord in default' within the meaning of s 27[4].

1 (1992) 24 HLR 578, CA.
2 *Lysaght v Edwards* (1876) 2 Ch D 499.
3 The contract of sale in *Jones v Miah* (ibid) incorporated the National Conditions of Sale (20th edn), General Condition 8 which specifies that the purchaser, if let into occupation prior to completion, is to be a licensee and not a tenant of the vendor pending completion. Cf Standard Conditions of Sale (1st edn), General Condition 5.2 to the same effect.
4 *Francis v Brown* (1998) 30 HLR 143, CA.

[2.35] This provision should be read with s 27(3), which imposes the liability to pay damages on the 'landlord in default', namely the landlord who unlawfully deprives the occupier of his occupation of the whole or part of the premises, either himself or through the agency of any person acting on his behalf[1]. This could have relevance where there are several superior interests other than the freehold, eg where the premises have been sublet. There may be several persons qualifying as 'landlords' within s 27(9)(c), but only the landlord in default is liable in damages under ss 27 and 28. If the landlord in default is the immediate landlord, this will not engage liability in any superior landlord, neither does the provision extend the immediate landlord's interest to include that of any superior landlord[2]. The quantification of the damages claim under s 28 is discussed below. Note, however, that for the purpose of quantifying the award of damages, the relevant interest is that of the landlord in default, and it is the difference in the value of *his* interest with and without a sitting tenant that will be relevant. It follows that the *quantum* of damages for eviction will depend on *who* evicts the tenant, and the nature of his interest in the property. This could produce quite arbitrary results. If the mesne tenant has a short lease, the fact that he (and not the freeholder) evicts, and is consequently the 'landlord in default', could greatly reduce the tenant's award of damages[3]. Where there are intermediate interests interposed between superior landlord and tenant, therefore, the tenant's entitlement to damages will depend to a certain extent on *who* carries out the eviction complained of.

1 See the HA 1988, s 27(1) and (3).
2 *Jones v Miah* (1992) 24 HLR 578, per Dillon LJ.
3 Ibid. The 'landlord in default' in *Jones v Miah* held a 20-year lease of a restaurant with sublet flats above. Were the mesne tenancy held by the immediate landlord to have a short residue unexpired, its value would be appropriately diminished, a fact which would impact on the value of the evicted tenant's damages entitlement under the HA 1988, s 28.

[2.36] Note that the landlord will be liable not only for his own actions, but where the eviction is carried out 'by any person acting on his behalf' (s 27(1)). This has been interpreted broadly and will engage liability in the landlord where eviction is by an independent contractor or sub-agent even if the latter's actions are not intended by the landlord[1]. Damages are only available under ss 27 and 28 against the landlord, however, and not his agent[2].

1 *Sampson v Wilson* (1996) Ch 39.
2 *Sampson v Wilson* [1996] Ch 39. Exemplary damages under the general law are not available against an agent unless he personally benefits from the eviction, *Ramdath v Daley* [1993] 1 EGLR 82.

Measure of damages

[2.37] By virtue of s 28, the measure of damages is the difference in value between the value of the landlord's interest determined on the assumption that the residential occupier:

(a) continues to have the same right to occupy (ie the same legal status of occupation, as licensee, assured tenant etc); and
(b) has ceased to have a right of occupation (ie vacant possession value).

[2.38] By virtue of s 28(2) the landlord's 'interest' means his interest in the building in which the premises in question are comprised (whether or not that building contains any other premises) together with its curtilage. The focus is therefore on the value of the landlord's interest in the whole building, both with and without the tenant in situ – and *not* on the value of the landlord's interest in the rented premises themselves. Further, for the purpose of assessing damages it is the value of the interest of the landlord *in default* which must be assessed with and without the sitting tenant – where there are intermediate leases this may be a mesne tenancy, and not necessarily the freehold reversion[1].

1 See above, para 2.35 ff where this problem is discussed in more detail.

[2.39] When calculating the value of the landlord's interest with vacant possession, the sole value of relevance is that of the landlord's freehold or leasehold interest per se. The value of any chattels or fixtures must be discounted, as must any business goodwill accruing to the premises[1].

1 *Jones v Miah* (1992) 24 HLR 578.

[2.40] The aim of fixing the level of damages at the difference between vacant possession and tenanted value is to rob the landlord of any financial benefit (the enhanced vacant possession value of his reversion) accruing as a consequence of the harassment or eviction complained of. Note that, for this purpose, the landlord's 'interest' means his interest in the building in which the premises concerned are comprised[1]. Thus, if the property comprises a block of flats, only one of which is let to a protected occupier, the illegal eviction of the latter may lead to a disproportionate increase in the value of the reversion on the block as a whole, as the eviction of the sole remaining tenant will facilitate a sale with vacant possession. The whole of the uplift in value may, it seems, be claimed in statutory damages. On the other hand, if there are (and after the eviction remain) several tenants in the building, the eviction of one of them may not lead to an increase in the value of the landlords reversion at all, and in this case an award of damages under s 28 would be inappropriate. In *Melville v Bruton*[2] a shorthold tenant who was unlawfully evicted from a house containing two other occupants was not entitled to damages under s 28. Evidence was given that when the interest of the other occupiers was taken into account, there would have been no difference in the value of the landlord's reversion after the eviction of the claimant. An award of £15,000 under s 28 was, therefore, set aside on appeal. The Court of Appeal emphasised that the calculation which s 28(1) requires is one that must take account of the *actual* situation in the premises that are being valued. It must not be made using a notional basis of valuation that assumes vacant possession of the premises following eviction.

1 HA 1988, s 28(2).
2 (1997) 29 HLR 319.

[2.41] The factual basis of the valuation must, therefore, encompass all factors impacting on the value of the landlord's reversion before and after the unlawful eviction, including the presence of other occupiers and their legal status, and the type of user or occupancy of the rest of the building. For example, if part of the building comprises business premises (for instance a shop with flat above) this would be relevant, as it is an integral part of the value of the landlord's interest in the building. Value attributable to goodwill alone, however, would not.

[2.42] For the purpose of valuing the damages claim, the respective values of the landlord's interest:

(a) subject to the tenants right to occupy; and
(b) with vacant possession,

must be quantified at the point in time immediately before the residential occupier ceased to occupy the premises as a residence. Clearly, the value of the landlord's interest with continued residential occupation will depend on the legal status, and consequent degree of security of tenure, enjoyed by the occupier. The presence of an assured tenant will depress the value of the reversion (and hence enhance the potential damages claim under s 28) to a greater extent than that of an assured shorthold tenant or an unprotected licensee. For example, where premises are let at a rack rent on an assured shorthold tenancy, there is unlikely to be any significant difference in value for the purposes of s 28[1]. Furthermore, if the tenant has agreed to surrender the tenancy, the landlord's interest must be valued on the basis of the period unexpired when eviction takes place, prior to the surrender taking effect[2]. Where the tenant is a joint tenant, the precarious nature of his tenure, in circumstances where his co-tenant has stated an intention to serve notice to quit ending the tenancy, is also a factor to be taken into account[3].

1 *Melville v Bruton* (1997) 29 HLR 319, 326. Cf *Miller v Eyo* (1998) 31 HLR 306, where an award of £18,000 to a fully assured tenant was upheld. The tenant here had signed an assured shorthold tenancy agreement but non-shorthold notice had been served, with the result that the tenancy was fully assured.
2 *King v Jackson* [1998] 1 EGLR 30 (shorthold tenant evicted six days before agreed surrender to take effect. Damages award of £11,000 quashed on appeal, and replaced with an award of £1,500 for breach of covenant for quiet enjoyment). Note that the agreement to surrender must, to be effective, normally be in writing signed by both parties (s 2 Law of Property (Miscellaneous Provisions) Act 1989). Here it was not, but the landlord had acted on it to his detriment and the tenant was held to be estopped from resiling from it.
3 *Wandsworth LBC v Osei-Bonsu* (1998) 31 HLR 515 at 528.

[2.43] When valuing damages the following assumptions must be made:

(1) That the landlord is selling his interest in the building on the open market to a willing buyer, namely a buyer uninfluenced by financial exigency or other constraints.
(2) That neither the occupier nor any member of his family wishes to buy.
(3) That it is unlawful to carry out substantial development of the building or its site, or to demolish the whole or part of any building on the land.

No method of valuation is prescribed. The courts have indicated their reluctance to impose strict requirements as to how the valuation is carried out, preferring instead to leave valuation matters to the skill and expertise of expert witnesses employed by the parties.

[2.44] Some guidance in applying the statutory guidelines was, however, given in *Tagro v Cafane*[1].

(1) The relevant date for valuation purposes is the time immediately before the occupier ceases to be in residence. This has the inevitable consequence that changes in market conditions between that date and the date of the hearing are inadmissible[2].
(2) The valuer is directed to make his valuation on the assumption that the landlord in default is selling his interest on the open market to a willing buyer. The Court of Appeal indicated in *Tagro* that this required the valuer to assume that he can sell it on the open market to a willing purchaser, and in so doing to

ignore any covenant against assignment which restricts alienation of the landlord in default's interest[3].

1 [1991] 2 All ER 235, CA.
2 Ibid at 241 per Lord Donaldson MR.
3 The lease here contained a covenant against assigning or subletting the whole or part of the premises. Nevertheless, the Court of Appeal held that if, bearing in mind that the mesne tenancy was protected by the Landlord and Tenant Act 1954, the surveyor when applying his local knowledge and professional expertise came to the conclusion that (notwithstanding that the lease could theoretically be terminated by notice to quit) it would in reality go on virtually indefinitely, then his valuation was not open to legal challenge. This approach is open to the objection, it is suggested, that it sits uneasily with the approach taken to the concept of the 'willing lessor' and 'willing lessee' in rent review cases, where it is clear that regard must be had both to the state of repair of the premises and the terms of the lease itself when valuing the rent a willing lessor would pay. Clearly, repairing obligations in the lease will be relevant to valuing the landlord's interest under s 28, and covenants against alienation should arguably also be relevant. Cf *F R Evans (Leeds) Ltd v English Electric Co Ltd* (1977) 245 Estates Gazette 657; *Dennis & Robinson Ltd v Kiossos Establishment* [1987] 1 EGLR 133, CA. See also [1991] Conv 297 (Rodgers).

[2.45] In *Jones v Miah*[1] the Court of Appeal indicated that the surrender value of the tenant's interest might provide a check on the quantum of damages, but no more than that. Evidence of sales of comparable premises with and without sitting tenants will clearly be of great importance. Alternatively, if the landlord's interest has recently been sold this might provide evidence of its current value. For example, in *Jones v Miah* the landlords in default had purchased the lease of a shop with a residential flat above for £85,000. Discounting goodwill and fixtures the value of the lease was put at £50,000. Evidence was produced that the defendants would have paid half this figure for the property with sitting tenants. The difference in value attributable to the unlawful evictions was therefore put at £25,000. Although the flat included four rooms, only three of which had tenants, the relevant value was that attributable to obtaining vacant possession – not the difference apportioned by reference to the number of rooms. The presence of the three protected tenants was what halved the value of the building, irrespective of the number of rooms involved. This gave a figure of £8,333 for each evicted tenant, representing the financial advantage obtained by the landlord in evicting them. This figure was rounded down to an award of £8,000 for each tenant under s 28. Note that the surrender value of the protected tenancies was, in this case, approximately £5,000; this being the sum the tenants had been advised to accept for surrendering their protected occupation rights.

1 (1992) 24 HLR 578.

Discount for development value

[2.46] Where the landlord is proposing redevelopment and has planning permission, the value of his reversion with vacant possession may be inflated by accrued development value. The HA 1988 therefore contains provisions intended to ensure that any additional value attributable to the possibility of 'substantial' development is not to be weighed against the landlord. Enhanced value attributable to non-substantial development will, however, count. 'Substantial' development is defined by s 28(6) to mean any development other than one for which permission is granted by a General Development Order currently in force or, where the dwelling is a flat within a larger building, a development by way of change of use of the whole or part of the building to residential use. Development value accruing by virtue of planning permission being obtained for a non-residential use is not, therefore, to be included in the damages equation. The inclusion, in the tenant's favour, of non-substantial development value was a compromise extracted during the Housing Bill's passage. As originally framed, the Bill allowed no development value to weigh in the tenant's favour, it being thought that if it were included in the damages equation, the resulting difference between tenanted and vacant possession value would be so great as to produce a damages award out of all proportion to the loss suffered by the tenant. This was criticised for failure to pursue the government's own stated aim of depriving landlords of the benefit of unlawful eviction – subsequent development being a common reason for harassment and illegal eviction. The HA 1988, s 28(6) represents a compromise between the two viewpoints.

OTHER CIVIL REMEDIES

[2.47] The statutory tort of unlawful eviction provides an additional remedy, and any liability arising (whether in tort, contract or otherwise) apart from s 27 is expressly preserved[1]. The statutory remedy is, moreover, expressly to be considered as in the nature of a liability in tort[2]. Section 27(5) further provides that the right of a residential occupier to enforce any liability which arises apart from the HA 1988, in respect of his loss of the right to occupy premises as his residence, remains unaffected. Given the fairly narrow ambit of the new tort, the existing remedies in tort and contract will probably retain considerable significance.

1 See s 27(4).
2 Ibid.

[2.48] In principle, general damages may be claimed (whether in contract or tort) for the tenant's loss of a protected right of occupation, special damages for financial loss and recompense consequent upon eviction, and also (in some situations) aggravated damages for the mental distress caused by the landlord's actions[1].

1 *McCall v Abelesz* [1976] QB 585 at 594, CA. Aggravated damages for mental distress will only be available in tort (eg trespass) and not in an action for breach of the covenant for quiet enjoyment: *Branchett v Beaney* [1992] 3 All ER 910, CA. Below para 2.55 ff.

[2.49] The award may encompass the value to the tenant of the unexpired term, namely the difference between the contractual or assessed rent to be paid during the residue of the term and the rental value of the premises. In the case of a fixed-term, this can be readily ascertained. Where the term is periodic the calculation is more difficult, but in the case of a statutory Rent Act tenancy it will represent the difference between the free market rent and the fair rent registered for the dwelling and payable (subject to registered increase) for the rest of the tenant's life. It might be noted that the relaxation of rent controls introduced by the HA 1988 will, in theory, greatly reduce the compensation available to an assured tenant on this basis. As rents are now unregulated, the difference between the assessed rent and the free market rent at the time of eviction may not be great – although it may still be significant in a period of inflation if the 12-month review period has just begun and an uplift in rent under s 12 is not due for almost a year. Considerable awards will still, however, be available to statutory Rent Act tenants to reflect the loss of their statutory right to live in premises for life, paying only an assessed rent considerably less than the market rent for the property. It may be more important for the assured tenant to be able to establish commission of the new statutory tort in s 27 (above) – although here, also, an assured or assured shorthold tenant will receive limited damages on the statutory basis as an assured shorthold tenancy does not devalue the landlord's reversion by as much as the presence of a sitting Rent Act tenant.

[2.50] Alternatively, he may wish to base his claim in the general law of tort (eg, if trespass is involved), where exemplary damages are available in appropriate cases. This re-emphasises the point (see above) that the weaker the security enjoyed by an occupier, the less effective the civil remedy available either under s 28 or at common law[1]. Note, also, that exemplary damages are not available against a landlord's *agent*, unless it can be shown on the balance of probabilities that the latter will personally benefit from the unlawful eviction[2]. The acts commonly involved in unlawful eviction and harassment (eg, cutting off electricity and gas supplies, removing personal effects, intimidation and abusive behaviour) may give rise to one or more of the following claims.

1 Above, paras 2.40–2.42. On quantification of damages claims in contract and tort see, inter alia, a helpful article by Clayton and Tomlinson, 'Damages for Loss of a Rent Act Tenancy' (1986) *Legal Action* 10.
2 See *Ramdath v Daley* [1993] 20 EG 123, CA; *Drane v Evangelou* [1978] 1 WLR 455. See generally *Rookes v Barnard* [1964] AC 1129.

Trespass

[2.51] Physical entry or interference with the demised premises will violate the tenant's inherent right to exclusive possession and ground an action in tort for trespass. Entry by the landlord or his agents and removal of a tenant's belongings[1], and entry in order to change locks on the door to the property[2] are common examples. For trespass to lie, however, there must be some physical interference with the property demised – merely cutting off gas or electricity supplies without entry is no trespass[3]. The tenant's remedy here must be pursued in contract for breach of the landlord's covenant for quiet enjoyment. Exemplary or punitive damages can be awarded where trespass is established, but not for mere breach of contract[4].

1 *Drane v Evangelou* [1978] 1 WLR 455, CA.
2 *Warder v Cooper* [1970] Ch 495; *Hume v Pratt* [1980] CLY 1647.
3 *Perera v Vandiyar* [1953] 1 WLR 672, CA.
4 See *Drane v Evangelou*, above.

Other tortious claims

[2.52] If violence is offered or inflicted by the landlord or his agents in the course of harassment the tenant will have an action for assault and in appropriate circumstances, battery. Assault is committed if the tenant is placed in fear of the immediate application of physical force to his person. Battery has now been defined as any touching of the tenant with hostile intent (see *Wilson v Pringle*[1]; the required element of hostility will be readily apparent in most situations involving eviction and harassment of tenants). Trespass, either to the person or the demised premises, is actionable per se without proof of loss. Considerable damages, including an exemplary element, can be awarded as eviction with violence is judicially regarded as the most heinous manifestation of unlawful eviction[2].

1 [1986] 2 All ER 440, CA.
2 See, eg *Andreiou v Reid* (1987) *Legal Action* 14, for threats with chisel and assault by 'heavies'.

[2.53] Quite apart from trespass, the facts alleged may ground an action for nuisance; eg, if the landlord retains adjoining property and uses it in a way which interferes with the reasonable enjoyment of the demised premises: *Guppys (Bridport) Ltd v Brookling*[1]. But the normal use of a residential flat cannot be a nuisance to neighbours. So excessive noise which is attributable to poor sound insulation will not ground an action in nuisance[2].

1 (1983) 269 Estates Gazette 846, 942, CA (rebuilding property around tenant's flat with a view to re-letting).
2 *Baxter v London Borough of Camden* [2000] Env LR 112, HL.

Breach of covenant for quiet enjoyment

[2.54] Most acts of harassment will also constitute breach of the landlord's implied covenant for quiet enjoyment. The latter is not an absolute covenant protecting the tenant from interference by anyone, but rather a qualified covenant protecting the tenant against interference with his quiet and peaceful enjoyment of the premises by the landlord or his agents[1]. The landlord impliedly promises not to interfere with the tenant's exercise and use of the premises during the term. For example, he will be in breach of covenant if he changes locks on doors[2], cuts off mains supplies[3], removes doors and windows[4] or indulges in abusive and intimidating behaviour intended to drive the tenant from the property[5]. No direct physical interference with the property need be shown[6]. However, the landlord merely covenants that the tenant's lawful possession of the premises will not be substantially interfered with, and the covenant does not give a warranty that the land is fit for use for a particular purpose. Accordingly, there was no breach of the covenant for quiet enjoyment where inadequate sound insulation was provided between adjoining flats, leading to excessive noise and disturbance to other occupiers[7]. Moreover, the covenant does not apply to things done before the tenancy is entered into, even if they have continuing consequences. Accordingly, the provision of inadequate soundproofing in a building which is subsequently let is an inherent defect for which the landlord assumes no responsibility[8].

1 *Kenny v Preen* [1963] 1 QB 499 at 511 per Pearson LJ.
2 *Warder v Cooper* [1970] Ch 495.
3 *Perera v Vandiyar* [1953] 1 WLR 672.
4 *Lavender v Betts* [1942] 2 All ER 72.
5 *Kenny v Preen* [1963] 1 QB 499.
6 *McCall v Abelesz* [1976] QB 585.
7 *Southwark LBC v Mills* [1999] 3 EGLR 35, HL.
8 *Baxter v London Borough of Camden* [2000] Env LR 112, HL.

[2.55] Breach of the covenant will give rise to a claim for damages and/or an injunction, but the court has no jurisdiction to award punitive damages[1]. Consequently, substantial damages may not be available if there has been no physical interference with the property (and hence no trespass), and the tenant cannot establish significant pecuniary or material loss arising from the landlord's actions. This will often be the case where mains services are discontinued externally, or the landlord merely writes threatening letters, as no trespass is involved[2]. The often low level of damages awards has been criticised, and was one factor motivating the introduction of the statutory claim in the HA 1988. Despite earlier doubts[3] it is now clear that aggravated damages for mental distress and injury to feelings are not available in an action for breach of the covenant for quiet enjoyment[4]. Damages for mental distress and injury to feelings *can*, however, be recovered in an action for, eg trespass. The landlord's conduct may also, if sufficiently serious, be in breach of the implied covenant against derogation from grant.

1 *Perera v Vandiyar* [1953] 1 WLR 672; *Kenny v Preen* [1963] 1 QB 499.
2 Ibid; *Perera v Vandiyar* [1953] 1 WLR 672; *Kenny v Preen* [1963] 1 QB 499.
3 *McCall v Abelesz* [1976] QB 585 at 594 per Lord Denning MR; *McMillan v Singh* (1984) 17 HLR 120, CA; *Sampson v Floyd* [1989] 2 EGLR 49, CA (supporting recoverability for mental distress). But cf *Perera v Vandiyar* [1953] 1 WLR 672 and *Kenny v Preen* [1963] 1 QB 499 to the opposite effect.
4 *Branchett v Beaney* [1992] 3 All ER 910, CA. The observations here were strictly obiter, however.

Interaction with statutory tort remedy

[2.56] The HA 1988, s 27(5) provides that the statutory tort of unlawful eviction does not affect the occupiers right to enforce any liability arising apart from the HA 1988, namely any pre-existing claim in contract or tort for trespass, breach of covenant, nuisance etc. However, it is expressly provided that damages shall not be awarded both under s 27 and pursuant to that other liability 'on account of the same loss'. This provision is intended to remove the possibility of the tenant receiving the benefit of double compensation, both at common law and under the HA 1988. The rule against double compensation has, however, proved difficult to interpret and apply in practice.

[2.57] By virtue of s 27(3) the statutory claim for damages is expressed to be 'in respect of [the occupier's] loss of the right to occupy the premises in question as his residence'. The HA 1988, s 27(5) would therefore bar, it seems, a claim for general damages in contract or tort for loss of rights of occupation if an award of damages under s 28 has been made (and vice versa)[1]. Where a statutory award has been made under ss 27 and 28, however, this will strip the landlord of his profit at the moment of eviction, and may (in the courts view) go beyond what is needed to compensate the tenant. In these circumstances the court will not award exemplary damages in addition to the statutory award under s 27[2]. If no award of exemplary damages can be made against the landlord, neither can exemplary damages be awarded against a joint tortfeasor; eg an agent or a purchaser who has evicted the tenant prior to exchanging contracts to purchase the premises with vacant possession[3]. In principle, however, an award of statutory damages should not preclude an award at common law for aggravated damages for distress or special damages for financial loss consequent upon the illegal eviction. These are not damages 'in respect of the ... loss of the right to occupy the premises' (s 27(3)). However, in *Nwokorie v Mason*[4] the Court of Appeal held that an award of aggravated damages for the humiliation and shame caused by the landlord's conduct, though appropriate, must be set off against the statutory award under s 28 – it was interpreted as an award of damages for the same loss ie the loss of the tenants right to occupy the premises as his residence[5]. This must be open to question, and may be distinguishable on the facts in *Nwokorie*, where the tenant had a restricted contract and lived in close proximity with the landlord. Damages awarded for breach of the covenant for quiet enjoyment are not subject to set off against statutory damages under s 28[6].

1 See *Mason v Nwokorie* [1993] 26 HLR 60, CA.
2 See *Francis v Brown* (1998) 30 HLR 143, 149–150.
3 The principle in *Broome v Cassell & Co* [1972] AC 1027, ie that awards of punitive damages against joint tortfeasors should reflect only the lowest figure for which any of the defendants could be liable. If no exemplary damages are awarded against the landlord, it follows that they cannot be awarded against other tortfeasors implicated in the eviction: *Francis v Brown* (above note 2).

4 (1993) 26 HLR 60, CA.
5 (1993) 26 HLR 60, at 68.
6 *Kaur v Gill* (1995) *The Times*, 15 June, CA.

[2.58] General damages and exemplary damages must be set off against statutory damages awarded against the landlord in default under s 27(5). Statutory damages can only be awarded against the landlord. However, if on the facts the landlords agent carrying out the eviction is liable as a joint tortfeasor, then common law damages will be recoverable against him, including aggravated and exemplary damages if appropriate. Any sums recoverable from other tortfeasors will be set off against the statutory damages recoverable by the occupier from the landlord. Thus in *Mehta v Royal Bank of Scotland*[1] statutory damages of £45,000 were awarded against the landlord for evicting a licensee of a hotel room. Compensatory, aggravated and exemplary damages of £27,000 were awarded against the landlord, his managing agent and receiver as joint tortfeasors. The common law damages were held to be recoverable from the managing agent and receiver. Statutory damages under the HA 1988, s 28 were held to be recoverable from the landlord alone, and were subject to a set off of the common law damages awarded against the managing agent and receiver.

1 (2000) 32 HLR 45.

D Eviction without due process

FORFEITURE

[2.59] The PEA 1977, s 2 provides that where any premises are let as a dwelling under a lease which includes a proviso for re-entry or forfeiture, it shall not be lawful to enforce the right to forfeit otherwise than by court proceedings while any person is lawfully residing in the premises. If the tenancy is protected under the RA 1977, forfeiture will not, in any event, entitle the landlord to possession[1]. Where the tenancy is an assured tenancy within the HA 1988, moreover, it is not possible to exercise a proviso for re-entry or forfeiture to terminate the tenancy – although the presence of an appropriately drafted forfeiture clause may entitle the landlord to bring proceedings for possession under the HA 1988 itself[2]. The provision in the PEA 1977, s 2 is of most significance, therefore, for tenants without security of tenure under the Rent Act or HA 1988.

1 RA 1977, ss 2 and 98. See below, Chapter 6.
2 See HA 1988, ss 5 and 7(6), discussed further below, Chapter 4, para 4.7 ff.

REQUIREMENT OF COURT ORDER

[2.60] The PEA 1977, s 3 prohibits the eviction without a court order of two groups of occupier:

(1) Those with tenancies not protected by the Rent Act and (now) the HA 1988 (protected or assured tenants can be lawfully evicted only by court order in any event).
(2) Tenants and/or licensees whose interest constitutes a restricted contract under the RA 1977, or alternatively a service occupancy. Restricted contracts are

protected only if entered into after the commencement of the Housing Act 1980, s 69.

[2.61] The HA 1988, s 30 extended the requirement of due process to apply to any premises occupied as a dwelling under a licence[1], and not simply those which formerly constituted restricted contracts. This protection does not extend, however, to 'excluded' tenancies or licences (see below). Breach of s 3 has been held to be an actionable tort, and there appears no reason why breach of the extended provisions should not also be so regarded[2]. A tenant retains the protection of s 3 after the grant of a possession order, until its lawful execution in accordance with the court rules. It will, therefore, be illegal to evict a tenant against whom a possession order has been obtained except by the due execution of a warrant for possession[3].

1 Whether periodic or otherwise. Cf the minimum notice to quit requirements in s 5(1A) apply only to periodic licences, a concept which has been restrictively interpreted by the courts – see *Norris v Checksfield* [1991] 4 All ER 327, CA.
2 *Warder v Cooper* [1970] Ch 495.
3 See *Haniff v Robinson* [1993] QB 419, CA.

EXCLUDED TENANCIES AND LICENCES

[2.62] The HA 1988, s 31 added a new s 3A to the PEA 1977 defining 'excluded tenancies and licences' to which the requirement of a court order for possession does not apply. Moreover, the minimum of four weeks' notice to quit in writing required by the PEA 1977, s 5 also does not apply in these cases[1] if the tenancy or licence was granted after the HA 1988's commencement. In these cases, the minimum notice period required at common law, based on the period of tenancy, will apply[2].

1 Section 5(1B), inserted by HA 1988, s 32(2). For s 5 and the notice to quit provisions, see below, para 2.73 et seq.
2 See HC Deb, Standing Committee G, 14th Sitting, 2 February 1988, col 542 (Minister of Housing).

[2.63] The interests excluded from the requirements of ss 3 and 5 are as follows.

Resident landlords sharing accommodation

[2.64] A tenancy or licence is excluded if under its terms the occupier has the use of any accommodation in common with the landlord or a member of the landlord's family, but only if, both at the time of grant and at the time the tenancy or licence came to an end, the landlord or a member of his family occupied as his principal home premises of which the whole or part of the shared accommodation formed part[1]. 'Accommodation', the sharing of which activates this provision, includes neither an area used for storage, nor a staircase, passage, corridor or other means of access. The exclusion will, however, apply if the sharing is of accommodation other than simply 'living' accommodation, and will therefore include the sharing of not only living rooms, kitchens etc, but also rooms where simultaneous use is not possible – eg bathrooms[2]. All that is required is that the landlord has the use of accommodation 'in common' with the tenant or licensee, whether or not in common also with others[3]. The sharing must be with the 'landlord' or members of his family, namely the landlord or licensor, or one out of joint landlords or licensors, or between a head lessor and lawful subtenant or sub licensee. Members of the owner's family are defined by reference to the Housing Act 1985, s 113 (secure tenancies).

1 PEA 1977, s 3A(2).
2 Cf for the purposes of assured tenancy protection HA 1988, s 3, below, para 3.69.
3 Ibid, s 3A(4), inserted by HA 1988, s 31.

[2.65] Consequently, there are now two classes of resident landlord situation: those where a resident landlord does not share accommodation with tenants or licensees, to whom the PEA 1977 requirements continue to apply; and those sharing accommodation, who will be exempt. Clearly, this may give rise to attempts to abuse resident landlord status to avoid the requirements of the PEA 1977, as amended[1].

1 See HC Deb, Standing Committee G, 14th Sitting, 2 February 1988, col 549 (Minister of Housing) for concern on this point.

Tenancy or licence granted as temporary expedient

[2.66] A tenancy or licence is also excluded if it was granted as a temporary expedient to a person who originally entered the premises (or any other premises) as a trespasser. The exclusion applies even where another tenancy or licence was granted prior to the current interest, so as to exclude a series of such grants, provided always that successive grants are in the nature of a 'temporary expedient'. The exclusion is aimed at temporary arrangements entered into; eg while an erstwhile trespasser seeks alternative accommodation[1].

1 PEA 1977, s 3A(6).

Holiday lets

[2.67] A tenancy or licence is excluded if it confers a right of occupation for the purposes of a holiday only. 'Holiday' is not defined and will presumably fall to be interpreted in the same manner as the exclusion from assured tenancy status in the HA 1988, Sch 1[1]. Previous case law on the 'holiday let' exclusion from Rent Act protection will be of assistance[2].

1 PEA 1977, s 3A(7).
2 See para 6.34 et seq, and, inter alia, *Francke v Hakmi* [1984] CLY 1906; *Buchmann v May* [1978] 2 All ER 993, CA.

Gratuitous tenancy or licence

[2.68] The PEA 1977, s 3A(7) also exempts a tenancy or licence that is purely gratuitous, ie is not granted for money or money's worth.

Hostel accommodation

[2.69] A licence to occupy hostel accommodation is excluded if granted by one of a variety of public bodies – a local authority, development corporation, the Commission for New Towns, an urban development corporation, a housing action trust, the Development Board for Rural Wales, the Housing Corporation, or a charitable housing trust or housing association. The Secretary of State has power to designate bodies falling within the exclusion by statutory instrument (the PEA 1977, s 3A(8) and (9)).

Scope of exclusions

[2.70] The above exclusions do not apply to tenancies granted before the HA 1988's commencement[1]. The exclusions will, however, apply to licences granted prior to commencement; licences granted to hostel dwellers and holiday lets. The aim is to avoid conferring extra protection on pre-commencement licences, which they did not previously enjoy[2].

1 PEA 1977, s 3(2C).
2 HC Deb, Standing Committee G, 14th Sitting, 2 February 1988, col 544.

AGRICULTURAL EMPLOYEES: POSSESSION ORDERS

[2.71] The PEA 1977, s 4 confers on the court power to suspend the execution of a possession order made against an agricultural employee occupying tied accommodation, but whose tenancy is not protected by the Rent (Agriculture) Act 1976 (R(A)A 1976). The court must grant suspension if the order is made within six months of the former tenancy coming to an end. The HA 1988, s 30(3) extends the power of suspension to licences granted to agricultural employees. This is not an extension of major significance, as the R(A)A 1976 protects most licences in any event. It will, however, confer additional protection on licensees of certain bodies not covered by the R(A)A 1976 which none the less provide tied accommodation; eg local authorities and housing associations. On the R(A)A 1976 and assured agricultural occupancies under the HA 1988, see further Chapter 8 below.

[2.72] The additional protection does not extend to 'excluded' licences within the categories outlined above.

MINIMUM NOTICE TO QUIT

General

[2.73] At common law a notice to quit a periodic tenancy can be oral, and the period of notice required will be determined by the periods of tenancy. Notice of at least one full period will generally be required at common law, except in the case of a yearly periodic tenancy, in which case six months' notice is required. Thus a week's notice is appropriate to determine a weekly periodic tenancy, one month's notice for a monthly tenancy and a quarter's notice for a quarterly tenancy[1]. The notice to quit must, moreover, be expressed to take effect at the end of a period of tenancy. Most residential tenancies are weekly or monthly, and the position of many residential occupiers at common law was, therefore, at best precarious. Accordingly, the PEA 1977 confers basic protection on licensees and tenants by prescribing a minimum period for a valid notice to quit of four weeks and statutory information to be included in the notice, which must itself be in writing. This is a *minimum* requirement. If on the facts notice to quit of a longer period is required, then this will apply; eg where the periods of tenancy are quarterly or yearly, or where there is no written agreement and the reasonable notice period implied at common law exceeds one month[2].

1 See inter alia *Queen's Club Gardens Estates Ltd v Bignell* [1924] 1 KB 117; *Lemon v Lardeur* [1946] KB 613, CA.
2 See *Mehta v Royal Bank of Scotland* (2000) 32 HLR 45 ('reasonable' notice period to determine long-term contractual licence of hotel room held to be four months).

[2.74] Where there is a joint tenancy, the protection of s 5 cannot be refused to one joint tenant where the other gives short notice that is accepted by the landlord. Thus protection still accrued to an occupier in *Hounslow LBC v Pilling*[1] where his co-tenant had given notice of three days' duration, which was accepted by the landlord pursuant to a clause in the tenancy allowing for such lesser period than four weeks' notice to quit by the tenant 'as the landlord may accept'. The notice was construed as a break clause, and therefore ineffective as both joint tenants had not concurred in giving it.

1 [1994] 1 All ER 432, CA.

Statutory requirements

[2.75] By virtue of the PEA 1977, s 5, no notice to quit premises let as a separate dwelling is valid unless given in writing and at least four weeks before it is to take effect. The notice must also include prescribed information[1]. In *National Trust v Knipe*[2] it was held that an agricultural holding which included a dwelling did not come within s 5, as the whole (ie land and dwellings) had been let as an agricultural holding, and not 'let as a dwelling'. This provision originally extended only to tenancies of dwellings, not licences[3]. The HA 1988, s 32 extended the minimum requirements as to notice to quit to apply to all periodic licences. They do not apply, however, to 'excluded' licences and tenancies; eg those granted by resident landlords sharing accommodation, or licences of hostel accommodation. In these cases, contractual notice in accordance with the period of licence or tenancy will presumably be necessary, in accordance with the common law requirements otherwise applicable.

1 See the Notice to Quit (Prescribed Information) Regs 1988 SI 1988/2201. This requirement only applies where notice is given by the landlord, not the tenant.
2 [1997] 4 All ER 627. But note that where (as is common) the land and farmhouse have been severed and let under separate tenancies (eg the land on a farm business tenancy and the house on a shorthold), the dwelling house will then be let as a dwelling so as to come under the PEA 1977, s 5. Any notice to quit a dwelling so let will have to comply with the statutory requirements in accordance with s 5 ibid.
3 See *Crane v Morris* [1965] 1 WLR 1104, CA – service occupier not protected unless an agricultural employee covered by the tied cottage legislation.

[2.76] It is now apparent that the extension of the minimum notice to quit requirements to periodic licences, as well as periodic tenancies, was not a radical departure. The notion of a 'periodic licence' is a relatively new one, and undefined in either the PEA 1977 or the 1988 HA. In *Norris v Checksfield*[1], however, the Court of Appeal held that it connotes a parallel situation to a periodic tenancy, and that s 5(1A) applies only to licences which are both:

(a) required to be determined by notice; and
(b) can also be properly described as periodic.

1 [1991] 4 All ER 327, CA.

[2.77] The mere fact that rent is paid periodically is of no significance, moreover, unless there is no other event (expressly provided for or implied) that will terminate the licence. The new provisions did not apply in *Norris*, therefore, to a service licence which was expressed to terminate automatically on termination of employment. The provision for periodic licences will not apply to most service licences in any event, as the latter are not 'periodic', being for one period only (the duration of the licensee's employment). By virtue of the HA 1988, s 45, any tenancy which is not periodic is deemed to be a fixed-term tenancy – by analogy, any licence which is not periodic must also be treated as for a fixed-term.

[2.78] The scope of s 5(1A) would appear, therefore, to be limited. It will apply to a service licence only where rent is paid periodically and the licence contains no term providing expressly for automatic determination on cesser of employment[1]. When the 'excluded' licences provided for in s 3A are also taken into account, the residual scope of the minimum notice requirements in relation to licences would appear very limited. Many residential licensees, other than service occupiers, will have a resident landlord sharing accommodation (living accommodation or otherwise), and will consequently be outside its ambit. The provision could apply, however, where a licensee has a periodic licence granted by a resident landlord with whom he does not share accommodation – an unlikely occurrence – or where a licensee is granted exclusive occupation of accommodation, with a non-resident landlord providing attendance and services; eg laundry cleaning and a maid service[2].

1 In *Norris v Checksfield* the licence contained express provision for its automatic termination on cesser of the licensee's employment with the licensor or employer.
2 Cf *Luganda v Service Hotels Ltd* [1969] 2 Ch 209, CA; *Marchant v Charters* [1977] 1 WLR 1181, CA.

CHAPTER 3

Assured tenancies

A Scope of assured tenancy regime

INTRODUCTION

[3.1] One of the central aims of the Housing Act 1988 (HA 1988) was to deregulate the rented housing market and concentrate the provision of rented private sector housing on the assured tenancy and its variants, the assured shorthold and assured agricultural occupancy. To this end, no protection under the Rent Act 1977 (RA 1977) accrues to tenancies or residential licenses granted on or after 15 January 1989, ie the commencement date of the HA 1988. The position of pre-existing tenants with Rent Act protection was in principle unaffected but, consistent with the HA 1988's aim of phasing out the Rent Acts as speedily as possible, transitional provisions were applied whereby the Rent Act protection for pre-existing tenancies can be lost in certain circumstances.

[3.2] Under the original assured tenancy scheme, unless the landlord expressly granted an assured shorthold tenancy, the tenancy was a 'fully' assured tenancy within the HA 1988. In order to grant an assured shorthold the landlord had to give the tenant notice at the time of grant that it was to be a shorthold, and the tenancy agreement had to be in writing for a fixed-term of not less than six months. These formalities did not apply for the creation of a fully assured tenancy. Under the original scheme, therefore, the 'fully' assured tenancy was the principal tenancy model, and landlords had to 'contract in' to an assured shorthold tenancy by serving the appropriate shorthold notice and complying with the other statutory formalities laid down in the HA 1988. In practice assured shortholds proved to be a very attractive medium for landlords letting residential property, as the tenant enjoys no security of tenure once the agreement has ended, and can be removed on the giving of two months notice under the terms of the HA 1988. Where a 'fully' assured tenancy has been granted, on the other hand, the tenant enjoys statutory security of tenure, and the landlord can only repossess the dwelling against his will if he can prove one of a number of statutory grounds for possession against the tenant. These are set out in the HA 1988, Sch 2[1].

1 See Chapter 4, para 4.20 ff below.

[3.3] Assured tenancies did not prove popular with private landlords, and fundamental changes were made by the Housing Act 1996 (HA 1996). These were aimed at further deregulating the market. From the commencement of the HA 1996, Pt 3, which came into force on 28 February 1997, any tenancy that satisfies the qualifying criteria for an assured tenancy will be deemed to be an assured shorthold[1]. This reversed the statutory presumption giving priority to the 'fully' assured tenancy under the original HA 1988 provisions. No shorthold notice need be given, and neither does the tenancy agreement have to be for a fixed-term or written. In the case of any assured tenancy granted on or after 28 February 1997 it can only be a 'fully' assured tenancy if the landlord gives notice on commencement that it is to be an assured tenancy (and not a shorthold), or it satisfies one of a number of other qualifying criteria set out in the HA 1988, Sch 2A[2]. The primary medium for letting private residential property is therefore now the assured shorthold, and not the 'fully' assured tenancy. It should be remembered, however, that although the security of tenure and rent provisions for the two tenancy models are fundamentally different, a tenancy has to satisfy the basic conditions for the grant of an assured tenancy before it can also be an assured shorthold. Additionally, although the parties are free to agree the terms of the tenancy, the HA 1988 regulates certain basic terms of all assured tenancies; eg in relation to assignment and subletting, and access for repairs. These are considered in this chapter. The security of tenure applicable to 'fully' assured tenancies is considered in Chapter 4, and assured shorthold tenancies in Chapter 5.

1 See the HA 1988, s 19A, added by the HA 1996, s 96.
2 These are considered in Chapter 5, para 5.18 ff below.

NO NEW PROTECTED TENANCIES

[3.4] The basic principle, set out in the HA 1988, s 34, is that any tenancy entered into on or after 15 January 1989 *cannot* be a protected tenancy within the RA 1977. Instead it will be either an assured tenancy or an assured shorthold within the HA 1988. However, s 34(1) gives three situations in which Rent Act protection will still apply to new tenancies granted after the commencement of the HA 1988. These are:

(1) Where the tenancy is entered into pursuant to a pre-commencement contract; eg an agreement for a lease, within the *Walsh v Lonsdale*[1] principle, entered into before 15 January 1989.

(2) Where there is a surrender and re-grant to a person who was, immediately before the new tenancy was granted, a protected or statutory Rent Act tenant. For this saving provision to apply, the re-grant must be by the person who was the landlord (or one of the joint landlords) under the protected or statutory tenancy immediately before the new tenancy was granted. The new tenancy will also retain its Rent Act status if the re-grant is to the original protected (or statutory) tenant jointly with others. The aim, clearly, is to prevent landlords depriving tenants of their protected status after commencement by forcing fresh tenancy agreements upon them. It should be noted that the preservation of Rent Act protection is not limited to the same or substantially the same premises. All that is required is that the identity of landlord and tenant are the same as under the original tenancy.
This was a deliberate policy applied by the HA 1988, to obviate concerns[2] that landlords may otherwise exploit the provision; eg by moving existing tenants from one property to another after the HA 1988's commencement[3]. The saving provision applies to preserve protected Rent Act status both for new tenancies of the same premises and for tenancies of other premises granted by the same landlord after the commencement of the HA 1988[4]. Applying this principle, the Court of Appeal in *Arogol Co Ltd v Rajah*[5] held that Rent Act protection contin-

ued to apply where a tenant with a pre-commencement tenancy of a single room subsequently took an enlarged tenancy of the whole floor. Since Rent Act protection is not limited to the same or substantially the same premises, but by virtue of s 34 extends to a tenancy granted by a person who was then a landlord to a person who immediately before the grant had been a protected tenant, the tenant's move to the entire ground floor of the flat in question did not constitute a surrender of the tenancy of the back room previously occupied and the creation of an assured tenancy of the entire floor. In this case the 'landlord' granting the fresh tenancy was the tenant's mother, who was the landlord within s 34 by succession[6]. In other cases, where the landlord's identity has changed prior to the new tenancy being granted, the tenant will come within s 34 (and retain Rent Act protection) if the landlord at the time of re-grant derives his title under the original landlord; eg if the re-grant is by a mesne tenant[7].

(3) Protected tenancy status is also preserved if the court, in possession proceedings brought by the landlord, directs that the protected tenant be granted a tenancy of suitable alternative accommodation and directs that the latter should be a protected tenancy[8]. This provision requires the court to have considered whether the grant of an assured tenancy will give the tenant the required security of tenure in the alternative accommodation offered. Only if, on the facts, it would not, can the court direct that the new tenancy of alternative accommodation be a Rent Act protected tenancy. So, in *Al Shakarchi v Laimond Properties Ltd*[9], where it was conceded that the assured tenancy of alternative accommodation offered by the landlord *would* give the tenant sufficient security, the court ruled that there was no obligation on it to make a direction under s 34(1)(c). Consequently, the new tenancy could be an assured tenancy. The court here ruled, further, that the saving provision for surrender and regrant in s 34(1)(b) (above) does not apply where the landlord goes to court and obtains a possession order, even if the identity of landlord and tenant under the proposed assured tenancy are the same as under the old tenancy.

1 (1882) 21 Ch D 9, CA.
2 See HC Deb, Standing Committee G, 2 February 1988, col 602.
3 At third reading in the House of Commons, HC Deb, 13 June 1988, vol 134, col 87.
4 See *Al Shakarchi v Laimond Properties Ltd* [1998] L&TR 90 CA, approving the earlier first instance decision in *Goringe v Twinsectra Ltd* (1994) (Staines County Court, unreported. See *Legal Action*, June 1994, p 11.
5 [2001] CA 21 March 2001.
6 For succession rights see below para 3.138 ff.
7 See HA 1988, s 45(1) (definition of 'landlord').
8 See RA 1977, Sch 16, Case 1 and Sch 15, Pt IV; and R(A)A 1976, Sch 4, Case 1.
9 (1998) L&TR 90, CA. And see *Arogol Co Ltd v Rajah* [2001] EWCA Civ 454, [2001] 5 C.L. 548 (CA).

[3.5] There was initially a question whether s 34(1) is permissive or mandatory, ie whether a tenancy falling within (1)–(3) above *must* of necessity be Rent Act protected or whether it *can* be so protected (but not necessarily). The uncertainty derived from the ambiguous wording of s 34(1) – 'a tenancy which is entered into on or after the commencement of [the HA 1988] *cannot* be a protected tenancy, unless ...' [author's italics]. The better view is that the section is mandatory – a tenancy granted in circumstances falling within (1)–(3) above *will* be protected, whether the agreement is expressed to be such or not. This was the original intent of the provision, and has now been judicially confirmed as the correct interpretation of s 34(1)[1].

1 *Al Shakarchi v Laimond Properties Ltd* (1998) L&TR 90 CA, per Roch LJ. See also Parl Debs (HC), vol 135, col 75, 87 and *Kotecha v Rimington* (1991) (Leicester County Court, unreported. See *Legal Action*, March 1991, p 15).

RENEWAL OF PROTECTED SHORTHOLDS

[3.6] By virtue of s 34(2), the saving provisions do not apply to a protected shorthold tenancy renewed (in whatever form) after commencement of HA 1988. If a protected shorthold tenancy had not expired at commencement, any renewal thereafter will not be a protected tenancy. If the fixed-term *had* expired, but the tenant has remained in possession as a statutory tenant without a further shorthold being granted, or if a further shorthold was granted before commencement to the same tenant, then likewise any renewal thereafter will not be a protected tenancy. For the avoidance of doubt, 'protected shorthold tenancies' for this purpose include any tenancy treated as such in possession proceedings under Case 19 of the RA 1977, namely any shorthold after the expiry of which there has been no further grant of a tenancy of the same property *except* to the (former) protected shortholder. This will apply, for instance, even if a fixed-term has continued as a statutory tenancy in the absence of notice of non-renewal[1]. It should also be appreciated that there is no requirement that the tenant vacate the premises on surrender and re-grant of a shorthold, provided the conduct and intention of the parties is clear. If it is, Case 19 will apply to the shorthold even if the prior (surrendered) tenancy was itself protected[2]. If a shorthold or protected tenancy to which Case 19 applies is renewed after commencement, the new tenancy will *not* be a protected shorthold. By virtue of s 34(3), it is deemed to be an assured shorthold tenancy.

1 See *Gent v de la Mare* [1988] 1 EGLR 104, CA.
2 See *Dibbs v Campbell* [1988] 30 EG 49, CA.

RESTRICTED CONTRACTS

[3.7] Special rules apply to restricted contracts formerly protected under the RA 1977. This category included any contract (whether tenancy or license) 'whereby one person grants to another person, in consideration of a rent which includes payment for the use of furniture or services, the right to occupy a dwelling as a residence'[1]. It therefore encompassed licenses of furnished accommodation, provided that the licensee enjoyed exclusive occupation of at least part of the premises[2], and licenses where the rent included payments for board, attendance or services. In addition, cases where (a) there was a resident landlord[3]; and (b) the tenant (albeit having exclusive occupation of some accommodation) had the right to share other accommodation in common with the landlord or others[4], were expressly brought within the restricted contract category. All restricted contracts created prior to commencement of the HA 1988 are subject to rent tribunal jurisdiction to determine a 'reasonable' rent, the tribunal having power also to suspend the operation of a possession order for up to three months (in the case of a post-Housing Act 1980 (HA 1980) license or tenancy) or longer if the contract was entered into prior to 29 November 1980[5].

1 RA 1977, s 19(2).
2 See ibid, s 19(6), implying the latter.
3 Ibid, s 20.

4 Ibid, s 21.
5 See RA 1977, ss 103–106 and HA 1980, s 69. Restricted contracts are considered further at paras 6.46 and 6.47 below.

[3.8] By virtue of the HA 1988, s 36(1), any license or tenancy granted *after* commencement of the HA 1988 cannot be a restricted contract unless entered into pursuant to a pre-commencement contract. Licenses of furnished accommodation will therefore in future be unprotected, save under the Protection from Eviction Act 1977 (PEA 1977). Tenancies excluded from assured tenancy status because of the resident landlord condition[1] will likewise enjoy no protection, and in this instance even the minimum requirement of four weeks' notice to quit and a court order[2] will not apply if the tenant shares accommodation with the (resident) landlord[3]. In future the most important question will, in most cases, simply be whether the tenant has a tenancy (which may then qualify as an assured tenancy) or a license (in which case he will enjoy no security or rent control).

1 See HA 1988, Sch 1, para 10.
2 PEA 1977, ss 3 and 5.
3 See HA 1988, s 31 and para 2.64 ff above.

[3.9] Even where a restricted contract was entered into *prior* to commencement of the HA 1988, it will cease to enjoy Rent Act protection in either of two situations:

(1) If the terms of the contract are varied after commencement in a way which affects the amount of the *rent* payable (s 36(2)(a)). In this case, the contract is deemed to be a new contract, and by virtue of s 36(1), restricted contract status will be lost. This will occur, however, only where the variation is voluntary – the contract is *not* deemed to have been renewed where the rent is varied by the rent tribunal, or the parties have varied the rent by agreement to bring it to the level registered for the dwelling[1]. Curiously, this militates against settlement by agreement without the involvement of the tribunal. The ease with which restricted contract protection can be lost under these provisions is illustrated by *Rowe v Matthews*[3], where a consensual variation in rent under a restricted contract in 1990 was held to come within s 36 – with the effect that the tenant was regarded as having entered into a new tenancy, and any protection afforded under the former restricted contract was removed.
(2) Where there is an agreed variation of any of the terms other than the rent payable then the sole question is whether the variation is such as to give rise to a new contract – in which case restricted contract status will no longer accrue[2].

1 See s 36(3), ibid.
2 Ibid, s 36(2)(b).
3 (2001) WL 272896.

HOUSING ASSOCIATION TENANCIES

[3.10] The RA 1977, Pt VI, applied the fair rent system to housing association tenancies, namely tenancies where the interest of the landlord belongs to a housing association, housing trust or housing corporation and the tenancy would be a protected tenancy but for that fact[1]. Such tenancies were also 'secure' tenancies within the Housing Act 1985 (HA 1985), for the purpose of security of tenure[2].

1 RA 1977, s 86(1) and (2).
2 See HA 1985, s 80(1).

[3.11] Any tenancy granted by a housing association after commencement of the HA 1988 cannot be a 'housing association tenancy' within the RA 1977, Pt VI[1]. Nor will it be a secure tenancy[2]. All housing association tenancies granted on or after 15 January 1989 will be on the assured tenancy basis (providing they qualify as such) with freedom from rent control (although market rents will not, in many cases, in practice be appropriate). Saving provisions identical to those for protected tenancies (para 3.4 above) preserve housing association tenancy status where there is a pre-commencement contract, where there is a re-grant (of the same or alternative accommodation) by the same landlord, or where the court gives possession using the suitable alternative accommodation grounds[3]. Special exception is made for secure tenancies granted to former owner-occupiers by an association pursuant to the HA 1985, Pt XVI (assistance for owners of defective housing)[4].

1 HA 1988, s 35(2).
2 Ibid, s 35(4).
3 See ibid, s 34(4).
4 Ibid, s 35(4) and Sch 17.

B Qualifying for protection

[3.12] For a tenancy to be 'assured' within the HA 1988, there must be a letting whereby 'a dwelling house is let as a separate dwelling'. This requirement is also a fundamental pre-requisite for the creation of a protected tenancy under the RA 1977[1]. Under both codes of protective legislation, the residential occupancy only acquires protected status if there is:

(a) a tenancy and not eg a license to occupy; and
(b) the letting is of a 'dwelling house' which has been let as a *separate* dwelling.

Each element of the statutory formulas been exhaustively considered by the courts, chiefly in cases decided under the RA 1977 and its predecessors. There are differences in the detailed rights and duties imposed on residential landlords and tenants under the two codes of statutory protection, which have very different policy objectives. Nevertheless, the core definitions for the protected status of the occupancy are the same. Although many of the cases were decided under the Rent Act, these will be considered here as the assured tenancy is now the primary tenancy structure for the creation of residential tenancies following the deregulation of the private rented housing market by the HA 1988.

1 RA 1977, s 1. For detailed analysis of the case law under previous rent legislation see *Megarry's Rent Acts* (10th edn, 1964) Chapter 3, pp 49–92 and (11th edn, 1988) pp 81–117.

ASSURED TENANCIES: DEFINITION

[3.13] Under the terms of the HA 1988, a tenancy must not only be of a dwelling house let as a separate dwelling; it will, furthermore, be an assured tenancy assured only if *and so long as* the following conditions are satisfied (s 1(1)):

(1) The tenant, or in the case of a joint tenancy each of the tenants, is an individual.
(2) The tenant, or at least one out of joint tenants, must occupy the dwelling as his principal home.

[3.14] A tenancy that meets these requirements will not be 'assured' if it is one of a number of exempt classes of agreement listed in the HA 1988, Sch 1 (see below). 'Old style' assured tenancies granted under the HA 1980 are converted by s 1(3) into 'new-style' assured tenancies to which the HA 1988 applies.

[3.15] The following elements of the statutory definition, which are largely derived from Rent Act jurisprudence, should be noted.

LET 'AS A SEPARATE DWELLING'

'Separate' dwelling

[3.16] The formula 'let as a separate dwelling' is adopted from the RA 1977 and has consistently been given a singular construction by the courts. Protection will accrue only if the letting is of a single unit of habitation, which at the time of letting is intended for occupation as a single residence (although not necessarily by the lessee himself); *Horford Investments Ltd v Lambert*[1], *St Catherine's College v Dorling*[2]. The fact that the lessee immediately sublets part of the premises is thus not relevant to the question of whether the dwelling is let as 'a' separate dwelling[3].

1 [1976] Ch 39, CA.
2 [1980] 1 WLR 66, CA.
3 *Regalian Securities Ltd v Ramsden* [1981] 1 WLR 611, HL; *Whitty v Scott-Russell* [1950] 1 All ER 884, CA.

[3.17] The purpose of the letting for these purposes is to be ascertained from the lease itself in the first instance, but if the latter gives no indication then the actual circumstances of the letting can be considered to ascertain the intention of the parties and, as a last resort, the court can consider the actual user at the material time (the rule in *Wolfe v Hogan*[1]). The material time for the purposes of the HA 1988, at which point the test must be satisfied, is the time of letting – a factor which can lead to entirely arbitrary results. If the letting is of one unit of habitation which is immediately converted for multiple occupation, the head lease will be assured, but if the property has already been converted to multiple units of habitation and let as such, it will not: *Horford Investments Ltd v Lambert*[2].

1 [1949] 2 KB 194 at 206, CA per Denning LJ.
2 [1976] Ch 39, especially at 48, for criticism by Russell LJ.

[3.18] Moreover, the motives and social objectives of the tenant are irrelevant. While the singular construction prevents the entrepreneur seeking protection of his head lease where he has sublet to multiple occupants, so as to enhance his profit (as in *Horford Investments Ltd*), it will also deprive the head lessee of protection where he simply wishes to pass on the benefit of rent control to subtenants (see *St Catherine's College v Dorling*). Similarly, the lease will not be assured if the premises are let by separate leases and the normal attributes of daily living (cooking, eating, sleeping etc) are distributed so that no one lease can be said to be of, in itself, a separate 'dwelling' – unless on the facts those lettings can be treated as one[1].

1 *Wimbush v Cibulia, Wimbush v Levinski* [1949] 2 All ER 432, CA.

[3.19] The arbitrary results which the singular construction of this basic definition gives rise to sit uneasily with the legislative policy of the Rent Act and presumably also (now) of the HA 1988 as judicially interpreted, namely 'to interfere with contract and property rights for a special purpose – the redress of the balance of advantage enjoyed in the world of housing shortage by the landlord over those who have to rent their houses' (see *Horford Investments Ltd*)[1].

1 [1976] Ch 39 at 52, per Scarman LJ. See also *Skinner v Geary* [1931] 2 KB at 560.

'Dwelling'

[3.20] The question of whether property is demised as a 'separate dwelling' involves two separate issues; it must be demised for use as a residence, in the required sense, and the physical attributes of the property must be considered to decide whether it comprises one, or several separate, units of habitation.

Attributes of habitation

[3.21] To be protected the premises must be let with the intent that the tenant should carry on there 'all the major activities of life, particularly sleeping, cooking and feeding'[1]. The tenancy will not be within the HA 1988 unless it was the tenant's 'home'. If so, it will be his 'dwelling'. Thus in *Curl v Angelo*[2] the lease of several rooms used as an annex to the tenant's hotel, and in which hotel guests slept, was not protected, because mere sleeping on the premises was not enough. It must be envisaged, in other words, that the premises should constitute the tenant's 'home' in the fullest sense of the term. In *Uratemp Ventures Ltd v Collins*[3] an assured tenancy arose where a hotel room was rented on terms that did not contemplate the introduction of cooking equipment by the occupier, and where no cooking facilities were provided by the landlord. The tenants brought their own cooking equipment into the room. The House of Lords held that the provision of cooking facilities was not an essential feature of a 'dwellinghouse' and that a tenancy would be of a 'dwelling' if it was where the tenant dwelt, lived or resided, ie it is the tenants' 'home'. The fact that the landlord did not provide cooking facilities did not alter the character of the premises as the tenants' 'home', and thus as a dwelling within the protection of HA 1988. It should be noted, however, that the tenancy agreement considered by the House of Lords did not expressly prohibit cooking by tenants in the rooms let – *query* it may be difficult to interpret the facts as giving rise to an assured tenancy where the tenant subsequently does so unlawfully in breach of the tenancy[4].

1 Wright v Howell (1947) 92 Sol Jo 26, CA.
2 [1948] 2 All ER 189, CA.
3 [2002] 1 All ER 46, HL, reversing [2001] 1 EGLR 156, CA.
4 In *Uratemp Ventures Ltd v Collins* (above n 3) one of the cases was remitted for rehearing at first instance by the court of appeal, as there was evidence that the landlord had expressly permitted the introduction of cooking equipment by the occupier of one of the hotel rooms in dispute (see [2000] 1 EGLR 156, CA).

Physical attributes

[3.22] Although the letting must be of a single unit of habitation, it is clearly established that this can comprise more than one building or dwelling[1]. Whether two adjacent properties can be treated as one dwelling is a question of fact and degree; they must, taken together, constitute a composite home (although not necessarily for the lessee himself)[2]. So, in *Metropolitan Properties Co (FGC) Ltd v Barder*[3] where the tenant took a lease of a single servant's bedroom across the corridor from his flat, both of which were let by the same landlord, the tenancy of the bedroom was unprotected. It was not let to the tenant as part of his existing accommodation, but rather the two premises were held under different contracts, made at different dates for different terms. The duration of the respective lettings will, it seems, be of considerable importance – in *Metropolitan Properties Ltd*, to hold the two premises to have been one dwelling would have meant that the quarterly tenancy of the bedroom could not be terminated until the term date of the 14-year lease of the flat. Note however that if both lettings are weekly tenancies there is no difficulty arising from the different methods or times for determining them[4]. If the facts indicate that two properties let by different agreements are intended as one residence, it is immaterial if the buildings are not adjacent (as in *Langford Property Co Ltd v Goldrich* where two self-contained flats, not adjacent, let by one tenancy for use as a composite home were held to be a 'separate dwelling').

1 *Langford Property Co Ltd v Goldrich* [1949] 1 KB 511; and see *Regalian Securities Ltd v Ramsden* [1981] 1 WLR 611, HL.
2 *Hampstead Way Investments Ltd v Lewis-Weare* [1985] 1 WLR 164 at 171, HL.
3 [1968] 1 All ER 536, CA.
4 See *Wimbush v Cibulia* [1949] 2 All ER 432, CA.

[3.23] It *is* essential, however, that the parties intend at the time of letting that the two properties be occupied as one residence, and if this is not physically possible at the time of grant, or reasonably soon thereafter, they cannot be treated as a single dwelling for the purposes of the HA 1988. Thus, in *Grosvenor (Mayfair) Estates v Amberton*[1], no protection accrued where two flats were let by one demise, but one was occupied by licensees whose early removal was not contemplated by the lease; it was merely a letting of two separate self-contained flats subject to the future possibility that they may be used as one at some unspecified future date. See also *Kavanagh v Lyroudias*[2] (no protection where two adjoining flats were let on separate leases, and the tenants slept in one flat and cooked in the other)[3].

1 (1982) 265 Estates Gazette 693.
2 [1985] 1 All ER 560, CA.
3 For criticism see P F Smith (1985) 48 Conv 228.

[3.24] It should be noted that 'dwellings' to which protection can accrue are not limited to buildings per se. There must, however, be a sufficient annexation of a structure to the land, so that it becomes part of the land itself, if it is to constitute a 'dwelling' for these purposes[1]. So in *R v Rent Officer of Nottinghamshire Registration Area, ex p Allen*[2] it was held that a mobile caravan could be a 'house' for the purposes of the Rent Act if it is rendered wholly immobile and ceases to be a moveable chattel; eg by having its wheels removed or being blocked in situ by a brick or concrete construction[3]. On the other hand, a houseboat that is moored will not be a 'dwelling', as the purpose of mooring it is to prevent it being carried away, and there is insufficient annexation if it can be easily moved. No assured tenancy arose, therefore, where a houseboat moored upstream of Battersea Bridge on the Thames was let for residential occupation[4]. Where a dwelling is let with land it will be protected, unless it is agricultural land exceeding two acres in extent (in which event the whole property demised can be protected only under the agricultural holding legislation)[5].

1 *Elitestone Ltd v Morris* [1997] 2 EGLR 115.
2 [1985] 2 EGLR 153.
3 See *Nutt v Read* [2000] 32 HLR 761.
4 *Chelsea Yacht and Boat Co Ltd v Pope* [2000] 2 EGLR 23.
5 HA 1988, Sch 2, para 6. See further para 3.81 and 3.82, below.

LET: REQUIREMENT OF TENANCY

Lease or licence?

[3.25] For an assured tenancy to arise, s 1(1) requires 'a *tenancy* under which a dwelling house is *let* as a separate dwelling'. The conferment of a mere licence to occupy residential property will not, therefore, attract the protection of the HA 1988, and neither will the more limited protection afforded by the Rent Act to restricted contracts in appropriate circumstances apply to licences granted after commencement. Despite the fact that the Law Commission has, on several occasions, advocated reform of protective legislation to remove the uncertainties inherent in the lease or licence distinction and to eradicate abuse[1], the licence will remain an effective device to avoid the protection of the assured tenancy code. Similarly, other arrangements such as deferred and rental purchase remain problematic[2].

1 Landlord and Tenant: Reform of the Law (Cm 162, 1987) paras 4.4–4.11.
2 On rental purchase schemes see below para 3.35.

[3.26] Although the view was expressed during the passage of the HA 1988 that such arrangements have no legitimate role to play in the rented housing market, the government resisted attempts to amend the Bill to abolish licences on the ground that one of the HA 1988's chief aims was to make such devices unnecessary by introducing more flexible forms of tenure, eg assured shortholds[1].

1 HC Deb, Standing Committee G, 4 February 1988, col 651 ff.

[3.27] The effectiveness of the licence to avoid protective legislation was considerably reduced by the House of Lords ruling in *Street v Mountford*[1]. The decision in *Street v Mountford* has generated a not inconsiderable volume of case law and learning, full consideration of which is beyond the scope of the present work[2]. It was there held that, despite the fact that an agreement is expressed as a licence, where 'residential occupation is offered and accepted with exclusive possession for a term at a rent, the result is a tenancy'[3]. Although the requirement of a monetary rent is not strictly necessary for a finding of tenancy[4], the necessity of a minimum rent of two-thirds of the dwelling's rateable value for assured tenancy status means that this additional trap for landlords is of no consequence in the present context.

1 [1985] AC 809.
2 The following, however, might be of assistance: J T Farrand, *Emmet on Title* (19th edn) 26.008–26.011; Anderson (1985) 48 MLR 712; Tromans (1985) CL 351; Clarke (1986) Conv 39; (1985) 101 LQR 467 (JMT). On the wider implications of Street, and non-exclusive possession agreements, see, inter alia, Street (1985) Conv 328; Clark (1986) Conv 39; Bridge (1986) Conv 344.
3 [1985] AC 809 at 826, per Lord Templeman.
4 See *Ashburn Anstalt v Arnold* [1989] Ch 1, CA.

Exceptional categories

[3.28] Where the agreement displays an intention to confer exclusive possession, a finding of tenancy will be avoided only in limited circumstances. In *Street v Mountford* it was recognised that there were exceptional cases where the grant of exclusive possession would not amount to the grant of a tenancy. The cases were categorised by Lord Templeman under the following headings, although it is recognised that these are only illustrative, and not exhaustive of the situations in which a finding of tenancy may be avoided[1].

1 See *Dellneed Ltd v Chin* [1987] 1 EGLR 75.

No intention to create legal relations

[3.29] The two hallmarks of a tenancy are an intention to create legal relations, coupled with the grant of exclusive possession. If there is no intention to create legal relations, a tenancy cannot arise, whether or not exclusive possession has been granted to the occupier. The commonest situations in which no intention to create legal relations will be present are where there is a familial relationship between the parties (see *Errington v Errington and Woods*[1]) or where the grant is 'an act of friendship or generosity' (the rule in *Facchini v Bryson*[2]). If the occupancy falls within one of these exceptional cases, regular payments for accommodation will not automatically create a tenancy rather than a license if there is no intention to create legal relations, although the absence of payment may be conclusive proof that a license rather than a tenancy has been granted.

1 [1952] 1 KB 290, CA. See also *Ward v Warnke* (1990) 22 HLR 496.
2 [1952] 1 TLR 1386 at 1388, per Denning LJ.

[3.30] The presence of a familial relationship between the landlord and occupier will not, in itself, be conclusive that there is no intention to create legal relations[1]. However, where the occupancy is rent-free, this will usually be taken by the courts as indicative of a lack of intent to create legal relations, and that a license and not a tenancy has been created. For example, in *Cobb v Lane*[2] a brother who occupied a house that his sister had purchased rent-free was held to be a licensee, and not a tenant at will. This decision was approved by Lord Templeman in *Street v Mountford*, as was that in *Errington v Errington*[3], where a son who contracted to buy his father's house in consideration of payment by him of his father's mortgage instalments, and who subsequently occupied the accommodation for his own exclusive use, was held to be a licensee. Although there was exclusive possession, there was no intention to create a tenancy. Following *Street v Mountford* it is the absence of a clear intention to create legal relations that rebuts the presumption of a tenancy and can sustain this decision.

1 *Ward v Warnke* (1990) 22 HLR 496.
2 [1952] 1 All ER 1199, CA.
3 [1952] 1 KB 290, CA.

[3.31] The second exception is where, prior to *Street v Mountford*, the courts had found that the landlord was motivated by 'friendship or generosity' when granting accommodation[1], and this had been found to negative the intention to create a tenancy because of a lack of intention to create legal relations. The cases are anomalous and difficult, but were approved in *Street v Mountford*. A classic example is provided by the decision in *Marcroft Wagons Ltd v Smith*[2] where the daughter of a deceased tenant was permitted to stay on at a preferential rent by the landlord for six months following her father's death. The landlord was 'acting in response to the ordinary decencies of human life'[3] and she was held to be a licensee rather than a tenant. Each case will depend on its facts. No intention to create legal relations was found in the more recent case of *Sharp v MacArthur*[4] where the landlord, as a favour, let the defendant into occupation of a property that was for sale, giving him a rent book as proof of his outgoings to be shown to the DHSS. Similarly in *Heslop v Burns*[5] friends of the owner who occupied a house rent-free were held to be licensees, and not tenants at will. The court found that the relationship between the parties was akin to a family arrangement (although they were not in fact related) and that the landlord had acted with extreme generosity, having formed a romantic attachment to one of the occupiers[6].

1 *Facchini v Bryson* [1952] 1 TLR 1486 per Denning LJ at 1389–90.
2 [1951]2 KB 496, CA.
3 [1951] 2 KB 496 at 502.
4 (1986) 19 HLR 364, CA.
5 [1974] 1 WLR 1241.
6 [1974] 1 WLR 1241 at 1244, 1252.

Exclusive possession referable to a legal relationship other than landlord and tenant

[3.32] 'Sometimes it may appear from the surrounding circumstances that the right to exclusive possession is referable to a legal relationship other than a tenancy. Legal relationships to which the grant of exclusive possession might be referable and which would or might negative the grant of an estate or interest in the land include occupancy under a contract for the sale of the land, occupancy pursuant to a contract of employment or occupancy referable to the holding of an office'[1].

1 *Street v Mountford* [1985] AC 809 at 826/827 per Lord Templeman.

[3.33] Where there is both exclusive possession and an intention to create legal relations, then only if there is another legal relationship will the presumption of a tenancy be rebutted. A classic example is the relationship between a vendor and a purchaser of land, although here it should be noted that a tenancy may still arise if exclusive possession is conferred before a binding contract of sale has been concluded[1].

1 See *Bretherton v Paton* (1986) 278 Estates Gazette 615, CA.

[3.34] Service occupiers whose occupation of accommodation is necessary for the performance of their employment will be licensees as their occupation (even if exclusive) will be deemed to be ancillary to performance of the contract of employment. On the other hand, if the accommodation occupied by an employee is owned by the employer, but its occupation is not strictly necessary for the performance of the contract of employment, then a tenancy will have been created[1].

1 *Royal Philanthropic Society v County* [1985] 2 EGLR 109, CA.

[3.35] In *Street v Mountford* Lord Templeman gave as a further example the case of a purchaser let into possession of accommodation pursuant to a contract for sale of the premises; occupation here will be referable to the relationship of vendor and purchaser, and the latter will not normally be a tenant. Occupation under a license with an option to purchase a lease will not create a tenancy as the occupation is referable to the equitable interest in the land[1]. However, in *Bretherton v Paton*[2] an oral agreement to allow an intending purchaser into occupation in order to carry out repairs, upon payment of the rates and insurance, on terms that the sale was to be completed on completion of the repairs, was held to have created a tenancy when the parties subsequently failed to agree a sale price. Another problem category is the 'rental purchase' agreement, ie where there is an agreement that the landlord will sell the property to the occupier for a sale price payable by instalments, completion being deferred until the full price has been paid. Rental purchase schemes have been used to avoid the effect of Rent Act protection, although their use has historically been limited to certain geographical areas[3]. In a genuine rental purchase agreement the occupier is not a tenant. However, if the parties never intended the contract for sale to be completed, the arrangement will be a sham, and the courts will be ready to find a tenancy has been created[4].

1 *Essex Plan Ltd v Broadminster* (1988) 56 P&CR 353.
2 [1986] 1 EGLR 172.
3 On rental purchase see, inter alia, B M Hoggett 'Houses on the Never-Never' (1972) Conv 325 and (1975) Conv 343. Also the Francis Report on the Rent Acts (Cmnd 4609, 1971) p 112.
4 See *Martin v Davies* [1972] 7 HLR 119.

Special categories

[3.36] Lord Templeman's list of 'exceptional' categories of letting is not in theory closed. Nevertheless, the courts have been reluctant to recognise additional special cases, in addition to those expressly recognised in *Street v Mountford* itself (above), in which a license can still be created despite a grant of exclusive possession. Several problematic situations have raised this question in the case law since 1985 – in particular lettings of hostel accommodation on short-term licenses, short-term lettings to the potentially homeless, and lettings of short-term accommodation scheduled for redevelopment in the near future.

Hostel accommodation

[3.37] The final exception specifically referred to by Lord Templeman, as providing a relationship that would negative the presumption of a tenancy even though exclusive possession had been granted, is where the occupier is the object of the landlord's charity[1]. This exception would seem to cover sheltered or supported housing schemes providing temporary accommodation to vulnerable groups, who would therefore occupy as licensees rather than assured or protected tenants. The cases are, however, difficult, and in *Westminster CC v Clark*[2] an occupier in this category (in that case an occupier of sheltered housing in a hostel for the homeless) was categorised as a licensee not on this basis, but on the more general ground that the landlord genuinely required to exercise control of the day to day management of occupancies in the building, including (if necessary) moving occupants from one room to another, as part of their responsibilities given the special needs and vulnerability of their clients. The occupants could not on the facts, therefore, assert exclusive possession of their individual bed sitting rooms. Neither was a term allowing the landlord to require occupants to move from one room to another a 'sham', as it was genuinely required given the special nature of the needs of the occupants and their proper management and care. The level of supervisory control retained by the landlord meant that no exclusive possession was granted to individual occupants, who therefore occupied as licensees not tenants.

1 *Street v Mountford* [1985] AC 809 at 818 per Lord Templeman.
2 [1992] 2 AC 288 HL.

Short-term lettings to the homeless

[3.38] A grant of exclusive possession may create a license outside the landlord–tenant relationship where the landlord is exercising statutory housing obligations; eg in the case of a local authority to make temporary accommodation available to the homeless pending an enquiry as to the housing status of the family for the purposes of the Housing Act 1996 (HA 1996), Pt VII (homelessness). In *Ogwr BC v Dykes*[1] the Court of Appeal held that, although granted exclusive possession while alternative accommodation was sought following a repossession, an occupier given council accommodation for 13 weeks was a licensee. Similarly, in *Mohamed v Manek*[2] the Court of Appeal held that a homeless man given the exclusive use of a room in a private bed and breakfast establishment, with shared access to a kitchen, was a licensee not a tenant. The court here ruled that accommodation made available for a very short period while homelessness enquiries are made cannot be construed as being let as a dwelling house under a full tenancy.

1 [1989] 1 WLR 295.
2 (1995) 27 HLR 439 CA. See also *West Wiltshire DC v Snelgrove* (1998) 30 HLR 57.

[3.39] The decision in *Ogwr BC v Dykes* is perhaps tenable on the basis that the letting was for a very short period, and thus the premises not let as a dwelling. Unfortunately, the Court of Appeal also relied upon a somewhat wider rationale, namely that the agreement could not be a tenancy because the landlord was exercising a statutory housing function under the HA 1985. On the other hand, in *Eastleigh BC v Walsh*[1] a family occupying temporary council accommodation pending a decision on their homelessness status were held to be tenants, not licensees. The occupancy agreement here expressly purported to create a tenancy, and was found by the House of Lords to be unambiguous, with the result that, as exclusive possession had also been granted, a tenancy and not a license had been created. In the public sector, the tenancy or license distinction is not normally decisive, as temporary lettings to the homeless under the HA 1996 cannot become 'secure' tenancies until the housing authority have notified the tenant that the tenancy is to be regarded as secure[2]. In *Eastleigh*, had the landlord served notice to quit terminating the tenancy at common law, the tenant would have had no defence to possession proceedings, as security of tenure would have been excluded by the relevant provisions of the HA 1985.

1 [1985] AC 809, HL.
2 HA 1985, Sch 1, para 4. See further Chapter 9, para 9.28 below.

[3.40] The decisions are unsatisfactory, and sit uneasily with the principles established in *Street v Mountford*, namely that the only intention relevant to construing the agreement is the intention to confer exclusive possession. The parties further intention as to the legal relationship which the agreement purports to create (tenancy or license) cannot in law be determinative of its legal status. The Court of Appeal refused to follow the wider rationale of *Ogwr BC v Dykes* in a later decision – *Family Housing Association v Jones*[1] – preferring to hold that a tenancy had been created where exclusive possession had been granted under a purported 'license' agreement to a temporarily homeless family. The two cases were distinguishable on their facts, but as *Family Housing Association v Jones* has subsequently been approved (on other grounds) in the House of Lords[2], the wider rationale of the decision in *Ogwr BC* must, it is suggested, be regarded as unsound.

1 [1990] 1 All ER 385.
2 In *Bruton v London Housing Trust* [1999] 3 All ER 481, see below.

Lettings of short-life accommodation

[3.41] Local authorities commonly 'license' property that has been acquired for redevelopment to registered social landlords so that it can be used for their charitable housing purposes pending redevelopment. This is an efficient use of housing resources, but is dependant upon the local authority being able to obtain vacant possession at short notice if demolition and redevelopment work is scheduled. Accordingly, the terms of the license will normally prohibit the letting of accommodation on assured tenancies by the head licensor. In *Family Housing Association v Jones*[1] local authority housing was licensed to the Family Housing Association for the temporary accommodation of homeless persons. It subsequently let a self-contained flat to Mrs Jones under a license agreement that stated that no exclusive possession was being granted and that the landlord retained a key. The Court of Appeal construed the 'license' here as a tenancy, on the basis that she was the only intended occupant of the flat, and that exclusive possession had in fact been granted. In *Bruton v London Housing Trust*[2] the House of Lords upheld this decision in a case involving the licensing of short-life accommodation at Oval House, SW2 by Lambeth Council to the London Housing Trust for its use (pending redevelopment by the Council) to provide short-term housing for homeless families. The Trust subsequently entered into an occupancy agreement with the claimant that was expressed to be a weekly 'license' on a temporary basis. On the facts, it was held that the agreement conferred exclusive possession and, this being the case, the characteristics identified for the creation of a tenancy in *Street v Mountford* existed. The agreement created a tenancy between the Trust and Bruton. The House of Lords refused to recognise a further exception to the principle in *Street v Mountford*, based upon either the identity of the landlord or the special circumstances, namely that the Trust was performing a socially valuable service. It follows that if an agreement is to constitute a license, and not a tenancy, the landlord must retain sufficient managerial control of the premises to negative any implication that exclusive possession has been granted. This was the case in *Westminster CC v Clarke* (above), where the landlord retained the right to move occupants from one part of the premises to another if operational needs so required. But in *Family Housing Association v Jones* it was held that the landlord merely retaining a key to the premises was insufficient if the context indicated that unrestricted access was not contemplated. Similarly, in *Bruton* a term reserving to the landlords a restricted right of entry at certain times and for certain purposes was held to be indicative of a grant of exclusive possession, cf the reservation of an *unrestricted* right of access for the provision of services might indicate otherwise.

1 [1990] 1 All ER 385.
2 [1999] 3 All ER 481, HL.

[3.42] The decision in *Bruton v London Housing Trust* is determinative only of the occupants status as a tenant vis a vis his immediate landlord, ie the intermediate licensor. The House of Lords expressed no view on the Council's right to repossess the property or on whether a secure tenancy had been created[1]. As between the intermediate licensor (the Housing Trust) and the occupant the tenancy would be an assured tenancy within the HA 1988. A subtenant who is let residential accommodation on an assured tenancy enjoys protection against the head landlord under the HA 1988, s 18, but only if the subtenancy was lawfully granted and the intermediate landlord is himself a *tenant* under a superior tenancy. If the terms on which short-life property is licensed to a social landlord prohibit subletting on assured or secure tenancies the fact that any agreement subsequently entered into creates a tenancy between the intermediate licensee and occupant (as in *Bruton*) will not necessarily confer protection on the latter vis a vis the head landlord.

1 See per Lord Hoffman at [1999] 3 All ER 481,489.

'SHAMS', CONTRACTING OUT AND CONSTRUCTION OF THE AGREEMENT

[3.43] The decision in *Street v Mountford* makes it more difficult to avoid protective legislation by creating licences outside the scope of the RA 1977 and HA 1988. Although the decision has considerable importance under the HA 1988, a measure of uncertainty will remain, as the question in many cases is whether the agreement between the parties is a 'sham' ie one purporting to deny exclusive possession to the occupier of residential premises when this was in fact clearly intended by the parties, and conferred on the 'licensee'. This is particularly the case given the readiness of the parties in many cases to draft occupation agreements in a manner which purports to deny exclusive occupation to the residential occupier, thus creating a licence to which the HA 1988 will not apply, rather than a tenancy. Although *Street v Mountford* ushered in a more objective approach to the interpretation of occupation agreements, it should be appreciated that distinguishing between licences and tenancies remains first and foremost a matter of contractual interpretation, an exercise in detecting the 'true' intention of the parties at the time of contract – and, especially, in detecting whether the agreement on its true construction confers on the occupier exclusive possession[1]. The court will disregard the parties' express intention as to the *type* of legal relationship they wish to create – the 'label' attached to the agreement. 'The only intention which is relevant is the intention demonstrated by the agreement to grant exclusive possession for a term at a rent'[2]. If this is granted, then the agreement creates a tenancy in law, whatever the parties call it.

1 *Street v Mountford* [1985] 2 All ER 289 at 299, per Lord Templeman.
2 Ibid at 300.

[3.44] Although the exercise remains, in theory, one of finding the parties' true intention at the time of contract, the courts have subsequently adopted a broad approach to construing occupation agreements and applying the *Street v Mountford* principles. In particular, the House of Lords in *Antoniades v Villiers* indicated that in considering one or more documents for the purpose of deciding whether a tenancy has been created, the court must consider the surrounding circumstances, including any relationship between the prospective occupiers, the course of negotiations and the nature and extent of the accommodation and the intended and actual mode of occupation of the accommodation[1].

1 [1988] 3 All ER 1058 at 1064 per Lord Templeman.

[3.45] The court is therefore entitled to look at the parties' conduct subsequent to the conclusion of the agreement, and especially at the exercise or otherwise of clauses in the agreement providing for the sharing of possession with the landlord and/or third parties, and aimed at denying a grant of exclusive possession. The Rent

Acts will not be allowed to influence the construction of the agreement. Nevertheless, the court will be astute to detect and frustrate sham devices and artificial transactions whose only aim is to disguise the grant of a tenancy and so evade the legislation[1]. Although astute to detect sham clauses, however, the court will approach the question in an even-handed and neutral manner, and only if some aspect of the agreement appears to be a pretence will it consider further whether it is 'sham' and an attempt at statutory evasion[2].

1 *Street v Mountford* [1985] 2 All ER 289 at 299. For an example see *Skipton Building Society v Clayton* (1993) 66 P&CR 223, CA.
2 *Stribling v Wickham* (1989) 21 HLR 381, CA.

'Sham' defined

[3.46] According to traditional legal theory, the essence of a sham arrangement lies in the fact that the parties have 'a common intention [here to grant exclusive possession of accommodation] that the acts or documents in question are not to create the legal rights and obligations which they give the appearance of creating'[1]. Where both parties intend a written tenancy agreement to be a 'sham' this will commonly be because of fraud or illegality on the part of either landlord or tenant, or both. In *Bhopal and Kaur v Guljit Waur*[2] the parties entered into an oral tenancy at a rent of £300 per month. Later, the landlord asked the tenant to sign a written agreement at £450 per month, so that he could show the agreement to his Bank. The tenant continued to pay £300 as formerly. The court held the written agreement to be a sham and unenforceable by the landlord's successor in title. Moreover, the tenant was not estopped from asserting its sham nature by reason of the possibility of fraud perpetrated by the landlord. *Query* whether the tenant would be estopped from asserting the sham doctrine where the illegality or fraud alleged benefited him as well as the landlord.

1 *Snook v London and West Riding Investments Ltd* [1967] 2 QB 786 at 802, CA.
2 (1999) L&TR 461.

[3.47] The sham doctrine requires an intention on the part of *both* parties to deceive. It is consequently of little utility in the landlord and tenant context, where it is unrealistic to attribute a clear intention of this sort to the tenant in what is – in economic terms – a contract of subordination. Its shortcomings have been highlighted in a number of decisions[1]. More recently, the courts have indicated that a *common* intention may not be required in appropriate cases, where clauses are clearly a 'pretence' or 'smoke screen' inserted by the landlord to disguise the true nature of the transaction, and to hide a grant of exclusive possession[2]. Indeed, according to Lord Templeman in *Antoniades v Villiers* 'it would have been more accurate and less liable to give rise to misunderstandings if I had substituted the word 'pretence' for the references to 'sham devices' and 'artificial transactions' in *Street v Mountford*'[3]. Moreover, it is now clear that the court will disregard individual terms of an agreement which are a pretence, and not part of the true bargain between the parties, even if the transaction viewed as a whole is not a 'sham' arrangement[4]. The court is not bound to give full effect to all the terms of the agreement in determining whether it is a licence or tenancy, only those which reflect the true bargain made between the parties. If, disregarding sham terms, the remaining agreement invests as a matter of law the rights and obligations of a tenant on the occupier, then it creates a tenancy irrespective of the label attached to it by the parties[5].

1 See *Mikeover Ltd v Brady* [1989] 3 All ER 618, CA; *Hilton v Plustistle Ltd* [1988] 3 All ER 1051, CA.
2 *Antoniades v Villiers* [1988] 3 All ER 1058 at 1067–8, per Lord Templeman.
3 Ibid at 1067.
4 *Aslan v Murphy* [1989] 3 All ER 130, CA.
5 See generally *Addiscombe Garden Estates Ltd v Crabbe* [1958] 1 QB 513, CA.

Indicia of sham intent

[3.48] All the terms of the agreement must be examined, but the courts have indicated that they will look closely at 'unusual' terms not commonly found in licence or tenancy agreements to establish whether they truly reflect the intention of the parties at the time of contract, or are merely inserted to give the appearance of non-exclusivity when exclusive possession is in fact offered and accepted. For example, in *Crancour v Da Silvaesa*[1] a clause requiring licensees of a bedsit to vacate the room between 10.30 am and 12 noon (and also to remove their belongings) each day was so extraordinary as to require close examination in order to ascertain whether it was a true statement of the nature of the occupation to be enjoyed by the 'licensees'. A clause permitting the landlord to move the licensee to another comparable room in the same building was not a sham, however, as there were legitimate circumstances in which a landlord might wish to rearrange the occupation arrangements of lodgers occupying bedsits in the building[2]. The court will look to the licence agreement itself in the first instance, but if it contains terms which ex facie give the appearance of being sham then the court will look to extrinsic evidence to ascertain the true intent of the parties[3]. Where the latter is the case, the sole question is whether there was at the time of grant an intention to grant exclusive possession, and not, for instance, whether the grantee is described as a 'lodger' enjoying attendance or services[4]. If the occupant is not a lodger, he will not inevitably be a tenant, despite dicta in *Street v Mountford* apparently to the contrary[5].

1 (1986) 278 Estates Gazette 618, CA.
2 (1986) 278 Estates Gazette 618 at 625, CA.
3 Ibid at 628.
4 See *Brooker Settled Estates Ltd v Ayers* (1987) 282 Estates Gazette 325, CA.
5 [1985] 2 All ER 289 at 293 per Lord Templeman.

[3.49] An occupier will be a 'lodger', and hence a licensee, if the landlord requires unrestricted access to the room to provide services (such as cleaning and changing linen), even when the lodger is not present[1]. The court must in principle focus on the rights and obligations of the parties under the tenancy agreement, and not on conduct subsequent to its being concluded. If the owner is contractually obliged to provide attendance or services, and retains a key to the premises for that purpose, then that is a strong indication that they are let on a license not a tenancy. The fact that the occupant chooses not to avail himself of the services to which he is entitled cannot subsequently convert a license into a tenancy[2]. The reservation by the landlord of a *restricted* right of access (eg between certain hours or on giving notice) will, on the other hand, be taken by the court as an implied recognition that exclusive possession has been granted, and that the grantee is a tenant[3]. Simply retaining keys to the premises will not be enough to negative a grant of exclusive possession, unless the landlord requires them to permit unlimited access to provide services contracted for, or bona fide to share occupation[4].

1 See *Abbeyfield (Harpenden) Society Ltd v Woods* [1968] 1 WLR 374, CA; *Marchant v Charters* [1977] 1 WLR 1181, CA.
2 *Uratemp Ventures Ltd v Collins* [2000] L&TR 369 reversed on different grounds [2002] 1 All ER 46, HL.

3 *Street v Mountford* [1985] 2 All ER 289 at 293. See also *Addiscombe Garden Estates Ltd v Crabbe* [1958] 1 QB 513, CA.
4 *Aslan v Murphy* [1989] 3 All ER 130, CA.

[3.50] The subsequent conduct of the parties is not strictly relevant in law, the sole question being the parties' common intention at the time of contract. Where, however, the landlord reserves a right to introduce further 'licensees' to share with the grantee at any time, but never in fact does so, it may prove difficult to establish that there was no intent to confer exclusive possession ab initio. So, in *Antoniades v Villiers*[1], there was held to be a joint tenancy, and not two separate licence agreements, where the landlord failed to exercise his supposed right to share occupation with the occupants of a one-bedroom flat. The flat was too small for sharing to be realistically envisaged, and the licensees were living together as man and wife – the clause was thus a 'sham', and not part of the true agreement between the parties, which was that exclusive possession (and hence a tenancy) should be granted. It is now clear that, to rebut the inference that exclusive possession has been granted, it will be necessary for the landlord to show a continuing intention on his part to exercise the clauses in question; he cannot confer exclusive possession for the time being, unless and until he requires the occupants to share either with himself or nominated occupants[2].

1 [1988] 3 All ER 1058, HL.
2 See *Aslan v Murphy* [1989] 3 All ER 130 at 137 per Lord Donaldson MR.

[3.51] As soon as exclusive possession is granted a tenancy is created in law, and it cannot be turned back into a licence by the subsequent exercise of sharing clauses in the agreement[1].

1 *Antoniades v Villiers* [1988] 3 All ER 1058, HL.

MULTIPLE OCCUPANCY

[3.52] In *Street v Mountford* the facts involved single occupancy under a purported licence agreement. More complex problems arise where two or more occupants are sharing premises and their status as licensees or tenants is called into issue. They may have exclusive possession of the premises between them, in which event they will be joint tenants of the whole and protected as such under the HA 1988. Alternatively, they may individually have exclusive possession of part of the premises (eg a bedroom) and share occupation of common parts, such as a living room and kitchen. In this event, the HA 1988, s 3 will apply to confer protection on each occupant – thus deeming there to be an assured tenancy of the part occupied exclusive of third parties (eg a bedroom) and restricting the landlord's right to vary the terms as to sharing[1]. The application of s 3 presupposes, however, a grant of exclusive possession of part of the premises, albeit with additional sharing rights.

1 See below, para 3.69.

[3.53] A third possibility is that multiple occupants may jointly share possession, but under agreements which deny them individually exclusive possession of any part of the premises. In this event s 3 will not apply. The question which arises – and to which in many cases there is no clear answer – is whether the occupants have jointly been given exclusive possession of the premises, and hence a tenancy, or whether they merely enjoy non-exclusive licences to share with each other and with further licensees introduced by the landlord. The position is further complicated by the application of the common law rules of joint tenancy. It is settled law that for a joint tenancy to arise there must be unity of possession, interest, time and title.

[3.54] The position was reviewed by the House of Lords in *AG Securities v Vaughan*[1]. The occupants were four young men who each signed separate licence agreements, and had taken up occupation separately at different times. The agreements were not identical (eg, they contained different terms as to rent) and each purported to deny the grantee exclusive possession of any part of the premises. The landlords retained the right to nominate licensees to replace occupants who left. The Court of Appeal had held them to be joint tenants of the whole premises. Reversing this decision, the House of Lords held that the four unities of possession, time, interest and title are not present in such an arrangement. Where a number of 'licensees' collectively enjoy exclusive possession of a dwelling under separate licence agreements which commence on different dates, and which give them rights to enjoy the whole between themselves, they cannot in law be joint tenants of the whole premises and fully protected[2]. The agreements were not interdependent – each occupant was separately liable for part of the rent, under an agreement which started at different times from those of other occupants and contained materially different terms. The arrangement, in other words, was 'a sensible and realistic one to provide accommodation for a shifting population of individuals who were genuinely prepared to share the flat with others introduced from time to time who would, initially at least, be strangers to them'[3].

1 [1988] 3 All ER 1058, HL.
2 See per Lord Oliver at [1988] 3 All ER 1074.
3 See ibid [1988] 3 All ER 1058 at 1061 per Lord Bridge. See also *Stribling v Wickham* [1989] 27 EG 81, CA.

[3.55] This decision should be compared with those in cases where joint applicants for accommodation sign separate licence agreements which are, on their proper construction, interdependent and create joint and several obligations, eg as to rent. Before *Street v Mountford* it had been possible to deny protection to joint applicants for accommodation by requiring them to sign separate 'licence' agreements, exclusive possession being denied by the element of sharing with the other 'licensee'[1].

1 *Somma v Hazlehurst* [1978] 1 WLR 1014, CA, overruled in *Street v Mountford.*

[3.56] This is no longer possible, especially if the court disregards terms as to sharing as 'sham'. So, in *Antoniades v Villiers*[1] joint tenancy arose where the two occupants jointly approached the landlord, signed identical agreements at the same time and entered into obligations which were intended to be joint (and not several). Lord Oliver indicated that, although each licensee was expressly liable for only half the rent, the two documents read together created a joint and several liability in each to pay the whole rent. Note, however, that if licence agreements genuinely reserve separate obligations, eg as to rent, then no unity of interest will be present and no joint tenancy can be implied. So, in *Mikeover Ltd v Brady*[2] two licensees signed separate, but identical, agreements which reserved payment by each of £86.66 per month for the right to share use of the rooms one with the other. When one of the licensees left the premises, the landlord refused to accept payment of the combined rent for both from the remaining occupant. Having regard to all the circumstances, and particularly to the conduct of the parties subsequent to contract, the Court of Appeal held that the agreements imposed separate – not joint – liability for rent. The obligations were not joint, there was no unity of interest, and hence no joint tenancy of the premises.

1 [1988] 3 All ER 1058 at 1074, HL, reversing the CA decision [1988] 2 All ER 173. See per Lord Oliver [1988] 3 All ER 1058 at 1074, the four unities, of interest, time, title and possession are not present in such an arrangement. It should be noted, however, that each individual licensee may be protected in some circumstances if he has exclusive possession of part (eg, a bedsit) and shares occupation of common parts – see the HA 1988, s 3 and p 71, below. The landlord in *AG Securities v Vaughan* had reserved a right to nominate licensees to share occupation up to a maximum of four at any one time, the licence agreement (further) expressly denying each licensee exclusive possession of any part of the flat. See also *Hadjiloucas v Crean* [1987] 3 All ER 1008. See also (1988) 138 NLJ 841 (H Lewis).
2 [1989] 3 All ER 618, CA.

PRE-ORDAINED SERIES OF TRANSACTIONS

[3.57] There is, finally, a wider issue involved in many cases of statutory avoidance. The parties cannot, by dividing what is in reality a grant of tenancy into several individual linked transactions, avoid the application of protective legislation by arranging matters so that no individual transaction can be impugned as 'sham'. In *Gisborne v Burton*[1] the Court of Appeal applied anti-avoidance principles enunciated in tax cases[2] to strike down a scheme whereby farmland was let to a nominee, then sublet to the tenant, with the intention of denying the latter protection under the Agricultural Holdings Act 1986 (AHA 1986). Under the agricultural legislation, subtenants of farmland enjoy no security of tenure if served notice to quit by a mesne tenant who has (in turn) received notice from the landlord[3]. The scheme in *Gisborne v Burton* was aimed at taking advantage of this anomaly to achieve a security-free letting. Dillon LJ indicated that the consequences of a pre-ordained series of transactions should be ascertained by considering the result of the series as a whole, and not by dissecting the scheme and considering each individual transaction separately. If there is a pre-ordained series of transactions, the sole intent and effect of which is to deprive the tenant of statutory rights to security of tenure etc, it will infringe this principle[4]. The subtenancy in *Gisborne* was therefore held to be a tenancy held directly of the landlord, and the mesne tenant was regarded as having acted as (at highest) the landlord's agent in its grant.

1 [1988] 3 All ER 760, CA See also Rodgers (1989) Conv 196–204; Martin (1989) NLJ 192.
2 See *Furniss v Dawson* [1984] 1 All ER 530, HL; *WT Ramsay Ltd v IRC* [1981] 1 All ER 865, HL.
3 See AHA 1986, s 26(1), Agricultural Holdings (Arbitration on Notices) Order1987, Art 16; SI 1987/710.
4 [1988] 3 All ER 760, CA.

[3.58] Quite clearly, this approach could prove useful in cases where no implication of 'sham' (in the traditional sense outlined above) is involved. Its scope in the context of the lease or licence type of case would appear to be limited, as there is only one transaction involved – not a series of transactions. It could arguably prove useful, however, where more complex schemes aimed at avoiding the legislation, or mitigating its full impact, are involved. Its application in cases involving the company let device would appear to be ruled out by recent decisions[1]. It could, however, prove of utility in the 'sharing' cases, and where joint tenancies are employed to evade the legislation (see below). Similarly, evasion of some of the restrictions on repossession in the HA 1988, and of tenants' pre-emption rights in the Landlord and Tenant Act 1987 (LTA 1987)[2], can be facilitated by the use of holding companies in which the landlord's interest is vested prior to letting. The new ground allowing for repossession of residential premises for reconstruction is, for example, unavailable if the landlord acquired his interest by purchase[3].

1 See *Hilton v Plustitle* [1988] 3 All ER 1051, CA; *Kaye v Massbetter Ltd* [1991] 2 EGLR 97, CA, discussed below.
2 See below, Chapter 4, para 4.10 ff and Chapter 13.
3 HA 1988, Sch 2, Ground 6; see also LTA 1954, s 30(2) applying a similar rule to restrict use of s 30(1)(g) ibid in relation to business premises.

[3.59] This can be sidestepped by transferring the landlord's interest to a holding company prior to letting and then transferring control of the premises by transfer of shares in the latter (and not by conveyance). The *Gisborne v Burton* principle could be useful in analysing schemes of this type. It should be stressed, however, that the existing 'sham' principles deal satisfactorily with many other arrangements encountered in the residential sector. For example, rental purchase schemes would not appear appropriate for the *Gisborne* approach[1].

1 See Hoggett (1972) 36 Conv 325, (1975) 39 Conv 343.

[3.60] Similarly, in *Quennell v Maltby*[1] the Court of Appeal was able to strike down the agreed transfer of a pre-existing mortgage (with priority over the tenants' interest) to the landlord by the use of 'sham' principles. Ralph Gibson LJ in *Gisborne*[2] viewed this as a case where the mortgagee and landlord colluded to deny the tenant Rent Act rights under the tenancy which had been granted to him – it was not a case of treating the tenant as entitled to rights under a tenancy which had *not* been granted to him.

1 [1979] 1 All ER 568.
2 [1988] 3 All ER 760 at 771, CA.

COMPANY LETS

[3.61] The HA 1988, s 1(1)(a) also requires that, for a tenancy to be assured, the tenant, or in the case of a joint tenancy *each* of the joint tenants, must be an individual. This would appear to give statutory sanction to the principle developed under the Rent Acts that a letting to a limited company cannot be protected (or, now, 'assured') because an incorporated body cannot 'reside' in a dwelling in the accepted sense[1]. In the context of the HA 1988 a letting to a company, or to joint tenants *one* of whom is a company, cannot by express statutory provision be an assured tenancy. In the absence, therefore, of willingness on the part of the courts to lift the veil of incorporation in landlord and tenant cases, and provided there is no implication of 'sham' (as to which see further below) the 'company let' will remain effective to avoid protective legislation[2]. Moreover, the requirement in the HA 1988, s 1(1)(a) that *all* joint tenants be individuals may facilitate even readier evasion of statutory protection. It may no longer be necessary to incorporate a company to which one lets in lieu of to the 'tenants'; a letting to individual tenants themselves will in principle not be assured if they are constituted joint tenants with a limited company. Attempts to abuse the requirements of s 1 by the use of 'controlled' company tenants would, it is suggested, fail; if not because the courts may lift the veil of incorporation and treat the corporate entity as the agent of the landlord (which is always a matter of uncertainty), then because the courts have recently demonstrated their willingness to strike down similar attempts to abuse tenant protection legislation by means of the joint tenancy rule[3]. *Query*, however, in the context of the agricultural and business tenancy legislation the decisions proceed on the basis that failure to serve notices claiming protection is a breach of trust[4] and that the tenants have usual partnership authority to serve statutory notices on behalf of all partners (including a 'controlled' company tenant). The context here is different; the question is whether assured tenancy *status* is appropriate ab initio, and principles of partnership and trust law would appear inappropriate. This might, however, be one area where the wider approach adopted in *Gisborne v Burton* (above) might be appropriate to frustrate statutory avoidance. The Law Commission has expressed concern at the use of joint tenancies to avoid protective legislation, and has suggested reform. It is therefore to be regretted that the HA 1988 perpetuated the scope for abuse and uncertainty in this area[5].

1 See, eg *Reidy v Walker* [1933] 2 KB 266; *Hiller v United Dairies (London) Ltd* [1934] 1 KB 57 at 63, CA; *Firstcross Ltd v East-West (Export/Import) Ltd* (1980) 255 Estates Gazette 355, CA. Note the converse situation where the letting is by a company with a disability in its memorandum of association prohibiting the grant of interests other than a licence. Such a device would probably now be ineffective: see Farrand (1976) 40 Conv (NS) 6; Pettit (1980) 44 Conv 112.
2 The efficacy of the company let to sidestep protective legislation has, indeed, been reaffirmed by the Court of Appeal: see *Estavest Investments Ltd v Commercial Express Travel Ltd* [1988] 49 EG 73; *Hilton v Plustitle* [1988] 3 All ER 1051; *Eaton Square Properties Ltd v O'Higgins* [2001] L&TR 15, CA.
3 See *Harris v Black* (1983) 46 P&CR 366, CA; *Featherstone v Staples* [1986] 2 All ER 461, CA; see also Rodgers (1985) 48 MLR 460, (1986) Conv 429.
4 *Harris v Black*, ibid.
5 Landlord and Tenant: Reform of the Law (Cm 162, 1987) paras 4.20–4.26.

Company lets and the sham doctrine

[3.62] Leaving aside questions of joint tenancy and more complex avoidance techniques, the utility of the company let as a means of avoiding the application of the Rent Acts has been reinforced in a number of recent decisions. These have indicated the courts' unwillingness to impugn such arrangements as 'sham', and their unwillingness to apply anti-avoidance principles developed under the taxing statutes to strike down such arrangements[1]. If the parties clearly intended the tenant to be a limited company, and that was the genuine intention of the parties, then the letting cannot be impugned as 'sham'[2]. So, in *Eaton Square Properties Ltd v O'Higgins*[3] the Court of Appeal refused to condemn as 'sham' an under lease to a limited company in circumstances where the lease had been taken in the company's name so that it could apply to the Inland Revenue to allow expenditure on refurbishment to be set off against corporation tax. Both here, and in the earlier case of *Hilton v Plustitle Ltd*[4]. the fact that the occupant gave a personal guarantee for the payment of rent was held to be irrelevant.

1 See *Gisborne v Burton* [1988] 3 All ER 760, CA. This approach was rejected, however, by the Court of Appeal in *Hilton v Plustitle Ltd* [1988] 3 All ER 1051.
2 *Kaye v Massbetter Ltd* [1991] 2 EGLR 97; affirming the decision in *Hilton v Plustitle Ltd* [1988] 3 All ER 1051. Note, however, that the decision in *Gisborne v Burton* (above) was not cited here.
3 [2001] L&TR 15, CA.
4 [1989] 1 EGLR 119.

ASSURED TENANCY OF 'ONLY OR PRINCIPAL HOME'

[3.63] The tenancy will be assured only if and so long as the tenant, or at least one out of joint tenants, occupies the dwelling as his 'only' or 'principal' home, s 1(1)(b). This formula is adopted from the HA 1985, s 81 ('secure' public sector tenancies) and prevents the tenant qualifying for assured tenancy protection in two properties – the 'two homes' tenant problem familiar under previous rent legislation[1]. An assured tenant will have to choose which of two potential homes he wishes to be protected, and make it his 'principal' home and residence. In the context of the HA 1985, it has been held that two houses can be occupied at the same time as a home, since actual physical occupation (i e 'residence') is not necessary for a dwelling to be a person's 'home', and that the question which of two 'homes' qualifies as a person's 'principal' home for these purposes is a question of fact for the county court judge[2]. 'Principal home' means more than simply 'principal residence' and all the facts, as well as actual occupation of the respective properties, will be relevant.

1 See *Hampstead Way Investments Ltd v Lewis-Weare* [1985] 1 WLR 164, HL.
2 *Crawley Borough Council v Sawyer* (1986) 20 HLR 98, CA.

'IF AND SO LONG AS'

[3.64] The tenancy will remain assured only if and so long as the qualifying conditions (above) in s 1 are met. For example, if the dwelling ceases to be let as a separate dwelling, or if a corporate entity becomes a joint tenant, or if the tenant ceases to reside in the property as his principal home, the protection of the HA 1988, Pt 1 will cease to apply. In this event, in particular, the restrictions on repossession in s 5 and Sch 1 will cease to apply, and the tenancy can be terminated by notice to quit in the normal way (although the residual protection of the PEA 1977 may continue to apply).

[3.65] The most common event terminating assured tenancy protection will doubtless be where the tenant (or in the case of a joint tenancy *all* of the tenants) ceases to occupy the dwelling house as his 'principal' residence. This raises a problem familiar under previous rent legislation: when does effective abandonment of occupation of the demised property as a *home* occur? It was clearly established under previous legislation that temporary absences would not jeopardize protected status. In *Gofor Investments Ltd v Roberts*[1], it was held that where a tenant is no longer physically resident in premises, he has to show animus revertendi (a de facto intention to return) together with sufficient corpus possessionis, ie a 'visible state of affairs', such as the maintenance of furniture or a caretaker, in which the tenant's animus revertendi finds expression. In other words, to retain his protected (or 'assured') status, the tenant must have a real hope of return, combined with the practical possibility of fulfilling it within a reasonable time[2]. If the premises are maintained in a habitable state, with furniture, it is still essential that the tenant maintains an intention to return to use the premises as his principal *home*; eg it will not suffice if the premises are maintained as a store for furniture without an intention to return[3]. Furniture, occasional visits for maintenance etc are only indicia of a bona fide intention to return and will not suffice if the dwelling is used merely as an occasional 'refuge of last resort' and office, the required intent being to carry on *all* the normal functions of home life there[4].

1 (1975) 29 P&CR 366, CA.
2 See especially ibid at 372, per Cairns LJ; also *Brown v Brash and Ambrose* [1948] 2 KB 247 at 255, per Asquith LJ.
3 *Duke v Porter* [1986] 2 EGLR 101, CA; cf *Brickfield Properties Ltd v Hughes* (1987) 20 HLR 108, CA.
4 See generally *Regalian Securities Ltd v Scheuer* (1982) 263 Estates Gazette 973, CA.

[3.66] While Rent Act authorities may be helpful, it should be noted that the HA 1988 requires the use of the premises as the tenant's *principal* home, not simply *a* home, as previously. The animus revertendi necessary to ensure assured tenancy protection will thus be to maintain the property as the tenant's *principal* home. This, it is suggested, will be more difficult to establish. Thus, in *Gofor Investments v Roberts* (above), Rent Act protection was maintained where the tenant intended to return in ten to twelve years' time; under the HA 1988, the tenant would have difficulty in these circumstances establishing that the demised premises remained his principal home.

LAND LET WITH DWELLING

[3.67] By virtue of the HA 1988, s 2(1), assured tenancy status applies where *land* is let with a dwelling, but only if the 'main' purpose of the letting is to provide 'a' home (note, not the 'principal' home) for the tenant, or for one out of joint tenants. As to 'main' purpose, in *Feyereisel v Turnidge*[1] it was said that, as statutory policy was to protect the tenant in his 'home', protection must be limited to cases where the land or other premises demised are an adjunct of the dwelling house and not vice versa; it is not enough simply to find a dwelling on the land demised by the lease. It should be noted also that, although s 2 refers to the provision of 'a' home, the dwelling must constitute the tenant's 'principal' home in the required sense if the tenancy is to qualify as an assured tenancy under s 1 (above). For these purposes, the dominant purpose of the letting falls to be assessed at the date of the application[2].

1 [1952] 2 QB 29, CA.
2 See *Russell v Booker* (1982) 5 HLR 10.

[3.68] Although the HA 1988 requires land let with a dwelling to be treated as part of the dwelling house for the purposes of statutory protection (s 2(1), above), protection will not apply if the tenancy falls within one of the classes of excluded agreements set out in Sch 1 (see s 2(2)). The principal exclusions of relevance are: Sch 1, para 4, exclusion of business tenancies; para 6, exclusion where dwelling is let with agricultural land exceeding two acres; and para 7, dwelling comprised in an agricultural holding and occupied as main farmhouse. Where land is let with a dwelling for business purposes, *any* amount of business use which is not de minimis will bring the tenancy within the Landlord and Tenant Act 1954 (LTA 1954)[1] and thus exclude application of the HA 1988. Where premises are let with land simpliciter the question will usually be whether the dwelling and land together constitute an agricultural holding (as defined by the AHA 1986, s 2). The question here is whether the *substantial* user is for agricultural purposes[2]. If it is, then the tenancy cannot be assured – even if the land let is less than two acres – provided that the dwelling is the main or only farmhouse[3]. It should be noted that no minimum area of land is required to constitute an agricultural holding, and even a building *without* land has been so held: see *Blackmore v Butler*[4] and *Hasell v McAulay*[5].

1 See LTA 1954, s 23.
2 See AHA 1986, s 1; also *Howkins v Jardine* [1951] 1 KB 614, CA; *Lord Monson v Bound* [1954] 3 All ER 228; *Dunn v Fidoe* [1950] 2 All ER 685, CA; and *Short v Greeves* [1988] 08 EG 109, CA.
3 HA 1988, Sch 1, para 7.
4 [1954] 2 QB 171, CA.
5 [1952] 2 All ER 825.

SHARING ANCILLARY ACCOMMODATION

[3.69] The HA 1988, s 3 contains provisions to deal with the situation where the tenant has exclusive use of part of the premises but shares occupation of common parts with occupiers other than the landlord (typically other tenants)[1]. For example, the tenant has the exclusive use of a bedsit, but shares a kitchen and lounge with other tenants (but not the landlord). The section applies where, by reason of the sharing of the shared accommodation, the separate accommodation occupied by the tenant would not itself qualify as a dwelling house let on an assured tenancy. In this situation s 3 applies to protect the tenant's occupation of the shared accommodation, but only where the tenancy agreement provides that the accommodation is to be shared with someone *other than the landlord*. The tenant is also deemed to enjoy an assured tenancy of the separate accommodation of which he has exclusive possession, and if the shared accommodation comprises 'living accommodation', the terms of the tenancy as to the use of the shared accommodation cannot be varied[2]. Rent Act jurisprudence on the meaning of 'living' accommodation would indicate that simultaneous use must be possible or envisaged. For example, a kitchen will qualify as 'living' accommodation for this purpose[3] but a bathroom will not as its simultaneous use by occupants is not normally envisaged[4]. Furthermore, s 10(2) provides that no order for possession of the shared accommodation can be made unless a like order is (or has been) made in respect of the separate accommodation let to the tenant. The landlord can apply for an order terminating the tenant's right to use shared accommodation, providing it is not 'living' accommodation[5].

1 These are modelled on RA 1977, s 22, which contain identical provision for Rent Act protected tenancies.
2 HA 1988, s 3(3). Any terms providing for the persons with whom the tenant is entitled to use shared accommodation to be varied, or their number increased, remain valid, however, ibid, s 3(4).
3 *Neale v Del Soto* [1954] KB 144.
4 *Goodrich v Paisner* [1957] AC 65.
5 HA 1988, s 10(3)(a).

[3.70] If the common parts are to be shared with the landlord s 3 does not apply, and in this case neither will the tenant have an assured tenancy of the separate accommodation. Clearly, this provides the landlord with a potential avenue to avoid the creation of an assured tenancy. The courts have, accordingly, been astute to ensure that the exclusion is limited to genuine cases where sharing with the landlord is envisaged, and where this is a contractual entitlement of the landlord which is clearly provided for in the tenancy agreement. For the exclusion to apply, the tenancy must expressly and clearly reserve to the landlord the right to re-enter and share common accommodation with other occupiers. The court will not imply a right for the landlord to share into a general clause obliging the tenant to share common parts of the premises with un named third parties[1]. The landlord can, similarly, apply for an order *varying* the tenant's use of shared accommodation (whether 'living' accommodation or not) by increasing the number of sharers entitled to use the accommodation, or varying the persons so entitled[2]. No variation can be ordered, however, unless it could (apart from the statutory power to vary) have been effected under the terms of the tenancy agreement[3].

1 *Miller v Eyo* (1998) 31 HLR 306. The tenant has to know with clarity whether or not he has the benefits of an assured tenancy, and this (in turn) depends on whether the landlord has a right to share so as to come within the exception to the HA 1988, s 3. See also *Gray v Brown* (1993) 25 HLR 144, decided under the RA 1977, s 22 (clause entitling landlord to introduce 'whosoever I choose' to share held not sufficient to reserve right of landlord to share, and not to come within the exception).

2 Ibid, s 10(3)(b).
3 Ibid, s 10(4).

[3.71] By virtue of the HA 1988, s 4, if part of the property is *sublet*, protection is not lost if sharing is allowed under the terms of the sublease. The tenancy will, as against the landlord, remain an assured tenancy. This saving provision does not, however, affect rights and liabilities between tenant and subtenant (see s 4(2)).

C Tenancies that cannot be assured tenancies

[3.72] The HA 1988, Sch 1 lists 13 types of tenancy, which cannot be assured, even if all the other qualifying conditions (above) are present. By virtue of s 1(2) a tenancy cannot be assured 'if and so long as' it falls within any paragraph in Sch 1, Pt I. If it ceases to be within one of the excepted categories, therefore, it could *become* assured if all the other qualifying conditions are met. Many of the exclusions in Sch 1 are identical to those exclusions from protection applicable under the RA 1977. Note, however, that housing association tenancies are not excepted from protection, with the consequence that all tenancies granted by housing associations on or after 15 January 1989 (with the exception of fully mutual housing associations)[1] are on an assured tenancy basis. Formerly they were excepted from the Rent Act[2] and treated as 'secure' tenancies, with special provision for 'fair rents' under the RA 1977, Pt VI. Similarly, there is no exclusion from the assured tenancy code for lettings with board and/or attendance[3].

1 See Sch 1, para 12(1)(h) ibid.
2 RA 1977, s 15 and HA 1988, Sch 17, para 99.
3 See also RA 1977, s 7 and *Otter v Norman* [1989] AC 129, HL.

[3.72] A fourteenth exception is provided by s 1(6), which makes special provision for exempt lettings to homeless persons under an arrangement with the relevant housing authorities. The excluded categories of tenancy will be discussed in the order in which they appear in Sch 1.

TENANCIES ENTERED INTO PRE-COMMENCEMENT

[3.73] A tenancy which is entered into before, or pursuant to a contract made before the commencement of the HA 1988 cannot be 'assured'[1]. By virtue of Sch 1, para 13, moreover, such a tenancy cannot in any event be 'assured' if it is a protected tenancy under the RA 1977, a housing association tenancy within the RA 1977, Pt VI, a secure tenancy or a protected agricultural occupancy under the Rent (Agriculture) Act 1976 (R(A)A 1976). Notwithstanding the general rule, note that certain pre-commencement tenancies can *become* assured tenancies after 15 January 1989. This will be the case if the tenancy is transferred from a public sector landlord to one in the private sector, so that the tenancy ceases to be a 'secure' one, for instance[2]. Similarly, assured tenancies granted under the HA 1980 are converted into 'new-style' assured tenancies by the HA 1988, s 1(3).

1 HA 1988, Sch 1, para 1.
2 That is because the 'landlord condition' in the HA 1985, s 79 ceases to be satisfied.

TENANCIES OF DWELLING HOUSES WITH HIGH RATEABLE VALUES OR HIGH RENTS

[3.74] A tenancy entered into before 1 April 1990 (or pursuant to a contract made before that date) cannot be 'assured' if it is of a dwelling house which had a rateable value on 31 March 1990 which exceeded £1,500 (if in Greater London) or £750 (elsewhere)[1]. A tenancy which is entered into on or after 1 April 1990 (otherwise than where the dwelling had a rateable value on 31 March 1990, pursuant to a contract made before that date) cannot be an 'assured' tenancy if the rent payable for the time being exceeds £25,000 a year[2].

1 HA 1988, Sch 1, para 2A (added by SI 1990/434).
2 Ibid, Sch 1, para 2 (added by SI 1990/434).

[3.75] The modified rule for post-1 April 1990 tenancies reflects the abolition of domestic rating. The rateable value limits for pre-1 April 1990 grants are the same as under the RA 1977, but the rules are simpler as the relevant figure is solely the rateable value on 31 March 1990 – compare this with the calculation of rateable values on whichever of the 'appropriate days' applied in the instant case under the RA 1977, s 25. Following the abolition of the domestic rating system, the exclusion post-1 April 1990 operates by reference to the *current* rent, with the consequence that dwellings can move in and out of protection with fluctuations in rent. The exclusion takes out of protection high-value properties, and goes to the social objectives of the security of tenure regime.

TENANCIES AT A LOW RENT

[3.76] A tenancy cannot be 'assured' if either:

(a) no rent is payable[1]; or
(b) the tenancy was granted before 1 April 1990 and the rent payable for the time being is less than two-thirds of the rateable value of the dwelling house on 31 March 1990[2]; or
(c) the tenancy was entered into on or after 1 April 1990 (otherwise than, where the property had a rateable value at 31 March 1990, pursuant to a contract made before that date) and the rent payable for the time being is payable at a rate of less than £1,000 a year (Greater London) or £250 a year (elsewhere)[3].

1 Ibid, Sch 1, para 3.
2 Ibid, Sch 1, para 3B (added by SI 1990/434).
3 Ibid, Sch 1, para 3A (as so added).

[3.77] This exclusion is intended to take out of the HA 1988 long tenancies granted at a low rent – to which a special regime applies under the Local Government and Housing Act 1989 and the Leasehold Reform Act 1967. The exclusion is similar to that in the RA 1977, s 5, but is simpler in that the necessary calculations are made by reference to the current rent payable for the tenancy and *not* the rateable value on the relevant 'appropriate day' when rating revaluation last took place.

Rent

[3.78] When calculating the rent there must be disregarded such part (if any) of the sums payable by the tenant as is expressed (in whatever terms) to be payable in respect of rates, services, management, repairs, maintenance or insurance *unless* it could not have been regarded by the parties to the tenancy as a part so payable[1]. The artificial allocation of rent to services and management etc, so as to bring the 'rent' figure down below the threshold for protection, will therefore be disregarded. Sums genuinely charged for service and repairs, etc, will not, however, be included when calculating the rent payable for this purpose, eg in the case of a long lease at a low rent with a service charge.

1 Ibid, Sch 1, para 3(2).

BUSINESS TENANCIES

[3.79] A tenancy to which Pt II of the LTA 1954, Pt II applies cannot be an assured tenancy[1]. This exclusion is the same as that applying under the RA 1977. The determining factor is whether the tenancy is within the LTA 1954. It should be appreciated that a tenancy can be within the business tenancy code in the LTA 1954 if there is *any* business user which is not de minimis[2]. Tenancies of premises with mixed business and residential user will therefore prima facie be business tenancies, and as such outside the protection of the HA 1988. Further, all that is required by the LTA 1954, s 23(1) is that the premises be occupied for the purposes of a business carried on by the tenant; it need not have been so occupied from the time of grant. It follows that a tenancy can come within the LTA 1954 if a business user develops. Note, however, that the reverse is not the case. For the HA 1988 to apply the premises must be 'let as a separate dwelling'. Mere abandonment of business use will take the tenancy outside the LTA 1954, but will not bring it automatically within the HA 1988[3]. Where a tenancy is initially within the latter, however, the development of a business user will take the tenancy outside the HA 1988, and into the protection of the business tenancy code. Note also that where there is mixed business and residential user the tenancy will lose its protection under the HA 1988; but a subtenancy may still be protected if exclusively for residential use[4].

1 Ibid, Sch 1, para 4.
2 See LTA 1954, s 23.
3 See *Wetherall v Smith* [1980] 2 All ER 530, CA; *Russell v Booker* (1982) 5 HLR 10.
4 HA 1988, s 18. See also RA 1977, s 137(3); *Wellcome Trust Ltd v Hamad* (1998) 30 HLR 1099.

LICENSED PREMISES

[3.80] A tenancy under which the dwelling house let consists of or comprises premises licensed for the sale of intoxicating liquors for consumption on the premises cannot be an assured tenancy[1]. This mirrors an identical exclusion to Rent Act protection[2].

1 HA 1988, Sch 1, para 5.
2 See RA 1977, s 11.

TENANCIES OF AGRICULTURAL LAND

[3.81] A tenancy under which agricultural land exceeding two acres is let together with the dwelling house cannot be an assured tenancy[1].

1 HA 1988, Sch 1, para 6.

[3.82] This exclusion will apply even if the primary purpose of the letting is residential, providing the land let exceeds two acres. This provision complements s 2(1)[1]. It provides that if the main purpose is not for the provision of a home for the tenant, then (even if the land is less than two acres) the letting shall not be treated as one under which a dwelling house is let as a separate dwelling. If the main purpose of the letting is to provide a home for the tenant then it will be protected, as the land is treated as part of the dwelling house[2]; but if the land let exceeds two acres it will be taken out of protection by Sch 1, para 6.

1 Above, para 3.67 ff.
2 HA 1988, s 2(1)(a).

TENANCIES OF AGRICULTURAL HOLDINGS

[3.83] A tenancy of a dwelling house cannot be assured if the dwelling is comprised in an agricultural holding[1] and is occupied by the person responsible for the control of the farming of the holding – whether as tenant, or servant or agent of the tenant[2]. It matters not that the land let with the dwelling does not exceed two acres; see also the exclusion in Sch 1, para 6 (above). Although uncommon, it is possible for a dwelling let with a very small parcel of land to constitute an agricultural holding, if the substantial user of the property let is agricultural[3]. If the property let constitutes an agricultural holding this in itself will take the tenancy outside the HA 1988, irrespective of the amount of land let with the dwelling. This exception to protection is identical to that in the RA 1977, s 10. Note that if a dwelling let as part of an agricultural holding is occupied by persons *other than* those responsible for farming the holding, the tenancy may be assured. In this event it will usually have been sublet for residential use, in which case the subtenancy will be assured, although the mesne tenancy will be that of an agricultural holding. The subtenant in this case may be protected vis a vis the landlord by provisions in the HA 1988, s 18, providing the subletting was lawful and not in breach of covenant[4].

1 Ibid, Sch 1, para 7.
2 Ibid, Sch 1, para 7(b).
3 See AHA 1986, s 1(2); Rodgers (1988) Conv 430.
4 See Chapter 4 below.

LETTINGS TO STUDENTS

[3.84] A tenancy granted to a person pursuing, or intending to pursue, a course of study at a specified educational institution cannot be assured if granted by that institution, or by another specified institution[1].

1 HA 1988, Sch 1, para 8.

[3.85] Lettings are only exempt from control if granted by educational institutions specified by statutory instrument, eg universities or colleges of higher education[1]. Lettings to students by private landlords are unaffected.

1 See SI 1988/2236.

HOLIDAY LETTINGS[1]

[3.86] The HA 1988 gives no definition of 'holiday' for these purposes, and familiar problems of identifying 'sham' holiday lets in the Rent Act context also apply in the assured tenancy context. If a tenancy expressly states that its purpose is for occupation for a holiday, that statement stands as evidence of the intention of the parties, unless the tenant (on whom the burden of proof lies) can establish that it does not correspond with the true purpose; see *Buchmann v May*[2]. This, of course, makes it difficult for a tenant to impugn as sham all but the most obviously artificial holiday let. As to the meaning of 'holiday' in this context, in *Francke v Hakmi*[3] it was said to connote 'a temporary suspension of one's normal activity not necessarily involving recreation', and it is this that the parties must have in view to bring the letting within the exclusion. Regrettably, perhaps, this exception from protection will remain a source of confusion and attempted evasion[4].

1 HA 1988, Sch 1, para 9.
2 [1978] 2 All ER 993, CA.
3 [1984] CLY 1906.
4 See generally T J Lyons [1984] Conv 286.

LETTINGS BY RESIDENT LANDLORDS[1]

[3.87] One of the principal aims of the HA 1988, at least in respect of private sector lettings, was to remove most of the remaining controls over new lettings by resident landlords[2]. Accordingly, by virtue of Sch 1, para 10, a tenancy granted by a resident landlord cannot be 'assured' within the HA 1988, Pt I. Moreover, if granted a tenancy or licence after the HA 1988's commencement an occupier with a resident landlord will not enjoy the more limited protection of a restricted contract, as was previously the case under RA 1977. The HA 1988, removed all the remaining restrictions on recovery of possession by resident landlords and rent control, and the former rent tribunal jurisdiction no longer applies to new lettings by residential landlords. It should be noted also that, although s 36 preserves restricted contract status (and rent tribunal jurisdiction) for lettings prior to commencement, this will be lost if there is an agreed variation of rent *or* a variation of other terms which suffices to give rise to a new contract.

1 HA 1988, Sch 1, para 10. See Chapter 6, paras 6.38 and 6.46 ff for the Rent Act provisions.
2 Housing – the Government's Proposals (Cm 214, 1987) para 3.14.

[3.88] The conditions for the application of the resident landlord exception mirror those of the RA 1977. The principal requirement laid down by HA 1988, Sch 1, para 10(1) is that the dwelling house let must form part only of a building which is not a purpose-built block of flats, and be granted by someone who at the time occupied as his only or principal home another dwelling house which also forms part of the same building or flat. This condition is satisfied if one out of joint landlords occupies as a resident landlord at the time of grant[1]. The second fundamental requirement[2] is that at all times since the tenancy's grant, the interest of the landlord must have vested in someone who is himself a resident landlord occupying a dwelling within the same building. Schedule 1, Pt III lays down complex provisions allowing for 'periods of disregard' where no resident landlord is in occupation; if these are complied with, the absence of a resident landlord will not bring in the protection of the assured tenancy code, a result which otherwise ensues if there is an interregnum during which no resident landlord is in situ. The disregards are intended to deal with the position where the landlord's interest is sold, or vests in either personal representatives on death or in 'trustees as such'. The basic rule[3] is that a period of non-residence of 28 days can be disregarded, extended to six months on giving notice of intended occupation. Where the landlord's interest vests in 'trustees as such', or in the probate judge on intestacy, the period of disregard is two years from the date of the death[4]. The same applies in the case of personal representatives[5].

1 Sch 1 para 10(2), giving statutory affect to *Cooper v Tait* (1984) 271 Estates Gazette 105, CA.
2 See HA 1988, Sch 1, para 10(1)(c).
3 See ibid, para 17(1).
4 Ibid, para 18.
5 Ibid, para 20.

Residence in same 'building'

[3.89] The forms that a structure can take are various – is the HA 1988 satisfied if the landlord lives in part of a converted row of terraced houses, an extension to an existing house, or one of two semi-detached houses? In *Bardrick v Haycock*[1], it was indicated that what constitutes a 'building' for these purposes is a question of fact, as the range of structures which the word encompasses is too wide to permit of a precise definition. It may be helpful, however, to recall that the mischief at which the exception is aimed is that of 'social embarrassment arising out of close proximity – close proximity which the landlord had accepted in the belief that he could bring it to an end at any time allowed by the contract of tenancy'[2]. On this basis an extension built on to the back of a house, in which the landlord resided, has been held not to be part of the same building[3]. In a similar situation, however, two outhouses built on to a house so as to form one building with a common garden *has* been held to qualify[4].

1 (1976) 31 P&CR 420, CA.
2 Ibid at 424, per Scarman LJ.
3 *Bardrick v Haycock* (1976) 31 P&CR 420, CA.
4 *Griffiths v English* (1982) 261 Estates Gazette 257, CA. See also *Humphery v Young* [1903] 1 KB 44, where two unconnected semi-detached houses were held on the facts not to constitute one building.

Purpose-built block of flats

[3.90] For these purposes a building is a 'purpose-built block of flats' (and so outside the exception) if *as constructed* it contained, 'and it contains' two or more flats[1]. It would appear, therefore, that the building must contain two flats both ab initio and at the date of application (although not necessarily continuously). 'Flat' is defined to mean a dwelling house which forms part only of a building and is separated horizontally (not vertically) from another dwelling house which forms part of the same building.

1 Schedule 1, para 22.

[3.91] These provisions add little by way of definition to the complex resident landlord provisions of the RA 1977, the learning on which may still, therefore, be of assistance[2].

1 For further discussion, see Farrand and Arden, *Rent Acts and Regulations* (2nd edn, 1981) pp 45–9; R. E. Megarry, *The Rent Acts* (11th edn, 1988), Chapter 8, especially p 191 ff.

MISCELLANEOUS EXCEPTIONS

[3.92] Crown tenancies, local authority lettings and shared ownership leases are excluded from assured tenancy protection[1].

1 See HA 1988, Sch 1, paras 1–14.

LETTINGS TO HOMELESS PERSONS

[3.93] By virtue of the HA 1988, s 1(6), if a private landlord assists a local authority to discharge its obligations under the HA 1985, Pt III to house the homeless in its area, by entering into an arrangement with the authority to grant tenancies to homeless persons in priority need, then any tenancy so granted cannot be an assured tenancy. If the conditions for assured tenancy status (above) are satisfied, however, the tenancy will become 'assured' 12 months after the local authority notifies the applicant for housing of its decision whether he is homeless or threatened with homelessness[1]. The intent is to assist local authorities by encouraging *temporary* lettings without security of tenure by arrangement with private sector landlords.

1 As required by HA 1985, s 64.

D Terms of the tenancy and rent

THE STATUTORY PERIODIC TENANCY

[3.94] The HA 1988 confers residential security on the tenant by providing that, on expiry of a fixed-term assured tenancy, a statutory periodic tenancy arises. Unlike the statutory Rent Act tenancy, this creates rights in rem and takes effect in possession immediately on expiry of a fixed-term[1]. A periodic assured tenancy, on the other hand, cannot be brought to an end except by a court order and in other limited circumstances[2]. The terms of the statutory periodic tenancy are governed by the HA 1988, which also lays down procedures for their variation by the Rent Assessment Committee. There is no mechanism for varying the terms of a *contractual* periodic assured tenancy, other than for rent reviews in accordance with the statutory review procedure (below).

1 HA 1988, s 5(2).
2 See Chapter 4, para 4.5 ff below.

TERMS OF THE STATUTORY PERIODIC TENANCY

[3.95] The terms of the statutory periodic tenancy are laid down in the HA 1988, s 5(3):

(1) *Parties*. The tenancy is deemed to have been granted by the person who was the landlord immediately before the fixed-term tenancy came to an end, to the person who was then the tenant under the tenancy[1].

(2) *Premises*. These are the premises which are the same dwelling house as was let under the fixed-term tenancy[2]. So, for instance, the statutory tenancy will take in all the premises originally let, even if on termination of the fixed-term the tenant is only occupying part of the dwelling. Variations in the tenancy agreement since its inception would, however, be relevant.

(3) *Periods of tenancy*. The periods of the statutory tenancy are the same as those for which rent was last payable under the fixed-term tenancy[3]. Note that if the periods at which rent is paid have been varied by agreement before expiry of the fixed-term, it is the period of payment in force immediately before its expiry which is relevant.

(4) *Other terms.* These are the same as those of the fixed-term tenancy *immediately before it came to an end*, except that any break clause is of no effect while the periodic tenancy is assured[4]. The direction that the terms are to be those of the old tenancy is expressly qualified, however, in that it takes effect 'subject to the following provisions of this Part of this Act' (ie the HA 1988, Pt I). The ensuring provisions imply clauses allowing, for instance, access to carry out repairs (s 16) and governing assignment and subletting (s 15). These are intended to apply to all statutory periodic tenancies, and will therefore override contrary provisions in the original tenancy. Further, it would seem that any term as to rent review in the original fixed-term will be replaced on termination of the fixed-term by the statutory rent review procedure set out in ss 13 and 14, and discussed below. The question is not free of doubt, however. The reference in s 5(3) to the tenancy taking effect on the same terms as the prior fixed-term would suggest that any provision by which the rent might be varied would become a term, also, of the statutory periodic tenancy. But this is expressly 'subject to the following provisions in this part of [the HA 1988]'. Section 13 puts in place a statutory procedure for review of proposed rent increases by the Rent Assessment Committee, in the case of statutory periodic tenancies. The question may arise, therefore, whether the statutory or contractual provision should apply. By virtue of s 13(1)(a) the statutory procedure applies to 'a statutory periodic tenancy other than' to tenancies granted by the Crown or local authorities. The better view, reading this provision with s 5(3)(e), would appear to be that the statutory procedure is intended to apply to *all* other statutory periodic tenancies, including those consequent upon a prior fixed-term which included express provision for rent review[5]. Compare this with the case where there is a contractual *periodic* tenancy; different considerations arise, and a review clause will clearly exclude the statutory mechanism. See below, para 3.106 ff.

1 Ibid, s 5(3)(b). See s 45(4) for the definitions of 'landlord' and 'tenant', both of which are wide.
2 Ibid, s 5(3)(c). Note that 'was let' may be problematical. Does this mean the premises as let at the commencement of the tenancy, or those conferred by the tenancy at its later termination? See further Megarry, *Rent Acts* (11th edn, 1988) vol 3, p 81.
3 Ibid, s 5(3)(d).
4 Ibid, s 5(3)(e), but this does not affect a proviso for re-entry or forfeiture: s 45(4) ibid.
5 The question is not, however, beyond doubt. Cf Adams and Clarke, *Rent Reviews and Variable Rents* (3rd edn) pp 520–1, and Megarry, *Rent Acts* (11th edn, 1988) vol 3, p 198 ff.

Variation of terms

[3.96] The terms of the statutory tenancy can be varied under s 6, not later than the first anniversary of expiry of the original tenancy, by the landlord or tenant serving notice in the prescribed form proposing different terms to those implied by the HA 1988[1]. The landlord can suggest a variation of rent to take account of the amended terms. Rent variations are otherwise dealt with separately[2]. The landlord or tenant can refer the proposed changes to the Rent Assessment Committee for approval, but must do so within three months of the notice proposing different terms being served, otherwise the proposed terms take effect[3].

1 HA 1988, s 6(2). For the prescribed form see the Assured Tenancies and Agricultural Occupancies (Forms) Regs 1997, SI 1997/194, Form 1 (Appendix, below).
2 See para 3.112 ff below.
3 Section 6(3). There is also a prescribed form for reference to the Rent Assessment Committee under this provision: see SI 1997/194, Form 2.

[3.97] The committee's function is to assess the new terms proposed and evaluate whether they are 'such terms as might reasonably be expected to be found in an assured periodic tenancy of the dwelling house concerned', being one granted by a willing landlord on the same terms, except those of which variation is sought, as the statutory periodic tenancy[1].

1 Ibid, s 6(4).

[3.98] The committee can in all cases, if it thinks it appropriate, vary the rent to take account of the varied terms of the tenancy, but in so doing must discount the fact that there is a sitting tenant[1].

1 Ibid, s 6(5) and (6).

Non-assignment clause and access for repairs

[3.99] Section 15 provides that it is an implied term of every *periodic* (note, not fixed-term) assured tenancy that the tenant will not sublet, assign or part with possession of the whole or any part of the dwelling without the landlord's consent. The bar on assignment is absolute, as s 15(2) expressly excludes s 19 of the Landlord and Tenant Act 1927 (LTA 1927); refusal of consent need not, therefore, be reasonable. Clearly, it will be important to insert a suitable non-assignment clause in fixed-term tenancies.

[3.100] The implied prohibition on assignment does not apply if a periodic tenancy contains an agreed non-assignment clause, or if a premium was paid on its grant. The statutorily implied term is excluded whether the agreed non-assignment clause is included in the tenancy itself or not, and whether or not the agreed clause prohibits or permits assignment absolutely or conditionally (see s 15(3)(a)). Semble if the agreed covenant is qualified by the requirement of consent the LTA 1927, s 19 will apply.

[3.101] It is also an implied term of every assured tenancy that the tenant will allow access to carry out reasonable repairs (s 16). It might also be noted that there is no bar as such on the payment of premiums (cf RA 1977, Pt IX, below para 7.71 ff).

CONTROL OF RENT

[3.102] Under the HA 1988, there are fewer restrictions on the rent that can lawfully be recovered by the landlord than under a Rent Act protected tenancy. There is no control at all of the rent payable for the initial grant of an assured tenancy – the parties are free to agree whatever rent they choose. However, the HA 1988, s 13 provides a special procedure for the determination of the rent by a Rent Assessment Committee where a subsequent increase in rent has been sought by the landlord. The statutory review procedure only applies where the landlord has served a formal notice of increase, and then only to periodic and statutory periodic assured tenancies. There is no provision for the registration of rents by the rent officer, and no discount of scarcity value in valuing the rent for an assured letting (cf 'fair' rents under the RA 1977, below Chapter 7). The assured tenancy regime is based on freedom of contract, and takes account of market forces in determining rent levels.

Scope of statutory review procedure

[3.103] By virtue of s 13(2) for the purpose of securing an *increase* in the rent under an assured tenancy the landlord may serve on the tenant a notice in prescribed form[1] proposing a new rent to take effect at the beginning of a new period of tenancy. The statutory procedure to vary the rent only applies, therefore, first to secure an *increase* in the rent. Any decrease in rent must be agreed by the parties, and secondly where the *landlord* seeks to raise the rent by notice of increase. It is not open to the tenant to initiate a review by the Rent Assessment Committee, even where the market for rented property has fallen and rents have fallen below that initially agreed. The tenant is obliged to pay the contractually agreed rent until the landlord seeks an increase.

1 See SI 1997/194 and Appendix, below, for the prescribed notice of income.

Tenancies to which applicable

[3.104] The statutory review procedure applies[1] to:

(a) 'a statutory periodic tenancy', other than one which cannot be an assured tenancy because granted by the Crown, a housing action trust or a local authority;[2] and
(b) 'any other periodic tenancy' which is an assured tenancy. It does not apply, however, to a periodic assured tenancy 'in relation to which there is a provision, for the time being binding on the tenant, under which the rent for a particular period of the tenancy will or *may* be greater than the rent for an earlier period' [author's italics].

1 See the HA 1988, s 13(1).
2 Ibid, Sch 1, paras 11 and 12.

[3.105] The statutory system of rent control does *not* apply, therefore, to fixed-term assured tenancies, or to periodic assured tenancies which include provision for rent increases. Neither does it apply to an assured shorthold tenancy during the original shorthold term, in relation to which separate provision for rent control is made by the HA 1988[1]. It *will* apply, however, to an assured shorthold tenancy which has expired and then continued as a periodic tenancy.

1 Ibid, s 22, below, Chapter 5.

Express provision for rent increase

[3.106] Hitherto, express contractual provisions for varying residential (as opposed to commercial) rents have been uncommon. This is hardly surprising, as the 'fair' rent registrable under the RA 1977 for a dwelling would override any contractually agreed higher rent. Under the HA 1988, however, a contractual provision for rent review in a periodic tenancy will be effective, and will exclude the statutory procedures, provided it complies with the requirements of s 13(1)(b). The following are required.

'A provision for the time being binding on the tenant'

[3.107] This will normally be a term of the initial tenancy, but need not be. Any agreement governing rent increases which is legally binding, even if made subsequent to the tenancy agreement itself, will operate to exclude ss 13 and 14. Any subsequent agreement as to rent variation must, however, take effect 'in relation to' the tenancy, eg as a variation thereof.

'Under which the rent for a particular period of the tenancy'

[3.108] This would appear to encompass a formula for rent increases for a new period of tenancy, which will then continue indefinitely to new periods until further varied (the normal position with periodic tenancies).

'Will or may be greater than the rent for an earlier period'

[3.109] The statutory procedure will clearly be excluded where the tenancy includes a clause laying down a formula for calculating a periodic increase or variation in rent, eg by reference to indexation of rent to the Retail Prices Index, or by valuation by an independent valuer in default of agreement. The provision in s 13(1)(b) is probably sufficiently wide, however, to include a clause allowing for a unilateral increase of rent by the landlord; eg on giving notice of specified length. In *Greater London Council v Connolly*[1] a clause providing that rent was 'liable to be increased or decreased on notice being given' was upheld, as the amount of rent could be calculated with certainty at the time when payment became due, and was therefore not uncertain – albeit the amount was dependent on a unilateral act of the landlord in giving notice of increase. *Query* whether a clause of this kind would also satisfy s 13(1)(b), being a provision, by the exercise of which the rent 'may be greater than the rent for an earlier period' of the tenancy. Whatever its form, the courts will seek to interpret a review clause benevolently and to give it effect[2].

1 [1970] 2 QB 100, CA.
2 See *Brown v Gould* [1971] 2 All ER 1505.

[3.110] The rent must be certain, but this does not mean it has to be certain at the date of the tenancy's grant. 'Rent is sufficiently certain if it can be calculated with certainty at the time when payment comes to be made'[1]. The tenancy must, however, either provide a mechanism by which the amount of rent may be calculated (whether by indexation, progressive rent increases or otherwise) or provide a means of determining any dispute as to quantum which may arise (eg by independent valuation). A clause which leaves the parties with 'a rent to be then agreed, such rent not to exceed a stated maximum' on review will be valid if on a proper construction it is just and necessary to imply a provision for the rent to be a fair rent[2]. On the other side of the line would be a clause leaving the rent on review undefined, save to reserve 'such a rental as may be agreed upon by the parties' without stipulating a maximum or minimum figure. This would, it is suggested, fail for uncertainty[3].

1 *Greater London Council v Connolly* [1970] 2 QB 100 at 109 per Lord Denning MR.
2 See *Corson v Rhuddlan Borough Council* [1990] 1 EGLR 255, CA. On principles of implication see generally *Foley v Classique Coaches Ltd* [1934] 2 KB 1, CA.
3 *King's Motors (Oxford) Ltd v Lax* [1969] 3 All ER 665; *Smith v Morgan* [1971] 2 All ER 1500.

[3.111] Note that the statutory rent review procedures will be excluded by the presence of a clause which 'may' result in a rent which is greater than for an earlier period. It is not necessary that an increase must, inevitably, follow from exercise of the clause in question. Any clause which can, in theory, lead to an increase in rent, and is not void for uncertainty, will suffice – but not a clause which provides solely for a *reduction* in rent. In practice, landlords will be well advised to choose one of a number of well-known methods of valuation, adapted from commercial lettings, where the drafting of review clauses has become an exact science[1]. The incorporation of an express review clause will be essential in a fixed-term assured tenancy, to which the statutory procedure has no application. In a periodic assured tenancy, the landlord will have to choose to rely on either an agreed review clause, or the statutory procedure under s 13, before granting the tenancy – he cannot have both. In the context of periodic tenancies, the statutory procedure has the merit of clarity, and may be preferable.

1 The possibilities include a clause indexing the rent by reference to the RPI, the provision of progressive rent increases at stated intervals ('progressive' rents) or valuation by an independent third party. See generally Clarke and Adams, *Rent Reviews and Variable Rents* (3rd edn) p 523 ff. Also D N Clarke, Rent Reviews in Residential Tenancies (1989) Conv 111.

Notice of increase

[3.112] To activate the statutory review procedure the landlord must serve notice proposing a new rent to take effect at the beginning of a new period of tenancy. This must normally be not earlier than the first anniversary of the date on which the first period of tenancy began, except where the statutory periodic tenancy arises on termination of a fixed-term assured tenancy[1]. In other words, one can require a rent increase after 12 months of tenancy, unless a fixed-term for less than a year is involved, in which case the rent can be varied on its termination and a statutory periodic tenancy arising. If the rent has previously been increased by notice under s 13, or by a determination of the Rent Assessment Committee under s 14, the date specified for the proposed increase must be not earlier than the first anniversary of the date on which the increased rent took effect[2].

1 See the HA 1988, s 13(2)(b). For the prescribed form of Notice of Increase see SI 1997/194.
2 Ibid, s 13(2)(c).

'Minimum period'

[3.113] Additionally, the date proposed for the variation to take effect must be not less than the 'minimum period' after service of the notice of increase[1]. This is defined by s 13(3) as six months in the case of a yearly tenancy, one month in the case of a tenancy of less than a month, and the period of tenancy in any other case.

1 Ibid, s 13(2)(a) .

[3.114] Notice of increase must be given in the prescribed form[1].

1 See Assured Tenancies and Agricultural Occupancies (Forms) Regs 1997, SI 1997/194 (Appendix, Form 4 or 4A, below).

Effect of notice

[3.115] The new rent specified in the notice takes effect on the date specified unless *either* the tenant refers it to the Rent Assessment Committee for adjudication, *or* the parties agree a variation of the rent which is different from that proposed or agree that the rent should remain unchanged[1]. The parties' right to agree a variation in the rent is expressly preserved by s 13(5), and is unaffected by the statutory review process. The initiative therefore rests squarely on the tenant, should he wish to challenge a proposed increase, to refer the matter to the committee before the date specified for its taking effect. There is a prescribed form for this purpose[2].

1 Ibid, s 13(4).
2 See SI 1997/194, Form No 5 (Appendix, below).

Determination by the Rent Assessment Committee

[3.116] On a reference to the Rent Assessment Committee, the latter must determine the rent at which the committee considers that the dwelling house concerned might reasonably be expected to be let in the open market by a willing landlord under an assured tenancy[1]. The proceedings will be governed by the procedure laid down for Rent Assessment Committee proceedings under the RA 1977, with some minor modifications[2].

1 HA 1988, s 14(1).
2 HA 1988, s 41(1) and SI 1988/2200, applying the Rent Assessment Committees (England and Wales) Regs 1971 (SI 1971/1065) to proceedings under the HA 1988.

[3.117] When valuing the open market rent certain assumptions must be made. The hypothetical assured tenancy is assumed to be subject to the same terms and periods as the subject tenancy, and it must be assumed that the same warning notices have been given for the purposes of the mandatory grounds for possession as were given in relation to the tenancy to which the application actually relates[1].

1 Ibid, s 14(1)(a)–(d), ie notices under Sch 2, Grounds 1–5, see Chapter 4, para 4.20 ff.

[3.118] Certain matters have to be disregarded when assessing the rent. These are set out in s 14(2).

Existing tenancy

[3.119] Any effect on rental value attributable to the granting of a tenancy to a sitting tenant must be disregarded[1].

1 Ibid, s 14(2)(a).

Tenant's improvements

[3.120] Any increase in the value of the dwelling house attributable to a 'relevant improvement' carried out by a person who at the time it was carried out was the tenant must be disregarded[1]. The disregard applies only if the improvement was carried out otherwise than pursuant to an obligation to the immediate landlord or (if it was) if it was carried out in accordance with the terms of a consent granted by the landlord to the improvement concerned.

1 Ibid, s 14(2)(b).

[3.121] Tenants' improvements (ie 'relevant' improvements) which must be disregarded, and the benefit of which will therefore accrue to the tenant, are more closely defined by s 14(3)[1]. They include only those made during the current tenancy itself, or (if made, for instance, during a previous tenancy) during the 21 years prior to the date of service of the notice of increase. In the latter case the disregard applies only if the property has been continuously occupied since the improvement concerned under assured tenancies, on the expiration of which the tenant has not quit the premises.

1 See Landlord and Tenant Act 1954, s 34, on which these provisions are based.

[3.122] Note that this is more restrictive than the rule for valuing a 'fair' rent under the RA 1977, where improvements carried out by the sitting tenant and any predecessor in title of his (whenever effected) must be disregarded[1].

1 RA 1977, s 70(3)(b).

Dilapidations

[3.123] The committee must disregard any *reduction* in the value of the dwelling house attributable to a failure by the tenant to comply with the terms of the tenancy[1]. In *N & D (London) Ltd v Gadsdon*[2] it was held that the disregard applies only to dilapidations arising from breaches of the current tenancy, and not to those occasioned by predecessors in title of the sitting tenant. Where the tenant has an assured tenancy by succession from either a Rent Act protected tenant, or a prior assured tenant, it follows that disrepair flowing from breaches of tenancy by the latter are not to be disregarded. This will lead to a depreciation in rental value. The onus is therefore on the landlord to enforce repairing obligations on the sitting tenant. Under the RA 1977, dilapidations attributable to breaches of tenancy by a regulated tenant *or his predecessors in title* were disregarded in assessing a 'fair' rent.

1 HA 1988, s 14(2)(c).
2 [1992] 1 EGLR 112.

Rates and service charges

[3.124] The committee is required to assume that rates are borne by the tenant, and the rent determined will accordingly be exclusive of rates, water charges, etc[1]. For the purposes of s 14, also, 'rent' does not include any variable service charge[2], but does include any sums payable by the tenant to the landlord for the use of furniture or for services, repairs, insurance and management costs, and maintenance – even if payable under separate agreements[3]. Variable service charges are assigned to a separate system of control under the Landlord and Tenant Act 1985 (LTA 1985)[4].

1 HA 1988, s 14(5). See s 45(1) ibid for definition of 'rates'. Domestic values will be inapplicable in any event, after 1 April 1990, following abolition of the domestic rating system and its replacement.
2 See LTA 1985, s 18, below Chapter 13.
3 HA 1988, s 14(4).
4 See below, Chapter 13 for consideration of variable service charges.

Variation of tenancy terms

[3.125] If the committee also has before it a reference to vary the terms of the tenancy (under s 6, above) it must decide that first and then assess the reviewed rent, bearing in mind the new terms[1]. The date on which the new terms are to take effect under the s 6 notice must not be later than the date in the rent increase notice under s 13. If it is, the machinery for hearing both references together does not apply[2].

1 Ibid, s 14(6).
2 See s 14(6) (b), ibid.

Effective date

[3.126] Unless the parties otherwise agree, the rent determined by the Rent Assessment Committee takes effect from the beginning of the new period of tenancy originally specified in the landlord's notice of increase. There is no provision for registration of rents, unlike fair rents assessed under the RA 1977. The HA 1988, s 42, however, requires the president of each Rent Assessment Committee to keep and make publicly available, on application, details of rents assessed by the committee[1]. The rent binds both parties to the tenancy, but does not attach to the dwelling house so as to restrict the rent levied for future lettings. In this, also, the HA 1988 differs from the approach taken under the RA 1977 to 'fair' rents (which take effect and bind the dwelling on registration; see Chapter 7, para 7.50 ff below).

1 And see the Assured Tenancies and Agricultural Occupancies (Rent Information) Order 1988, SI 1988/2199.

[3.127] The committee has jurisdiction to fix a later date for its award to take effect, if it is satisfied that 'undue hardship' would result from its taking effect from the date in the landlord's notice of increase. The substituted date must not be later than the date the rent is determined by the committee[1]. There is no appeal from the committee's decision (except on a point of law). The parties are free to agree a rent, even while committee proceedings are pending or in progress. The committee is, by s 14(8), not required to continue with its determination of the rent if landlord and tenant give notice in writing and they no longer require such determination, or if the tenancy has come to an end.

1 Ibid, s 14(7).

RENT BOOKS

[3.128] The LTA 1985, s 4 requires tenants occupying premises in return for weekly rent payments to be given rent books containing certain prescribed information[1]. This applies to assured tenancies and assured agricultural occupancies, as well as to Rent Act tenancies. A form, with prescribed information to be inserted into rent books, has been prescribed specifically for assured tenancies and agricultural occupancies[2].

1 The information to be supplied is contained in LTA 1985, s 5 and regulations made hereunder.
2 See SI 1988/2198.

INFORMATION AS TO LANDLORD'S ADDRESS, ETC

[3.129] The Landlord and Tenant Act 1987 (LTA 1987) contains provisions requiring a landlord of residential premises to furnish information to tenants. By the LTA 1987, s 47, any written demand for rent or service charge payments must contain the name and address of the landlord and (if that address is not in England or Wales) an address in England or Wales at which notice (including notices in proceedings) may be served. If the demand fails to include the required information, then any amount demanded which consists of a service charge is to be treated as not due until the stipulated information has been supplied[1].

1 LTA 1987, s 47(2).

[3.130] Further, by the LTA 1987, s 48, the landlord of a dwelling must by notice furnish the tenant with an address in England and Wales at which notices (including notices in proceedings) may be served on him by the tenant. The penalty for non-compliance in this instance is more severe. If the landlord fails to give notice in accordance with s 48(1) then any rent or service charge otherwise due from the tenant 'shall be treated as not being due from the tenant to the landlord at any time before the landlord does comply' with that provision[1].

1 Ibid, s 48(2).

[3.131] The only saving is for periods when a receiver or manager has been appointed by the court inter alia to receive rents and service charge payments from tenants[1].

1 Ibid, s 48(3).

[3.132] These provisions apply whenever there is a letting of 'premises' which include or consist of a dwelling[1]. This phrase has been given a wide meaning, to include not only a dwelling per se but the subject matter of a letting; eg an agricultural holding which includes a dwelling[2]. These provisions have also been held to apply to tenancies created or in existence before the LTA 1987 came into force, and to any rent which was in arrears before that date[3]. The effect of non-compliance with s 48 is to render the rent not lawfully due until a notice with the prescribed information has been served. It will be irrecoverable in proceedings, and (moreover) non-payment cannot furnish a ground for possession under, for instance, the HA 1988, Sch 2, Ground 8, Ground 10 or Ground 11. In *Dallhold Estates (UK) Pty Ltd v Lindsey Trading Properties Inc*[4], however, the court refused to give to s 48(2) the extended meaning there argued for, viz that failure to give notice under s 48(1) should have the effect that rent which would otherwise have been due is irrecoverable for all time. Once notice complying with s 48(1) has been given, all rent contracted for becomes lawfully due from the tenant and recoverable, including payments due prior to notification under s 48 having been given.

1 Ibid, s 46(1).
2 *Dallhold Estates (UK) Pty Ltd v Lindsey Trading Properties Inc* [1994] 17 EG 148, CA. See also *Maunsell v Olins* [1975] AC 373.
3 See *Hussain v Singh* [1993] 31 EG 75, CA.
4 [1992] 1 EGLR 88, esp at 92 per Chadwick J; revsd on other grounds [1994] 17 EG 148, CA.

THE RENT ASSESSMENT COMMITTEE: INFORMATION POWERS, PUBLICITY OF AWARDS

[3.133] Under the RA 1977, the Rent Assessment Committee fulfilled an appellate role, hearing appeals from determinations of a fair rent by the rent officer[1]. As we have seen, its role under the HA 1988 in relation to assured tenancies is different, as it now has first instance jurisdiction to determine rent and vary terms of tenancies under the assured tenancy regime. The rent officer has no function under the HA 1988 in relation to these matters, although he now has extensive duties in relation to housing benefit. There is now no jurisdiction to hear appeals against determinations on rent or terms, appeal against the Rent Assessment Committee's decision being limited to points of law only.

1 See RA 1977, Sch 11, paras 7–9.

Powers to require information

[3.134] The HA 1988, s 41 gives the committee power to require information from landlord or tenant, if such is 'reasonably' required to enable it to carry out its functions. A request for information must be made by 14 days' notice given in prescribed form[1]. Default is constituted a criminal offence by s 41(3), punishable on summary conviction with a fine. Moreover, special provision is made for offences committed by a body corporate, engaging personal liability in any director or other officer by whose knowledge, connivance or neglect, the default in complying with an information request has occurred. The committee itself has no power to prosecute defaulters: it was felt that existing provisions conferring on local authorities power to do so in such cases were adequate[2].

1 HA 1988, s 41(2).
2 Local Government Act 1972, s 222. And see Parl Debs (HL) Standing Committee G, 4 February 1988, col 626.

Publicity of awards

[3.135] The determination of market rents for assured tenancies and shorthold rents is, under the 1988 Act, essentially a comparative exercise. To sustain this comparative function, the HA 1988, s 42 requires the president of each committee to keep a public record of information with respect to rents under assured tenancies and agricultural occupancies which have been referred to the Rent Assessment Committee. The information to be so kept is specified in an order made by the Secretary of State[2]. During committee proceedings on the HA 1988, a government assurance was given that the power given by s 42(1) to discontinue this function would not be exercised[1]. The reference to assured tenancies in s 42(1) is also intended to encompass assured shorthold tenancies, information as to rents of which will therefore also have to be registered[3].

1 See Parl Debs (HL) Standing Committee G, 4 February 1988, col 429.
2 See SI 1988/2199.
3 Ibid, col 630. See below, Chapter 11.

[3.136] Clearly, without information of this type it would be impossible to determine the appropriate rent for a shorthold tenancy by reference to the rents obtaining for shorthold tenancies of similar dwelling houses in the locality, as required by the HA 1988, s 22(3).

DISTRESS FOR RENT: RESTRICTIONS

[3.137] By virtue of the HA 1988, s 19, no distress for unpaid rent of a dwelling let on an assured tenancy can be levied except with the leave of the county court.

On an application for leave to levy distress, the court has power to suspend, adjourn, stay or postpone distress in the same manner as in possession proceedings under one of the discretionary grounds for possession[1]. This provision re-enacts in the assured tenancy context the restrictions on distress for rent applicable to regulated tenancies and contained in the RA 1977, s 147. It should be noted, however, that these restrictions do not apply to distress levied under the County Courts Act 1984, s 102.

1 See below para 4.17 ff.

E Succession to assured tenancies

[3.138] The HA 1988, s 17 provides for succession to an assured tenancy, but on more restricted grounds than is provided for in the statutory succession scheme for protected and statutory Rent Act tenancies. Succession to an assured tenancy under the HA 1988 can occur only once and only in favour of the tenant's spouse. If one succession has already taken place in a deceased tenant's favour, the deceased's spouse has no further right to succession on the tenant's later death. The succession scheme for assured tenants differs in material respects to that applicable to Rent Act protected and statutory tenancies, and is more limited[1].

1 As to which see Chapter 6 para 6.56 ff.

ENTITLEMENT OF SPOUSE

[3.139] By virtue of s 17(1), three conditions must be satisfied before a succession entitlement arises:

(1) The *sole* tenant under an assured periodic tenancy dies. If the spouse is a joint tenant with the deceased, he or she will take by virtue of the right of survivorship (jus accrescendi), and not under the HA 1988.
(2) Immediately before the tenant's death, his or her spouse must have occupied the dwelling house as his or her principal home. It should be noted that there is no further requirement that the successor has resided *with* the tenant at the dwelling; cf the revised rules for protected Rent Act tenancy succession[1].
(3) The tenant must not himself have been a successor (as defined by s 17(2) and (3)), ie only one succession can take place.

1 See para 6.71 ff, below.

[3.140] If these conditions are satisfied, the tenancy vests on death by virtue of s 17 in the spouse, and not under the tenant's will or intestacy. As a consequence, the ground for possession in Sch 2, Ground 7 will be inapplicable. This avoids the problems encountered under the Rent Act succession provisions (above) where a contractual tenancy subsisting at death might devolve to someone other than the successor entitled, and go into abeyance while the successor occupies the dwelling[1]. Under the HA 1988 no such conflict between contractual and statutory rights can arise – the existing tenancy vests by statute in the qualifying successor as a periodic assured tenancy.

1 See *Moodie v Hosegood* [1952] AC 61, HL.

ONE SUCCESSION ONLY

[3.141] For the purposes of the one-succession rule the deceased tenant is deemed to himself have been a successor in two situations:

(1) If the tenancy became vested in him either by succession under the HA 1988 itself or under the will or intestacy of the former tenant.
(2) If the tenancy was at some time a joint tenancy under which he has become sole tenant by jus accrescendi (ie survivorship)[1].

1 HA 1988, s 17(2)(b).

[3.142] The second rule is unlikely to be commonly invoked in practice, for it can refer only to cases where the tenant holds on a joint tenancy with a third party other than his or her spouse or has remarried. If the tenant's spouse is a joint tenant, he or she will take by right of survivorship, recourse to s 17 being unnecessary. Where there *is* a joint tenancy with someone other than the tenant's spouse, however, the effect may be to deprive the spouse of succession rights on the tenant's death. It should be noted that the tenant is deemed to be a successor, thus barring succession under s 17, if these conditions are satisfied in relation to a prior tenancy of the same (or substantially the same) dwelling house – but only if at all times since then tenant has been the tenant (either solely or jointly with others) of substantially the same dwelling under the new tenancy[1].

1 Ibid, s 17(3).

'SPOUSE'

[3.143] By virtue of s 17(4), a spouse entitled to succession includes not only the de jure spouse of the tenant at the latter's death, but also 'a person who was living with the tenant as his or her wife or husband' at that date. The position of cohabitees generated considerable case law under the original Rent Act succession scheme, the question there being whether a cohabitee qualified for succession as a member of the tenant's family[1]. The wider definition of spouses in the HA 1988 (like the parallel amendment to the Rent Act scheme for protected and statutory tenancies introduced by the HA 1988[2]) removes uncertainty by promoting cohabitees to the status of 'spouse' for the purposes of statutory succession. By contrast, under the HA 1985 cohabitation as de facto husband and wife is not treated as a spousal relationship for the purposes of succession to public sector secure tenancies. Here a cohabitant can merely qualify as a member of the deceased tenant's wider 'family', and as a non-spousal claimant must satisfy a residence condition to be entitled to succession[3].

1 See, eg *Gammans v Ekins* [1950] 2 KB 328, CA; *Hawes v Evenden* [1953] 1 WLR 1169, CA; *Dyson Holdings Ltd v Fox* [1976] QB 503, CA; *Helby v Rafferty* [1978] 3 All ER 1016, CA; *Watson v Lucas* [1980] 3 All ER 647, CA; *Chios Property Investment Co Ltd v Lopez* [1988] 05 EG 57, CA.
2 See below, para 6.65 ff.
3 See HA 1985, s 113, and below Chapter 9, para 9.56 ff.

'As his or her husband or wife'

[3.144] Similar terminology is used to define qualifying cohabitees in other statutes, notably in the sphere of matrimonial law; eg the Domestic Violence and Matrimonial Proceedings Act 1976 (DVMPA 1976), s 1(2). Because of the different context, decisions on this cannot be regarded as of authority, although they may be of illustrative assistance. Thus, in *Adeoso v Adeoso*[1] (a decision under the DVMPA 1976), a married couple who, following matrimonial breakdown, continued to live separately in a two-bedroom flat but shared outgoings, were treated as living together 'as husband and wife' for the purposes of the DVMPA 1976. The test here adopted was whether they were living together 'as if they were husband and wife'. Thus it is thought that the fact that one cohabitee is already married should not invalidate a claim for succession[2]. Note, however, that the parties in *Adeoso v Adeoso* were married, the question there being whether they *continued* to reside 'as' husband and wife – the question in the succession context is often the opposite, namely whether a non-marital relationship in circumstances where the parties have never married signifies cohabiting 'as husband and wife'[3]. In *Sterling Housing Association v Fitzpatrick*[4], a decision under the RA 1977, the House of Lords ruled that same sex partners cannot be construed as 'living together as husband and wife', but that a same sex partner could qualify for succession to a protected Rent Act tenancy as a member of the tenant's wider family. If applied in the context of succession to an assured tenancy, this decision means that a cohabitating same sex partner will never qualify for succession to an assured tenancy, as succession is expressly limited by the HA 1988, s 17 to spouses and persons 'living together as husband and wife'. There is no succession for non-spousal members of the tenant's family. The position is clearly anomalous, and in need of clarification and reform.

1 [1980] 1 WLR 1535, CA.
2 See *Watson v Lucas* [1980] 3 All ER 647, CA.
3 And see further below, para 6.65 ff.
4 (2000) 32 HLR 178 HL. See also Chapter 9, para 9.60 ff.

MORE THAN QUALIFYING SUCCESSOR

[3.145] The inclusion of de facto spouses could lead to a situation where more than one potential successor exists at the tenant's death; eg, a wife or husband of the tenant, and the tenant's cohabitee. In this eventuality, s 17(5) provides that the decision as to who shall succeed lies with the county court, in default of agreement. It should be noted that the court need not be a party to any agreement between potential successors[1]. See the HA 1985, s 89(2) whereby succession to a public sector 'secure' tenancy is determined by the landlord in default of agreement.

1 See *Dealex Properties Ltd v Brooks* [1966] 1 QB 542, CA; *General Management Ltd v Locke* (1980) 255 Estates Gazette 155, CA.

CHAPTER 4

Assured security of tenure

A Assured tenancies: recovery of possession

RESIDENTIAL SECURITY

[4.1] Security of tenure was provided under the Rent Acts by leaving the landlord's right to terminate a residential tenancy at common law (eg by notice to quit) intact, but then conferring on the tenant a personal right of occupancy, following termination, based on the statutory tenancy – a personal right of occupancy vested in the tenant. The court was then prohibited from making an order for possession, bringing the statutory tenancy to an end, except on the grounds in the Rent Act 1977 (RA 1977), Sch 15. As has already been noted, the Housing Act 1988 (HA 1988) operates in an altogether different manner[1]. It firstly interferes with the landlord's right to terminate the contractual tenancy, by providing:

(a) that a periodic assured tenancy cannot be brought to an end without an order of the court; and
(b) that a fixed-term assured tenancy can be terminated, pursuant to a 'break' clause, only in limited circumstances.

1 See Chapter 1, para 1.18 ff, above.

[4.2] Where the landlord terminates a fixed-term tenancy, a statutory periodic tenancy will arise under the HA 1988, s 5 and this in turn can be terminated only by a court order obtained under the HA 1988, Sch 2. The statutory periodic tenancy that arises under s 5 is a tenancy taking effect in possession (ie a tenancy properly so-called) unlike the Rent Act statutory tenancy, which was merely a personal right of occupancy vested by statute in the tenant. This difference of approach has a number of important consequences, both for the tenant's legal rights and obligations, and for the organisation of the statutory provisions governing assured security of tenure[1]. The approach of the HA 1988 is to prevent the *initial* contractual tenancy being terminated by the landlord except in accordance with the terms of the HA 1988, and in the case of certain fixed-term tenancies to impose a new contractual tenancy by statute, which in turn must be terminated in accordance with the HA 1988. The RA 1977 operated to confer security at the *later* stage, following lawful termination of the contractual tenancy, by restricting the landlord's right to terminate the occupier's statutory tenancy and attendant statutory right of occupancy.

1 For example, the statutory periodic tenancy may, in certain circumstances, be assignable, and capable of transmission on death by will or on intestacy. See further Chapter 1, para 1.20 ff, above.

[4.3] It might also be added that, under the Housing Act 1980 (HA 1980), security of tenure for old-style 'assured' tenants was based on the Landlord and Tenant Act 1954 (LTA 1954), Pt II. Although some of the grounds in the HA 1988, Sch 2 are based on the provisions in the LTA 1954 applicable to business lettings, the assured tenancy provisions operate in a fundamentally different manner from the LTA 1954.

TERMINATION OF ASSURED TENANCIES

[4.4] By virtue of the HA 1988, s 5(1) an assured tenancy can be brought to an end *by the landlord* only in the circumstances set out below. The prohibitions on termination explained below operate only where the landlord seeks to determine the tenancy. The HA 1988 places no restriction on the tenant's ability to terminate an assured tenancy by any of the recognised methods available under the general law. A notice to quit by the tenant will therefore be effective, as will a surrender of the tenancy. Note, moreover, that one out of joint tenants can give an effective notice to quit a periodic assured tenancy[1]. The tenant's ability to terminate is, however, restricted by anti-avoidance provisions in s 5(5). These nullify any surrender, notice to quit, or any other document bringing the tenancy to an end at any time while it is an assured tenancy, where the document or notice in question was given or executed either before or at the time the assured tenancy was granted. This prevents the landlord obtaining a deed of surrender or tenant's notice to quit at the time of grant, thus sidestepping the security provisions of the HA 1988. It does not, however, invalidate any surrender or notice to quit given at any time *after* the grant of the tenancy in question; neither will it invalidate a prior surrender or notice to quit if, at the material time, the tenancy has ceased to be an 'assured' tenancy[2].

In *Bankway Properties Ltd v Penfold-Dunsford*[3] it was held that a rent review clause entitling the landlord to increase rent to £25,000 (a figure above the rent limit for assured tenancy protection) was merely a device to enable the landlord to obtain possession of the premises free from the restrictions in ss 5 to 7 of the 1988 Act. It was repugnant to the statutory provisions, in that the parties had clearly intended to grant an assured tenancy, and was an unlawful contracting out of the statute and unenforceable.

The HA 1988 distinguishes between periodic and fixed-term assured tenancies.

1 *Greenwich LBC v McGrady* (1982) 6 HLR 36, CA; *Hammersmith and Fulham LBC v Monk* [1992] 1 All ER 1, HL.
2 For instance because the tenant has ceased to reside in the dwelling as his only or principal home. See Chapter 3, para 3.64 ff above.
3 [2001] 2 EGLR 36, CA.

Periodic assured tenancies

[4.5] A periodic assured tenancy can be brought to an end by the landlord only by an order of the court obtained under the HA 1988. Notice to quit, in addition to notice of proceedings, is not only unnecessary – if given it will be of no effect[1]. A possession order, if obtained, will both entitle the landlord to possession and, by inference, terminate the 'contractual' tenancy[2].

1 HA 1988, s 5(1). See also Parl Debs (HL) vol 500, col 1362.
2 The latter effect is not expressly stipulated in s 5(1) ibid, but must follow as a matter of inference from the drafting of the relevant provisions in the HA 1988. It would be odd were the HA 1988 to entitle the landlord to possession while leaving the contractual periodic tenancy intact.

Fixed-term assured tenancies

[4.6] The provisions governing the termination of fixed-term tenancies are more complex, and in some regards more problematic. Many fixed-term assured tenancies will be assured shortholds, in relation to which additional problems arise where termination is sought during the fixed (shorthold) term of tenancy. These are discussed separately in Chapter 5, below[1].

1 See Chapter 5, para 5.30 ff below.

[4.7] A fixed-term assured tenancy can only be brought to an end by the landlord either by a court order or 'in the case of a fixed-term tenancy which contains power for the landlord to determine the tenancy in certain circumstances, by the exercise of that power'[1]. By virtue of s 45(4), however, this does *not* include a proviso for re-entry or forfeiture. Although the relevant provisions are obscurely drafted, it is clear that a 'break' clause, if exercised by the landlord, will be effective to determine a fixed-term tenancy; a forfeiture clause cannot, however, be exercised to terminate the tenancy while it is assured. It may, therefore, be important to distinguish between the two in certain cases.

1 HA 1988, s 5(1).

[4.8] The HA 1988 itself refers to a power to determine 'in certain circumstances'. It would seem, therefore, that a break clause giving the landlord power to give notice terminating the tenancy if stipulated conditions are met, or on certain occasions (eg at stated intervals during the tenancy) would be within s 5(1). A clause giving an unlimited and unrestricted right to break the tenancy by notice may not. Similarly, a clause giving the landlord a right to 'break' the term if the tenant is in breach of any of the terms of the agreement is likely to be construed by the courts as a proviso for re-entry and forfeiture, and not as a break clause within the meaning of s 5(1)[1]. As an assured tenancy cannot be brought to an end by re-entry or forfeiture, it follows that statutory rights to relief from forfeiture[2] under the general law will be inapplicable in possession proceedings under the HA 1988[3]. This may be disadvantageous to a subtenant or mortgagee, who would otherwise be entitled to relief under the Law of Property Act 1925, s 146(4). The HA 1988 makes special provision for the protection of an assured subtenant where a mesne tenancy is terminated[4], but no such protection is afforded to mortgagees or other third parties with an interest in the property.

1 See *Plymouth Corpn v Harvey* [1971] 1 WLR 549.
2 The Law of Property Act 1925, s 146(1)–(4).
3 See *Artesian Residential Investments Ltd v Beck* [1999] 2 EGLR 30 (assured tenant not entitled to relief against forfeiture under the County Courts Act 1984, s 138)
4 HA 1988, s 17.

[4.9] If an assured tenancy is terminated by the exercise of a break clause, this will not in itself entitle the landlord to possession. The tenant will normally be entitled to remain in possession, as a statutory periodic tenancy will arise under the HA 1988, s 5(2). The latter provides that if a fixed-term assured tenancy comes to an end *otherwise* than by virtue of an order of the court[1] or a surrender or other action on the part of the tenant[2], then the tenant shall be entitled to remain in possession of the dwelling house let under that tenancy, and his right to possession shall depend upon a statutory periodic tenancy arising under s 5(1). By virtue of s 5(4) the statutory periodic tenancy will not arise if, on the coming to an end of the fixed-term tenancy, the tenant is entitled by virtue of the *grant* of another tenancy, to possession of the same or substantially the same dwelling house as was let to him under the former fixed-term tenancy. The statutory tenancy will therefore arise under s 5(2) in two of the commonest situations in which a fixed-term tenancy ends, namely:

(a) where it expires by effluxion of time at the end of the contractual term; and
(b) where it is terminated during the contractual term pursuant to a break clause in the lease[3].

The statutory periodic tenancy itself can then be terminated only by court order on one of the grounds in the HA 1988, Sch 2, or by surrender or notice to quit by the tenant. No notice need be served by the tenant to claim security. Cf the requirements as to notice under the HA 1980 for 'old-style' assured tenancies and under the LTA 1954, Pt II (business lettings).

1 Section 7(6) ibid places additional restrictions on the landlord's ability to terminate by obtaining a court order, which will be relevant here – see below, para 4.11 ff.
2 For instance notice to quit by the tenant or one out of joint tenants. On surrender see *Dibbs v Campbell* [1988] 2 EGLR 122, CA and *Bridge* (1989) Conv 98.
3 Providing always that the clause satisfies the requirements of the HA 1988, s 5(1), ie it gives the landlord power to determine 'in certain circumstances' only. If it does not, the clause will in principle be ineffective to end the tenancy under s 5(1) ibid.

ORDERS FOR POSSESSION

General

[4.10] The HA 1988, s 7(1) stipulates that the court shall not make an order for possession of a dwelling house let on an assured tenancy except on one or more of the grounds set out in Sch 2. Like its similarly phrased predecessor (see the RA 1977, s 98(1)), this provision would, it is suggested, void any executory agreement to give up possession should the tenant subsequently seek to enforce his right to security of tenure, and likewise an agreement to surrender would clearly be unenforceable[1]. It would not, however, affect a consent order for possession, to which different considerations apply[2]. The grounds for possession in Sch 2 differ markedly from those applicable to the original 'assured' tenancy under the HA 1980, and are a mixture of familiar Rent Act cases for possession, and the grounds of opposition found in the LTA 1954, s 30 applicable to business leases. The emphasis and balance is also different to RA 1977, in that the mandatory grounds are set out first and now include several matters previously constituting discretionary cases for possession under the RA 1977, Sch 15. A preoccupation with financial matters is signaled by the inclusion of no fewer than three grounds for possession based on non-payment of rent, and the grounds (in general terms) reinforce the landlord's prerogative to exploit property for commercial reward to a greater extent than did the RA 1977. For example, the landlord now has mandatory grounds where redevelopment is in prospect, or where a mortgagee wishes to sell with vacant possession.

1 See eg *Appleton v Aspin* [1988] 04 EG 123, CA noted in (1988) Conv 212–216 (S Bridge).
2 See *Syed Hussain v Abdullah Sahib* [1985] 1 WLR 1392, PC.

Fixed-term tenancies

[4.11] The court's power to make possession orders for dwellings let on a fixed-term assured tenancy is further restricted. By virtue of s 7(6), the court cannot make an order for possession unless the ground for possession relied on is either Ground 2 (pre-existing mortgage, with mortgagee exercising power of sale) or Ground 8 (three months' arrears of rent), or one of the discretionary grounds for possession (other than Grounds 9 or 16). Furthermore, the terms of the tenancy must make provision for the tenancy to be terminated on one of those grounds – although this can 'take the form of a provision for re-entry, for forfeiture, for determination by notice or otherwise'. These further restrictions are central to the assured tenancy concept, for they provide the 'assurance' that the tenant will have security of tenure during the fixed period of tenancy agreed with the landlord, with limited exceptions based on obligations to a pre-existing mortgagee or failure to pay rent.

[4.12] Note that, by virtue of s 7(7) the court has power to make an order for possession of a dwelling on grounds relating to a fixed-term tenancy which has come to an end, and where an order is made in such circumstances any statutory periodic tenancy which has arisen on the ending of the fixed-term tenancy shall end (without notice and regardless of the period of tenancy) on the day on which the order takes effect.

[4.13] The form a leasehold provision must take in order to invoke s 7(6) is a matter of some difficulty. The section refers to provision being made 'by proviso for re-entry, for forfeiture, for determination by notice or otherwise'. A forfeiture clause or break clause will therefore suffice, provided it identifies the grounds to be relied on sufficiently clearly, and provided that ground is one of those allowed by s 7(6) during the fixed-term. For the avoidance of doubt it is probably preferable for any break or forfeiture clause to refer specifically to the permitted grounds in the HA 1988, Sch 2, particularly if the mandatory grounds (Grounds 2 and 8) are to be available. A forfeiture clause in standard form, for instance, would not suffice under s 7(6) to make Ground 8 available to the landlord, as the latter requires two months' arrears of rent both at the date of notice of proceedings and the subsequent hearing[1]. These provisions cause particular difficulty with regard to termination of shorthold tenancies, and a more detailed consideration is given in that context below[2].

1 See *McDonald v Tipping* (1991) Leicester CC (unreported), discussed below at para 5.37. And for the form of forfeiture clause (1989) 139 NLJ 104, 160, 326.
2 See Chapter 5, para 5.30 ff below.

[4.14] Note that a proviso for re-entry or forfeiture, though effective to activate the right to possession under s 7(6), will not ground an action for forfeiture under the general law at any time while the tenancy remains an assured tenancy within the meaning of the HA 1988[1].

1 HA 1988, ss 5(1) and 45(4).

NOTICE OF PROCEEDINGS

[4.15] Before commencing proceedings for possession the landlord must serve notice of proceedings in accordance with s 8. The court cannot entertain proceedings for possession of a dwelling let on an assured tenancy unless the landlord (or in the case of joint landlords one of them) has served notice of proceedings in accordance with s 8, and an order for possession cannot be made on any of the grounds in the HA 1988, Sch 2 unless that ground and particulars of it are specified in the notice. The ground for possession in the notice can, however, be added to or altered with the leave of the court[1]. Notice of proceedings can be dispensed with if the court considers it 'just and equitable' to do so, but cannot be dispensed with if the landlord is seeking to rely on Ground 8 (two months' rent arrears)[2]. This, it is suggested, will be a question of fact for the court (cf the court's discretion to dispense with written notice at the commencement of tenancy if mandatory grounds are to be relied on; the RA 1977, Sch 15, Case 11, and the HA 1988, Sch 2, Grounds 1–5). The landlord's notice of proceedings must give at least *two weeks'* notice of the commencement of proceedings, unless Grounds 1, 2, 5–7, 9 or 16 are at issue – for example if the landlord is relying on the availability of alternative accommodation – in which event at least *two months'* notice must be given[3]. If the tenancy is periodic, moreover, the notice must expire on a term date of the tenancy. If Ground 14 is specified (nuisance or illegal or immoral user of the premises) the requirement is only that the notice of proceedings specifies a date not earlier than its service[4].

1 HA 1988, s 8(2).
2 See s 8(1)(b) and (5).
3 See s 8(3) and (4A), amended by HA 1996, s 151.
4 Section 8(4) as amended by the HA 1996, s 151.

[4.16] The possession proceedings must not begin earlier than the date specified in the notice of proceedings, and not later than 12 months from the date of the notice. A prescribed form is provided for in the Assured Tenancies and Agricultural Occupancies (Forms) Regulations 1997[1] and the notice must be given in this form or a form 'substantially to the same effect'. Moreover, the court cannot make an order for possession unless the ground relied on and particulars of it are specified in the notice of proceedings[2]. So, in *Mountain v Hastings*[3] possession was refused where the landlord had served notice specifying only 'Landlord intends to seek possession ... Ground 8, at least three months' rent unpaid.' The words used must fully set out the substance of the ground and give the tenant the information that the HA 1988 requires, so as to enable him to consider what he should do, and what is in his power to protect against the loss of his home. The notice here omitted to inform the tenant that the three months' rent in issue must be (a) lawfully due, and (b) owing both at the date of service of the notice *and* at the date of the hearing. It was therefore bad in law. Note also that where Ground 14A (domestic violence) is relied on and the tenant's partner has left the dwelling, a copy of the notice of proceedings must be served on the partner (as well as the tenant) before the court can entertain possession proceedings – unless the court considers it just and equitable to dispense with service on the partner[4].

1 See SI 1997/194 Form 3.
2 Ibid, s 8(2).
3 (1993) 25 HLR 427, CA.
4 HA 1988, s 8A, added by HA 1996, s 150.

DISCRETIONARY GROUNDS FOR POSSESSION: SUSPENSION POWERS

[4.17] In cases involving the discretionary grounds for possession only, the court can suspend proceedings or stay execution of a possession order on terms as to payment of rent on such conditions as it thinks fit[1]. It should be noted, however, that when granting a postponement, stay or suspension, the court must (unless it considers it would cause exceptional hardship to the tenant or be unreasonable) impose conditions with regard to the payment of rent arrears and mesne profits (s 9(3)).

If these conditions are complied with, the court can rescind or discharge the possession order if it thinks fit to do so (s 9(4)). The power of suspension etc can also be exercised in favour of a spouse of an assured tenant who enjoys rights of occupation under the Family Law Act 1996, Pt IV[2].

1 See s 9 and cf also RA 1977, s 100.
2 See the Matrimonial Homes Act 1983 (MHA 1983), s 1(6) and HA 1988, s 9(5). But note that the MHA 1983 applies to confer rights of occupation only if the dwelling has, on the facts, become the matrimonial home: see *Hall v King* (1987) 283 Estates Gazette 1400, CA.

MANDATORY GROUNDS FOR POSSESSION

[4.18] These are contained in the HA 1988, Sch 2, Pt I. If one of the grounds is established, then by virtue of s 7(3) the court must order possession, and has no discretion to suspend a possession order.

[4.19] As with the mandatory Rent Act cases for possession, the majority of the assured tenancy grounds for possession require the service of notice, prior to grant of the tenancy, to the effect that the letting is subject to the availability of the ground relied on. Thus Grounds 1–5 below are only available to the landlord if notice was served before the vacancy was granted. Detailed provisions for the giving of notice on grant are contained in the HA 1988, Sch 2, Pt IV. This provides that in the case of joint landlords, the requirement is satisfied if notice prior to grant is given by at least one (joint) landlord[1]. If notice has been validly given, it will also suffice for the purposes of a second or subsequent tenancy of substantially the same dwelling house, provided it was granted on expiry of the original tenancy to the same tenant[2]. A reference to notice being given not later than at the beginning of the tenancy in Grounds 2–5 is a reference to its being given not later than the day on which the tenancy was entered into[3] and not, for instance, any antecedent date from which the grant is expressed to commence. This follows logically from the rule in *Roberts v Church Comrs for England*[4] that a lease cannot vest a term retrospectively in the tenant, and that it takes effect in law from the date it is entered into.

1 Schedule 2, para 7.
2 Ibid, para 8.
3 Ibid, para 11.
4 [1972] 1 QB 278, CA. And see *Keen v Holland* [1984] 1 All ER 75, CA; *Panayi v Roberts* (1993) 25 HLR 421, CA (assured shorthold notice).

B The grounds for possession

MANDATORY GROUNDS FOR POSSESSION

Landlord requiring premises for own use

[4.20] *Ground 1: Not later than the beginning of the tenancy the landlord gave notice in writing to the tenant that possession might be recovered on this ground or the court is of the opinion that it is just and equitable to dispense with the requirement of notice and (in either case):*

(a) *at some time before the beginning of the tenancy, the landlord who is seeking possession or, in the case of joint landlords seeking possession, at least one of them occupied the dwelling house as his only or principal home; or*

(b) *the landlord who is seeking possession or, in the case of joint landlords seeking possession, at least one of them requires the dwelling house as his or his spouse's only or principal home and neither the landlord (or, in the case of joint landlords, any one of them) nor any other person who, as landlord, derived title under the landlord who gave the notice mentioned above, acquired the reversion on the tenancy for money or money's worth.*

[4.21] This ground provides two alternative grounds for possession and encapsulates both former Case 9 and Case 11 in the RA 1977, Sch 15. It gives those who were owner-occupiers before the grant of an assured tenancy a mandatory right of repossession. Note that there is no limitation as to the length of time of the occupier's prior occupation, or when it took place[1]. In the case of joint landlords, prior residence by one expressly suffices (thus confirming *Tilling v Whiteman*)[2]. It should also be noted that there is *no* requirement that the owner-occupier or landlord prove the dwelling is needed for occupation by himself or a member of his family (cf the old RA 1977, Case 11). It would appear, therefore, that this ground would be available to an owner occupier wishing to sell with vacant possession.

1 See *Pocock v Steel* [1985] 1 WLR 229, CA and the Rent (Amendment) Act 1985.
2 [1980] AC 1, HL decided under the RA 1977, Case 11.

[4.22] Notice in writing must be given to the tenant, before grant of the tenancy, that possession might be recovered under the ground. This condition can be dispensed with if the court considers it 'just and equitable' to do so, and Rent Act jurisprudence on the scope of this discretion will prove useful. The courts have shown a willingness to exercise this discretion if an oral notice has been given, but if no notice at all has been given the landlord is unlikely to succeed, for the tenant must appreciate the position when he takes the property[1].

1 See *Bradshaw v Baldwin-Wiseman* [1985] 1 EGLR 123, CA. Cf *Fernandes v Parvardin* (1982) 264 Estates Gazette 49, CA.

[4.23] The landlord who is not a previous owner-occupier can also use this ground, but only if he requires the dwelling as his or his spouse's 'principal' home[1]. Also, he must not have acquired his interest for money or money's worth. No prior residence is required in this instance. This is a restricted version of the old ground in the RA 1977, Case 9, although it applies to spouses only (not children or parents as under Case 9) and no hardship test applies as formerly. Notice in writing of the availability of this ground must be given on the grant of the tenancy.

1 Note, not a residence as formerly under the RA 1977, Case 9.

Dwelling subject to existing mortgage

[4.24] *Ground 2: The dwelling house is subject to a mortgage granted before the beginning of the tenancy and:*

(a) *the mortgagee is entitled to exercise a power of sale conferred on him by the mortgage or by section 101 of the Law of Property Act 1925; and*

(b) *the mortgagee requires possession of the dwelling house for the purpose of disposing of it with vacant possession in exercise of that power; and*
(c) *either notice was given as mentioned in Ground 1 above or the court is satisfied that it is just and equitable to dispense with the requirement of notice; and for the purposes of this ground 'mortgage' includes a charge and 'mortgagee' shall be construed accordingly.*

[4.25] Ground 2 gives the landlord a mandatory ground where, at the time of the letting, the property was subject to a pre-existing mortgage, and the mortgagee wishes to sell with vacant possession pursuant to his power of sale. A Ground 1 notice must have been given by the landlord at the time of grant for this ground to be available – unless the court considers it just and equitable to dispense with the requirement of notice. Mortgagees will presumably wish to obligate a potential landlord to serve the appropriate notice by making this a condition of the mortgage itself. There is no guidance as to how the discretion to dispense with notice will operate in this context; under the parallel RA 1977 ground (Case 11, see below para 6.156 ff), the criterion applied was usually prejudice to the tenant, or the lack of it, arising from non-compliance. *Query*, will hardship to the mortgagee be relevant? See *Dudley and District Benefit Building Society v Emerson*[1] for the right of a mortgagee to repossess where the mortgage excludes the mortgagor's right to create leases. A mortgagee would, accordingly, not be bound by assured tenancies created subsequently in breach of the mortgage agreement. Neither would a tenant, in such circumstances, be entitled to an adjournment or relief under the Administration of Justice Act 1970, s 36, for letting property in breach of the mortgage agreement has been judicially construed as irremediable[2]. Relief is available only where the breach of obligation can be remedied.

1 [1949] Ch 707, CA.
2 See *Britannia Building Society v Earl* [1990] 2 All ER 469, CA.

[4.26] Ground 2 will be of use where the mortgagor's statutory right to create leases[1] is not excluded.

1 Law of Property Act 1925, s 101.

Holiday lettings

[4.27] *Ground 3: The tenancy is a fixed-term tenancy for a term not exceeding eight months and:*

(a) *not later than the beginning of the tenancy the landlord gave notice in writing to the tenant that possession might be recovered on this ground; and*
(b) *at some time within the period of twelve months ending with the beginning of the tenancy, the dwelling house was occupied under a right to occupy it for a holiday.*

[4.28] This ground mirrors that in the RA 1977, Case 13, and allows repossession of out-of-season holiday lets. As formerly, notice must be given at the commencement of the tenancy, which itself must be for a term certain of not more than eight months. Any second or subsequent tenancy in relation to which the notice has effect is to be treated as commencing on the date of the initial tenancy in respect of which notice was originally given (the HA 1988, Sch 2, Pt IV, para 10).

Student lettings

[4.29] *Ground 4: The tenancy is a fixed tenancy for a term not exceeding 12 months and:*

(a) not later than the beginning of the tenancy the landlord gave notice in writing to the tenant that possession might be recovered on this ground; and
(b) at some time within the period of 12 months ending with the beginning of the tenancy, the dwelling house was let on a tenancy falling within paragraph 8 of Schedule 1 to this Act.

[4.30] This ground facilitates repossession of student accommodation let by educational institutions or by landlords who let to such bodies for the purpose of further subletting by the latter to students. The assured tenancy must be for a term certain not exceeding 12 months, and notice of the application of the ground for possession must be given at the outset. This ground is modelled on the RA 1977, Case 14. As with Ground 3 (above), any second or subsequent tenancy is to be treated as commencing on grant of the original tenancy in respect of which notice is given (Sch 2, para 10).

Lettings to ministers of religion

[4.31] *Ground 5: The dwelling house is held for the purpose of being available for occupation by a minister of religion as a residence from which to perform the duties of his office and:*

(a) not later than the beginning of the tenancy the landlord gave notice in writing to the tenant that possession might be recovered on this ground; and
(b) the court is satisfied that the dwelling house is required for occupation by a minister of religion as such a residence.

[4.32] This ground is modelled on the RA 1977, Case 15, and allows repossession where: (a) notice that the ground is applicable has been served prior to letting; and (b) the dwelling is required for a minister of religion.

Demolition or reconstruction of dwelling

[4.33] *Ground 6: The landlord who is seeking possession or, if that landlord is a registered social landlord or charitable housing trust, a superior landlord intends to demolish or reconstruct the whole or a substantial part of the dwelling house or to carry out substantial works on the dwelling house or any part thereof or any building of which it forms part and the following conditions are fulfilled:*

(a) the intended work cannot reasonably be carried out without the tenant giving up possession of the dwelling house because:
  (i) the tenant is not willing to agree to such a variation of the terms of the tenancy as would give such access and other facilities as would permit the intended work to be carried out, or
  (ii) the nature of the intended work is such that no such variation is practicable, or
  (iii) the tenant is not willing to accept an assured tenancy of such part only of the dwelling house (in this sub-paragraph referred to as 'the reduced part') as would leave in the possession of his landlord so much of the dwelling house as would be

reasonable to enable the intended work to be carried out and, where appropriate, as would give such access and other facilities over the reduced part as would permit the intended work to be carried out, or

(iv) the nature of the intended work is such that such a tenancy is not practicable; and

(b) either the landlord seeking possession acquired his interest in the dwelling house before the grant of the tenancy or that interest was in existence at the time of that grant and neither that landlord (or, in the case of joint landlords, any of them) nor any other person who, alone or jointly with others, has acquired that interest since that time acquired it for money or money's worth; and

(c) the assured tenancy on which the dwelling house is let did not come into being by virtue of any provision of Schedule 2 to the RA 1977, as amended by Part I of Schedule 4 to this Act or, as the case may be, section 4 of the Rent (Agriculture) Act 1976, as amended by Part II of that Schedule.

For the purposes of this ground, if, immediately before the grant of the tenancy, the tenant to whom it was granted or, if it was granted to joint tenants, any of them was the tenant or one of the joint tenants of the dwelling house concerned under an earlier assured tenancy (or as the case may be, under a tenancy to which Schedule 10 of the Local Government and Housing Act 1989 applied) any reference in paragraph (b) above to the grant of the tenancy is a reference to the grant of that earlier assured tenancy (or as the case may be, to the grant of the tenancy to which the said Schedule 10 applied).

For the purposes of this ground 'registered housing association' has the same meaning as in the Housing Associations Act 1985 and 'charitable housing trust' means a housing trust, within the meaning of that Act, which is a charity, within the meaning of the Charities Act 1993.

[4.34] This ground reflects the policy applied to business leases by of the LTA 1954, s 30(1)(f) (reconstruction of business premises) and was not available under the RA 1977[1]. A similar ground, again reflecting the LTA 1954 approach, is also provided for public sector 'secure' tenancies[2]. It gives the landlord a mandatory right to repossess if he 'intends to demolish or reconstruct the whole or a substantial part of the dwelling house or to carry out substantial works on the dwelling house or any part thereof or any building of which it forms part'.

1 See generally M Haley, *Statutory Regulation of Business Tenancies* (OUP 2000) at p 215 ff.
2 HA 1985, Sch 2, Ground 10, below para 10.53 ff.

[4.35] The following conditions must also be satisfied:

(1) The landlord must not have acquired his interest as such by purchase.
(2) Either the tenant is not willing to agree to a variation of the tenancy to give the landlord access to carry out the work, or such variation is not practicable.
(3) Having regard to these factors, the landlord must not be able to carry out the work without obtaining possession.

'Possession' has, in this context, been interpreted under the LTA 1954 to mean 'legal possession', not factual possession, ie the landlord must show he cannot obtain possession to do the work intended under the terms of the current tenancy, which must therefore be terminated (the rule in *Heath v Drown*[1]). The matter turns, in most cases, on the terms of the tenancy as to entry for repairs and improvements, and previous case law under the LTA 1954 may prove of assistance in the present context. For instance, the landlord will require possession in the required sense if the lease allows access to carry out repairs and the proposed work of reconstruction constitutes an improvement (not simply repair)[2]. It should also be noted that s 16 implies into every assured tenancy a term that the tenant will allow access and all reasonable facilities for executing repairs to the dwelling house.

1 [1973] AC 498, HL.
2 See inter alia *Price v Esso Petroleum Co Ltd*, (1980) 255 Estates Gazette, 243, CA; *Leathwoods v Total Oil (Great Britain) Ltd* [1985] 2 EGLR 237, CA; and *Cerex Jewels Ltd v Peachey Property Corpn plc* [1986] 2 EGLR 65, CA.

Intention to demolish or reconstruct

[4.36] The landlord, to use this ground, must establish that he has a settled intention to carry out work of demolition and/or reconstruction and that he has a reasonable prospect of carrying out his planned redevelopment. This is a question of fact, to be decided at the date of hearing[1]. Thus it will be necessary to establish that steps have been taken to obtain necessary planning consents and, if the landlord is a company, that a board resolution to carry out the works has been obtained. Decisions on the provisions of the LTA 1954, s 30(1)(f) and (g), on which the ground is based, will be of assistance; for example, the principle in the leading case of *Cunliffe v Goodman*[2] was applied in the context of 'old-style' assured residential tenancies in *Wansbeck District Council v Marley*[3].

1 See *Betty's Cafes Ltd v Phillips Furnishing Stores Ltd* [1959] AC 20; *Cunliffe v Goodman* [1950] 2 KB 237, CA, decided under the LTA 1954. And see further *Europark (Midlands) Ltd v Town Centre Securities plc* (1985) 274 Estates Gazette 289; *A Levy & Son Ltd v Martin Brent Developments Ltd* [1987] 2 EGLR 93; *Capocci v Groble* [1987] 2 EGLR 102, CA.
2 [1950] 2 KB 237.
3 (1987) 20 HLR 247, CA.

Landlord by purchase, not grant

[4.37] By virtue of Ground 6, para (b), the ground is *not* available to a landlord (or one out of joint landlords) if he did not acquire the reversionary estate before the grant of the assured tenancy in question, *or* if he did acquire it subsequently, if he acquired it by purchase for money or money's worth. The intent is to avoid the use of this ground by speculators acquiring the freehold interest during the currency of an assured tenancy (see the LTA 1954, s 30(2)). The exclusion would not apply, however, where the reversionary interest is vested in a corporate body, control of which is transferred by purchase of shares[1]. Where the landlord has renewed the tenancy (thereby becoming a landlord by grant, not purchase) after acquiring the reversionary estate, the ground will not be available if the tenancy is of the same dwelling house and is granted to the sitting tenant either alone or as one of joint tenants[2].

1 See HC Debs, vol 134, col 1025 ff, for concern on this point.
2 This would appear to be the effect of the penultimate paragraph of Ground 6 (above). Cf *Northcote Laundry Ltd v Fredrick Donnelly Ltd* [1968] 1 WLR 562, CA.

Assured tenants by succession

[4.38] Note that this ground does not apply where the current tenant holds an assured tenancy by succession under the RA 1977 or Rent (Agriculture) Act 1976

(R(A)A 1976). This prevents the tenancy, though now assured, becoming vulnerable to a ground previously unavailable under the Rent Act against the successor's predecessor.

Compensation for disturbance

[4.39] By virtue of s 11, where a landlord acquires possession in reliance on Ground 6, he must pay the tenant a sum 'equal to the reasonable expenses likely to be incurred by the tenant in removing from the dwelling house'. This is to be decided by agreement or, in default of agreement, by the county court deciding what amounts to reasonable removal expenses. Cf the LTA 1954, s 37, which entitles a business tenant to recover compensation based on the ratable value of the holding (depending on length of occupation) where possession is recovered under the parallel provisions of the business tenancies code. Unlike the comparable provisions in the LTA 1954, however, the compensation here is intended to compensate solely for removal expenses and not loss of business goodwill.

Devolution on death of tenant

[4.40] *Ground 7: The tenancy is a periodic tenancy (including a statutory periodic tenancy) which has devolved under the will or intestacy of the former tenant and the proceedings for the recovery of possession are begun not later than 12 months after the death of the former tenant or, if the court so directs, after the date on which, in the opinion of the court, the landlord or, in the case of joint landlords, any one of them became aware of the former tenant's death.*

For the purposes of this ground, the acceptance by the landlord of rent from a new tenant after the death of the former tenant shall not be regarded as creating a new periodic tenancy, unless the landlord agrees in writing to a change (as compared with the tenancy before the death) in the amount of the rent, the period of the tenancy, the premises which are let or any other term of the tenancy.

[4.41] This ground gives the landlord a mandatory right to possession where a periodic tenancy (including a statutory periodic tenancy) has devolved under the will or intestacy of the former tenant, provided proceedings are commenced within 12 months of the date on which the landlord (or one of joint landlords) became aware of the tenant's death.

[4.42] Court proceedings for possession must be begun within 12 months of the landlord becoming aware of the tenant's death. It will not suffice if notice of proceedings is served within the 12 months period allowed, but court proceedings commence after its expiry[1]. This Ground does not affect the statutory periodic tenancy which vests in certain close relatives by virtue of the HA 1988 itself; eg if they are assured tenants by succession following the death of a Rent Act tenant. There is a statutory right to one succession, by spouses only, to assured tenancies granted under the HA 1988[2], and this also remains unaffected by this ground. For the purposes of this ground the acceptance of rent after the death of a former tenant is deemed not to create a fresh periodic tenancy. The intent is to ensure that succession takes place *only* in accordance with the terms of the HA 1988, and not de facto by devolution under the tenant's will or intestacy. Devolution of an unexpired *fixed* (not periodic) term is, however, unaffected.

1 *Osada v Shepping* [2000] 2 EGLR 38.
2 HA 1988, s 17. See also Chapter 3 above, para 3.138 ff.

Arrears of rent

[4.43] *Ground 8: Both at the date of the service of the notice under section 8 of this Act relating to the proceedings for possession and at the date of the hearing:*

(a) if rent is payable weekly or fortnightly, at least eight weeks' rent is unpaid;
(b) if rent is payable monthly, at least two months' rent is unpaid;
(c) if rent is payable quarterly, at least one quarter's rent is more than three months in arrears; and
(d) if rent is payable yearly, at least three months' rent is more than three months in arrears;

and for the purpose of this ground 'rent' means rent lawfully due from the tenant.

[4.44] Ground 8 was amended by the HA 1996[1]. Rent arrears are a mandatory ground of possession under the assured tenancy regime. Previously it was one of the principal discretionary grounds for Rent Act protected and statutory tenancies[2].

If two months' rent is unpaid at the date on which notice of proceedings is served, the ground will be unavailable if rent is subsequently paid so as to reduce the amount outstanding to less than two months' rent prior to the subsequent hearing. For this ground to apply, rent must be 'lawfully due' from the tenant. *Query*, therefore, if the tenant withholds rent to pay for landlord's repairs, within the rule in *Lee-Parker v Izzet*[3]. Presumably rent would not then be 'lawfully due' and the ground inapplicable[4]. Note also that, pursuant to the Landlord and Tenant Act 1987 (LTA 1987), s 48, rent becomes lawfully due only when the landlord has furnished the tenant with notice of his address for the service and receipt of notices and other communications[5]. Rent due and unpaid prior to this will not be 'lawfully due' and will not ground proceedings under Ground 8[6]. In *Rogan v Woodfield Building Services Ltd*[7] it was held, however, that the landlord's notice does not have to include words expressly stating that the address given is one at which notices may be served by the tenant. Accordingly, a shorthold notice, or a notice terminating a shorthold tenancy, can satisfy LTA 1987, s 48[8]. Section 48 applies to tenancies created or in existence before the LTA 1987 came into effect and to rent which was in arrears before that date[9]. This Ground is, of course, open to the criticism that it exposes the tenant's security to the vagaries of technical rules as to the legality of rent demands, without a residual discretion in the court to decide the matter on the merits of the tenant's position. Furthermore, the ground may be available even if non-payment is out of the tenant's control. In *Marath v MacGillivray*[10] it was held that, where rent was paid by the local housing authority, non-payment by the latter did not provide a defence for the tenant to proceedings under Ground 8.

1 HA 1996, s 101.
2 The RA 1977, Sch 15, Case 1.
3 [1971] 1 WLR 1688.
4 See ibid at 1693, per Goff J.
5 See *Dallhold Estates (UK) Ltd v Lindsey Trading Properties Inc* [1992] 23 EG 112 revsd [1994] 17 EG 148, CA.
6 For examples see, *Westminster CC v Isaac* (1993) 12 *Legal Action* 11 and *Barnsley Metropolitan BC v Crossland* (1993) ibid (address on rent giro book insufficient) (county court).
7 (1995) 27 HLR 78.

8 See *Marath v McGillivray* (1996) 28 HLR 484 (notice under HA 1988, s 20 on grant of shorthold sufficient); *Drew-Morgan v Hamid-Zadeh* (1999) L&TR 503 (notice of termination of shorthold under HA 1988, s 21).
9 See *Hussain v Singh* [1993] 31 EG 75, CA. The LTA 1987 came into force on 1 February 1988.
10 (1996) 28 HLR 484. Note the Court of Appeal's comments upon the possibility of collusion between the landlord and housing authority.

DISCRETIONARY GROUNDS FOR POSSESSION

[4.45] The HA 1988, Sch 2, Pt II sets out a further eight discretionary grounds for possession. If one of the discretionary grounds is made out, the court may make an order for possession only if 'it considers it reasonable do so so' (s 7(4)). Previous authority on the construction of the analogous provisions of the RA 1977 will, of course, be of assistance[1]. Whether it is reasonable to grant possession is a question of fact for the county court, and clearly factors of relevant hardship to either party will be particularly relevant[2]. The extent of the tenant's breach and whether it was deliberate and/or avoidable are relevant factors. The court can also take into account the tenant's conduct over and above (for example) his inexcusable failure to pay rent, including the making of false allegations against the landlord[3]. Reasonableness falls to be determined as at the date of hearing.

1 See RA 1977, s 98(1) and Sch 15, Pt 1. The authorities are numerous; see further Megarry's *Rent Acts* (11th edn 1988) pp 387–393 for detailed considerations of the case law under previous rent legislation.
2 See *Cumming v Danson* [1942] 2 All ER 653, CA; *Cresswell v Hodgson* [1951] 2 KB 92, CA; and *Coombs v Parry* (1987) 19 HLR 384, CA.
3 *Drew-Morgan v Hamid Zadeh* (1999) L&TR 503.

Suitable alternative accommodation

[4.46] *Ground 9: Suitable alternative accommodation is available for the tenant or will be available for him when the order for possession takes effect.*

[4.47] Ground 9 gives the landlord a discretionary ground for possession where suitable alternative accommodation is available for the tenant, or will be available for him, when the order for possession takes effect. In the Housing Bill 1988, as originally framed, this was to be the principal mandatory ground for possession, a proposal which was severely criticised as it would have enabled landlords to move tenants from property to property without restraint, and have completely undermined the security of tenants whose landlords own multiple dwellings[1]. Accordingly, alternative accommodation was removed from the mandatory grounds and now provides the principal discretionary ground for possession, the same place it previously enjoyed in the Rent Act scheme of protection[2].

1 See HC Debs, Standing Committee G, 19 January 1988, col 299 ff.
2 RA 1977, s 98(1); see Parl Debs (HC) vol 134, col 1019 ff.

'Suitability' of alternative accommodation

[4.48] Suitability is defined in Sch 2, Pt III in similar terms as previously (see the RA 1977, Sch 15, Pt IV), namely by reference to the tenant's needs as to the extent and character of the property, and equivalence of terms and security of tenure with the existing tenancy. So, the alternative premises must be let on an assured tenancy other than a shorthold, and no notice under mandatory Grounds 1–5 must have been given. This condition is satisfied if the premises are offered not on an assured tenancy but 'on terms which will in the opinion of the court afford to the tenant security of tenure reasonably equivalent to that afforded by Chapter I of Part I of [the HA 1988]'[1].

1 Schedule 2, Pt III, para 2.

[4.49] As well as equivalence of security, the alternative accommodation must be reasonably suited to the needs of the tenant and his family as regards proximity to place of work, and having regard to the rent and the extent of accommodation offered by the local housing authority to persons whose needs are similar to those of the tenant or his family. This second requirement will also be met, however, if the landlord can show that the alternative premises are reasonably suitable to the means of the tenant and to the needs of him and his family as regards extent and character[1]. A certificate from the local housing authority is conclusive evidence of the extent of accommodation and the rental it would charge to provide suitable alternative accommodation[2]. Furthermore, if the authority is itself able to provide accommodation, a certificate from it certifying that it will make suitable alternative accommodation available to the tenant is conclusive evidence of its availability for the purposes of Ground 9[3]. Rent Act case law will be of assistance in interpreting these provisions. Under the RA 1977, it was clearly established that suitability must be judged by reference solely to the tenant's *housing needs*, and not by considering the relative advantages and disadvantages of the alternative premises and those originally demised[4]. It is, however, permissible to compare the environment which the tenant has hitherto enjoyed with that of the alternative accommodation offered in order to establish whether it will afford the particular tenant concerned an opportunity to live in conditions suitable to the style of life he leads[5]. So more spacious accommodation may not be 'suitable' if it is situated in a noisy, busy area or thoroughfare, whereas the tenancy is of a dwelling in a quiet residential area[6]. The relevance of environmental matters, such as noise and smell, does not extend to cultural or spiritual considerations, and factors such as proximity of alternative accommodation to the tenant's friends and place of worship will not influence its suitability in terms of housing need[7].

1 Schedule 2, Pt III, para 3(1).
2 Ibid, Pt III, para 3(2).
3 Ibid, Pt III, para 1.
4 See *Hill v Rochard* [1983] 1 WLR 478, CA; advantages enjoyed with the demised property – here a paddock, out buildings and stable – held not relevant if the alternative accommodation offered is otherwise suitable to the tenant's housing needs.
5 See *Redspring Ltd v Francis* [1973] 1 WLR 134, CA; *Hill v Rochard* [1983] 1 WLR 478, CA.
6 As in *Redspring Ltd v Francis* [1973] 1 WLR 134, CA.
7 *Siddiqui v Rashid* [1980] 1 WLR 1018, CA.

[4.50] Two further principles derived from Rent Act jurisprudence have relevance:

(1) By virtue of the rule in *Mykolyshyn v Noah*[1], the alternative accommodation offered, if suitable, can constitute part of the premises originally demised. The courts treat the whole premises, and that part offered as alternative accommodation, as distinct in law, thus enabling the landlord to repossess any part of the property which is surplus to the tenant's needs using this ground.
(2) Suitable alternative accommodation must be available to the tenant *at the date of the hearing*. The fact that the tenant had alternative accommodation available

at an antecedent date is irrelevant if he in fact has none at the date of hearing. Thus, in *Fennbend Ltd v Millar*[2], a landlord was (surprisingly perhaps) not entitled to an interlocutory injunction to prevent the tenant disposing of a freehold house which he owned, and which would have clearly constituted suitable alternative accommodation for the purposes of this ground if not sold prior to hearing.

1 [1970] 1 WLR 1217, CA.
2 (1988) 20 HLR 19, CA.

Reasonableness of order for possession

[4.51] If alternative accommodation is 'suitable', the landlord must still establish that it is reasonable on the facts to make an order for possession. Considerations of relative hardship to landlord and tenant will be of considerable importance. So, for instance, the fact that the tenant has lived in the property for many years may be relevant, especially if the landlord does not need it for his own personal occupation, and will weigh against a possession order being made[1]. This important additional protection for tenants would have been lost had, as originally intended, the availability of alternative accommodation constituted a mandatory ground for possession.

1 As in *Battlespring Ltd v Gates* (1983) 268 Estates Gazette 355, CA.

Compensation for disturbance

[4.52] By virtue of s 11, if the landlord obtains possession relying on this ground, the tenant is entitled to recover by way of compensation a sum equal to the reasonable expenses likely to be incurred by him in removing from the dwelling house. Compensation for disturbance is available only under this ground and Ground 6 ('Reconstruction or demolition of dwelling', para 4.39 ff above).

[4.53] Many of the remaining discretionary grounds mirror, in the assured tenancy context, the discretionary grounds under the RA 1977, Sch 15. These allow repossession in the circumstances covered by Grounds 10–16.

Rent arrears

[4.54] *Ground 10: Some rent lawfully due from the tenant:*

(a) is unpaid on the date on which the proceedings for possession are begun; and
(b) except where subsection (1)(b) of section 8 of this Act applies, was in arrears at the date of the service of the notice under that section relating to those proceedings.

[4.55] We have seen that Ground 8 gives a mandatory ground for possession where two months' rent is unpaid both at the date of notice of proceedings *and* at the date of the hearing. This is supplemented by Ground 10, which gives a discretionary ground if *some* rent (no amount is specified) is lawfully due but unpaid on the dates on which possession proceedings are begun *and* was in arrears at the date on which notice of proceedings was originally served. This ground would apply, for instance, if some rent were paid following notice of proceedings to bring the amount outstanding down below the threshold for the applicability of Ground 8. It would appear, also, that this ground would apply however small the amount outstanding ('*some* rent . . . is unpaid') even if de minimis (although it may not be reasonable to order possession in such cases).

Persistent delay in paying rent

[4.56] *Ground 11: Whether or not any rent is in arrears on the date on which proceedings for possession are begun, the tenant has persistently delayed paying rent which has become lawfully due.*

[4.57] This ground applies whether or not any rent is in arrears at the date on which possession proceedings are begun, and enables repossession where the tenant has 'persistently' delayed paying rent which has become lawfully due. This is clearly a question of fact for the county court, but late payment on, at the very least, two occasions is envisaged.

Breach of tenancy

[4.58] *Ground 12: Any obligation of the tenancy (other than one related to the payment of rent) has been broken or not performed.*

[4.59] This ground applies where any obligation of the tenancy – other than as to payment of rent – has been broken or not performed; eg, failure to carry out tenant's repairs or to pay service charges. Acceptance of rent in knowledge of breach would not, it is suggested, necessarily waive the landlord's right to rely on this ground (cf waiver in forfeiture proceedings)[1].

1 See *Oak Property Co Ltd v Chapman* [1947] KB 886, CA; *Henry Smith's Charity Trustees v Willson* [1983] QB 316, CA.

Deterioration of dwelling house

[4.60] *Ground 13: The condition of the dwelling house or any of the common parts has deteriorated owing to acts of waste by, or the neglect or default of, the tenant or any other person residing in the dwelling house and, in the case of an act of waste by, or the neglect or default of, a person lodging with the tenant or a subtenant of his, the tenant has not taken such steps as he ought reasonably to have taken for the removal of the lodger or subtenant.*

For the purposes of this ground, 'common parts' means any part of a building comprising the dwelling house and any other premises which the tenant is entitled under the terms of the tenancy to use in common with the occupiers of other dwelling houses in which the landlord has an estate or interest.

[4.61] This ground applies where the condition of the dwelling house or any common parts has deteriorated owing to acts of waste by and/or neglect or default of, the tenant or any other person residing in the dwelling. In the case of waste or neglect attributable to a person lodging with the tenant, or to a subtenant, the ground applies only if the tenant has failed to take reasonable steps to obtain the removal of the offending lodger or subtenant. This ground was also available under the RA 1977[1], in which context it was clearly established that proof of a breach of a tenancy obligation was not necessary for its application[2].

There seems no reason why this should not also hold good for the parallel ground in the HA 1988.

1 See the RA 1977, Sch 15, Case 3.
2 See *Lowe v Lendrum* (1950) 159 Estates Gazette 423.

Nuisance and illegal or immoral user

[4.62] *Ground 14: The tenant or a person residing in or visiting the dwelling house:*

(a) has been guilty of conduct causing or likely to cause a nuisance or annoyance to a person residing, visiting or otherwise engaging in a lawful activity in the locality; or
(b) has been convicted of:
   (i) using the dwelling house or allowing it to be used for illegal or immoral purposes, or
   (ii) an arrestable offence committed in, or in the locality of, the dwelling house.

[4.63] This ground applies if the tenant (or any person residing in the dwelling concerned) has been guilty of conduct which is a nuisance or annoyance to adjoining occupiers, or has been convicted of using the dwelling house (or allowing it to be used) for immoral or illegal purposes (cf also the RA 1977, Sch 15, Case 2). In the case of nuisance or annoyance, if the complainant has property in the vicinity it does not have to be 'adjoining' in the sense of being physically proximate or adjacent, provided it is near enough to suffer from the tenant's actions[1]. This ground was considerably widened by amendments introduced by the HA 1996[2]. The wider grounds in the revised Ground 14 can be relied upon by the landlord where the tenancy agreement itself contains a version of the original ground in the HA 1988 as the court will not construe the agreement as disabling the landlord from applying any statutory change to the permitted grounds for possession[3].

1 See *Cobstone Investments Ltd v Maxim* [1985] QB 140, CA.
2 HA 1996, s 148, substituting a new Ground 14 to the HA 1988, Sch 2.
3 See *North British Housing Association v Sheridan* [1999] 2 EGLR 138 (tenant committing acts of violence in vicinity of demised premises).

Domestic violence

[4.64] *Ground 14A: The dwelling house was occupied (whether alone or with others) by a married couple or a couple living together as husband and wife and:*

(a) one or both of the partners is a tenant of the dwelling house;
(b) the landlord who is seeking possession is a registered social landlord or a charitable housing trust;
(c) one partner has left the dwelling house because of violence or threats of violence by the other towards:
   (i) that partner, or
   (ii) a member of the family of that partner who was residing with that partner immediately before the partner left; and
(d) the court is satisfied that the partner who has left is unlikely to return.

[4.65] This ground was added by the HA 1996[1]. Note that, while giving wide possession grounds in cases of domestic violence, it can only be used by registered social landlords and charitable housing trusts. The ground can be used where violence, or threats of violence, has been offered not only to a tenant and/or his partner, but also to a member of the partner's family. For this purpose a 'member of the family' of the tenant or partner includes a spouse of that person, or non-married partner if he and that person live together as husband and wife, or the parent, grandparent, child, grandchild, brother, sister, uncle, aunt, nephew or niece of the tenant or partner[2].

1 HA 1996, s 149.
2 HA 1996, s 62.

Deterioration of furniture

[4.66] *Ground 15: The condition of any furniture provided for use under the tenancy has, in the opinion of the court, deteriorated owing to ill-treatment by the tenant or any other person residing in the dwelling house and, in the case of ill-treatment by a person lodging with the tenant or by a subtenant of his, the tenant has not taken such steps as he ought reasonably to have taken for the removal of the lodger or subtenant.*

[4.67] This ground applies where furniture provided for use under the tenancy has deteriorated owing to ill-treatment by the tenant or by a lodger or subtenant. In the case of the latter, the tenant must also have failed to take reasonable steps to obtain the removal of the lodger or subtenant concerned (see also the RA 1977, Sch 15, Case 4).

Termination of employment

[4.68] *Ground 16: The dwelling house was let to the tenant in consequence of his employment by the landlord seeking possession or a previous landlord under the tenancy and the tenant has ceased to be in that employment.*

[4.69] This ground applies where the dwelling house was let to the tenant in consequence of his employment by the landlord who is seeking possession (or a previous landlord), and the tenant has ceased to be in that employment. The ground does not apply if the employee is occupying tied accommodation and is employed by the landlord in agriculture (s 25(2)). It might be noted that the equivalent provision of the RA 1977[1] required the landlord to establish, additionally, that the residence was required for occupation by a replacement employee. This further limitation does not apply to assured tenancies under the HA 1988.

1 See RA 1977, Sch 15, Case 8.

Tenancy obtained by false statement.

[4.70] *Ground 17: The tenant is the person, or one of the persons, to whom the tenancy was granted and the landlord was induced to grant the tenancy by a false statement made knowingly or recklessly by:*

(a) the tenant; or
(b) a person acting at the tenant's instigation.

[4.71] This ground was added by the HA 1996[1]. It applies to give the landlord a discretionary ground for possession if it later appears that the grant of the tenancy was procured as a result of false statements made either knowingly, or with reckless disregard for their accuracy. Examples might include false credit references produced by the tenant as security for payment of rent, or false representations as to the tenant's employment status. Note that the ground requires that the misrepresentation 'induced' the landlord to grant the tenancy. Whether this is the case will be a question of fact, not law, but it would seem to presuppose that the misrepresentation must be as to some material factor motivating the landlord's decision to grant the tenancy, and without which the tenancy would not have been granted.

1 HA 1996, s 102.

COMPENSATION FOR MISREPRESENTATION

[4.72] If the landlord obtains possession on one of the grounds in Sch 2 and it subsequently appears to the court that the order was obtained by misrepresentation or concealment of material facts, the court may order the landlord to pay to the tenant 'such sum as appears sufficient as compensation for damage or loss sustained by the tenant as a result of the order' (s 12). Previously, under the RA 1977[1], compensation for misrepresentation was available only if the landlord had relied on Case 8 or 9, ie where the tenant's employment had ceased or the landlord required the dwelling for himself or a member of his family. It now applies in all cases and would allow the tenant to claim compensation, for instance, for the increased cost of renting alternative premises at a higher rent. This remedy should be compared with the provisions concerning compensation for unlawful eviction and loss of protected occupation rights (see Chapter 2, para 2.48 ff above) where the issues as to quantum are similar.

1 See 1977 Act, s 102.

C Derivative and joint interests

SUBTENANCIES AND REVERSIONARY INTERESTS

[4.73] The HA 1988, s 18(1) protects subtenants whose interests, as between themselves and their immediate landlord, constitute an assured tenancy. It is provided that if a dwelling is lawfully let on an assured tenancy and the landlord is himself a tenant under a superior tenancy which comes to an end, then the assured tenancy shall continue in existence as a tenancy held directly of 'the person whose interest would, apart from the continuance of the assured tenancy, entitle him to actual possession of the dwelling house at that time'. This will be the person entitled to possession as a result of the order, the subtenancy falling at common law with the tenancy – often the head landlord, but not necessarily if there is a chain of subleases. Section 18 should be compared with the complex provisions of the RA 1977, s 137, which confers protection on protected and statutory subtenants.

[4.74] For the purposes of the assured tenancy code, the following points should be noted:

(1) The dwelling must be lawfully sublet for the protection to apply and *not*, for instance, sublet in breach of covenant. It should be noted here that if the head lease is itself 'assured', there may be an implied covenant against subletting without consent by virtue of the HA 1988, s 15 (see para 3.99 ff above).

(2) The head lease which is terminated need not itself be an assured tenancy. The RA 1977, s 137 principally protected subtenants of a Rent Act tenant, but s 137(3) also extended protection to subtenants where *part* of the premises had been sublet by a tenant who was not himself within the RA 1977. The latter provision was of limited utility, however, as the tenant subletting part would normally qualify as a resident landlord, and the 'subtenancy' would probably be no more than a restricted contract[1]. The phrasing of the HA 1988, s 18 is altogether less obscure. It will clearly apply where the whole is sublet, and whether or not the superior lease is itself assured. Indeed, if the whole *is* sublet, the superior tenancy cannot by definition be assured, as the residence qualification in s 1(1)(b) will not be met. The provision will also apply, however, where the superior tenancy is itself a business lease or agricultural tenancy[2].

(3) Whatever the problems under the RA 1977, it is clear from the terms of s 18(1) that the subtenant continues to hold the assured tenancy under the sublease originally granted to him, the identity of the immediate landlord being the only import of the section. The terms and conditions of the subtenancy remain in force and will be enforceable by and against the head landlord. It would seem, also, that any notice given for the purposes of the mandatory grounds for possession by a tenant to a subtenant would retain their validity, and be exercisable by the head landlord. The latter is constituted landlord by s 18(1) and should, in principle, be able to use the mandatory grounds if they were available to his predecessor. However, this could lead to curious results; eg, the tenant giving notice under Ground 1, when granting a subtenancy, indicating that the property might be wanted for his own use, and the ground then being relied on later by the head landlord to repossess for *his* own use and occupation. Ultimately, this question turns on whether the term 'landlord' as used in Grounds 1–5 ('the landlord gave notice' etc) is interpreted restrictively to include solely the particular landlord who gave notice, and who alone can therefore use the grounds for possession, or generically to mean simply the person who at the time of notice and (later) possession proceedings happens *in law* to be the landlord. There is, as yet, no judicial guidance on this.

1 See Farrand and Arden *Rent Acts and Regulations* (2nd edn, 1981) p 159.

2 See also *Maunsell v Olins* [1975] AC 373, HL revised by the R(A)A 1976 (Sch 8, para 20); *Pittalis v Grant* [1989] 2 All ER 622, CA And see generally, Farrand and Arden, op cit, pp 158–160; Martin, *Security of Tenure under the Rent Act* (1986) Chapter 9; also Martin (1976) 40 Conv (NS) 96 and Smith (1976) 40 Conv (NS) 197. On mixed business and residential lettings see Martin (1989) 139 NLJ 1260 and Rodgers (1990) Conv 204.

[4.75] The protection of s 18(1) does *not* apply if the interest of the head landlord is one which, by virtue of Sch 2, precludes assured tenancy status; eg, if the head lease was granted by the Crown or by a local authority, and the dwelling was then sublet on an assured tenancy to the subtenant now claiming protection (s 18(2)). Although the subtenant may be protected as between himself and the tenant, his interest cannot be assured as between himself and the ultimate landlord.

REVERSIONARY TENANCIES

[4.76] By virtue of s 18(3), if the landlord grants a reversionary lease so as to begin on or *after* (a) the date on which a fixed-term assured tenancy continues as a statutory periodic tenancy; or (b) the date on which a periodic assured tenancy could be lawfully terminated, then the reversionary lease takes effect as if it had been granted subject to the tenant's (statutory) periodic tenancy. This is necessary, in part, to block potential avoidance of the HA 1988 by this avenue.

JOINT TENANCIES

[4.77] The HA 1988, s 45(3) deals expressly with joint proprietorship, something most earlier protective legislation failed to do[1]. It is provided that any reference in the HA 1988 to the landlord or tenant is a reference to all persons jointly constituting landlord and/or tenant. In so providing the HA 1988 gives statutory force to the joint tenancy rule at common law, namely that all co-owners must join together to effect a legal act affecting the leasehold interest. In the case of periodic tenancies, this has meant that all tenants must concur in renewal (see *Doe D Aslin v Summersett*[2]) although the Rent Act statutory tenancy – being a mere right in personam – has been held capable of vesting in one out of joint tenants[3]. Similarly, to surrender a tenancy before its expiry date, all joint tenants must concur, and no single joint tenant can validly surrender the tenancy before its contractual term date[4]. The difficulties that a strict application of the joint tenancy rule might cause are mitigated by s 1(1)(b), which expressly provides that a tenancy remains 'assured' if and so long as '*one* of the joint tenants occupies the dwelling house as his only or principal home'. But note the possibility of one out of joint tenants terminating a periodic tenancy by notice to quit served *on the landlord*[5]. This will, however, be effective only if the notice (properly construed) is a notice to quit and not a purported surrender. If it purports to terminate the tenancy other than at the end of a period of tenancy, and in accordance with the common law rules, it will be construed as a surrender, and effective only if *both* joint tenants concur in giving it[6]. It will not be construed as a surrender, however, simply because it was given by arrangement and with the agreement of the landlord[7]. For other examples of express provision for one out of joint tenants or landlords to act, see, inter alia, s 21(1)(b) (one out of joint landlords entitled to serve notice of repossession in shorthold cases), s 34(1) (saving of pre-commencement protected tenancies), Sch 2, Ground 1 (one of joint landlords in prior occupation as owner occupier) and Ground 6 (bar on use of reconstruction ground where one of joint landlords acquired reversion by purchase). In cases where no specific provision is made joint tenants must act together; eg, in serving notices to initiate a Rent Assessment Committee review of rent or terms[8]. Section 45(3) goes some way to meet Law Commission criticism, and recommendations of a unified approach to joint tenancy rules and protective legislation[9].

1 For judicial criticism on these grounds, see *Howson v Buxton* (1928) 97 LJKB 749, CA.
2 (1830) 1 B&Ad 135.
3 *Lloyd v Sadler* [1978] 2 All ER 529, CA.
4 *Leek and Moorlands Building Society v Clark* [1952] 2 QB 788, CA.
5 *Greenwich LBC v McGrady* (1982) 6 HLR 36, CA confirmed by the House of Lords in *Hammersmith and Fulham LBC v Monk* [1992] 1 All ER 1, HL (the principle in which would appear to be unaffected by s 5(1) and (2) and s 45(3)). See also s 5(2)(b), continuing protection in the case of a fixed-term, unless the tenancy is ended by 'surrender or other action of the tenant', ie all joint tenants acting together (s 45(3)).
6 *Hounslow LBC v Pilling* [1994] 1 All ER 432, CA.
7 See *Barrett v Morgan* [2000] 2 EGLR 8 (HL)
8 See ss 13(2) and 6(2) read with HA 1988, s 45(3).
9 On problems of joint ownership, see generally Martin (1978) 42 Conv 436; Webb (1983) 47 Conv 194; Rodgers (1985) 48 MLR 460 and (1986) 50 Conv 429. For the Law Commission's criticisms see Landlord and Tenant: Reform of the Law (Cm 145, 1987) paras 4.20–4.26.

CHAPTER 5

Assured shorthold tenancies

A Introduction

[5.1] The 'assured shorthold' scheme introduced by the Housing Act 1988 (HA 1988) was presented as an extension of the existing shorthold concept, originally introduced by the Housing Act 1980 (HA 1980) ('protected' shorthold tenancies). This was aimed at further liberalising the market for short-term accommodation, while at the same time removing some of the legal technicalities associated with 'protected' shortholds under the HA 1980[1]. In many respects, however, the assured shorthold was a different legal creature altogether, and at the very least represented a radical extension of the 'shorthold' concept. The minimum period of letting was reduced from twelve to six months, but with no maximum duration (cf the five years' maximum for shortholds under the HA 1980). The tenant's lack of security was not counterbalanced by a right to registration of a fair rent, although an assured shorthold tenant can seek registration of an 'appropriate' rent, which in most cases will be at, or very near, free market levels (see below). Furthermore, upon termination of the initial shorthold, the assured shorthold tenancy can continue indefinitely as a statutory periodic tenancy, subject to termination at any time on a minimum of two months' notice. The assured shorthold may not be 'short' at all, but of considerable duration.

1 See HC Deb, 30 November 1987, col 623, per the Secretary of State; and Housing: The Government's Proposals (Cm 214, 1987), para 3.11ff.

[5.2] The assured shorthold regime was further liberalised by the Housing Act 1996 (HA 1996). This removed the requirement for a written tenancy agreement, and for the tenancy to be for a fixed period of at least six months, for all tenancies entered into on or after 28 February 1997. Neither does the landlord now have to give a prescribed shorthold notice to the tenant informing him the tenancy is to be a shorthold. As a consequence of the changes made by the HA 1996, all private sector tenancies entered into on or after 28 February 1997, whether fixed-term or periodic, will be assured shorthold tenancies *unless* the landlord notifies the tenant that the tenancy is to be a fully assured tenancy. In practice, this means that fully assured tenancies will be granted principally now by registered social landlords. Most other new private sector tenancies will be assured shortholds. Because of the changes introduced in the HA 1996 it is important to distinguish between assured shortholds granted before 28 February 1997, and those granted on or after that date. Those granted before 28 February 1997 must be for a fixed period of at least six months, and shorthold notice must have been given prior to grant. This does not apply for those shortholds granted on or after 28 February 1997.

B Assured shortholds granted before 28 February 1997

QUALIFYING CONDITIONS

[5.3] The HA 1988, s 20(1) provides that to qualify as an 'assured shorthold', an assured tenancy granted before 28 February 1997 must have fulfilled three requirements:

(1) It must be a fixed-term tenancy granted for a term certain of not less than six months.
(2) A notice in prescribed form, informing the tenant that the letting is to be a shorthold, must have been served before the tenancy was entered into. The appropriate statutory notice was prescribed by the Assured Tenancies and Agricultural Occupancies (Forms) Regulations 1988[1].
(3) It must be a tenancy in respect of which there is no power for the landlord to determine the tenancy at any time earlier than six months from the beginning of the tenancy[2].

1 SI 1988/2203.
2 Section 20(1)(b): see further para 5.33 ff below.

'Term certain of not less than six months'

[5.4] The grant must be of a fixed-term tenancy that is also a term certain of not less than six months. It should be noted that no maximum duration for the initial fixed-term is stipulated, although many landlords may, it is suggested, have been tempted to grant short terms in the first instance. If a longer initial term was contemplated, it should be remembered that the requirements of the Law of Property Act 1925, ss 52 and 54 must have been complied with, namely to be validly granted, a term for three years or more must be created by deed under seal.

'Fixed-term tenancy'

[5.5] By virtue of s 45(1) any tenancy other than a periodic tenancy will qualify as a fixed-term for the purposes of the shorthold provisions.

'Tenancy'

[5.6] This includes an agreement for a tenancy (s 45(1)), and also a subtenancy or agreement for a subtenancy. Note that to create an enforceable agreement for a tenancy, the requirements of the Law of Property (Miscellaneous Provisions) Act 1989 (LPA 1989), s 2 will have to be complied with, namely the agreement will have to be in writing signed by both parties, unless it is for the grant of a tenancy of less than three years (in which event the formalities of the LPA 1989 are dispensed with)[1]. Where an assured shorthold is granted by way of a subtenancy, the protective provisions of s 18 will apply on termination of the mesne tenancy during the currency of the fixed-term (see para 4.73 ff above).

1 See the LPA 1989, s 2(1) and (5).

'Granted'

[5.7] The requirement of 'grant' in s 20(1) would, it is suggested, exclude a tenancy that is periodic ab initio (even if a half-yearly periodic term). The express inclusion of an agreement for a tenancy in the definition of a 'tenancy' for the purposes of s 20 (above) would validate an agreement for a shorthold term rendered enforceable by the rule in *Walsh v Lonsdale*[1]. Tenancies at will and at sufferance are clearly excluded.

1 (1882) 21 Ch D 9, CA (note that there was a question whether this would have sufficed for a protected shorthold tenancy – see Farrand and Arden *Rent Acts and Regulations* (2nd edn, 1981) p 316.

'Term certain'

[5.8] A lease which contains a break clause entitling the landlord to terminate the term at any time earlier than six months from the beginning of the tenancy (eg by giving notice) will not qualify as an assured shorthold[1]. A break clause exercisable by the landlord could be included in an assured shorthold tenancy, but must be expressly limited so as not to be exercisable during the first six months of the term. The inclusion of a clause not so limited in application will take the tenancy outside the shorthold provisions, in which event it will be, an assured tenancy simpliciter. A break clause exercisable by the tenant does not, however, have to be thus limited in application, and can be exercisable within the initial six months of tenancy without infringing the shorthold provisions. Note, however, that under the HA 1988 the assured shorthold tenant has no statutory right to give notice terminating the tenancy during the fixed shorthold term. Cf the position under the HA 1980, where the tenant had an absolute right to terminate a protected shorthold (this provision does not appear in the assured shorthold scheme).

1 Section 20(1)(b).

[5.9] Whatever the complications associated with 'break' clauses, it is clear that a forfeiture clause in common form will not have the effect of taking the tenancy outside the shorthold provisions, even if exercisable during the first six months of tenancy[1].

1 See s 20(1)(b), as interpreted with s 45(4) ibid, and see also *Patterson v Aggio* (1987) 284 Estates Gazette 508, CA noted by Martin (1987) Conv 448.

'Not less than six months'

[5.10] For the purpose of calculating the length of the term, a lease is granted at the date of execution, for it cannot retrospectively vest a term of years in the tenant[1]. It was not possible to avoid the minimum six-month grant by backdating, even to a tenant already in possession prior to grant[2]. The parties are free, however, to define the duration of the letting by reference to a date earlier than that of the lease, and can validly create contractual obligations in respect of some prior period; eg, as to break clauses or the tenant's obligation to pay rent (see *Bradshaw v Pawley*[3], *Colton v Becollda Property Investments Ltd*[4]). But for the purpose of calculating the length of a term for statutory purposes, as here, the commencement date cannot be earlier than the date of the lease. Breach of covenant prior to execution of the lease will similarly not constitute a breach of the lease entitling a landlord to forfeit (*Bradshaw v Pawley*[5]). Where the lease is expressed to commence at some date prior to execution, the parties cannot raise an estoppel to vary its legal effect, for example by arguing that both parties agreed a shorthold was to be granted, when in fact the term was for less than six months. The doctrine of estoppel by convention, endorsed in *Amalgamated Investment and Property Co Ltd v Texas Commerce International Bank Ltd*[6], applies only to common assumptions of fact, not law, and cannot vary the effect of protective legislation[7]. Backdating the grant of an assured shorthold – or attempting to do so – would also inevitably have involved non-compliance with the requirement for shorthold notice to be served at the time of grant (see below) and have infringed the notice requirements in s 20(2).

1 *Roberts v Church Comrs for England* [1972] 1 QB 278, CA.
2 See generally *Keen v Holland* [1984] 1 All ER 75, CA.
3 [1980] 1 WLR 10.
4 [1950] 1 KB 216 at 231, CA.
5 [1980] 1 WLR 10 especially at 14, per Sir R Megarry V-C.
6 [1981] 3 All ER 577, CA.
7 See *Keen v Holland* [1984] 1 All ER 75, CA, noted at (1984) Conv 315 (Rodgers) and in a helpful article by NDM Parry (1985) Sol Jo 182.

Notice in prescribed form

[5.11] For the tenancy to be an assured shorthold, notice in prescribed form must have been served before the assured tenancy was entered into. It must state that the tenancy is to be an assured shorthold (s 20(2)). A similar requirement applied to protected shortholds[1]. The shorthold notice could be served by one out of joint landlords (s 20(6)). The notice could be served on the same day as the tenancy was entered into, provided it can be shown to have been given at a point in time before the tenancy's commencement[2]. Although straightforward, service of the shorthold notice proved problematic in several cases, and was one of the requirements dispensed with for shortholds granted after commencement of the HA 1996 (below).

1 HA 1980, s 52(1)(b).
2 *Bedding v McCarthy* (1993) 27 HLR 103. The s 20 notice here was given in the morning, and the tenants went into possession in the afternoon of the same day. The Court of Appeal held that the notice had been validly given, and also rejected the tenant's further argument that the shorthold period (a fixed-term of six months) was of less than six months duration because of the notice being served on the day the tenancy commenced.

[5.12] The prefatory notice must have been served in the prescribed form, or in a notice 'substantially to the same effect', and must accurately convey the information required by the prescribed form. Subject to this, however, the courts will make enquiry to ascertain whether mistakes in the notice are material, and as such invalidate the notice. In *York v Casey*[1] Ralph Gibson LJ endorsed a two stage test for the validity of statutory notices:

(1) The court must see whether the error in the notice is obvious or evident (if it is, then it will be excused, and the notice will stand).
(2) It must ascertain whether, notwithstanding the error in the notice, it is sufficiently clear when read in its context to leave a reasonable recipient in no reasonable doubt as to the terms of the notice. The notice must, for this purpose, be read side by side with the assured shorthold tenancy agreement and any covering letter delivered with it.

1 [1998] 2 EGLR 25. The Court of Appeal here applied the test formulated by the House of Lords for commercial lease notices in *Mannai Investments Ltd v Eagle Star Insurance* (1998) 1 EGLR 57, HL.

[5.13] In *York v Casey* (above) the termination date given in the notice was an evident error (it was before the commencement date of the tenancy), and mistakenly identifying a sole landlord, when in fact joint landlords had granted the tenancy, was also excused as a mistake which would not confuse a reasonable tenant. The notice was effective to create an assured shorthold tenancy. In *Panayi v Roberts*[1] it was held, on the other hand, that the notice must accurately specify the termination date of the fixed shorthold term. In exceptional cases, where the landlord makes an 'evident error', a benevolent construction might be allowed, ie where the error would have been evident to a person with the ordinary qualities of the addressee tenant (eg where '1793' was inserted in error for '1993' in the notice)[2]. But apart from this, a strict interpretation will be applied. So in *Panayi* the landlord unwittingly created a fully assured tenancy where the shorthold notice mistakenly stipulated 6 May 1991 as the termination date, when the shorthold tenancy (to which the notice related) was expressed to terminate on 7 November 1991. The mistaken substitution of 'May' for 'November' in the shorthold notice was not an evident error, and therefore s 20(1)(c) and 20(2) had not been complied with. In contrast, however, where an assured shorthold notice specified that the tenancy would commence on 29 May 1993 and end on 28 May 1993 it was held that the mistaken termination date was an 'evident error' which did not invalidate the notice, and that an assured shorthold (and not a fully assured tenancy) had been created[3].

1 [1993] 2 EGLR 51, CA.
2 Ibid at 52 per Mann LJ.
3 See *Brewer v Andrews* (1997) 30 HLR 203.

[5.14] Changes in the tenancy's commencement date could also prove problematic, especially if the shorthold notice had already been served, or was not amended to reflect the term finally agreed. The problems here are illustrated by the decision in *Clickex Ltd v McCann*[1]. The shorthold notice here specified that the tenancy was to be a six-month shorthold commencing on 21 December 1995, and was served on 20 December. The landlord later scratched out the commencement date in the tenancy agreement and substituted 8 January 1996 as the start date (this was the date the tenants entered into possession). The error in the notice was here held not to be evident or excusable, as a reasonable tenant would be left in doubt as to whether the tenancy was to end on 23 June or 7 July 1996 (that is, six months from 21 December 1995 or 8 January 1996). Finally, a shorthold notice which fails to include the notes and advice contained in the prescribed form is not a 'form substantially to the same effect' as the prescribed shorthold form, with the consequence that a notice omitting this information will be ineffective, and a fully assured tenancy will have been granted[2].

1 [1999] 2 EGLR 63, CA.
2 See *Manel v Memon* (2000) 5 CL 431, CA.

[5.15] Note that, even prior to the HA 1996, an assured shorthold tenancy could come into being in several situations without a shorthold notice having been given. One is where the tenant is in possession pursuant to a previous tenancy which was a protected shorthold, and which is renewed after commencement[1]. Another is where an assured shorthold tenancy comes to an end, and the tenant remains in possession pursuant to a statutory periodic tenancy – the latter is 'deemed' to be an assured shorthold by s 20(4). Finally, the HA 1988, s 39(7) provides that where a tenant with a Rent Act protected or statutory tenancy dies after 15 January 1989, then if the original tenancy was a Protected Shorthold in respect of which Case 19 was available against the former tenant then any successor (other than the tenant's spouse) takes an assured shorthold tenancy by way of statutory succession, and not an assured tenancy (as would otherwise be the case)[2].

1 HA 1988, s 34(2) and (3).
2 See generally Chapter 3 above.

C Assured shortholds granted on or after 28 February 1997

SCOPE OF ASSURED SHORTHOLD TENANCY PROVISIONS

[5.16] The HA 1996 introduced a new s 19A to the HA 1988[1]. Under s 19A any assured tenancy entered into on or after 28 February 1997 (otherwise than in pursuance of a contract made before that date), and any statutory periodic tenancy which arises on the coming to an end of such a tenancy is an assured shorthold tenancy – unless it falls within one of the exceptions set out in the HA 1988, Sch 2A. As a consequence, all private sector residential lettings after commencement of the HA 1996 will be assured shortholds unless the tenancy comes within one of the excepted classes in Sch 2A (see below). In these cases, and these only, the tenancy will be a fully assured tenancy. There is no requirement for the tenancy to be a fixed-term of minimum duration, neither need it be in writing, and there is no requirement for service of a shorthold notice in prescribed form. The stated policy objective of these provisions was to simplify the rules governing assured shorthold tenancies, and to remove the pitfalls (described above) which many landlords had encountered despite the apparent simplicity of the shorthold concept. The legal effect, however, is that assured shorthold tenancies are now the primary vehicle for lettings in the private sector. Full assured tenancy status is reserved for a limited number of excepted categories of tenancy, and cases where the parties 'contract in' to the assured tenancy code; eg where the landlord is a registered social landlord wishing to give longer term security to its tenants.

1 HA 1996, s 96, Sch 7.

DUTY TO PROVIDE STATEMENT OF TERMS

[5.17] Where the tenancy is created post-commencement of the HA 1996, it does not have to be in writing. However, s 20A places the landlord under a duty to provide a written statement of the terms of the tenancy, if they are not evidenced in writing. The landlord's duty is triggered by the tenant serving written notice requiring the information provided for in the HA 1996. The duty is limited to providing a written statement of the following basic terms:

(1) The date on which the tenancy began or, if it is a statutory periodic tenancy, the date on which the tenancy came into being.
(2) The rent payable under the tenancy and the dates on which the rent is payable.
(3) Any term providing for a review of the rent payable under the tenancy.
(4) In the case of a fixed-term tenancy, the length of the fixed-term.

If the landlord fails to comply within 28 days with a written notice requiring a statement of the terms of the tenancy, without reasonable excuse, he is guilty of an offence and liable on summary conviction to a fine not exceeding level four on the standard scale.

CASES WHERE FULLY ASSURED TENANCY CREATED

[5.18] Where an assured tenancy is granted on or after 28 February 1997, it will be an assured shorthold in all cases, unless it falls within one of the cases set out in the HA 1988, Sch 2A. A 'fully' assured tenancy can only be created if the tenancy comes within one of these cases. The cases provided for in Sch 2A are as follows:

'Contracting in' to assured tenancy status

[5.19] An assured tenancy will not be an assured shorthold if, before the assured tenancy is entered into, a notice is served by the landlord on the person who is to be the tenant under the tenancy, stating that the tenancy to which it relates is not to be an assured shorthold[1]. No form is prescribed for the landlords notice. A fully assured tenancy can also be created where the landlord serves notice that the tenancy is not to be an assured shorthold tenancy after it has been entered into[2]. This means that the landlord can, effectively, convert an assured shorthold tenancy into a fully assured tenancy during its term, by giving notice. Note that, although no form is prescribed for the landlord's notice, the statutory requirement is that it states that the tenancy *is not to be an assured shorthold tenancy* ie it is exclusionary in nature. *Query* whether a notice stating that the tenancy was *to be* an assured tenancy, rather than that it was *not* to an assured shorthold, would be effective to exclude the shorthold provisions and create a fully assured tenancy. Shortholds and fully assured tenancies are simply different variants of assured tenancy, and a notice in these terms may not be effective to clearly exclude the assured shorthold tenancy provisions.

1 HA 1988, Sch 2A, para 1, inserted by the HA 1996, Sch 7.
2 Ibid, Sch 2A, para 2.

[5.20] The parties can also create a fully assured tenancy by making appropriate provision in the tenancy agreement itself. A fully assured tenancy will be created where the tenancy contains a provision to the effect that the tenancy is not an assured shorthold tenancy[1].

1 Ibid, Sch 2A, para 3.

Statutory succession by way of assured tenancy

[5.21] The next case applies where a tenant with a Rent Act protected or statutory tenancy dies. If he or she leaves a spouse living at his or her death, then the latter will succeed and the succession tenancy will remain within the Rent Act 1977 (RA 1977). If there is no spouse alive at the tenants death, however, the RA 1977, Sch 1 makes provision for other close family members to succeed, provided they have lived with the tenant for two years prior to his death. In this case, unlike that of the spouse, the succession tenancy is an assured tenancy. An assured tenancy arising on succession in these circumstances will be a fully assured tenancy, and not an assured shorthold[1]. The position is unaffected by the changes made by the HA 1996. The statutory succession provisions are described in Chapter 3 above.

1 Ibid, Sch 2A.

Former secure tenants

[5.22] A secure tenancy will cease to be 'secure' if the landlord's interest is transferred by the local authority to a private sector landlord. In this case the 'landlord condition' for secure tenancy status ceases to be satisfied[1]. An example would be where the local authority disposes of housing stock under a large scale voluntary transfer, using powers under the Housing Act 1985 (HA 1985), s 32 ff, or where a transfer is made by a housing action trust into the private sector. Tenants affected by such a transfer will become assured tenants. They will remain 'fully' assured tenants where the transfer takes place post-commencement of the HA 1996[2]. Although they become, on transfer of the landlords interest, assured tenants, they retain their 'right to buy' under the provisions in the HA 1985 for the preserved right to buy.

1 See Chapter 9, para 9.14 ff.
2 Ibid, Sch 2A, para 5.

Long residential tenancies

[5.23] Where a long residential lease comes to an end, the tenant has security of tenure under the Landlord and Tenant Act 1954, Pt I. The security of tenure provisions following termination were changed as a result of the amendments in the Local Government and Housing Act 1989, Sch 10 which came into effect on 15 January 1999[1]. On termination of a long lease before 15 January 1999 the tenant would remain in possession with a statutory tenancy within the RA 1977. On termination of a long lease on or after 15 January 1999 the tenant will instead enjoy an assured tenancy within the HA 1988, Pt I. An assured tenancy arising on termination of a long lease will be a 'fully' assured tenancy, and not an assured shorthold tenancy[2].

1 Local Government and Housing Act 1989, s 186 and Sch 10. See further Chapter 11, para 11.3 ff below.
2 HA 1988, Sch 2A, para 6.

Replacement of an existing assured tenancy

[5.24] The next case deals with the situation where there is an existing fully assured tenancy, and the landlord grants a new tenancy, after commencement of the HA 1996, to the existing tenant. Where an assured tenancy is granted on or after 28 February 1997, to a person who (alone or jointly with others) was, immediately before the tenancy was granted, the tenant under an assured tenancy other than an assured shorthold, then the new tenancy will be 'fully' assured unless the tenant gives notice that it is to be an assured shorthold tenancy[1]. The replacement tenancy must be granted by the person who was the landlord (or in the case of joint landlords one of them) under the old tenancy. Note however, that the exception does not require the replacement tenancy to be of the same premises. This case will enable the landlord to move an assured tenant from one dwelling to another, without the tenancy of the new premises becoming thereby an assured shorthold. To this extent the case is intended to encourage and facilitate tenancy exchanges and the rearrangement of the landlord's housing stock without impairing sitting assured tenants' residential security and tenancy rights.

1 Ibid, Sch 2A, para 7.

Fixed-term assured tenancies

[5.25] Where a fixed-term assured tenancy comes to an end, a statutory periodic tenancy will arise under the HA 1988, s 5 provided the tenant is then residing at the dwelling as his only or principal home. The periodic tenancy will remain a fully assured tenant, notwithstanding the changes in the shorthold tenancy regime outlined above[1].

1 Ibid, Sch 2A, para 8.

Tied agricultural cottages

[5.26] The final exception applies to tied agricultural accommodation[1]. An assured tenancy which is an agricultural occupancy satisfying the conditions for protection as such will not become a shorthold tenancy if notice is served before it is entered into specifying that it is not to be a shorthold tenancy. A notice in prescribed form is specified for this purpose. This case is considered more fully in the context of agricultural tied cottages in Chapter 8 below.

1 Ibid, Sch 2A, para 9.

ASSURED TENANCY CONDITIONS

[5.27] It should be remembered that, whether the tenancy is created before or after 28 February 1997, it must (in addition to the shorthold requirements, above) also fulfil the conditions for the grant of an assured tenancy simpliciter under the HA 1988. Thus, no assured shorthold can be granted if one of the exclusions in Sch 1 applies; eg, if it is a letting of holiday or student accommodation, or by a resident landlord. It should also be noted that where an assured tenancy created before 28 February 1997 is renewed and one of the tenants under the new tenancy was a party to the original tenancy, the new tenancy cannot be an assured shorthold (s 20(3)). This saving provision, however, applies only if the new tenancy is granted by the person who was, *immediately before* the beginning of the tenancy, the landlord under the assured tenancy concerned, s 20(3)(b). A similar saving provision applies to assured tenancies arising by surrender and regrant after 28 February 1997, preventing the renewal tenancy becoming an assured shorthold (see above para 5.24).

DURATION OF SHORTHOLD

Post-Housing Act 1996 tenancies

[5.28] There is now no requirement that the shorthold term be created in a fixed-term tenancy. Any assured tenancy granted on or after 28 February 1997 will be a shorthold, whether periodic or fixed-term, unless it comes within the exceptions outlined above. Where the tenancy is periodic, however, the tenant effectively enjoys six months security of tenure, as the court cannot make a possession order to take effect earlier that six months from the beginning of the tenancy[1]. The tenancy will , if periodic, continue until terminated by two months' notice in accordance with the terms of the HA 1988, and throughout its term remains a assured shorthold tenancy – whatever its ultimate duration. If a fixed-term assured shorthold is granted, on the other hand, the tenancy will continue on expiry as a statutory periodic tenancy by virtue of s 5. The 'continuation' tenancy is deemed to be a shorthold unless it falls within one of the exceptions in Sch 2A; eg the landlord gives notice that it is to be a fully assured tenancy.

1 HA 1988, s 21(5), added by the HA 1996 s 99.

Pre-Housing Act 1996 tenancies

[5.29] All assured shortholds granted before 28 February 1997 will be fixed-term tenancies. By virtue of ss 5(2) and 20(4) on the expiry of the fixed-term shorthold tenancy the tenant is entitled to remain in possession, as a statutory periodic tenancy arises which is also deemed to be an assured shorthold. In *Lower Street Properties v Jones*[1] the Court of Appeal held that s 20(4) can operate more than once, and that each subsequent tenancy will be an assured shorthold even though the formalities have not been complied with. The same principle would apply, it is suggested, on successive grants following an 'informal' shorthold granted after 28 February 1997 under the HA 1996 provisions. This was a considerable improvement on the position regarding protected shorthold tenancies under the HA 1980, under which a continuation tenancy might attract protection as a statutory Rent Act tenancy subject to the continued availability of Case 19, a position fraught with uncertainty[2]. It is plain that many assured shortholds created under the HA 1988 provisions before 28 February 1997 may not be 'short' at all. Indeed, they may be of considerable duration. Many such tenancies will have continued after the initial term date as assured periodic shorthold tenancies, and may last for considerable periods of time with no security of tenure. As with post-HA 1996 shortholds, it should be noted that the statutory periodic tenancy, or new tenancy (if expressly granted), will not be a shorthold if before it commences the landlord serves notice that it is not to be an assured shorthold tenancy[3].

1 (1996) 28 HLR 877.
2 See PF Smith (1982) Conv 28, 34; Farrand and Arden *Rent Acts and Regulations* (2nd edn, 1981) p 317.
3 Ibid, s 20(5) – a facility which, it is suggested, is not likely to be commonly used.

D Termination during fixed shorthold term

[5.30] The chief drawback with the original protected shorthold regime was the complexity of the procedure for terminating the tenancy following expiry of the fixed-term. The landlord could include a proviso for re-entry in the tenancy agreement and forfeit for breach of tenancy during the fixed-term, without infringing the shorthold provisions[1]. The tenancy could not, however, include a 'break' clause entitling the landlord to terminate by notice during the fixed shorthold term.

1 See HA 1980, s 52(1)(a).

[5.31] The assured shorthold provisions provide a much simpler procedure for termination following expiry of a fixed shorthold term[1]. The position where the landlord wishes to terminate the tenancy *during* a fixed-term is, however, problematic. Although the initial shorthold term can be as short as six months, there may be advantages to a landlord in granting a longer fixed-term – especially if he has the security of knowing he can repossess during that term by invoking a break clause in the tenancy agreement, or by way of forfeiture for breach of tenancy. A longer shorthold term may be advantageous in that the landlord can contractually commit the tenant to payment of the rent and performance of other tenancy obligations for a guaranteed period, while at the same time leaving himself the option of prematurely ending the tenancy by inserting a suitable break clause in the tenancy agreement, together (of course) with a proviso for re-entry and forfeiture. An assured shorthold tenant has no statutory right to terminate by notice during the fixed-term[2]. The landlord can theoretically tie the tenant into a longer shorthold term, at a suitable rent, while reserving to himself the option prematurely to bring it to an end by exercising a break clause in the tenancy agreement.

1 See below, para 5.52 ff.
2 Cf the position for protected shorthold tenants, who enjoyed a statutory right to terminate under HA 1980, s 53.

[5.32] Although long fixed-term assured shortholds are not uncommon, the landlord's right to exercise either a forfeiture or break clause during the currency of the fixed-term is problematic. This is due to the inordinately obscure provisions to be found in the HA 1988, ss 5(1)–(2), 7(6) and 45. The problems these provisions create apply to fixed-terms whether granted before or after 28 February 1997, when the HA 1996 came into force. Where there is pre-HA 1996 shorthold that contains a break clause, the question will often be whether it is a fully assured tenancy or an assured shorthold. In the case of a post-HA 1996 shorthold, the presence of a break clause exercisable during the first six months of the tenancy does not take it outside the assured shorthold tenancy regime, but the court cannot make a possession order to take effect until six months have elapsed since the grant of the original tenancy[1], and the clause will therefore be ineffective to give an immediate right to possession – although it may lawfully terminate the contractual fixed-term itself. The position where (a) a forfeiture clause and (b) a break clause are exercised during a fixed shorthold term must be considered separately.

1 HA 1988, s 21(5).

Proviso for re-entry and forfeiture

[5.33] In order to qualify as an assured shorthold, a pre-HA 1996 tenancy must[1] be one 'in respect of which there is no power for the landlord to determine the tenancy at any time earlier than six months from the beginning of the tenancy'. A power to determine, as statutorily defined[2], does not include a proviso for re-entry or forfeiture. It follows, therefore, that a forfeiture clause could be inserted without taking the tenancy outside the shorthold provisions. The provision in s 20(1)(b) was aimed, rather, at break clauses exercisable before the expiry of six months of tenancy had elapsed. A proviso for re-entry or forfeiture, if included, did not have to be limited so as not to be exercisable during the first six months of tenancy. In the case of a post-HA 1996 fixed-term shorthold, there is no requirement that the tenancy agreement omit a power for the landlord to determine during the first six months of tenancy. A break clause can be included without taking the agreement outside the shorthold provisions, although the courts power to order possession is controlled in the first six months of tenancy. The operation of forfeiture clauses is controlled in the same way, however, as in pre-HA 1996 shortholds, under the provisions in the HA 1988, ss 5, 7 and 45.

1 HA 1988, s 21(1)(b).
2 HA 1988, s 45(4) ibid.

[5.34] The precise effect that the exercise of a proviso for re-entry will have is problematic. It would appear from the terms of the HA 1988 that a forfeiture clause, if included, cannot be exercised as such to terminate the tenancy. The shorthold is, of course, a species of assured tenancy, and the general rules in the HA 1988, Pt I apply to assured shortholds, as to other assured tenancies. Section 5(1) provides that an assured tenancy can be terminated only by court order or additionally, if it is a fixed-term, by the exercise of a power for the landlord to determine the tenancy in certain circumstances; this does not include a forfeiture clause[1]. It must follow, therefore, that a proviso for re-entry or forfeiture cannot in itself be used to terminate the shorthold during the fixed-term – albeit that its inclusion does not invalidate the shorthold status of the tenancy.

1 See HA 1988, s 45(4).

[5.35] It does not follow, however, that a proviso for re-entry or forfeiture, if included, has no legal effect whatever. It may, if appropriately drafted, enable the landlord to terminate the tenancy by obtaining a court order during the fixed-term. This is clear from a consideration of the effect of s 7(6) ibid. The latter provision provides that the court cannot make an order for possession at any time when a dwelling is let on an assured fixed-term tenancy unless *two* conditions are satisfied:

(1) The ground relied on must be either Ground 2 (mortgagee exercising power of sale) or Ground 8 (two months' rent arrears), or one of the discretionary grounds for possession, other than Grounds 9 or 16; eg Ground 10 (unspecified rent arrears), Ground 11 (persistent delay in paying rent) or Ground 12 (other breach of tenancy).
(2) The terms of the tenancy must, moreover, make provision for the tenancy to be brought to an end 'on the ground in question'. Section 7(6)(b) goes on to provide that the tenancy may so provide 'whether that provision takes the form of a provision for re-entry, for forfeiture, for determination by notice or otherwise'.

[5.36] It is clear that s 7(6) envisages a forfeiture clause sufficing to enable a landlord to ground possession proceedings under the HA 1988, invoking one of the specified grounds for possession. The critical obscurity is, it is suggested, in the wording to the proviso in s 7(6)(b), for it is by no means clear what *form* the proviso for forfeiture or re-entry must take if it is to satisfy the statutory criteria and enable the landlord to initiate possession proceedings under the HA 1988. Is it essential for the clause to refer specifically to the permitted grounds for possession in the HA 1988 (ie Grounds 2 or 8, and the discretionary grounds other than Grounds 9 or 16)? Or will a more generally drafted forfeiture clause satisfy the criteria in s 7(6)(b)? The drafting of the sub-section itself – 'whether that provision takes the form . . . or otherwise' – might suggest that a forfeiture clause drafted in standard terms, and without specific reference to the HA 1988, would suffice. Clearly, however, if the landlord wished to rely on Ground 2 or, as is more likely, Ground 8 (mandatory ground for two months' rent arrears), this would have to be specifically provided for in the terms of the forfeiture clause inserted into the shorthold agreement. Most standard forfeiture clauses would probably suffice to invoke the discretionary grounds for possession, eg Ground 10 (for unspecified rent arrears) or Ground 12 (other breaches of tenancy).

[5.37] It should be appreciated, however, that the provision in s 7(6)(b) is equally capable of a narrower interpretation, namely that the forfeiture clause in the tenancy agreement must refer to the specific grounds in Sch 2 – 'on the ground in question'. The provisions have been judicially considered and a narrow view of the effect of s 7(6)(b) taken, namely that the forfeiture clause in the tenancy agreement must make specific reference to the grounds in Sch 2 relied upon by the landlord. Possession was therefore refused where a shorthold tenancy contained a standard form forfeiture clause providing for re-entry and forfeiture if the rent reserved was unpaid for 21 days after becoming due and payable. The agreement did not refer specifically to Grounds 10 or 11 (those relied on), nor did it adopt the wording of either of those grounds in the HA 1988. It therefore failed to trigger the landlord's right to possession under Sch 2 to the latter[1]. Neither, for the reasons outlined above, could a clause in this form ground forfeiture proceedings at common law, owing to the restrictions on possession during an assured tenancy, contained in the HA 1988, s 5.

1 *McDonald v Tipping* (1991) Leicester County Court. HHJ Orrell (unreported). And see 'Termination of Assured Shorthold Tenancies' (1991) Sol Jo 728. (Rodgers), (1992) Legal Action 3–92, p 15 (Madge). For correspondence as to the effect of a forfeiture clause in these circumstances see (1989) 139 NLJ 104, 160 and 326.

[5.38] The statutory provisions are clearly deficient in failing to make clear what form a proviso for re-entry or forfeiture must take. A counsel of caution would dictate that the shorthold agreement should contain a proviso for re-entry drafted so as to refer *either* specifically to each of the relevant grounds for possession allowed by s 7(6)(a) and available to terminate the tenancy during the fixed-term *or* to the grounds for possession set out in the HA 1988, Sch 2. If it does so there would appear no good reason why a suitably drafted clause should not still come within ss 20(1) and 45(4), thus allowing the landlord to take possession proceedings during the fixed-term and (in the case of a pre-HA 1996 tenancy) also preserving the shorthold status of the tenancy.

[5.39] It would appear to follow from ss 5 and 7 that, as a fixed-term assured shorthold tenancy cannot be terminated by forfeiture during its fixed-term, relief from forfeiture will be unavailable to the tenant. The tenancy can be terminated *only* under the provisions in the HA 1988, Sch 2, in which event suspensory powers are exercisable if the discretionary grounds are invoked but not, for instance if Ground 8 (one of the mandatory grounds for possession) is made out. The tenant's statutory right to relief from forfeiture under the general law will not, it is suggested, be applicable, as the landlord is not in this situation seeking to 'enforce against a lessee a right of re-entry or forfeiture' for non-payment of rent[1]. The landlord is proceeding under the statutory possession provisions in the HA 1988, albeit that his ability to do so may have been triggered by the inclusion in the tenancy agreement of a suitably worded proviso for re-entry. The matter is not beyond doubt, however, and a contrary view has been taken at first instance on at least one occasion[2].

1 County Courts Act 1984, s 138(1).
2 See *Patel v Patel* (1991) Wandsworth County Court. HHJ White (unreported). This was not, however, an assured shorthold tenancy, but concerned a fixed-term fully assured tenancy.

Break clauses and termination by notice

[5.40] The problems surrounding forfeiture clauses (above) are less pressing if the landlord can validly include a 'break' clause entitling him to terminate the tenancy by notice during its fixed-term. Although a shorthold tenancy clearly can include a break clause, the relevant statutory provisions (discussed above in relation to forfeiture clauses) cause similar problems where premature termination is sought by exercising a break clause in the agreement. Although there may be some doubt as to whether a lease with a break clause can be termed a 'term certain', it is clearly intended to be viewed as such for the purposes of the HA 1988. In the case of pre-HA 1996 tenancies, s 20(1)(b) specifically provides that a tenancy can be a shorthold only if it is for a fixed-term of not less than six months, and there is no power for the landlord to determine the tenancy 'at any time earlier than six months from the beginning of the tenancy'. By s 45(4) this includes a break clause but not a forfeiture clause. A break clause could therefore be included provided it was expressly inoperable during the first six months of the term. In the case of a post-HA 1996 tenancy, the clause may be operable in the first six months, but by virtue of s 21(5) the court cannot grant a possession order to take effect until at least six months of tenancy have elapsed.

[5.41] In both cases problems arise, however, when one considers the precise legal effect that exercise of the 'break' will have, and the form the break clause must itself take. As with forfeiture clauses the relevant provisions are to be found in the HA 1988, ss 5, 7(6), 20(1) and 45, and these apply to both pre- and post-HA 1996 shortholds. The provisions are difficult to interpret but their effect would appear to be as follows:

(1) Section 5(1) allows a fixed-term assured tenancy to be brought to an end where it 'contains power for the landlord to determine the tenancy in certain circumstances'. By reference to s 45(4) this encompasses a break clause but not a forfeiture clause.
(2) If the landlord gives notice to terminate, in reliance on such a provision in the tenancy agreement, the tenancy will not necessarily thereby terminate. By virtue of s 5(2) ibid a statutory periodic tenancy will arise. This is because s 5(2) provides that the tenant is entitled to remain in possession under a periodic statutory tenancy whenever an assured fixed-term tenancy comes to an end other than by order of the court or the surrender or other act of the tenant. In the case of both pre- and post-HA 1996 shortholds the new tenancy that arises on the coming to an end of the original shorthold is statutorily deemed to be an assured shorthold tenancy[1].
(3) Section 5(2) is, however, expressed to be 'subject to s 7 and Ch 11 below' – Ch 11 contains the shorthold provisions in ss 20–22.
(4) We have already seen that s 7(6) provides that a fixed-term assured shorthold tenancy can be terminated during its fixed-term only by a court order obtained under specific Sch 2 grounds[2] and that these grounds must be specified in the tenancy agreement itself; eg by provision for 'determination by notice or otherwise'. This could clearly encompass their inclusion in a break clause, thus triggering the availability of possession proceedings on the specified grounds, much in the same manner as if such provision were made in a forfeiture clause in the tenancy agreement.
(5) At this point, however, an interpretative problem arises. Once the break has been effected by notice, is the tenancy to be treated, by virtue of s 5(2), as a periodic shorthold tenancy; in this event can it then be terminated by two months' notice in the usual way?[3] Or, as appears to be intended by the wording of s 7(6), can a break clause be effective to terminate a fixed-term shorthold

only if it specifies the permitted grounds in Sch 2 and is given pursuant to one of them; eg Ground 8 (two months' rent arrears)?

1 See s 19A(b) (post-HA 1996 shortholds) and the HA 1988, s 20(4) HA 1988 (pre-HA 1996 shortholds).
2 See above, para 5.35 ff.
3 See below para 5.52 ff.

[5.42] The better view would seem to be that the exercise of a 'break' will terminate the tenancy under s 5(1)[1]. If the tenant remains in possession then a statutory periodic tenancy will arise[2], and this will be 'deemed' a shorthold[3]. The exercise of the break clause cannot *of itself* ground possession proceedings, however, unless the required Sch 2 grounds are specified in the clause and relied upon to obtain an order for possession[4]. Having become a statutory periodic tenancy following a 'break' notice, however, then like any other shorthold tenancy which has continued beyond its term date it can be terminated by two months' notice in accordance with the HA 1988, s 21[5]. Where the tenancy includes a break clause, service of a s 21 notice can operate both as statutory notice of requiring possession and as contractual notice under the break clause (provided it complies strictly with the contractual requirements laid down in the tenancy agreement). Thus, in *Aylward v Fawaz*[6] where a break clause allowed one month's notice to break a 12-month assured shorthold tenancy, exercisable after the first six months of tenancy, and the landlord served a s 21 notice requiring possession 'after 14 August 1996' (a date two months from service of the latter) it was held that the notice complied both with s 21 and with the contractual break provision, and sufficed to bring the tenancy to an end in accordance with the HA 1988.

1 This appears to have been accepted without argument in *Aylward v Fawaz* (1997) 29 HLR 408.
2 Ibid, s 5(2).
3 Ibid, s 20(4).
4 See ss 5(2) and 7(6) ibid.
5 This view is supported by the terminology of s 5(2) ibid, which in providing for a periodic tenancy to arise on termination expresses itself to be 'subject to s 7 and Ch II [the shorthold provisions] of the Act.'
6 (1997) 29 HLR 408.

[5.43] The position remains unsatisfactory, and cannot be regarded as free of doubt. Clearly, if (as suggested above may be the correct interpretation) the landlord can end a fixed-term shorthold by serving a break notice, thereby turning the tenancy into a periodic tenancy, this would appear to render s 7(6) redundant in relation to shorthold tenancies, which are in practice one of the commonest forms of fixed-term tenancy. Any fixed-term shorthold could, once six months of tenancy has expired[1] (and providing of course that the agreement contains an appropriate break clause) be converted into a statutory periodic tenancy and terminated on two months notice without reference to any of any of the Sch 2 grounds for possession, without the additional restrictions in s 7(6) applying. The latter will, it is suggested, be relevant only where the landlord seeks to terminate a shorthold by court order while it remains an assured fixed-term tenancy; eg pursuant to a forfeiture clause drafted in appropriate terms. Where the lease contains a break clause he will not, apparently, need to do so. Clearly, the statutory provisions are in need of clarification and amendment.

1 and before the expiry of six months in the case of a post-HA 1996 assured shorthold.

E Control of shorthold rents

[5.44] By virtue of s 22(1), the tenant can refer the rent payable to the Rent Assessment Committee for adjudication if he considers the rent he is paying is 'significantly higher' than the rent payable under similar tenancies of similar dwelling houses in the locality[1]. The geographical 'locality' relevant for this purpose is not defined and its definition will, presumably, be a question of fact to be decided by the committee[2]. The committee is to fix the rent at that level which, in its opinion, the landlord might reasonably be expected to obtain under the assured shorthold in question. The expectation is that this will not be a fair rent level, but a market rent, which takes account of the limited degree of contractual security that the tenant has been offered. The lack of statutory security of tenure under an assured shorthold is a potent disincentive to the use of the rent control provisions (below) by a tenant other than one with a fixed-term shorthold of long duration. Note also that the rent fixing machinery relates to the tenancy, not the dwelling, and so has no effect on subsequent tenancies[3].

1 There is a prescribed form for the reference: see form 6 in the Assured Tenancies and Agricultural Occupancies (Forms) Regulations 1997, SI 1997/194 (Appendix, below).
2 Cf RA 1977, s 70, and decisions there under, especially *Metropolitan Property Holdings Ltd v Finegold* [1985] 1 WLR 349 ('Locality' to be viewed in a common sense manner, connoting a substantial and not limited area).
3 Compare with the 'fair rent' provisions in the RA 1977, s 70 which bind the property, not the tenancy.

Exclusion of committee's jurisdiction

[5.45] The Rent Assessment Committee's jurisdiction to control shorthold rents is excluded by s 22(2) and (3) in a number of situations. The breadth of the exclusions considerably limits the jurisdiction to control shorthold rents. The committee's jurisdiction is excluded in the following circumstances:

(1) If the rent payable is a rent previously determined by the committee.
(2) If the tenancy is a post-HA 1996 shorthold, and more than six months have elapsed since the beginning of the tenancy (or in the case of a replacement tenancy since the beginning of the original tenancy)[1]. Semble this would apply not only to a periodic shorthold, but also in the case of a fixed-term shorthold of more than six months duration, limiting the right to a reference to the initial six months of the term granted.
(3) If the tenancy is a pre-HA 1996 assured shorthold that has continued after expiry of the initial fixed-term (s 20(2)). In this case the right to go to the Rent Assessment Committee arises only during the first fixed-term. It cannot be used during any further fixed-term, although if on expiry of the first term a periodic tenancy arises, landlord and tenant can use the assured tenancy provisions (ss 13 and 14) to increase the rent[2].

1 HA 1988, s 22(2)(aa).
2 See HC Deb, Standing Committee G, 26 January 1988, col 469 ff. 'Where a second fixed-term is granted, a landlord who has allowed a tenant to stay on in that way will have established a firm relationship with his tenant and it would not be appropriate for the tenant to be able to use the s 20 mechanism to get the rent reduced' (ibid, col 465).

[5.46] The effect of the exclusions is that the right to refer a shorthold rent to the Rent Assessment Committee under s 22 can only be exercised once, and then (a) only during the original term in the case of a pre-HA 1996 shorthold, and (b) only during the first six months of the tenancy in the case of a post-HA 1996 shorthold.

Powers of the Rent Assessment Committee

[5.47] The Rent Assessment Committee must not make a determination unless it considers that there is a sufficient number of similar dwelling houses in the locality let on assured tenancies (whether shorthold or not)[1]. This is a question of fact for the committee[2]. It is not clear whether the 'sufficiency' referred to is of the number of dwelling houses in the locality itself, or a sufficiency from which the committee can make a comparison for the purposes of giving a determination. The better view, it is suggested, is that the required sufficiency refers to the need for there to be a sufficient number of dwellings etc for the purpose of making the comparison needed to evaluate the existing rent, and whether it is significantly higher than others in the locality. This being the case, if the committee considers that there are insufficient assured tenancies or shortholds for comparison purposes in the locality, there is effectively no control of rent unless the tenancy continues as a periodic term, in which case s 13 can be invoked. *Query* whether housing association rents in the locality (which are likely to be lower) can be taken into account for comparison purposes under s 22. Section 22(3)(b) directs the committee to have regard to 'the level of rents payable under the tenancies referred to in s 22(3)(a)' – namely assured tenancies 'whether shorthold or not'. This would suggest that they can be taken into account. But the reference to 'the landlord' in s 22(1) might suggest that it is the circumstances of the particular tenancy under consideration that are relevant, and these may be materially different in the case of private sector and housing association lettings.

1 HA 1988, s 22(3)(a).
2 Cf RA 1977, s 70(2), below para 7.23 ff.

[5.48] The committee must not make a determination unless it considers the rent in question to be 'significantly higher' than the rent the landlord might reasonably be expected to obtain under the tenancy, having regard to the level of rents paid under comparable assured tenancies or assured shortholds in the locality[1]. The rent can be reduced, therefore, only if it is considered excessive. What is to be considered 'significantly' higher for this purpose is not defined and will be a question of fact for the committee.

1 Ibid s 22(3)(b).

Effect of control

[5.49] The process involved on shorthold rent references is essentially comparative in nature, and does not preclude higher rents than those currently prevalent being charged for shorthold lets, provided that they are not excessive ('significantly' higher) in comparison with other shorthold rents. The committee's function might fairly be described as one of averaging rent increases, rather than one of rent control by reference to fixed objective criteria, as was the case under the RA 1977, s 70 with regard to regulated tenancies.

[5.50] If the Rent Assessment Committee makes a determination, any excess rent over the sum awarded is irrecoverable, and no notice of increase (under s 13, for periodic 'continuation' tenancies) can be served for 12 months after the determination takes effect. The determination takes effect on such date as the committee may direct, but not earlier than the date of application.

Lifting of rent control

[5.51] By virtue of s 23, the Secretary of State has power to direct (by statutory instrument) that the Rent Assessment Committee shall not have jurisdiction to exercise its powers in relation to shorthold rents in designated areas of the country. No orders have been made under this provision.

F Security of tenure

TERMINATION OF ASSURED SHORTHOLDS

[5.52] An assured shorthold is a species of assured tenancy, and the grounds for possession in Sch 2 apply, as to other assured tenancies[1]. Additionally, the HA 1988, s 21 gives (in effect) another mandatory ground for possession, separate and distinct from the grounds in Sch 2[2], entitling a landlord to possession if *two* conditions are met:

(1) The assured shorthold term must have expired and no further assured tenancy (whether shorthold or not) must for the time being be in existence, other than an assured shorthold periodic tenancy (whether statutory or not)[3]. Semble, if a second fixed-term shorthold has replaced the first (rather than a periodic continuation tenancy) the tenant's security is assured until the end of the agreed term – the grounds for possession apply only if the tenancy is a statutory periodic tenancy (there is, however, no rent control if a second fixed-term is granted; see above). The restrictions on possession set out in s 7(6) (above) will apply during the second, and subsequent, fixed-terms.

(2) The landlord (or one out of joint landlords) must give to the tenant not less than two months' written notice that he requires possession[4]. This can be given at any time before, at, or after, termination of the original shorthold term[5]. If a statutory periodic tenancy is not to arise on expiry of the fixed shorthold term, then notice will have to be given at least two months before the expiry of the fixed-term. Once a statutory periodic tenancy has arisen, however, by virtue of s 5(2) ibid, it can be terminated at any time thereafter on giving two months' notice pursuant to s 21.

1 HA 1988, s 21(1).
2 See *Panayi and Pyrkos v Roberts* (1993) 25 HLR 421.
3 Ibid, s 21(1)(a), as amended, Local Government and Housing Act 1989, Sch 11, para 103.
4 HA 1988, s 21(1)(b). Prior to amendments in the HA 1996, the notice did not need to be in writing, although as a counsel of caution it was preferable to serve written notice. HA 1996, s 98 now requires the notice to be given in writing. There is not, however, a prescribed form.
5 Ibid, s 21(2) and (4).

[5.53] Two points should be noted:

(1) The two-month notice period laid down by s 21(4) is a minimum only, and does not abrogate a longer notice period if required at common law[1]. It follows that to validly terminate a statutory periodic tenancy the notice of termination must end on a term date of the tenancy[2] as well as being of a minimum two months' duration. Thus a weekly or monthly tenant will be entitled to longer notice under section 21 than required for notice to quit at common law. Quarterly, half-yearly, and yearly tenancies will still require a quarter or six months' notice to terminate, however. It should also be noted that only one notice need be

served. There is no requirement to serve a separate notice to quit. The landlord cannot start possession proceedings until the period specified in the notice requiring possession has expired[3].

(2) It is not necessary for the landlord to serve a section 8 notice of seeking possession. This is only required if the landlord is seeking possession under the Sch 2 grounds. Section 21 provides a separate freestanding procedure for regaining possession of property let on an assured shorthold tenancy, and it is not necessary to serve (in addition to the s 21 notice) a notice of seeking possession[4].

1 See generally, HC Deb, Standing Committee G, 12th sitting, 28 January 1988, cols 461 ff.
2 Ibid s 21(4).
3 *Lower Street Properties v Jones* [1996] EGCS 37 (proceeding invalid because commenced one day before the end of the period stated in the s 21 notice requiring possession).
4 *Panayi and Pyrkos v Roberts* (1993) 25 HLR 421.

[5.54] The court has no discretion to refuse possession if the s 21 conditions are fulfilled. If the court orders possession, any statutory periodic tenancy which has arisen on expiry of the assured shorthold shall end (regardless of the period) on the day on which the order takes effect[1]. The only ground for postponement is that in the HA 1980, s 89(1), which allows the court to order a postponement of the giving up of possession, but only to a date not later than six weeks after the making of the order. A postponement can only be granted if it appears to the court that exceptional hardship would be caused by requiring possession to be given up on that day. In any other case possession must not be postponed (whether by variation or suspension of the order for possession or stay of execution) to a date later than 14 days after the making of the order. This procedure was challenged under the Human Rights Act 1998 in *Poplar Housing & Regeneration Community Association v Donoghue*[2], on the basis that the court's lack of discretion to refine possession breached the tenants right (under Art 8 of the European Convention on Human Rights) to respect for the home. The court of appeal, while holding that the eviction impacted on her family life and engaged Article 8, held however, that the legal procedures for terminating shortholds were proportionate to the social policy objectives laid down by Parliament. The limited role given to the court under section 21(4) was a legislative policy decision with which the court would not interfere[3]. The procedures for terminating shortholds did not, therefore, infringe the Human Rights Act.

1 See s 21(3) ibid.
2 [2001] 3 WLR 183, CA.
3 See [2001] 3 WLR 183, CA at 202–203.

Accelerated procedure for possession

[5.55] Where there is a written tenancy agreement and the proper notices have been served, an accelerated procedure for possession is available allowing the landlord to proceed by way of originating application. The accelerated procedure only applies in limited circumstances[1]:

(1) The tenancy must be an assured shorthold and not a protected, statutory or housing association tenancy under the RA 1977.

(2) It must not immediately follow an assured tenancy that was not itself an assured shorthold tenancy. If a periodic statutory tenancy arises on expiry of a fixed-term shorthold this is, as we have seen, statutorily deemed to be an assured

shorthold, and the accelerated procedure will be applicable on its later termination. If there is a re-grant to a tenant with an *assured* tenancy, however, then the procedure will *not* apply, even if the re-grant is of a written assured shorthold tenancy[2].

(3) In the case of a pre-HA 1996 tenancy, then the tenancy must be in writing and satisfy the requirements of s 20(1). In particular, shorthold notice in prescribed form must have been served before the tenancy was granted[3]. It has already been noted that an assured shorthold could arise in some circumstances *without* the need for a prescribed shorthold notice to be given on letting[4]; eg where there was a protected shorthold tenancy which is renewed after 15 January 1989, or where a succession takes place to a statutory tenancy which was subject to case 19 in the RA 1977, Sch 15 (protected shortholds)[5]. The accelerated procedure will not be available in these circumstances. In the case of post-HA 1996 shortholds, there is no need for service of written shorthold notice on grant, but the agreement must be in writing for the accelerated procedure to apply.

(4) Written notice requiring possession must have been given in accordance with the HA 1988, s 21(2)[6].

1 See order 49, rule 6A(3), County Court Rules 1981 (added by SI (1993/2175). The accelerated procedure was introduced for possession actions begun on or after 1 November 1993.

2 Note *Manel v Meman* (2000) 5 CL 431 where the landlord's notice was not sufficient. The court of appeal expressed concern that the accelerated procedure had been followed even though the tenant's reply had raised allegations of non-compliance.

3 Order 49, rule 6A(3)(c) ibid. Note, however, that this is the case only where the shorthold grant 'immediately follows' termination of the prior assured tenancy. This will be a question of fact for the county court.

4 See above para 5.15 ff.

5 See HA 1988, s 39(7). Any successor other than the deceased tenant's spouse takes an assured shorthold tenancy by way of succession.

6 See above para 5.52 ff.

[5.56] Where these conditions are met, the landlord can proceed by originating application and supporting affidavit, in accordance with order 49, rule 6A of the County Court Rules[1]. The accelerated procedure can only be used, however, if the only purpose of the proceedings is to recover possession. It cannot be used if the landlord wishes to make any other claim; eg for arrears of rent. Neither can it be used where the Assured Shorthold is brought to an end by forfeiture[2]. Once the originating application has been served, the tenant has 14 days to file a reply. The judge can, after considering the landlord's application and the reply (if any) order possession without requiring the attendance of the parties. Indeed, he is directed to do so 'without delay', unless he is *not* satisfied that the relevant statutory notices were served, or that the application was itself properly served[3]. If he is not so satisfied a hearing date will be fixed, allowing not less than 14 days' notice of hearing to the parties. Where the tenant seeks a postponement of possession on grounds of exceptional hardship (under the HA 1980, s 89 above) the court may direct a hearing limited to that issue, and in this case it must take place before the date on which possession is to be given up. If satisfied that hardship would be caused by the giving of possession on the date specified in the order for possession, the court can vary the date on which possession is to be given up[4].

1 See Order 49, rule 6A(11)–(18) for the detailed rules of procedure.

2 HA 1988, s 45(4).

3 Order 49, rule 6A(17) ibid.

4 Order 49, rule 6A(17), added by the Civil Procedure (Amendment No 4) Order 2000, SI 2000/2092.

UTILITY OF ASSURED SHORTHOLD PROVISIONS

[5.57] The assured shorthold offers an attractive legal regime for landlords, whether or not the letting envisaged is of short duration. In the case of a fixed-term it allows for indefinite continuation once the initial term has expired, subject always to an immediate right to repossess on giving two months' notice. Following the changes made by the HA 1996 the landlord can, as an alternative, grant a periodic shorthold, in which case possession cannot be obtained during the first six months of tenancy, but thereafter can be gained at any time on giving two months notice – whatever the ultimate duration of tenancy. In these circumstances, it is difficult to see any advantage to a potential landlord in granting a fully assured tenancy, rather than an assured shorthold; he can grant a fixed-term six-month assured shorthold, or a periodic shorthold, and allow it to continue indefinitely once the initial six months have expired, ensuring thereby that the tenant enjoys no security of tenure, while attracting little effective rent control. Prior to the HA 1996, there may have been circumstances in which an owner-occupier might wish to use a fully assured tenancy subject to mandatory Ground 1, where a periodic tenancy might have given the landlord greater flexibility. As shortholds can now be periodic, the only potential advantage of the fully assured tenancy is the possibility of terminating the tenancy during the first six months of tenancy.

[5.58] Although primarily intended to encourage short-term lettings of residential property, the assured shorthold provisions, in their current form, effectively present a landlord with three options for letting:

(1) He can grant a periodic assured tenancy. Unless the conditions in Sch 2A apply (discussed above) this will be an assured shorthold tenancy. The landlord will be unable to obtain possession for six months from grant, but thereafter the tenancy remains a shorthold whatever the ultimate length of the term. It can be terminated at any time after the initial six months by service of two months' notice requiring possession in accordance with s 21 (above). Furthermore, the provisions for reference of shorthold rents to the Rent Assessment Committee only apply during the first six months of the term. Once this period has elapsed, therefore, the level of rent payable is only reviewable in accordance with the provisions for fully assured tenancies, under the HA 1988, ss 13 and 14. The only redress this gives the tenant is the right to refer a proposed *increase* to the Rent Assessment Committee[1]. He cannot, of his own initiative , refer the rent for an adjudication. As a consequence, once the initial six-month period has elapsed, the landlord will potentially have a security-free letting with no rent control on the shorthold basis – whatever the ultimate length of tenancy.

(2) He can grant a short fixed-term shorthold; eg for six months[2]. If the tenant remains in possession paying rent after expiry of the fixed-term, a statutory periodic tenancy will arise. This will also be an assured shorthold tenancy[3] and the shorthold ground for possession will continue to be available – whatever the ultimate length of the letting. In the case of a pre-HA 1996 shorthold, the statutory periodic tenancy which arises on termination of the fixed-term will only be deemed a shorthold if the tenant and landlord are the same as at the coming to an end of the fixed shorthold term[4]. In this case, therefore, a change of tenant during the 'continuation' assured tenancy may put its shorthold status at risk. This is irrelevant in the case of a post-HA 1996 shorthold, as all periodic tenancies are, in any event, deemed to be shortholds unless the exceptions

discussed above apply. Once the fixed shorthold term has expired, the landlord will have the double benefit of lack of rent control during the 'continuation' periodic tenancy, as the shorthold rent control provisions only apply during the initial fixed-term (above), as well as a security-free letting. Note, however, that the statutory periodic tenancy will be on the same terms as the fixed-term (s 5(3)), except that 'any term which makes provision for determination by the landlord or the tenant shall not have effect while the tenancy remains an assured tenancy' (s 5(3)(e) ibid). A break clause in the original tenancy will cease to have effect, therefore, but not semble a proviso for re-entry or forfeiture (see s 45(4) ibid). Once the tenancy has become periodic, the more limited rent review provisions for assured tenancies in ss 13 and 14 will become applicable. It should be noted that these only apply where the tenancy agreement contains no provision for variation of rent. It follows that if the initial shorthold term contained express provisions for the review of rent or for an increase of rent by notice (in whatever form), this will continue to have effect by virtue of s 5(3), thus disapplying the statutory rent review machinery.

(3) The landlord can grant a longer fixed-term, thereby contractually committing the tenant to payment of rent and performance of other leasehold obligations for a longer period. At the same time, by inserting into the agreement a suitably drafted break clause and proviso for re-entry, the landlord can reserve to himself the right to terminate the tenancy prematurely, while not extending the same benefit to his tenants. The shorthold rent provisions can be used only once during the fixed-term by the tenant to secure a variation of the rent, and are, in any event, of limited scope (see above para 5.44 ff). Furthermore, where the tenancy is for a considerable period, a rent review provision can be included to increase the rent as appropriate. Such a provision would be statutorily implied into any statutory periodic tenancy arising on termination, although it may be preferable to review rents at the commencement of each of a series of fixed-term grants, as the statutory rent review machinery will be inapplicable where a review clause has been included in the tenancy agreement.

1 See Chapter 3 para 3.102 ff, above.
2 Following the HA 1996 amendments, the fixed period can now be of less than six months, but in this case a statutory periodic tenancy will arise on termination of the fixed-term, and possession cannot be granted until six months have elapsed (HA 1988, s 21(5)). There would therefore seem to be little incentive to grant a fixed-term for less than six months, if the landlord wishes to use a fixed-term, rather than periodic, tenancy.
3 HA 1988, s 19A(b), inserted by HA 1996, s 96(1).
4 Ibid, s 20(4).

CHAPTER 6

Residential security under the Rent Act 1977

[6.1] The Rent Act 1977 (RA 1977) consolidated earlier Rent Acts. Although superseded by the assured tenancies scheme introduced by the Housing Act 1988 (HA 1988), it continues, as amended, to govern the majority of private sector residential tenancies (other than long leases) granted before the coming into force of the HA 1988 on 15 January 1989. The policy behind the Rent Act scheme was intended to confer security of tenure on residential tenants by restricting the landlords right to possession except in limited 'cases' set out in Schedule 15 of the 1977 Act. It also aimed to avoid exploitation of tenants by landlords extorting premiums for the grant or renewal of a tenancy, and provided for a system of rent registration based on 'fair rents' fixed by a rent officer, disregarding the scarcity value of housing for rent. The net result of the protection granted by the Acts was to confer on protected and statutory Rent Act tenants what has been judicially described as a 'status of irremoveability'.

A Protected tenancies

[6.2] Tenancies entitled to the full protection of the RA 1977 are described as protected tenancies[1]. A protected tenancy may subsequently become a statutory tenancy entitling the tenant to the same protection as that afforded under the original protected tenancy[2]. Both protected and statutory tenancies are subject to the rent control provisions of the RA 1977 and are therefore described as regulated tenancies[3]. Some categories of tenancy known as restricted contracts were specifically excluded from full Rent Act security of tenure but were entitled to rent control[4].

1 RA 1977, s 1.
2 See RA 1977, ss 2 and 3, discussed below at para 6.48 ff.
3 See RA 1977, s 18(1).
4 See RA 1977, s 19(2), discussed below at para 6.46.

IDENTIFYING A PROTECTED TENANCY

[6.3] For a residential tenancy to qualify for full Rent Act protection, the following conditions must be satisfied:

(1) Was the original tenancy granted before 15 January 1989 or do the transitional provisions of the HA 1988 apply[1]?

(2) The letting must come within the definition set out in RA 1977, s 1, which requires that the accommodation is a dwelling house that is let as a separate dwelling.
(3) The rateable value and/or the rent payable in respect of the dwelling house must be within the Rent Act limits for protection to accrue[2].

1 See HA 1988, s 34, discussed below at para 3.4 ff.
2 See RA 1977, ss 4 and 5.

[6.4] If these conditions are satisfied, and the tenancy is not one that is specifically excluded from protection by the RA 1977, ss 4–16A, the tenancy will be protected. The RA 1977, ss 4–16A contain a number of excluded categories of letting where protection does not accrue, even if the other qualifying conditions (above) are satisfied – these are chiefly based on policy consideration eg holiday lets and lettings with board and attendance.

DEFINITION OF A PROTECTED TENANCY

[6.5] The RA 1977, s 1 provides that a protected tenancy must be a tenancy of a dwelling house let as a separate dwelling[1]. If a tenancy comes within this definition and is not excluded from protection on any other grounds, it will have full Rent Act protection. The same terminology is employed in the HA 1988 to define assured tenancies. These basic concepts, and the extensive case law they have generated, are discussed above in Chapter 3, para 3.12 ff to which reference should also be made.

1 Cf the formula was retained in the HA 1988, s 1(1), to define assured tenancies granted after the commencement of that Act.

'A tenancy'

[6.6] Entitlement to Rent Act protection requires there to have been a tenancy as opposed to a mere licence, restricted contract, or some other category of occupation such as trespass, and this is underlined by the use of the word 'let' later in the statutory definition. The only statutory definition of tenancy found in the RA 1977 is to the effect that a tenancy includes a subtenancy[1]. There is no requirement that, in order to be a protected tenancy, the letting must be in writing. The tenancy may be oral or even (in appropriate cases) arise by implication of law. In short, any form of tenancy may qualify for Rent Act protection, whether periodic, fixed-term or implied by law, and whether made orally or in writing.

1 See RA 1977, s 152(1).

[6.7] A tenancy confers an estate in land giving the tenant the right to exclude all third parties, including the landlord, from possession for the duration of the lease, in return for which a rent is normally payable[1]. This contrasts with a licence which does no more than grant a personal right to an occupier to do some act which would otherwise constitute a trespass[2]. A licence cannot be protected by the RA 1977. However, providing all the other criteria of a regulated tenancy are present, a tenancy at sufferance, a tenancy at will and a tenancy by estoppel are each capable of being protected tenancies[3], as is an agreement for a lease capable of specific performance in accordance with the long-established principle in *Walsh v Lonsdale*[4].

1 While absence of payment of rent may be evidence that no more than a licence has been created (*Soldiers' Sailors' and Airmen's Families Association v Merton Corpn* [1966] 1 WLR 736) it was held by the Court of Appeal in *Ashburn Anstalt v Arnold* [1989] Ch 1 at 9 that reservation of rent is not essential for the creation of a tenancy.
2 See definition of a licence offered by Vaughan CJ in *Thomas v Sorrell* (1673) Vaugh 330 at 351, Ex Ch.
3 In most cases such tenancies will not be created because other factors such as too low a rent being reserved will prevent protection. For further discussion see R E Megarry *The Rent Acts* (11th edn, 1988), pp 66 and 67.
4 (1882) 21 Ch D 9, CA.

[6.8] In order to grant a tenancy, the landlord must be competent to grant such an estate in land. If this is not the case, the occupier will be no more than a licensee or at best, a tenancy by estoppel may have been created which would bind only the landlord by estoppel[1]. In addition, there must be an intention to create legal relations if a tenancy is to arise.

1 See *Edward H Lewis & Son Ltd v Morelli* (1948) 65 TLR 56, CA; and *Stratford v Syrett* [1958] 1 QB 107, CA.

[6.9] The modern leading authority on the distinction between a lease and a licence is now found in the House of Lords' decision of *Street v Mountford*[1]. The significance of the distinction is that tenancies alone are entitled to the statutory security of tenure and rent control of, respectively, the RA 1977 or the HA 1988, depending on whether the tenancy was granted on or after 15 January 1989, or before that date. The decision in *Street v Mountford* has been the subject of extensive judicial analysis since 1985, and is considered fully in Chapter 3, para 3.25 ff.

1 [1985] AC 809, [1985] 2 All ER 289.

Dwelling house

[6.10] A dwelling house can be a house or part of a house, including a flat[1] or even a single room[2]. Indeed, the concept of a 'dwelling house' is not limited to buildings. A temporary or mobile structure can be a dwelling house with Rent Act protection, provided there is a sufficient annexation to the land, so that it becomes part of the land itself[3]. In *R v Rent Officer of Nottinghamshire Registration Area, ex p Allen*[4] it was held that a mobile caravan could be a 'house' for the purposes of the Rent Act if it is rendered wholly immobile and ceases to be a moveable chattel, eg by having its wheels removed or being blocked in situ by a brick or concrete construction[5]. On the other hand, a houseboat that is moored will not be a 'dwelling', as the purpose of mooring it is to prevent it being carried away, and there is insufficient annexation if it can be easily moved. No assured tenancy arose, therefore, where a houseboat moored upstream of Battersea Bridge on the Thames, was let for residential occupation[6]. Where a dwelling is let with land it will be protected, unless it is agricultural land exceeding two acres in extent (in which event the whole property demised can be protected only under the agricultural holding legislation)[7].

1 *Langford Property Co Ltd v Goldrich* [1949] 1 KB 511 at 517, CA.
2 See *Field v Gover* [1944] KB 200, CA, and *Curl v Angelo* [1948] 2 All ER 189, CA.
3 *Elitestone Ltd v Morris* [1997] 2 EGLR 115.
4 [1985] 2 EGLR 153.
5 See *Nutt v Read* [2000] 32 HLR 761.
6 *Chelsea Yacht and Boat Co Ltd v Pope* [2000] 2 EGLR 23.
7 RA 1977, s 26, below paras 6.28 and 6.29.

Let 'as a separate dwelling'

[6.11] Providing there is a letting, it must also be shown that its purpose is residential. Thus the terms of the tenancy must be considered and will be decisive[1]. If they do not contemplate a residential user then a regulated tenancy will not have been created even if the premises are being used as a dwelling with the landlord's knowledge, unless the landlord actively consented to the change of use[2].

1 See *Ponder v Hillman* [1969] 1 WLR 1261 where property being used as a residence but described in the lease as 'all that shop and premises' with no mention of residential user, was not a regulated tenancy.
2 *Wolfe v Hogan* [1949] 2 KB 194, CA.

[6.12] Where the terms of the lease contemplate a mixed user that is partly residential, the property would not normally fall within the protection of the RA 1977. Unless the business user element is minimal, mixed business and residential user tenancies will normally fall within the protection of the Landlord and Tenant Act 1954, Pt II. Even where business use has ceased, leaving the property solely as a residence, Rent Act protection is unlikely to arise[1]. Similar principles apply where the user is mixed residential and agricultural with protection falling within the agricultural holdings legislation. Decline in this use will not necessarily cause the letting to fall within Rent Act protection, however[2].

1 See *Pulleng v Curran* (1980) 44 P&CR 58, CA.
2 See *Russell v Booker* (1982) 263 Estates Gazette 513, CA.

[6.13] There must be evidence of a new contract with sole residential use having arisen, either expressly or by implication of law, if Rent Act protection is to apply[1].

1 See *Wolfe v Hogan* [1949] 2 KB 194, CA.

'A'

[6.14] The house must be let as one single dwelling and not more than one. In *Horford Investments Ltd v Lambert*[1] a house already converted into separate accommodation units, but let as a whole, was not a letting protected by the Rent Act as it was not let as a separate dwelling, although the subletting of the individual units could create protected tenancies. Similarly in *St Catherine's College v Dorling*[2] a house not yet specifically converted into separate dwelling units but containing separate bedrooms intended to be let individually by the college to students, was not let to the college as 'a' separate dwelling. Conversely, a letting of more than one dwelling house as a home may constitute a separate dwelling[3]. However, if the different properties were not let together as a single unit, but have been let to the same tenant at different times under different agreements, they may not be protected, even where the rent for both is paid as a whole[4].

1 [1976] Ch 39, CA.
2 [1979] 3 All ER 250, [1980] 1 WLR 66, CA.
3 *Langford Property Co Ltd v Goldrich* [1949] 1 KB 511, CA.
4 See *Metropolitan Properties Co Ltd v Barder* [1968] 1 WLR 286, CA which involved a flat and a separate room which were not together found to constitute a separate dwelling. But see also *Verity v Waring* [1953] CPL 423, CA, where different parts of a house let to a tenant at different times were held to constitute a separate dwelling.

'Separate'

[6.16] In order to attract Rent Act protection, the dwelling house must have been let as a 'separate' dwelling. A tenant must have exclusive possession of some part of the accommodation for a tenancy to exist, but this may be coupled with the right to share other parts of it. The RA 1977, ss 21 and 22 deal with sharing, and make provision for situations in which a protected tenancy may still be created. By virtue of s 21 a tenant who shares 'living accommodation' with his landlord is not fully protected but will have the benefit of a restricted contract. The courts have drawn a distinction between the sharing of 'living accommodation' which includes kitchens and sitting rooms where simultaneous use by different occupiers is envisaged, and sharing other accommodation, such as bathrooms, where it is not[1]. The reservation of a right to share living accommodation in the tenancy agreement is the critical factor, not the actual user. The agreement must have clearly reserved a right to share to the landlord, if the grant of a fully protected tenancy was to be avoided. Thus in *Gray v Brown*[2] it was held that a clause entitling the landlord to introduce 'whosoever I choose' to share the premises was insufficient to reserve a right to the landlord to share, and did not trigger the application of the exception to full protection afforded by s 21. The introduction of the resident landlord provisions of the Rent Act 1974 (now contained in the RA 1977, s 12 and Sch 2 and discussed below) reduced the significance of the case law as tenants of resident landlords now had restricted contracts. However, in the case of unfurnished tenancies granted by a resident landlord before the Rent Act 1974, these may still be protected tenancies (rather than restricted contracts) where landlord and tenant share no 'living accommodation'.

1 See *Goodrich v Paisner* [1957] AC 65, HL.
2 [1993] 25 HLR 144. And see *Miller v Eyo* (1998) 31 HLR 306.

[6.17] A tenant who shares with other tenants will, by virtue of the RA 1977, s 22, still be protected providing he occupies 'separate accommodation'. No distinction has been drawn in this context between 'living' and other accommodation. A tenant who has exclusive possession of a bedroom but has the right to share a living room, kitchen and bathroom with other tenants will have a regulated tenancy. Section 22 also renders ineffective any term of the tenancy which permits the landlord to terminate or modify the tenant's use of shared 'living accommodation', other than to increase the number of persons with whom it is shared or by means of a possession order which also relates to the separate accommodation. The HA 1988 makes similar provision for sharing arrangements, in relation to the grant of an assured tenancy[1].

1 See Chapter 3, para 3.69 ff.

'Dwelling'

[6.18] The premises must be let as a 'dwelling'. This requires that residential use be envisaged by the agreement and undertaken by the occupier, although the tenancy will be protected during the contractual period even if the tenant does not actually reside there[1]. It follows that, although a limited company is incapable of 'residing', accommodation may be let to a company 'as a separate dwelling' if it is used as a residence; eg by its employees or subtenants. Whereas an assured tenant can only be an individual, a limited company may be a protected tenant[2]. However, a statutory tenancy cannot arise in favour of a limited company on termination of the contractual term, as it cannot fulfil the residence requirement set out in the RA 1977, s 2.

1 Compare the position with regard to statutory tenancies, discussed below para 6.50 ff.
2 See HA 1988, s1(1)(a) which provides that a company cannot be an assured tenant as the tenant must be an individual.

[6.19] For a property to constitute a dwelling the tenant must undertake all the normal daily activities of normal life there. If it is capable of being used for eating, sleeping and cooking and this is the intended use foreseen by the agreement, then it is likely to constitute a dwelling[1]. Thus in *Wright v Howell*[2] a tenant who did not sleep on the premises which had neither cooking facilities nor water, was not protected. Yet accommodation comprising two rooms in a house which was just rented as sleeping accommodation by a hotelier for guests and employees was not a dwelling on the basis that sleeping alone without undertaking any other normal residential activities was insufficient to show the accommodation had been let as a dwelling[3]. By virtue of the RA 1977, s 26, protection will extend to land let together with the dwelling house as it is treated as part of the dwelling house. Thus any garden, garages or outhouses will come within the protected tenancy[4] providing the additional land does not exclude the letting from Rent Act protection, eg if it is agricultural land exceeding two acres in extent, or if the property infringes the rateable value limits for protection[4].

1 See *Uratempt Ventures Ltd v Collins* [2002] 1 All ER 46, HL.
2 (1947) 92 Sol Jo 26, CA, discussed in *Curl v Angelo* [1948] 2 All ER 189, CA.
3 Ibid *Curl v Angelo* .
4 *Langford Property Co Ltd v Batten* [1951] AC 223, HL.
5 See RA 1977, s 26(1).

TENANCIES EXCLUDED FROM RENT ACT PROTECTION

[6.20] If a tenancy falls within the criteria set out above, it may still fail to be protected as it is specifically excluded from protection by the RA 1977. The exclusions are principally contained in ss 4–16 and in the main comprise categories of premises, landlord or tenant in respect of which, for policy reasons, Rent Act protection was considered inappropriate. Although excluded from full protection, lettings within some of the categories below might give rise to 'restricted contracts', with more limited protection based on the rent tribunal's jurisdiction to suspend possession orders and rent control[1].

1 See RA 1977, ss 77 and 78 whereby the rent tribunal can substitute a 'reasonable rent' as opposed to the fair rent available to protected tenancies.

Rateable value or rental limits

[6.21] With the aim of excluding expensive properties, Rent Act protection has traditionally been excluded where the rateable value of the accommodation exceeds prescribed levels. Consequently the abolition of the rating system and its replacement with firstly the Community Charge, and latterly the Council Tax have required the substitution of rental limits for those tenancies entered into on or after 1 April 1990. Tenancies entered into before this date (and those entered into after this date but pursuant to a contract made before, where the property had a rateable value as at 31 March 1990), will be excluded if the demised premises had a rateable value that exceeded the prescribed limits 'on the appropriate day'. The RA 1977, s 25(3) defines the appropriate day as 23 March 1965 or if the property did not appear in the valuation list at that date, the date when it did so appear.

[6.22] The relevant rateable value is that which relates to the whole of the property included in the letting and thus will be the aggregate value assessed by inclusion of any land or other buildings demised as part of the tenancy in addition to the dwelling house. Conversely, if the demise comprises part of a house, the rateable value will have to be appropriately apportioned[1] in order to ascertain whether or not the tenancy is excluded. The limits set are aimed at excluding the most expensive properties and the vast majority of rented properties would fall within them. They are detailed in s 4 and distinguish between properties in Greater London (where the higher figure shown in each subsection is relevant) and elsewhere. The rules are unfortunately rather complex[2] and are as follows:

(1) Where the appropriate day fell on or after 1 April 1973, the rateable value limits are £1,500 or £750.
(2) Where the appropriate day fell on or after 22 March 1973 but before 1 April 1973, the limits are £600 and £300 providing the new rateable value on 1 April 1973 also exceeded £1,500 and £750 respectively.
(3) Where the appropriate day fell before 22 March 1973, the limit involves the rateable value exceeding £400 or £200 at this time, and £600 and £300 on 22 March 1973 and also exceeding £1,500 and £750 on 1 April 1973.

1 See s 25(1) and (2), ibid.
2 This is due in the main to the rating revaluation exercise in 1973.

[6.23] By s 25(4), where the valuation list is altered after the appropriate day, with retrospective effect from no later than the appropriate day, then the altered value is taken. However, if the revised valuation takes place after the appropriate day, then the old valuation will remain the relevant value[1]. The rateable value will be deemed to fall within the limits unless the contrary is proved[2] with jurisdiction relating to any disputes being reserved to the county court[3]. However, in the recent case of *Guestheath Ltd v Mirza*[4] landlords who at first admitted that the tenancy was protected, but later challenged this in court on the ground that the property was excluded from protection by virtue of its rateable value, were not estoppel from denying that the tenant was protected as they had not influenced him by encouragement or representation.

1 See *Rodwell v Gwynne Trusts Ltd* [1970] 1 WLR 327, HL, where the revised lower valuation took effect only nine days after the appropriate day but could not therefore be substituted resulting in the tenancy not being protected despite the new valuation being within the prescribed limit. See also *Guestheath Ltd v Mirza* (1990) 22 HLR 399.
2 RA 1977, s 4(3).
3 Ibid, s 25(2).
4 (1990) 22 HLR 399.

[6.24] Tenancies entered into after 1 April 1990 are subject to a simpler test, although the purpose of excluding more expensive properties remains the same. By RA 1977, s 4(4)[1] a tenancy is not protected if the rent payable for the time being is payable at a rate exceeding £25,000[2] a year. Rent is deemed not to include any sum expressed to be payable in respect of rates, services, repairs, and maintenance or insurance 'unless it could have been regarded by the parties as a sum so payable'. Section 4(6) retains the presumption that a tenancy falls within this limit unless the contrary is shown but it should be noted that the tenancy may fall in or out of protection with an appropriate rent variation.

1 Sub-ss (4)–(7) inserted by the References to Rating (Housing) Regulations 1990, SI 1990/434.
2 This sum may be replaced by order of the Secretary of State by statutory instrument (s 4(7)).

[6.25] In practice, following the HA 1988, there will be very few tenancies claiming Rent Act protection granted after 1 April 1990, although, as has been discussed above, the same test has been preserved for assured tenancies.

Tenancies at a low rent

[6.26] A tenancy will not be protected if either no rent is payable or the current annual rent is less than two-thirds of the rateable value on the appropriate day[1]. Where the tenancy was granted on or after 1 April 1990 (unless granted pursuant to a contract entered into before that date), the tenancy will not be protected where the annual rent payable is £1,000 or less in Greater London or £250 or less elsewhere[2]. Services rendered as payment for accommodation in both cases may constitute 'rent' for this purpose only if their value is quantifiable. Thus although long leases are not specifically excluded from Rent Act protection, the majority of long leases are at a low rent less than two-thirds of the rateable value or below the rental limits set out above and will not be protected. Section 5(4) defines rent in connection with long tenancies exceeding 21 years as excluding sums payable in respect of rates, services, repairs, and maintenance or insurance. However, with respect to short tenancies, all money payable by the tenant to the landlord will be regarded as rent for the purpose of s 5[3]. As the test for protection relates to the *current* rent payable, a tenancy may fall in and out of protection with an appropriate rent variation. A landlord may therefore attempt to avoid protection by reserving the right in the contractual tenancy to reduce the rent, and then exercising it to reduce the rent below the protection limit. Registration of the rent would not necessarily assist the tenant as in *Williams v Khan*[4] the view was taken that the 'rent payable' referred to in s 5 was the contractual rent and not the registered rent. Former controlled tenancies whose rents may be less than two-thirds of the rateable value were converted to regulated tenancies following the Housing Act 1980 (HA 1980) and are subject to special rules which ensure they are none the less protected[5].

1 RA 1977, s 5. Note that 'appropriate day' has the meaning described above in relation to rateable value calculations.
2 RA 1977, s 2A. These sums may be substituted from time to time by the Secretary of State by statutory instrument.
3 See *Sidney Trading Co Ltd v Finsbury Borough Council* [1952] 1 All ER 460.
4 (1980) 43 P&CR 1, CA.
5 See RA 1977, Sch 17, para 5 as amended by HA 1980, Sch 25, para 59.

Shared ownership leases

[6.27] The next exclusion is set out in the RA 1977, s 5A[1] and relates to certain shared ownership leases either granted pursuant to the Housing Act 1985 (HA 1985), Pt V or granted by housing associations and meeting the requirements set out in s 2A. These are principally leases of 99 years or longer granted at a premium in relation to at least 25 per cent of the dwelling house and on terms permitting the lessee to acquire further shares. Under such schemes, the tenant rents the remainder of the premises but cannot become a protected tenant of it. Thus the terms of the shared ownership lease, including the rent provisions, will prevail.

1 Added by the Housing and Planning Act 1986, s 18 and Sch 4.

Tenancy of a dwelling let together with other land

[6.28] This exclusion is found in the RA 1977, s 6. It is subject to s 26, which has been discussed above and covers the converse situation to that described here. Where a dwelling house is 'let together with' other land, which is not agricultural land of more than two acres, s 26 provides that the tenancy is protected. If, on the other hand, the agreement primarily relates to the letting of land that happens to include a dwelling house, then the letting will not be protected as it is excluded by virtue of s 6.

[6.29] This provides for exclusion where the tenancy is a letting of a house together with land other than the site of the dwelling house. Thus in order to ascertain whether or not a tenancy of a house let with land is protected, it is necessary to decide the dominant purpose of the letting as at the date of the application relating to the dispute[1]. Thus in *Feyereisel v Turnidge*[2] a bungalow let together with a caravan site was not a protected tenancy as the letting of the bungalow was ancillary to the letting of the site. In any event, where the letting of the land relates to business user which is more than minimal, the letting will not be protected but instead will attract the security of tenure afforded by the Landlord and Tenant Act 1954, Pt II.

1 See *Russell v Booker* (1982) 263 Estates Gazette 513, CA.
2 [1952] 2 QB 29, CA.

Board and attendance

[6.30] The RA 1977, s 7 excludes from protection a tenancy where a part of the rent comprises payment for board or attendance. In the case of attendance (but not board) it must account for a substantial part of the rent. A tenancy excluded by s 7 may nevertheless have constituted a restricted contract, although in the case of board even the limited protection of a restricted contract was excluded where the board was 'substantial'. The RA 1977 gave no definition of the meaning of 'board' and 'attendance'.

(1) *Board.* A morning cup of tea was not considered to constitute board in *Wilkes v Goodwin*[1], but in *Otter v Norman*[2] a full continental breakfast prepared and provided by the landlords was held by the House of Lords to constitute 'board'. It was there held that 'board' implied a requirement of preparation of the meal and the provision of crockery and cutlery. Landlords who merely provided a packet of cereal or other groceries could not be said to be providing their tenants with board. A letting with board would give rise to a restricted contract, although if a substantial portion of the rent was attributable to the board provided even this protection was excluded.
(2) *Attendance.* If attendance is substantial, a restricted contract arises, whereas attendance that is less than substantial leaves the tenancy fully protected.

'Attendance' involves a landlord providing services such as room cleaning, and supplying and laundering bed linen to the tenant personally. Services that are provided in common to all occupiers, such as cleaning of common parts, are not 'attendance' in the required sense. In *Palser v Grinling*[3] it was held that a broad non-arithmetical approach should be adopted to whether attendance was 'substantial', although each case must turn on its own facts.

1 [1923] 2 KB 86, CA.
2 [1989] AC 129, HL, (1988) 51 MLR 645 (C P Rodgers).
3 [1948] AC 291, HL.

[6.31] The board and attendance exception was frequently used to avoid granting protected tenancies under the RA 1977. Following the deregulation of the rented market by the HA 1988 the use of board and attendance as a technique for avoiding protective legislation is now less common.

Student lettings

[6.32] The RA 1977, s 8 provides that lettings to students by certain specified educational institutions will not be protected tenancies although they may be restricted contracts. Whether or not the tenancy falls within this excepted category is to be determined by the facts at the grant of the tenancy. The private landlord who lets to students is not therefore within this special category, although a letting to the institution upon terms that the accommodation is to be sublet only as student lettings may be of indirect benefit to private landlords. Although the head lease may be a protected tenancy, the institution cannot become a statutory tenant. As the students would not be protected tenants in relation to the head lessee, they cannot become protected tenants on determination of the head lessee's interest vis-a-vis the head landlord[1].

1 See RA 1977, s 137.

[6.33] It should also be noted that a letting to an educational institution may in certain circumstances create a business tenancy giving security of tenure under the Landlord and Tenant Act 1954, Pt II[1].

1 See *Groveside Properties Ltd v Westminster Medical School* (1983) 47 P&CR 507, CA, and see case note by J E Martin (1984) Conv 57.

Holiday lettings

[6.34] The RA 1977, s 9 provides that holiday lets are a further exceptional category of tenancy that cannot be protected. Neither can they be restricted contracts[1]. Where the purpose of the tenancy is to grant the tenant the right to occupy the dwelling house for a holiday, no protected tenancy will arise.

1 See RA 1977, s 19(7).

[6.35] Lack of statutory definition of the meaning of 'holiday' has enabled attempts to be made to evade Rent Act protection by the use of so-called holiday let agreements where the true purpose of the letting is not connected with a holiday. In *Buchmann v May*[1] it was held that the onus of proof is on the tenant to show that the holiday let agreement was in fact a sham. Nurses who signed a holiday agreement but whose landlord was aware that they were working as student nurses and not on holiday succeeded in discharging this burden of proof in *R v Rent Officer for the London Borough of Camden, ex p Plant*[2].

1 [1978] 2 All ER 993, CA.
2 (1980) 257 Estates Gazette 713.

Agricultural tenancies

[6.36] A tenancy will not be protected if the dwelling house forms part of an agricultural holding and is occupied by the person responsible for the control of the farming of the holding and it will instead be governed by the Agricultural Holdings Act 1986[1].

1 RA 1977, s 10. For the definition of 'agricultural holding' see the Agricultural Holdings Act 1986, s 1(2) and specialist works on agricultural holdings: inter alia Muir Watt and Moss *Agricultural Holdings* (14th edn, 1998) p 155 ff; Rodgers *Agricultural Law* (2nd edn, 1998), Chapter 5, p 111 ff.

Licensed premises

[6.37] A dwelling house that consists of or comprises premises licensed to sell intoxicating liquors for consumption on the premises cannot be a regulated tenancy. Neither will they be a business tenancy as they are specifically excluded from this protection by the Landlord and Tenant Act 1954, s 43(1).

Resident landlords

[6.38] The RA 1977, s 12 provides that resident landlords grant restricted contracts, not protected tenancies. Consequently the pre-15 January 1989 tenant of a resident landlord does not enjoy full security of tenure and will not become a statutory tenant on determination of their tenancy. However, they can register the rent and, where the tenancy is granted after the HA 1980, the tenant is also protected to the extent that the landlord cannot evict him without a court order and possession may be suspended by the court for a maximum period of three months[1]. Since the RA 1974, no distinction was drawn between furnished and unfurnished lettings by resident landlords. Both grant restricted contracts. However, an unfurnished tenancy granted by a resident landlord before the RA 1974 (not now commonly encountered) will be a protected tenancy providing landlord and tenant do not share living accommodation.

1 See HA 1980, s 65 which affects tenancies granted on or after 28 November 1980.

[6.39] A resident landlord is one who grants a tenancy of accommodation which forms part of a building which is not a purpose-built block of flats, and who has himself resided throughout the tenancy in a dwelling house situated in another part of that building. There is no requirement that any accommodation be shared and thus a tenancy of a self-contained flat situated in a house converted into flats where the landlord resides in another flat of the converted building will be a restricted contract and not a protected tenancy[1]. The landlord in that situation is as much a resident landlord as a landlord who has let out a room in his home. Purpose-built flats are excepted, although the letting by a landlord of part of a flat that he occupies as his residence within a purpose-built block fell within the resident landlord definition. 'Building' is not defined and whether the dwellings of landlord and tenant form part of the same building will be a matter of fact for the court to decide[2].

1 In *Barnes v Gorsuch* (1981) 43 P&CR 294, CA, a Victorian house converted into flats was not constructed as a 'purpose-built' block and did not satisfy the statutory definition.
2 Contrast the decisions of *Bardrick v Haycock* (1976) 31 P&CR 420, CA, and *Griffiths v English* (1982) 261 Estates Gazette 257, CA.

[6.40] The landlord must also occupy a dwelling in another part of the building 'as his residence' and the residence test will be the same as that for statutory tenants discussed below. A company cannot therefore be a resident landlord but it may be possible for a 'two-home' landlord to establish residence as the amount of residence required is a matter of fact and degree[1]. If sufficient residence is established, this will deprive tenants of full Rent Act protection. Residence by one of joint landlords is sufficient to create a restricted contract and not a protected tenancy[2].

1 See *Hampstead Way Investments Ltd v Lewis-Weare* [1985] 1 WLR 164 where the House of Lords reviewed the case law relating to the two-home statutory tenant, which would seem also to apply to the residence required for a landlord to be a resident landlord.
2 See *Cooper v Tait* (1984) 15 HLR 98, CA.

Crown lettings

[6.41] Following an amendment introduced by the HA 1980, s 73 and which has retrospective effect, tenancies where the immediate landlord is the Crown or a government department, originally excluded from Rent Act protection, can now be protected tenancies, but only where they are under the management of the Crown Estate Commissioners[1]. Any exclusion from protection under this section ceases upon the Crown assigning its interest to another landlord. Conversely, a tenancy could lose protection upon assignment by a landlord to the Crown or a government department.

1 See RA 1977, s 13 as amended.

[6.42] A subtenancy of a Crown letting could in any event be protected as against the immediate landlord.

[6.43] The RA 1977, ss 14 to 16 excludes from Rent Act protection tenancies where the immediate landlord is a local authority, housing association or housing co-operative as such tenancies will either be 'secure' and governed by the HA 1985, Pt IV, or assured and governed by the HA 1988.

Other exclusions

[6.44] 'Old-style' assured tenancies granted pursuant to the HA 1980 were formerly excluded from Rent Act protection by the RA 1977, s 16A. However, this has now been repealed by the HA 1988, which converted such tenancies to new-style assured tenancies[1].

1 See HA 1988, ss 1(3) and 37, Sch 18.

[6.45] Business tenancies which are governed by the Landlord and Tenant Act 1954, Pt II cannot be protected[1]. As discussed above, this will now include mixed user tenancies which could formerly be controlled tenancies providing there is some business user, as premises occupied for this purpose will not be 'let as a dwelling' as required by the RA 1977, s 1 unless the business user is minimal[2].

1 RA 1977, s 24.
2 See *Royal Life Saving Society v Page* [1978] 1 WLR 1329, and *Cheryl Investments Ltd v Saldanha* [1978] 1 WLR 1329, CA.

RESTRICTED CONTRACTS

[6.46] A limited code of protection was applied to restricted contracts. These were formerly known as 'Part IV contracts', as the provisions conferring limited security were contained in the Rent Act 1968, Pt IV. This is now of largely historic relevance, as restricted contracts can no longer be created after the commencement of the HA 1988, and (as we have seen) the latter contains transitional provisions aimed at phasing out this category of letting[1]. The RA 1977, s 19 defines a restricted contract as a contract 'whereby one person grants to another person, in consideration of a rent which includes payment for the use of furniture or for services, the right to occupy a dwelling as a residence'[2]. The use of the word 'contract' as opposed to 'tenancy' coupled with the wider definition of lessor and lessee found in s 19(8) means that some licences were also embraced by the restricted contract code[3]. Section 19(6) stipulates that the right to occupy part of a house may constitute a restricted contract where there is exclusive occupation of that part whether or not there is also shared use of other parts of the accommodation. The RA 1977[4] gives a very broad definition of 'services' to include attendance, the provision of heating and lighting, the supply of hot water and any other privilege or facility connected with the dwelling other than that needed for the purpose of access, the cold water supply or sanitary accommodation. Rent must be payable, although there is no minimum rent. The rateable value limits applicable to protected tenancies apply, however.

1 HA 1988, s 36 above para 3.7 ff.
2 Section 19 has been repealed except for contracts entered into before 15 January 1988, and in relation to contracts which remain restricted under the transitional saving provisions in the HA 1988, s 36 (as to which see paras 3.8 and 3.9 above); HA 1988, s 140(2) and Sch 18.
3 *Luganda v Service Hotels Ltd* [1969] 2 Ch 209
4 See RA 1977, s 19(8).

[6.47] Prior to the Rent Act 1974 (RA 1974), all furnished tenancies were restricted contracts. The RA 1974 brought furnished tenancies into full protection, with the result that the restricted contract code henceforth enjoyed more limited application. The main category of restricted contract were tenancies granted by a resident landlord, for which full protection was excluded by the RA 1974. Other examples of lettings prior to 15 January 1989 which gave rise to a restricted contract (rather than a fully protected tenancy) include student lettings, lettings with board and lettings with substantial attendance[1]. A limited measure of security of tenure applied[2], in that the rent tribunal had power to suspend the operation of any notice to quit given by the landlord. The security of tenure provisions were an adjunct of the rent control function of the tribunal in relation to restricted contracts, and were intended to ensure that the occupier's security was not prejudiced by a notice to quit given following his application to the tribunal for a reduction in rent. If a notice to quit were served by the landlord at any time before the tribunal gave its decision, or within a period of six months thereafter, the tribunal had power to suspend its taking effect for a period up to six months[3]. The HA 1980 abolished the rent tribunal jurisdiction for restricted contracts entered into on or after 28 November 1980[4]. For contracts entered into on or after this date the rent tribunal jurisdiction was replaced by a more limited power for the court, in possession proceedings, to suspend, stay or postpone the operation of an order for possession for a period up to three months[5].

1 These are discussed at paras 6.30 and 6.31, above.
2 See RA 1977, ss 103–106.
3 See RA 1977, s 103(1).
4 See HA 1980, s 69.
5 The rules applicable to restricted contracts entered into on or after 28 November 1980 are now to be found in the RA 1977, s 106A. They confer a much more limited degree of security than that applicable to restricted contracts entered into before the HA 1980 came into force.

B Statutory tenancies

[6.48] If a protected tenancy, either fixed-term or periodic, comes to an end, whether by effluxion of time, forfeiture or notice to quit, then the RA 1977, s 2 provides that the person who immediately before termination was the protected tenant, will become the statutory tenant 'if and so long as he occupies the dwelling house as his residence'. The statutory tenancy confers a personal right on the tenant to continue to occupy the premises as a residence on the terms and conditions set out in the RA 1977, s 3. This does not constitute a legal or equitable interest in the land, although by virtue of statute, it binds the landlord and his successors in title. The statutory tenancy cannot be assigned unless the landlord agrees in writing that another person should be deemed to be the statutory tenant of the property[1], even if the contractual tenancy was assignable.

1 See RA 1977, Sch 1, para 13.

[6.49] The effect of a statutory tenancy arising under s 2 is to prevent the landlord repossessing the premises other than on the statutory grounds for possession contained in the RA 1977, Sch 15 (see below para 6.86 ff). Whether or not the residence condition has been – and is being – fulfilled is therefore of critical importance to a landlord wishing to repossess the property.

OCCUPATION AS A RESIDENCE

[6.50] The critical condition needed to be fulfilled is that the tenant who was the protected tenant immediately before the determination of the tenancy must occupy the dwelling house as his residence. If the tenant is not in residence, then no statutory tenancy will arise or if the residence ceases later, then the statutory tenancy ceases and the landlord may regain possession.

[6.51] As noted above, a company which was the contractual protected tenant cannot become a statutory tenant as it cannot 'reside'. This ensures that where a protected tenancy will determine at the end of the fixed-term period or by forfeiture, no statutory tenancy will arise. Consequently, the company let has been used by landlords to attempt to avoid full Rent Act protection, by insisting that the tenancy is taken in the name of the company, often set up by an intending occupier purely for the purpose of obtaining the accommodation. The company then nominally lets the intending occupier into occupation as a licensee. Where the company rents the accommodation for its employees or guests, the occupiers will usually be genuine licensees. In any event, providing the tenancy agreement contains a covenant against subletting, it will not normally be possible for any individual whom the company has let into occupation to claim any protection against the head landlord as they will not be the lawful subtenant of the company[1]. Even where such a scheme was set up to avoid Rent Act protection, the argument that this should be regarded as a sham agreement failed in *Hilton v Plustitle Ltd*[2]. Here, the Court of Appeal refused to look at the series of transactions used to avoid Rent Act protection[3], and found that a company which had been set up by a person wanting to rent accommodation solely for that purpose, where the occupier paid the rent personally, was a legitimate means of Rent Act avoidance as opposed to evasion.

1 See RA 1977, s 137.
2 [1989] 1 WLR 149. And see to the same effect, *Kaye v Massbetter Ltd* [1991] 2 EGLR 97.
3 In *Gisborne v Burton* [1989] QB 390, CA, the tax doctrine of *WT Ramsay Ltd v IRC* [1982] AC 300, HL, was applied to an attempt to avoid the agricultural holdings legislation and considered a series of transactions which were individually quite legitimate taken as a whole amounted to a sham agreement designed to avoid security of tenure. See generally Martin (1988) 138 NLJ 792–795 and Rodgers (1989) Conv 196.

[6.52] Where the occupier is an individual, the question may arise as to whether they do occupy the property as their residence. Continued residence may exist despite a temporary absence although the burden of proof lies with the tenant. There must be a manifestation of both animus revertendi and corpus possessionis: an intention to return, and sufficient physical occupation of the accommodation; eg by means of the tenant's personal possessions or occupation by a licensee on behalf of the tenant. One without the other, however, will not suffice. In *Brown v Brash and Ambrose*[1] a tenant who was unable to occupy the accommodation due to a term of imprisonment and whose common law wife and children thereafter left taking most of the furniture, was held no longer to reside there despite an intention to return. Yet in *Colin Smith Music Ltd v Ridge*[2] occupation of accommodation by a common law wife and children of a statutory tenant who left and had no intention to return meant that the statutory tenancy had ceased. Whether there is sufficient animus revertendi and corpus possessionis is a question of fact and degree in each case. Prolonged absences may not jeopardise the statutory tenancy providing there is a real intention to return and a practical or real possibility of fulfilling this intention within a reasonable time[3]. The reason for the absence might also be significant, it having been said that illness, education, employment, or government service might be considered more sympathetically[4].

1 [1948] 2 KB 247, CA.
2 [1975] 1 WLR 463, CA.
3 See *Gofor Investments Ltd v Roberts* (1975) 29 P & CR 366, CA, where an absence with intention to return after the tenant's children had been educated, leaving furniture and other belongings in the accommodation did not prejudice the statutory tenancy.
4 Ibid at 373.

OCCUPATION BY A SPOUSE

[6.53] Occupation by a tenant's spouse as their residence will constitute occupation sufficient to ensure a statutory tenancy arises or continues in the absence of the tenant for this purpose by virtue of the Matrimonial Homes Act 1983 (MHA 1983), s 1(6). This is the case even in the absence of an intention to return by the tenant. A spouse is also able to make payments of rent as if they were the tenant by virtue of the MHA 1983, s 1(5), although the original tenant remains liable for the rent. As noted above, occupation by a common law spouse is not sufficient[1] at the present time although there are proposals to extend occupation rights to include cohabitants[2]. The provisions of the MHA 1983 relate only to the matrimonial home and thus a spouse's occupation will not be sufficient to preserve a statutory tenancy in relation to any other property. It should also be noted that the provisions can be relied upon only until decree absolute and any application to transfer the tenancy should be made prior to this[3].

1 See *Colin Smith Music Ltd v Ridge*, above.
2 See 'Domestic Violence and Occupation of the Family Home', Pt IV, 1992, Law Commission Report No 207.
3 See *Lewis v Lewis* [1985] AC 828, HL, for the effect of this upon the court's ability to transfer a statutory tenancy. A transfer of tenancy order may only be made under Matrimonial Causes Act 1973, s 25 and MHA 1983, Sch 1, para 1, following divorce if the tenancy is still subsisting.

'TWO-HOMES' TENANTS

[6.54] Unlike the provisions relating to secure tenancies and assured tenancies which have succeeded it, the Rent Act does not stipulate that a statutory tenant must occupy the property as their only or principal home, but rather that they occupy it as 'a' residence. A tenant may therefore be a statutory tenant of a second home providing it is used as a home and not merely a place used when convenient and rarely[1]. The most recent review of the law in this area was in *Hampstead Way Investments Ltd v Lewis-Weare*[2] when the House of Lords reiterated that whether a tenant with two homes was 'residing' in one or both, was a question of fact and degree. In that case a statutory tenant of a flat, following their marriage, moved to a house close by with his wife. His stepson occupied the flat but he continued to sleep there five times a week after working a night shift and paid the rent and other outgoings. He continued to keep his clothes there and to have mail sent to that address but he did not eat there. The court, while confirming the principle that a tenant with two homes may be a statutory tenant[3], found that he did not occupy the flat as his residence, but rather for a more limited purpose which was not sufficient to constitute residence.

1 See *Zetie v Cohen* (1958) 172 Estates Gazette 371, CA.
2 [1985] 1 WLR 164, HL.
3 This was established in *Langford Property Co Ltd v Tureman* [1949] 1 KB 29, CA.

TERMS OF THE STATUTORY TENANCY

[6.55] The RA 1977, s 3 provides that a statutory tenancy takes effect on the terms and conditions of the original tenancy in so far as they are consistent with the Act. However, as discussed above, a statutory tenancy is not generally assignable even though the original tenancy permitted assignment. Subletting is permissible if the original contract did not contain a covenant against it, although if the whole of the property is sublet the statutory tenancy will be lost as there is no residence by the tenant. The notice provisions are modified and a statutory tenant must give at least four weeks' notice if the contractual notice period was less, or three months' notice if no notice period was required. A landlord does not have to give notice to quit to a statutory tenant, however, but may proceed directly to recover possession[1]. Access to the premises is specifically preserved for the landlord in s 3(2) for the purpose of carrying out repairs which are the landlord's responsibility.

1 See RA 1977, s 3(4).

STATUTORY SUCCESSION

[6.56] Where a protected or statutory Rent Act tenant dies, the tenant's spouse, or some other member of the tenant's family, may be entitled to a statutory tenancy by way of succession under the RA 1977, s 2(1) and Sch 1. The succession scheme for Rent Act tenants was amended by the HA 1988, s 39 and Sch 4 so that only a spouse of the deceased will take a statutory Rent Act tenancy. Other family members can only take an assured tenancy by way of succession to the deceased tenant. The amended Rent Act succession scheme applies in all situations where a protected or statutory tenant *dies* after the commencement of the HA 1988, or where the first successor to such a tenancy dies after commencement[1].

1 HA 1988, s 39(2).

Entitlement to succession

[6.57] The succession provisions are complex. However, in outline, the amended RA 1977, Sch 1 provides as follows:

(1) The surviving spouse of a protected or statutory tenant becomes the statutory tenant of the dwelling house by succession if and so long as he or she occupies the dwelling house as a residence. No qualifying period of residence is required (cf the position of other family members, below). For this purpose, a person living with the deceased tenant 'as his or her wife or husband' is to be *treated* as the spouse of the tenant[1].

(2) Where the tenant is survived by a family member other than his or her spouse, the latter is entitled only to an *assured* tenancy by succession, and then only if he or she has lived in the dwelling house with the deceased for a period of two years immediately prior to the latter's death. The requirement of residence in the dwelling subject to tenancy, and not simply with the deceased tenant, requires the claimant to have resided with the deceased for two years, as a member of the latter's family, where the deceased was a protected tenant at the time of his death[2]. It follows that if both the deceased and the successor moved to the premises during the two years before the tenant's death, no succession rights accrue – even if they were living together elsewhere prior to this and have done so for the requisite two years.

(3) A second succession is possible, but on more restricted grounds than obtained before the amendments introduced by the HA 1988. Where the surviving *spouse* of the deceased tenant dies, a member of both the first successor's family and the original tenant's family can succeed to an assured tenancy by succession. No succession is possible where the first succession was by a family member other than the deceased's spouse, and the successor must be a member of both the tenant's and the first successor's families. Moreover, the second successor must also have resided with the first successor in the dwelling house for two years prior to the latter's death.

1 The HA 1988, Sch 4, para 2 introduced this amendment in order to remove the uncertainty surrounding the position of the common law or de facto spouse – a situation which has exercised the courts on numerous occasions (see further para 6.66 below).

2 See *Waltham Forest BC v Thomas* [1992] 3 All ER 244 HL overruling *South Northants DC v Power* [1987] 1 WLR 1433 CA, both decisions on the public sector succession provisions (HA 1985, s 87, below Chapter 9, para 9.58 ff). The phrasing of RA 1977, Sch 1, para 3, as amended by HA 1988, is clearer than that of HA 1985 (on which the *Waltham Forest BC* decision was made) and clearly excludes succession where the deceased tenant and the claimant moved to the premises during the two-year qualifying period before the tenant's death.

[6.58] Where more than one member of the deceased's family is qualified to succeed to the tenancy, succession is to be by whichever one of them is decided by agreement or, in default, by the county court[1].

1 RA 1977, Sch 1, para 6, as amended by HA 1988, Sch 4, para 6.

Assured tenancy by succession

[6.59] The assured tenancy to which a successor other than a spouse becomes entitled, differs in a number of respects from the statutory tenancy enjoyed by a surviving spouse.

[6.60] By virtue of s 39(5) and (6), the assured tenancy by succession is a periodic tenancy that takes effect in possession immediately after the death of the protected or statutory tenant on whose death the successor became entitled. It is therefore a property right, unlike a statutory Rent Act tenancy, which confers merely personal rights of occupation. However, like any other assured tenancy, being periodic, the statutory bar on assignment will apply[1]. Likewise, the tenancy will cease to be assured if the successor ceases to occupy the dwelling house as his principal home – in which event the restrictions on repossession set out in s 5 and Sch 2 will also cease to apply. Unlike a statutory tenancy, on the other hand, an assured tenancy by succession will vest in the successor's executors or personal representatives. As no further succession is possible under the entitlement rules, however, the tenancy can be brought to an end by notice to quit. The landlord need not invoke Sch 2, Ground 7 of the HA 1988 to bring the tenancy to an end, as the tenancy will not be 'assured' once the successor has died, and the restrictions on possession in s 5 will therefore not apply.

1 See HA 1988, s 15 and para 3.99 ff above.

[6.61] Likewise, if the tenancy vests in any third party under the tenant's will or on intestacy, it can be terminated by notice to quit, thus ensuring that succession takes place only in accordance with the rules in the RA 1977, Sch 1 (as amended). In this situation, the contractual tenancy goes into abeyance, unless lawfully terminated by the landlord, while the statutory tenancy subsists[1]. If not previously terminated by notice to quit or passage of time, it will 'revive' on cessation of the statutory tenancy, eg on the tenant's widow's death. In the case of an *assured* tenancy by succession, however, the scope for the operation of the 'abeyance' principle is more restricted. It clearly cannot apply on the death of an assured tenant by succession simpliciter, as no further succession to the periodic tenancy is possible. It might, however, apply where a protected tenant with a fixed-term dies and a family member succeeds to an assured tenancy by succession, the latter terminating before the end of the fixed contractual term.

1 See *Moodie v Hosegood* [1952] AC 61, HL.

[6.62] The assured tenancy by succession is deemed to have been granted to the successor by the person who was the immediate landlord of the original tenant at the time of his death. The premises let are the same dwelling house as the latter occupied immediately before his death[1]. By virtue of s 45(1), a 'dwelling house' may be a house or part of a house. The successor will receive an assured tenancy only of such part of the premises as the original tenant was occupying as a dwelling at the time of his death, namely such premises as he was occupying for the major activities of daily living, including sleeping, cooking and eating[2]. Such use need not, it seems, have been by the tenant to whom the property was initially let.

1 Section 39(6)(b) and (c).
2 See *Wright v Howell* (1947) 92 Sol Jo 26, CA; *Curl v Angelo* [1948] 2 All ER 189, CA.

[6.63] The *period of tenancy* is the same as the periods at which rent was last paid by the original tenant under his tenancy, and the other terms of the tenancy (eg as to repairs) are the same as those obtaining immediately before the tenant's death[1]. There is no control of rents as such (cf if the successor is a widow or widower of the tenant, a fair rent under the RA 1977 can be registered) and the rent can be increased to market levels using the machinery in ss 13 and 14[2]. As far as other terms are concerned, if the term is periodic there is no provision for variation[3]. However, if the predecessor had a fixed-term, s 39(9) applies the variation provisions for assured tenancies (contained in RA 1977, s 6) thus enabling either party to propose variation within one year of the statutory periodic tenancy commencing. Such variation must be proposed by notice, and is subject to rent assessment committee jurisdiction (if invoked) in the normal way.

1 Section 39(6)(d) and (e).
2 See Chapter 3, para 3.109 ff above.
3 See s 39(6)(d) and (e).

[6.64] If the landlord could, immediately before the original tenant's death, have invoked Case 19 in the RA 1977, Sch 15 to gain possession of the premises (mandatory repossession of protected shorthold lets), then by virtue of the HA 1988, s 39(7) the assured periodic tenancy is deemed to be an assured shorthold tenancy. This will be so even if the conditions for a shorthold grant[1] have not been fulfilled. As a consequence, the landlord will be entitled to repossess on giving at least two months' notice, whatever the duration of the succession tenancy. This contingency may arise, for instance, where the tenant dies after the shorthold term has expired and he was holding over as a protected tenant, subject to the availability of Case 19[2].

1 See HA 1988, s 20 and Chapter 5, above.
2 See *Gent v de la Mare* [1988] 18 EG 63, CA.

Definition of 'family' for succession purposes

[6.65] This issue has given rise to much litigation, in large measure concerned with the status of the de facto spouse under the previous Rent Act rules. 'Family' is not defined in either the RA 1977 or HA 1988; see also the HA 1985, s 113, which for the purposes of the parallel public section provisions stipulates a person to be a member of another's family if he is the spouse of that person, 'he and that person live together as husband and wife', or he is that person's parent, grandparent, child, grandchild, brother, sister, uncle, aunt, nephew or niece. In the absence of a clear definition in the private sector provisions, Lord Denning MR indicated in *Dyson Holdings Ltd v Fox*[1] that the concept of the 'family' should be viewed in a non-technical sense:

'It is not used in the sense in which it would be used by a studious and unworldly lawyer, but in the sense in which it would be used by a man who is "base, common and popular", to use Shakespeare's words in *Henry V*, Act IV.' As such, the family embraces not only blood relationships and those created by the marriage ceremony, but can include de facto as well as de jure relationships – provided they display a sufficient degree of stability and permanence that the ordinary man would regard the parties as members of the same family[2]. This question falls to be determined as at the date of the tenant's death.

1 [1976] QB 503 at 508, CA.
2 Ibid, per James LJ; *Brock v Wollams* [1949] 2 KB 388 at 395, per Cohen LJ.

[6.66] Under the amended provisions, as has been seen, a person living with the original tenant 'as his or her wife or husband' is now deemed to be the tenant's spouse. It follows that no specific period of residence need be proved to qualify for succession. Under the old law, cohabitees could qualify only if their relationship displayed sufficient permanence and stability that they could be said to be otherwise members of the tenant's family. Thus, a cohabitee who lived with the tenant for 21 years in a childless relationship qualified for succession in *Dyson Holdings Ltd v Fox*[1] whereas in *Helby v Rafferty*[2] a claim failed where a male cohabitee had lived with the tenant for five years before her death, but the parties had no intention of marrying and did not hold themselves out as married (the relationship lacked the necessary permanence). The presence or absence of children could, in appropriate circumstances, be an important indicator to the permanence or otherwise of the relationship[3].

1 [1976] QB 503, CA.
2 [1978] 3 All ER 1016, CA.
3 See *Gammans v Ekins* [1950] 2 KB 328, CA, and *Hawes v Evenden* [1953] 1 WLR 1169, CA.

[6.67] The ambit of the requirement that the successor and tenant live together 'as' husband and wife is not altogether clear. Clearly, as no period of residence with the tenant need now be established, it cannot be the case that the permanence or otherwise of the relationship remains relevant. It is suggested that, provided that the normal attributes of family life are evident, the length of time for which the relationship has endured should not be relevant – a couple can live as husband and wife for a day, if not more. Some of the Rent Act case law would, on this test, be differently decided under the current rules, eg *Helby v Rafferty*[1] and *Gammans v Ekins*[2] (several years' cohabitation but no children). Other of the extant decisions would be similarly decided under the new test, but on the simpler ground of communal living with the normal attributes of marriage, eg *Hawes v Evenden*[3] (12 years' cohabitation with children); *Dyson Holdings Ltd v Fox*[4] and *Chios Property Investment Co Ltd v Lopez*[5] (two years' cohabitation with intention of later marriage – the shortest period allowed for succession on the old rules). Quite clearly, the presence or absence of children need not be a relevant factor under the new provisions.

1 [1978] 3 All ER 1016.
2 [1950] 2 KB 328, CA.
3 [1953] 1 WLR 1169, CA.
4 [1976] QB 503, CA.
5 (1988) 20 HLR 120, CA.

[6.68] One final problem may arise: can a couple be living 'as husband and wife' if one of them is already married to someone else? In *Watson v Lucas*[1] a married claimant lived with the tenant, a widow, for 19 years prior to her death, and the couple publicly held themselves out as married, although they continued to use their original surnames. Here the claim was upheld on the ground that being married was not a bar to becoming a member of another family, as had occurred here. Remaining married and keeping one's own name could, it was said, be indicators of impermanence or instability, but were here outweighed by other factors. It would be curious were the new rules to produce a different result. It follows that one should be living 'as husband and wife' for these purposes, even if the attainment of the legal status of marriage is impossible because one party is already married, although not (it is thought) where impossibility results from some other disability, such as the parties being within the prohibited degrees of relationship. In other words, the test should (it is suggested) be to ask whether the parties are living 'as if' they are husband and wife, and not simply 'as' such[2].

1 [1980] 3 All ER 647, CA.
2 Similar terminology is used in other statutes, notably in the sphere of matrimonial law, eg Domestic Violence and Matrimonial Proceedings Act 1976, s 1(2). Because of the different context, decisions on the latter cannot be regarded as authoritative, although they may be illustrative. See, inter alia, *Adeoso v Adeoso* [1980] 1 WLR 1535, CA, where a similar approach to that suggested here was taken with regard to the application of the Domestic Violence and Matrimonial Proceedings Act 1976, s 1(2) in a de facto marriage contract context.

Other family members

[6.69] To come within the second category of potential successor, a claimant has to show a legal relationship by blood or marriage to the tenant, eg brother, sister, stepchild, stepfather, or an in-law relationship[1]. The furthest the courts have been willing to go in recognising de facto familial relationships beyond this (apart from cohabitees) is to allow succession by a child adopted de facto by the tenant, but not legally, while very young[2]. Beyond this, however, the courts draw a distinction between being a member of a family, and merely a member of a household, the latter being insufficient. Two parties who are neither related by blood nor legally related cannot, by behaving as brother and sister, artificially establish a familial nexus between them, even if their relationship is tantamount to that alleged[3]. Similarly, where two parties form a platonic aunt-nephew, brother-sister or similar relationship, the necessary familial nexus will be absent (*Carega Properties SA v Sharratt*[4]). The length of time for which such a relationship has endured is irrelevant. Thus, in *Sefton Holdings Ltd v Cairns*[5], a *de facto* 'sister' relationship which had endured for no fewer than 45 years was held to be insufficient.

1 See *Ross v Collins* [1964] 1 All ER 861 at 866, CA, per Russell LJ.
2 *Brock v Wollams* [1949] 2 KB 388.
3 See *Ross v Collins* [1964] 1 All ER 861, CA.
4 [1979] 2 All ER 1084, HL.
5 [1988] 14 EG 58, CA.

[6.70] The position of homosexual or lesbian partners is problematic. In *Sterling Housing Association v Fitzpatrick*[1] the House of Lords held that same sex partners cannot be construed as 'living together as husband and wife', and that a same sex partner cannot take by way of succession as a spouse. However, it was also there held that a homosexual partner could succeed as a member of the tenant's wider family, provided a stable and established relationship of a familial nature can be established on the facts. This is arguably discriminatory, as the entitlement will only be to an assured tenancy by succession, rather than (as would be the case for a spouse) a statutory Rent Act tenancy with rent control and Rent Act security of tenure. The position is also different to that obtaining for succession to secure public sector tenancies on death, and to the succession provisions for assured tenancies (see Chapter 3, para 3.144 ff and Chapter 9, para 9.60 ff). The law on succession rights is undoubtedly in need of urgent review and rationalisation.

1 (2000) 32 HLR 178 HL.

Residence 'with' the tenant

[6.71] For the purposes of the residence requirement for succession, spouses (including cohabitees) and other family members are treated differently. A spouse or cohabitee need only show residence in the dwelling concerned, with no minimum time limit; any other family member must prove that he 'resided with' the tenant for the two years prior to the latter's death, and also that this residence was in the dwelling subject to the tenant's tenancy. This difference of approach was retained by the HA 1988.

'Residing with'

[6.72] The courts draw a distinction between 'residing with' the tenant and merely 'living at' the premises. The words 'residing with' import some measure of factual community of family living and companionship[1]. The issue is one of fact and degree, to be decided by looking at all the relevant circumstances objectively. A close personal relationship with the tenant will not of itself suffice, and a connection with the property is also required:

> 'The person claiming to succeed to the tenancy ... must fairly and truly be said to have been residing with the predecessor in those premises in the sense that the successor lived and shared for living purposes the whole of the premises to which he or she claims to have succeeded[2].'

1 *Foreman v Beagley* [1969] 1 WLR 1387 at 1392, per Sachs LJ. And for a review of the authorities see (1991) Conv 432 (Brierley).
2 *Edmunds v Jones* [1957] 1 WLR 1118n at 1120, per Evershed MR.

[6.73] So a subtenant sharing some rooms with the tenant will not be entitled, although a successor sharing living accommodation, but not as a subtenant, may[1]. The successor must also establish an intent to reside and make his home there, though not indefinitely. The element of intent is, though relevant, only one factor to be taken into account when assessing the facts objectively[2]. An intention to reside will not be negatived, similarly, by temporary absences provided sufficient animus revertendi can be established[3]. The authorities were reviewed in *Swanbrae Ltd v Elliott*[4]. Here the claimant cared for her elderly mother during her final illness for the last six months of her life, and slept for three or four nights each week in a spare room (instead of at her own home nearby). The fact that she had a permanent home elsewhere in which she intended to live for the foreseeable future was not fatal to her claim, but the fact that she moved in with the tenant for a limited time and for a limited purpose was. According to Swinton Thomas J, the requirements of residence 'with' the tenant does not require the successor to dwell permanently, in the sense of indefinitely, with the tenant, but it does require something more than to dwell transiently, and has the connotation of having a settled home, ie the successor must establish that he 'has become in a true sense part of the household'. Furthermore, although a successor may maintain a claim if he has a home elsewhere, the court indicated that such cases will be rare[5].

1 *Collier v Stoneman* [1957] 1 WLR 1108.
2 *Swanbrae Ltd v Elliott* (1986) 281 Estates Gazette 916, CA.
3 See *Middleton v Bull* [1951] WN 517; *Tomkins v Rowley* (1949) 153 Estates Gazette 442. Similarly, temporary absences by the tenant prior to his death will not invalidate the successor's claim if he has the necessary animus to reside there. *Hedgedale v Hards* [1991] 1 EGLR 118.
4 (1986) 281 Estates Gazette 916, CA. Cf *Hildebrand v Moon* [1989] 2 EGLR 100.
5 Ibid at 920, per Kerr LJ; see also *Hampstead Way Investments Ltd v Lewis-Weare* [1985] 1 WLR 164, HL.

[6.74] The succession scheme was amended by the HA 1988 to require that the successor reside with the tenant for two years *in the same dwelling*. This means that even if a settled household *is* established, the claim will fail if the parties moved to the premises in question within the last two years of the tenant's life. The 1988 amendment gave statutory effect to the decision in *South Northamptonshire District Council v Power*[1] made on the parallel provisions in the HA 1985, s 87 governing succession to public sector 'secure' tenancies. In the context of the public sector provisions, the House of Lords held in *Waltham Forest London Borough Council v Thomas*[2] that the wording of s 87 ibid merely required a successor to be living with the deceased tenant in a dwelling of which he had a secure tenancy at his death, providing they had lived (elsewhere) as one household for the requisite period of time. The wording of the RA 1977, Sch 1, para 3 (as amended) is, however, more stringent: it requires the successor to be 'residing with him [the tenant] in the dwelling house at the time of and for the period of two years immediately before his death'. The better view, it is suggested, is that this would exclude the successor in circumstances akin to those in *Waltham Forest London Borough Council v Thomas*, where the parties have lived together as one household for two years, but moved to the subject dwelling within that time and had been living there at the tenant's death. The succession provisions are, accordingly, somewhat more favourable for secure tenancies than for private sector Rent Act tenancies.

1 *South Northamptonshire District Council v Power* [1987] 3 All ER 831, CA. See alsogenerally on both the 'family' and 'residence' requirements (above) articles by Hill (1987) Conv 349 and Martin (1988) Conv 197–200, discussing the impact of the HA 1988 provisions on these decisions.
2 *Waltham Forest London Borough Council v Thomas* [1992] 3 All ER 244, overruling *South Northamptonshire District Council v Power* (above, n 1).

SUBTENANCIES

Introduction

[6.75] A subtenancy is capable of being protected by the RA 1977 as between tenant and subtenant and providing the necessary requirements discussed above are met, the Act clearly extends to subtenancies[1]. This is so even if the head tenancy is not itself Rent Act protected. However, the position of a Rent Act protected subtenant becomes less straightforward where the mesne tenancy has been determined and the question of the legal relationship between the head landlord and the subtenant falls to be considered.

1 See definition of 'tenancy' in RA 1977, s 152(1).

[6.76] At common law the general rule is that the subtenancy will be extinguished with the determination of the tenancy itself[1]. However, there are various exceptions to this rule. Thus s 146(4), Law of Property Act 1925 enables a subtenant to apply to the court for relief from forfeiture where the mesne tenancy has itself been forfeited. A Rent Act protected subtenant could apply for relief in these circumstances. Similarly, a subtenancy is preserved on surrender of the mesne tenancy, and the subtenant is in the same position as if no surrender had occurred[2].

1 See *Bendall v McWhirter* [1952] 2 QB 466, CA.
2 Law of Property Act 1925, s 150. *Doe D Palk v Marchetti* (1831) 109 ER 953.

[6.77] Additional protection is provided by the RA 1977, s 137, although the extent of the protection depends on whether the head tenancy was itself Rent Act protected and also on the manner in which it was determined. This provision has generated a complex and fraught case law, the interpretation of which is not without difficulty. Its importance is, however, of diminishing relevance. It only applies to subtenancies granted before the commencement of the HA 1988: any subtenancy granted on or after 15 January 1989 will not (as between tenant and subtenant) be Rent Act protected, but be an assured tenancy and protected by the discrete rules for assured subtenants[1]. Furthermore, protection under s 137 can only arise if the subletting was lawful ie permitted within the terms of the head tenancy. An unlawful subtenant will have no rights as against the head landlord and such a subtenancy will not survive determination of the head tenancy unless the unlawful subletting has been waived[2].

1 Above Chapter 4.
2 For a discussion of waiver in the Rent Act context, see *Chrisdell Ltd v Johnson* (1987) 54 P& CR 257, CA, and *Metropolitan Properties Co Ltd v Cordery* (1979) 39 P&CR 10, CA.

[6.78] Where a lawful subletting had taken place before the coming into force of the HA 1988, the tenant was required to notify the landlord under the terms of the RA 1977[1].

1 RA 1977, s 139 required tenants who sublet any part of premises on a protected tenancy to notify their landlord in writing of the particulars of the subtenancy within 14 days. This was intended to ensure that head landlords who may become bound by a subtenancy were made aware of their existence.

Subtenant of a protected or statutory Rent Act tenant

[6.79] Where the head tenancy is either a Rent Act protected or statutory tenancy, s 137(1) and (2) protects the subtenant's residential security on termination of the mesne tenancy, whereupon the subtenant is promoted to become the tenant of the head landlord on the terms of the original subtenancy. Although it is clear that the head tenancy must be Rent Act protected for s 137 to apply[1], it was not clear whether the subtenancy had to be a fully protected Rent Act tenancy. The provision required the subtenancy to fall within the Rent Act, but there was a question whether a subtenancy that was a restricted contract could fall within these provisions[2].

1 Note that the provisions were expressly excluded where the original tenancy was a protected shorthold tenancy, HA 1980, s 54; and that a head tenancy which is a long tenancy of a dwelling house at a low rent but which apart from the low rent would be either a protected tenancy or an assured tenancy under HA 1988, Pt I, is by s 137(5) specifically included in the definition of 'statutorily protected tenancy'.

2 For a full discussion of this point see Martin J, *Residential Security* (1989) pp 145–6. Logically, as a restricted contract would almost certainly involve the mesne tenant being a resident landlord, it would not be possible for the subtenant to retain the same status as required by s 137(2) as the head landlord would not fulfil the resident landlord conditions. The legislative history of this provision also militates against such an interpretation.

[6.80] Another difficult issue arose where the mesne tenant was a statutory tenant who had sublet the *whole* of the dwelling. Having done so and consequently ceased to occupy the property as a residence, he would fail to fulfil the requirement (see s 2 of the RA 1977, above para 6.50 ff) for the statutory mesne tenancy to continue. As a result, conceptual difficulties arise as to the legal status of the subtenancy. This matter was discussed in *Henry Smith's Charity Trustees v Willson*[1] when Slade LJ took the view obiter that such a subletting was not without effect.

1 [1983] QB 316, CA; [1983] Conv 248 (J Martin).

[6.81] The limitations to the application of s 137(1) and (2) derive from the decision of *Leith Properties Ltd v Byrne*[1]. In this case a protected tenant whose tenancy did not contain a covenant against subletting, sublet the whole property without the landlord's consent. The head landlord sought possession under the discretionary ground contained in Sch 15, Case 6 which permits the court to order possession where a tenant sublets the whole premises without the landlord's consent. The Court of Appeal held that possession could be granted under this ground notwithstanding the fact that the subletting was not in breach of the tenancy agreement and was not therefore unlawful. It further held that although s 137 applied to the subtenant, protection was afforded to him only subject to the RA 1977, and that where the landlord could recover possession as against the mesne tenant under Case 6, it gave a ground for possession against the subtenant also, providing the court was of the view that it was reasonable to make a possession order as generally required by s 98(1). It is arguable that this reasoning could be extended to other grounds for possession contained in Sch 15 available to the landlord against the mesne tenant, leaving the subtenant relying on s 137(1) very vulnerable[2], although the court would in all cases have to decide whether it was reasonable to make a possession order in accordance with the provisions of s 98(1) which may safeguard the 'innocent' lawful subtenant.

1 [1983] QB 433, CA; [1983] Conv 155 (J Martin).
2 For a full discussion of this issue see Martin J, *Residential Security* (1989) pp 147–9.

Subtenants of part of commercial premises

[6.82] Particular problems arose where commercial premises were let to a business tenant, and a self-contained part (eg a self-contained flat above a shop) was then sublet to a residential tenant. The position of a protected or statutory subtenant in these circumstances is governed by RA 1977, s 137(3). This provides:

> 'Where a dwelling house:
>
> (a) forms part of premises which have been let as a whole on a superior tenancy but do not constitute a dwelling house let on a statutorily protected tenancy; and
> (b) is itself subject to a protected or statutory tenancy, then, from the coming to an end of the superior tenancy, this Act shall apply in relation to the dwelling house as if, in lieu of the superior tenancy, there had been separate

tenancies of the dwelling house and of the remainder of the premises, for the like purposes as under the superior tenancy, and at rents equal to the just proportion of the rent under the superior tenancy.'

[6.83] The section only applies where the subtenancy relates to part of the premises, and operates in a complex fashion. On the determination of the superior tenancy, two notional tenancies are implied, one in relation to the sublet part of the premises, and one in relation to the remainder 'at rents equal to the just proportion of the rent under the superior tenancy'. The effect of this is that provided the implied notional tenancy of the sublet part would have been protected even though the actual tenancy was not, eg because the superior tenancy exceeded the rateable value limits but the notional tenancy of part does not, then s 137(3) will govern the situation as if the notional superior protected tenancy had actually been granted, notionally making the superior landlord protected and within the rules discussed in the section above.

[6.84] A good deal of confusion arose because of the court's attempt to reconcile the protection afforded by s 137(3) with the basic requirement that, for Rent Act protection to accrue, there should normally be a letting of a dwelling house as a separate dwelling. Much of the difficulty has stemmed from the majority decision of the House of Lords in *Maunsell v Olins*[1], where it was held that a residential subtenancy granted by an agricultural tenant was not protected, as the mesne tenancy was not itself of premises constituting a dwelling. This interpretation limited the application of s 137(3) to cases where the superior tenancy was residential or at least had a dual purpose, as the word 'premises' was construed as being limited to dwelling houses. This decision was reversed by statute, an amendment to the subsection now expressly providing that 'premises' includes an agricultural holding. Unfortunately, in *Pittalis v Grant*[2] the court of appeal felt constrained to follow this reasoning in a case concerning the more common situation, where part of commercial premises let under the Landlord and Tenant Act 1954, Pt II have been sublet for residential use eg a flat above a shop or office premises. In *Maunsell v Olins* it was held that a flat originally let together with a shop was not within s 137(3) as the property was not a dwelling house and therefore not 'premises' within the meaning of the sub-section. This reasoning was subsequently followed in *Bromley Park Garden Estates Ltd v George*[3] and *London Regional Transport v Brandt*[4]. In the latter it was held that the subtenant also could not invoke the protection of the Law of Property Act 1925, s 139, and enjoyed no protection whatever against the head landlord following surrender of the intermediate business tenancy.

1 [1975] AC 373, HL.
2 [1989] QB 605, CA. See Rodgers (1990) Conv 204; Martin (1989) 139 NLJ 1260.
3 [1991] 2 EGLR 95, CA.
4 (1997) 29 HLR 193, CA

[6.85] The unfairness of these decisions, together with the partial statutory reversal of the decision in *Maunsell v Olins*, has long called for a review of the operation of s 137(3). This has now been accomplished in three consolidated appeals heard by the court of appeal in *Wellcome Trust Ltd v Hamad*[1] concerning the subletting of a flat above shop premises let on a commercial lease. In each case, the head lease was of premises let on a long lease within the Landlord and Tenant Act 1954 Pt II, and Rent Act protected subtenancies had subsequently been granted of the residential parts of the buildings let. The court of appeal held that a Rent Act protected subtenant has security of tenure against eviction following termination of a commercial head lease. The lease is treated as if there had been separate leases of the commercial part of the property and the dwelling let under the subtenancy. The court refused to follow *Pittalis v Grant* on the basis that it had been decided per incuriam[2]. In each of the three appeals the premises sublet was a dwelling house, and it therefore qualified for the protection of s 137(3). A similar result was arrived at in *Laimond Properties Ltd v Al-Shakarchi*[3], where the head tenancy was an assured tenancy, but the subtenancy had been granted before the HA 1988 came into force and was therefore a protected subtenancy within the RA 1977. On termination of the head tenancy the subtenant was held to be protected against the head landlord by the RA 1977, s 137(3). Although there are two lines of court of appeal authority, therefore, it is unlikely that *Pittalis v Grant* will be relied upon in future.

1 [1998] QB 638, CA.
2 For example, the court of appeal had overlooked the case law on the principles discussed in *Maunsell v Olins*, and had not reviewed the history of the modern Rent Acts or considered the statutory exception introduced to reverse the decision in *Maunsell* on its facts.
3 (1998) 30 HLR 1099; J.Martin [1999] Conv 248

C Protected and statutory tenancies: recovery of possession

RESTRICTIONS ON ORDER FOR POSSESSION

[6.86] Following termination of a protected or statutory residential tenancy, the tenant enjoys protection from eviction otherwise than by court order. Once a tenancy has been terminated at common law, eg by notice to quit in the case of a periodic residential tenancy, the RA 1977 places an additional hurdle in the way of the landlord seeking possession by requiring a court order for possession based on one of the grounds for possession set out in the RA 1977, s 98 and Sch 15. The tenant remains entitled to security under the RA 1977, following termination of the tenancy, until an order for possession has been granted by the court.

[6.87] By virtue of the RA 1977, s 98(1), the court cannot make an order for possession of a dwelling house which is for the time being let on a protected tenancy or subject to a statutory tenancy, unless:

(a) the court considers it reasonable to make such an order; and either
   (i) the court is satisfied that suitable alternative accommodation is available for the tenant, or will be available for him when the order takes effect, or
   (ii) the circumstances are as specified in any of the cases for possession set out in the RA 1977, Sch 15, Pt I (ie the discretionary cases see below); or
(b) the landlord would be entitled to recover possession of the dwelling house concerned but for the provision in s 98(1) aforesaid, and the circumstances of the case are as specified in any of the cases for possession set out in Sch 15, Pt II ibid (ie the mandatory cases for possession, see below).

[6.88] Section 98 is mandatory, and its application cannot be varied by agreement. So, for instance, this provision will void any executory agreement to give up possession, should the tenant subsequently seek to enforce his right to security of tenure under the RA 1977[1]. Similarly it will, it is suggested, void an executory *agreement* to surrender a protected or statutory tenancy to which the RA 1977 otherwise applies[2]. It would not, however, affect a consent order for possession, to which different considerations apply, or a concession by the tenant in possession proceedings that the Rent Act does not apply[3]. It has been held, however, that a term in the tenancy agreement which purports to give the landlord the right to share possession or introduce others to share with the tenant – so as to deprive him of exclusive possession and thereby convert an otherwise protected tenancy into an unprotected licence or other insecure interest – will be contrary to the policy of s 98 and accordingly void[4].

1 *Appleton v Aspin* [1988] 04 EG 123, CA (executory agreement not to enforce right to security of tenure against purchaser of dwelling from the landlord void).
2 Cf surrender of tenancy which will terminate the tenancy, and is therefore not to be readily implied. See *Chamberlaine v Scally* [1992] EGCS 90, CA.
3 *Syed Hussain v Abdullah Sahib & Co* [1985] 1 WLR 1392, PC. Cf *R v Newcastle-upon-Tyne County Court, ex p Thompson* [1988] 2 EGLR 119.
4 *Antoniades v Villiers* [1988] 3 All ER 1058, HL.

[6.89] The grounds for possession available to the landlord are subdivided into discretionary and mandatory grounds, and set out in the RA 1977, Sch 15, Pt I and Pt II respectively. The grounds are considered further below, at para 6.106 ff.

OTHER MODES OF TERMINATION

[6.90] A protected or statutory tenancy may be brought to an end in the following circumstances, without the need for an order for possession based on the cases for possession in RA 1977, Sch 15. Section 98 does not apply in the following situations.

Surrender of tenancy

[6.91] Surrender may be express (ie by deed) or implied, as where there is unequivocal conduct on the part of both parties which is inconsistent with the continuance of an existing tenancy. In cases of express surrender, it is not necessary for the tenant to yield up possession for surrender of a protected tenancy to be effective. In the leading case of *Dibbs v Campbell*[1] the landlord purported to grant a protected shorthold tenancy, but failed to comply with the shorthold requirements and therefore created a fully protected tenancy. In order to rectify this omission, the tenant was persuaded to execute a deed of surrender, whereupon a fresh protected shorthold tenancy was granted by the landlord. The tenant remained in possession throughout. The tenant subsequently claimed that he had acquired a statutory tenancy which, not being a protected shorthold, could not be terminated using the RA 1977, Sch 15, Case 19 (the shorthold ground, see below). The Court of Appeal here held, however, that just as the tenant could effectively surrender a protected tenancy by operation of law by giving up possession, so also an effective surrender could be made by signing a deed of surrender in clear terms. This decision, which is not without its critics[2], may be supported on its special facts, in that there was no implication of 'sham' in the purported surrender there effected, and that it represented the bona fide intention of the parties.

1 [1988] 2 EGLR 122, CA.
2 For criticism of the decision in *Dibbs v Campbell ibid* see Martin, *Residential Security*, (1989) p 114, Bridge [1989] Conv 98.

[6.92] An implied surrender by operation of law will occur where there is unequivocal conduct on the part of both parties which is inconsistent with the continuance of an existing tenancy, eg a yielding up of possession by the tenant in circumstances which indicate that the tenant unequivocally accepts that the tenancy has been terminated[1]. Because a finding of implied surrender will have serious implications for the tenant's security of tenure, the courts are loath to imply surrender unless there has been a long period of absence from the premises with large arrears of rent owing. So, in *Chamberlaine v Scally*[2] the tenant successfully resisted any implication of surrender, in circumstances where she had retained the key to the flat demised, left behind her personal effects, fed her pets in the flat, and informed the landlord that a possible reconciliation might occur between her and her partner (who remained in residence). Furthermore, there were no arrears of rent at the point in time when the landlord decided that there had been a surrender by abandonment of the premises. The tenant's conduct was therefore equivocal, in the sense that her belongings and her pets were still at the premises, and she visited to attend to them and retained a key for this purpose. The court will not imply an unequivocal surrender by operation of law where the tenant's absence is merely accompanied by a statement of future intention, eg that he intends to disappear and does not intend to pay rent owing. Statements of this kind, even if made to the landlord himself, are merely statements of future intention, and will not be sufficiently clear to amount to a surrender of an existing protected tenancy[3].

1 See *Tarjomani v Panther Securities Ltd* (1982) 46 P & CR 32; Woodfall, Law of Landlord and Tenant, vol 1, 1–1849.
2 [1992] EGCS 90.
3 *Love and Lugg v Herrity* (1990) 23 HLR 217, CA.

[6.93] Surrender by operation of law would also occur where the tenant ceases to be a protected tenant, but retains possession as, eg a licensee[1]. The court will closely scrutinise any transaction which has this effect, to establish its bona fides. Furthermore, as already noted, an executory agreement by which the tenant agrees to share possession during the currency of his tenure, thereby converting his interest into an unprotected licence, will be viewed by the court as contrary to the policy of s 98 and accordingly void[2].

1 *Foster v Robinson* [1951] 1 KB 149, CA.
2 *Antoniades v Villiers* [1988] 3 All ER 1058, HL.

Rescission of contract of tenancy

[6.94] A protected or statutory tenancy can be terminated if rescission is available under the general law; eg for fraudulent misrepresentation made by the tenant when obtaining the tenancy[1]. The grounds for possession in Sch 15 have no application in such circumstances.

1 See *Killick v Roberts* [1991] 4 All ER 289, CA.

Overcrowding and public health

[6.95] For reasons of public policy, the legislation concerning overcrowding and dwellings unfit for human habitation overrides the tenant's security of tenure under the Rent Act. Accordingly a protected or statutory tenancy can be terminated without reference to the grounds for possession in the following circumstances:

(1) The RA 1977, s 101 provides that, at any time when a dwelling house is overcrowded within the meaning of the HA 1985, Pt VIII, nothing in the Rent Act shall prevent the immediate landlord or the occupier from obtaining possession of the dwelling house.
(2) Further, by virtue of the HA 1985, s 276 nothing in the Rent Act shall prevent the recovery of possession by a landlord while a closing order under the HA 1985 is in force. This will be the case even if the condition of the premises giving rise to the closing order is attributable to fault or breach of covenant of the landlord[1].

1 See *Buswell v Goodwin* [1971] 1 WLR 92, CA.

[6.96] The public health legislation overrides the tenant's security during such period as the dwelling is overcrowded or subject to a closing order within the meaning of the HA 1985. If the dwelling ceases to be overcrowded within the meaning of the HA 1985, or ceases to be subject to a closing order there under, the security of tenure provisions of the Rent Act will resume their application.

Change of user

[6.97] A protected or statutory tenancy may lose its protection under the RA 1977 if the tenant ceases to occupy the premises as his residence, but adopts a changed user which brings the property within one of the other codes of statutory protection, eg that appropriate to business tenancies or agricultural holdings[1]. If a tenancy comes within the code appropriate to business tenancies (the Landlord and Tenant Act 1954, Pt II) or agricultural holdings (the Agricultural Holdings Act 1986) this will exclude it from Rent Act protection. Rent Act protection can be unilaterally lost by change of user, but the tenancy will only come within one of the alternative schemes of statutory protection if there has been consent by the landlord to the change of use. To come within the Landlord and Tenant Act 1954 or the Agricultural Holdings Act 1986 the tenant must establish that there is a new contract of tenancy providing for the change of use, or that the original agreement has been validly varied.

1 See RA 1977, ss 10 and 24. On change of user generally see Martin [1983] Conv p 390 ff.

[6.98] The user prescribed in the terms of the lease is what counts. If it is departed from through the parties making a new contract or varying the existing contract so as to permit or provide for a change of user, then the new user may be treated as the material one; but nothing short of a new contract or variation of the contract will suffice[1].

1 *Court v Robinson* [1951] 2 KB 60.

[6.99] For a variation to take place it is settled law that the landlord must have actual knowledge of the change of use, and must have consented to the new user, eg the use of the former dwelling for business purposes. Mere acceptance of rent with knowledge of the changed use will have no effect 'unless it can be inferred, as a matter of fact, that the landlord has affirmatively assented to the change of user'[1]. If a change of use takes place in circumstances which bring it within the protection of either the Landlord and Tenant Act 1954 or the Agricultural Holdings Act 1986, then this will automatically take it outside the protection of the RA 1977. The landlord will, of course, be able to seek possession under the terms of the statutory code applicable to business lettings and/or agricultural holdings (whichever applies).

1 *Wolfe v Hogan* [1949] 2 KB 194 at 206, CA.

MANDATORY AND DISCRETIONARY GROUNDS FOR POSSESSION

[6.100] The RA 197, s 98 divides the grounds for possession available to the landlord into two classes, namely:

(1) *Discretionary grounds*. These are specified in the RA 1977, Sch 15, Pt 1. The court can make an order for possession under these cases only if it considers it reasonable to do so.
(2) *Mandatory grounds*. These are set out in Sch 15, Pt II. If the landlord makes out a mandatory ground for possession the court *must* make an order for possession. The issue of reasonableness does not apply.

In addition to (1) and (2) above the court must make an order for possession if suitable alternative accommodation is available for the tenant, or will be available for him when the order takes effect. This ground is contained in s 98(1) itself (and not Sch 15). The availability of suitable alternative accommodation effectively provides another discretionary ground for possession, as s 98(1) specifies that the court must not make an order for possession unless it considers it reasonable to do so in all the circumstances.

Discretionary grounds: 'reasonableness' of possession order

[6.101] The reasonableness or otherwise of making an order for possession is a question of fact for the trial judge, to be assessed taking into account all the surrounding circumstances and evidence in the case. Reasonableness falls to be determined as at the date of the hearing. The judge must take into account all the relevant circumstances existing at the date of the hearing, and approach the issue in a common-sense, broad manner, giving such weight as he thinks fit to the various factors in the situation before him. Similarly, the relative weight to be given to the various factors put before the court is a matter for the court's discretion, although the judge must not exclude from consideration matters which he ought to take into account[1]. Clearly, factors of relative hardship to either party will be particularly relevant, although no question of assessing greater hardship arises in this context, cf RA 1977, Sch 15, Case 9 (below)[2]. It may prove easier to establish reasonableness where suitable alternative accommodation is pleaded, and is available for the tenant at the time of the hearing or when the possession order is to take effect -but there is no established rule to this effect[3]. The conduct of the parties may be relevant – and particularly past and prospective breaches of tenancy by the tenant[4]. It is important that the tenant should be given notice that he will be expected to leave, and the lack of a letter before action or similar warning can, accordingly, affect the issue of reasonableness under s 98 of the RA 1977, s 98[5]. The nature of the premises may also be relevant – as for instance where the landlord of a Grade I listed building required possession to facilitate a scheme of renovation for some seventeenth-century buildings of which the property demised formed an integral part[6].

1 *Cumming v Danson* [1942] 2 All ER 653 at 655 (Lord Greene MR).
2 See *Cresswell v Hodgson* [1951] 2 KB 92; *Coombs v Parry* (1987) 19 HLR 384, CA.
3 *Cumming v Danson* [1942] 2 All ER 653 (above).
4 For instance *Bell London and Provincial Properties Ltd v Reuben* [1947] KB 157, CA.
5 *White v Wareing* [1992] 1 EGLR 271, CA (invalid notice to quit sufficient warning, and relevant to issue of reasonableness under s 98(1)).
6 *Dame Margaret Hungerford Charity Trustees v Beazley* [1993] EGCS 90.

[6.102] If the court considers the landlord's need for possession to be reasonable (as required for instance by Case 9 below) it does not necessarily follow that it is also reasonable for the court to order possession. The two issues are not identical and must be considered separately. If the court considers the landlord to have a reasonable need for possession, it must then go on to consider whether it is reasonable for the court to gratify his need for possession[1]. The reasonableness of making an order for possession is a question of fact for the trial judge in the light of all the circumstances and evidence. The exercise of his discretion will not be interfered with by the Court of Appeal unless the trial judge has made an error of law[2]. Nevertheless, an appeal against the exercise of the judge's discretion under s 98(1) will rarely be vexatious or an abuse of process, because of the special circumstances arising under s 98 and the cases in Sch 15 ibid[3]. Regardless of whether or not there is a good chance of success upon appeal, there must be genuine grounds for appeal which are capable of being sensibly and responsibly argued – it is not a relevant criterion to study the chances on appeal, provided the grounds of appeal are not on their face unsustainable and therefore frivolous[4].

1 *Shrimpton v Rabbits* (1924) 131 LT 478. For Case 9 see below.
2 See eg *Dame Margaret Hungerford Charity Trustees v Beazley* [1993] EGCS 90; *Televantos v McCulloch* [1991] 1 EGLR 123, CA.
3 *Law Land plc v Sinclair* (1991) 24 HLR 57, CA.
4 See *Law Land plc v Sinclair* ibid.

Possession orders

Discretionary cases for possession

[6.103] In cases involving the discretionary cases for possession only the RA 1977, s 100 gives the court an extended discretion to:

(a) adjourn the proceedings for possession for such period or periods as it thinks fit; or
(b) on the making of an order for possession, or at any time before the execution of such an order, power to stay or suspend execution of the order; or
(c) on the making of an order for possession or at any time before the execution of such an order, a power to postpone the date of possession for such period or period as the court thinks fit[1].

1 RA 1977, s 100(1) and (2).

[6.104] Where the court adjourns the proceedings, or stays, suspends or postpones a possession order, pursuant to these provisions, the court must – unless it considers that to do so would cause exceptional hardship to the tenant or would otherwise be unreasonable – impose conditions with regard to the payment of arrears of rents (if any) and rent or payments in respect of occupation after termination of the tenancy (mesne profits). The court may also impose 'such other conditions as it thinks fit'[1]. Although wide, this does not give the court an unrestricted discretion to impose conditions unrelated to the tenant's breach of tenancy agreement. In *Raeuchle v Laimond Properties Ltd*[2]. It was held that the court only has power to impose terms which relate to payment of rent arrears or mesne profits: the terms imposed cannot relate to other judgement debts due from the tenant (in this case damages for trespass to neighbouring property also owned by the landlord)[3]. If the conditions imposed (above) are complied with the court may if it thinks fit discharge or rescind a possession order previously made[4]. If the tenant fails to comply with the conditions imposed – eg in an adjournment – the landlord will subsequently be free to apply for an order for possession[5]. The order for possession may be a conditional or an absolute order. Where an absolute order is made, the tenancy terminates forthwith. So, if the tenant dies after the making of an absolute order but before it takes effect, no successor is entitled to succeed to the tenancy under the RA 1977[6]. A conditional order, on the other hand, does not terminate the tenancy immediately. The tenancy subsists with the result that a successor *will* be entitled if the tenant dies subsequent to the making of the order but before it takes effect[7]. Where an order has been made, whether conditional or absolute, the tenant retains the protection of the Protection from Eviction legislation and must be evicted by process of the court if unwilling to give up possession. Accordingly, eviction otherwise than by the execution of a warrant for possession can give rise to a substantial liability of damages under the relevant protection from eviction provisions[8].

1 Ibid s 100(3). The court should not, however, use this discretion to suspend a possession order on terms involving payment of arrears over an almost indefinite period: *Taj v Ali* [2002] 3 EGLR 35.
2 [2000] L&TR 345, CA
3 When considering the exercise of its discretion to suspend under s 100(3) , the court here had taken into account the damages awarded for trespass against the tenant, which were considerable, and accordingly refused to suspend the possession order on terms as to repayment of arrears. The decision not to suspend was set aside on appeal.
4 Ibid, s 100(4).
5 *Mills v Allen* [1953] 2 QB 341, CA.
6 See *American Economic Laundry Ltd v Little* [1951] 1 KB 400, CA.
7 *Sherrin v Brand* [1956] 1 QB 403, CA.
8 See *Haniff v Robinson* [1993] 1 All ER 185 CA (damages of £28,800 awarded under HA 1988, s 27(8)). As to which see Chapter 2, para 2.17 ff.

Mandatory cases for possession

[6.105] The court's wide powers to suspend, stay and adjourn possession proceedings (above) do not apply to the mandatory cases for possession in the RA 1977, Sch 15 Pt II. Instead, by virtue of the HA 1980, s 89 the court has very limited powers when making an order for possession. The giving up of possession shall not be postponed (whether by the order for possession itself or by any variation, suspension or stay of execution) to a date later than 14 days after the making of the order. If it appears to the court that exceptional hardship would be caused by requiring possession to be given up by that date, the court can postpone possession for a longer period, but in any event such postponement must not be to a date later than six weeks after the making of the order[1].

1 HA 1980, s 89(1). On the scope of s 89(1), see *Bain & Co v Church Comrs for England* [1989] 1 WLR 24, where it was held to apply to the county court jurisdiction, and not in possession proceedings in the High Court.

D The cases for possession

SUITABLE ALTERNATIVE ACCOMMODATION

[6.106] By virtue of the RA 1977, s 98(1) the court may make an order for possession if it is satisfied that suitable alternative accommodation is available for the tenant, or will be available for him when the order for possession takes effect. The court must, additionally, consider it reasonable to make such an order on the facts before it. Although dealt with under a separate heading, s 98(1) in effect confers a discretionary ground for possession on the landlord, in addition to those set out in Sch 15, Pt I[1].

1 For the discretionary cases see para 6.117 ff below.

[6.107] The accommodation need not be offered by the landlord himself. A certificate of the local housing authority for the district in which the dwelling house in question is situated, certifying that the authority will provide suitable alternative accommodation for the tenant by a specified date, is conclusive evidence that the suitable alternative accommodation will be available for him by that date[1]. If no local authority certificate is provided, then 'suitability' falls to be assessed by reference to statutory criteria set out in the RA 1977, Sch 15, Pt IV. Broadly, these provisions require two tests to be satisfied: premises must be 'suitable' in that they provide reasonably equivalent security for the tenant to that currently obtaining under the protected or statutory tenancy in question, and secondly the accommodation must be reasonably suitable for the tenant's needs as to the extent and character of the property offered.

1 RA 1977, Sch 15, para 3.

Equivalence of security and terms

[6.108] Where no local authority certificate is produced to the court, accommodation shall be deemed to be suitable if it consists of either:

(a) premises which are to be let as a separate dwelling such that they will then be let on a protected tenancy, other than a protected tenancy under which the landlord might recover possession under one of the mandatory cases for possession in the RA 1977, Sch 15, Pt II; or
(b) the premises offered are to be let as a separate dwelling on terms which will in the opinion of the court afford to the tenant 'security of tenure reasonably equivalent' to that afforded by a protected Rent Act tenancy. The 'reasonably equivalent security' requirement will be met by an offer of a public sector secure tenancy, by a Rent Act protected tenancy, or by a long residential tenancy. If an assured tenancy is offered, the court may instead direct that the tenant be offered a protected tenancy, in which event the latter will take effect as a protected tenancy within the RA 1977 notwithstanding its grant after 15 January 1989[1].

1 See HA 1988, s 34(1). There is no obligation on the court to do so, however: see *Al Shakarcer v Laimond Properties Ltd* (1998) WTR 90, CA, and further para 3.4 above.

Equivalence of suitability to tenant's needs, etc

[6.109] By virtue of Sch 15, para 5 the accommodation offered must be reasonably suitable to the needs of the tenant *and his family* as regards proximity to place of work. It must also be either:

(a) similar as regards rental and extent to the accommodation afforded by dwelling houses provided in the neighbourhood by any local housing authority for persons whose needs as regard extent are, in the opinion of the court, similar to those of the tenant and his family; or
(b) it must be reasonably suitable to the means of the tenant, and to the needs of the tenant and his family as regards *extent and character.*

[6.110] If any furniture was provided for use under the protected or statutory tenancy in question then furniture must be provided for the tenant's use which is either similar to that provided or is reasonably suitable to the needs of the tenant and his family. A certificate from the local housing authority is conclusive evidence of the extent of the accommodation and rental it would charge to provide suitable alternative accommodation[1]. The authority's certificate should not, however, go beyond this and compare local authority accommodation with that offered by the landlord. It should set out the extent of the accommodation which would be provided by the authority. It is then for the judge alone to decide whether or not the accommodation offered is similar as regards extent and character, etc to the local authority accommodation specified in the certificate. The certificate should provide dimensions if possible, but will not be void if it fails to do so[2].

1 RA 1977, Sch 15, para 5(2).
2 *Jones & Massey v Cook and Cook* (1990) 22 HLR 319.

[6.111] When assessing suitability as regards the extent and character of the accommodation offered, it is clearly established that suitability must be judged by reference solely to the tenant's *housing* needs and not by considering the relative advantages and disadvantages of the alternative premises and those originally let[1]. So, if considerable advantages were enjoyed with the demised property, repossession of which is being sought by the landlord, this will not be relevant if the alternative accommodation offered is otherwise suitable to the tenant's housing needs. Environmental factors have, however, been held to be relevant. It is therefore permissible to compare the environment which the tenant has hitherto enjoyed with that of the alternative accommodation offered, in order to establish whether the latter will be reasonably suitable to the tenant's needs as regards extent and *character.* The accommodation offered must be reasonably suitable in that it gives the tenant an opportunity to live in conditions suitable to the style of life which he leads[2]. For example, in *Redspring Ltd v Francis*[3] more spacious accommodation was not deemed 'suitable' as it was situated in a noisy, busy thoroughfare, whereas the original tenancy was of a dwelling in a quiet residential area. Environmental considerations will, moreover, be directly relevant to the issue of reasonableness under s 98, quite apart from their relevance under Sch 15, para 5. In *Downcar Investments v Plews*[4] it was held that environmental considerations are directly relevant to the general issue of reasonableness under s 98, and should carry no less weight than any other consideration in assessing the reasonableness or otherwise of a possession order. The county court is not obliged to give less weight to environmental considerations when assessing overall reasonableness than to other factors. The question of what weight to give to particular factors is a question of fact for the judge to decide on the facts of each individual case. In *Downcar Investments*, possession was refused where the flat occupied by the tenant was in a quiet road in a pleasant part of Hampstead near good-quality shops, and the alternative accommodation offered was on a busy commercial road with a railway to the back and front of the property and two public houses nearby. The tenant had a small child, and had refused the alternative accommodation offered as she would not feel safe living there with an infant. The relevance of environmental matters such as noise and smell does not extend to cultural or spiritual considerations, however, and factors such as the proximity of alternative accommodation to the tenant's friends and place of worship do not influence suitability in terms of housing need[5]

1 *Hill v Rochard* [1983] 1 WLR 478, CA.
2 *Redspring Ltd v Francis* [1973] 1 WLR 134, CA; *Hill v Rochard* [1983] 1 WLR 478.
3 [1973] 1 WLR 134, CA.
4 (1993) 25 HLR 639, CA.
5 *Siddiqui v Rashid* [1980] 1 WLR 1018, CA.

[6.112] The accommodation must also be suitable for the needs of the tenant's 'family' as regards extent and character. 'Family' in this context has been held to have the same meaning as is applied under the rules governing succession to statutory tenancies[1]. The needs of a person living with the tenant as his or her wife or husband will therefore be relevant, as will the needs of the de jure spouse and others with a legal relationship by blood or marriage to the tenant – eg brothers, sisters, children and stepchildren. The needs of members of the tenant's 'household', as opposed to members of his family, will not however be relevant. Consequently the needs of a resident housekeeper and her family are not relevant to the issue of suitability[2], and neither will be the needs of friends of the tenant resident with him[3].

1 *Kavanagh v Lyroudias* [1985] 1 All ER 560, CA. For the position on succession see para 6.65 ff above.
2 *Darnell v Millward* [1951] 1 All ER 88, CA.
3 *Kavanagh v Lyroudias* [1985] 1 All ER 560.

Alternative accommodation of part dwelling

[6.113] If otherwise suitable, the alternative accommodation offered can constitute part of the premises demised. The landlord is therefore able, using this ground, to repossess any part of the property which is surplus to the tenant's housing needs – providing, always, that the accommodation occupied by the tenant is suitable within the meaning of the provisions outlined above and that it is reasonable in the circumstances to make an order for possession[1].

1 See *Mykolyshyn v Noah* [1970] 1 WLR 1217, CA.

Availability at date of hearing

[6.114] Suitable alternative accommodation must be available to the tenant at the date of the *hearing*[1]. The fact that the tenant had alternative accommodation available to him at an earlier date is therefore irrelevant, if he in fact has none at the date of the hearing. It was held, further, in *Fennbend Ltd v Millar*[2] that an interlocutory injunction will not be granted to prevent the tenant disposing of any freehold property which he owns, and which would otherwise constitute suitable alternative accommodation for the purposes of this ground if not sold prior to the hearing of the landlord's application for a possession order.

1 RA 1977, s 98(1).
2 (1988) 20 HLR 19.

Overcrowding

[6.115] By virtue of Sch 15, para 6, accommodation shall not be deemed to be suitable to the needs of the tenant and his family if the result of their occupation of that accommodation would be that it would be an overcrowded dwelling house for the purposes of the HA 1985, Pt X. This would appear to be an absolute rule, applicable even if the tenant's current accommodation is also overcrowded within the meaning of the HA 1985 (or more so) or is, eg unfit for human habitation within the meaning of the HA 1985, Pt IX[1].

1 See HA 1985, ss 264 and 604.

Reasonableness of order for possession

[6.116] If alternative accommodation is suitable within the meaning of Sch 15, Pt IV (above) the landlord must still establish that it is reasonable on the facts, to make an order for possession. Factors of relative hardship to landlord and tenant will be particularly relevant, eg the fact that the tenant has lived in the property for many years will weigh heavily against a possession order being made, especially if the landlord does not wish to occupy the premises himself[1]. 'Reasonableness', and the factors relevant to its assessment, are discussed above (see para 6.101 ff).

1 *Battlespring Ltd v Gates* (1983) 268 Estates Gazette 355, CA.

DISCRETIONARY GROUNDS FOR POSSESSION

[6.117] The RA 1977, Sch 15, Pt I sets out ten grounds for possession (referred to in Sch 15 as 'cases' for possession) available where a dwelling house is subject to a protected or statutory tenancy within the RA 1977. In addition to proving the availability, on the facts, of one or more of the cases for possession, the landlord must also establish that it is reasonable for the court to make an order for possession[1]. The factors relevant to the issue of reasonableness have already been discussed (see above para 6.101 ff). In particular it does not follow that if the landlord is being reasonable in seeking possession, that it will necessarily be 'reasonable' for the court to gratify that wish by making an order for possession[2]. The reasonableness or otherwise of the making of an order for possession is a discrete issue, to be considered separately once the availability of one or more of the cases for possession (below) has been established.

1 RA 1977, s 98(1).
2 *Shrimpton v Rabbits* (1924) 131 LT 478.

Breach of obligation by tenant

[6.118] *Case 1: Where any rent lawfully due from the tenant has not been paid, or any obligation of the protected or statutory tenancy ... has been broken or not performed.*

[6.119] This case gives the landlord a discretionary ground for possession where the tenant has a poor record of breach of tenancy as regards payment of rent or other terms of his protected and/or statutory tenancy. The court has wide powers under the RA 1977, s 100[1] to suspend, stay or adjourn possession proceedings on terms as to payment of arrears of rent, and the landlord is unlikely to obtain possession under this case in cases of isolated breach of tenancy or non-payment of rent. No order for possession will be made, eg if unpaid rent is tendered before the hearing – even though the Common Law Procedure Act 1852, s 212 (which gives an automatic right to relief in such circumstances in forfeiture proceedings) does not apply to statutory tenancies under the RA 1977[2]. For Case 1 to apply the breach must exist at the date of commencement of proceedings, but unless there is a long history of rent arrears and/or breach of other terms or conditions of the tenancy the court is unlikely to order possession – the suspension or stay of proceedings, or postponement of an order for possession on terms as to payment of arrears and undertakings as to compliance in future with tenancy obligations, is the common practice.

1 Above para 6.103 ff.
2 See *Bird v Hildage* [1948] 1 KB 91, CA.

[6.120] The following points should, additionally, be noted.

Bankruptcy of tenant

[6.121] It was held in *Cadogan Estates Ltd v McMahon*[1] that where a tenancy agreement contains a proviso for re-entry in the event of the tenant's bankruptcy, this constitutes an obligation of the statutory tenancy on the tenant's part not to become bankrupt. If the tenant subsequently becomes bankrupt after becoming a statutory tenant, then his bankruptcy will constitute a breach of an obligation of the previously protected tenancy within the meaning of the RA 1977, Case 1, and provides a ground for possession under Case 1. The tenancy here contained a proviso for re-entry for bankruptcy, but the covenants in the tenancy agreement contained no express obligation as to bankruptcy. Case 1 was nevertheless held applicable, the obligation arising from the proviso for re-entry being sufficient.

1 [2001] 1 EGLR 47, HL.

Rent 'lawfully due'

[6.122] By virtue of the Landlord and Tenant Act 1987, s 48 rent is not to be treated as lawfully due from the tenant at any time before the landlord has, by notice, furnished the tenant with an address in England and Wales at which notices (including notices in proceedings) may be served on him by the tenant[1]. Until notice complying with s 48(1) has been served, therefore, no proceedings for non-payment of rent – including proceedings under Case 1 – can be brought. Note however that once notice under s 48 has been served, rent then becomes due after service and is recoverable in respect of periods before notice has been given. Non-compliance with s 48 aforesaid does not, therefore, render rent irrecoverable for periods prior to service of notice under the Landlord and Tenant Act 1987, s 48[2].

1 As required by Landlord and Tenant Act 1987, s 48(1).
2 See *Dallhold Estates (UK) Pty Ltd v Lindsey Trading Properties Inc* [1992] 23 EG 112; on appeal [1994] 17 EG 148, CA (decision at first instance reversed on the facts); *Hussain v Singh* [1993] 2 EGLR 70, CA.

Forfeiture, waiver, etc

[6.123] Neither the Law of Property Act 1925, s 146, nor the Common Law Procedure Act 1852, ss 210–212 apply to a statutory tenancy under the RA 1977.

Consequently the distinction found in the general law between remedial and irremediable breaches of tenancy has no strict relevance, although the tenant's willingness (or otherwise) to remedy breaches of tenancy will be relevant to the question of the reasonableness of an order for possession under s 98. Similarly the distinction between once and for all breaches and continuing breaches of tenancy – of importance in the general law of forfeiture – has no strict relevance under Case 1. The latter applies whether the breach is of a once and for all nature (such as subletting without the landlord's consent[1]) and also where the breach is of a continuing nature, such as breach of a covenant against business user[2] or a covenant restricting user to the tenant and his family or 'the tenant's staff or directors'[3]. Acceptance of rent with knowledge of the tenant's breach will not bar proceedings under Case 1, as the doctrine of waiver is inapplicable to statutory tenancies – but continued acceptance of rent with full knowledge of the breach of tenancy concerned may affect the issue of reasonableness under s 98(1) and, therefore, preclude a possession order being made[4]. Note also that if there are breaches of the landlord's statutory repairing obligations, or of repairing covenants[5], the tenant may have an equitable right of set off to any claim for rent arrears – but only if the tenant's claim relates wholly to the period before proceedings for possession commenced[6]. Further, on the issue of reasonableness the court must take account of any well-founded complaint made by the tenant about the inconvenience he or she was suffering as a result of the landlord's breach of repairing covenant, and that he/she was entitled to damages in excess of the rent withheld, and in respect of which possession proceedings have been brought[7].

1 *Roberts v Macilwraith-Christie* [1987] 1 EGLR 224, CA.
2 *Florent v Horez* (1983) 48 P&CR 166, CA.
3 *Blanway Investments Ltd v Lynch* (1993) 25 HLR 378, CA.
4 See *Henry Smith's Charity Trustees v Willson* [1983] QB 316. See also *Oak Property Co Ltd v Chapman* [1947] KB 886, CA.
5 See Landlord and Tenant Act 1985, s 11.
6 *Televantos v McCulloch* [1991] 1 EGLR 123. For principles of equitable set off, see *British Anzani (Felixstowe) Ltd v International Marine Management (UK) Ltd* [1980] QB 137.
7 *Televantos v McCulloch* [1991] 1 EGLR 123.

Nuisance, annoyance, or immoral or illegal user

[6.124] *Case 2: Where the tenant or any person residing or lodging with him or any sub-tenant of his has been guilty of conduct which is a nuisance or annoyance to adjoining occupiers, or has been convicted of using the dwelling house or allowing the dwelling house to be used for immoral or illegal purposes.*

Annoyance

[6.125] Annoyance connotes any behaviour which would trouble a reasonable person occupying a dwelling house in the vicinity. It is therefore wider than 'nuisance', a concept which involves some physical interference with neighbouring property[1]. Where nuisance is established an order for possession can be made even if the nuisance in question has been abated, provided it is on the facts reasonable for an order for possession to be made, eg if the nuisance is likely to recur[2].

1 *Florent v Horez* (1983) 48 P&CR 166, CA (Turkish Cypriot organisation operating from demised premises an annoyance).
2 See *Florent v Horez* (1983) 48 P&CR 166, CA.

[6.126] For Case 2 to be applicable the nuisance or annoyance must affect *adjoining* occupiers. 'Adjoining' does not mean contiguous or physically adjacent, and premises will be 'adjoining' if the complainant has property which is near enough to be affected by the user complained of[1].

1 *Cobstone Investments Ltd v Maxim* [1985] QB 140, CA.

'Illegal or immoral purposes'

[6.127] A conviction for immoral or illegal use of the premises will suffice for Case 2, even if the user concerned involves no annoyance or nuisance to neighbouring occupiers. Note however that the premises must be *used for* immoral or illegal purposes – it will not suffice if the premises are merely the scene of immoral or illegal activities, and are not used for the purpose of committing them per se. For example, the commission of an offence accidentally on the premises will not suffice[1]. Similarly, it has been held that the possession of restricted or proscribed drugs, such as cannabis resin, without knowledge that the drugs are on the premises, does not constitute 'using' the dwelling for illegal purposes[2]. It would be otherwise, however, were the premises being used to store proscribed drugs for illegal distribution.

1 *Waller & Son Ltd v Thomas* [1921] 1 KB 541.
2 *Abrahams v Wilson* [1971] 2 All ER 1114, CA.

Deterioration owing to waste, neglect or default

[6.128] *Case 3: Where the condition of the dwelling house has, in the opinion of the court, deteriorated owing to acts of waste by, or the neglect or default of, the tenant or any person residing or lodging with him or any sub-tenant of his and, in the case of any act of waste by, or the neglect or default of, a person lodging with the tenant or a subtenant of his, where the court is satisfied that the tenant has not, before the making of the order in question, taken such steps as he ought reasonably to have taken for the removal of the lodger or sub-tenant as the case may be.*

[6.129] Case 3 will apply where there is no breach of tenancy, but nevertheless acts of 'waste' are causing a deterioration in the condition of the dwelling house. The case applies whether there is waste properly so-called – such as unauthorised improvements or alterations – and also where deterioration is occasioned by the neglect or default of the tenant or any subtenant or lodger. It will apply, for instance, where there is a failure to take reasonable precautions to prevent damage to the dwelling by inclement weather. The case applies, moreover, where the waste and/or neglect complained of is to the garden of the dwelling; for a 'dwelling house', statutorily defined, includes land let with the dwelling as well as the house itself[1].

1 See *Holloway v Povey* (1984) 271 Estates Gazette 195 (allowing garden to run wild with neglect).

Deterioration of furniture owing to ill treatment

[6.130] *Case 4: Where the condition of any furniture provided for use under the tenancy has, in the opinion of the court, deteriorated owing to ill treatment by the tenant or any person residing or lodging with him or any sub-tenant of his and, in the case of any ill treatment by a person lodging with the tenant or a sub-tenant of his, where the court is sat-*

isfied that the tenant has not, before the making of the order in question, taken such steps as he ought reasonably to have taken for the removal of the lodger or sub-tenant as the case may be.

Tenant's notice to quit

[6.131] *Case 5: Where the tenant has given notice to quit and, in consequence of that notice, the landlord has contracted to sell or let the dwelling house or has taken any other steps as the result of which he would, in the opinion of the court, be seriously prejudiced if he could not obtain possession.*

[6.132] This ground may be relied upon where the tenant has given a valid notice to quit[1] but not where the parties have concluded a mere agreement to surrender the tenancy[2]. Case 5 covers the situation where the tenant, having given a valid notice to quit, changes his mind and seeks to enforce his statutory right to security of tenure. Note that the ground may be relied upon only where the landlord has concluded a binding contract of sale, and not where he merely intends to sell[3]. *Query* this ground would not apply where there is an improperly constituted contract of sale, in circumstances where a purchaser may have a remedy in equity based on eg proprietary estoppel or rectification[4].

1 For the requirements as to which see Protection from Eviction Act 1977, s 5; Chapter 2, para 2.75 ff above.
2 *De Vries v Sparks* (1927) 137 LT 441.
3 For contract requirements, see now Law of Property (Miscellaneous Provisions) Act 1989, s 2 (written contract signed by both parties).
4 For example where there is no written agreement post-1989. For proprietary estoppel see inter alia *Pascoe v Turner* [1979] 1 WLR 431; *Re Basham* [1987] 1 All ER 405.

Unauthorised assignment or subletting

[6.133] *Case 6: Where without the consent of the landlord the tenant has . . . assigned or sublet the whole of the dwelling house or sublet part of the dwelling house, the remainder already being sublet.*

[6.134] Case 6 applies whether or not the assignment or subletting in question is in breach of a covenant against assignment or subletting in the tenancy agreement. It will be recalled that a statutory tenancy cannot be assigned; a statutory tenant may, however, sublet part of the premises, although if he sublets the whole his statutory tenancy will cease as he will cease to 'reside' within the meaning of the RA 1977, s 2[1]. In this situation Case 6 will be available to recover possession against the subtenant, the mesne tenant having ceased to enjoy the protection of the RA 1977[2].

1 See para 6.50 ff above. And see generally Martin, *Residential Security* (1989) p 42 ff.
2 *Chrisdell Ltd v Johnson* (1987) 54 P&CR 257, CA.

[6.135] Case 6 is applicable even if subletting is not in breach of a term of the tenancy agreement (if it were Case 1 would also be applicable – see above). If possession is sought against a lawful subtenant the latter will have additional rights under the RA 1977, s 137[1], but it was held in *Leith Properties Ltd v Byrne*[2] that the court may order possession under Case 6 notwithstanding, as s 98(1) overrides the subtenant's rights under s 137. Whether the subletting is lawful or otherwise will, however, go to the issue of reasonableness, which latter must be decided as between the subtenant and the head landlord.

1 See para 6.75 ff above.
2 [1983] QB 433, CA.

[6.136] Consent (if given) need not be in writing, and can be implied from the conduct of the parties. It suffices, moreover, if consent was given at any time before commencement of possession proceedings[1].

1 *Hyde v Pimley* [1952] 2 QB 506, CA.

[6.137] The purpose of Case 6 has been judicially described as to protect the landlord against finding someone wholly unknown to him irrevocably installed in his property[1].

1 *Hyde v Pimley* [1952] 2 QB 506, CA.

Dwelling required for landlord's employee

[6.138] *Case 8: Where the dwelling house is reasonably required by the landlord for occupation as a residence for some person engaged in his whole time employment, or in the whole time employment of some tenant from him or with whom, conditional on housing being provided, a contract for such employment has been entered into and the tenant was in the employment of the landlord or a former landlord, and the dwelling house was let to him in consequence of that employment and he has ceased to be in that employment.*

[6.139] By virtue of the RA 1977, s 102 the payment of compensation may be ordered by the court where a landlord obtains an order for possession under Case 8 by misrepresentation or concealment of material facts. *Query* whether Case 8 is available where there are joint landlords, only one of whom was the employer of the original tenant and is the prospective employer of the proposed new occupier[1].

1 See Martin, *Residential Security* (1989) p 100 to the effect that it is probably available in such circumstances. And for problems in establishing the employment status of the intended occupier, and the material time at which it must be proved see Pettit, *Private Sector Tenancies* (2nd edn) pp 206–7.

Dwelling required for occupation by landlord or family

[6.140] *Case 9: Where the dwelling house is reasonably required by the landlord for occupation as a residence for :*

(a) himself; or
(b) any son or daughter of his over 18 years of age; or
(c) his father or mother; or
(d) if the dwelling house is let on or subject to a regulated tenancy, the father or mother of his wife or husband, and the landlord did not become landlord by purchasing the dwelling house or any interest therein after —
  (i) 7th November 1956 in the case of a tenancy which was then a controlled tenancy;
  (ii) 8th March 1973 in the case of a tenancy which became a regulated tenancy by virtue of . . . the Counter-Inflation Act 1973;
  (iii) 24th May 1974 in the case of a regulated furnished tenancy; or
  (iv) 3rd March 1965 in the case of any other tenancy.

[6.141] Schedule 15, Pt III further provides:

> A court shall not make an order for possession of a dwelling house by reason only that the circumstances of the case fall within Case 9 . . . if the court is satisfied that, having regard to all the circumstances of the case, including the question whether other accommodation is available for the landlord or the tenant, greater hardship would be caused by granting the order than by refusing to grant it.

[6.142] This ground enables the landlord to recover possession where he reasonably requires the dwelling for occupation by himself or members of his immediate family. Case 9 has generated a not inconsiderable body of case law over the years[1]. By virtue of the RA 1977, s 102 the court has power to award compensation if the landlord obtains possession in reliance on Case 9 by material misrepresentations or concealment of relevant facts. The onus is on the landlord to establish that he 'reasonably requires' the dwelling for occupation within the terms of Case 9; the onus of proving greater hardship, if pleaded, falls on the other hand to the tenant[2].

1 See Megarry's *Rent Acts* (11th edn) pp 423ff, for a thorough review of the jurisprudence. Also Pettit, *Private Sector Tenancies* (2nd edn) pp 207–15; Martin, *Residential Security* (1989) pp 100–2.
2 *Manaton v Edwards* [1985] 2 EGLR 159, CA.

[6.143] The following features of Case 9 should be noted.

Requirement as residence

[6.144] Whether the dwelling is reasonably required by the landlord is a question of fact, and the relevant time for establishing whether he reasonably requires the property is the date of the hearing. In *Kennealy v Dunne*[1] it was indicated that for a dwelling house to be 'reasonably required' it must be the subject of a genuine and present need on the part of the landlord. The words 'reasonably required' connote something more than desire, although at the same time something much less than absolute necessity will do[2]. An immediate pressing need for possession is not required, provided the landlord can establish that the property is reasonably required for his occupation, or that of a member of his family, within the reasonably ascertainable immediate future[3]. The fact that the landlord, or other members of his family for whom the property is required, has other accommodation may be relevant, as may the fact that the dwelling let is too large for the landlord to occupy himself. If, on a balance of probabilities, the court concludes that the landlord does not want the dwelling as a residence for himself (eg because it is too large), and is seeking possession to sell it with vacant possession, Case 9 will not be available[4].

1 [1977] 2 All ER 16 per Stephenson LJ.
2 Ibid at 43. And see *Aitken v Shaw* 1933 SLT (Sh Ct) 21.
3 *Kidder v Birch* (1982) 46 P&CR 362, CA.
4 As in *Ghelani v Bowie* [1988] 2 EGLR 130, CA.

[6.145] By virtue of the rule in *Baker v Lewis*[1] Case 9 can be used where the reversion is owned by two or more joint landlords, both of whom intend to reside in the dwelling. Case 9 is not, however, applicable where only one out of joint landlords reasonably requires the premises as his residence, or as a residence for a member of his family – the rule in *McIntyre v Hardcastle*[2]. Personal representatives or trustees cannot use Case 9, for residence in the dwelling will normally constitute a breach of trust on their part if they have no beneficial interest, unless the facts are exceptional, eg as where the personal representatives were trustees for the landlord's children and, having adopted the latter, planned to live in the house with them as a family home[3]. The courts have signalled a relaxation in the strict application of the rule in *McIntyre v Hardcastle*, limiting the strict interpretation of Case 9 favoured in *McIntyre* and *Baker v Lewis* to paragraph (a) in Case 9, ie where the landlord requires possession for occupation by himself. Thus in *Potsos v Theodotou*[4] Case 9 applied where a husband and wife were joint landlords, and wanted possession of a dwelling for occupation by the natural (ie biological) son of one of them, in circumstances where the latter was neither the biological nor adopted son of the other joint landlord. The Court of Appeal favoured a purposive approach to Case 9, ie that it was intended to allow a landlord to recover possession for the immediate families of both husband and wife and should be construed accordingly. The rule in *McIntyre v Hardcastle* was therefore inapplicable, and should be limited to cases where possession is sought for the occupation of the landlords themselves and not members of their family, or the families of either of them. Case 9 will also be applicable where the landlord holds the reversion on trust for himself and a beneficiary as joint tenants in equity, with an undertaking to transfer the reversion into their joint names when the beneficiary attains majority. In *Bostock v Tacher de la Pagerie*[5] it was held that Case 9 applied to allow repossession for occupation by the landlord or trustee's daughter, even though the latter would have become landlord had a transfer been executed on request, in accordance with the terms of the declaration of trust. Had the trust been executed, and the landlord and beneficiary been jointly invested with the legal estate in the dwelling, the rule in *McIntyre v Hardcastle* would have applied and Case 9 would have been inapplicable.

1 [1947] KB 186, CA.
2 [1948] 2 KB 82, CA.
3 *Patel v Patel* [1982] 1 All ER 68, CA.
4 [1991] 2 EGLR 93, CA.
5 [1987] 1 EGLR 104, CA.

Landlord by purchase

[6.146] The restriction on the use of Case 9 by a 'landlord by purchase' is intended to prevent the eviction of a sitting tenant by a landlord who has purchased the reversion over his head. A similar restriction applies in proceedings to repossess business premises where the reversion has been sold subject to tenancy[1].

1 See Landlord and Tenant Act 1954, s 30(2) restricting the availability of s 30(1)(g) ibid.

[6.147] A person inheriting property by will is not a landlord by purchase and can therefore use Case 9[1]. Similarly, where the reversion was vested in the landlord's daughter by assent, as part of a family arrangement under which she bought out the share of the landlord's other children, she was held *not* to be a landlord by purchase – notwithstanding that valuable consideration was paid to buy out the share of the landlord's other offspring[2]. 'Purchase' is to be construed in its ordinary everyday sense, and the payment of money when acquiring a dwelling does not necessarily mean it has been acquired by 'purchase'. The proper test is to ask whether an ordinary and reasonable person would call the transaction by which the reversion is acquired a 'purchase and sale' of the dwelling concerned[3]. If the transaction, on its proper construction, is a purchase and sale, then Case 9 will be inapplicable even if the landlord purchased the reversion with finance provided by the original landlord's estate[4]. Note that if the landlord transfers an interest in the dwelling to his successor by will, Case 9 will be applicable[5].

1 *Baker v Lewis* [1947], KB 186, CA.
2 *Thomas v Fryer* [1970] 1 WLR 845, CA.
3 *Amaddio v Dalton* (1991) 23 HLR 332, CA.
4 As in *Amaddio v Dalton* (1991) 23 HLR 332.
5 See *Baker v Lewis* [1947] KB 186. In *Amaddio v Dalton* (above n 3) the testator had only a life interest and could therefore only express a wish that the property go to the landlord.

[6.148] If the transaction by which the reversion is acquired is, on its proper construction, a *gift* then Case 9 remains applicable. For example, in *Mansukhani v Sharkey*[1] Case 9 remained applicable where a husband and wife transferred the reversion on a residential flat to their son 'in consideration of mutual love and affection' with a covenant that the latter would continue to pay the mortgage instalments. There was nothing to suggest that the parties negotiated the transfer as a sale in consideration of the covenant to continue payment of mortgage instalments; the reference to love and affection strongly suggested a gift, and the covenants in the conveyance were held to be consistent with a gift of mortgaged property. The son had not become a landlord by purchase, and was therefore entitled to use Case 9 when subsequently seeking possession of the dwelling.

1 (1992) 24 HLR 600, CA.

The 'greater hardship' test

[6.149] The burden is on the tenant to prove greater hardship[1]. Hardship to not only the landlord and tenant themselves, but also to all those concerned on either side will be relevant. The correct approach was laid down in *Harte v Frampton*[2].

1 *Robinson v Donovan* [1946] 2 All ER 731, CA.
2 [1948] 1 KB 73 at 79, CA.

[6.150] The court should take into account hardship to all who may be affected by the grant or refusal of an order for possession – relatives, dependents, lodgers, guests and the stranger within the gates – but should weigh such hardship with due regard to the status of the persons affected and their proximity to the landlord or tenant, and the extent to which consequently hardship to them would be hardship to him.

[6.151] Hardship to third parties can be taken into account, provided they are in a close personal or family relationship to landlord or tenant. Hardship to a wife or child of either party will be of importance, and hardship to a parent has been held relevant – but hardship to more distant relatives will carry little weight unless the circumstances are exceptional. The effect of a decision to give or refuse possession on the health of either party can be a relevant factor, although medical evidence as to the likely effect of the court's decision will require close scrutiny[1]. The availability of other accommodation must be considered, but as long as it is considered it need not necessarily be the prevailing circumstance[2]. The court will not normally interfere with the county court judge's finding of fact as to hardship unless it is perverse or one which no reasonable judge could reach on the facts[3]. In *Baker v MacIver*[4] it was held that, while the fact that the tenant would have to move should not be taken in itself as evidence of hardship, it will be a relevant factor that the landlord has alternative accommodation available to him, and the tenant has no such alternative accommodation. The fact that the tenant's alternative accommodation would not have the same statutory protection as the existing tenancy may also be relevant. The comparative balance of hardship cannot be litigated through the higher courts, but if the evidence all falls one way then the court can intervene. If there is evidence of hardship on one side and none on the other, the county court judge can come to only one conclusion, and if he finds hardship where none exists on the evidence he commits an error of law. If, however, there is evidence which in law can amount to hardship on both sides, then the county court is the conclusive judge of what is the *greater* hardship on the facts before it[5].

1 See generally *Thomas v Fryer* [1970] 2 All ER 1, CA. And see *Rhodes v Cornford* [1947] All ER 601, CA; *Addington v Sims* (1952) 159 Estates Gazette 663.
2 *Sims v Wilson* [1946] 2 All ER 261, CA.
3 *Hodges v Blee* (1987) 20 HLR 32, CA.
4 (1990) 22 HLR 328, CA.
5 See the discussion in *Baker v MacIver* (1990) 22 HLR 328, and the principle in *Coplans v King* [1947] 2 All ER 393, CA.

[6.152] The Court of Appeal is entitled to take into account any change of circumstances which has occurred since the hearing at first instance, and can in its discretion make a possession order on appeal where possession was refused in the county court. The court will not exercise its discretion to award possession, however, unless it has enough evidence of the changed circumstances on which to assess the relative hardship to landlord and tenant[1]. On the other hand, if possession was ordered at first instance the Court of Appeal's proper function is to consider whether on the facts a possession order was rightly made having regard solely to the circumstances obtaining at the date of the order[2].

1 *Coombs v Parry* (1987) 19 HLR 384, CA (cottage on estate becoming vacant after hearing and available to landlord).
2 See *Alexander v Mohamadzadeh* (1985) 18 HLR 90, CA; *Manaton v Edwards* [1985] 2 EGLR 159, CA.

Subletting of part at excessive rent

[6.153] *Case 10: Where the court is satisfied that the rent charged by the tenant :*

(a) for any sublet part of the dwelling house which is a dwelling house let on a protected tenancy or subject to a statutory tenancy is or was in excess of the maximum rent for the time being recoverable for that part, having regard to . . . Part III of this Act; or

(b) for any sublet part of the dwelling house which is subject to a restricted contract is or was in excess of the maximum (if any) which it is lawful for the lessor, within the meaning of Part V of this Act to require or receive having regard to the provisions of that Part.

[6.154] This case applies when there is a subletting of part by a tenant with a regulated tenancy, and the subtenant is charged a rent in excess of that permissible under the rent control provisions in the RA 1977. The rules in the RA 1977, Pt III, discussed below in Chapter 7, make it illegal for a landlord to receive rent above prescribed limits for a letting on a regulated tenancy; Case 10 complements this by giving the head landlord a right to possession where the tenant is himself subletting part of the property demised and receiving an excessive rent.

MANDATORY GROUNDS FOR POSSESSION

[6.155] The RA 1977, Sch 15, Pt II contains ten cases pursuant to which the landlord of a protected or statutory tenant may recover possession mandatorily. By virtue of s 98(2) the court must make an order for possession if the landlord makes out one of these grounds for possession – the court has no jurisdiction to consider the reasonableness or otherwise of the making of a possession order on the facts; cf the discretionary cases for possession set out in Sch 15, Pt I (above). Cases 11, 12, 16–18 and 20 in Sch 15, Pt II are also available against the successor to a protected or statutory tenant who succeeds to an assured tenancy after 15 January 1989[1], in addition to the assured tenancy grounds otherwise applicable[2]. Special rules apply if the assured tenancy to which the successor became entitled is an assured agricultural occupancy[3]. Further, in relation to an assured tenancy to which a successor has become entitled by succession, any notice given to the predecessor for the purposes of Case 13, Case 14 or Case 15, Sch 15 is to be treated as having been given for the purposes of the corresponding grounds for possession applicable to assured tenancies[4].

1 That is, under the succession rules as amended by HA 1988, Sch 4. See Chapter 5 above.
2 See HA 1988, Sch 4, para 13.
3 See Sch 4, para 14 ibid. Rent (Agriculture) Act 1976, Sch 4, Case XI and Case XII apply in addition to the assured tenancy grounds.
4 That is, HA 1988, Sch 2, Grounds 3–5.

Owner-occupier requiring possession

[6.156] *Case 11: Where a person (in this Case referred to as 'the owner-occupier') who let the dwelling house on a regulated tenancy had, at any time before the letting, occupied it as his residence, and:*

(a) not later than the relevant date the landlord gave notice in writing to the tenant that possession might be recovered under this Case; and
(b) the dwelling house has not since [specified dates set out in paragraphs (i) to (iii)] been let by the owner-occupier on a protected tenancy with respect to which the condition mentioned in paragraph (a) was not satisfied; and
(c) the court is of the opinion that, of the conditions set out in Part V of this Schedule, one of those in paragraphs (a) and (c) to (f) is satisfied.

If the court is of the opinion that notwithstanding that the condition in paragraph (a) or (b) above is not complied with, it is just and equitable to make an order for possession of the dwelling house, the court may dispense with the requirement of either or both of those paragraphs, as the case may require.

The giving of a notice before 14th August 1974 under section 79 of the Rent Act 1968 shall be treated, in the case of a regulated furnished tenancy, as compliance with paragraph (a) of this Case.

The conditions referred to in para (c) above are the following:

(a) the dwelling house is required as a residence for the owner or any member of his family who resided with the owner when he last occupied the dwelling house as a residence;
(b) the owner has retired from regular employment and requires the dwelling house as a residence;

(c) *the owner has died and the dwelling house is required as a residence for a member of his family who was residing with him at the time of his death;*
(d) *the owner has died and the dwelling house is required by a successor in title as his residence or for the purpose of disposing of it with vacant possession;*
(e) *the dwelling house is subject to a mortgage made by deed and granted before the tenancy, and the mortgagee is entitled to exercise a power of sale conferred on him by the mortgage or by section 101 of the Law of Property Act 1925, and requires the dwelling house for the purpose of disposing of it with vacant possession in exercise of that power; and*
(f) *he dwelling house is not reasonably suitable to the needs of the owner having regard to his place of work and he requires it for the purpose of disposing of it with vacant possession and of using the proceeds of that disposal in acquiring, as his residence, a dwelling house which is more suitable to those needs.*

[6.157] Case 11 cannot be relied upon unless written notice has been served on the tenant – normally not later than the grant of the tenancy in question – although the court has power to dispense with this requirement if it is just and equitable to do so on the facts of the case. No form is prescribed for the notice, which can therefore be in any form provided it fairly draws the attention of the tenant to the fact that the landlord will be able to resume possession under the case stipulated (in this case, Case 11)[1]. The purpose of Case 11 is to encourage lettings by an owner-occupier who is, for some reason, likely to be absent (eg for the purposes of his work abroad) and who wishes to let in the secure knowledge that he can regain possession on his return. The text of Case 11 above is given as amended by the HA 1980, which considerably widened its scope and application.

1 *Springfield Investments Ltd v Bell* (1990) 22 HLR 440 (decided under Sch 15, Case 16). A certificate of fair rent given to the tenant with the keys, with the terms of Case 16 written on the reverse, was here held sufficient. Case 16 (like Case 11) refers to 'notice in writing' being given, not 'a notice in writing'.

'Relevant date' for service of notice

[6.158] Except in certain special cases defined in Sch 15, Pt III, the 'relevant date' for the service of notice for the purposes of Case 11 means the date of the commencement of the regulated tenancy in question[1]. Although notice must be in writing to comply with Case 11, no prescribed form of notice is required.

1 Sch 15, Pt III, para 2. The special cases referred to apply where the protected tenancy was created before 8 December 1965, or where it became regulated by virtue of Counter-Inflation Act 1973. See Sch 15, Pt III, para 2(a) and (b).

Notice-dispensing power

[6.159] Both conditions (a) and (b) in Case 11 (above) can be dispensed with if the court considers that it is just and equitable to make an order for possession of the dwelling house. The court therefore has a discretion to dispense with the requirement of service of written notice prior to letting, and the requirement that all tenancies under which the dwelling has been let be ones in respect of which notice has been given under Case 11 – *provided*, always, that it is just and equitable in the circumstances to order possession.

[6.160] For the purposes of Case 11 written notice which has been posted, but never received by the tenant, has not been 'given' and does not satisfy the terms of

Case 11[1]. Where written notice had been sent by the landlord, but not received, the court held in *Minay v Sentongo* that it was just and equitable to exercise its discretion to dispense with notice under Case 11, and to order possession[2]. Similarly in *Fernandes v Parvardin*[3] the requirement of written notice was dispensed with where oral notice had been given to the tenant at the time of letting that possession would be required. The Court of Appeal were divided, however, as to the scope of the dispensing power. According to Stevenson LJ a wide view should be taken enabling the county court judge to take into account all the circumstances, including anything that might make it unjust or inequitable to award possession, including greater hardship to the relative parties. Donaldson LJ preferred a narrower view, namely that the court is wholly concerned to see solely what injustice or inequity flows from the failure to comply precisely with the terms of Case 11 as to notice. On either view, however, there was no suggestion on the facts in *Fernandes v Parvardin* that there was any misunderstanding on the part of the tenant as to the applicability of Case 11, and therefore the dispensing power was exercised. Where no notice has been given, however, either oral or written, the court is unlikely to exercise the dispensing power in the landlord's favour and Case 11 will be inapplicable. In *Bradshaw v Baldwin-Wiseman*[4] the Court of Appeal held that it was not the intention of Parliament to apply Case 11 to a letting which was not intended in the first place to be a temporary letting, and which was a tenancy which was intended to carry Rent Act security. Accordingly, where it is apparent from the facts that there was never any intention to create a Case 11 tenancy, it cannot be just and equitable to dispense with written notice in accordance with para (a) above. The court here favoured the wider approach to construction of the dispensing power, as formulated by Stephenson LJ in *Fernandes v Parvardin* . The words 'just and equitable' are of wide import, and the court should look at all the circumstances of the case – those affecting the landlord or his successors in title, those affecting the tenant, *and* those in which failure to give notice arose. It was here held that it is only if, having considered all those circumstances, the court considers it would be just and equitable to give possession that it should do so, because it must be borne in mind that by failing to give written notice the tenant may have been led into a wholly false position[5]. For example, it would not be just and equitable to dispense with the notice requirement merely because the tenant has signed what purported to be a licence agreement, and therefore knew that his occupation would be temporary, in circumstances where the agreement in question created in law a tenancy to which the Rent Act applies[6]. The essential prerequisite for exercise of the dispensing power is that the tenant appreciates the position when he takes the tenancy[7].

1 *Minay v Sentongo* (1982) 45 P&CR 190, CA, and see *Sun Alliance and London Assurance Co Ltd v Hayman* [1975] 1 WLR 177, CA.
2 (1982) 45 P&CR 190.
3 (1982) 5 HLR 33.
4 (1985) 17 HLR 260. Cf *Jones v White* [1993] EGCS 178, CA.
5 See (1985) 17 HLR 260 at 267 per Griffiths LJ.
6 *Ibie v Trubshaw* (1990) 22 HLR 191.
7 *Bradshaw v Baldwin-Wiseman* [1985] 1 EGLR 123, 17 HLR 260, CA. And see *RJ Dunnell Property Investments Ltd v Thorpe* (1989) 21 HLR 559 (decided under the parallel requirements for Case 19 *infra*).

Prior residence by landlord

[6.161] The opening words of Case 11 require the landlord, at any time before the letting, to have occupied the dwelling 'as his residence'. There is no limitation as to the length of time of the occupier's prior occupation, or when it took place. In *Pocock v Steel*[1] it was held that the landlord's residence must be immediately prior to the grant of the tenancy to which Case 11 applies. This decision was reversed by the Rent (Amendment) Act 1985, which amended Case 11 to make it clear that the landlord's residence can be at any time before the letting concerned. Case 11 therefore applies where there is a series of lettings, providing notice under Case 11 was given in respect of each – although this requirement can be dispensed with if it is just and equitable to do so on the facts. Note also that Case 11 merely requires the landlord to have occupied the dwelling as his 'residence', and not as his home. The landlord's prior occupation can be temporary or intermittent[2] and there is nothing in Case 11 which imports permanent residence as a home as a prerequisite for its application. The two-homes cases – such as *Hampstead Way Investments Ltd v Lewis-Weare*[3] do not provide an exact analogy, and different considerations apply where it is a question of whether the landlord had at any time occupied premises as his 'residence' within the meaning of Case 11. Temporary or intermittent residence – which may suffice for the purpose of Case 11 – by no means necessarily involves occupation as a home within the meaning of the 'two-homes' case[4]. For example, in *Davies v Peterson*[5] residence was established where the landlord (who worked and lived in Sierra Leone) visited the UK for three to five weeks each year and wanted to repossess the dwelling concerned for use from time to time for holidays etc. Similarly in *Mistry v Isidore*[6] the requirements of Case 11 were satisfied where the landlord merely slept in the flat in question for five nights a week, for a period of eight weeks before letting it, even though there were no facilities for cooking or washing at the property and he kept most of his belongings elsewhere. The question of residence is one of fact and degree. The court in *Mistry* considered the facts to be very near the borderline, however. Although it is not necessary to occupy premises on a daily basis in order to establish occupation 'as a residence', the landlord's presence must be sufficiently long and continuous to show that there is genuine occupation as a residence[7].

1 [1985] 1 WLR 229, CA.
2 *Naish v Curzon* (1985) 51 P&CR 229, CA.
3 [1985] 1 WLR 164, HL.
4 *Mistry v Isidore* [1990] 2 EGLR 97; CA.
5 (1988) 21 HLR 63, CA, following *Naish v Curzon* (1985) 51 P&CR 229, CA.
6 [1990] 2 EGLR 97, CA.
7 *Ibie v Trubshaw* (1990) 22 HLR 191, CA (landlord failed where he visited his girlfriend and two children and, occasionally, stayed overnight).

Requirement as residence

[6.162] The landlord need not show that he intends to occupy the property as his only or main residence if he successfully regains possession[1]. Where the reversion is held by joint landlords, moreover, Case 11 is applicable where one of joint landlords wishes to resume occupation. In *Tilling v Whiteman*[2] the House of Lords held that Case 11 was satisfied in circumstances where one of joint landlords wished to resume occupation, and to use the premises as his residence. It was there held that different considerations apply to those under Case 9 (above) where, as we have seen, intended residence by all joint landlords is required if the case is to be available[3]. The policy of Case 11 is different, namely to encourage letting, and the decisions on Case 9 were distinguished accordingly. Whether the landlord's intended residence suffices for the purposes of Case 11 is ultimately a question of fact and degree for the county court. Case 11 will not be available, however, where the landlord intends to re-let or sell the property without returning to occupy it as his residence[4].

1 *Naish v Curzon* (1985) 51 P&CR 229, CA; *Davies v Peterson* (1988) 21 HLR 63, CA; *Whitworth v Lipton* [1993] EGCS 172 (intent to occupy as residence until dwelling could be sold held sufficient for Case 11).
2 [1980] AC 1.
3 The rule in *McIntyre v Hardcastle* [1948] 2 KB 82, CA.
4 See *Ghelani v Bowie* [1988] 2 EGLR 130, CA.

Retirement homes

[6.163] *Case 12: Where the landlord (in this case referred to as 'the owner') intends to occupy the dwelling house as his residence at such time as he might retire from regular employment and has let it on a regulated tenancy before he has so retired and:*

(a) not later than the relevant date the landlord gave notice in writing to the tenant that possession might be recovered under this Case; and
(b) the dwelling house has not since 14th August 1974 been let by the owner on a protected tenancy with respect to which the condition mentioned in paragraph (a) was not satisfied; and
(c) the court is of the opinion that of the conditions set out in Part V of this Schedule one of those in paragraph (b) to (e) is satisfied.

If the court is of the opinion that, notwithstanding that the condition in paragraph (a) or (b) above is not complied with, it is just and equitable to make an order for possession of the dwelling house, the court may dispense with the requirements of either or both of those paragraphs as the case may require.

[6.164] The conditions in Sch 15, Pt V, referred to in Case 12, para (c), require principally that the owner has retired from regular employment and requires the dwelling house as his residence[1]. Conditions in Pt V, (c) to (e) aforesaid are as set out above in relation to Case 11. The court has power to dispense with the requirement of written notice, as under Case 11, and similar considerations apply to those already discussed (see above para 6.159 ff).

1 RA 1977, Sch 15, Pt V, para 2(b).

Out of season holiday lets

[6.165] *Case 13: Where the dwelling house is let under a tenancy for a term of years certain not exceeding 8 months and:*

(a) not later than the relevant date the landlord gave notice in writing to the tenant that possession might be recovered under this Case; and
(b) the dwelling house was at some time within the period of 12 months ending on the relevant date, occupied under a right to occupy it for a holiday.

For the purposes of this Case a tenancy shall be treated as being for a term of years certain notwithstanding that it is liable to determination by re-entry or on the happening of any event other than the giving of notice by the landlord to determine the term.

[6.166] This ground is intended to encourage the letting of holiday accommodation out of season. Providing the terms of Case 13 are satisfied, it is not a prerequisite for its application that the landlord intends to re-let for holiday purposes upon obtaining possession.

[6.167] As with Case 11 (above) the court has power to dispense with the requirement of written notice where it is just and equitable so to do. For the grounds on which this discretion may be exercised see the discussion above in the context of Case 11[1].

1 See para 6.159 ff above.

[6.168] For Case 13 to apply the dwelling house must at some time within the 12 months prior to letting have been occupied 'under a right to occupy it for a holiday'. There is a question whether prior occupation for holiday purposes by the landlord himself will suffice for this purpose. The better view would appear to be that such occupation will not suffice. The landlord will occupy by right of ownership and not under 'a right to occupy it' for a holiday[1]. No statutory definition of 'holiday' is given; cf the scope of the holiday let exception to Rent Act protection and the jurisprudence relative thereto[2]. Similar provision is made for out of season holiday lets in the grounds for possession appropriate to assured tenancies granted after 15 January 1989.

1 See to this effect Pettit, *Private Sector Tenancies* (2nd edn) p 210; Martin, *Residential Security* (1989) p 107 ff.
2 Above, para 6.34 ff.

Lettings of student accommodation

[6.169] *Case 14: Where the dwelling house is let under a tenancy for a term of years certain not exceeding 12 months and:*

(a) not later than the relevant date the landlord gave notice in writing to the tenant that possession might be recovered under this Case; and
(b) at some time within the period of 12 months ending on the relevant date, the dwelling house was subject to such a tenancy as is referred to in section 8(1) of this Act.

For the purposes of this Case a tenancy shall be treated as being for a term of years certain notwithstanding that it is liable to determination by re-entry or on the happening of any event other than the giving of notice by the landlord to determine the term.

[6.170] The purpose of this case is to facilitate vacation lettings of student accommodation, and thereby to encourage the maximum utilisation of student accommodation. Student accommodation let by specified institutions is exempt from Rent Act protection by virtue of the RA 1977, s 8. Note however that, for the purposes of Case 14, a vacation letting need not be by an institutional landlord provided the accommodation concerned has been sublet within the last 12 months. This covers the case where student accommodation is sublet by a private landlord who has, in turn, rented the accommodation from an institution to which s 8 applies[1].

1 See Martin, *Residential Security* (1989) at p 108.

Occupation by minister of religion

[6.171] *Case 15: Where the dwelling house is held for the purpose of being available for occupation by a minister of religion as a residence from which to perform the duties of his office and:*

(a) not later than the relevant date the tenant was given notice in writing that possession might be recovered under this Case; and
(b) the court is satisfied that the dwelling house is required for occupation by a minister of religion as such a residence.

[6.172] As with Cases 13 and 14 (above) the court has no power to dispense with the service of written notice prior to letting if Case 15 is to be applicable.

Dwelling houses formerly occupied by persons employed in agriculture

[6.173] A special code applies to lettings of tied accommodation, and this is considered separately in Chapter 8 below. Cases 16, 17 and 18 apply to facilitate the recovery of possession of dwelling houses which are not tied cottages, but which were once occupied by an agricultural employee, or are a redundant farmhouse at the time of the letting, and are now required by the landlord in order to provide accommodation for an agricultural employee. As with the other mandatory cases notice must be given of the availability of the relevant case at the time of letting[1].

1 For Cases 16–18 see para 8.67 ff below.

Protected shorthold tenancies

[6.174] *Case 19: Where the dwelling house was let under a protected shorthold tenancy (or is treated under section 55 of the Housing Act 1980 as having been so let) and:*

(a) there either has been no grant of a further tenancy of the dwelling house since the end of the protected shorthold tenancy or, if there was such a grant, it was to a person who immediately before the grant was in possession of the dwelling house as a protected or statutory tenant; and
(b) the proceedings for possession were commenced after appropriate notice by the landlord to the tenant and not later than 3 months after the expiry of the notice.

A notice is appropriate for this Case if:

(a) it is in writing and states that proceedings for possession under this Case may be brought after its expiry; and
(b) it expires not earlier than 3 months after it is served nor, if, when it is served, the tenancy is a periodic tenancy, before that periodic tenancy could be brought to an end by a notice to quit served by the landlord on the same day;
(c) it is served:
  (i) in the period of 3 months immediately preceding the date on which the protected shorthold tenancy comes to an end; or
  (ii) if that date has passed, in the period of 3 months immediately preceding any anniversary of that date; and
(d) in a case where a previous notice has been served by the landlord on the tenant in respect of the dwelling house, and that notice was an appropriate notice, it is served not earlier than 3 months after the expiry of the previous notice.

[6.175] The HA 1980, s 55 added this case for possession in order to guarantee the landlord's mandatory right to repossession on expiry of a protected shorthold tenancy. By virtue of the HA 1980, s 55(2), Case 19 can apply to a tenancy which fails to satisfy the qualifying conditions for protected shorthold status because the landlord failed to give the tenant a valid notice that the tenancy is to be a protected shorthold tenancy before its grant. The power to extend the scope of Case 19 under s 55(2) ibid, however, applies only if the court is satisfied that it is just and equitable to make an order for possession, in which event it may treat the tenancy under which the dwelling house was let as a protected shorthold tenancy[1].

1 See for example, *RJ Dunnell Property Investments v Thorpe* (1989) 21 HLR 559.

[6.176] Case 19 will be available on expiry of the fixed-term, but it also continues to apply during any statutory tenancy which arises following expiry of the original shorthold term. Case 19 can be used by the landlord to claim possession both against a tenant who remains in possession after expiry as a statutory tenant, and against any member of the tenant's family who succeeds to the statutory tenancy on death[1]. Moreover, Case 19 will continue to apply until there is a grant of tenancy to a person who is not, immediately before the grant, in possession of the dwelling house as a protected or statutory tenant[2].

1 But note HA 1988, s 39(7). A successor who would be an assured tenant rates an assured shorthold tenancy ie a family member other than the deceased tenant's spouse.
2 See Pettit, *Private Sector Tenancies* (2nd edn) at p 222.

[6.177] Where a protected shorthold tenant is granted a fresh fixed-term or periodic tenancy of the dwelling after the shorthold tenancy has ended, the landlord's right to possession under Case 19 is preserved, albeit the new tenancy is not itself a protected shorthold. This will be the case whether the tenant is granted a fresh contractual tenancy, or whether – as in *Gent v de la Mare*[1] and *Ridehalgh v Horsefield*[2] – the tenant holds over in possession as a statutory tenant on expiry of the shorthold term.

1 [1998] 1 EGLR 104, CA.
2 (1992) 24 HLR 453, CA.

[6.178] The procedure for repossessing property let on a protected shorthold tenancy is somewhat problematic. The landlord must give three months' notice of intended proceedings, and this must, moreover, be given within three months of the term date of the tenancy or its anniversary thereafter. It follows that, where the tenant remains in possession as a statutory tenant following expiry of the shorthold term, there is an annual three-month 'window of opportunity' during which proceedings under Case 19 can be instituted. The timing of the landlord's notice is therefore a matter of considerable importance and complexity[1]. Not surprisingly, a more straightforward procedure for recovering possession was adopted in the HA 1988 for assured shorthold tenancies[2].

1 See Pettit, *Private Sector Tenancies* (2nd edn) 222–3, PF Smith (1982) Conv. 29.
2 HA 1988, s 21(1), above Chapter 5.

Lettings by members of the armed forces

[6.179] *Case 20: Where the dwelling house was let by a person (in this case referred to as 'the owner') at any time after the commencement of section 67 of the Housing Act 1980 and:*

(a) at the time when the owner acquired the dwelling house he was a member of the regular armed forces of the Crown;

(b) at the relevant date the owner was a member of the regular armed forces of the Crown;
(c) not later than the relevant date the owner gave notice in writing to the tenant that possession might be recovered under this Case;
(d) the dwelling house has not, since the commencement of section 67 of the Act of 1980 been let by the owner on a protected tenancy with respect to which the condition mentioned in paragraph (c) above was not satisfied; and
(e) the court is of the opinion that :
(i) the dwelling house is required as a residence for the owner; or
(ii) of the conditions set out in Part V of this Schedule one of those in paragraphs (c) to (f) is satisfied.

If the court is of the opinion that, notwithstanding that the condition in paragraph (c) or (d) above is not complied with, it is just and equitable to make an order for possession of the dwelling house, the court may dispense with the requirements of either or both of these paragraphs, as the case may require.

[6.180] For the purpose of this Case 'regular armed forces of the Crown' has the same meaning as in the House of Commons Disqualification Act 1975, s 1.

[6.181] The conditions in Sch 15, Pt V referred to above have already been discussed in the context of Case 11. The court can, if it considers it just and equitable to make an order for possession, dispense with compliance with conditions (c) and (d) in Case 20. The circumstances in which the court's discretion is likely to be exercised have already been discussed in the context of Case 11.

[6.182] This case applies to lettings after 28 November 1980 by a landlord who, both at the time when he acquired the dwelling house, and at the time of letting, was a member of the regular armed forces. There is no requirement (cf Case 11 above) that the landlord had resided in the dwelling prior to its being let.

CHAPTER 7

Rent regulation under the Rent Act 1977

[7.1] Rents under private sector lettings made before January 1989, when the Housing Act 1988 (HA 1988) came into force, continue to be governed by the Rent Act 1977 (RA 1977), as do many housing association tenancies granted before that date. The RA 1977 provides for the registration by the rent officer of a 'fair rent' for a dwelling let on a regulated tenancy. The RA 1977 also provided separately (in Pt V) for the statutory control of rents paid under restricted contracts, under the jurisdiction of the rent tribunal. As the agreed variation of a rent paid for a restricted contract will now, by virtue of the HA 1988, s 36(2), result in the ending of the restricted contract (and hence of Rent Act protection), this is now of limited significance.

A Regulated tenancies

INTRODUCTION: THE 'FAIR RENT' SCHEME

[7.2] Successive Rent Acts, starting with the Rent and Mortgage Interest (Restrictions) Act 1915, have imposed restrictions on residential rents. The early legislation applied only to unfurnished lettings and applied a crude system of rent *control*, in that the rent for most dwellings was fixed at the rent obtaining at the time the legislation was introduced. The introduction of rent *registration* in the Rent Act 1965, and the introduction of fair rents, signaled the adoption of a more sophisticated approach to rental valuations aimed at removing any scarcity element reflected in rentals, but otherwise allowing them to change to reflect other relevant factors. The rent registration provisions applied a variant of current-value pricing for establishing 'moderated' rents, using as the starting point the rents of individual dwellings[1]. This type of rent mechanism results in higher rents than those generated by, eg the historic-cost pricing model used to fix public sector rents, in which income from rents and subsidies is pooled to meet aggregate housing expenditure. The use of current value pricing also has implications for housing subsidy, in that where it is used to fix rents by reference to market-based criteria, subsidies are directed towards individual tenants in the form of income related benefits (such as rent rebates or, more recently, housing benefit).

1 See generally Malpass P and Murie A, *Housing Policy and Practice* (2nd edn 1994) at 193–4.

[7.3] The fair rent provisions applied a sophisticated form of current value pricing for determining residential rents, and the legislation contains comprehensive guidance for rent officers on how to assess fair rents. The 'fair' rent must be established in accordance with a formula set out in the RA 1977, s 70. This has three elements. The general clause in s 70(1) requires the rent officer to have regard to all the circumstances (other than the personal circumstances of the tenant), and in particular to the age, character, locality and state of repair of the dwelling, the quality and quantity of furniture provided by the landlord (if any) and any premium lawfully required or received for the grant or assignment of the tenancy. He is then directed to assume an equilibrium of demand and supply (the scarcity disregard, s 70(2)), and to value out of the rent a number of statutory disregards, such as tenants improvements (s 70(3)). The most controversial aspect of the fair rent formula concerns the relevance (or otherwise) of scarcity value and the use of market comparables, such as rents for assured and assured shorthold lettings, in fixing fair rents under the RA 1977. Section 70(2) provides that, when determining the rent, 'it shall be assumed that the number of persons seeking to become . . . tenants of similar dwelling houses in the locality on the terms (other than those relating to rent) of the regulated tenancy is not substantially greater than the number of such dwelling houses in the locality which are available for letting on such terms.' The breadth of the geographical area of the market to be considered (the 'locality') is not specified. For this purpose, however, the courts have assumed that the rent officer should look for 'broad, overall, general scarcity' affecting a substantial (and not a limited) area[1].

1 *Metropolitan Properties Ltd v Finegold* [1975] 1 WLR 349.

[7.4] Although the valuation criteria are closely defined, the overall concept of 'fairness' reflected in the fair rent formula has to some extent remained elusive. Both rent registration, and earlier attempts at rent 'control', were based on the assumption that there will always be a shortage of accommodation to rent, and that the law should intervene to protect poorer sections of society by restricting a landlords' ability to charge rents at levels inflated by the imbalance of demand and supply. This assumption is clearly evident in the terms in which the scarcity disregard in the RA 1977, s 70(2) was drafted. That this must always be the case is no longer necessarily true, however, following the increase in the private sector rental market after the HA 1988. A deregulating measure, the HA 1988 adopted the radical strategy of attempting to stimulate the private rented market by removing all rent restrictions for tenancies granted after it came into force. As we have seen, tenants with 'assured' tenancies under the HA 1988 enjoy statutory security of tenure, but there is no provision for the registration of fair rents for assured tenancies, and no legal limit on the initial rent that can be lawfully recovered by the landlord[1].

1 See Chapter 3, para 3.102 ff above. Proposed increases in rent can be referred to the rent assessment committee for an adjudication, but this can only be done in response to a notice of increase served by the landlord – the tenant cannot take the initiative if no increase is proposed. If a reference is made, the committee has jurisdiction to fix a market rent in accordance with criteria laid down in the HA 1988, s 14.

[7.5] The deregulation of the housing market has required the courts to reconsider the relationship of 'fair' rents with market rents, principally with market rents under assured and assured shorthold tenancies. This is of considerable importance for those tenants who still have protected tenancies governed by the RA 1977. Fair rents have substantially increased on re-registrations in recent years, prompting legislative intervention to cap excessive increases[1]. The mean average rental for assured shorthold tenancies in 1990 was £63 per week, compared with £24 for a regulated tenancy with a registered 'fair' rent. By 1996/7 the mean rental for a shorthold had risen to £94 per week, and for a regulated tenancy to £42 weekly[2]. The mean registered rent awarded on reregistrations increased from £2,222 pa in 1994 to £3,104 in the first quarter of 1999, and in London from £2,698 to £3,914, the average increase being 15% and (in London) 19%[3]. The fair rent provisions continue to apply to a substantial number of regulated tenancies granted before the HA 1988, Pt I came into force, and in some transitional cases to tenancies granted after that date eg on succession to a regulated tenancy following the tenant's death. Admittedly, the number of regulated tenancies with registered rents had fallen from 322,000 (18 per cent of all private sector tenancies) in 1990 to 128,000 (6 per cent) in 1996/7, a figure which has shrunk further since then. In 1997 there were approximately 240,000 regulated tenancies to which the fair rent provisions were relevant – approximately 11 per cent of all private sector tenancies. To this figure must be added 287,000 secure tenancies held of Registered Social Landlords for which the rent officer registers the maximum rent that can be charged[4]. The Fair Rent provisions therefore retain considerable importance.

1 The Rent Acts (Maximum Fair Rents) Order 1999, SI 1999/6. See below at para 7.41 ff.
2 *Housing and Construction Statistics 1986–1996* (Stationery Office, 1997), Table 11.4 at p 179.
3 *Housing Statistics* September quarter 2001 (Stationery Office, 2001), table 13.
4 See generally *Housing and Construction Statistics 1986–1996* (Stationery Office, 1997), Table 11.4 p 179, and DETR Press Release 1101/98.

RENT 'LIMITS': PROTECTED AND STATUTORY TENANCIES

[7.6] The basic principle applicable to regulated tenancies is that the rent recoverable by the landlord cannot exceed the registered fair rent. There is no obligation on the parties, however, to apply to the rent officer for the registration of the rent, and they are free to agree a rent if they so choose. To protect the tenant where no registration has been made, the RA 1977 imposes a rent 'limit' during the contractual period of tenancy, ie while the tenancy remains a protected tenancy. Once the tenancy has become statutory (eg following a notice to quit or the expiry of a fixed-term) a separate rent 'limit' will apply.

[7.7] While the tenancy remains contractual, the rent recoverable is limited to the rent registered for the dwelling under the RA 1977, Pt IV[1]. If the contractually agreed rent exceeds the rent limit (ie the registered fair rent) then any excess is irrecoverable from the tenant[2]. If it is less than the registered rent, however, then the contractual rent alone is recoverable. The registered rent cannot be recovered until the tenancy has been terminated and converted into a statutory tenancy. This can be achieved by the service of a notice of increase of rent under s 49 – if the contractual tenancy could have been ended by the service of a notice to quit given by the landlord at the same time, then the notice of increase operates to convert the tenancy into a statutory tenancy[3]. In this event the rent limits in s 45 (below) will then apply, and the registered fair rent will become effective from that date.

1 RA 1977, s 44(1).
2 Section 44(2) *ibid*.
3 Section 49(4) ibid. The notice of increase must be in prescribed form, and the tenancy must have been capable of termination by notice to quit before the date specified in the notice of increase.

[7.8] Where no rent has been registered, the landlord can in principle recover the contractually agreed rent without restriction. Section 51 seeks to protect the tenant, however, by providing for the use of formal 'rent agreements' if the contractual rent is to be increased by agreement, or an increased rent is to be charged on re-grant of a fresh regulated tenancy of the premises[1]. The rent agreement must be in writing signed by both landlord and tenant, and must contain a prominent statement[2] that the tenant's security of tenure under the RA 1977 will not be affected if he refuses to sign it, and that its conclusion does not affect his right to apply for the registration of a fair rent. This statement must be set out at the head of the agreement[3]. If these requirements are not met, any increase in rent thereunder, over the rent previously payable, is irrecoverable[4]. The intention of these provisions is to bring the tenant's statutory rights to his attention and encourage registration of the rent, although there is little evidence they are adhered to in practice.

1 Section 51(1) ibid.
2 'A statement not less conspicuous than those used in any other part of the agreement' (s 51(4)(b) ibid).
3 See s 51(4) ibid.
4 Section 54(1) and (2) ibid.

[7.9] The existing tenancy may have already become a statutory tenancy – a notice to quit may have expired, the tenancy may have been a fixed-term that has ended or a notice of increase of rent (above) may have been served. By virtue of the RA 1977, s 45 the rent limit during a statutory period of tenancy is prima facie the registered fair rent. If the rent payable for any statutory period would exceed the registered rent, then the excess is irrecoverable from the tenant[1]. If the contractual rent is *less* than the registered rent, it can be increased up to the amount of the registered rent by service of a statutory notice of increase that states the date from which the increase is to take effect[2]. The notice of increase must, to be effective, be in the statutorily-prescribed form, or a form to the like effect[3]. The date specified, from which the increase is to take effect, must be not earlier than the date of registration of the rent and not earlier than four weeks from service of the notice. Increases were formerly subject to phasing, but this has now been abolished[4].

1 Section 45(2)(a) ibid.
2 Section 45(2)(b) ibid.
3 See SI 1980/1697 (Sch).
4 HA 1988, Sch 17, para 22.

[7.10] Provision is made for the recoverable rent to be increased or decreased in the event of the amount of any rates borne by the landlord changing during the statutory period[1]. Similarly, the recoverable rent can be increased or decreased to reflect any change in the circumstances relating to the provision of services by the landlord, or the use of furniture by the tenant[2]. In this event, any question as to the quantum of any variation of rent is referable to the county court in default of agreement[3].

1 RA 1977, s 46(1).
2 Section 47(1) ibid.
3 Section 47(2) ibid.

Recovery of excess

[7.11] Any amount paid by way of rent *in excess* of the rent limits imposed by the RA 1977 is recoverable from the landlord who received it or his personal representatives, and can be deducted by the tenant from any rent payable to the landlord[1]. The tenant cannot recover any amount, however, at any time after the expiry of two years *or* where there is a breach of the rent agreement provisions, after the expiry of one year[2]. Recoverability is thus limited, in most cases, to two years' excess rent.

1 Section 57(1) and (2) ibid.
2 See s 57(3) ibid (as amended by HA 1980, s 68(3)), and see s 54 as to rent agreements (above).

QUANTIFYING A FAIR RENT

[7.12] The 'fair' rent must be established in accordance with the formula in the RA 1977, s 70. The operation of the provisions for valuing fair rents, and particularly the direction in s 70(2) to disregard scarcity, has occasioned a not inconsiderable degree of controversy.

Factors to be taken into account

[7.13] By virtue of s 70(1) when determining what rent would be a fair rent for a dwelling house under a regulated tenancy, regard must be had to all the circumstances (other than personal circumstances of landlord or tenant) and in particular to the following.

The age, character, locality and state of repair of the dwelling house

[7.14] The rent officer or rent assessment committee are entitled to take into account any inherent amenities or advantages a house enjoys by reason of its location, but *not* any increase in rental value accruing simply because there is a shortage of rented accommodation in the locality pushing rents up beyond the otherwise market figure[1]. So in *Metropolitan Property Holdings Ltd v Finegold*[2] the amenity advantages of a block of flats near a school for American children in London, which made the area more attractive for American families, was allowable to increase the fair rent for dwellings therein. A set off for scarcity, under s 70(2) (below) will not result simply because the amenity advantages of a district attract more people to live there. Distinguishing this from scarcity value simpliciter will not, however, always be easy. When assessing the state of repair of the dwelling, the rent officer or committee must have regard to the value of repairing covenants in the lease of the dwelling concerned, as well as to the physical condition of the premises[3].

1 *Metropolitan Property Holdings Ltd v Finegold* [1975] 1 WLR 349 at 352.
2 [1975] 1 WLR 349 at 352.
3 *Sturolson & Co v Mauroux* [1988] 1 EGLR 66, CA.

The quality, quantity and condition of furniture provided (if any)

[7.15] A term that the tenant can provide his own furniture in place of the landlord's, which will be removed for the duration of the letting, will be included under this head[1].

1 *R v London Rent Assessment Panel, ex p Mota* [1988] 1 EGLR 89.

Premiums

[7.16] With regard to any premiums paid by the tenant for grant, renewal, continuance or assignment of the tenancy, the taking of a premium will normally be unlawful under the RA 1977, Pt X. In some cases, however, if the tenancy has been brought into protection by statute a premium may lawfully have been taken, and this can be reflected in a higher fair rent[1].

1 See *Crown Estate Comrs v Connor* [1986] 2 EGLR 97.

'All the circumstances'

[7.17] The rent officer's remit is not confined to the items above. He must, in addition, have regard to 'all the circumstances' when fixing a fair rent for a dwelling house let on a regulated tenancy. This does not, however, give him an unfettered discretion as to what to consider. 'All the circumstances' must mean all the relevant circumstances; what circumstances are relevant and what are not, when valuation is being exercised, is one of the decisions which will call for the use of the valuer's professional skill and experience[1]. Factors materially affecting the rental value of the premises (other than scarcity) will be relevant, eg the terms of the tenancy, and the landlord's statutory obligations as to repair and fitness for habitation of the dwelling (see the Landlord and Tenant Act 1985, ss 8 and 11).

1 *Mason v Skilling* [1974] 1 WLR 1437 at 1443, HL (Lord Kilbrandon).

Factors to be disregarded (other than scarcity value)

Disregard of personal circumstances

[7.18] Considerations of financial exigency affecting either landlord or tenant must be disregarded when arriving at a fair rent. Moreover, in *Mason v Skilling*[1] it was held that the tenant's security of tenure (his 'irremoveability') is a personal circumstance to be disregarded. If a capital valuation of the premises is adduced in support of the landlord's case, it must therefore be calculated on a vacant possession basis. Any legal status (other than that of landlord or tenant) accruing to the parties will also be a personal circumstance, eg the charitable status of the landlord and fiscal advantages consequent thereon[2].

1 [1974] 1 WLR 1437.
2 See *Royal British Legion Housing Association Ltd v East Midlands Rent Assessment Panel* [1989] 1 EGLR 131.

[7.19] Additionally, a number of statutory disregards are specified in s 70(3) ibid, by virtue of which the following factors *must* be disregarded in all cases when arriving at a fair rent.

Disrepair

[7.20] The rent officer must disregard any disrepair or other defect attributable to a failure by the tenant under the regulated tenancy or any predecessor in title of his to comply with the terms of the tenancy. Disrepair occasioned by the tenant's default is to be discounted only if it occurred during the regulated tenancy, and not (for example) during his prior occupation in some other legal capacity. Disrepair attributable to a predecessor in title is also to be disregarded, but only if it occurred while the predecessor was (at the time) holding under the regulated tenancy now vested in the current tenant[1]. The disregard would apply, therefore, where the tenant has taken by way of lawful assignment or statutory succession from a protected tenant. The disregard in s 70(3)(a) should be compared with that applied in the valuation of rents for assured tenancies granted under the HA 1988[2]. Under the HA 1988 no disregard is made for disrepair occasioned other than by the tenant himself during the assured tenancy. Disrepair arising from a predecessor in title's breach of covenant is not to be disregarded[3]. This can create anomalies where succession to a protected tenancy takes place. A spouse of the deceased tenant takes a statutory Rent Act tenancy by way of succession, and would be subject to the disregard in the RA 1977, s 70(3)(a). Any other family member, however, would take an *assured* tenancy by succession[4] and consequently be subject to the rules in the HA 1988 s 14(2). The latter would be entitled to a reduction in rent to reflect disrepair occasioned by his predecessor in title whereas a successor spouse would not[5].

1 For the problems this can engender see *Henry Smith's Charity Trustees v Hemmings* (1981) 265 Estates Gazette 383, CA.
2 See HA 1988, s 14(2)(c).
3 *N&D (London) Ltd v Gadsdon* [1992] 1 EGLR 112.
4 RA 1977, Sch 1, para 6, amended by HA 1988, Sch 4, para 6.
5 *N&D (London) Ltd v Gadsdon* (above n 3) provides a good example (rent reduced to £5 per month because house uninhabitable due to previous tenant's breach of repairing obligations. The previous registered fair rent had been £30 per week. Applying market rent rules in HA 1988, s 14 (above Chapter 3, para 3.116 ff) the house was not lettable and had no rental value. If the successor had been the deceased tenant's spouse, rather than his son, the disrepair would have been disregarded under the RA 1977, s 70(3)).

Improvements

[7.21] Any improvements carried out by the tenant or a predecessor in title must be disregarded. Improvements carried out pursuant to the terms of the tenancy are not disregarded[1].

1 RA 1977, s 70(3)(b).

Furniture

[7.22] If furniture is provided by the landlord, any improvement to the furniture so provided by either the tenant or his predecessor in title must be disregarded. Conversely, any deterioration in the condition of furniture so provided is to be disregarded whether occasioned by ill treatment by the tenant or any lodger, subtenant or other person residing with the tenant[1].

1 RA 1977, s 70(3)(e).

Disregard of scarcity value

[7.23] The direction to the rent officer to disregard any scarcity value when determining the rent for a dwelling is central to the policy of the fair rent provisions. The presence of scarcity value, attributable to an excess of demand for housing over supply, accounts for the higher rents obtained for free market rentals over fair rents under the RA 1977. The interpretation of the relevant provisions is not, however, without difficulty. By virtue of the RA 1977, s 70(2) when determining the rent, it shall be assumed that the number of persons seeking to become tenants of similar dwelling houses in the locality on the terms (other than those relating to rent) of the regulated tenancy is not substantially greater than the number of such dwelling houses in the locality which are available for letting on such terms.

[7.24] This applies a unilateral disregard: when the state of the market is such that demand exceeds the supply of rented accommodation, any enhancement in market rental values attributable solely to that scarcity must be discounted. If, however, supply exceeds the demand in the locality for rented housing (thus depressing rents)[1] the statutory disregard does not apply, and the imbalance in the market will reduce the level of fair rents registrable under the RA 1977. Section 70(2) requires fair rents to be determined 'on the hypothetical basis that the housing letting market in the locality is in a state of equilibrium, in respect that the number of comparable houses available for letting does not substantially exceed the number of persons seeking to become tenants'[2].

1 An unlikely, though not impossible, eventuality.
2 *Western Heritable Investment Co v Husband* [1983] 2 AC 849 at 856 per Lord Keith.

[7.25] Note that the disregard is of scarcity value due to the *number* of houses for rent in the locality being less than demand, and not of any inherent 'amenity' value due to other factors making an area more (or less) attractive as a place of residence.

[7.26]

> 'If a house has inherent amenities and advantages by all means let them be reflected in the rent under [s 70(1)]; but if the market rent would be influenced simply by the fact that in the locality there is a shortage, and in the locality rents are being forced up beyond the market figure, then that element of market rent must not be included when the fair rent is being considered'[1].

1 *Metropolitan Property Holdings Ltd v Finegold* [1975] 1 WLR 349 at 352 per Lord Widgery CJ.

'Locality'

[7.27] For this purpose the rent officer or committee should look for 'broad, overall, general scarcity' affecting a substantial (and not a limited) area[1]. There is no statutory guidance as to *how* scarcity is to be valued out of the rent.

1 *Ibid*, [1975] 1 WLR 349.

METHODS OF VALUING A FAIR RENT

Older modes of valuation

[7.28] As long as they adhere to the broad statutory framework outlined above, rent officers and rent assessment committees have considerable latitude to choose *how* to arrive at a fair rent. They may adopt any method of valuation that is not unlawful or unreasonable[1]. The most obvious, and appropriate, method is to have regard to the registered rents of comparable dwellings let on similar terms in the locality. When a sufficient number of registered rents were available as comparables, this was hitherto the preferred method of valuation[2]. Following the introduction of assured tenancies by the HA 1988, with the deregulation of rents for new lettings, the number of registered fair rents available as comparables has inevitably decreased. This has focused attention on potential alternative modes of valuation, and especially on the use of assured and shorthold rents as comparables for valuing fair rents.

1 *Mason v Skilling* [1974] 1 WLR 1437 at 1439 per Lord Reid.
2 Per Lord Reid, *Mason v Skilling* [1974] 1 WLR 1437 at 1439. And see *Tormes Property Co Ltd v Landau* [1971] 1 QB 261.

[7.29] In the past the chief alternative to the use of comparables was to ascertain a free market rental and then apply a discount to take account of scarcity. This approach was endorsed by the House of Lords in *Western Heritable Investment Co v Husband*, who indicated that where reliance is placed on rents actually being paid in the market, a discounting procedure should be applied to those (market) rents in order to eliminate from them the element which is attributable to the relative scarcity of houses available for letting[1]. With an increase in the number of lettings at free market rentals following the HA 1988, this may in future be a more appropriate means of arriving at a 'fair' rent figure. 'Market rent less scarcity' cannot however, be regarded as the exclusive or primary formula for use since the emergence of a real rented market post-HA 1988[2].

1 [1983] 2 AC 849 at 856.
2 See *Aspley Hall Estate Ltd v Nottingham Rent Officers* [1992] 2 EGLR 187 (East Midlands Rent Assessment Panel). The committee here held that they were entitled to take into account and mitigate any clear unfairness caused by an application of the 'market rent less scarcity' formula.

[7.30] A third method of valuation involves calculating a rate of return on the capital value of the dwelling with vacant possession, and then applying a discount for scarcity. This cannot, however, provide a reliable guide to the appropriate fair rent, especially where comparable registered rents are available to the rent officer[1]. 'A fair rent should be fair to the landlord as well as fair to the tenant'[2], and he is entitled to consider capital value when estimating the fair rent. In *Tormes Property Co Ltd v Landau*[3], however, Lord Parker LJ indicated that the 'contractors theory' and its variants, based on a return on capital valuations, could at best only produce a check or guide on fair rent levels, and nothing more.

1 See *Tormes Property Co Ltd v Landau* [1971] 1 QB 261.
2 *Mason v Skilling* [1974] 1 WLR 1437 at 1440 per Lord Reid.
3 [1971] 1 QB 261 at 266.

Use of market rent comparables

[7.31] Where market rents are used as the basis of valuation, the amount to be deducted for scarcity has always been a question of fact for the rent officer, to be determined by his expert evaluation of the extent of housing shortage in the locality. This will rarely be interfered with by the courts. So, in *Western Heritable Ltd v Husband*[1] the rent assessment committee arrived at a fair rent by taking the capital value of a dwelling with vacant possession and applying to that a rate of 6 per cent to represent an annual return to the landlord. From the resulting figure it made deductions for repairs and a deduction of 40 per cent to reflect the fact that houses in the area were in high scarcity. The discount of 40 per cent, although high, was upheld by the House of Lords as a question of fact for the committee. Historically the discount from market rent has tended to be more in the range of 10 to 20 per cent, depending on the facts and the housing situation in the locality.

1 [1983] 2 AC 849, esp at 856.

[7.32] The argument presented by landlords in post-HA 1988 cases has been a simple one. The increase in the availability of accommodation for rent, following deregulation of the market, means that a 'fair' rent, as legally defined in s 70(1) (above), should equal the free market rental, taking account of the statutory disregards and any discount for scarcity value (if it can be proved to exist). This issue first came to prominence with the first instance decision in *BTE Ltd v Merseyside and Cheshire Rent Assessment Committee*[1]. Hutchinson J accepted that, when using comparables to fix a fair rent, 'in general and subject to the scarcity value qualification, the object must be to arrive at what is the fair market rent for the property'[2]. This decision aroused considerable interest, and its rationale was subsequently accepted and extended by the higher courts in *Spath Holme Ltd v Chairman of the Greater Manchester and Lancashire Rent Assessment Committee*[3] and *Curtis v London Rent Assessment Committee*[4]. It is arguable, however, that the *BTE Ltd* decision should have been treated with greater circumspection[5]. In the first place, the decision of the rent assessment committee was quashed because, having accepted the landlord's evidence of market lettings, it then rejected his arguments because it considered there to be a paucity of accommodation to let 'at a reasonable rent'. The imposition of the criteria of 'reasonableness' on comparable rents was arbitrary and outside the terms of s 70, and for this reason alone the committee's determination was unsound. The court's observations as to the relevance of free market rents were therefore strictly obiter. Secondly, the operation of s 70(2) clearly *does* depend upon scarcity existing as a fact, in the view of the committee, in the case before it.

1 [1992] 16 Eg 111.
2 [1992] 16 Eg 111 at 112.
3 [1995] 2 EGLR 80.
4 [1997] 4 All ER 842.
5 For criticism see Rodgers (1999) Conv 201–231, NP Gravells [1998] JHL 67.

[7.33] In *Curtis v London Rent Assessment Committee*[1] the Court of Appeal extended the reasoning in *BTE Ltd* , holding that the statutory disregard for scarcity, on its proper construction, necessitated the conclusion that a fair rent is a market rent, adjusted for scarcity and the other statutory disregards. In so doing, it strongly endorsed the earlier approach taken by Morritt LJ in *Spath Holme*[2], and by Hutchinson J in *BTE Ltd*[3]. It does not follow, however, that a market rent will always be 'fair'. Indeed, this approach to some extent begs the question – what role remains for the other statutory factors (those in s 70(1)) in determining the 'fairness' of the rent? As the Court of Appeal itself recognised, the concept of 'fairness' is elusive if not tied to particular criteria.

1 [1997] 4 All ER 842, 862 per Auld LJ.
2 (1996) 28 HLR 107, 118–9.
3 (1991) 24 HLR 514 at 516–7.

Choice of valuation method

[7.34] Until the *Spath Holme* and *Curtis* decisions, the courts had always taken the view that, as long as they adhered to the broad statutory framework outlined above, rent officers should be given considerable latitude to choose *how* to arrive at a fair rent. Indeed, in *Mason v Skilling*, the House of Lords went as far as to hold that they could adopt any method of valuation that is not unlawful or unreasonable[1]. Until the controversy surrounding the use of assured rents as comparables arose in *BTE Ltd v Merseyside and Cheshire Rent Assessment Committee*, the most commonly used method was to have regard to the registered rents of comparable dwellings let on similar terms in the locality. Indeed, the courts had endorsed this approach by holding that where a sufficient number of registered rents are available as comparables, this was to be the preferred method of valuation[2]. This was an inevitable consequence of the fact that there would often be no reliable evidence of free market rental levels in the locality[3]. Rent officers were always, however, entitled to adopt other methods if appropriate. Following the deregulation of rents for new lettings on assured tenancies in 1989, the number of registered fair rents available as comparables has inevitably been decreasing. This explains the move in the more recent cases to examine whether alternative modes of valuation may now be preferable.

1 [1974] 1WLR 1437 at 1439 Lord Reid.
2 *Mason v Skilling* [1974] 1 WLR 1437 at 143 per Lord Reid. See also *Tormes Property Co Ltd v Landau* [1971] 1 QB 261
3 See generally Davey, M A *Farewell to Fair Rents* [1992] JSW&FL 497.

[7.35] The first judicial guidance on the *choice* of valuation methods in the post-HA 1988 context was given at first instance in *Spath Holme Ltd v Greater Manchester and Lancashire Rent Assessment Committee*, when Harrison J laid down six principles governing the choice of valuation method to be employed[1]. These were approved by the Court of Appeal in both *Spath Holme* itself, and in *Curtis v London Rent Assessment Committee*. The *Spath Holme* principles, if adhered to, allow the rent officer considerable latitude in choosing the appropriate method of valuation in individual cases. Harrison J recognized that the method adopted might vary according to the particular circumstances of each case. The committee must consider the methods suggested to them by the parties, and must give adequate reasons for their choice of method. But subject to these requirements, they are free to adopt the method that appears to them, on the evidence, to be the most appropriate, provided it is not one that is either unlawful or unreasonable. He went on, however, to add the significant qualification that, where the committee departed substantially from market rents – in this case rentals recently agreed for assured tenancies of similar flats within the same block – they would have to show weighty reasons for doing so. This formulation of the relevant valuation principles is uncontroversial, and would leave the rent officer considerable latitude to adopt the best method, or combination of methods, available to him in the instant case. The additional caveat – that the committee would have to show weighty reasons to depart from recent market comparables – was justified by the special facts of *Spath Holme* , in which the fair rent registrations challenged were in the same block of flats as more recent lettings on otherwise identical terms on assured tenancies.

1 [1994] 27 HLR 243, aff'd [1995] 2 EGLR 80 (CA). For the discussion of the guidelines in the Court of Appeal see [1995] 2 EGLR 80 at 82 (Morritt LJ).

[7.36] The Court of Appeal endorsed Harrison J's valuation principles in *Curtis v London Rent Assessment Committee*, but went further by adding the all important caveat that, while there may be more than one route to determining a fair rent, *every route* must have the market rent for the dwelling concerned as its starting point. In so doing, the court[1] reinterpreted the principles of 'fairness' set out in the RA 1977 to require the starting point in s 70(1) to be the market rent in every case. The reasoning used to justify this change of approach focused, once again, on the statutory disregard for scarcity – the court considered that the required assumption of a hypothetical absence of scarcity must presuppose that the starting point in s 70(1) is the market rent. This is open to question. Section 70 does not expressly mention market rents at all, let alone establish them as the starting point in the valuation process. Moreover, this approach ignores the fact that all fair rents registered since the *Spath Holme Ltd* decision in 1995 will have been arrived at using market comparables with a built in adjustment for scarcity. There would therefore appear to be no good reason why they should not be admissible as comparables in future valuations, even if pre-1995 fair rent registrations are not.

1 [1997] 4 All ER at 864 per Auld LJ.

[7.37] The change of emphasis in *Curtis* narrows the range of choice available to rent officers when considering the choice of an appropriate valuation method. The courts have in the past endorsed the use of the contractors method of valuation to calculate a fair return on capital investment to the landlord. But it does not have market rent as its starting point. Presumably, post-*Curtis* this method can only be adopted as a 'check' on fair rent levels established by the use of free market comparables. Yet it was approved by the House of Lords in *Mason v Skilling*[1] and while its use as a sole valuation method may, in modern circumstances, be difficult to justify, there seems no reason why it should not be used in combination with others eg in combination with market rent comparables, where it might be used as a check on the level of 'fair' rents generated. This was the use of it envisaged in *Tormes Property Co Ltd v Landau*[2], where its use as a check on fair rents achieved by the use of registered comparables was endorsed. The Court of Appeal in *Curtis* expressly held that, where there are existing market rent comparables available, enabling the identification of a market rent as a starting point, there is no need to refer to registered rent comparables at all – 'still less to engage in an arid exercise of verifying ... their soundness as current indicators of an adjusted market rent'. While this undoubtedly limits the rent officer to using market rent comparables alone, it does not necessarily prevent him checking the 'fairness' of the rental, adjusted for scarcity, by the use of some variant of the contractor's theory.

1 [1974] 1 WLR 1437 at 1440 per Lord Reid.
2 [1971] 1 QB 261 at 266.

[7.38] Where market rent comparables are produced by the parties, therefore, these must be the starting point in the valuation in every case. However, the evaluation of scarcity (or the lack of it) remains a question of fact for the professional skill and judgment of the rent officer. This still leaves him a limited amount of room for the application of his specialist knowledge of the local housing market. A key question remains, however, as to the degree of latitude the courts have left to the rent officer when assessing the evidence of comparable rents put before him. This was tested in three appeals brought in 1999 by the Northumberland and Durham Property Trust against determinations made by the London Rent Assessment Panel[1]. The courts indicated, in all three appeals, that the scope for the rent officer to ignore market comparables is now very narrow. He should not refuse to consider market comparables simply because they are not closely comparable and may need to be adjusted. Neither is there any obligation on the landlord to prove that the comparables he is adducing are compelling. The panel should be particularly wary of rejecting comparable market rents, even if they need adjustment to give a 'true' comparison, especially if comparable registered fair rents also need adjustment. This is because, in the courts' view, open market rents should in principle provide a more reliable starting point for the valuation. The rent officer or (on appeal) rent assessment panel must, moreover, explain their reasoning on any discount for scarcity that is actually made.

1 The decisions are reported at [1998] 24 Eg 128 (Latham J) and [1998] 3 EGLR 85 (Keene J).

[7.39] It must be appreciated that, when discussing market comparables, the courts have failed to draw a clear distinction between fully assured tenancies and assured shorthold tenancies. In practice many market comparables put forward by landlords in fair rent valuations are of rents obtained for assured *shorthold* lettings[1]. Shorthold tenants enjoy no security of tenure beyond the initial contractual shorthold term, which can be as little as six months, or beyond the first six months of a periodic shorthold[2]. The disparities in the legal rights and obligations of the parties to an assured shorthold and a regulated tenancy are obvious. Perhaps less obvious, but just as significant, is the fact that many shorthold rents contain an inbuilt 'premium' to compensate the landlord for the fact that the dwelling may be vacant for periods between short term lets, and to reflect the distinct clientele to whom this type of letting is often attractive – transient tenants in good employment looking for flexible short term letting arrangements. There are strong grounds, therefore, for arguing that many shorthold rents cannot be truly 'comparable' and that they should not be used in valuing fair rents under the RA 1977. The courts' failure to address this point assumes considerable significance as a consequence of changes introduced by the Housing Act 1996 (HA 1996), as most private sector lettings will in future be on shortholds and not fully assured tenancies[3]. Any assured tenancy which is granted on or after 28 February 1997, or which comes into being on the expiration of a fixed-term assured shorthold granted on or after that date, will (with limited exceptions) be an assured shorthold tenancy. The principal exception will be where the landlord gives notice at the time of grant that the tenancy is to be an assured tenancy, or where the tenancy agreement contains a stipulation to that effect – a facility which will be used primarily by housing associations and other 'social' landlords, who may wish to continue granting fully assured tenancies[4]. Most tenancies granted by private landlords will be assured shortholds. It is likely to be increasingly the case, therefore, that the majority of 'market' comparables produced by private landlords will be examples of shorthold rents. Assured tenancy comparables will retain some relevance for valuing fair rents for dwellings let by social landlords, but are unlikely to be widely used in the private sector. It follows that the decisions in *Curtis* and *Spath Holme Ltd* will legitimate the widespread use of shorthold rents as market 'comparables'. This will generate additional pressure for further substantial uplifts in registered fair rents.

1 The comparables produced to the rent assessment committee in *Curtis v London Rent Assessment Committee* were, eg, of seven assured shorthold tenancies of similar or identical dwellings in the same block or one in an adjacent street (see [1997] 4 All ER 842, 860). Evidence of both assured tenancies and assured shorthold rents was produced before the committee in the *Spath Holme Ltd* litigation.

2 HA 1988, s 21(4) enables the landlord to give two months notice of termination at any stage after the expiry of the contractual fixed-term, or (in the case of a periodic tenancy) after six months. See Chapter 5 above.

3 See Chapter 5 above.

4 See HA 1988 Sch 2A, paras 1 and 2 (inserted by HA 1996, s 99). Registered social landlords are precluded from using assured shortholds other than for temporary or transient arrangements (such as for relocation of tenants during refurbishment work to a dwelling) by the statutory guidance on housing management (the 'Tenants Guarantee') issued by the Housing Corporation under the HA 1996, s 36.

[7.40] Another distortion complicating the use of market rents as comparables arises from the taking of premiums on grant. Under the RA 1977, s 70(1), any premiums paid for the grant, renewal or assignment of a residential tenancy must be taken into account when valuing a 'fair' rent. Clearly, the taking of a premium on grant will directly affect the level of rent eg if rent is capitalised in the form of a substantial initial premium, the periodic rental thereafter will normally be substantially smaller to reflect this. The taking of a premium on the grant of a regulated tenancy will normally have been unlawful, however, under the RA 1977, Pt X. In some cases, if the tenancy had been brought into protection by statute a premium may lawfully have been taken, and this can legitimately be reflected in a higher fair rent[1]. Significantly, however, there are no legal restrictions on the taking of premiums on the grant of an assured tenancy or assured shorthold under the HA 1988. Where evidence of market rents under assured tenancies are brought forward as comparables, therefore, any distortion occasioned by the taking of a premium on grant should be adjusted out of the rent if a true comparator is to be arrived at. Unfortunately, the RA 1977 directs the rent officer to take into account any premium paid on the grant of the tenancy of the subject dwelling, but says nothing of the effect of premiums on the rentals of *comparable* tenancies brought in evidence. Market rent comparables distorted by the taking of a premium would, presumably, fall to be adjusted under the general clause in s 70(1) namely the direction to the rent officer to have regard to 'all the relevant circumstances'. *Query*, however, if the only available evidence of comparable market rents is that of rents distorted by the taking of a premium on grant, the rent officer would be entitled to reject these as not truly comparable on the facts, notwithstanding the ruling in *Curtis v London Rent Assessment Committee*. A careful enquiry of the facts will be required, as market rents distorted by the taking of premiums cannot in principle provide reliable comparables for valuing 'fair' rents.

1 See *Crown Estate v Connor* [1986] 2 EGLR 97.

LIMITING FAIR RENT INCREASES

[7.41] Registered fair rents have increased substantially over the last decade, reflecting the increased volume of rented accommodation available for letting in many areas, and the new guidelines on the use of market comparables issued by the courts. The scale of increases in the early 1990s, following the litigation in *BTE Ltd v Merseyside and Cheshire Rent Assessment Committee*, initially prompted the issue of a consultation document by the Department of the Environment in 1992[1]. Government statistics now show that from April to September 1997, in 86 per cent of cases where a fair rent was registered, the increase was over 5 per cent higher than the increase in the retail prices index (RPI)[2]. This prompted proposals to 'cap' fair rent increases by linking them to the retail prices index. The Rent Acts (Maximum Fair Rents) Order 1999 (RAO 1999)[3] now limits fair rent registrations to the increase in RPI plus 7.5 per cent for the first re registration, and RPI plus 5 per cent for subsequent re-registrations. There is, however, no limit on the fair rent registrable on a first registration[4]. The rent limits do not apply if the rent officer or rent assessment committee consider that repairs or improvements carried out by the landlord have improved the property such that the new rent should be at least 15 per cent more than the existing registered rent. The 'capping' regulations were initially declared ultra vires and void by the Court of Appeal in *R v Secretary of State for the Environment Transport and the Regions ex parte Spath Holme Ltd*[5], on the basis that the enabling legislation used to introduce them (the Landlord and Tenant Act 1985) was limited to measures introduced for counter inflation purposes[6]. This decision was subsequently reversed on appeal to the House of Lords and the Regulations upheld[7]. The effect of the House of Lords ruling is that the RAO 1999 has been continually in force since 1 February 1999. However, rent assessment committees refused to reopen cases decided between 20 January 2000 (when the Court of Appeal quashed the RAO 1999) and 7 December 2000 (when the RAO 1999 was subsequently upheld by the House of Lords), which were made without reference to the terms of the 1999 Regulations. The Department of the Environment, Transport and the Regions (DETR) subsequently issued a further Guidance Note to the effect that rent assessment committee decisions made between these dates are of no effect, because they failed to take account of the RAO 1999, and must be deleted from the rent register[8]. The registered fair rent will revert to that previously determined by the rent officer. The parties can appeal against the rent officer's determination to the rent assessment committee a second time, but (of course) on this subsequent appeal the committee's decision will be subject to the terms of the 1999 Regulations.

1 'Rent Act Tenants: Rent Increases'. (Department of the Environment, 1992).
2 'Limiting Fair Rent Increases: A Consultation Document' (DETR, 1998) quoted at para 2.4.
3 SI 1999/6. And see *Spare Holme Ltd v North Western Rent Assessment Committee* [2001] 3 EGLR 30 (capping order applies to cap the original registered rent and not the rent level which would have been obtained two years previously).
4 SI 1999/6, introduced under the Landlord and Tenant Act 1995, s 31. The restrictions are more severe than those originally proposed, which would have limited increases to RPI plus 10 per cent on first re-registration. See 'Limiting Fair Rent Increases: A Consultation Document' op.cit at paras. 2.6–2.9.
5 [2000] 1 All ER 884 CA.
6 The relevant provision in the Landlord and Tenant Act 1985 (a consolidating measure) originated in the Counter Inflation Act 1973, s 11, and was re enacted in the Housing Rents and Subsidies Act 1975, s 11 before being consolidated in the Landlord and Tenant Act 1985.
7 [2001] 1 All ER 195 HL.
8 The Rent Acts (Maximum Fair Rent) Order 1999 – further guidance note for the rent service (DETR, May 2001).

[7.42] The 1999 Regulations provide a crude mechanism for limiting excessive rent increases. Rent officers will still be required, however, to produce initial rent valuations using the existing fair rent formula, in accordance with the guidelines laid down by the courts. This would appear an unnecessary and overly complex way of fixing fair rents on re-registration[1].

1 If fair rent increases are to be moderated in a way which minimises the effects of the rulings in *Curtis* and *Spath Holme Ltd*, it would surely have been preferable to amend the statutory rent formula itself: see further Rodgers (1999) Conv 201, 226.

REGISTRATION OF RENTS

[7.43] Applications for the registration of fair rents are determined by rent officers. The rent officer service was originally organised around registration areas based on counties, London boroughs and the City of London. The administration of the service was reformed in 1999, and has now been reconstituted as a national service independent of the local authorities[1]. The volume of work generated by the fair rent system is in decline, and rent officers now have additional functions in relation to housing benefit; eg to determine whether claimants are being asked to pay higher rents than a landlord might reasonably obtain in market conditions, and to determine the 'reference rent' for calculating housing benefit. They also have responsibility for determining whether claimants are being housed in accommodation that is too spacious for their needs, by reference to space requirements laid down in the relevant regulations, and whether any element of the rent is ineligible for housing benefit[2].

1 Administration of the Rent Officer Scheme (England) Order 1999, SI 1999/2403.
2 See the Housing Benefit (General) Regulations 1997, as amended. HA 1996, s 122 and Rent Officers (Housing Benefit Functions) Order 1997, SI 1997/1984.

[7.44] By virtue of the RA 1977, s 66, rent officers are under a duty to prepare and keep up to date a register of fair rents for regulated tenancies in their registration area. This is a public document, and must be made available for inspection in accordance with the terms of the relevant rent officer scheme.

Application for registration of fair rent

[7.45] Application must be made to the rent officer in the prescribed form[1] specifying the rent that it is sought to register, and (where the rent includes sums paid for services provided by the landlord) giving details of any services provided by the landlord for which payment is sought to be included in the rent[2].

1 See the Rent Regulation (Forms etc) Regulations 1980, SI 1980/1697.
2 Ra 1977, s 67(2). If the proposed rent is not stated the application will be invalidated: *Chapman v Earl* [1968] 1 WLR 1315.

[7.46] An application for registration can be made by the landlord *or* the tenant individually, or jointly by the landlord and the tenant under a regulated tenancy[1]. Where the reversion is held by joint landlords, or the tenancy is vested in joint tenants, it would appear that an application made by one (out of joint landlords or tenants) will be valid if it is expressed to be made on behalf of all[2].

1 Ibid, s 67(1) ibid.
2 See *R v Rent Officer for the London Borough of Camden, ex p Felix* (1988) 21 HLR 34.

[7.47] The procedure to be adopted by the rent officer following application is provided for in the RA 1977, Sch 11[1]. He may, and normally will, require the production of further information as to the particulars set out in the application. Unless the application is a joint one by landlord and tenant, he must serve written notice on the parties inviting them:

(a) to make written representations; and
(b) to indicate whether they wish him to hold a consultation with both landlord and tenant as to the rent which ought to be registered[2].

If there are no representations, or if the application is jointly by landlord and tenant, the officer will make such inquiries as he thinks fit and (if he considers it a fair rent) register the rent mentioned in the application[3]. If there *are* representations, or if he disagrees with the rent applied for, then the rent officer must hold a 'consultation' with the parties as to what rent ought to be registered for the dwelling house. He must give at least seven-days' notice of the time and place of the consultation, and each party is entitled to be represented by counsel or a solicitor[4]. The consultation will otherwise be conducted on informal lines, and the rent officer has considerable latitude as to the evidence to be admitted in determining the rent; his statutory duty is merely 'to consider in consultation with the landlord and the tenant' what rent ought to be registered for the dwelling in question[5].

1 RA 1977, Sch 11, paras 1–7.
2 Ibid, Sch 11, para 3(1).
3 Ibid, Sch 11, paras 2 and 3A.
4 Ibid, Sch 11, para 4(2) and (3); at least 14-days' notice must be given if the landlord has proposed a rent which includes an element of payment for services.
5 Ibid, Sch 11, para 4(2) ibid.

[7.48] The precise ambit of his duty was considered in *R v Brighton Rent Officers, ex p Elliott*[1], where the rent officer, having disclosed that he would rely on comparable properties when fixing the rent, refused to disclose in advance of the consultation which comparables he intended to use. It was there held that the function of the consultation under Sch 11, para 4 is merely to enable the rent officer to approach his decision having heard the parties' views about the case; he is not expected to decide the issue during the course of the consultation, neither need he come to it with a preconceived idea of what the rent ought to be. He is not under a duty to disclose to the parties what comparable properties he will rely on before he comes to the consultation. Stressing the informal nature of the exercise, Lord Widgery CJ observed that 'an important function . . . of the consultation is to enable the rent officer to pick up the atmosphere of the matter, make contact with the parties, listen to their observations, and thus, one hopes, come to a conclusion which reflects what the parties have to say'[2].

1 (1975) 29 P & CR 456.
2 (1975) 29 P&CR 456 at 460.

[7.49] After considering what rent ought to be registered, or whether a different rent ought to be registered, the rent officer will determine a fair rent and register it as the rent for the dwelling house. He must notify the parties accordingly by a notice which also informs them that if they make an objection in writing within 28 days he will refer the matter to a Rent Assessment Committee[1].

1 Schedule 11, paras 5A and 6. The period of 28 days can be extended.

Effect of registration

[7.50] Once registered, the fair rent registered operates in rem and attaches to the dwelling to which it applies until the registration is cancelled or varied in accordance with the RA 1977. By virtue of s 44 it becomes the recoverable rent limit for any contractual period of a regulated tenancy of the dwelling house in respect of which it is registered. Once a fair rent is registered it remains the recoverable rent for the dwelling house in respect of which the rent is payable until either the demised premises undergo such a change in their structure as to render them no longer the dwelling house referred to in s 44 or there is a new registration consequent on a fresh application (pursuant to s 67(3) or s 68(4))[1]. Once the rent has been registered, no application for re-registration can be made by the landlord alone or the tenant alone before the expiry of two years from the date on which the rent was registered (or confirmed by the Rent Assessment Committee on appeal)[2]. There are limited exceptions, considered below, allowing for variation within this period, but the basic principle is that the rent registered can be varied (on application to the rent officer) only at intervals of not less than two years, and if not varied or cancelled will continue to apply to the dwelling if re-let on a regulated tenancy. Any tenancy granted on or after 15 January 1989 will (with limited exceptions) be an assured tenancy within the HA 1988, in which event the rent limit will cease to apply. The registered rent will continue to be relevant, however, in those cases falling within the transitional provisions where a regulated tenancy can still be granted after 15 January 1989, and also where a dwelling with a registered rent was re-let prior to that date on a regulated tenancy within the RA 1977.

1 *Rakhit v Carty* [1990] 2 QB 315 at 326, CA.
2 RA 1977, s 67(3).

[7.51] The amount registered as the rent must include any sums paid to the landlord for the use of furniture or for services, irrespective of whether they are payable under the tenancy agreement or under separate agreements with the landlord[1]. The rent is registered exclusive of rates, although if they are borne by the landlord this fact is noted on the register[2]. The amount of any rates so borne is added to the rent limit for the relevant rental period and will be recoverable without the need for a formal notice of increase[3].

1 RA 1977, s71(1). This is an anti-avoidance measure to prevent the landlord charging excessively for services and thus indirectly enhancing the rent recoverable.
2 Ibid s 71(2). Rates were, in any event, replaced by the Council Tax under the Local Government Finance Act 1992.
3 Ibid, s 71(3) .

[7.52] Where, under a regulated tenancy, the sums paid by the tenant include variable amounts for services provided by the landlord or for any works of maintenance and/or repair carried out by the landlord, then a variable rent can be registered. The rent officer (or Rent Assessment Committee on appeal) must first be satisfied that the terms as to variation are reasonable, in which event the rent will be registered as an amount variable in accordance with the relevant terms of the tenancy[1]. If the rent officer is not satisfied that the terms are reasonable he must place a value on the services provided and include this in a fixed registered rent[2].

1 Ibid, s 71(4). Service charges do not have to be included in the registered rent, however, if they are provided under a separate agreement with a management company which is not the landlord's agent: *Eaton Square Properties v Ogilvie* [2000] 1 EGLR 73 (London rent assessment committee).
2 See *Firstcross Ltd v Teasdale* (1982) 47 P&CR 228.

[7.53] The registration of a rent takes effect, if determined by the rent officer, from the date when it is registered. If it is determined by the Rent Assessment Committee then the registration takes effect from the date the committee makes its decision[1]. As from the date when the registration takes affect any previous registration of rent for the dwelling ceases to have effect[2]. The date of registration (or confirmation of an existing registered rent) must be noted on the register. An application merely to confirm an existing registered rent will be invalid[3]. The rent officer may, however, when considering a valid application to increase or decrease the registered rent, consider the existing registered rent still to be the fair rent in the circumstances and confirm the registration. If the rent for the time being registered is confirmed, the confirmation takes effect from the date when it is noted on the register by the rent officer or (where confirmed by the Rent Assessment Committee) from the date the committee makes its decision[4].

1 RA 1977, s 72(1).
2 Ibid, s 72(5).
3 See *R v Chief Rent Officer for Royal Borough of Kensington and Chelsea, ex p Moberley* [1986] 1 EGLR 168; [1986] Conv 274 (Martin).
4 RA 1977, s 72(2).

Variation or cancellation of registered rent

[7.54] As already observed, once registered the registered rent remains the recoverable rent for the dwelling house under a regulated tenancy, unless and until one of three events occurs: either the structure of the building alters so that it is no longer the dwelling in respect of which the registration is applicable, *or* an application to vary the rent is made under s 67(3) and is successful, *or* an application to cancel the rent registered is made under s 73, and results in cancellation.

Change of circumstances

[7.55] By virtue of s 44 the registered rent becomes the limit of rent 'recoverable for any contractual period of a regulated tenancy *of the dwelling house*'[author's italics]. If a change of circumstances occurs which means the property ceases to be the dwelling house in respect of which the rent was registered, then the registration becomes inoperative. It had previously been thought that re-letting on a furnished tenancy premises which had previously been let unfurnished was a change of circumstances rendering the registered rent inoperative[1]. In *Rakhit v Carty*[2], however, the Court of Appeal ruled that the provision of furniture as a term of the tenancy does not affect the recoverable rent until the registered rent is increased and that rent is registered. For a registration to become ineffective there must be change of a structural nature to the property, such that it ceases to be the dwelling house in respect of which the rent was registered. So the tenant here succeeded in a counterclaim for overpaid rent, where unknown to the current landlord a rent of £550 per annum had been registered in 1974 for an unfurnished letting by a previous landlord, and the same flat had been relet (furnished) in 1987 at £450 per month. The necessity of the landlord inspecting the register prior to reletting was emphasised by the court.

1 See *Kent v Millmead Properties Ltd* (1982)44 P&CR 353, *CA and Cheniston Investments Ltd v Waddock* [1988] 2 EGLR 136, CA.
2 [1990] 2 QB 315. The court declined to follow *Kent v Millmead Properties Ltd* (1982) 44 P & CR 353 on the basis that the decision was per incuriam RA 1977, s 67(3) not having been considered in the latter.

Application to vary

[7.56] Unless made jointly, an application to vary the rent cannot be made until two years from the date when the registration took effect. An application by the landlord alone can, however, be made within the last three months of the two-year period[1]. Section 67(3) makes provision for an application to re-register the rent within the two-year period in certain limited circumstances, *namely* where there has been a change in either:

(a) the condition of the dwelling house;
(b) the terms of the tenancy;
(c) the quality, quantity and condition of furniture provided under the tenancy[2]; or
(d) any other circumstances taken into consideration when the rent was previously registered or confirmed.

The change of circumstances must, moreover, be such that the registered rent is no longer a fair rent. Where an application to vary within two years is made under s 67(3), the rent officer must first ask himself whether there have been changes in the condition of the house or other factors enumerated in s 67(3). Only if there have been changes coming within (a)–(d) above does the right to a review arise at all. If there have, he must then go on to ask a second question, namely whether the registered rent is not, as a consequence of those changes, any longer a fair rent. If he so decides, he is not limited (when reassessing the rent) to awarding an increase confined to those factors which follow from the change which gave rise to a right of review under s 67(7) in mid-term. He must make an assessment of the fair rent under s 70 in the normal manner, under no additional limitations beyond those in s 70[3]. For example, inflation would be relevant once a change of circumstances has been established, but would not suffice to trigger a review under s 67(3)[4]. It has been held for these purposes that carrying out substantial repairs to the dwelling can constitute a change in its condition justifying a mid-term re-registration of the fair rent for the dwelling[5].

1 RA 1977, s 67(3) and (4). An application by the landlord within the last three months will not take effect until two years have expired: s 72.
2 Deterioration by fair wear and tear is excluded.
3 See generally *London Housing and Commercial Properties Ltd v Cowan* [1977] QB 148 per Lord Widgery CJ at 151–3.
4 See *Wareing v White* [1985] 1 EGLR 125, CA; *R v London Rent Assessment Panel, ex p Chelmsford Building Co Ltd* [1986] 1 EGLR 175.
5 See *R v Rent Officer for the West Sussex Registration Area* [2001] 2 EGLR 63, CA.

Cancellation of registered rent

[7.57] The RA 1977, s 73 provides for the cancellation of a registered rent in specified circumstances. If two years have elapsed since registration, and the dwelling house is not for the time being subject to a regulated tenancy, an application to cancel the registration can be made by the landlord under s 73(1A)[1]. This is now of little consequence, as a new letting after 15 January 1989 will in any event be on an assured tenancy, not a regulated tenancy, unless the exceptional circumstances in which a regulated tenancy can still be granted apply. An application to cancel the registered rent can also be made where a rent agreement has been made by landlord and tenant, to take effect after the end of the two-year period, and the application is made jointly by the parties[2]. This is rarely encountered in practice.

1 Added by HA 1980, s 62. The application is, strictly speaking, by the person who would be the landlord were a regulated tenancy in existence, namely the holder of the immediate reversion of such a tenancy.
2 RA 1977, s 73(1). For rent agreements see s 54 and para 7.8 ff above.

APPEAL TO THE RENT ASSESSMENT COMMITTEE

[7.58] Where a rent has been registered by the rent officer, he must notify the landlord and tenant by notice accordingly. The notice of registration (or confirmation) of the rent must inform the parties that, if an objection is made in writing to the rent awarded, the matter will then be referred to the Rent Assessment Committee[1]. It[2] will then consider the appeal and either confirm or vary the rent registered. Appeal from the committee lies to the courts on points of law only.

1 RA 1977, Sch 11, paras 5A and 6. The rent officer and/or the committee can allow a longer period for objections if they so wish.
2 For the constitution and composition of Rent Assessment Committees generally see RA 1977, Sch 10. For the applicable procedural rules and prescribed forms see further SI 1988/2200.

[7.59] In considering a reference the committee has power, by giving notice, to require either party to provide such further information within a period of not less than 14 days as they may reasonably require[1]. Non-compliance with a notice for further information is a summary offence punishable by a fine[2]. The committee must also give the parties notice specifying a period of not less than seven days during which they can either make representations in writing or request permission to make oral representations to the committee. If either party chooses to request the right to make oral representations, then the committee must give him an opportunity to be heard either in person, or by a solicitor or counsel, or some other person representing him[3]. After making such enquiries as it thinks fit (including, usually, visiting the premises) and considering the information supplied by the parties, the committee will either confirm the fair rent registered by the rent officer, or if it does not appear to it to be a fair rent, it must determine a fair rent for the dwelling. The parties must then be notified of the decision and its date. If a new fair rent has been determined or existing fair rent confirmed, this must be noted on the register of rents kept by the rent officer[4].

1 RA 1977, Sch 11, para 7(1).
2 Ibid, Sch 11, para 7(2), ie by a fine not exceeding level 3 on the standard scale.
3 Ibid, Sch 11, para 8.
4 Ibid, Sch 11, para 9.

[7.60] The rules of natural justice apply to Rent Assessment Committee proceedings, and the committee is obliged (on request) to give reasons for its decision[1]. The character and extent of the reasons which must be given depend on the nature of the problem the committee has had to resolve. If it simply disagrees with the valuations produced by each party, and on its own expert knowledge preferred another figure, it is not obliged to justify its own valuation – save to deal with any substantial points raised by the parties and the view the committee took of them[2]. In *Guppy's Properties Ltd v Knott (No 3)*[3] it was held that the committee is not required to state its method of valuation – its reasons must merely be intelligible and, where it decided to rely on its own skill and knowledge, it is not required to explain in detail how that figure was reached. It must explain why evidence presented to it has been rejected but need not explain its own valuation in detail[4].

1 Tribunals and Inquiries Act 1993, s 10(1).
2 *Metropolitan Property Holdings Ltd v Laufer* (1974) 29 P & CR 172. See also *Guppys (Bridport) Ltd v Sandoe* (1975) 30 P&CR 69, *Mason v Skilling* [1974] 1 WLR 1437.
3 (1981) 258 Estates Gazette 1083.
4 For further consideration of the committee's duty see, inter alia, *Waddington v Surrey and Sussex Rent Assessment Committee* (1982) 264 Estates Gazette 717, *R v London Rent Assessment Committee, ex p St George's Court Ltd* (1982) 265 Estates Gazette 984, *R v London Rent Assessment Panel, ex p Chelmsford Building Co Ltd* [1986] 1 EGLR 175.

[7.61] The Rent Assessment Committee's determination takes effect from the date of registration[1]. Rents registered by the Rent Assessment Committee on appeal tend to be higher than those awarded by the rent officer. The delays encountered in the committee proceedings may make this to some extent inevitable due to changes in the rental market during the intervening period since the initial registration.

1 RA 1977, s 72(4).

B Restricted contracts

INTRODUCTION

[7.63] The RA 1977, Pt V contains provisions enabling either party to a restricted contract (landlord or tenant) to apply to the rent tribunal for the registration of the rent under the restricted contract[1]. By RA 1977, s 79 the president of every rent assessment panel is required to keep an up-to-date register of rents for restricted contracts awarded by the panel for dwellings in its jurisdiction. Since 1980 the rent tribunal's functions are carried out by the Rent Assessment Committee, specially constituted as a rent tribunal for the purpose of hearing applications under the RA 1977, Pt V[2]. The procedures to be followed by the tribunal are laid down by statutory instrument[3] but are characterised by greater informality than proceedings under the RA 1977, Pt IV; eg there is no prescribed form for applications, and the rules of evidence do not apply. The powers of the tribunal are set out in the RA 1977, s 78(2). After making such enquiry as it thinks fit, and after giving each party to the contract an opportunity to be heard or make written submissions, the tribunal can do one of three things:

(a) it can approve the rent payable under the contract; or
(b) it can reduce or increase the rent to such sum as they may, in all the circumstances, think 'reasonable'; or
(c) it may, if it thinks fit in all the circumstances, dismiss the reference.

1 RA 1977, ss 77 and 78.
2 HA 1980, s 72.
3 See SI 1980/1700 as amended.

[7.64] The rent as approved, reduced or increased will be entered in the register kept for the purposes of Pt V.

REASONABLE RENT

[7.66] The rent to be ascertained by the tribunal is the 'reasonable' rent for the grant of a restricted contract of the dwelling in question. No detailed guidance is given in the Act as to how the 'reasonableness' or otherwise of the rent is to be ascertained, cf the detailed guidance to rent officers given by s 70 as to the determination of 'fair' rents under the RA 1977, Pt IV. Although often equated in popular currency with fair rents, tribunal awards tend to be of higher rents. In particular, while it must be assumed that scarcity value and the tenant's personal circumstances are to be discounted, and usually are so discounted by tribunals, there is no express requirement that this will be done[1]. There is little judicial guidance as to the proper construction of s 78(2)[2].

1 See the express disregards in the RA 1977, s 70(1) and (2) for fair rents (above para 7.18 ff).
2 See, eg *Ponsford v HMS Aerosols Ltd* [1979] AC 63, HL.

RESIDUAL IMPORTANCE OF TRIBUNAL JURISDICTION

[7.67] In practice, it is now very unlikely that many applications under this part of the Rent Act will arise. Under the HA 1988, s 36(1) no new restricted contract can be created after 15 January 1989. Moreover, even for pre-commencement restricted contracts, Rent Act protection will be lost if the terms of the contract are varied by agreement after 15 January 1989 in a way which affects the amount of the rent payable[1]. Where this occurs the contract is deemed to be a new contract, with the result that its restricted contract status will be lost under s 36(1). Variation of the rent by the tribunal will not have this effect, neither will a variation by agreement which increases the rent to the rent registered for the dwelling. However, any other agreed variation in rent will remove protection[2], and this will greatly accelerate the decline in the number of contracts to which Pt V theoretically applies. Moreover, since changes introduced in the Housing Act 1980 (HA 1980)[3] tenants who *do* still have restricted contracts enjoy very little security of tenure if they refer their rent to a rent tribunal. The tribunal now has no power to suspend notices to quit, and the court can delay the operation of a possession order for only three months. It seems likely, therefore, that the rent tribunal jurisdiction will be little used in future – even where theoretically applicable – and it will not be further discussed here[4].

1 HA 1988, s 36(2)(a).
2 See *Rowe v Matthews* (2001) WL 272896, and above Ch 3 para 3.7 ff.
3 HA 1980, s 69. This provision removed the tribunal's power to suspend notices to quit in relation to contracts entered into after 28 November 1980, and replaced it with a more limited power vested in the county court to suspend a possession order for a maximum of three months. See further Chapter 3, para 3.7 ff.
4 For detailed discussion see Megarry, *The Rent Acts* (11th edn, 1988) vol 1, p 764 ff; Martin, *Residential Security* (1989) pp 166–71; Hill and Redman, *Law of Landlord and Tenant*, (18th edn) at C 128 ff; Farrand and Arden, *Rent Acts and Regulations* (2nd edn, 1981), p 132 ff; Pettit, *Private Sector Tenancies* (2nd edn, 1981) pp 105 ff and 161 ff.

C Housing association tenancies

FAIR RENT: REGISTRATION

[7.68] Lettings by housing associations on or after 15 January 1989 will be assured tenancies, and governed by the HA 1988. For housing association tenancies granted before 15 January 1989, the RA 1977, Pt VI made provision for the registration of a fair rent by the rent officer, and the keeping of a separate part of the register for registered housing association rents[1]. Determination of fair rents for housing association tenancies constituted a significant proportion of the work of the rent officer service. The provisions in Pt VI apply to any tenancy (other than a co-ownership tenancy) where the interest of the landlord belongs to a housing association or housing trust, to the Housing Corporation, and the tenancy would (if not excluded by the RA 1977, ss 15 and 16) otherwise be a protected tenancy[2]. The rent is to be assessed by the rent officer having regard to the same considerations applicable to 'fair' rents for regulated tenancies under Pt IV[3].

1 RA 1977, s 87(1).
2 RA 1977, s 86(2).
3 Ibid, s 87(2) ibid applying ss 67, 70 and 72 for the purpose of quantifying housing association rents.

RENT LIMIT

[7.69] When the rent has been determined and registered it becomes the 'rent limit' for the dwelling house. Any excess payable under the tenancy over the rent limit is irrecoverable from the tenant[1]. Where no rent is registered, the rent limit is the rent recoverable under the tenancy, or (if the dwelling has been let in the foregoing three years) the rent at which it was last let before the current tenancy commenced[2]. Where the rent limit is increased – either by registration or variation of the rent registered – then the rent payable can be increased by written notice of at least four weeks' duration, effective from the beginning of a new rental period. This procedure (laid down in s 93) is somewhat more straightforward than the provisions applicable to private sector regulated tenancies.

1 Ibid.
2 Ibid, s 88(4).

[7.70] The fair rent provisions do not apply to tenancies granted on or after 15 January 1989. These will be assured tenancies, and no statutory rent limit applies under the HA 1988[1].

1 See Chapter 3, para 3.102 ff.

D Illegal premiums

GENERAL

[7.71] Clearly, there would be little merit in controlling the rent recoverable for a regulated tenancy if the rent restrictions could be circumvented by the taking of a capital sum on grant, followed by a low rent during the tenancy. Consequently, the taking of premiums ('key money') was prohibited on the grant or assignment of a protected tenancy by the RA 1977, Pt IX. As there is no control of rents for assured tenancies under the HA 1988, there is no bar on the taking of a premium on the grant of an assured tenancy. As it is no longer possible to grant a protected tenancy within the RA 1977[1], the rules restricting the taking of premiums on grant are of reduced significance. They will still have relevance, however, where a tenancy is granted after 15 January 1989 to a sitting tenant with a pre-existing Rent Act tenancy, or where other of the transitional provisions still facilitate the grant (after 15 January 1989) of a protected Rent Act tenancy[2]. The rules restricting the taking of premiums on the *assignment* of a protected tenancy probably now have greater relevance than those restricting premiums on grant.

1 See HA 1988, s 34(1).
2 See HA 1988, s 34(1) and Chapter 3 para 3.4 ff above.

PREMIUMS ON GRANT OF PROTECTED TENANCIES

[7.72] By virtue of the RA 1977, s 119 it is an offence for any person to require, as a condition of the grant, renewal, or continuance of a protected tenancy, the payment of any premium in addition to the rent, or the making of a loan. The court has power to order a person convicted of taking a loan or premium, in contravention of s 119, to repay the amount taken[1]. Section 122 contains similar provisions making it an offence to take a premium or loan for the grant, continuance or renewal of a restricted contract.

1 RA 1977, s 119(4).

[7.73] To prevent avoidance, 'premium' is given a wide meaning by s 128, and includes not only any fine or other pecuniary consideration in addition to rent, but also any sum paid by way of a deposit – unless the latter does not exceed one-sixth of the annual rent and is reasonable in relation to the potential liability for which it is paid[1]. For the same reason, payments in respect of furniture are closely controlled. By virtue of s 123 where the purchase of furniture has been required as a condition of the grant, renewal or assignment of a protected tenancy then if the price exceeds the 'reasonable price' of the furniture the excess is to be treated as a premium. The quantum of the 'reasonable price' is a question of fact for the trial judge, and represents the price which an incoming tenant would be willing to pay for the furniture concerned to the outgoing tenant[2]. This is, clearly, an imprecise yardstick and leaves much to the discretion of the court to assess on the facts. It is an offence to offer furniture at a price which the vendor knows, or ought reasonably to know, is unreasonably high, or to fail to provide an inventory itemising the prices of individual items[3]. The local authority have, in theory, powers of entry and inspection under s 124 to enforce these provisions[4].

1 Ibid s 128(1)(c). Deposits to cover breakages and rent arrears will therefore be legal if these conditions are met.
2 See *Eales v Dale* [1954] 1 QB 539, CA.
3 RA 1977, s 124(1).
4 Ibid, s 124(2)–(8).

[7.74] The payment of rent in advance is, in the interests of anti-avoidance, also carefully controlled. Section 126 provides that any requirement stipulating that rent be paid before the beginning of the rental period in respect of which it is payable shall be void. Similarly void will be any requirement by which rent is to be paid earlier than six months before the end of the rental period in respect of which it is payable (if that period is more than six months). It matters not whether the condition is imposed as a condition of the grant, renewal or continuance of the tenancy, or under the terms of the tenancy itself. Rent is irrecoverable from the tenant for any period to which a prohibited requirement relates[1]. The tenant, moreover, has a right to the recovery of sums paid, exercisable against the landlord for up to two years from the date of payment[2]. It is an offence, punishable by a fine, to impose a requirement of the kind prohibited by s 126 (above)[3].

1 Ibid s 126(3).
2 Ibid, s 126(4)–(7) .
3 Ibid, s 126(4).

[7.75] It is illegal for 'any person' to receive a premium for the grant, assignment or renewal of a protected tenancy, and liability is potentially applicable to persons other than the landlord. In the leading case of *Farrell v Alexander*[1], the phrase 'any person' was held to consist of words of wide generality, and wide enough to include landlords, tenants, agents or middlemen[2]. There was, in this case, an infringement of s 119 where the payment of an inflated price for furniture to the outgoing tenant was made a condition for the simultaneous grant of a protected tenancy by the landlord. The receiving of any pecuniary consideration, in the form of a monetary benefit to the landlord, will constitute a premium, including in one case, the sale of a house at an undervalue of £500 to a nominee of the landlord, in return for the grant of a protected tenancy[3].

1 [1977] AC 59, HL. Overruling *Remmington v Larchin* [1921] 3 KB 404, CA; *Zimmerman v Grossman* [1972] 1 QB 167, CA.
2 [1977] AC 59 at 71 per Lord Wllberforce. And see, for a further example, *Saleh v Robinson* [1988] 2 EGLR 126.

3 See *Elmdene Estates Ltd v White* [1960] 1 All ER 306 especially at 311; 'there is, I think, a pecuniary consideration whenever the benefit obtained by the landlord or the detriment suffered by the tenant is expressed in terms of money' (Lord Radcliffe).

[7.76] Quite apart from criminal liability RA 1977, s 125 gives a general right to recover any premium or loan unlawfully required or received from the recipient. There is no time limit within which proceedings for the recovery of sums paid must be commenced.

PREMIUMS ON ASSIGNMENT

Protected tenancies

[7.77] By virtue of the RA 1977, s 120(1) any person[1] who, as a condition of the assignment of a protected tenancy, requires the payment of any premium or the making of a loan is guilty of an offence. It is also an offence to *receive* a premium for the assignment of a protected tenancy[2]. The bar on assignment applies to a tenancy while it is a protected tenancy; once the tenancy has become statutory (eg following notice to quit) assignment is, in any event, not possible, and the rules as to premiums etc cease to have relevance[3]. Notwithstanding the bar on premiums, an outgoing tenant is legitimately entitled to pass on certain costs to an incoming assignee. The rules are relaxed by s 120(3) to entitle the assignor to recover the reasonable cost of structural alterations[4], and of providing fixtures, and any post-assignment outgoings discharged by the assignor. The assignor is also entitled to recover a reasonable amount for business and/or professional goodwill where part of the premises assigned has been used by him for business, shop, office or professional purposes[5]. The penalties for contravention of the bar on taking premiums and loans on assignment are broadly the same as those under s 119, discussed above.

1 See *Farrell v Alexander* [1977] AC 59, above para 7.75.
2 RA 1977, s 120(2).
3 Being a personal right of occupation only, the statutory tenancy cannot be assigned. Further, it is a criminal offence to demand any payment as a condition for giving up possession of a statutory tenancy (RA 1977, Sch 1, para 12).
4 Recoverability is not limited to expenditure incurred after the tenancy which is the subject of the assignment granted – see *Steele v McMahon* [1990] 2 EGLR 114.
5 Ibid, s 120(3)(d).

Long leases

[7.78] It will be appreciated from the above account that the taking of premiums on the grant or assignment of a tenancy is illegal only if the tenancy is within the RA 1977. Most long leases at a low ground rent are not within Rent Act protection, the rent reserved being insufficient to come within the threshold for protection[1]. The taking of a premium for the assignment of a long lease will not, therefore, be illegal in most cases.

1 That is two-thirds of the rateable value of the dwelling (RA 1977, s 5). See Chapter 6, para 6.26 ff.

Assignment of long leases: the problem defined

[7.79] The rules banning the charging of a premium on the grant or assignment of a protected tenancy (above) can, however, work an injustice in the case of long leases. If the tenant has a long lease at a ground rent sufficiently low to take the tenancy outside Rent Act protection, but the ground rent and service charge payments increase during its currency, the 'rent' for the purposes of the RA 1977 may rise above the threshold for protection. Having paid a premium on grant, a long leaseholder may then be precluded from charging a premium on assignment of the remainder of his term. He will have an unmarketable lease, the capital value of which cannot be realised. This problem affects only leases granted prior to commencement of the HA 1988, as the latter imposes no restriction on the charging of premiums for an assured tenancy.

[7.80] In an attempt to remedy this injustice, the RA 1977, s 127 exempted from Pt IX any tenancy which was both a long tenancy (within the meaning of the Landlord and Tenant Act 1954, Pt I) and a protected tenancy, provided three conditions were satisfied: the tenancy must not be terminable within the first 20 years; the rent payable (excluding rates, service and maintenance charges) must not be liable to variation in that time; and the terms of the tenancy must not inhibit assignment or underletting. The HA 1980 added two more classes of exempt tenancy[1]:

(1) Leases (not necessarily long) granted *before* 16 July 1980 which were granted initially at a low rent, with assignment permitted, and a premium lawfully paid on grant. This exemption was aimed at leases where service charges have risen, thus bringing the tenancy above the threshold for Rent Act protection. Unless the service charge element in the rent is 'expressed' in the lease to be payable in respect of, inter alia, repairs, maintenance or services, then it counts as rent for these purposes and is not disregarded, see RA 1977, s 5(4).
(2) Long leases granted *after* 15 July 1980 which were not terminable within 20 years, and which were assignable, provided that the basic ground rent (excluding service charges) must not be reviewable at less than six-yearly intervals and must be stated to be incapable on review of exceeding the two-thirds rateable value limit.

1 See HA 1980, ss 78 and 79 for definition of 'premium' for these purposes. Also Farrand and Arden *Rent Acts and Regulations* (2nd edn 1982) p 150ff for the detailed changes introduced by the HA 1980 .

[7.81] Owing to the complexity of these provisions, some doubt remained whether all classes of long lease, on assignment of which premiums *should* be permitted, were catered for. To remove any residual difficulties, and replace the existing provisions with clearer guidelines, the HA 1988, s 115 replaced much of the old law with a simpler formula to be applied to all long leases[1]. It should be added that these rules apply only to protected tenancies – there is no bar on the charging of premiums on assignment of an assured tenancy (whatever its length) granted after the HA 1988's commencement.

1 See RA 1977, s 127, as amended by HA 1988, s 115.

Premiums on assignment: special rules

[7.82] Where a tenancy is both a long tenancy (ie for a term certain of at least 21 years) *and* a protected tenancy, then with regard to any premium or loan received or paid after 15 January 1989[1], the Rent Act bar on premiums shall not apply (and be deemed never to have applied), provided two conditions are satisfied:

(1) The landlord must have no power to determine the tenancy at any time within 20 years of its grant. The presence of a power of re-entry or forfeiture for breach of any term or condition of the tenancy will not take the lease outside this proviso[2], but a break clause exercisable at the landlord's option would do so.
(2) The terms of the tenancy must not inhibit both the assignment and the underletting of the whole of the premises comprised in the tenancy. The one exception is that a bar on assignment or underletting during the last seven years of the term is disregarded – such a restriction is, of course, commonly found in long leases and, if not catered for, would have greatly restricted the scope of these provisions.

1 That is, after the commencement of the HA 1988.
2 See s 127(3), added by HA 1988, s 115(2).

[7.83] For these purposes, by virtue of s 127(5), a term of the tenancy 'inhibits' an assignment or underletting if it either:

(a) precludes it altogether (eg, a non-assignment clause not qualified by reference to the landlord's consent); or
(b) permits it subject to consent but excludes the Law of Property Act 1925, s 144. The latter prohibits the exacting of a fine or money payment for consent or license to assign, unless excluded by the lease itself. This provision therefore covers clauses under which the landlord can exact payment for consent, and which therefore constitute an inhibition to assignment; or
(c) permits it subject to consent but requires in connection with a request for consent the making of an offer to surrender the tenancy. The legitimacy of this device for avoiding the requirement of reasonableness in relation to consent (otherwise required by the Landlord and Tenant Act 1927, s 19(1)) was recognised in *Bocardo SA v S & M Hotels Ltd*[1], and it effectively enables the landlord to put an absolute bar on assignment and obtain some or all of any premium payable thereon.

1 [1980] 1 WLR 17, CA.

[7.84] It follows that a non-assignment clause which permits assignment or underletting subject to consent – but which is not otherwise qualified by reference to surrender and under which no payment can be exacted for consent – does not 'inhibit' assignment in the required sense. Even if the tenancy is protected, therefore, a premium can lawfully be charged on assignment with consent.

[7.85] It should be noted that the charging of premiums is allowable under s 127, as amended, only if the lease is a long lease within the meaning of the Local Government and Housing Act 1989, Sch 10 namely a tenancy granted for a term of years certain of exceeding 21 years[1]. It is immaterial whether the tenancy is protected ab initio or becomes so by rent increase.

1 See 1954 Act, s 2(4). And see Chapter 11 below.

[7.86] The only category of lease *shorter* than 21 years where a premium is lawful is short leases granted prior to 16 July 1980 on payment of a premium, where rent or service charge increases have brought them into protection (above). Although concern was expressed during the HA 1988's passage that this category may lose protection under the new rules[1], they would appear to be unaffected, as the HA 1988 left s 127(3A) and (3B) in situ, repealing only sub-s (3C) and (3D), which formerly dealt with long leases[2].

1 See Parl Debs (HC) Standing Committee G, 8 March 1988, cols 1406–07.
2 See HA 1988, s 115(3), introducing new s 127(3A) and (3B) to RA 1977.

Part premium if condition is unsatisfied

[7.87] If any of the conditions in s 127(2) for the charging of a lawful premium are not satisfied, it remains the case that a part premium calculated in accordance with RA 1977, Sch 18, Pt II can lawfully be paid on assignment. Broadly, this permits the tenant to recover on assignment a fraction of the premium he himself paid on grant, calculated by reference to the unexpired residue of the term as a fraction of the original term granted. For example, a part premium will be allowable if the lease includes a break clause (contrary to s 127(2)(a) (above)) or a prohibition on assignment which is absolute or excludes the Law of Property Act 1925, s 144, provided an initial premium was paid by the tenant on grant.

CHAPTER 8

Farm cottages

A Introduction

[8.1] Agricultural workers in tied accommodation are commonly either service occupiers, or pay rent lower than the threshold to attract Rent Act protection[1]. The Rent (Agriculture) Act 1976 (R(A)A 1976) introduced statutory protection and rent control, modelled on the Rent Acts, guaranteeing security of tenure after an occupier's employment ceases, subject to the landlord's right to re-let to another agricultural employee if alternative accommodation is available for the protected occupier. The regime under the R(A)A 1976 was replaced by the Housing Act 1988 (HA 1988) for new lettings on or after 15 January 1989. All occupancies granted after that date will be 'assured' agricultural occupancies governed by the HA 1988. In broad terms, the 'assured' occupier will enjoy similar security of tenure to that available under the R(A)A 1976, but restriction of rents on 'fair rent' principles no longer applies. The landlord is free to demand a market rent, with increases being subject to review by the Rent Assessment Committee[2].

1 RA 1977, s 5(1).
2 HA 1988, ss 13 and 14.

[8.2] The R(A)A 1976 continues to apply to most occupancies created prior to the commencement of the HA 1988. The protection afforded by the R(A)A 1976 is, moreover, retrospective and applies to occupancies granted prior to its commencement, as if it had 'at all material times' been in force[1]. The existence of separate regimes for occupancies created prior to 15 January 1989, and those created on or after that date, is a source of considerable complexity. The transitional provisions in the HA 1988 are somewhat complex, and may give rise to anomalies; eg not all occupancies created prior to 15 January 1989 will be governed by the R(A)A 1976. For this reason they are separately dealt with below.

1 *Skinner v Cooper* [1979] 2 All ER 836, CA.

B Protected agricultural occupancies

QUALIFYING FOR PROTECTION

[8.3] The R(A)A 1976 employs complex terminology to define occupancies to which protection extends. The occupier must have been granted a 'relevant licence or tenancy' of property in 'qualifying ownership', and the occupier must usually be a 'qualifying worker'. If these conditions are met the employee becomes a 'protected occupier in his own right'. On termination of his contractual tenancy or licence he will be a 'statutory tenant in his own right.' The code of protection for 'protected' agricultural occupiers, contained in the R(A)A 1976, continues to apply where the tenancy or licence was granted *prior* to commencement of the HA 1988 on 15 January 1989.

Protected occupiers in their own right

[8.4] By virtue of the R(A)A 1976, s 2(1), an employee will be a 'protected occupier in his own right' if three conditions are satisfied:

(1) He has a 'relevant licence or tenancy'.
(2) The dwelling is in 'qualifying ownership', or has been at any time during the subsistence of the tenancy or licence[1].
(3) The occupier is a 'qualifying worker', or he *has been* a qualifying worker *at any time* during the subsistence of the licence or tenancy[2]. Once the occupier has become a 'qualifying worker' his protected status will be unaffected by his ceasing to be employed in agriculture, or employed by his landlord. Once satisfied, the qualifying worker condition cannot be disapplied[3].

An occupier will qualify for protection if he satisfies (1) and (2) but has been incapable of whole time work in agriculture as a consequence of a qualifying injury or disease[4]. Similarly, he will remain a protected occupier in his own right where, first, there has been a surrender and re-grant in circumstances where he was, prior to re-grant, a protected occupier; and secondly where the licence or tenancy was granted in consideration of his giving up possession of another dwelling house of which he was a protected occupier[5].

1 Whether or not it was at that time a 'relevant' licence or tenancy: s 2(1) ibid.
2 Ibid, s 2(1)(b).
3 Cf the agricultural worker condition for 'assured' occupancy protection under the HA 1988, which clearly can cease to be fulfilled. See para 8.36 ff below.
4 R(A)A 1976, s 2(2) and (4).
5 Ibid, s 2(3) and (4).

Relevant tenancy or licence

[8.5] The R(A)A 1976 applies whenever a qualifying worker (see below) has exclusive occupation of a dwelling house as a separate dwelling. Occupation can be under either a licence or tenancy, though if the employee has a licence, it is a prerequisite of protection that he has exclusive occupation of the property as a dwelling[1]. If the occupier has a tenancy, the qualifying conditions of the Rent Act 1977 (RA 1977) are modified. A 'relevant tenancy' is one under which a dwelling house is let as a separate dwelling[2]. It will qualify for protection under the R(A)A 1976, however, even if the rent is less than the threshold for full Rent Act protection[3], and if the dwelling is comprised in an agricultural holding[4]. A tenancy will be outside the R(A)A 1976 if it is a bona fide term that the landlord provides the tenant with board or attendance, but meals provided by the landlord in the course of the occupier's employment do not constitute 'board' for this purpose[5]. Apart from these modifications the qualifying conditions for full protection under the RA 1977 must be satisfied, and apply whether the occupier's interest is a licence or tenancy. A 'protected' occupancy cannot arise, for instance, if the landlord's interest belongs to the Crown or a local authority, or the landlord is a resident landlord within the meaning of the RA 1977[6].

1 Ibid, Sch 2, para 1.
2 See RA 1977, s 2; HA 1988, s 1(1). This formula has been used in successive Rent Acts, and has generated a not inconsiderable body of case law, as to which see above Chapter 3, para 3.12 ff.
3 That is, less than two-thirds the rateable value of the dwelling on the relevant date, as otherwise required by RA 1977, s 5, where the tenancy was granted prior to 1 April 1990.
4 R(A)A 1976, Sch 2, para 3.
5 Ibid, Sch 2, para 3(3) and (4).
6 See RA 1977, ss 13, 14 and 17, and see paras 6.36 et seq above for the relevant exceptions to full Rent Act protection.

Qualifying ownership

[8.6] A dwelling is in 'qualifying ownership' for the purposes of the R(A)A 1976 at any time if, at that time, the occupier is employed in agriculture and the occupier's employer is *either* the owner of the dwelling house *or* has made arrangements with the owner for it to be used as housing accommodation for persons employed by him in agriculture[1].

1 R(A)A 1976, Sch 3, para 3.

Qualifying worker

[8.7] For protection to accrue, the occupier must have been a 'qualifying worker' at some time during the subsistence of the tenancy or licence – not necessarily, note, at the date on which protection is claimed[1]. By virtue of Sch 3, para 1, a person is a qualifying worker if, *at any time*, he has worked whole time in agriculture, or has worked in agriculture as a permit worker, for not less than 91 out of the last 104 weeks. For the purpose of calculating the number of weeks worked in agriculture, a week will 'count' if the number of hours for which he works for his employer is not less than 35 hours[2]. Certain weeks will count towards the occupier's entitlement even if he does not work during them. These are:

(a) any week during which, by agreement with his employer, he works less than the standard 35 hours[3];
(b) any week during which he is absent from work in agriculture by reason of taking a holiday to which he is entitled;
(c) any week in which he is absent from work in agriculture with the consent of his employer;
(d) any week during which he is absent in consequence of an injury or disease (whether a 'qualifying' injury or disease or not)[4].

Where an occupier is suffering from a 'qualifying' injury or disease, any week of absence will count as a week of whole time work in agriculture, whether or not that person is employed in agriculture as a whole time worker[5].

1 Ibid, s 2(1).
2 Ibid, Sch 3, paras 4(2) and 12.
3 Ibid, Sch 3, para 4(3).
4 For exceptions (ii)–(iv) see Sch 3, para 4(4) ibid.
5 Ibid, Sch 3, para 4(5).

[8.8] Note that the qualifying employment need not be with the same employer – if an agricultural worker *at any time* works for 91 out of the previous 104 weeks full time in agriculture, he achieves the *status* of 'qualifying worker'. If he is offered accommodation thereafter on terms that constitute a 'relevant licence or tenancy', and the premises are in 'qualifying ownership', the protection of the R(A)A 1976 will apply ab initio. It is therefore important for an employer offering accommodation to agricultural employees to ascertain the precise nature of their previous employment status at the outset. It is also important to note that, once a protected agricultural occupancy has arisen, it will continue to be protected notwithstanding the occupier later ceases to be employed full time in agriculture – indeed, he may cease to be employed at all. Once the agricultural worker condition has been satisfied it gives the occupier an ongoing *status* that confers protection. Likewise, as soon as the occupier becomes a 'protected agricultural occupier' this status attaches to the property irrespective of his future employment record, provided he continues to occupy the dwelling as his residence. Although, in most cases to which the R(A)A 1976 applies in practice, the occupier will have completed 91 weeks' work with the same employer, by whom the accommodation has also been provided, potentially the scope of the Act is considerably wider.

Permit workers

[8.9] Special provision is made for this category of employee. An employee is entitled to count towards his entitlement any week during which he has worked in agriculture as a 'permit worker'[1]. Where an employee is suffering from a physical or mental incapacity which prevents him earning the minimum rate of pay prescribed by an Agricultural Wages Order, the Agricultural Wages Board may grant him a permit, exempting his employment from the statutory restrictions otherwise applicable under the terms of the Agricultural Wages Act 1948[2]. Any week worked as a permit worker can be counted irrespective of whether 35 hours are worked or not. In this way, therefore, the Act ensures its benefits are extended to incapacitated employees who are unable to comply with the more stringent qualifying conditions applicable to others. As with other employees, weeks during which absence is due to holiday leave, agreed absence or injury, may be counted towards the 91-week qualifying period.

1 Ibid, Sch 3, para 1 and Sch 3, para 5.
2 See the Agricultural Wages Act 1948, s 5.

Employees suffering 'qualifying disease or injury'

[8.10] Again, special provision is made for this category of employee. An employee can count towards his entitlement any week in which he is incapable of work by reason of any qualifying injury or disease[1], namely an injury caused by an accident arising out of and in the course of his agricultural employment, or an injury prescribed in relation to agricultural workers under the Social Security legislation[2]. Furthermore, where an occupier suffers a qualifying injury or disease during the course of his employment, rendering him incapable of whole time work in agriculture, he will be a protected occupier irrespective of whether he has 91 weeks' work in agriculture or not[3]. Workers suffering injuries in the course of their employment therefore enjoy the residential security conferred by the R(A)A 1976 irrespective of the length of their employment. The R(A)A 1976 will apply if an injury is sustained during the early part of an occupier's agricultural career. Moreover, while he is unable to work, as a consequence, weeks will count towards his statutory entitlement so that after 91 weeks he will achieve the status of 'protected occupier'. This will ensure continual protection under the R(A)A 1976 if, on his return to health, he subsequently ceases to be employed in agriculture or is employed by a different employer who offers him tied accommodation. Anomalously, however, if one returns to health during the initial 91-week qualifying period, statutory protection will cease to apply until the qualifying period has elapsed. The concession of automatic protection applies only 'if and so long as' the occupier is incapable of whole time work in agriculture, or work as a permit worker, in consequence of a qualifying injury or disease[4].

1 R(A)A 1976, Sch 3, para 4(5).
2 Ibid, Sch 3, para 2(1).
3 Ibid, s 2(2).
4 Ibid, s 2(2) .

Employment in 'agriculture'

[8.11] An occupier must be employed in agriculture pursuant to a contract of employment or apprenticeship, whether express or implied, written or oral[1]. The protection of the R(A)A 1976 does not extend, therefore, to self-employed agricultural contractors. Although self employment is sometimes encountered in practice, it has never provided a ready means to avoid the security of tenure provisions of the HA 1988 or the R(A)A 1976[2]. The occupier must also be employed, for the requisite period of time (above), in 'agriculture' as statutorily defined.

1 Ibid, Sch 3, para 1.
2 The courts apply a 'multiple test' to distinguish between an employment contract and a contract for services, which involves looking at both the degree of control which the employer exerts over the worker's work, and the degree to which he is integrated into the employer's business: *Ready Mix Concrete (South East) Ltd v Minister of Pensions* (1978)2QB 397. The test is one of substance, not form, and will depend on a variety of factors, in particular whether there is mutuality of obligations between the parties under the contract (ie to provide and accept work on a regular basis): see *O'Kelly v Trusthouse Forte plc* [1984] QB 90. This makes it difficult to avoid the legislation by merely adopting the form of a self-employed contracting arrangement, when in substance there is a relationship with mutuality more akin to employment. See further the specialist works; eg Williams, *Agricultural Law Tax and Finance* (Sweet & Maxwell Ltd, 1990, loose-leaf) at B2.5 and PR Williams and M Johnstone, *Farm Cottages: Security of Tenure* (Burges Salmon, 2001) at 16.3.

[8.12] 'Agriculture' is defined by the R(A)A 1976 in terms which differ in material respects from the definition contained in the Agricultural Holdings Act 1986[1]. By virtue of the R(A)A 1976, s 1 'agriculture' includes dairy-farming and livestock keeping and breeding, the production of any consumable produce grown for sale or consumption (or use in another trade or business), the use of land as grazing, meadow or pasture land, as orchards or osier land, the use of land for market gardens or nurseries[2], and also forestry. This definition, it should be noted, is inclusive but not exhaustive. Decisions on the analogous provisions of the Agricultural Holdings Act 1986, the General Rate Act 1967, the Rating Act 1971 and the Town and Country Planning Acts are thus of assistance, if not strictly authority[3]. The definition was apparently not intended to encompass every rural activity, but was intended to include all operations involved in farming land for commercial purposes[4]. Arable farming is therefore included, though not specified, but not (apparently) growing crops and weeds for testing commercial weed killers[5]. Grazing is an agricultural activity, even though the animals concerned may not be 'livestock' within the statutory definition of the latter, eg racehorses[6].

1 Agricultural Holdings Act 1986, s 1. See generally Rodgers, *Agricultural Law* (2nd edn, 1998) at Chapter 5, p 112 ff. Scammel and Densham's *Law of Agricultural Holdings* (8th edn) at Chapter 2. Muir, Watt and Moss *Agricultural Holdings* (14th edn) at Chapter 8, para 8.18 ff.

2 As to which see *Short v Greeves* [1988] 1 EGLR 1, CA; (1988) NLJ 329 (Wilkinson); (1988) Conv 430 (Rodgers) and (1988) 14 EG 51 (Muir Watt).
3 See Agricultural Holdings Act 1986, s 1, General Rate Act 1967, s 26(3), Town and Country Planning Act 1990, s 336(1).
4 *Lord Glendyne v Rapley* [1978] 1 WLR 601, CA.
5 *McClinton v McFall* (1974) 232 EG 707, CA. Cf *Dow Agrochemicals Ltd v EA Lane (North Lynn) Ltd* (1965) 192 EG 737, CCA.
6 See *Hemens v Whitsbury Farm and Stud Ltd* [1987] 1 All ER 430, 436, CA; affd [1988] 1 All ER 72, HL; and see *Belmont Farm Ltd v Minister of Housing and Local Government* (1962) 13 P&CR 417; *Bracey v Read*[1963] Ch 88; *University of Reading v Johnson-Houghton* [1985] 2 EGLR 113; (1986) Conv. 275 (Rodgers).

[8.13] 'Livestock' includes, by virtue of s 1(2), any animal which is kept for the production of food, wool, skins or fur, or for the purposes of its use in the carrying on of any agricultural activity. For the purpose of this definition 'animal' includes birds, but not fish, thus seemingly excluding fish farming from the scope of 'agriculture' in this context[1]. By contrast, mink farming would clearly be within the statutory definition. Pheasants and other game reared primarily for sport are not livestock, and gamekeepers employed for this purpose are not protected by either the R(A)A 1976 or the HA 1988[2]. 'Animals reared for sport or entertainment or for their decorative qualities cannot . . . be regarded as being reared in the course of the activity of farming'[3]. Racehorses are thus not livestock within the definition[4].

1 Cf *Jones v Bateman* (1974) 232 EG 1392, CA; *Wallace v Perth and Kinross Assessor* 1975 SLT 118; *Gunter v Newtown Oyster Fishery Ltd* (1977) 244 EG 140; *Cresswell v British Oxygen Co Ltd* [1980] 3 All ER 443, CA and other rating decisions.
2 See *Lord Glendyne v Rapley* [1978] 1 WLR 601, CA; *Earl of Normanton v Giles* (1978) 248 EG 869, CA, also *Reeve v Atterby* [1978] CLY 73.
3 *Forth Stud Ltd v East Lothian Assessor* [1969] RA 35, 46 per Lord Avondale.
4 *Hemens v Whitsbury Farm and Stud Ltd* [1987] 1 All ER 430.

[8.14] Note that an employee employed in general farm work, such as a farm mechanic, will be employed in 'agricultural' work even though his contractual duties may not, taken alone, be agricultural by definition. The definition in the R(A)A 1976, s 1 is directed towards including *all* operations, including repair and maintenance of farm machinery, which are involved in farming land for commercial purposes[1]. Cf a shop assistant working in a farm shop, whose duties are not in themselves 'agricultural', will not, it seems, be employed in agriculture' for the purposes of the R(A)A 1976, s 1[2]. Protection will not automatically be lost if the occupier ceases to be employed in agriculture and commences a non-agricultural user of the premises, eg by using the dwelling to run a jobbing builder's premises[3]. Such user may, however, constitute a breach of the terms of the statutory tenancy.

1 *McPhail v Greensmith* (6 August 1987, unreported) Lexis transcript.
2 *Baird v Newell* [11992] CLY 113 (County Court).
3 See *Durman v Bell* [1988] 2 EGLR 117, CA.

Statutory tenants in their own right

[8.15] Where an occupier satisfies the agricultural worker condition and becomes a 'protected occupier in his own right' then, on termination of the protected occupancy, he becomes a 'statutory tenant in his own right'[1]. The statutory tenancy subsists only if and so long as the occupier occupies the dwelling house as his residence[2]. It confers merely a personal right of occupation, not a tenancy vesting in possession, and will therefore terminate on the tenant's later death without successors, or on his vacating the dwelling without sufficient animus revertendi, ie without a settled intention to return, together with a 'visible state of affairs', such as the maintenance of furniture, in which that intention finds expression[3]. In this respect the R(A)A 1976 differs from the code for 'assured' agricultural occupancies under the HA 1988, which latter confers a tenancy vesting in possession on those employees occupying tied accommodation to which it applies[4]. The statutory tenancy arises automatically when the protected occupancy is terminated, whether by notice to quit, by a notice of rent increase[5], 'or otherwise'[6]; eg by the tenant accepting a registered 'fair' rent fixed by the rent officer[7]. A single succession to the statutory tenancy is provided for by the R(A)A 1976[8]. Where the occupier's license to occupy the dwelling house is, on the facts, an integral term of his contract of employment, it will come to an end when his employment ceases. At that point in time it will become a statutory tenancy under the R(A)A 1976, no formal or informal notice seeking possession being necessary. No *separate* licence to occupy can be inferred from the lack of notice from the landlord seeking possession on cesser of employment[9].

1 R(A)A 1976, ss 2(4) and 4(1).
2 Ibid, s 4(1).
3 See *Gofor Investments Ltd v Roberts* (1975) 29 P&CR 366, *Duke v Porter* [1986] 2 EGLR 101, *Brickfield Properties Ltd v Hughes* [1987] 20 HLR 108.
4 See below para 8.48 ff.
5 That is, pursuant to s 16(3), see below.
6 Ibid s 4(1).
7 *Durman v Bell* [1988] 2 EGLR 117, CA. Here the protected tenancy ceased, and statutory tenancy commenced, by operation of law upon the parties impliedly agreeing to a statutory tenancy.
8 See below pp ... ff and R(A)A 1976, ss 3 and 4.
9 *Burgoyne v Griffiths* [1991] 1 EGLR 14

THE STATUTORY TENANCY

Control of rent

[8.16] Following termination of his employment, the landlord may wish to charge a protected occupier an economic rent for the accommodation provided. The parties can at any time agree a rent payable under the statutory tenancy. By virtue of the R(A)A 1976, s 11(3), however, a rent 'ceiling' is applied, in that the agreed rent cannot exceed either the registered fair rent for the dwelling or (if no rent is registered) the weekly or other periodic equivalent of a rent fixed at one and a half times the rateable value of the dwelling[1]. The 'fair rent' provisions of the RA 1977, Pt IV are applied to tied cottages by the R(A)A 1976, s 13 enabling either party to apply for the registration of a 'fair rent' for the dwelling, quantified in accordance with the RA 1977[2].

1 Ibid, s 12(7) and (9).
2 See RA 1977, s 70.

[8.17] If no rent has been registered, and the agreed rent is less than the periodic equivalent of one and a half times the rateable value of the dwelling, the rent can be increased to this level by a notice of increase under s 12(2). Where a fair rent *has* been registered, the agreed rent can be raised to the level of the registered rent by a notice of increase under s 14(2)[1]. An agreed rent is irrecoverable from the tenant in so far as it exceeds the rent ceiling imposed by the R(A)A 1976[2]. Note that 'assured' agricultural occupancies granted after commencement of the HA 1988 enjoy no rent control on fair rent principles.

1 See R(A)A 1976, s 15.
2 See s 11(3) and (8) ibid.

Other terms of the statutory tenancy

[8.18] The statutory tenancy arises immediately upon termination of the occupier's contractual licence or tenancy. The terms of the statutory tenancy are set out in the R(A)A 1976, s 10 and Sch 5. No rent is payable under a statutory tenancy until there is an agreed rent or notice of increase under ss 12 or 14[1]. Rent under a statutory tenancy is payable weekly in arrears, subject to agreement to the contrary[2]. A covenant to pay rent in accordance with the provisions of the R(A)A 1976 is implied[3].

1 Ibid, s 10(2).
2 Ibid, s 10(3) ibid. If rent was paid under the protected tenancy on a different basis, that will prevail.
3 Ibid, s 10(5).

[8.19] With regard to other obligations, the general principle is that, as long as the statutory tenant retains possession, all the terms of the original contract remain enforceable by the parties inter se[1]. Subject to this, Sch 5 makes special provision for the following:

(1) *Licences.* Where the original contract was a licence, the statutory tenancy is a weekly tenancy, and includes all terms which would have been implied if it had been a contract of tenancy; eg the landlord's covenant for quiet enjoyment[2].
(2) *Non-contractual arrangements.* The landlord must continue to supply any facilities or services which he previously supplied, but not under the contract, provided these are reasonably necessary for any person occupying the dwelling house as a statutory tenant[3]; eg the supply of electricity or water supplies by the landlord from his own installations.
(3) *Repairing obligations.* The Landlord and Tenant Act 1985, s 11 applies[4]. This implies a covenant on the part of the landlord to keep the structure and exterior of the property in repair, as well as installations for the supply of water, gas and electricity.
(4) *Non-assignment and user.* It is a condition of the statutory tenancy that the tenant will not use the dwelling house, or any part of it, for purposes other than those of a private dwelling house[5]. This obligation will be breached by significant business use of the premises, but such breach can be waived by the landlord and made good, in which event the court may refuse as a matter of discretion to order possession[6]. The tenant cannot assign, sublet or part with possession of the dwelling house or any part of it[7].
(5) *Access.* The tenant must allow reasonable access for the execution of repairs. Likewise the landlord must afford such right of access to the premises as is reasonable in all the circumstances; eg over adjoining land not subject to the statutory tenancy[8].
(6) *Notice to quit.* The tenant must give at least four weeks' notice to quit, if the original tenancy or licence failed to make provision in this regard[9].

1 Ibid, Sch 5, para 2.
2 Ibid, Sch 5, paras 3 and 4.
3 Ibid, Sch 5, para 5.

4 Ibid, Sch 5, para 6(1) and (2).
5 Ibid, Sch 5, para 7(i).
6 See *Durman v Bell* [1988] 2 EGLR 117, CA.
7 R(A)A 1976, Sch 5, para 7(2).
8 Ibid, Sch 5, paras 8 and 9.
9 Ibid, Sch 5, para 10.

[8.20] Schedule 5, para 12 entitles the parties to vary the terms of the statutory tenancy, provided they do so by agreement in writing. Certain basic terms cannot, however, be varied in this way; eg the application of Landlord and Tenant Act 1985, s 11 or a substantial addition to the land and premises which the tenant is entitled to occupy, or variation of the circumstances in which the tenant can give notice to quit[1].

1 Ibid, Sch 5, para 12(3) and (4).

SECURITY OF TENURE

[8.21] The security of tenure provisions are modelled closely on those of the RA 1977. By virtue of s 6(1) a court cannot make an order for possession of a dwelling house subject to a protected or statutory occupancy unless one of the 'cases' in Sch 4 is made out. The cases are similar to those in the RA 1977 and are divided into mandatory and discretionary cases for possession. In the case of a discretionary ground, the court cannot make an order for possession unless it considers it reasonable to do so[1]. Moreover, where one of the discretionary grounds is relied on the court has power to stay or suspend execution of an order for possession, or to postpone the date of possession for such a period or periods as it thinks fit[2]. The court also has discretionary power to adjourn the proceedings[3].

1 Ibid, s 7(2). And see generally para 6.101 ff above.
2 Ibid, s 7(3).
3 Ibid, s 7(2A). And see s 7(4) for the court's power to order a suspension or postponement subject to such conditions as to payment of arrears of rent etc as it thinks fit.

[8.22] The discretionary grounds for possession are contained in the R(A)A 1976, Sch 4, Pt 1. A major policy consideration underlying the legislation is that security of tenure should not interfere with the efficient organisation of agriculture by tying up agricultural accommodation indefinitely, thus preventing its use for housing new employees. Cases 1 and 2 to Sch 4 therefore permit repossession where suitable alternative accommodation is provided either by the landlord or the housing authority. Although this ground is discretionary, it is reinforced in the agricultural context by the R(A)A 1976, s 27, which enables an agricultural landlord to apply to the housing authority on the ground that it ought 'in the interests of efficient agriculture' to provide suitable alternative accommodation for a protected occupier. Section 29 establishes agricultural dwelling house advisory committees to advise housing authorities on the merits of applications and the interests of efficient agriculture. Agricultural landlords therefore enjoy powers of compulsion, lacking under the RA 1977, to compel housing authorities to consider providing alternative accommodation[1].

1 See further para 8.60 ff below.

[8.23] The 'suitability' of alternative accommodation is to be judged by criteria similar to those applicable under the RA 1977. Where the landlord offers alternative accommodation it must be 'suitable' by reference to the tenant's needs as to the character and extent of the property, and equivalence of terms and security of tenure with the existing property[1]. If alternative accommodation is offered by the housing authority, Case 2 will be satisfied if either:

(a) an offer of suitable accommodation is made, giving the tenant not less than 14 days in which to accept it;
(b) the housing authority notifies the tenant that it has received, from a third party, an offer of alternative accommodation, and the tenant has accepted within the time allowed; or
(c) the landlord shows that the tenant did not accept the offer, and in so doing acted unreasonably in refusing the housing authority's offer of alternative accommodation.

1 See Sch 4, Case 1, paras 2, 3 and 4 ibid.

[8.24] The other discretionary grounds mirror those available under the RA 1977. Possession can be obtained if rent lawfully due is unpaid or other obligations of the tenant have been breached[1], if the tenant or his lodger or subtenant has been guilty of conduct which is a nuisance or annoyance to adjoining occupiers[2], or if the condition of the dwelling house or furniture provided by the landlord has deteriorated owing to the neglect or default of the tenant[3]. A further discretionary ground applies where the tenant has, without the consent of the landlord, assigned, sublet or parted with possession of the dwelling house or any part of it[4], and where the premises have been sublet (with or without consent) at a rent exceeding the maximum recoverable under the R(A)A 1976 or the RA 1977[5]. Where the tenant has given notice to quit, and the landlord has contracted to sell or let the dwelling house, or taken other steps as a result of which he would be seriously prejudiced by being unable to obtain possession, the landlord has a discretionary ground for possession[6]. This ground does not apply, however, where the tenancy has been terminated not by notice to quit, but by the tenant giving notice to terminate his employment. A further discretionary ground applies where the dwelling is reasonably required by the landlord as a residence for himself, his son or daughter, parents or grandparents, provided he did not become landlord by purchasing the reversion in the dwelling house after 12 April 1976[7]. This ground is subject to a further requirement, namely that the court must be satisfied that no greater hardship would be caused by granting possession than by refusing it[8].

1 Ibid, Sch 4, Case III.
2 Ibid, Sch 4, Case IV.
3 Ibid, Sch 4, Cases V and VI.
4 Ibid, Sch 4, Case VIII.
5 Ibid, Sch 4, Case X.
6 Ibid, Sch 4, Case VII.
7 Ibid, Sch 4, Case IX.
8 Ibid, Sch 4, Case IX, para 2. Cf RA 1977, Sch 15, Case 9.

[8.25] The mandatory grounds for possession are contained in the R(A)A 1976, Sch 4, Pt II. Where the landlord makes out a mandatory ground, the court does not have an overriding discretion to refuse to make a possession order[1]. The mandatory grounds provide for the following cases:

(1) Where the person granting the tenancy was an owner-occupier and the court is satisfied that the dwelling house is required as a residence for the original

occupier or a member of his family who resided with him when he last occupied the dwelling as a residence[2]. Notice must have been given at the commencement of the tenancy that possession might be recovered under this ground.

(2) Where the person granting the original tenancy had acquired the dwelling with a view to occupying it as a residence upon retirement, and he now requires it as a retirement home, or (if he has died) it is so required by a member of his family who was residing with him at the date of his death[3]. Notice must have been given on commencement of the tenancy if this ground is to be available.

(3) Where the dwelling house is overcrowded in circumstances rendering the occupier guilty of an offence under the housing legislation[4].

1 R(A)A 1976, s 6(6).
2 Ibid, Sch 4, Case XI.
3 Ibid, Sch 4, Case XII.
4 Ibid, Sch 4, Case XIII.

SUBTENANTS

[8.26] Subtenants are protected by the R(A)A 1976, s 9. Broadly, where a statutory tenancy is terminated, any subtenant who has been lawfully sublet the dwelling house or any part of it is protected and becomes a direct tenant of the landlord on the same terms as the statutory tenant – provided, always, that he qualifies as a protected occupier or statutory tenant under the R(A)A 1976[1].

1 Ibid, s 9(2).

SUCCESSION RIGHTS

[8.27] The R(A)A 1976, s 4 provides for one succession to a protected occupancy. The succession provisions have been amended, however, where the protected occupier dies after the commencement of the HA 1988. Succession rights accrue in either of two situations:

(1) If the original occupier died leaving a spouse who was residing with him at his death, then if the latter is not a protected occupier in his own right, he becomes the statutory tenant if and so long as he occupies the dwelling as his residence. The HA 1988, Sch 4, Pt II amends the R(A)A 1976[1] to provide that a cohabitee will be so treated if he or she 'was living with the original occupier as his or her wife or husband'. This mirrors the similar changes made to the succession scheme for protected and statutory Rent Act tenancies by the HA 1988, and removes the uncertainty surrounding the position of common-law spouses and cohabitees[2]. If there is more than one person who fulfils this requirement, then in default of agreement it is for the county court to decide who shall be statutory tenant[3].

(2) If the occupier had no spouse living with him in the dwelling at his death, then an *assured* tenancy by succession is conferred on any member of his family who was residing with him in the dwelling house at the time of, and for the two years immediately preceding, his death. The requirement of residence in the dwelling house itself, rather than simply with the deceased occupier, was added by the HA 1988, Sch 4, para 10. The latter also extended the qualifying period of residence from six months to two years. If more than one family member fulfils this

requirement, the assured tenant shall be, in default of agreement, such one as the court directs.

1 Ibid, s 4(5).
2 As to which see inter alia, *Dyson Holdings Ltd v Fox* [1976] QB 503, *Helloy v Rafferty* [1978] 3 All ER 1016, *Chios Property Investments Co Ltd v Lopez* [1988] 05 EG 57.
3 Section 4 (5B) inserted by HA 1988, Sch 4, para 12.

[8.28] It should be noted that the HA 1988 provides that in the case of deaths occurring after its commencement, family members other than spouses shall occupy by virtue of an assured tenancy by succession[1], cf the statutory tenancy by succession enjoyed by widows or widowers, and previously enjoyed by other family members. The effect, broadly, is to confer greater security of tenure on the former than the latter from the date of the HA 1988's commencement. There will also be no control of rents on fair rent principles where a family member (other than a spouse) succeeds to an assured tenancy by succession. Existing statutory tenancies by succession remain unaffected, however.

1 Ibid, Sch 4, para 11(b).

C Transitional provisions

[8.29] A license or tenancy granted after the commencement of the HA 1988 will normally be an 'assured' agricultural occupancy (below). Protected occupancy status under the R(A)A 1976 is preserved by the HA 1988[1] for licenses and tenancies granted on or after 15 January 1989 in one of three situations only, namely:

(1) If they are entered into pursuant to a contract entered into prior to the commencement of the HA 1988. Semble, this would include occupancies granted as a term of a contract of employment entered into prior to the HA 1988's commencement.
(2) If the tenancy or license is granted to a person who immediately before its grant was the protected or statutory occupier of tied accommodation. The occupier's protected status is therefore continued in the event of surrender and re-grant, provided the re-grant is by the person who was landlord or licensor (or one out of joint landlords or joint licensors) under the previous protected occupancy or statutory tenancy.
(3) Prior to the grant of the tenancy, an order for possession was granted under the R(A)A 1976, Sch 4, Case 1 (ie suitable alternative accommodation) and the premises occupied are suitable alternative accommodation provided by the landlord, the tenancy of which the court directed should be a protected tenancy[2].

1 See HA 1988, s 34(1) and (4).
2 Ibid, s 34 (1)(c)(i).

[8.30] It will be appreciated that the transitional provisions define those tenancies and licenses which *can* remain protected under the R(A)A 1976, without stating clearly those which will fall to be protected instead by the HA 1988. Under both Acts[1] protection accrues only once the agricultural worker condition has been satisfied namely, when the occupier is a qualifying worker who has worked whole time in agriculture (or has thus worked as a permit worker) for 91 out of the last 104 weeks[2].

1 R(A)A 1976, s 2(1) ; HA 1988, s 24(1).
2 R(A)A 1976, Sch 3, para 1; HA 1988, Sch 3, para 2.

[8.31] A problem may arise where an agricultural worker was granted a tenancy or license prior to 15 January 1989 (the commencement date of the HA 1988) but satisfied the agricultural worker condition *after* that date; eg he may have entered into a tenancy or license 90 weeks before 15 January 1989. At the commencement of the HA 1988 regime he was not a qualifying worker; but he will become protected *after* commencement of the HA 1988, having then completed 91 weeks' employment in agriculture[1]. Does the employee have in these circumstances a 'protected' or an 'assured' agricultural occupancy, namely does the R(A)A 1976 apply, or the assured tenancy code of the HA 1988? The better view, it is suggested, is that the R(A)A 1976 will continue to apply in such circumstances, albeit that its protection may have accrued after the commencement of the HA 1988. The occupancy will have been granted pursuant to a contract made before the commencement of the HA 1988, and so will be covered by the saving provisions in s 34 ibid[2]. Although there is no provision which expressly *excludes* protection under the HA 1988, an assured agricultural occupancy cannot arise in these circumstances. For protection under the HA 1988 there must be an assured tenancy, or an interest which *would* be such if certain factors (eg a low rent) were discarded. But the HA 1988, Sch 1, para 1 specifies that a tenancy entered into before, or pursuant to a contract made before, 15 January 1989 *cannot* be an assured tenancy. Reading the assured agricultural occupancy provisions with the HA 1988, Sch 1[3], then it is clear that an occupancy granted prior to 15 January 1989, but which becomes protected only after that date, will confer on the occupier the more extensive protection of the R(A)A 1976, and not that of the HA 1988.

1 In the example given, protection will accrue one week after 15 January 1989.
2 See HA 1988, s 34(4)(a).
3 That is, s 24(2) and Sch 1, para 1 ibid.

D Assured agricultural occupancies

[8.32] The HA 1988 introduced a new regime – 'assured' agricultural occupancies – applicable to licenses and tenancies granted after the commencement of Part I of the HA 1988. The broad features of the new regime are a reduced degree of security of tenure for agricultural occupiers, and the absence of rent control once the occupier's employment has ceased, other than the limited control on rents afforded to assured tenants by the HA 1988, ss 13 and 14.

QUALIFYING FOR PROTECTION

[8.33] A tenancy or licence will be an 'assured agricultural occupancy' if two conditions are satisfied[1]. For these purposes, any assured agricultural occupancy which is not an assured tenancy, ie a licence, shall be treated as if it were an assured tenancy and the provisions of HA 1988, Pt I will apply accordingly[2]. The two qualifying conditions are:

(1) that the licence or tenancy:
 (a) is an assured tenancy other than an assured shorthold tenancy. The protection will not apply, therefore, where the landlord grants an assured

shorthold tenancy of agricultural accommodation[3]. The limited rent control provided for shortholds, based on comparability of rents, may be problematical given the probable lack of comparable shorthold lettings 'in the locality', suggesting (perhaps) a fruitful avenue of avoidance for agricultural landlords[4];

(b) is not an assured tenancy by virtue only of the fact that it is granted at a low rent or the dwelling is comprised in an agricultural holding and is occupied by the person responsible for the farming of the holding[5]; or

(c) the occupancy is conferred by a licence under which a person has exclusive possession of a dwelling house and which, if it conferred a sufficient interest in land, would be a tenancy falling within (a) or (b) above. Notwithstanding the House of Lords' ruling in *Street v Mountford*[6] many such occupancies will remain licences, given the grant of exclusive possession, owing to the service occupancy element present.

(2) The 'agricultural worker condition', as defined by the HA 1988, Sch 3, must be satisfied for the time being with respect to the dwelling house subject to the licence or tenancy[7]. This condition, which is discussed further below, requires that the worker have worked in agriculture for 91 out of the last 104 weeks before protection under the HA 1988 applies.

1 HA 1988, s 24.
2 Ibid, s 24(3).
3 See, ibid, Pt I, Ch II, ss 20–23. Also see generally Chapter 5 above.
4 Section 22(3). See further PR Williams and M Johnstone in *Agricultural Law Tax and Finance* (ed Lennon and Mackay, Sweet & Maxwell loose-leaf) at B151ff.
5 Schedule 1, paras 3, 3A and 7. By virtue of s 24(2)(b) and Sch 1, para 3A (added by SI 1990/434) a tenancy will not be 'assured' if entered into after 1 April 1990 and the rent payable is for the time being less than £1000 per annum (Greater London) or £250 (elsewhere). If entered into before 1 April 1990 a tenancy will not be assured if the rent for the time being is less than two-thirds the ratable value of the dwelling for the time being (Sch 1, para 3(c)).
6 [1985] 2 All ER 289, HL.
7 HA 1988, s 24(1)(b).

[8.34] The assured agricultural occupancy under the HA 1988 is merely a variant of the assured tenancy regime applicable to all private sector lettings after 15 January 1989. This is reflected in the qualifying conditions – the tenancy or licence must either *be* an assured tenancy, or be such that it *would* be one if the dwelling were let at a low rent etc. There is no control of rents on fair rent principles, however, and the landlord is free to charge a market rent on commencement of the agreement if he wishes. Previously the amount recoverable by agreement was limited by the R(A)A 1976[1]. If a market rent is now charged, the occupier retains his assured agricultural occupancy under the HA 1988. This is unlikely to arise in practice, as most farmers make no charge for tied accommodation.

1 By virtue of the R(A)A 1976, s 11 any agreed rent is irrecoverable insofar as it exceeds either the registered rent or (if more) one and a half times the rateable value of the dwelling. See para 8.16 ff.

[8.35] Nevertheless, the legal implications of exacting a rent in such circumstances should be appreciated:

(1) If a tenancy is granted to an employee who has not been employed in agriculture for 91 out of the last 104 weeks, then if he is charged a rent of less than two-thirds the rateable value of the property for the time being, or if the dwelling was let on or after 1 April 1990, a rent less than the relevant rent limit[1], he will enjoy no protection under the HA 1988. He will, however, *become* an

assured agricultural occupant as soon as he has 91 weeks' qualifying employment (see below)[2]. The same result ensued under the R(A)A 1976, leading to the creation of a protected agricultural occupancy once 91 weeks' qualifying employment has elapsed.

(2) If tied accommodation is let to an agricultural worker for a rent of *more* than two-thirds the rateable value of the dwelling, or if the tenancy was granted after 1 April 1990 more than £1,000 per annum (London) or £250 per annum (elsewhere), the full protection of the assured tenancy code under the HA 1988, Pt I will apply – unless one of the relevant exclusions in Sch 1 applies, so as to prevent an assured tenancy arising[3]. The same employee would, under the old regime, have enjoyed protection under the RA 1977.

(3) Once an employee granted an assured tenancy has completed 91 weeks' qualifying employment, his interest will cease to be an assured tenancy simpliciter and will *become* an assured agricultural occupancy[4]. Although fully protected in the intervening period, the employee will at this point find himself in exactly the same position as an agricultural employee who has paid rent or a licence fee ab initio of *less* than two-thirds the rateable value of the dwelling or less than the rent threshold applicable to lettings after 1 April 1990. He therefore receives no return for having paid a full rent from the outset. The position under the HA 1988 might be compared with that obtaining under the R(A)A 1976. Under the old regime an employee paying a full rent would have been fully protected by the RA 1977, and would have remained so even after the qualifying period of employment had elapsed – a protected occupancy under the R(A)A 1976 arose only where the rent paid was less than two-thirds the rateable value of the dwelling[5]. Although the tenancy would in such circumstances be a regulated tenancy under the RA 1977, however, the local authority rehousing provisions[6] remained available to the landlord or farmer by virtue of the R(A)A 1976, s 27(2). This approach, it is suggested, has more to commend it than that adopted by the HA 1988.

(4) Although a landlord or farmer is in theory free to charge a full rent when letting to an employee, it must be appreciated that the Agricultural Wages Orders formerly limited the amount which may be deducted from an employee's wages by way of rent. This means that it is unlikely in practice that an employee will be paying a rent sufficiently large to lead to the creation of an assured tenancy – although an assured agricultural occupancy will in such cases arise once the period of qualifying employment has been completed.

1 That is, less than two-thirds rateable value; or less than £1000 per annum (London) or £250 (elsewhere) if the tenancy is granted on or after 1 April 1990.

2 The tenancy will then be within the HA 1988, s 24(2)(b), namely it is a tenancy which is not assured solely because Sch 1, para 3 (tenancy at a low rent) is not satisfied. Section 24(1)(b) (agricultural worker condition) will also now be satisfied.

3 See Sch 1, para 6 (letting of land exceeding two acres with dwelling house) and (letting of dwelling house occupied by person controlling farming of agricultural holding).

4 This conclusion follows inevitably from the interaction of s 24(2)(a) and s 24(1).

5 R(A)A 1976, Sch 2, para 2.

6 see below para 8.60 ff.

THE AGRICULTURAL WORKER CONDITION

[8.36] This definition has two functions:

(1) It limits the scope of protection by defining those agricultural employees on whom an assured agricultural occupancy is conferred.

(2) It triggers the distinctive security of tenure provisions applicable to agricultural occupancies, as opposed to other forms of assured tenancy.

[8.37] If at any time the agricultural worker condition ceases to be fulfilled, the tenancy will cease to be an assured agricultural occupancy[1]. It then becomes a normal assured tenancy, and the special security of tenure provisions requisite to agricultural occupation cease to apply – in particular Ground 16 becomes available giving the landlord a discretionary ground for possession upon cessation of the occupier's employment (as to which see below).

1 HA 1988, s 24(1)(a) – 'the agricultural worker condition is for *the time being* fulfilled etc' [author's italics].

'Agricultural worker' – the statutory definition

[8.38] By virtue of the HA 1988, Sch 3, para 2, two requirements must be met before the condition is satisfied:

(1) *The landlord condition.* The dwelling house must be, or have been, in 'qualifying ownership' at any time during the subsistence of the tenancy or licence. 'Qualifying ownership' is defined by reference to the R(A)A 1976, Sch 3, para 3 which requires that the occupier must be employed in agriculture, and his employer must be either the owner of the dwelling house or someone who has made arrangements with the owner for it to be used to house agricultural workers.
(2) *The occupier condition.* The occupier (or one out of joint occupants) must be a 'qualifying worker', or have been a qualifying worker at any time during the subsistence of the licence or tenancy. An occupier is a qualifying worker for these purposes if, at the relevant time, he has worked the whole time in agriculture, or has worked in agriculture as a permit worker for not less than 91 out of the past 104 weeks[1]. Alternatively, the occupier must be incapable of whole time work in agriculture, or of permit work, by reason of a qualifying injury or disease suffered in the course of his agricultural employment with the landlord (see the R(A)A 1976, Sch 2, para 2).

1 R(A)A 1976, Sch 3, para 1.

Extension to qualifying spouses and members of occupier's family

[8.39] Where a qualifying worker has died, the agricultural worker condition is deemed to be satisfied if the occupier is either the 'qualifying widow or widower' of the previous occupier, or is a 'qualifying member of that previous occupier's family'[1]. A widow or widower qualifies under this provision if he or she was residing with the previous occupier in the dwelling house immediately before his or her death[2]. In the case of other members of his family, they qualify only if there was at the occupier's death no qualifying widow or widower, and the member of the family concerned was residing in the dwelling house with the occupier at the time of, and for two years before, his or her death[3]. If there is more than one member of the occupier's family who qualifies, then in default of agreement, that member of the deceased's family who the county court so decides shall be the qualifying occupier for the purposes of the Act[4]. For these purposes, someone living with the deceased occupier 'as' his or her husband or wife is deemed to be his or her spouse.

1 HA 1988, Sch 3, para 3(1).
2 Ibid, para 3(2).
3 Ibid, para 3(3).
4 Ibid, paras 3 and 4.

[8.40] One succession to an assured agricultural occupancy is, therefore, possible, subject to the same conditions as apply to succession to protected occupancies under the R(A)A 1976 (as amended) where the occupier dies after the commencement of the HA 1988[1]. The spouse succeeding to an assured occupancy granted after commencement will have only an assured tenancy, however, whereas a protected or statutory tenancy by succession is available if the occupancy was originally granted pre-commencement.

1 See para 8.27 ff above.

Substitutionary licences or tenancies

[8.41] The agricultural worker condition is satisfied, and the occupier protected, if the tenancy or licence which he currently enjoys was granted in consideration of his giving up possession of another dwelling house in respect of which, at the time of surrender, the condition was satisfied[1]. In other words, the occupier who vacates voluntarily to enable his employer to re-let to, eg, a replacement employee, does not thereby lose his assured occupancy status. Similarly, the latter is preserved where there is a surrender and re-grant of a licence or tenancy in relation to the same dwelling, thus protecting the occupier's status, even though the agricultural worker condition is not satisfied at the time of the re-grant[2].

1 HA 1988, Sch 3, para 4.
2 Ibid, para 5.

Cessation of agricultural worker condition

[8.42] It will be noted that the assured agricultural occupancy will continue only if the agricultural worker condition is *for the time being* fulfilled with respect to the dwelling house[1]. It is envisaged, clearly, that the condition can *cease* to be satisfied, in which event the distinctive protection of the assured agricultural occupancy provisions will cease to apply. In that event, also, the landlord would cease to have the benefit of the local authority's obligation to consider rehousing agricultural employees[2]. In this respect the assured agricultural occupancy provisions differ from the parallel provisions of the R(A)A 1976, which make no provision for the cessation of 'protected' agricultural occupancy status if the occupier ceases to be a qualifying worker[3].

1 HA 1988, s 24(1)(b). See also s 25(1)(a) ibid.
2 R(A)A 1976, s 27, discussed below para 8.60 ff.
3 See s 2(1)(a) and (b) ibid.

[8.43] Interpretation of the provisions providing for cessation of the agricultural worker condition is not without difficulty. It might be thought that the condition ceases to be satisfied upon an employee retiring, or ceasing to be employed in agriculture for upwards of 13 weeks, or on moving to part-time work. This is not, however, the case. By virtue of the HA 1988, Sch 3, para 2(b), the agricultural worker condition is satisfied if the occupier has been a qualifying worker *at any time* during the subsistence of the tenancy or licence. Once the occupier has satisfied the condition by completing 91 weeks' work in agriculture out of the last 104 he will remain protected – even if he retires, moves to part-time work or is dismissed. Once the condition is satisfied, the assured agricultural occupancy effectively acts in rem, and binds the dwelling irrespective of the personal employment status, thereafter, of the occupier[1]. In this respect the HA 1988 follows the same policy as that of the R(A)A 1976.

1 HA 1988, s 5(2).

[8.44] The agricultural worker condition will cease to be satisfied, as envisaged by the HA 1988, only in very limited circumstances. These arise from the distinctive nature of the assured occupancy as a variant of the fully assured tenancy. By virtue of the HA 1988, s 5 a periodic assured tenancy cannot be brought to an end without a court order and, furthermore, on termination of a fixed-term assured tenancy a statutory periodic tenancy arises. By virtue of s 5(3)(a) the latter takes effect in possession, immediately on the coming to an end of the fixed-term tenancy. It is not merely a right in personam, as is the statutory tenancy under the RA 1977 or the R(A)A 1976. Being an interest in possession the statutory tenancy can be assigned or devised by will, and can pass on intestacy. The HA 1988 implies an absolute covenant against assignment in all periodic lettings of residential accommodation, but not where a fixed-term assured tenancy is granted. It follows that the agricultural worker condition could *cease* to be satisfied if a fixed-term tenancy of tied agricultural accommodation were assigned to a non-qualifying worker, or any other person not satisfying the requirement of 91 weeks' work in agriculture. Similarly, it could cease to be satisfied if, on the tenant's death, the tenancy was vested in a third party (other than a spouse with succession rights) and the latter was a non-qualifying person.

[8.45] Where a periodic assured tenancy devolves under the will or intestacy of the former tenant, the 1988 Act gives the landlord a mandatory ground for possession, providing proceedings are begun not less than 12 months after the tenant's death[1]. Cessation of the agricultural worker condition will be of most importance, then, where a fixed-term tenancy has been granted to an agricultural employee and is subsequently assigned, devised by will, or passed on insolvency, to a non-qualifying occupant. It might be noted that a similar result was achieved by the R(A)A 1976, but by different means. The R(A)A 1976, s 4 conferred on the occupier a statutory tenancy, following termination of his licence or tenancy, but this was a personal right which continued only if and so long as he (the occupier) occupied the dwelling house 'as his residence'. On his ceasing to do so, the statutory tenancy ceases automatically. The inclusion of provisions in the HA 1988 cesser of the assured agricultural occupancy is a necessary consequence of the nature of the assured tenancy as an interest in rem.

1 See Sch 2, Ground 7 ibid.

Cesser of agricultural worker condition: effects

[8.46] As we have seen, an assured agricultural occupancy can be either:

(a) an assured tenancy;
(b) a tenancy which would be assured if not let (for instance) at a low rent; or
(c) a licence giving exclusive possession.

By virtue of s 24(3) assured agricultural occupancies which are *not* assured tenancies, (ie (b) and (c) above) are to be treated as assured tenancies. It follows that if a tenancy at a low rent, or a licence, ceases to be an assured agricultural occupancy, for instance due to cesser of the agricultural worker condition, the deeming provision in s 24(3) will cease to apply. Where an agricultural employee has a tenancy at a low rent or a licence, therefore, cesser of the agricultural worker condition will entitle the landlord to repossess following notice to quit, unhampered by the restrictions on possession in the HA 1988. If the tenancy was an assured tenancy, the rent payable being above the rateable value or rent thresholds, the HA 1988 will continue to apply. In this event, however, Sch 2, Ground 16 will become available to the landlord (in addition to the other grounds for possession) and will give a discretionary ground for possession on the basis that the dwelling house was let in consequence of the tenant's employment, which latter has now ceased. If a fixed-term occupancy has been assigned in breach of a covenant against assignment or underletting, the landlord will also be able to invoke Ground 12, breach of obligation other than as to rent.

SECURITY OF TENURE AND RENT CONTROL

[8.47] As we have seen, the assured agricultural occupancy is a variant of the assured tenancy provided for in the HA 1988, Pt I. The general provisions applicable to assured tenancies apply, also, to assured agricultural occupancies. Protection is assured for agricultural occupants by conferring on the occupier a statutory periodic tenancy, but varying its terms and the grounds for possession to confer special protection.

Statutory periodic tenancy

[8.48] On termination of the original licence[1] or tenancy, a 'statutory periodic tenancy' arises[2]. By virtue of the HA 1988, s 5(3) this takes effect in possession immediately on the coming to an end of the former tenancy, and subject to the same terms as those of the former tenancy. If the occupancy was pursuant to a periodic tenancy, rather than a fixed-term, the tenancy cannot be brought to an end by the landlord except by obtaining a court order[3].

1 A license that constitutes an assured agricultural occupancy is deemed to be an assured tenancy for the purposes of the HA 1988, Pt I.

2 HA 1988, s 5(2). The statutory periodic tenancy will not arise if the tenancy was ended by a court order or a surrender.

3 Ibid, s 5(1).

[8.49] Prima facie, if the former tenancy was a fixed-term the periods of tenancy will be the same as those for which rent was last payable[1]. Clearly, however, no rent will have been payable under many agricultural occupancies. The HA 1988[2] therefore provides that, in this event, the periods of tenancy shall be monthly, beginning on the day following the expiry or termination of the licence or tenancy. It is an implied term of every *periodic* assured tenancy that, except with the landlord's consent, the tenant will not assign the tenancy, or sublet, or part with possession of the whole or part of the dwelling[3]. This will be implied in all statutory periodic tenancies, but will not be implied into a fixed-term, or where a premium is paid on grant. It is not an incident of the implied covenant that the landlord has to establish the reasonableness of any refusal of consent to assign etc[4]. There is also an implied term in every assured tenancy that the tenant shall afford access to the landlord, and all reasonable facilities, for executing repairs[5].

1 Ibid, s 5(3)(d).
2 Ibid, s 25(1).
3 Ibid, s 15(1)(3).
4 Ibid, s 15(2), ie Landlord and Tenant Act 1927, s 19 does not apply.
5 Ibid, s 16.

Control of rent

[8.50] One of the characteristics of 'assured' occupancies, when compared with 'protected' occupancies under the R(A)A 1976, is the absence of rent control on fair rent principles. The HA 1988 places no restriction on the rent which may be agreed between the parties at the outset. Section 13 provides, however, a procedure by which proposed rent *increases* can be controlled once a statutory periodic tenancy has arisen, or where a periodic tenancy itself has no rent review clause. The rent control provisions have no application in the case of a fixed-term[1].

1 It follows that the parties can, in effect, contract out of the rent control provisions of the HA 1988 by making their own provision for rent review in the tenancy agreement: see Chapter 3, para 3.103 ff above.

[8.51] To obtain an increase in rent, the landlord must serve a notice of increase, to take effect at the beginning of a new period of tenancy[1]. The latter must be a date not earlier than the first anniversary of the commencement of the tenancy, except where a statutory periodic tenancy has arisen on determination of a fixed-term[2]. There is also a requirement that notice of increase be of at least the 'minimum period' prescribed by the Act – six months in the case of a yearly tenancy, one month in the case of a tenancy of less than a month, and the period of tenancy in any other case[3]. The proposed date for rent increase must also be not less than 12 months from the date on which the last increase of rent took effect[4]. The tenant can refer a proposed rent increase to the Rent Assessment Committee for adjudication at any time before it comes into effect[5]. In default of reference, the rent proposed takes effect on the date proposed in the landlord's notice of increase[6]. The rent review provisions are considered in more detail in Chapter 3, para 3.102 ff above, to which reference should be made.

1 HA 1988, s 13(2). The notice must be in prescribed form, for which see the Assured Tenancies and Agricultural Occupancies (Forms) Regulations 1997, SI 1997/104 (Appendix, below).
2 Ibid, s 13(2)(b).
3 Ibid, s 13(3).
4 Ibid, s 13(1)(c).
5 Notice in prescribed form, referring the matter to the Rent Assessment Committee, must be served on the landlord: s 13(4), ibid. For the prescribed form see SI 1997/104, Form 5.
6 Ibid, s 13(4).

[8.52] It should be appreciated that the rent control procedure applies only where the landlord seeks an increase – it is not open to the tenant to seek a *reduction* in rent, unless the landlord has served a notice of increase. In many cases, an assured agricultural occupant will have paid no rent during his period of employment. The HA 1988 enables the landlord to increase the rent to a free market level by notice of increase. There are, moreover, no provisions for the phasing of rent increases analogous to those previously available under the R(A)A 1976. The only saving provision is s 14(7), which enables the committee to delay implementation of a rent increase, following adjudication, where it would cause 'undue hardship' if it came into effect on the date proposed in the landlord's notice of increase.

Grounds for possession[1]

[8.53] By virtue of s 7(1), the court cannot grant an order for possession of a dwelling house let on an assured tenancy unless one or more of the grounds set out in Sch 2 are satisfied. All the grounds for possession in the HA 1988, Sch 2 apply, as to other assured tenancies, with the one important exception that Ground 16 (namely repossession on cesser of employment) does not apply (see s 25(2)). As the aim of the HA 1988 is to prevent arbitrary eviction of agricultural workers from tied cottages upon termination of employment, this exception is of the first importance. Most landlords will wish to seek possession after terminating the occupier's employment, and the availability of Ground 16 would thus remove any security of tenure whatsoever from tied accommodation. Note, however, that Ground 16 is excluded only while the agricultural occupancy lasts. If the agricultural worker condition ceases to be fulfilled, the statutory periodic tenancy ceases to be an 'assured agricultural occupancy'. At this point Ground 16 will come back in, enabling the landlord to claim that the dwelling was let to the occupant by virtue of his employment and that he has ceased to be so employed. Ground 16 is discretionary, it will be recalled, and not mandatory. Notice given to terminate employment, if given by a tenant under an assured agricultural occupancy, does not constitute notice to quit and his security is not thereby prejudiced (s 25(4)). An *actual* notice to quit, however, does have effect to terminate the occupancy (see s 25(5)). This provision preserves the tenant's right to terminate the occupancy voluntarily, in which event the security of tenure provisions are inapplicable. The normal common law requirements for a valid and effective notice to quit will apply.

1 See above Chapter 4 for a more detailed treatment of the security of tenure provisions applicable to assured tenancies.

E Assured shorthold tenancies

SHORTHOLDS AND TIED COTTAGE LEGISLATION

[8.54] Many farm cottages will be let on assured shorthold tenancies. Shortholds are commonly used where cottages are let to farm workers who would otherwise qualify for an assured agricultural occupancy under the HA 1988. The two codes are mutually exclusive. If a tenancy or licence is an assured shorthold tenancy, it cannot be an assured agricultural occupancy within the meaning of the HA 1988, s 24. It will not, therefore , be within the tied cottage provisions discussed above, but will be subject to the separate code for shortholds set out in the HA 1988, Pt I, Ch II.

[8.55] The interaction of the assured shorthold provisions with the tied cottage legislation gives rise to several anomalies which are potentially problematic. As we have seen[1] in the case of assured shortholds granted before the Housing Act 1996 (HA 1996) came into force (ie before 28 February 1997) three qualifying conditions had to be satisfied[2]:

(1) The tenancy must have been granted for a fixed-term certain of not less than six months.
(2) A notice in prescribed form, informing the tenant that the tenancy was a shorthold, must have been served before the tenancy was entered into[3].
(3) The tenancy must have been one in respect of which there is no power for the landlord to determine the tenancy at any time earlier than six months from the beginning of the tenancy.

1 See Chapter 5 above.
2 HA 1988, s 20(1).
3 For the prescribed form see SI 1988/2203.

[8.56] A tenancy granted in circumstances where any of these conditions was not met would not be an assured shorthold – in this case it would either be a fully assured tenancy or, if the agricultural worker condition were met, it might be an assured agricultural occupancy. Despite the relatively straightforward nature of these requirements, they nevertheless proved potent to trap the unwary landlord on numerous occasions. A landlord might fall foul of the letting rules in a number of ways; eg where no prescribed notice was served, where the notice was served but only after the creation of the tenancy, where a break clause was included which was operable during the first six months, or where the dates in the tenancy agreement and the prescribed notice were inaccurate and incompatible[1]. The backdating of a tenancy agreement could also cause difficulties, if less than six months were left unexpired at the date of grant[2]. The HA 1996 accordingly simplified the rules for granting shortholds on or after 28 February 1997[3].

1 *Panayi v Roberts* [1993] 2 EGLR 51.
2 See *Keen v Holland* [1984] 1 All ER 75. And, on the qualifying conditions pre-HA 1996 see Rodgers, *Private Sector Housing Law* (Butterworths, 1995) p 302 ff; Hill and Redmans *Law of Landlord and Tenant.*
3 See further Chapter 5, above.

GRANTING AN ASSURED SHORTHOLD TENANCY

General

[8.57] Any assured tenancy which is granted on or after 28 February 1996[1], or which comes into being on termination of a fixed-term assured shorthold granted on or after that date, will be an assured shorthold tenancy unless it falls within one of the exceptions set out in the HA 1988, Sch 2A. As a consequence, any residential tenancy at a rent above the qualifying threshold (more than £250 per annum outside London, or more than £1000 per annum in Greater London) will normally be an assured shorthold, whether periodic or fixed-term – unless the landlord gives notice at the time of grant that it is to be an assured tenancy, or the tenancy agreement contains a stipulation to that effect[2]. The tenancy does not have to be a fixed-term, and no prescribed shorthold notice need be given by the landlord. In the case of a periodic tenancy, the tenant is afforded limited protection in that the court cannot make a possession order to take effect earlier than 6 months from the beginning of the tenancy[3].

1 That is, the date on which HA 1996, s 96 came into force.
2 HA 1988, Sch 2A, paras 1 and 2 (inserted by HA 1996, Sch 7).
3 HA 1988, s 21(5), inserted by HA 1996, s 99.

[8.58] Where the letting is to an agricultural worker, however, special rules apply:

(1) The requirement to serve a prescribed shorthold notice on grant has been preserved (see below).
(2) Following relaxation of the rules by the HA 1996, it is now possible to grant an assured shorthold tenancy to a tenant who previously enjoyed a fully assured tenancy: the tenant must give notice prior to grant, stating that the tenancy is to be an assured shorthold[1]. This facility does not apply to agricultural occupancies, however. It follows that an existing assured agricultural occupancy cannot be replaced with a shorthold.
(3) Where there is an existing assured shorthold tenancy, the import of these special rules is that a landlord granting a second assured shorthold to an existing farm worker, who satisfies the agricultural worker condition, must serve a fresh shorthold notice prior to grant. If he does not, the second tenancy will be (or become, on completion of the agricultural worker condition) an assured agricultural occupancy with full security of tenure.

1 HA 1988, Sch 2A, para 7(1)(c) and 7(2).

Agricultural workers

[8.59] By virtue of the HA 1988, Sch 2A, para 9 an assured tenancy will *not* be an assured shorthold if it is one in the case of which the agricultural worker condition is *for the time being* fulfilled with respect to the dwelling house subject to the tenancy[1]. However, this does not apply if, before it was entered into, a notice in prescribed form stating that the tenancy is to be a shorthold tenancy, is served on the tenant by the person who is to be the landlord[2]. It follows that, if the proposed tenant is a farm worker who has completed 91 weeks work in agriculture out of the previous 104, and who therefore satisfies the agricultural worker condition, the landlord must serve a prescribed shorthold notice before commencement if the tenancy is to be an assured shorthold. However, it should be appreciated, when letting to farm worker tenants, that the agricultural worker condition might *become* satisfied at some point after the tenancy is created; eg on the tenant completing 91 weeks work in agriculture. At this point, if no shorthold notice has been given, the tenancy will cease to be an assured shorthold and become an assured tenancy or assured agricultural occupancy with, as a consequence, considerably greater security of tenure. It follows that, when letting to farm workers, the landlord will be well advised to serve a prescribed shorthold notice on grant. This will prevent the tenancy later ceasing to be a shorthold, and becoming an assured agricultural occupancy, if and when the tenant subsequently satisfies the agricultural worker condition for tied cottage protection. If the landlord serves the shorthold notice, the tenancy will remain an assured shorthold by virtue of the HA 1988, Sch 2A, para 9(2). Different considerations apply, of course, when letting farm cottage accommodation to non-farm workers.

1 For the agricultural worker condition see above para 8.36 ff.
2 HA 1988, Sch 2A, para 9(2).

F Rehousing former agricultural workers

[8.60] It would clearly be contrary to the needs of efficient agricultural production if property needed to house essential workers were rendered indefinitely unavailable to an agricultural employer, and the protection of former employees extended indefinitely. Of the grounds for possession, the availability of suitable alternative accommodation will be of particular importance to agricultural employers, enabling the relocation of former employees in alternative accommodation and the freeing of formerly tied accommodation for letting to essential workers. The suitability of alternative accommodation is assessed for assured agricultural occupancies in the same manner as with other assured tenancies, namely in accordance with the HA 1988, Sch 2, Pt III. The availability of alternative accommodation also furnishes one of the principal grounds for possession under the R(A)A 1976[1]. The security of the 'assured' agricultural occupier under the HA 1988 is, in this respect, broadly similar, as this ground for possession remains discretionary.

1 R(A)A 1976, Sch 4, Cases 1 and 2, above para 8.22 ff.

[8.61] The agricultural occupancy provisions differ markedly from the regime applicable to other residential lettings, in that they enable an estate owner who is himself unable to provide accommodation to make application to the housing authorities, and to compel the latter to consider making accommodation available. This is, apparently, another facet of the underlying legislative policy of promoting the efficient organisation of agriculture[1].

1 See *R v Agricultural Dwelling House Advisory Committee for Bedfordshire, Cambridgeshire and Northamptonshire, ex p Brough* (1986) 282 EG 1542, 1545 per Hodgson J.

[8.62] R(A)A 1976, s 27 enables a landlord to apply to the relevant housing authority on the ground that vacant possession is, or will be, needed of a dwelling house which is subject to either a protected or assured occupancy, in order to house a person who is, or is to be, employed by the landlord in agriculture. The latter must establish that he is himself unable to provide, by any reasonable means, suitable alternative accommodation himself, and that its provision by the authority would be 'in the interests of efficient agriculture' (the key concept).

[8.63] In assessing the merits of the application, and in particular the requirements of efficient agriculture, the authority can obtain advice from the Agricultural Dwelling House Advisory Committee for the area concerned. The latter are constituted under the R(A)A 1976, s 29 specifically for this purpose, and are established in the area of each Agricultural Wages Committee. The committee must tender its advice in writing making copies available to both landlord and tenant[1]. Although its ruling is advisory only, and not binding on the authority, it can be quashed by certiorari if insufficient or inadequate reasons are given. The committee's rulings are influential and invariably followed by housing authorities, and can therefore lead directly to a later decision adverse to the parties' rights. For this reason they can be subjected to judicial review[2]. If the housing authority is satisfied that the landlord's case is made out, it has a statutory duty to use its 'best endeavours' to provide suitable alternative accommodation[3]. When assessing the priority of the landlord's claim on its resources, the authority must give account to the urgency of the case, the competing claims on the accommodation which they can provide and the resources at their disposal. They must, moreover, treat an ex-employee as an applicant in a special category, and not simply by reference to a 'priority needs category' established under the HA 1985[4].

1 R(A)A 1976, s 28(4).
2 See *R v Agricultural Dwelling House Advisory Committee for Bedfordshire, Cambridgeshire and Northamptonshire, ex p Brough* (1986) 282 EG 1542.

3 R(A)A 1976, s 28(7).
4 See generally *R v East Hertfordshire District Council, ex p Dallhold Resources Management (UK) Pty Ltd* (1989) 22 HLR 77 (Pill J).

[8.64] The rehousing provisions of the R(A)A 1976 are applied to assured agricultural occupancies by the HA 1988, s 26. Coupled with the wider grounds for possession applicable to assured tenancies, this will further enhance the landlord's ability to repossess dwellings for re-letting to agricultural employees, where the occupancy was granted on or after 15 January 1989, and commensurately reduce the protection afforded to former employees.

G Availability of premises for tied lettings

[8.65] The effect of the security regime for assured tenancies and assured agricultural occupancies is to reinforce the subjection of the tenant's need for secure accommodation to the policy interest of encouraging the efficient organisation of agriculture. Where a dwelling has been let on an assured tenancy, it will be easier to repossess for occupation by other workers than was formerly the case. Where accommodation was let *prior* to the commencement of the HA 1988, its repossession may be more problematical. Two situations in particular merit attention.

[8.66] First, a landlord may have let accommodation to an agricultural employee before 15 January 1989, but at a full rent, thus precluding a protected agricultural occupancy arising. The R(A)A 1976, s 27(2) ensures that the landlord is in no less favourable a position providing that the rehousing provisions (above) apply in cases where a tenancy *would* constitute a protected occupancy, but does not, solely because granted at a market rent. This provision does not apply where other factors come in to prevent a protected occupancy arising; eg if the agricultural worker condition is not fully satisfied.

[8.67] Secondly, where a dwelling has been let with full Rent Act protection, its repossession for use in housing agricultural workers may be possible in two situations:

(1) The RA 1977, Sch 15, Case 16 gives a mandatory ground for possession when a house was at one time occupied by a worker employed in agriculture, but the present tenant (or her husband if a widow) is not and never has been employed by the landlord. Possession can be granted if the landlord proves the house is required for occupation by an agricultural employee. Case 16 can be used, however, only if the tenant was given, at the time of letting, notice in writing that possession might be recovered under this case. In *Fowler v Minchin*[1] the Court of Appeal interpreted this to mean that the notice given must state clearly that possession might be recovered under the provisions of the RA 1977. It must make it clear that a situation would obtain which would be compulsory as far as the tenant was concerned. A written agreement whereby the tenant undertook to vacate on 28 days' notice was therefore insufficient, amounting to no more than a voluntary undertaking to vacate by the tenant[2]. A copy of a certificate of fair rent obtained by the landlord for the dwelling will suffice, however, if it draws attention to Case 16 and the possibility of possession being required under that case[3].

(2) Case 18 further provides that where the prior occupier was responsible for farming a holding of which the dwelling formed part, and the present tenant has never been employed by the landlord in agriculture, possession can be obtained if the court is satisfied that the house is required for occupation by some person employed by the landlord in connection with agriculture; eg an agricultural employee. Written notice that possession might be sought under this case must, again, be given to the tenant at the time of letting.

1 (1987) 282 EG 1534.
2 For criticism see further Bridge (1988) Conv 457.
3 See *Springfield Investments Ltd v Bell* [1991] 1 EGLR 115 CA

[8.68] Provisions analogous to Cases 16 and 18 are not available under the assured tenancy code, and landlords envisaging a need to repossess to house employees will have to rely on the assured shorthold tenancy – the only drawback being that either a minimum let of six months will be required or (if a periodic tenancy is granted) that possession will be unavailable for the first six months of the tenancy[1].

1 See generally Chapter 5, above.

CHAPTER 9

Public sector secure tenancies

A Introduction

BACKGROUND

[9.1] Most private sector tenancies have been regulated by statute, in different ways, since the early years of the twentieth century. However, it was not until the passage of the Housing Act 1980 (HA 1980) that statutory protection was conferred upon public sector tenants. The HA 1980 introduced a 'tenant's charter' which conferred rights to security of tenure on public sector tenants holding 'secure' tenancies of certain categories of public sector body – principally local housing authorities and new town corporations. Although the HA 1980 will mainly be remembered for the introduction of the 'right to buy' provisions for public sector tenants, the Tenant's Charter also conferred on those who opted to stay in the public rented sector extensive statutory rights and full security of tenure, including the right to exchange tenancies, to carry out improvements and to take lodgers. The statutory code for public sector tenancies is now contained in the Housing Act 1985 (HA 1985), Pt IV, which has been successively amended, most notably by the Housing Act 1988 (HA 1988) and the Housing Act 1996 (HA 1996).

SCOPE OF PUBLIC SECTOR PROTECTION

[9.2] The protection of the HA 1985 applies where the tenancy is granted by a 'public sector landlord' (ie a local authority, new town corporation or urban development corporation, or a housing action trust). The definition of 'public sector landlord' is considered further below. The position of tenants of registered social landlords is more difficult to classify. Before the passage of the HA 1988, all tenancies granted by registered social landlords were 'secure' tenancies for the purposes of the security of tenure provisions under the HA 1985. Additionally the Rent Act 1977 (RA 1977), Pt VI applied the fair rent system to housing association tenancies ie tenancies where the interest of the landlord belonged to a housing association or trust or the housing corporation and the tenancy would be a protected tenancy but for that fact[1]. However, as a result of policies enacted by the HA 1988, Pt I the legal status of all tenancies granted by registered social landlords on or after 15 January 1989 was fundamentally changed. Any tenancy granted by a housing association or other registered social landlord on or after 15 January 1989 cannot be a 'housing association tenancy' within the RA 1977, Pt VI[2], neither can it be a secure tenancy[3]. All lettings by registered social landlords after the commencement of the HA 1988, Pt I will be assured tenancies (providing that they qualify as such) with freedom from rent control – although market rents will not, in most cases, be appropriate in practice. Saving provisions identical to those for protected Rent Act tenancies (see Chapter 5 above) preserve the secure tenancy status of tenancies granted by registered social landlords prior to 15 January 1989; eg where there is a re-grant of the same or alternative accommodation by the same landlord, or where the court gives possession using the suitable alternative accommodation ground for possession under the HA 1985[4].

1 RA 1977, s 86(1) and (2).
2 HA 1988, s 35 (2).
3 HA 1988, s 35(4).
4 HA 1988, s 34(4).

[9.3] The HA 1988, s 35(4) limits public sector 'secure' tenancies to those to which the HA 1985 applies – to situations where the landlord's interest belongs to a local authority, new town corporation, urban development corporation or a housing action trust set up under the HA 1988, Pt III. Tenancies granted on or after 15 January 1989 can be 'secure' only if the landlord's interest belongs to one of these categories of body. Lettings by housing cooperatives[1] granted on or after 15 January 1989 remain 'secure', although housing association tenancies in general will now be on the assured tenancy basis. Housing association tenancies preserve the secure tenancy status for post-15 January 1989 tenancies in limited circumstances; eg a housing association tenant who accepts a new tenancy of alternative accommodation from the same landlord will hold a housing association tenancy, and not an assured tenancy, by virtue of the surrender and re-grant conditions. Such a tenancy will also remain 'secure' within the security of tenure provisions of the HA 1985. Both 'secure' and 'housing association tenancy' status will also be preserved where statutory succession takes place to a pre-existing housing association tenancy on or after 15 January 1989[2].

1 Within the meaning of the HA 1985, s 27B.
2 See further para 9.55 ff below.

[9.4] In general, tenancies granted on or after 15 January 1989 by a registered social landlord will be assured tenancies and not 'secure'. Tenancies granted by a registered social landlord before 15 January 1989 will be 'secure' tenancies within the HA 1985. Tenancies of a non-registered social landlord will, similarly, be assured tenancies within the HA 1988, Pt I, if granted on or after this date. If granted before 15 January 1989, they will normally be private sector protected tenancies within the RA 1977.

THE HOUSING ACT 1996

[9.5] The HA 1996, Pt V introduced provisions giving local housing authorities and other public sector landlords new powers to deal with anti-social behaviour by tenants and their families. Local authorities and housing action trusts can introduce introductory tenancies schemes under which new tenants do not acquire a secure tenancy for a period of 12 months from grant. During the 12-month 'trial period' the new tenant has no security of tenure and the other statutory rights of secure tenants (such as the right to exchange, carry out improvements or take lodgers) do not apply. The landlord can recover possession under a special procedure laid down in the HA 1996 if the new tenant proves unsatisfactory. The HA 1996 also introduced a new ground for possession for domestic violence, and broadened the existing grounds for possession for anti-social behaviour and nuisance to cover misbehaviour in the locality of the tenant's home and nuisance occasioned by visitors to the tenant's property. Public sector landlords were also given a new power to apply for an injunction to restrain breaches of the tenancy agreement and to prevent anti-social behaviour by public sector tenants.

B Introductory tenancies

INTRODUCTORY TENANCY REGIME

[9.6] The introductory tenancy provisions in the HA 1996, Pt V apply if (and only if) a local housing authority or a housing action trust has elected to operate an 'introductory tenancy regime'[1]. When such an election is in force, any new tenancy or licence[2] will remain introductory for a trial period, and will not become a fully secure tenancy until its expiration. The trial period is normally one year, during which time the tenancy remains an introductory tenancy. It becomes a secure tenancy at the end of the 12-month trial period, unless it has ceased to be an introductory tenancy before the end of the trial period. The HA 1996[3] stipulates four situations in which a tenancy can cease to be an introductory tenancy before the end of the trial period, namely:

(1) A tenancy will cease to be an introductory tenancy if the circumstances are such that the tenancy would not otherwise be a secure tenancy; eg because the tenant no longer occupies the dwelling as his home, or alternatively as his 'only or principal' home.
(2) It may cease to be an introductory tenancy if, before the end of the trial period, a person or body other than a local housing authority or housing action trust becomes the landlord under the tenancy. This might be the case where the local authority makes a large-scale voluntary transfer to a private landlord or registered social landlord and the property transferred includes a dwelling occupied by an introductory tenant.
(3) A tenancy will cease to be an introductory tenancy if the landlord decides to revoke its election to operate an introductory tenancy regime.
(4) The tenancy will cease to be an introductory tenancy if, before the end of the trial period, the tenant dies and there is no one qualified to succeed to the tenancy under the terms of the statutory succession scheme for secure tenancies[4].

1 HA 1996, s 124 (1).
2 Ibid, s 126 brings licences, as well as periodic tenancies, within the introductory tenancy regime.
3 Ibid, s 125(5).
4 As to which see para 9.55 ff below.

[9.7] The 12-month trial period runs from the date on which the tenancy was entered into, or (if later) the date on which the tenant was first entitled to possession under the tenancy, where the tenancy was granted by a local housing authority or housing action trust[1]. If the tenancy was adopted by the local housing authority or a housing action trust, the trial period runs from the date of adoption. In this case, where the tenant was formerly a tenant under another introductory tenancy (eg held of a different local authority) or held on an assured shorthold tenancy from a registered social landlord, the prior tenancy period will count towards the trial period provided it ended immediately before the date on which the latter commenced[2].

1 HA 1996, s 125(2).
2 Ibid, s 125(3).

[9.8] At the end of the trial period, unless previously terminated, the tenancy will become a fully secure tenancy. Not surprisingly, therefore, the terms on which the introductory tenancy is held resemble those for a fully secure tenancy. Where the introductory tenant dies during the trial period, a statutory succession is allowed by the tenant's spouse or another member of the tenant's family, subject to qualification requirements which parallel those for fully secure tenancies under the HA 1985[1]. Similarly, with limited exceptions (eg for assignments made in matrimonial proceedings under the Matrimonial Causes Act 1973 (MCA 1973), s 24 (Property Adjustment Orders) or under the Children Act 1989 (CA 1989, Sch 1), an introductory tenancy is not capable of being assigned[2]. Every local housing authority or housing action trust which lets dwelling houses under introductory tenancies must publish information about its introductory tenancies and supply the tenant with not only a copy of its published information concerning its introductory tenancies scheme, but also with a written statement of the terms of the tenancy in so far as they are not expressed in a written tenancy agreement nor implied by law[3]. The introductory tenant's rights to consultation on matters of housing management mirror those in the HA 1985, and the Secretary of State may, by regulation[4], extend the secure tenant's repair scheme to introductory tenancies[5].

1 HA 1996, ss 131–133.
2 Ibid, s 134.
3 Ibid, s 136.
4 That is, by regulation made under the HA 1985, s 96.
5 HA 1996, s 135.

TERMINATING AN INTRODUCTORY TENANCY

[9.9] Where the local authority finds the tenant to be unsuitable for the grant of a secure tenancy they can terminate the introductory tenancy before the end of the trial period. An introductory tenancy can only be brought to an end by the landlord obtaining an order for possession of the dwelling house from the court[1]. However, the landlord does not have to prove that a ground for possession exists; neither does it have to prove that it is acting reasonably in seeking possession. The only requirement is that the landlord complies with a special written notice procedure provided for in the HA 1996, s 128. This provides that the court cannot entertain proceedings for the possession of a dwelling house let under an introductory tenancy unless the landlord has first served on the tenant a notice of proceedings informing him that the court will be asked to make an order for possession, and setting out the reasons for the landlord's decision to apply for a possession order. The notice must specify a date after which possession proceedings may be begun by the landlord, and this must be a date not earlier than a date on which the tenancy could be brought to an end by notice to quit (eg in the case of a weekly or monthly tenancy this will be a date at least four weeks from the date of service of the notice ending on a term date of the tenancy[2]).

1 HA 1996, s 127(1).
2 See the Protection from Eviction Act 1977, s 5.

[9.10] Although the court has no power to review the reasons for the landlord's decision to evict, the HA 1996 lays down a bespoke review procedure for introductory tenancies under which the tenant is entitled to ask the local authority to review its decision to evict[1]. The landlord's notice of proceedings must inform the tenant of his right to request a review of the landlord's decision and of the time within which any review must be requested. The tenant can request a review of the landlord's decision, provided his request is made within 14 days beginning on the day on which the notice of proceedings is served. If this is done the landlord must review its decision in accordance with procedures laid down in regulations made under the HA 1996[2]. The review must be carried out by somebody of sufficiently senior status other than the local authority officer who took the decision to evict, and the review must be carried out (and the tenant notified), before the date specified in the notice of proceedings as the date after which possession proceedings may be began. The tenant is entitled to be represented, although an oral hearing will only be held if the tenant seeks one. The compatibility of the review process with the Human Rights Act 1998 was considered in *McLellan v Bracknell Forest DC*[3]. It was here held that the possession regime for introductory tenancies did not infringe Art 6 of the European Convention on Human Rights (the due process requirement). The review process was not inherently unfair since the reviewing officer was in a position similar to that of a planning inspector deciding planning appeals, and the court considered the scope of the power to judicially review his decisions sufficient to satisfy the Convention right. The court stressed, however, that it should be the norm for the council to spell out how the review procedure was operated, its independence and the way the hearing was conducted. The court must also, on judicial review, be given the reason for taking the decision to continue with the eviction proceedings. While not inherently unfair and incompatible with Art 8, the review procedure must be operated in each case in a manner which is both reasonable and proportionate. A separate challenge under Art 8 (right to respect for one's home) also failed, in that the extent of the interference with the claimant's right was considered proportionate, and was relevant and corresponded to a pressing social need.

1 HA 1996, s 129.
2 See the Introductory Tenants (Review) Regulations 1997, SI 1997/72.
3 [2002] 1 All ER 899, CA.

[9.11] If the local authority's review upholds its previous decision to evict, the court cannot review the reasons for its decision in subsequent possession proceedings. In *Manchester CC v Cochrane*[1] the Court of Appeal ruled that the court must order possession if s 128 is satisfied, even where (as in this case) the tenant alleged a breach of natural justice in the way in which the council's review had been conducted. It has no power to review the council's decision. The local authority's decision is, however, subject to judicial review if there has been a breach of the relevant administrative law principles (eg the tenant alleges bias or the local authority has taken into account irrelevant factors in making its decision). In *Cochrane* the court indicated that, where it considered there was a reasonable prospect of the tenant successfully challenging the decision, it was entitled to adjourn the possession proceedings to enable the tenant to apply for judicial review. The court criticised the provisions in the HA 1996 for reviewing decisions to seek possession, comparing them unfavourably with the court's power to consider appeals on points of law arising from council reviews of decisions on homelessness[2], and suggested that the HA 1996 be amended to introduce a similar appeal on points of law for decisions to terminate introductory tenancies.

1 (1999) L&TR 190, CA.
2 HA 1996, s 204.

[9.12] The landlord may seek possession at any time during the introductory 12-month trial period. Provision is made for the case where possession proceedings are commenced before the end of the trial period, but where it expired before the proceedings are finally disposed of. In this event, the tenancy remains an introductory tenancy until it comes to an end on a date on which the tenant is to give up possession pursuant to an order of the court or the proceedings are otherwise finally determined[1].

1 HA 1996, s 130(2).

C Secure tenancies defined

[9.13] By virtue of the HA 1985, s 79(1) 'a tenancy under which a dwelling house is let as a separate dwelling is a secure tenancy at any time when the conditions described in ss 80 and 81 as the landlord condition and the tenant condition are satisfied'. It will be immediately apparent that the secure tenancy provisions envisage that a tenancy may move in or out of the protection of the HA 1985 if either the 'landlord condition' or 'tenant condition' ceases to be satisfied for the time being; eg if the landlord's reversion is transferred to a non-public body such that the landlord condition ceases to be satisfied, or if the tenant ceases to occupy the dwelling as his only or principal home such that the tenant condition ceases to be satisfied.

THE LANDLORD CONDITION

[9.14] This is concerned with the type of landlord holding the reversion out of which the tenancy has been granted. By virtue of the HA 1985, s 80 the landlord condition requires that the interest of the landlord belongs at all times to a local authority, a new town corporation, a housing action trust, an urban development corporation, the Development Board for Rural Wales, a housing trust which is a charity, or a housing cooperative to which the HA 1985 applies[1]. If a cooperative housing association ceases to be a registered social landlord, within the meaning of the HA 1985, its tenants will thereby become secure tenants and it must, within 21 days of ceasing to be a registered social landlord, notify its tenants accordingly[2]. Where there is more than one joint landlord, the landlord condition is satisfied if one out of two or more joint landlords comply with it[3].

1 HA 1985, s 80(1).
2 HA 1985, s 80(3).
3 See *R v Plymouth CC ex parte Freeman* (1987) 19 HLR 328.

THE TENANT CONDITION

[9.15] This requires that the tenant is an individual, and occupies the dwelling house as his 'only or principal home' or, where the tenancy is a joint tenancy, that each of the joint tenants is an individual and at least one of them occupies the dwelling house as his only or principal home[1]. It follows from the requirement that each tenant be an individual, that a company letting or a letting to joint tenants of whom one is a limited company or other corporate body, cannot be a secure tenancy, (cf the position in the private sector where the use of company lets is one means frequently used to avoid the creation of a fully assured or protected tenancy[2]). The requirement that secure tenancy status only extends to tenants occupying a 'dwelling house' as their only or principal 'home' mirrors that applied in the private sector by the RA 1977 and the HA 1988, and these expressions will in principle carry the same meaning in the present context[3]. Thus, if the tenant has only a bedroom, and carries out cooking and other attributes of daily living elsewhere (for instance in premises he owns or rents from a different landlord) the letting will not be of a 'dwelling house' and will not be a secure tenancy.

1 HA 1985, s 81.
2 See Chapter 3, para 3.61 ff above.
3 For a discussion of the extensive case law see Chapter 3, para 3.20 ff above. Note in particular the implications of *Uratemp Ventures Ltd v Collins* [2002] 1 All ER 46, HL.

[9.16] If any of the requirements of the tenant condition cease to be satisfied, the tenancy will thereupon cease to be 'secure'. Thus, if the tenant ceases to occupy the dwelling house as his only or principal home, the tenancy will cease to have secure status. The reference in s 81 to occupation as the tenant's 'principal' home removes the possibility of the tenant qualifying for secure tenancy status in two properties – the 'two homes' tenant problem familiar under the RA 1977[1]. A secure tenant will have to choose which of two potential homes he wishes to be protected and make it his principal home and residence. In this context it has been held that two houses can be occupied at the same time as a home since actual physical occupation is not necessary for a dwelling to be a person's 'home', and that the question as to which of 'two homes' qualifies as the person's principal home for these purposes is a question of fact for the County Court Judge[2]. 'Principal home' means more than simply 'principal residence', and all the facts; eg whether all of the daily attributes of normal living are carried out at the property, as well as the actual occupation of the respective properties (if more than one is at issue) will be relevant.

1 See *Hampstead Way Investments Ltd v Lewis-Weare* (1985) 1WLR 164.
2 See *Crawley BC v Sawyer* (1986) 20 HLR 98.

[9.17] If the tenant effectively abandons his occupation of the demised property as a home then the tenancy will cease to have secure status. Continuous occupation is not necessary, and it is clearly established that temporary absences will not jeopardise the tenancy's status. Where the tenant is no longer physically resident in premises he has to show an animus revertendi (an intention to return) together with sufficient corpus possessionis (a visible state of affairs such as the maintenance of furniture or a caretaker in which his intention to return finds expression). So, where a tenant abandons the premises permanently leaving no possessions indicative of an intention to return, following which the landlords peaceably re-enter, changing the locks, secure tenancy status will be lost[1]. But if the premises are maintained in a habitable state with furniture, the tenant maintaining an intention to return to use it as his principal home, then the security of the HA 1985 will not be lost[2]. Identical issues arise under the private sector protective provisions in the RA 1977 and the HA 1988, and reference should be made to the discussion of the extensive case law on abandonment in Chapter 3 above, para 3.64 ff. It follows from the terms of the tenancy condition (above) that a secure periodic tenancy is a personal right of occupation and therefore cannot be an asset forming part of the estate of a bankrupt tenant[3].

1 *R v London Borough of Croydon Council ex parte Toth* (1997) 20 HLR 576.
2 See *Duke v Porter* (1986) 2 EGLR 101, cf *Brickfield Properties Ltd v Hughes* (1987) 20 HLR 108.
3 See *City of London Corporation v Brown* (1989) 22 HLR 32.

PROTECTION OF LICENCES

[9.18] By virtue of the HA 1985, s 79 (3) the secure tenancy provisions apply in relation to a licence to occupy a dwelling house (whether or not granted for a consideration) in the same manner as they apply to a tenancy. The protection of the HA 1985 does not extend, however, to a licence granted as a 'temporary expedient' to a person who entered a dwelling house or any other land as a trespasser (whether or not before the grant of the licence, another licence to occupy that or another dwelling house had been granted to him)[1]. The extension of statutory protection to licences removes the importance (problematic under the Rent Acts) of the distinction between residential tenancies and licences. Nevertheless, s 79(3) has a narrow application. It does not abrogate the common law rules distinguishing tenancies and licences. The scope of this provision was considered by the House of Lords in *Westminster CC v Clarke*[2], a case concerning the occupation rights of a licensee of a bedsit in a local authority-owned hostel for homeless men with special needs. All occupants were required to sign a licence agreement, one of the terms of which empowered the local authority to require licensees to move from one bedsit to another, as the management needs of the hostel required. The House of Lords held that a licence can only be within s 79(3) if it confers exclusive possession of the premises on the occupant. The licence in this case did not, as managerial control was retained by the landlord who in the circumstances could at any time exercise his contractual right to require the licensee to move and occupy another part of the hostel.

1 See HA 1985, s 79(4).
2 [1992] 2 AC 288.

[9.19] Similarly, short-term arrangements under which the landlord retains rights of access to a dwelling that is scheduled for demolition or imminent reconstruction have also been held to lack the requisite exclusive possession to found a secure tenancy. This was the case in *Shepherds Bush Housing Association v Hat's Co-operative*[1] where short-term licences were granted by a property developer with a view to providing temporary accommodation before imminent redevelopment commenced, and in *Camden LBC v Shortlife Community Housing*[2] in similar circumstances. The House of Lords has held, in *London and Quadrant Housing Trust v Bruton*[3], that a secure tenancy can be created as between a licensee and subtenant occupying premises with exclusive possession, even if the licensee itself has no power to grant tenancies as between itself and the head landlord. In that case a subtenancy was found to have arisen in circumstances where the licensee had taken possession of the premises concerned under a licence, one of the terms of which expressly prohibited the grant of subtenancies to residential occupiers.

1 (1991) 24 HLR 176.
2 (1992) 25 HLR 330.
3 [2000] AC 406.

TRESPASSERS AND 'TOLERATED TRESPASSERS'

[9.20] Where the occupant entered the dwelling as a trespasser the court will be loath to imply the grant of a new tenancy with secure status unless on the facts it is clear that the landlord intended to do so; eg by demanding and accepting rent in circumstances which impute a clear intention to create a new tenancy. So in *Westminster CC v Basson*[1] no secure tenancy was held to have arisen in circumstances where the landlord made it clear to an unlawful occupant that she had to leave, and that any payments received by the council would be used as occupation charges only, despite the fact that the landlord had mistakenly issued a rent book[2].

1 (1990) 23 HLR 225.
2 Cf *Tower Hamlets LBC v Ayinde* (1994) 26 HLR 631 and *Southwark LBC v Logan* (1995) 29 HLR 40.

[9.21] In *Burrows v Brent LBC*[1] the House of Lords held that a secure tenant against whom a suspended possession order had been made became a 'tolerated trespasser' if allowed to remain in possession after the terms of the suspended order had been breached, thereby automatically bringing the tenancy to an end. The court will not impute to the landlord an intention to grant a secure tenancy or licence to a tenant against who a possession order has formerly been made, and which has come into effect on its terms being breached (for instance by failure to adhere to the repayment of rent arrears by instalments) even though he has been allowed to remain in possession by agreement. The secure tenancy effectively goes into 'limbo' while the occupant remains in possession as a tolerated trespasser, and can be revived if the possession order is subsequently discharged. This effectively creates a new category of occupation right with anomalous consequences[2]. While the secure tenancy is in limbo the tenant cannot enforce the repairing covenants in the tenancy agreement. If, however, the possession order is discharged, thereby retrospectively reviving the tenancy, the effect will be to retrospectively revive the landlord's repairing obligations during the limbo period, potentially rendering it liable in damages for breach of its repairing covenants[3]. On the other hand, until the possession order is executed, the tolerated trespasser is entitled to exclusive occupation vis-à-vis third parties and the landlord, and as such has a sufficient interest to bring proceedings for nuisance[4].

1 (1996) 29 HLR 167.
2 The tolerated trespasser concept has been criticised by the Law Commission, which has suggested its review and reform: *Reform of Housing Law: A Scoping Paper* (Law Commission, 2001).
3 See *Lambeth LBC v Hawa Rogers* (2000) L&TR 319, CA.
4 *Pemberton v Southwark LBC* [2000] 3 All ER 924.

TENANCIES THAT CANNOT BE 'SECURE'

[9.22] The HA 1985, Sch 1 lists a number of types of tenancy and/or licence that, even if the qualifying conditions are otherwise met, cannot be secure tenancies. If the tenancy is excluded from the HA 1985, Pt IV by these provisions the tenant cannot, as he is not a 'secure tenant', exercise the statutory right to buy, or any of the other statutory rights accruing to secure tenancies. The following are excluded from the HA 1985[1].

1 See HA 1985, s 79, Sch 1.

Long leases

[9.23] A tenancy cannot be a secure tenancy if it is a long tenancy, ie a tenancy granted for a term certain exceeding 21 years, whether or not it is (or may become) terminable before the end of the term by notice given by the tenant or by re-entry or forfeiture[1].

1 See HA 1995, s 115, Sch 1, para 1.

Introductory tenancies

[9.24] The tenancy cannot be a secure tenancy if it is an introductory tenancy granted under the provisions introduced in the HA 1996, and discussed above. Neither can a tenancy be 'secure' if it was originally an introductory tenancy granted by a local authority under an introductory tenancy scheme, but has ceased to be an introductory tenancy because the tenant has died and there is no qualifying successor or the tenant has ceased to occupy the dwelling house as his only or principal home.

Premises occupied in connection with employment

[9.25] A tenancy is not a secure tenancy if the tenant is an employee of the landlord, or of inter alia a local authority (other than the landlord), and his contract of employment requires him to occupy the dwelling house for the better performance of his duty. When property is let to an employee within this exception, it may be re-let within a period of three years. In this case, except where the landlord is a local housing authority, the new tenancy becomes a secure tenancy when the periods during which it is re-let aggregate more than three years in total[1].

1 HA 1985, Sch 1, para 2(4) and 2(4)A.

[9.26] The key requirement is for the contract of employment to require occupation of the dwelling as a term of employment. In *Hughes v Greenwich LBC*[1] the exception did not apply in circumstances where a schoolteacher lived in a property within the curtilage of the school and his contract of employment did not require occupation of the residence as a term of his employment. The court refused to imply a term into the agreement that the dwelling was let as a term of the contract of employment, in circumstances where its occupation was not necessary to the better performance of his employment duties. However, if the tenant's employment has ceased some time earlier and he has been allowed to remain in occupation of a dwelling (perhaps awaiting the availability of other tied accommodation with new employers) the court may conclude that the connection of his former employment with the letting has been severed. In these circumstances he may obtain a secure tenancy even though the tenancy, when it commenced, was not 'secure'[2]. It follows that the status of the tenancy is not irrevocably fixed as insecure on commencement, as circumstances may change during its duration rendering it secure at a later date.

1 (1994) 26 HLR 99.
2 See *Greenfield v Berkshire CC* (1996) 28 HLR 691.

Land acquired for development[1]

[9.27] A tenancy will not be a secure tenancy if the dwelling house concerned is on land that has been acquired for development, and it is used by the landlord pending development as temporary housing accommodation. This exception is intended to allow the use of land awaiting redevelopment for 'short-life' occupancy without creating a secure tenancy. Provided the land is originally acquired for the purposes of development there is no restriction on the length of time before re-development commences, during which the exception will apply[2]. The exception will not apply, however, where no development is pending, owing to the development proposals and an application for planning permission having been dismissed by the local planning authority[3]. The landlord acquiring the property for redevelopment need not be the same body as that which grants the tenancy of the dwelling house for the exception to apply[4].

1 HA 1985, Sch 1, para 3.
2 See *Attley v Cherwell DC* (1989) 21 HLR 613; ten-year fixed-term of dwelling on land intended for redevelopment held to be within the exception.
3 *Lillieshall Road Housing Co-operative Ltd v Brennan* (1991) 24 HLR 195.
4 *Hyde Housing Association Ltd v Harrison* (1991) 1 EGLR 51.

Accommodation for homeless persons[1]

[9.28] A local housing authority is under a statutory duty, under the HA 1996, Pt VII to ensure that housing accommodation is made available to a homeless family while it carries out its duty to review their homeless status, whether they have a priority need and whether they did or did not become intentionally homeless. This exception is intended to enable the local housing authority to grant short-term accommodation to homeless families to whom it potentially has a statutory duty to house, without creating a secure tenancy in the interim. Accordingly, a tenancy granted in pursuance of any function under the HA 1996, Pt VII (homelessness) is not a secure tenancy unless the local housing authority concerned have notified the tenant that the tenancy is to be regarded as a secure tenancy[2]. The local authority may enter into an arrangement with a private landlord or housing association to provide accommodation to homeless families pending a decision on their homelessness status. Where this is the case, and short-term accommodation is provided by a private landlord, a tenancy granted pursuant to the arrangement to a person specified by the local authority cannot be an assured tenancy until the expiry of a period of 12 months beginning with the date on which the applicant was notified of the local authority's decision on homelessness, or if there is a review of that decision within 12 months of the date on which he is notified of the decision on review or the appeal is finally determined[3]. The tenancy will become assured, however, if during the 12-month period the tenant is notified by the landlord (or in the case of joint landlords by at least one of them) that the tenancy is to be regarded as an assured shorthold tenancy or an assured tenancy. If the landlord is a registered social landlord, it cannot serve notice making the tenancy an assured tenancy other than an assured shorthold tenancy. In any other case, where a tenancy is granted pursuant to an arrangement with the local authority by a registered social landlord to a person specified by the authority, the tenancy must be an assured shorthold tenancy, and the landlord cannot convert it into an assured tenancy unless the accommodation is allocated to the tenant under the HA 1996, Pt VI[4].

1 HA 1985, Sch 1, para 4.
2 Ibid, Sch 1, para 4.
3 HA 1996, s 209(2).
4 Ibid, s 209(3).

Temporary accommodation for persons taking up employment[1]

[9.29] This exception is intended to facilitate the grant of temporary accommodation to persons taking up employment within a local authority district, without the risk of thereby creating a secure tenancy. The exception provides that a tenancy is not a secure tenancy if:

(a) the person to whom the tenancy was granted was not, immediately before the grant, resident in the local authority district in which the dwelling is situated;
(b) before the grant of the tenancy, the tenant obtained employment (or an offer of employment) in the district or its 'surrounding area'. By surrounding area in relation to a district is meant the area consisting of each local authority district that adjoins it[2]; and
(c) the tenancy was granted to the tenant to enable him to meet his need for temporary accommodation in the district or its surrounding area in order to work there, and to enable him to find permanent accommodation there.

1 HA 1985, Sch 1, para 5.
2 Ibid, Sch 1, para 5(2).

[9.30] The landlord must give written notice of the circumstances in which the exception applies and that in its opinion the proposed tenancy will fall within the exception. Where the landlord is a local housing authority, a tenancy granted within the exception will only become a secure tenancy if at any time the authority notifies the tenant that the tenancy is to be regarded henceforth as a secure tenancy. In all other cases, the tenancy will become a secure tenancy on the expiry of one year from the grant or on earlier notification by the landlord to the tenant that the tenancy is to be regarded as a secure tenancy[1].

1 See HA 1985, Sch 1, para 5(1A) and (1B).

Short-term arrangements

[9.31] This exception applies where a dwelling is leased to the landlord with vacant possession for use as temporary housing accommodation. A tenancy is not a secure tenancy in these circumstances if the terms on which it has been leased to the landlord enabled the lessor to obtain vacant possession from the landlord on the expiry of a specific period or when required by the lessor (for instance, pursuant to a break clause in the head lease) and the lessor is itself not a body capable of granting secure tenancies. For this exception to apply the landlord must have no interest in the dwelling house other than under the lease in question or as a mortgagee[1].

1 HA 1985, Sch 1, para 6.

Temporary accommodation during works[1]

[9.32] This exception is intended to ensure that where temporary accommodation is granted to an occupier, while work is being carried out to his own home, that he will not become a secure tenant of the temporary accommodation concerned. Accordingly, the HA 1985 specifies that a tenancy is not a secure tenancy if the dwelling house has been made available for occupation by the tenant (or a predecessor in title of his) while works are being carried out on the dwelling house that he previously occupied as his home. It is a pre-condition for the application of this exception, however, that the tenant or predecessor was not a secure tenant of the other dwelling house at the time he ceased to occupy it as his home.

1 HA 1985, Sch 1, para 7.

Agricultural holdings

[9.33] A tenancy will not be a secure tenancy if the dwelling house concerned is comprised in an agricultural holding and is occupied by the person responsible for the control of the farming of the holding, whether as tenant or servant or agent of the tenant concerned. Neither will it be a secure tenancy if the dwelling house is comprised in a holding held under a farm business tenancy and is occupied by the person responsible for the control or management of the holding. This exclusion is intended to ensure that agricultural holdings owned by public bodies, such as county council smallholdings, cannot be secure tenancies protected by the HA 1985. They will be entitled to the security of tenure and protective provisions provided in the Agricultural Holdings Act 1986 and (in the case of tenancies granted on or after 1 September 1995) by the Agricultural Tenancies Act 1995[1].

1 See further Muir Watt *Agricultural Holdings* (14th edn, 1998) Chapter 1 and Rodgers *Agricultural Law* (2nd edn, 1998) Chapters 3 and 6.

Licensed premises

[9.34] A tenancy will not be secure if the dwelling consists of or includes premises licensed for the sale of intoxicating liquor for consumption on the premises[1].

1 HA 1985, Sch 1, para 9.

Student lettings[1]

[9.35] A letting whereby a tenancy of a dwelling house is granted to a student is not a secure tenancy if it is granted for the purpose of enabling the tenant to attend the designated course at an educational establishment. Prior to the grant of the tenancy, the landlord must give the tenant written notice of the circumstances in which the exception applies and that in his opinion the proposed tenancy would fall within the exception. The notice must, furthermore, specify the educational establishment at which the person concerned proposes to attend. Except where the landlord is a local housing authority, a tenancy granted under this exception will become a secure tenancy at the end of a period of six months following the tenant ceasing to attend the designated course concerned, or in any other case at the end of a period of six months after the grant of a tenancy[2].

1 HA 1985, Sch 1, para 10.
2 Ibid, Sch 1, para 10(3).

Business tenancies

[9.36] A tenancy will not be a secure tenancy if it is a tenancy to which the Landlord and Tenant Act 1954 (LTA 1954), Pt II applies[1].

1 As to which see LTA 1954, s 23 and Haley M, *Statutory Regulation of Business Tenancies* (OUP, 1999) Chapter 1.

Alms houses

[9.37] This exception applies to licences granted by alms house charities[1]. Any licence granted by or on behalf of a charity which is authorised under its trusts to maintain the dwelling house as an alms house, and has no power under its trusts to grant a tenancy of a dwelling, cannot be a secure tenancy if the dwelling house is an alms house.

1 HA 1985, Sch 1, para 12.

D Benefits of secure tenancy status

RIGHTS OF SECURE TENANTS

[9.38] The HA 1985, Pt IV confers extensive rights on public sector 'secure' tenants. These include the right to have repairs carried out, to carry out improvements, to take in lodgers and to statutory succession by close family members of a deceased tenant. Perhaps the most important is the 'right to buy' conferred by the HA 1985, Pt V. The right to enfranchise represents an important extension of the residential security rights conferred on secure tenants by the HA 1985. It is therefore considered separately, alongside security of tenure, in Chapter 10 below.

IMPROVEMENTS

[9.39] By virtue of the HA 1985, s 97 it is a term of every secure tenancy that the tenant will not make any improvement without the written consent of the landlord. However, the HA 1985 effectively gives the tenant the qualified right to carry out improvements by regulating the terms on which the landlord's consent can be withheld. 'Improvements' are defined to include any alteration in or addition to a dwelling house, and includes any addition or alteration to the landlord's fixtures and fittings, any addition or alteration connected with the provision of services, the erection of a wireless or TV aerial and the carrying out of external decorating work[1]. The landlord's consent to improvements must not be unreasonably withheld, and if unreasonably withheld shall be treated as given[2]. It is for the landlord to show that a withholding of consent was reasonable, if any question arises that the landlord's consent has been unreasonably withheld[3]. If the landlord refuses consent, he must give the tenant a written statement of the reason why consent was refused[4]. If the tenant has applied in writing for consent to improvements, and if the landlord neither gives nor refuses consent within a reasonable time, the landlord's consent shall be taken to have been withheld[5]. The landlord's consent may be given subject to conditions, but here again if the conditions are alleged to be unreasonable, the onus is on the landlord to show that it was reasonable. Furthermore, if the tenant has made a written application for consent and the landlord's consent is subject to an unreasonable condition, consent shall be taken to have been unreasonably withheld[6]. However, if the landlord imposes a reasonable condition on the carrying out of improvements and the tenant subsequently fails to comply with it in the manner in which the improvements are carried out, this will be treated for the purposes of the HA 1985 as a breach by the tenant of the terms of his tenancy, and may provide grounds for possession proceedings under Sch 2, para 1[7].

1 See HA 1985, s 97(2).
2 Ibid, s 97(3).
3 See s 98(1).
4 Ibid, s 98(4).
5 See s 98(4)(b).
6 See s 99(2) and (3) ibid.
7 See s 99(4).

[9.40] Limited provision is made for compensation to be paid in respect of improvements to a former secure tenant or a qualifying successor to the tenancy, on the tenancy's later termination[1]. The compensation rights discussed here are only exercisable in respect of improvements where the work was begun not earlier than the commencement of the Leasehold Reform, Housing and Urban Development Act 1993 (LRHUDA 1993), s 122. Compensation is only payable if the landlord (or a predecessor in title of the landlord) has given written consent to the improvement or is to be treated as having given consent, and if at the time when the tenancy comes to an end the landlord is a local authority and the tenancy is, at that time, a secure tenancy within the meaning of the HA 1985[2]. The amount of compensation is prescribed by regulations made under the HA 1985, s 99A[3]. The statutory compensation scheme applies in addition to discretionary powers granted by the HA 1985, s 100 enabling public sector landlords to make discretionary payments to tenants who have improved their dwellings. The HA 1985 also contains provision requiring the landlord to disregard tenant's improvements when considering increases in the rent for a dwelling held under a secure tenancy[4].

1 HA 1985, s 99A, introduced by the LRHUDA 1993, s 122.
2 Ibid, s 99A(1).
3 See the Secure Tenants of Local Authorities (Compensation for Improvements) Regulations 1994, SI 1994/613.
4 HA 1985, s 101.

REPAIRS

[9.41] The Tenants' Charter gave secure tenants the right to carry out certain repairs and then to claim the costs involved from their landlord. The system which existed until 1993 was somewhat complex, and was replaced by new provisions introduced by the LRHUDA 1993, s 121. Under the new provisions, now contained in the HA 1985, s 96, regulations may be made entitling secure tenants of local housing authorities to have 'qualifying repairs' carried out at their landlord's expense. Under regulations made under these provisions[1], secure tenants of local housing authorities have the right to have certain specified repairs, principally urgent repairs of a structural nature, carried out following a tenant's notice. There is provision in the regulations for the tenant to require the landlord to arrange for the work to be done by a different contractor if the landlord is in default in having the work carried out expeditiously, and if the work is not carried out within a reasonable time there is provision for compensation to be paid to the tenant. The landlord has a right of set off if the tenant is in default; eg if the tenant owes rent arrears.

1 See the Secure Tenants of Local Housing Authorities (Right to Repair) Regulations 1994, SI 1994/133.

INFORMATION AND CONSULTATION RIGHTS

[9.42] The HA 1985, Pt IV contains a number of provisions giving public sector tenants consultation rights in matters of housing management. Every public sector body letting dwelling houses on secure tenancies must publish information about the terms of its tenancies, the application of the right to buy and of its statutory repairing obligations under the Landlord and Tenant Act 1985 (LTA 1985), ss 11–16[1]. The landlord must supply the tenant with a copy of the information for secure tenants published by it under these provisions, and with a written statement of the terms of the tenancy in so far as they are neither expressed in a written tenancy agreement nor implied by law. The tenant must be supplied with a written statement of the terms of the tenancy on its commencement, or as soon as practicable thereafter[2]. The HA 1985 also confers consultation rights on matters of 'housing management', requiring tenants to be informed of the landlord's proposals and enabling tenants to make their views known to the authority within a specified period. The consultation rights require the authority, before making any decision on the matter in question, to consider any representations made to it in accordance with the statutory consultation arrangements[3]. 'Housing management' is defined to include any matter which relates to the management, maintenance, improvement or demolition of dwelling houses let by the authority under secure tenancies, or the provision of services or amenities in connection with dwellings let on secure tenancies – but it excludes any question as to the rent payable or to charges for services or facilities provided by the authority[4]. If the local authority is proposing to transfer its housing stock to a private or independent sector landlord under a large-scale voluntary transfer, special consultation provisions apply under the HA 1985, s 106A. This requires the landlord to consult with tenants and give full information of the proposed transfer and its legal implications, eg in terms of changes in tenancy status and application of the 'preserved' right to buy in accordance with detailed provisions in the HA 1985, Sch 3A[5]. The transfer will require approval by the Secretary of State before it can be completed. The Secretary of State cannot give consent for a large-scale voluntary transfer if it appears to him that a majority of the tenants of the dwelling houses to which the application relates do not wish the disposal to proceed[6].

1 HA 1985, s 104(1).
2 Ibid, s 104(2).
3 Ibid, s 105.
4 Ibid, s 105(2).
5 Ibid, Sch 3A, para 2.
6 Ibid, Sch 3A, para 5.

[9.43] The HA 1985, ss 102 and 103 give secure tenants enhanced consultation rights where changes in the terms of the tenancy are proposed by the landlord, and supersede the common law rules in this regard. The terms of secure tenancy can only be varied in one of three ways:

(1) By agreement between the landlord and the tenant.
(2) Where the change relates to rent or service payments in accordance with a provision in the lease or tenancy agreement providing for such changes.
(3) In accordance with the statutory notice procedure for variation of periodic tenancies laid down by s 103.

[9.44] This provides that the terms of a periodic (but not, note, a fixed-term) secure tenancy can be varied by the landlord by a notice of variation served on the tenant. Before doing so, however, the landlord must serve on the tenant a preliminary notice informing him of the landlord's intention to give notice of variation, specifying the proposed variations and their effect, and inviting the tenant to comment on the proposed variation within a specified time. The time allowed must be considered by the landlord to be reasonable. The landlord must consider any comments made by the tenant before serving notice of variation. This procedure applies to facilitate variation of any terms of the tenancy except for a variation of the rent or service payments in respect of services, facilities or rates. These can only be varied in accordance with the terms of the tenancy or by agreement between the parties. In *Palmer v Sandwell Metropolitan Borough*[1], it was held that when a landlord served notice of a proposed increase in rent, the tenant not formally responding, the fact that the tenant continued living in the dwelling and paid the rent did not ipso facto imply his agreement to the variation in the terms of the tenancy.

1 (1987) 20 HLR 74.

ASSIGNMENT AND SUBLETTING

Bar on assignment and subletting

[9.45] A secure tenancy is not capable of being assigned, except in the limited situations discussed below[1]. A statutory bar on assignment applies to any periodic tenancy and to a fixed-term tenancy granted on or after 5 November 1982. In *Burton v Camden LBC*[2] a wide interpretation of the statutory bar was adopted, to the effect that an 'assignment' for this purpose includes a deed of release executed by one joint tenant, as a consequence of which the tenancy vests in the remaining occupant. The legal result there was to vest a tenancy previously held by A and B in A alone. The other way to achieve the same result would, of course, be for A and B to formally assign the tenancy to A. Both transactions would produce the same result in law, and therefore the execution of a deed of release was held to be caught by the statutory bar on assignments and therefore void. If a secure tenancy for a fixed-term, granted before 5 November 1982, is assigned other than in the circumstances allowed for by the exceptions discussed below, then it ceases to be a secure tenancy and cannot subsequently become a secure tenancy again[3].

1 1985 Act, s 91(1).
2 [2000] 32 HLR 625, HL.
3 See HA 1985, s 91(2).

[9.46] Where it applies, the statutory bar on assignment overrides the terms of the tenancy agreement and the rules providing for assignment by operation of law in certain circumstances; eg to prevent a periodic tenancy passing to the tenant's trustee in bankruptcy as part of his estate[1]. The three situations in which assignment is allowed are listed below.

1 See *City of London Corporation v Brown* (1990) 22 HLR 32.

Assignment by way of exchange

[9.47] Every secure tenant has the right, with the written consent of the landlord, to assign the tenancy to another secure tenant or to an assured tenant of a registered social landlord, by way of exchange[1]. The tenant must first obtain the landlord's written consent, but this may only be withheld on the grounds set out in the HA 1985, Sch 3. If consent is withheld by the landlord on any other ground, then consent is treated as being given[2]. The landlord cannot, furthermore, rely on any of the Sch 3 grounds for refusing consent unless he has, within 42 days from the tenant's application for consent, served a notice on the tenant specifying the ground and giving particulars of it[3].

1 See HA 1985, s 92(1).
2 See s 92(2) and (3) ibid.
3 Ibid, s 91(4).

[9.48] The grounds set out in Sch 3 on which a landlord can withhold consent are:

(1) Either the tenant or the proposed assignee is obliged to give up possession under an order of the court or will be so obliged at a date specified in a court order.
(2) Possession proceedings have begun against the tenant or proposed assignee, or notice of intended possession proceedings have been served on the tenant or

proposed assignee, under Sch 2, Pt I, Grounds 1–6[1]. These are the grounds for possession applicable where the court may order possession if it considers it reasonable on the facts, without the landlord having to establish that suitable alternative accommodation is available for the tenant; eg that rent lawfully due from the tenant has not been paid or that some other obligation of the tenancy has been broken (Ground 1), or that the condition of the dwelling house has deteriorated owing to the neglect, default or acts of waste of the tenant or other residents (Ground 3).

(3) The accommodation afforded by the dwelling house is substantially more extensive than is reasonably required by the proposed assignee.

(4) The extent of accommodation afforded by the dwelling house is not reasonably suitable to the needs of the proposed assignee and his family.

(5) The dwelling house in question forms part of or is within the curtilage of a building held by the landlord mainly for purposes other than housing, and the dwelling was let to the tenant (or a predecessor in title) because of his employment by the landlord, a local authority or other specified landlord[2].

(6) The landlord is a charity and the proposed assignee's occupation of the dwelling house would conflict with the charity's objects.

(7) Where the dwelling house is adapted to make it suitable for occupation by physically disabled persons, and the proposed exchange by way of assignment would result in it being occupied by someone who is not disabled.

(8) The landlord is a registered social landlord (ie a housing association or trust) which lets dwellings only for occupation by persons whose circumstances (other than merely financial circumstances) make it difficult for them to satisfy their need for housing, and the assignment would result in the dwelling being occupied by someone whose needs no longer fulfil this purpose.

(9) The dwelling house is one of a group of dwellings which it is the practice of the landlord to let for occupation by persons with special needs, and there are social services or special facilities provided in close proximity to the dwelling houses in order to assist persons with special needs, in circumstances where if the assignment were made there would no longer be a person with those special needs residing in the dwelling house.

(10) The dwelling house is the subject of a management agreement under which the manager is a housing association of which at least half the members are tenants of dwelling houses subject to the management agreement, at least half the tenants of the dwelling houses are members of the association and the proposed assignee is not, and is not willing to become, a member of the housing association.

1 As to which see Chapter 10, para 10.31 ff.

2 That is, a new town corporation housing action trust, the Development Board for Rural Wales, an urban development corporation or the governors of an aided school; see the HA 1985, Sch 3, Ground 5.

Property adjustment orders in connection with matrimonial proceedings

[9.49] The statutory bar prohibiting an express assignment does not apply to an assignment under the Matrimonial Causes Act 1973, s 24[1]. This exception also applies to property adjustment orders made after overseas divorce[2] and to assignments made under an order for financial relief against parents under the Children Act 1989[3]. As assignment to the secure tenant's spouse under these provisions will trigger the application of the statutory concession provisions of the HA 1985. A tenant to whom the tenancy is assigned pursuant to, for instance, a property adjustment order made under the MCA 1973 is only a successor if the other party to the marriage was a successor within the meaning of the HA 1985[4].

1 See HA 1985, s 91(3)(b).
2 See the Matrimonial and Family Proceedings Act 1984, s 17.
3 See CA 1989, Sch 1, para 1.
4 See HA 1985, s 88(2).

Assignment to a qualified successor

[9.50] The bar on assignment does not apply where the tenancy is assigned to somebody who would be qualified to succeed to the tenancy, if the tenant died immediately before the assignment[1]. In this situation the statutory succession provisions will be operated by the assignment, with the result that no further succession will be possible following the later death of the assignee or successor[2]. As we shall see, to qualify as a potential successor the successor or assignee must either be the tenant's spouse or, if he is another member of the tenant's family he must have resided with the tenant for a period of 12 months ending with the tenant's death. In the case of an assignment by way of exchange to a successor, the relevant qualifying period is the period of 12 months ending with the date of the assignment. For example, where a successor who was not married to the tenant claimed to have lived with him as his de facto wife, the period of 12 months required for qualifying residence as a member of the tenant's family was calculated backwards from the date of assignment[3]. The claimant here failed to qualify where, being the tenant's ex-wife, she had retained a secure tenancy of a different flat throughout the relevant period and had only intermittently cohabited with the secure tenant.

1 See HA 1985, s 91(3)C.
2 Ibid, s 88(1)(d) and below para 9.61 ff.
3 See *Westminster CC v Peart* (1991) 24 HLR 389.

Lodgers

[9.51] It is a term of every secure tenancy that the tenant can allow any person to reside as a lodger in the dwelling house[1]. A 'lodger' is a licensee who does not occupy any part of the premises with exclusive possession, in circumstances where the owner provides services that require him having access to that part of the premises[2].

1 See HA 1985, s 93(1).
2 See *Street v Mountford* [1985] AC 809 and Chapter 3, above.

Subletting

[9.52] A secure tenant cannot, without the landlord's written consent, sublet or part with possession of part of the dwelling house[1]. If, in breach of the statutory implied term against subletting, the tenant under a secure tenancy parts with possession of the dwelling house or sublets the whole of it (or sublets first part of it and then the remainder) the tenancy ceases to be a secure tenancy and cannot subsequently become a secure tenancy again[2]. In this event the statutory security of tenure afforded by the HA 1995, Pt IV will cease to apply, and the landlord can terminate the tenancy by taking the necessary steps to bring the contractual tenancy to an end; eg by serving notice to quit in the case of the periodic tenancy – provided, of course, that the basic provisions of the Protection from Eviction Act 1977 (PEA 1977) are complied with[3].

1 See HA 1985, s 93(1)(b).
2 See s 93(2) ibid.
3 See PEA 1977, s 5, above, Chapter 2.

[9.53] The landlord must not unreasonably refuse consent to sublet, and if consent is unreasonably withheld it is to be treated as having been given. The landlord's consent to subletting is regulated by provisions set out solely in the HA 1985 (the provisions of the Landlord and Tenant Act 1988 do not apply to secure tenancies)[1]. The landlord's consent shall not be unreasonably withheld, and if the question arises whether the withholding of consent was reasonable or not the onus is on the landlord to show that it was not unreasonable[2]. In deciding whether to give consent the landlord is entitled to consider whether giving consent to subletting would lead to overcrowding of the dwelling house, or the effect which any work which the landlord proposes to carry out to the dwelling house would have on the accommodation likely to be used by the subtenant who would reside there if the consent were granted. The landlord is not, however, entitled to impose conditions upon the grant of consent, and if consent purports to be given subject to a condition it is to be treated as given unconditionally[3]. If the tenant has made a written application for consent, then if the landlord refuses to give consent he must give the tenant a written statement of the reasons why consent has been refused. Furthermore, if a landlord neither gives nor refuses to give consent within a reasonable time, consent shall be taken to have been withheld[4].

1 See the Landlord and Tenant Act 1988, s 5(3).
2 See HA 1985, s 94(2).
3 Ibid, s 94(5).
4 Ibid, s 94(6).

[9.54] Where the landlord alleges that the tenant has sublet or parted with possession of the dwelling in breach of the statutory implied terms, it will not suffice to show that the tenant has ceased to occupy for intermittent periods, perhaps allowing someone else into occupation for part of the time. The landlord must show that the tenant has parted with possession in the permanent and legal sense required by the HA 1985, s 93 if he is to establish that the tenant has sublet the whole of the premises[1].

1 See *Hussey v Camden LBC* (1994) 27 HLR 5 and *Monmouth BC v Marlog* (1994) 27 HLR 30.

STATUTORY SUCCESSION

[9.55] The HA 1985 allows for one succession on the death of a secure tenant. Succession rights are limited to the secure tenant's spouse or another member of the tenant's family who resided with the deceased tenant. Where, as is common, the tenancy is vested in husband and wife as joint tenants, the death of one partner will result in the joint tenancy vesting by operation of law (the survivorship rule) in the remaining spouse. This counts as one succession under the terms of the HA 1985 precluding further succession under the HA 1985 to other family members, on the subsequent death of the surviving spouse.

Qualifying for succession

[9.56] A person is qualified to succeed to a secure tenancy if he (a) occupies the dwelling house as his 'only or principal home' at the time of the tenant's death and (b) is either the tenant's spouse, or another member of the tenant's family and has resided with the tenant throughout the period of 12 months ending with the tenant's death[1]. In either case the tenant must not himself be a 'successor' (see below para 9.61 ff).

1 See HA 1985, s 87.

[9.57] A potential successor may occupy two houses at the same time as a 'home', and the question which of two 'homes' qualifies as the person's 'principal' home for the purposes of the qualifying conditions for succession is a question of fact for the County Court Judge[1]. 'Principal home' means more than simply 'principal residence' and all the facts, as well as the actual occupation of the respective properties, will be relevant[2]. Where the deceased tenant is survived by a spouse, no qualifying period of residence is required and the tenant's spouse is to be preferred to any other member of the tenant's family who may potentially qualify[3]. If the deceased tenant is not survived by a qualifying spouse, but there are two or more other family members to whom succession rights accrue, then the preference is to be as agreed between them, or if there is no agreement amongst the potential successors, the successor is to be selected by the landlord[4]. The HA 1985 provides for succession by an individual person only, and not (for instance) by more than one potential successor as joint tenants.

1 See *Crawley BC v Sawyer* (1986) 20 HLR 98.
2 For further discussion see also the qualifying condition for assured tenancy status in the HA 1988, s 1(1) HA; above Chapter 3.
3 HA 1985, s 89(2).
4 Ibid, s 89(2)(b).

[9.58] Where succession rights are claimed by some other member of the tenant's family, the HA 1985 imposes a period of qualifying residence. In order to qualify to succeed to the tenancy, a non-spouse member of the tenant's family must have resided with the tenant throughout the period of 12 months ending with the tenant's death. In *Waltham Forest LBC v Thomas* [1] the Housing of Lords held that the successor must reside with the tenant for the requisite period of 12 months, but not necessarily in the same dwelling as that to which the succession is claimed. In *Waltham Forest* the secure tenant and his brother had rented the same premises for two-and-a-half years under a secure tenancy, and moved to a new property ten days before the tenant's death. The brother's claim to succeed to the secure tenancy of the latter was upheld as he had resided with the deceased tenant for considerably longer than the statutory residence period required by the HA 1985, even though that residence was in different dwellings. The residence rule for succession to a secure tenancy is, accordingly, more generous than the succession regime applied to Rent Act protected and statutory tenancies, where residence in the same dwelling for the whole of the qualifying period (in the case of a Rent Act tenancy for two years) is required[2]. A similar rule was applied to public sector secure tenancies prior to the *Waltham Forest* decision; see *South Northamptonshire DC v Power*[3]. This approach was overruled by the House of Lords in the *Waltham Forest* case, who adopted a more liberal interpretation of the HA 1985, s 87.

1 (1992) 24HLR 622.

2 RA 1977, Sch 4, para 1 as amended.
3 (1987) 1 WLR 1433.

[9.59] Where a family member, other than a spouse, wishes to succeed to the tenancy the burden of proof lies on the claimant to show that they are both a family member, that they lived with the deceased tenant for the required period of 12 months, and that the dwelling was their only principal home during this time[1]. A person is a member of the former tenant's 'family' for the purposes of the HA 1985 if he and the deceased tenant lived together 'as husband and wife', or if the would-be successor is the deceased tenant's parent, grandparent, child, grandchild, brother, sister, uncle, aunt, nephew or niece[2]. A stepchild is to be treated as a child of the deceased tenant for these purposes, and an illegitimate child as legitimate. Similarly relationships by marriage are to be treated as relationships by blood[3]. In the case of a would-be successor who is a cohabitee, not a spouse, the claimant will have to show not only that he or she lived with the deceased tenant for 12 months, but that throughout the 12-month qualifying period he did so 'as the deceased tenant's husband or wife'[4]. This can give rise to difficult questions of fact where the deceased tenant and would be successor had lived together for more than 12 months, but a de facto cohabitation in the fullest sense allegedly endured for only part of that period. It should be added that, under the parallel RA 1977 succession scheme, de facto relationships as now regarded as spousal, entitling the partner to take a statutory tenancy as a husband or wife without proof of the qualifying residence period. Non-married cohabitants are treated less generously under the HA 1985 for the purposes of succession to secure tenancies.

1 See *Peabody Donation Fund Governors v Grant* (1982) 6 HLR 41.
2 See HA 1985, s 113(1). In the case of children, the Court of Appeal held in *Kingston BC v Prince* (1999) 3 IHLR 794 that a 13-year-old child could succeed to a secure tenancy.
3 Ibid, s 113(2).
4 See *Westminster CC v Peart* (1991) 24 HLR 389.

[9.60] The requirement that cohabitants reside and live together 'as husband and wife' was construed in *Harrogate BC v Simpson*[1] to mean that a lesbian or homosexual co-resident cannot qualify as a member of the tenant's 'family', and cannot succeed to a secure tenancy. In *S v United Kingdom*[2] the European Court of Human Rights dismissed the surviving partner's claim that this was an infringement of her right to respect for her family life and home under the European Convention on Human Rights, Art 8. This gives rise to several anomalies in the respective treatment of same sex partners for succession purposes, particularly following the House of Lords ruling in *Fitzpatrick v Sterling Housing Association*[3] on the parallel provisions governing succession to private sector tenancies under the RA 1977. The House of Lords there ruled that same-sex partners cannot be construed as 'living together as husband or wife' but that a same-sex partner could qualify as a member of the tenant's wider 'family', entitling him or her to take an assured tenancy by succession under the amended RA 1977 provisions. In the case of a secure tenancy, however, a same-sex partner will never qualify for succession: following *Fitzpatrick* he or she cannot qualify as a de facto spouse, and thus as a member of the extended 'family' within the HA 1985 definition, and the HA 1985 defines the other categories of the deceased tenants 'family' in express terms which rule out extending it to same-sex relationships.

1 (1986) 2 FLR 91.
2 (1986) DR 274.
3 (2000) 32 HLR 178.

One succession only

[9.61] There is no right to succession if the deceased tenant was himself a successor. The HA 1985, s 88 provides that the tenant is himself a successor in the following circumstances:

(a) if the successor himself took succession to a periodic tenancy under the terms of the HA 1985 (ie under s 89); or
(b) the successor was a joint tenant and has become the sole tenant eg on the death of his or her spouse where the secure tenancy was originally held by both as a joint tenancy; or
(c) the tenancy was a periodic tenancy arising at the end of a term certain, by virtue of s 86, and the first tenancy (ie the fixed term) was granted to another person or jointly to the deceased tenant and another persons; or
(d) the tenant became a secure tenant on the tenancy being assigned to him.

[9.62] The principle that a tenant is himself a 'successor' if the secure tenancy was assigned to him is subject to two exceptions, and in these cases the right to succession is preserved for members of the deceased tenant's family. The first is where the tenancy was assigned by virtue of a property adjustment order made in divorce proceedings under the MCA 1973, s 24. In this case the tenant to whom the tenancy was assigned is to be treated as a successor only if, on the facts, the other party to the marriage was a successor. The other exception applies where the tenant took the secure tenancy as an assignee as a consequence of exercising his statutory right to exchange tenancies in accordance with the HA 1985, s 92[1]. In this case the deceased tenant is a successor only if he was a successor in relation to the tenancy that he himself assigned under the statutory right of exchange[2].

1 As to which see above para 9.47 ff.
2 HA 1985, s 88(3).

[9.63] The HA 1985 provides for an automatic succession by a qualifying successor following the tenant's death. The landlord may, however, grant a new secure tenancy to a potential successor outside the framework of the HA 1985 succession provisions, in which case the new tenancy will not count as one 'succession' and will itself carry succession rights under the HA 1985, Pt IV[1]. The HA 1985, s 88(4) does provide, however, that where within six months of the coming to an end of a secure periodic tenancy the tenant became a tenant under another secure periodic tenancy of the same dwelling house, or in the case of a different dwelling house one granted by the same landlord, then if the tenant was a successor in relation to the former tenancy he is also to be treated as a successor in relation to the latter tenancy – unless the tenancy agreement for the latter expressly provides otherwise. This is intended to ensure that a tenant who is himself a successor is to be treated as such even if granted a new tenancy of a different dwelling by the same landlord or of the same dwelling where the identity of the landlord changes. The grant of a new secure tenancy in these circumstances will not trigger the creation of additional succession rights accruing to the new tenancy.

1 See *Epping Forest DC v Pomphrett* (1990) 22 HLR 475 (no statutory succession where landlord agreed to grant a new secure tenancy to the deceased tenant's widow, and statutory succession rights exercisable on her later death to transmit the tenancy to another member of her family).

Devolution of secure tenancy

[9.64] Where the deceased tenant held a periodic tenancy, then where there is a person qualified to succeed the tenant the tenancy vests in that person automatically by virtue of the HA 1985, s 89. As noted above, if there is more than one person qualified to succeed, then preference is given to the tenant's spouse, and as between other family members preference is to be given in accordance with any agreement reached between them or (in default) as selected by the landlord. If there is no person qualified to succeed the tenant, the tenancy ceases to be a secure tenancy when it is vested or otherwise disposed of in the course of the administration of the tenant's estate[1]. There are exceptions where the vesting or disposal is made pursuant to a property adjustment order in matrimonial proceedings under the MCA 1973 or in accordance with an order made under the Matrimonial and Family Proceedings Act 1984 or the CA 1989, Sch 1. Having ceased to be a secure tenancy, the tenancy cannot subsequently become a secure tenancy again[2].

1 See HA 1985, s 89(3).
2 Ibid, s 89(4).

[9.65] Where the deceased held a fixed-term secure tenancy then the tenancy will remain a secure tenancy if the remainder of the fixed term becomes vested in a person qualifying to succeed to the tenant under the rules outlined above[1]. It will, however, cease to be a secure tenancy if it is vested or otherwise disposed of in the course of the administration of the tenant's estate to someone who is not entitled to succeed. A fixed-term tenancy that ceases to be a secure tenancy, in these circumstances, cannot subsequently become a secure tenancy[2]. Having ceased to be as secure tenancy the various statutory rights conferred on secure tenants by the HA 1985, Pt IV will cease to apply for the remainder of the fixed term.

1 HA 1985, s 90(3)(b).
2 Ibid, s 90(4).

CHAPTER 10

Secure tenancies: residential security and the right to buy

[10.1] The passage of the Housing Act 1980 (HA 1980) fundamentally altered the position of public sector tenants, by giving them rights to residential security similar to those enjoyed in the private sector, and extending to them the 'right to buy' ie the right to purchase the freehold on their homes and become owner-occupiers. These rights are now contained in the Housing Act 1985 (HA 1985), Pts IV and V.

A Security of tenure

[10.2] Under the HA 1985, Pt IV public sector secure tenants are given extensive security of tenure. The HA 1985 abrogates the common law methods of termination available to the landlord, replacing them with a statutory procedure to be followed if the landlord wishes to obtain possession in circumstances where the tenant is unwilling to voluntarily surrender possession. This involves the service of a statutorily prescribed notice warning the tenant that the landlord intends to seek possession, specifying the grounds for possession to be relied upon and giving particulars of the facts alleged to give rise to the right to possession. If the tenancy is periodic, it cannot be brought to an end by notice to quit, and in the case of a fixed-term tenancy the HA 1985 limits the effect of the exercise of any right of re-entry contained in the agreement[1].

1 HA 1985, s 86. See below para 10.4 ff.

PERIODIC TENANCIES

[10.3] A secure tenancy that is a weekly or other periodic tenancy cannot be brought to an end by the landlord except by obtaining an order for possession in the county court, and the tenancy terminates on the date specified in the order on which the tenant is to give up possession[1]. The court can only make an order for possession on one or more of the grounds specified in the HA 1985, Sch 2. These are considered below.

1 Ibid, s 82(1) and (2).

FIXED-TERM TENANCIES

[10.4] The rules for terminating fixed-term tenancies (rarely encountered in the public sector) are somewhat more complex. If the agreement contains a proviso for re-entry and forfeiture (eg for non-payment of rent for a specified period) the court cannot order possession in pursuance of that provision. However, where the court *would* have made such an order on the facts it can instead make an order terminating the tenancy on a date specified in the order, in which event the HA 1985, s 86 applies[1]. By virtue of s 86, a periodic tenancy automatically arises, and this is only terminable in accordance with the statutory procedures prescribed by the HA 1985[2]. The statutory periodic tenancy also arises whenever a fixed-term expires by effluxion of time at the end of its term[3], unless the tenant is granted another secure tenancy of the same dwelling house (whether periodic or fixed-term) to begin when the first tenancy ends. The periods of the tenancy are the same as those for which rent was last paid under the first tenancy, and the terms of the statutory periodic tenancy are otherwise the same as those applicable to the prior fixed-term, except that they do not include any provision for re-entry or forfeiture[4].

1 Ibid, s 82(3).
2 *Hammersmith and Fulham LBC v Harrison* [1982] 2 All ER 588, 597.
3 Ibid, s 86(1)(b).
4 Ibid, s 86(2).

[10.5] Whether arising by virtue of a court order under s 82(3), or on effluxion of time at common law, the statutory periodic tenancy can only be terminated in accordance with the possession procedures laid down in the HA 1985. Where the landlord has instituted possession proceedings during the fixed-term and obtained a court order under s 82(3) terminating the fixed-term, the net result will be to convert the fixed-term into a statutory periodic tenancy, and *that* tenancy will have to be ended by serving the statutory notice seeking possession and establishing one or more of the Sch 2 grounds. Note, however, that where a notice of seeking possession has been served with respect to a fixed-term secure tenancy, it also has effect with regard to any periodic tenancy arising by virtue of the termination of the fixed-term[1]. It will not be necessary to serve a fresh notice to ground proceedings to terminate the subsequent periodic tenancy.

1 Ibid, s 83(6).

NOTICE SEEKING POSSESSION

[10.6] If he wishes to recover possession the landlord must first serve a statutory notice complying with the HA 1985, s 83. The court cannot entertain proceedings for possession of a dwelling house let under a secure tenancy, or for the termination of a secure tenancy, unless this has been done. The court does, however, have power to dispense with the requirement of prior notice if it is just and equitable to do so[1]. The purpose of the s 83 notice is to warn the tenant of impending proceedings, and of the grounds on which it will be based, and to give him an opportunity to rectify them if possession proceedings are to be avoided. The procedure is not dissimilar to that required for the termination of private sector assured tenancies, although there are important differences in the formal requirements for a valid notice and in its effect. The notice of seeking possession is the foundation stone on which any subsequent possession proceedings must be based. The court cannot make an order for possession on any of the grounds set out in the HA 1985, Sch 2 unless the ground in question is specified in the notice, although the grounds so specified may be altered or added to with the leave of the court[2].

1 This power was added by amendments introduced by HA 1996, s 147, substituting a new HA 1985, s 83 and 83A, and brings the procedure under s 83 more closely into conformity with that for private sector tenancies under the HA 1988, s 8 (as to which see above Chapter 4).
2 Ibid, s 84(3).

Requirements: General

[10.7] The notice must comply with the following[1]:

(a) it must be in a prescribed form[2];
(b) it must specify the ground (or grounds) on which the court will be asked to make an order for possession of the dwelling house or for the termination of the tenancy; and
(c) it must give particulars of that ground.

1 Ibid, s 83(2).
2 See Secure Tenancies (Notices) Regs 1987 SI 1987/755, amended SI 1997/71, 1997/377.

[10.8] The requirement to give particulars of the ground relied upon accords with the warning function the notice is intended to fulfil. The HA 1985 does not, however, specify the amount of information, or detail, which has to be supplied by the landlord. If insufficient particulars are given, the validity of the notice given may be open to challenge, and with it subsequent possession proceedings grounded upon it. Where unpaid rent is the ground relied upon, the landlord must specify the amount of rent arrears relied upon[1], although there is no requirement that the amounts alleged as unpaid be accurate, provided the landlord acts in good faith (and to the best of his knowledge) in giving them[2]. In case of alleged disrepair the items alleged should be specified if the notice is not to be open to challenge. The court has the power to permit the amendment of a s 83 notice to add to or vary the grounds relied upon, and this has been held to extend to permitting amendments or additions to the particulars given in the notice relative to the grounds relied upon[3].

1 *Torridge DC v Jones* [1985] 2 EGLR 54, CA.
2 See *Dudley MBC v Bailey* [1991] 1 EGLR 53.
3 See, eg *Camden LBC v Oppong* (1996) 28 HLR 701.

Periodic tenancies

[10.9] Additional requirements are specified for a valid notice of seeking possession where the tenancy is periodic[1].

(1) The notice must specify the date after which proceedings for possession of the dwelling house may be begun. This must be a date not earlier than that on which the tenancy could have been brought to an end by notice to quit given by the landlord on the same date as the notice seeking possession[2]. In the case of a weekly or monthly tenant, a minimum of four weeks notice will therefore be required[3], and in the case of a quarterly tenant a full quarters notice ending on a term date.
(2) The notice ceases to be in force 12 months after the date specified in the notice as that after which proceedings may be begun.

The court cannot entertain possession proceedings unless they are begun after the date specified in the notice, and at a time when the notice remains in force[4], ie within the 12-month period following the date in the notice specified as that after which proceedings might be begun.

1 See s 83(4) ibid.
2 Ibid, s 83(5).
3 Protection from Eviction Act 1977, s 5, above Chapter 2, para 2.73 ff.
4 Ibid, s 83A(2).

Nuisance and domestic violence

[10.10] Special rules apply where the ground relied upon by the landlord is Ground 2 (the tenant is alleged to be guilty of causing a nuisance or other anti-social behaviour) or Ground 2A (he is guilty of domestic violence).

(1) *Ground 2.* The notice shall state that proceedings may be begun immediately. The tenant is not entitled to the warning period prior to proceedings being commenced, as under the other grounds in Schedule 2 (above). The notice must specify the date sought by the landlord as the date on which the tenant is to give up possession of the dwelling house, and will cease to be in force 12 months after the date so specified[1].
(2) *Ground 2A.* Where this is relied upon by the landlord, and the partner who has left the dwelling as a consequence of the violence alleged is not formally a tenant of the dwelling house, then the court cannot entertain proceedings for possession unless it is satisfied that the landlord has served a copy of the notice on the partner or has taken reasonable steps to do so[2]. The intent is to ensure that the victim of the domestic violence in issue has notice of the proceedings to terminate the tenancy, so that he or she can take appropriate steps to protect his or her position regarding the matrimonial home. For similar reasons, where possession proceedings are amended to plead Ground 2A they cannot be continued until the court has satisfied itself that the absent partner has been served a notice specifying the grounds and particulars relied upon, and informing him or her that possession proceedings have been begun[3].

1 Ibid, s 83(3).
2 Ibid, s 83A(3).
3 see s 83A(4) and (6) ibid.

LOSS OF RESIDENTIAL SECURITY

[10.11] The above rules apply to possession proceedings instigated by the landlord where there is breach of the tenancy agreement or some other malfeasance by the tenant falling within the grounds for possession set out in the HA 1985, Sch 2. They apply whenever the tenancy remains a secure tenancy and the tenant enjoys the long-term security that status confers. The tenant may, however, lose his security of tenure in several other ways.

[10.12] The tenant will only remain 'secure' if and so long as he occupies the dwelling house as his only or principal home. If he ceases to occupy the premises he will lose his protected status if the statutory residence conditions are no longer met[1]. The courts have interpreted these liberally, however, permitting fairly lengthy absences from the home if the tenant can show a settled intention to return to live there, coupled with some physical manifestation of that intention which justifies the conclusion that he still regards the premises as his principal home. Prolonged absence by the tenant can be indicative of a cessation of occupation, and if so the burden of proof shifts to the tenant to prove otherwise. To do so the tenant will need to show that his return within a reasonable time was realistic and practical. In *Amoah v Barking and Dagenham LBC*[2] the court held that a secure tenant who had been sentenced to 12 years imprisonment for possession of Class A drugs remained a secure tenant, in circumstances where his stepdaughter held the key and looked after the home, and his furniture and other personal effects remained stored there pending his release. There was a realistic and bona fide intention to return to the home and to treat it as his principal residence, and a possession order obtained by the landlords was set aside on appeal.

1 See *Preston BC v Fairclough* (1982) 8 HLR 70, CA.
2 [2001] 82 P&CR D6.

[10.13] Similarly the rules regarding notice of seeking possession have no application to a notice to quit served by the tenant to terminating a periodic tenancy. The tenant can bring a periodic secure tenancy to an end by serving four weeks notice to quit in writing[1]. If he serves a notice to quit, he cannot then rely upon the security of tenure provisions in the HA 1985[2]. Where, as is common, the tenancy is held by joint tenants, then one joint tenant is entitled to serve notice to quit terminating the tenancy without consulting his co-tenants, thus bringing the tenancy to an end[3]. The giving of notice to quit is not a dispositive act, merely an indication that the joint tenant is not willing to consent to the tenancy continuing beyond the date at which it could otherwise expire ie the end of the current period of tenancy[4]. Once terminated, the secure tenancy cannot subsequently be revived[5], the other joint tenants will have no further right to security of tenure, and the landlord will be free to recover possession.

1 Protection from Eviction Act 1977, s 5.
2 *Greenwich LBC v McGrady* (1982) 81 LGR 288, CA.
3 *Hammersmith LBC v Monk* [1992] AC 478, *Bates v Greenwich* LBC [1999] 4 All ER 944.
4 *Newlon Housing Association v Alsulaimen* [1998] 4 All ER 1 HL per Lord Hoffman at p 4–5.
5 *Newlon Housing Association v Alsulaimen* op cit per Lord Hoffman at p 6.

B Recovering possession

THE GROUNDS FOR POSSESSION

[10.14] The court cannot make an order for possession of a dwelling house let on a secure tenancy except on one or more of the grounds set out in the HA 1985, Sch 2[1]. The ground (or grounds) relied upon by the landlord must be specified in the notice of seeking possession, and the court cannot make an order on any of those grounds unless they are specified in the notice. The grounds so specified can, however, be amended or added to with the leave of the court[2]. The court has wide power to add to the grounds specified in the s 83 notice, or to alter a ground specified in the notice. Although not expressly referred to, it is implicit in the statutory power to vary the s 83 notice that the court also has power to vary or add to the *particulars* of any ground specified in the notice; eg to give further and better particulars of alleged rent arrears or disrepair. As the validity of the preliminary s 83 notice is fundamentally important to ground any subsequent possession proceedings, it follows that the power to vary its terms effectively places the tenants security of tenure at the discretion of the court. The Court of Appeal has an important role in reviewing the exercise of this discretion by county courts in possession cases[3]. Where the ground relied upon is Ground 2 (nuisance or anti-social behaviour) the notice must specify a date on which the tenant is to give up possession of the dwelling, and the court cannot make a possession order requiring the tenant to give up possession before the date so specified in the s 83 notice[4].

1 Ibid, s 84(1).
2 Ibid, s 83(3) ibid , substituted by HA 1996, s 147(2).
3 See *Camden LBC v Oppong* (1996) 28 HLR 701. CA.
4 Ibid, s 84(4).

THREE CATEGORIES OF GROUNDS FOR POSSESSION

[10.15] The HA 1985 divides the grounds set out in Sch 2 into three distinct categories.

Discretionary grounds

[10.16] The court cannot make an order for possession on the grounds set out in Grounds 1–8 unless it considers it reasonable to make the order[1]. This confers an overriding discretion on the court, exercisable in much the same manner as that applicable to the discretionary cases for possession under the Rent Act 1977 (RA 1977). The factors relevant to the courts interpretation of 'reasonableness' in this context are considered below. Grounds 1–8 are principally concerned with breach of tenancy or other malfeasance by the tenant; eg breach of covenant, nuisance or anti-social behaviour by the tenant, deterioration in the condition of the dwelling or of furniture supplied by the landlord.

1 Ibid, s 84(2)(a).

Mandatory grounds where suitable alternative accommodation is available

[10.17] The court cannot make an order for possession under Grounds 9–11 unless it is also satisfied that suitable alternative accommodation will be available for the tenant when the order takes effect[1]. These grounds are mandatory in the sense that, if the ground itself is made out, and the landlord establishes that suitable alternative accommodation is available, the court has no overriding discretion to refuse possession. The accommodation must be suitable for the needs not only of the tenant himself, but also of any member of his family living with him[2]. In *Wandsworth LBC v Fadayomi*[3] the Court of Appeal held that a member of the tenant's family living with him at the premises (in this case the tenant's estranged wife) would have an interest in the possession proceedings, as a member of the family for whom the alternative accommodation was required to be suitable, and should therefore be given leave to be joined as a party to the proceedings and intervene as a defendant.

1 Ibid, s 84(2)(b).
2 See Sch 2, Pt IV, para 2, ibid, considered further below at para 10.25 ff.
3 [1987] 1 WLR 1473.

Discretionary grounds where suitable alternative accommodation is also required

[10.18] The court cannot make an order for possession under Grounds 12–16 unless it considers it reasonable to make the order and is satisfied that suitable alternative accommodation will be available to the tent when the order takes effect[1]. These grounds principally apply to specially adapted property; eg sheltered accommodation for the disabled or special needs tenants.

1 Ibid, s 84(2)(c).

REASONABLENESS

[10.19] The discretionary grounds for possession, Grounds 1–8 and Grounds 12–16, are subject to an overriding requirement that possession can only be ordered if the court considers it reasonable to make the order[1]. This confers a wide discretion on the court in possession proceedings brought under these grounds, not dissimilar to that applicable in possession proceedings brought under the RA 1977. The grounds available to the landlord in relation to secure tenancies are, however, somewhat wider (especially in relation to nuisance, domestic violence and anti-social behaviour) and the factors relevant to reasonableness in individual cases will frequently differ from those relevant in possession claims against private sector tenants. The discretion is not absolute, moreover, and its exercise is subject to several fundamental principles:

(1) The question to be determined is the reasonableness in the particular case of ordering possession. The court cannot widen its enquiry to consider the rectitude of a policy rule adopted by the local authority in relation to its housing stock. So, in *Barking and Dagenham LBC v Hyatt*[2] the Court of Appeal held that it was wrong of the trial judge to consider the propriety of the council's rule prohibiting the siting of caravans in the gardens of council dwellings, when considering reasonableness in relation to a possession claim based on breach of a standard tenancy term to this effect inserted in all of its secure tenancy agreements.
(2) The impact of the making of a possession order on the tenant's right to be rehoused under the homelessness legislation[3] is a matter for the local authority to assess, and not one for the court to consider when deciding whether it is reasonable to order possession. 'It is not the function of the court to decide whether or not a person is intentionally homeless. That is the function of the local authority and had been entrusted to the local authority by Parliament. Those who are on the housing list who have an equal or greater claim to public housing would . . . justly be indignant to find that the court did not think it reasonable . . . to make an order for possession merely because the effect of the order would result in the occupant having to be considered by the local authority as homeless or intentionally homeless'[4]. For example, in *Bristol CC v Mousah*[5] , where proceedings had been brought based on the use of premises for drug dealing in breach of the tenancy, it was improper to refuse an order for possession on the ground that it would be unreasonable because, as a single man, the tenant would be unlikely to be rehoused as a homeless person.
(3) It is not permissible, in cases brought under Grounds 1–8, for the court to require that suitable alternative accommodation be provided for the tenant or

his family. The sole issue is reasonableness. The court is not entitled to refuse possession on grounds of reasonableness unless the landlord can show he will provide suitable alternative accommodation[6].

1 Ibid, s 84(2).
2 (1992) 24 hlr 406, CA.
3 Now HA 1996, Pt VII.
4 *Shrewsbury and Atcham BC v Evans* (1998) 30 HLR 123, 132 (Beldam LJ).
5 (1998) 30 HLR 32, CA.
6 See *Darlington BC v Sterling* (1997) 29 HLR 309, CA.

[10.20] Subject to this, the court has a wide discretion, and can take into account a wide range of relevant factors when deciding whether it is reasonable to order possession and deciding what weight to give them. The weight to be given to the various factors considered is a question of fact for the court of first instance, whose decisions will rarely be overturned on appeal[1]. The fact that the tenant is in breach of the tenancy agreement, though relevant, will not be a decisive factor. The court will, however, weigh the seriousness of the breach and, where a most serious breach of the tenancy agreement has been committed, it will invariably be reasonable to order possession unless there are exceptional circumstances[2].

1 See *Haringey LBC v Stewart* [1991] 2 EGLR 252.
2 *Bristol CC v Mousah* (1998) 30 HLR 32, CA (use of premises for supply of illegal drugs in breach of tenancy agreement). Cf *Tower Hamlets BC v Kellum* [2000] CLY 3925 (not reasonable to order possession because there was not evidence of persistent criminality in using the premises for drug related crime, and the tenant here had lived there for seven years before committing the offences alleged).

[10.21] In *Woodspring DC v Taylor*[1] it was held that it was not reasonable to make an order for possession against tenants who had a previously good rent record, and who has fallen into arrears because of a combination of bad health and redundancy, in circumstances where they were (at the time of the order) receiving benefits to pay the current rent and arrears by instalments. The court must have regard to the potential income available through the benefit system to pay current rent and accrued arrears, as well as the personal circumstances and health of the tenant. For example, it will not be reasonable to order possession in a case where rent arrears are alleged if the tenant agrees to have all future rent paid in the form of housing benefit direct to the landlord[2]. Similarly, where the tenant is already in receipt of housing benefit the court is unlikely to consider it reasonable to order possession against a responsible tenant where a pattern of regularly accruing arrears is generated – and then paid off – by the benefit system itself[3].

1 (1982) 4 HLR 95, CA.
2 Second *WRVS Housing Society v Blair* (1987) 19 HLR 104. The tenant here also suffered a psychiatric illness, a factor the court was entitled to take in to account when assessing reasonableness.
3 See *Brent LBC v Marks* (1999) 31 HLR 343, CA.

[10.22] In *Haringey LBC v Stewart*[1], on the other hand, it was held to be reasonable to order possession in circumstances where the tenant had failed in a counterclaim for disrepair, but had failed to set aside sufficient funds to pay the outstanding rent arrears should his counter claim fail. Where the non-payment of other charges in breach of the tenancy agreement – eg water rates – is used to ground possession proceedings, the fact that most of the moneys due will ultimately go to a private utility is irrelevant, and cannot be considered in regard to reasonableness[2].

1 [1991] 2 EGLR 252.
2 *Lambeth LBC v Thomas* (1990) 30 HLR 89, CA.

[10.23] Where the tenant has exercised the 'right to buy' by serving notice under the HA 1985, Pt V, this does not prevent the landlord from seeking possession. The tenant remains a secure tenant until the grant of the freehold title to him, and his right to buy is defeasible until then by a possession order made under the HA 1985[1]. The landlord can seek possession on any of the grounds set out in Schedule 2, but if the ground pleaded requires the court to consider the reasonableness of making a possession order, then the fact that the tenant has exercised his right to buy is a factor to be taken into account[2].

1 *Bristol CC v Lovell* (1999) L&TR 66 HL.
2 *Enfield LBC v McKeon* [1986] 2 All ER 730, CA.

[10.24] Where a term of the tenancy, other than as to payment of rent, has been broken this will be a material factor, but is not decisive. The court will consider all the circumstances. In *Wandsworth LBC v Hargreaves*[1] the court was entitled to rule that it was not reasonable to order possession against a tenant who had taken no active part in events leading to a serious fire caused by visitors to his flat, who had thrown petrol bombs from the window and caused £14,000 worth of damage to the flat. There had been no further problems since the tenant's return to the premises following their refurbishment, another relevant factor. On the other hand, where the tenant is guilty of behaviour amounting to a nuisance or annoyance to neighbours in the locality, the fact that the behaviour is continuing at the time of the hearing and that the tenant has shown no intention of mending his ways is a 'highly relevant fact' to be taken into account, as is the obligation which the council has to other residents in the locality[2]. Similarly, in *Sheffield CC v Jepson*[3], it was held that the judge was entitled to conclude that it was reasonable to order possession where the tenant had kept a dog in breach of the express terms of the tenancy agreement, and refused to remedy the breach by removing the pet. In *Sheffield CC v Green*[4] the Court of Appeal indicated that where there was an admitted breach of the tenancy agreement and a declared intention to continue with the breach, the landlord should only be refused possession in a very special case. This was another case of a secure tenant keeping dogs at the premises in breach of the terms of the tenancy, and the court refused to overturn the possession order granted at first instance despite evidence that the tenant had acquired the dog for protection and that it was of an advanced age.

1 (1995) 27 HLR 142, CA.
2 *Woking BC v Bistram* (1995) 27 HLR 1, CA.
3 (1993) 25 HLR 299, CA.
4 (1994) 26 HLR 349, CA.

SUITABLE ALTERNATIVE ACCOMMODATION

[10.25] Where the landlord is relying on any of Grounds 9–16, the court cannot make an order for possession unless satisfied that suitable alternative accommodation will be available for the tenant when the order takes effect[1]. Regard must be had to the criteria in Sch 2, Pt IV as to the suitability of any alternative accommodation that may be offered or available. These aim to ensure that the future security of tenure enjoyed by the tenant is roughly equivalent to that under the secure tenancy which is to be terminated, and that the physical attributes of the alternative accommodation make it suitable for the needs of the tenant and his family. For these purposes accommodation is suitable if it consists of premises that are to be let:

(a) as a separate dwelling under a secure tenancy; or

(b) as a separate dwelling under a protected tenancy, not being a tenancy under which the landlord might recover possession under one of the mandatory Rent Act grounds for possession[2]; or
(c) as a separate dwelling under an assured tenancy that is neither an assured shorthold, nor an assured tenancy under which the mandatory grounds for possession are available to the landlord[3].

1 Ibid, s 84(2).
2 That is, Cases 11 et seq in the RA 1977, Sch 15, as to which see above Chapter 6, para 6.156 ff.
3 That is, those in the HA 1988, Sch 2, Grounds 1–5, above Chapter 4, para 4.20 ff. Note that accommodation can be suitable for these purposes if mandatory Grounds 6–8 are available to the landlord (eg in cases of rent arrears, provided for in Ground 8).

[10.26] In addition, the court must, in all cases, consider that the accommodation is reasonably suitable to the needs of the tenant and his family. When determining this the court must have regard to a number of factors set out in Sch 2, Pt IV, para 2. Regard must be had to:

(1) The nature of the accommodation which it is the practice of the landlord to rent to persons with similar needs.
(2) The distance of the accommodation available from the place of work or education of the tenant or any member of his family.
(3) Its distance from the home of any other member of the tenant's family, in cases where the proximity of the tenant is essential to that other family members well-being. For example, where the tenant has an elderly parent living nearby who is dependant on him for nursing care or other welfare needs.
(4) The needs of the tenant's family as regards extent of accommodation, and the means of the tenant and his family. The weight to be given to the different needs of the tenant and his family is a question of fact and a matter of degree in each case. The fact that the tenant has a garden with the existing secure tenancy has been held to be a relevant factor, and should be taken into account with all other relevant circumstances where the alternative accommodation offered lacks a garden[1].
(5) The terms of the tenancy under which the accommodation is available, and those of the secure tenancy.
(6) If furniture was provided by the landlord for use under the secure tenancy, whether furniture is to be provided for use in the other accommodation, and if so the nature of the furniture offered and provided.

If the local housing authority provide a certificate that it will provided suitable accommodation for the tenant by a specified date set out in the certificate, then this is conclusive evidence that suitable accommodation will be available for him by that date[2].

1 *Enfield LBC v French* (1985) 17 HLR 211. The Court of Appeal dismissed the tenant's appeal against a possession order here, however, having regard to all the relevant circumstances (including the lack of a garden) as to the suitability for the tenant's needs of the one-bed roomed flat offered by the Council.
2 HA 1985, Sch 2, Pt IV, para 4. This paragraph does not apply, however, where the landlord is itself a local housing authority – it will be applicable only where some other public body is the landlord seeking possession in the proceedings concerned; eg a housing trust or housing association.

ORDERS FOR POSSESSION

[10.27] Where possession is sought under any of the discretionary grounds for possession[1], the court has wide powers to adjourn or stay the proceedings or to suspend the order for possession. By virtue of the HA 1985, s 85(1) the court may adjourn the proceedings for such a period as it thinks fit. Further, under s 85(2) the court may, if a possession order is made on any of the discretionary grounds, stay or suspend the execution of the order, or postpone the date for possession. This power is exercisable at any time before the execution of the possession order. Where the court exercises its powers of adjournment, stay, suspension or postponement, it *must* impose conditions with respect to the payment of accrued rent arrears and (if the tenancy has terminated) mesne profits for continued occupation, unless it considers that to do so would cause exceptional hardship to the tenant or be otherwise unreasonable. The court can impose such other conditions as it thinks fit[2]. When considering whether to make an immediate or suspended order, the court has a wide discretion, and can take into account all relevant circumstances, including whether the wider public interest of the local community would be served by suspending the order[3].

1 That is, HA 1985, Sch 2, Grounds 1–8 and 12–16.
2 Ibid, s 85(3).
3 *Greenwich LBC v Grogan* (2001) 33 HLR 12. (The tenant here claimed that ordering immediate possession would return him to a life of crime. The Court of Appeal held that, although the local authority had a duty to its existing tenants on the estate, it was in the interests of the local community that order be suspended for 12 months to give the tenant a chance to lead an honest life.)

[10.28] Where the landlord has obtained an order for possession, the tenancy terminates on the date on which the tenant is to give up possession under the order[1]. Where possession has been postponed under the order, therefore, the postponed date for possession is the date on which the tenancy will end. Similarly, where the order has been suspended on terms, the tenancy will automatically terminate upon the tenant breaching the terms of the suspended order[2]. At this point the tenant will become a 'tolerated trespasser' if allowed to remain in possession with the landlords agreement. The public sector possession procedures are unique, however, in allowing the court to 'revive' a tenancy even after its formal termination. The power to postpone possession was held in *Burrows v Brent LBC*[3] to be exercisable after the date for possession specified in the court order, and even if the tenancy had already terminated; eg because of the tenants failure to adhere to the terms of a suspended order for possession.

1 See s 82(2) ibid.
2 *Thompson v Elmbridge BC* [1987] 1 WLR 1448, *Burrows v Brent LBC* [1996] 4 All ER 577, HL.
3 [1996] 4 All ER 577, HL.

[10.29] Where the conditions of a suspended or postponed order are complied with, the court has power under s 85(4) to discharge or rescind the order for possession. Where it does so, then if the tenant has in the meantime become a tolerated trespasser, the effect will be to 'revive' the secure tenancy. The tenancy will not, however, be automatically revived where the tenant has later discharged accrued rent arrears in accordance with the terms of a suspended order. A further court order under s 85 is required varying the conditions of the original possession order or postponing the date of possession[1]. Where the court discharges the possession order so as to revive the former secure tenancy, this also has the effect of retrospectively reviving the landlords repairing obligations during the 'limbo' period, so that he may be liable in damages for breaches of his repairing covenants occurring after the tenancy had formerly terminated[2].

1 See *Marshall v Bradford MBC* (2000) WL 395270.
2 *Lambeth LBC v Hawa Rogers* (2000) L&TR 319, CA.

[10.30] Once a warrant for possession has been executed the court has no further power to stay or suspend it under s 85(2)[1]. A warrant for possession can only be set aside on much narrower grounds; eg if it has been obtained by fraud, or where there has been oppression in the execution of the warrant[2].

1 *Tower Hamlets LBC v Azad* (1998) 30 HLR 241, CA. The application to suspend was here made on the same day as (but one hour after) the warrant was executed. The court held that there was no power to suspend possession and so 'revive' the tenancy.
2 See *Hammersmith and Fulham LBC v Hill* (1995) 27 HLR 368, CA.

[10.30A] The restrictions on granting possession orders restrict the courts power to make a consent order against a secure tenant. If the ground for possession pleaded is one of the discretionary grounds, the court must consider it reasonable to make the order claimed before it can do so, and this applies equally to consent orders. Unless the order contains an admission about matters on which the jurisdiction to make the order rests, such as the reasonableness of making it in the circumstances, then the tenant can appeal against the order and any subsequent warrant for possession[1]. So, in *Foley v Birmingham CC*[2] a consent order made against the tenant on grounds of nuisance (HA 1985, Sch 32, Ground 2) was set aside where the tenant had never expressly or impliedly admitted the nuisance alleged at the premises, and the judge had not considered whether it was reasonable to make the order. By contrast, where the tenancy has ceased to be a secure tenancy (eg because the residence requirement is no longer satisfied by the tenant) these conditions need not be considered as a pre-requisite to a consent order being made, and it will be difficult for the tenant to appeal against the making of an order for possession by consent if he has admitted that the protection of the HA 1985, Pt IV no longer applies[3].

1 *Hounslow LBC v McBride* (1999) 31 HLR 143, CA.
2 (2000) WL 37116593, CA.
3 See *Bruce v Worthing BC* (1993) 26 HLR 223, CA.

C The grounds for possession

DISCRETIONARY GROUNDS

Rent arrears or other breach of covenant

[10.31] *Ground 1: Rent lawfully due from the tenant has not been paid or an obligation of the tenancy has been broken or not performed.*

[10.32] This ground is very commonly used to base possession claims. The court will take into account all the circumstances. If the tenant has only recently fallen into rent arrears and is suffering ill health the court is unlikely to consider it reasonable to order possession[1]. On the other hand, if the tenant is counterclaiming for breach of repairing covenant, and that he is withholding rent for this reason, the court may consider it reasonable to order possession if the tenant has failed to put aside the rent payments withheld against the eventuality that the counterclaim will fail, and makes no proposals to pay off the arrears[2]. This is exceptional, however, as normally it will be considered reasonable to suspend the order on payment of arrears by instalments. The jurisdiction is similar to that applicable under the RA 1977 in cases of rent arrears, and is exercised in a similar fashion[3].

1 *Woodspring DC v Taylor* (1981) 1 HLR 50, CA.
2 *Haringey LBC v Stewart* (1991) 23 HLR 557, CA.
3 See Chapter 6, para 6.118 ff above.

[10.33] Where a breach of tenancy other than non-payment of rent is alleged, the court will give due weight to the prospect of further breaches and the tenant's undertakings in this regard. It will be unlikely to refuse to order possession if the tenant is unwilling to give undertakings to rectify the breach alleged. In this type of case the landlord will only be refused possession in an exceptional case, and it matters not that the tenant's alleged breach of tenancy does not amount to a nuisance or annoyance to neighbours[1].

1 See *Sheffield CC v Green* (1994) 26 HLR 349, CA (tenant keeping dogs in breach of tenancy, allegedly for his protection).

Nuisance and/or annoyance

[10.34] *Ground 2: The tenant or a person residing in or visiting the dwelling house:*

(a) has been guilty of conduct causing or likely to cause a nuisance or annoyance to a person residing, visiting or otherwise engaging in a lawful activity in the locality; or
(b) has been convicted of:
  (i) using the dwelling house or allowing it to be used for immoral or illegal purposes, or
  (ii) an arrestable offence committed in, or in the locality of the dwelling house.

[10.35] This ground was considerably widened as a result of amendments made by the Housing Act 1996 (HA 1996), s 144, and intended to widen local authority powers to tackle anti-social behaviour by some council tenants. In the context of the original Ground 2 it had been held to cover foul and abusive language directed at neighbouring tenants[1], as well as aggressive behaviour, throwing stones, lighting fires, throwing knives and assaults[2]. Where the ground is made out, the issue of reasonableness will be critical, and the fact that the behaviour alleged is continuing will be an important factor indicating that it is reasonable to order possession. The behaviour complained of must affect those in the 'locality', a phrase which has been given a wide meaning by the courts so as to cover all those working or living in the neighbourhood who are sufficiently close to be affected by the conduct[3].

1 *Woking DC v Bistram* (1995) 27 HLR 1, CA.
2 *Darlington BV v Sterling* (1997) 29 HLR 309, CA.
3 *Northampton BC v Lovatt* [1998] 1 EGLR 15 (possession ordered where the nearest victim of the tenant's sons unruly behaviour was over 100 metres from her home).

[10.36] The tenant will be held responsible for the actions of a minor child. In *Kensington and Chelsea RLBC v Simmonds*[1] the court ordered possession against a tenant whose teenage sons were guilty of directing racial abuse at neighbours, even though she claimed to be unable to control them. The court said it had to consider not only the interests of the tenant, but also those of neighbours, and it would be intolerable if the latter were deprived of relief because the tenant was incapable of controlling her own children.

1 (1997) 29 HLR 507, CA.

[10.37] The revised Ground 2 is potentially very wide. It certainly requires no fault, or even knowledge, on the part of the tenant for the ground to be established, if the conduct complained of is that not of the tenant himself but of other residents or visitors to the dwelling. So in *Bryant v Portsmouth CC*[1] the tenant had a possession order made against her for breach of the terms of the tenancy because she had 'allowed' her two grandsons to cause a nuisance to neighbours, where she had failed to control them over a long period of time. The Court of Appeal said there were sound policy reasons why the ground should be construed to cover cases where the tenant could not prevent her husband or family from intimidating the neighbourhood, as it would be illogical not to be able to dispossess simply because the tenancy was held in the mother's name. The need to prove that it is reasonable to order possession provides a check on the jurisdiction and means that the court can deal with individual cases appropriately. If, for instance, there is no evidence of persistent criminality in a case where it is alleged that the premises have been used for drug-related crime, the court may take the view that it is not reasonable to order possession, even though the terms of Ground 2 have been made out[2].

1 (2000) 32 HLR 906, CA.
2 See *Tower Hamlets LBC v Kellum* (2000) CLY 3925, cf *Bristol CC v Mousah* (1998) 30 HLR 32.

Domestic violence by partner

[10.38] *Ground 2A: The dwelling house was occupied (whether alone or with others) by a married couple or a couple living together as husband and wife and:*

(a) one or both of the partners is a tenant of the dwelling house;
(b) one partner has left because of violence or threats of violence by the other towards:
  (i) that partner, or
  (ii) a member of the family of that partner who was residing with that partner immediately before that partner left; and
(c) the court is satisfied that the partner who has left is unlikely to return.

[10.39] This ground was introduced in 1997[1] as part of the policy initiative to enable public sector landlords to control anti-social behaviour by council tenants. It is designed to enable the landlord to recover possession where a partner has been forced to leave the dwelling because of violence by the other partner either towards him or herself or a child or other member of the family living there. In practice the ground may be difficult to establish, as the courts have insisted that the violence (or threats of violence) alleged must be the real and effective reason for the decision of the partner to leave[2]. It is not sufficient for violence to feature as one factor amongst several causes motivating one of the partners to leave. Where this ground is used, and the partner who has left is not the tenant, the landlord has to satisfy the court that it has served copies of the notice seeking possession on that partner, or taken all reasonable steps to do so[3].

1 Added by the HA 1996, s 145 with effect form 12 February 1997: see SI 1997/66.
2 *Camden LBC v Mallett* (2001) 33 HLR 20.
3 HA 1985, s 83A.

Deterioration in the condition of the dwelling

[10.40] *Ground 3: The condition of the dwelling house or of any common parts has deteriorated owing to acts of waste by, or the neglect or default of, the tenant or a person residing in the dwelling house and, in the case of an act of waste by, or the neglect or default of, a person lodging with the tenant or a subtenant of his, the tenant has not taken such steps as he ought reasonably to have taken for the removal of the lodger or subtenant.*

[10.41] This ground is similar to the corresponding case for possession against a private sector tenant under the RA 1977[1]. It is, however, somewhat wider, in that Ground 3 applies where damage has been caused to common parts of the dwelling, not just the demised premises themselves, and it may therefore apply where the dwelling is a flat in a block, and common parts (such as staircases) have been damaged by the tenant or his lodgers. Where the damage alleged is by a lodger or subtenant it is not necessary to show fault (eg lack of supervision) on the part of the tenant for the ground to apply – merely that the tenant has not taken such steps as he ought reasonably have done to remove the lodger or subtenant in question.

1 RA 1977, Sch 15, Case 3, above para 6.128 ff.

Deterioration in the condition of furniture

[10.42] *Ground 4: The condition of furniture provided by the landlord for use under the tenancy, or for use in the common parts, has deteriorated owing to ill treatment by the tenant or a person residing in the dwelling house and, in the case of ill treatment by a person lodging with the tenant or a subtenant of his, the tenant has not taken such steps as he ought reasonably to have taken for the removal of the lodger or subtenant.*

[10.43] This ground is identical to that applicable to private sector protected tenants under the RA 1977[1]. While private sector landlords frequently provide furniture for use by the tenant under the terms of a tenancy, it is very uncommon for public sector landlords to do so. Correspondingly, this ground is little used in practice. As under Ground 3 (above) the damage complained of may be caused by a lodger or subtenant living with the tenant. In this event, it is not necessary to prove fault on the part of the tenant – merely that he has failed to take reasonable steps to remove the lodger or subtenant.

1 RA 1977, Sch 15, Case 4, above para 6.130 ff.

Tenancy obtained by false statement

[10.44] *Ground 5: The tenant is the person, or one of the persons, to whom the tenancy was granted and the landlord was induced to grant the tenancy by a false statement made knowingly or recklessly by:*

(a) the tenant; or
(b) a person acting at the tenant's instigation.

[10.45] The policy underlying this ground is to discourage deceitful applications for rented public housing , and the ground was widened in 1997 to include misrepresentations made by a third party acting on the tenants behalf; eg by giving a false or fraudulent reference[1]. Very often, the misrepresentation will be as to the tenant's existing housing status when applying for council accommodation; eg failing to disclose existing tenancies of alternative accommodation, or ownership of another dwelling in which the tenant resides. This type of malpractice prejudices honest applicants for housing on the council waiting list, and this is a factor the court will take into account when assessing whether it is reasonable to order possession. Because of the seriousness of the allegation involved, however, where Ground 5 is invoked the burden of proof is akin to the criminal standard ie the landlord must establish beyond reasonable doubt that the tenant is guilty of the conduct alleged[2]. Where the tenant is found to have deliberately lied to obtain council accommodation, the court will only consider the effect of the homelessness legislation in exceptional circumstances[3]. The fact that the tenant will be intentionally homeless if evicted, and thus ineligible for rehousing under the homelessness legislation, is therefore unlikely to prevent the court concluding that it is reasonable to order possession.

1 HA 1996, s 146.
2 See *Rushcliffe BC v Watson* (1992) 24 HLR 124, CA.
3 *Shrewsbury and Atcham BC v Evans* (1998) 30 HLR 123, CA.

Premium paid on assignment by exchange

[10.46] *Ground 6: The tenancy was assigned to the tenant, or to a predecessor in title of his who is a member of his family and is residing in the dwelling house, by an assignment made by virtue of section 92 (assignment by way of exchange) and a premium was paid either in connection with that assignment or the assignment which the tenant or predecessor himself made by virtue of that section.*

In this paragraph 'premium' means any fine or other like sum and any other pecuniary consideration in addition to rent.

[10.47] This ground enables the landlord to seek to recover possession where the tenant has taken a financial inducement or premium when assigning the tenancy under the right to exchange[1]. The object is to prevent a 'market' arising where tenants exercise their statutory right to exchange tenancies. Note that 'premiums' are very widely defined, and the taking of any pecuniary consideration will potentially bring this ground into play.

1 As to which see Chapter 9, above.

Tied accommodation in a non-residential building

[10.48] *Ground 7: The dwelling house forms part of, or is within the curtilage of, a building which, or so much of it as is held by the landlord, is held mainly for purposes other than housing purposes and consists mainly of accommodation other than housing accommodation, and:*

(a) the dwelling house was let to the tenant or a predecessor in title of his in consequence of the tenant or predecessor being in the employment of the landlord, or of a local authority, new town corporation or other named public sector landlords]; and
(b) the tenant or a person residing in the dwelling house has been guilty of conduct such that, having regard to the purpose for which the building is used, it would not be right for him to continue in occupation of the dwelling house.

[10.49] This ground enables the landlord to recover possession from an occupant of tied accommodation ie accommodation rented to him in consequence of his being employed by the local authority or some other public sector landlord. The dwelling must be part of premises used mainly for non-housing purposes; eg a flat within a school building occupied by a caretaker or teacher. To trigger the application of the ground, the tenant must be guilty of conduct which, having regard to the purpose for which the premises are used, makes it no longer 'right' for him to continue to occupy the dwelling. This imports a moral judgement of the tenant's behaviour, but it is not thought it adds anything materially to the courts overriding duty to decide whether it is 'reasonable' to order possession on the facts of the particular case.

Temporary accommodation during works

[10.50] *Ground 8: The dwelling house was made available for occupation by the tenant (or a predecessor in title of his) while works were carried out on the dwelling house which he previously occupied as his only or principal home and:*

(a) *the tenant (or predecessor) was a secure tenant of the other dwelling house at the time when he ceased to occupy it as his home;*
(b) *the tenant (or predecessor) accepted the tenancy of the dwelling house of which possession is sought on the understanding that he would give up occupation when , on completion of the works, the other dwelling house was again available for occupation by him under a secure tenancy; and*
(c) *the works have been completed and the other dwelling house is so available.*

[10.51] This ground is intended to deal with the case where the landlord offers a tenant temporary accommodation while repair work is being carried out to his existing home. The ground only applies where the tenant was a secure tenant of his existing home, although it is not a pre-requisite for its application that he be a secure tenant of the particular landlord granting the temporary accommodation. It will not apply, however, where temporary public sector accommodation is offered to a private sector tenant in these circumstances. The ground enables the landlord to recover possession of the temporary accommodation if the tenant refuses to vacate once the repair work to his original home is completed.

MANDATORY GROUNDS: SUITABLE ALTERNATIVE ACCOMMODATION MUST BE AVAILABLE

Overcrowding

[10.52] *Ground 9: The dwelling house is overcrowded within the meaning of [HA 1985] Part X, in such circumstances as to render the occupier guilty of an offence.*

[10.53] Where this ground is made out, it is not necessary for the court to consider it reasonable to make an order for possession. It suffices if overcrowding which satisfies the criteria in the HA 1985, Pt X is proved to exist. In order to recover possession the landlord will have to establish that suitable alternative accommodation is available for the tenant and his family.

Redevelopment

[10.53] *Ground 10: The landlord intends, within a reasonable time of obtaining possession of the dwelling house:*

(a) to demolish or reconstruct the building or part of the building comprising the dwelling house; or
(b) to carry out work on that building or on land let together with, and thus treated as part of, the dwelling house;

and cannot reasonably do so without obtaining possession of the dwelling house.

[10.54] The landlord must establish that it has a settled and firm intention to carry out the development in question. A similar ground for possession is available to landlords of business premises under the Landlord and Tenant Act 1954[1], and the same criteria will be applied to establish whether the necessary intention is established as apply in that context[2]. In *Wansbeck DC v Marley*[3] the landlord failed to repossess a cottage where it was unable to produce any council minutes or resolution to show what works were intended and that possession would be needed before they could be carried out. The council wanted to erect a building in the garden of the cottage with a doorway linking into the dwelling. The Court of Appeal held that the council had to prove not only a settled intention to carry out the development, but also that the work could not reasonably be carried out without obtaining possession. The production of oral evidence from a council officer was insufficient evidence of either, and possession was refused.

1 Landlord and Tenant Act 1954, s 30(1)(f). See further M Haley, *Statutory Regulation of Business Tenancies* (Oxford, 2000) at p 215 ff. A similar ground also applies in possession proceedings for assured tenancies under the HA 1988, Pt 1; see the HA 1988, Sch 2, Ground 6, above, Chapter 4.
2 See in particular *Heath v Drown* [1973] AC 498 HL. The authorities under the Landlord and Tenant Act 1954 are discussed in the context of the parallel ground for assured tenancies at Chapter 4, para 4.33 ff to which reference should be made.
3 (1998) 20 HLR 247, CA.

Redevelopment schemes

[10.55] *Ground 10A: The dwelling house is in an area which is the subject of a redevelopment scheme approved by the Secretary of State or the [Housing Corporation] in accordance with Part V of [the HA 1985, Sch 2] and the landlord intends within a reasonable time of obtaining possession to dispose of the dwelling house in accordance with the scheme; or part of the dwelling house is in such an area and the landlord intends within a reasonable time of obtaining possession to dispose of that part in accordance with the scheme and for that purpose reasonably require possession of the dwelling house.*

[10.56] This ground gives the landlord a mandatory right to possession where the dwelling, or part of it, is within the area of a redevelopment scheme. The landlord must prove it has a settled intention to dispose of the dwelling in accordance with the terms of the scheme, and (it is suggested) similar considerations as to proof of intention apply as under Ground 10 (above).

Charitable landlords

[10.57] *Ground 11: The landlord is a charity and the tenant's continued occupation of the dwelling house would conflict with the objects of the charity.*

[10.58] This ground is restricted to charitable landlords only, and may apply, for instance, where the landlord's charitable status and objects limit it to letting social housing to specific classes of beneficiary, and the tenant's personal circumstances have changed so that he no longer meets the charity's qualifications to receiving housing.

DISCRETIONARY GROUNDS: SUITABLE ALTERNATIVE ACCOMMODATION MUST BE AVAILABLE

Tied non-housing accommodation

[10.59] *Ground 12: The dwelling house forms part of, or is within the curtilage of, a building which is . . . held mainly for purposes other than housing purposes and consists mainly of accommodation other than housing accommodation, or is situated in a cemetery, and:*

(a) the dwelling house was let to the tenant or a predecessor in title of his in consequence of the tenant or predecessor being in the employment of the landlord or of [a local authority or other specified public bodies] and that employment has ceased; and
(b) the landlord reasonably requires the dwelling house for occupation as a residence for some person either engaged in the employment of the landlord, or of such a body or with whom a contract for such employment has been entered into conditional on housing being provided.

[10.60] This ground enables the landlord to prepossess certain types of tied accommodation, if he can show that it is reasonably required for housing another employee for whom the landlord is contractually obliged to provide accommodation. For the ground to be available the tenant's own employment with the landlord must have ceased. The landlord, must, in addition, satisfy the court that it is reasonable to make an order for possession and that suitable alternative accommodation is available for the tenant.

Special accommodation for the disabled

[10.61] *Ground 13: The dwelling house has features which are substantially different from those of ordinary dwelling houses and which are designed to make it suitable for occupation by a physically disabled person who requires accommodation of a kind provided by the dwelling house and:*

(a) there is no longer such a person residing in the dwelling house; and
(b) the landlord requires it for occupation (whether alone or with members of his family) by such a person.

[10.62] This ground enables a landlord to recover possession of premises which have been designed for the physically disabled, where there is no longer a physically disabled person living there. This might be because the tenant has died and been succeeded as secure tenant by a relative who is not disabled, or a disabled joint tenant may have quit the premises leaving a sole remaining joint tenant in occupation who is not disabled. For the ground to apply the premises must have *features* which are *substantially different* from those of ordinary dwelling houses. The building must be designed in such a way as to be especially suitable for disabled occupants. This would be indicated by the presence of widened doors, access ramps, cooking facilities at special heights etc, but not simply by the installation of an indoor downstairs lavatory (which is common in non-adapted premises)[1].

1 See *Wansbeck DC v Freeman* (1984) 10 HLR 54, CA.

Special accommodation let by registered social landlords and housing trusts

[10.63] *Ground 14: The landlord is a housing association or housing trust which lets dwelling houses only for occupation (whether alone or with others) by persons whose circumstances (other than merely financial circumstances) make it especially difficult for them to satisfy their need for housing and:*

(a) either there is no longer such a person residing in the dwelling house or the tenant has received from the local housing authority an offer of accommodation in premises which are to be let as a separate dwelling under a secure tenancy; and
(b) the landlord requires the dwelling house for occupation . . . by such a person.

[10.64] This ground is similar to Ground 13, but is only available to housing association landlords and housing trusts. It applies where the social landlord lets accommodation only for letting to special needs groups whose circumstances make it difficult for them to obtain housing elsewhere. The accommodation need not be physically adapted for special client groups for this ground to be applicable cf Ground 13 above, where this is a requirement.

Special needs tenants

[10.65] *Ground 15: The dwelling house is one of a group of dwelling houses which it is the practice of the landlord to let for occupation by persons with special needs and:*

(a) a social service or special facility is provided in close proximity to the group of dwelling houses in order to assist persons with those special needs;
(b) there is no longer a person with those special needs residing in the dwelling house; and
(c) the landlord requires the dwelling house for occupation (whether alone or with members of his family) by a person who has those special needs.

[10.66] This ground applies where the property let is one out of a group of dwellings let to tenants with special needs, and enables the landlord to recover possession where the house is no longer occupied by a person with those special needs. For the ground to apply, the property must be part of a 'group' of dwelling houses, in the sense that they are linked by a common call facility or warden system and are in close proximity to each other[1]. It will not suffice if the dwelling is simply one of an specially adapted or design type that is scattered throughout the landlord's housing stock. The HA 1985 does not specify those special needs groups for which the landlord must provide, and this ground will be available to the landlord whatever the needs of the tenant group it serves. The landlord must establish that the property is required for another tenant with the special needs for which it was initially provided, as well as the availability of suitable alternative accommodation for the displaced tenant.

1 See *Martin v Motherwell DC* 1991 SLT (Lands Tribunal) 4.

Statutory succession: Accommodation too extensive

[10.67] *Ground 16: The accommodation afforded by the dwelling house is more extensive than is reasonably required by the tenant and:*

(a) the tenancy vested in the tenant by virtue of [statutory succession under the HA 1985], the tenant being qualified to succeed . . . as a member of the tenants family other than a spouse; and
(b) notice of the proceedings for possession was served [or where no such notice was served the proceedings for possession were begun] not more than six months but less than 12 months after the date of the previous tenants death.

The matters to be taken into account by the court in determining whether it is reasonable to make an order for possession on this ground included:

(a) the age of the tenant;
(b) the period during which the tenant has occupied the dwelling house as his only or principal home; and
(c) any financial or other support given by the tenant to the previous tenant.

[10.68] This ground can be used by the landlord where there has been a succession to a secure tenancy by a qualified successor other than the deceased tenant's spouse, where the accommodation is more extensive than is reasonably required by the new tenant. Note that the notice of proceedings under s 83 must be served not less than 6 and not more than 12 months after the deceased tenant's death. The ground will only be available where the tenancy is periodic: where the deceased had a fixed-term tenancy the residue unexpired will pass to his successor otherwise than under the HA 1985.

D The right to buy

INTRODUCTION

[10.69] The right to buy (RTB) was introduced as part of the 'Tenants Charter' in the HA 1980, and gives secure tenants of local authorities and other public sector landlords a right to enfranchise and buy the freehold in their homes. These rights are now set out in the HA 1985, Pt V. Under the original legislation the RTB was granted to a secure tenant of a local authority, a registered non-charitable social landlord and tenants of certain other public sector landlords (such as new town corporations) provided in each case the tenant had lived in the dwelling for a qualifying period of at least two years. Substantial discounts on the market value of the dwelling are given by the HA 1985 in order to promote the scheme to tenants on low incomes or with limited capital.

[10.70] The RTB is excluded in a number of cases set out in the HA 1985, Sch 5, and this means in practice that most tenants of registered social landlords do not enjoy the RTB. Since 1989 most tenants of social landlords, such as housing associations, are granted assured tenancies under the HA 1988, Pt 1 and not secure tenancies. Assured tenants do not enjoy the RTB under the HA 1985. The only exceptions where tenants of registered social landlords enjoy the RTB are:

(1) Former public sector secure tenants whose property has been transferred into the private sector; eg under a large scale voluntary transfer to a housing association or housing trust, or under the former 'Tenants Choice' scheme. Such tenants become assured tenants on transfer, but continue to enjoy a 'preserved right to buy' under the HA 1985[1].
(2) Secure tenants of non-charitable registered social landlords.

1 That is, under HA 1985, s 171A–171H.

[10.71] The HA 1996 extended a new 'right to acquire' to assured and secure tenants of all registered social landlords, but only in respect of dwellings built or acquired by the landlord after the HA 1996 came into force ie on or after 1 April 1997. Assured and/or secure tenants of dwellings built or acquired before commencement will still not enjoy the right to acquire the freehold in their homes. However, the 1996 Act introduced a voluntary purchase scheme under which social landlords are permitted to offer substantial discounts to tenants in these categories as an inducement to purchase the freehold on their houses[1].

1 The voluntary scheme administered by the Housing Corporation is underpinned by powers in the HA 1996, s 21 to make grants to registered social landlords in respect of discounts made to purchasers otherwise than in exercise of the statutory right to acquire, ie where the purchaser is offered sale voluntarily by the landlord rather than under the mandatory procedures of RTB or the right to acquire.

QUALIFYING FOR THE RIGHT TO BUY

The basic right

[10.72] The HA 1985 confers the RTB on a secure tenant, so that if for any reason a tenancy cannot be 'secure' the RTB will not apply[1]. The right given where the RTB applies is, in the case of a house where the landlord is the freehold owner, the right to acquire the freehold; and in the case of a flat (or a house where the landlord is not the freeholder) the right to acquire a long lease of the dwelling house. Any provision in a superior lease of the property held by the landlord (or a superior landlord) which purports to restrict or prohibit the exercise of the RTB is void[2]. The tenant must remain a secure tenant up to the completion of the purchase, otherwise the right to buy will be lost[3]. This status may be lost, and with it the RTB; eg if the tenant ceases to reside in the dwelling as his only or principal home. Similarly, where the tenant remains a secure tenant until completion of the RTB, the tenant's RTB remains defeasible by a possession order granted to the landlord. Even if the tenant has completed all the formal stages to exercise the RTB, the court can adjourn any proceedings for an injunction to force the landlord to convey the freehold, pending the hearing of possession proceedings brought under the HA 1985.

1 HA 1985, s 118(1).
2 Ibid, s 179.
3 *Sutton LBC v Swan* (1985) 18 HLR 140, CA.

[10.73] The nature of the RTB as a species of property right has proved problematic. It is now clear that the RTB is not a property right vesting in the tenant independently of the secure tenancy in relation to which it arises. It is a creature of statute and is entirely dependant upon the continued existence of the secure tenancy of the dwelling in question, to which it is incidental[1]. The tenant does not acquire any equitable or proprietory interest in the dwelling whatsoever under the

RTB until the grant of the freehold is actually made[2]. It has been judicially described as 'analogous to a personal equity'[3]. It follows that the RTB will be lost where one out of joint secure tenants (eg a husband or wife) serves a unilateral notice of termination ending the secure tenancy before the conveyance of the freehold is made under the RTB, even if all the formal stages short of conveyance have been completed[4]. As no equitable interest or title arises in the purchaser until completion under the RTB, the service of notice to quit by a joint tenant does not constitute a disposal of a property interest for the purposes of, eg, the matrimonial causes legislation[5]. The RTB cannot be exercised where the landlord has obtained a possession order, whether the order is immediate or suspended on terms under the HA 1985, s 85[6]. Neither can the RTB be exercised by a person who has a bankruptcy petition pending against him, is an undischarged bankrupt or has made a composition with his creditors the terms of which remain unfulfilled.

1 See *Sutton LBC v Swan* (1985) 18 HLR 140, *Jennings v Epping Forest LBC* (1992) 25 HLR 241 and *Bradford Metropolitan City Council v McMahon* [1993] 4 All ER 237.
2 See *Bristol CC v Lovell* (1999) L&TR 66 HL, overruling *Dance v Welwyn Hatfield DC* (1990) 22 HLR 339, CA.
3 *Bradford Metropolitan City Council v McMahon* [1993] 4 All ER 237 at 245 per Balcombe LJ.
4 *Bates v Greenwich LBC* [1999] 4 All ER 944 (husband unable to complete RTB where his wife, a joint tenant, served notice of termination prior to the RTB conveyance).
5 That is, the Matrimonial Causes Act 1973, s 37. If divorce proceedings are in progress, the unilateral destruction of the secure tenancy can best be avoided by the extraction of a letter of undertaking not to serve notice to quit from the non-resident secure tenant, which can then be served on the landlord. In the absence of an undertaking, an application can be made for an injunction, which can then be served on the landlord: see the comments of Thorpe LJ in *Bates v Greenwich LBC*, above n 5, at [1999] 4 All ER at p 953.
6 Ibid, s 121. For suspension and postponement of possession orders see above para 10.27 ff.

[10.74] Where there is a joint tenancy, the RTB belongs jointly to each tenant or to such one of them as they shall agree between them – and this is the case whether or not each of the joint tenants occupies the dwelling as his or her principal home[1]. This relaxes the residence qualification, in that only the person exercising the RTB, or at least one of the joint tenants to whom it is by agreement to belong, must occupy the dwelling as his only or principal home.

1 Ibid, s 118(2).

[10.75] Where the tenant exercises the RTB he will acquire any land that was let with the dwelling. The only exception is agricultural land that exceeds two acres in extent, which will not be treated as part of the dwelling for these purposes.

Qualifying residence period

[10.76] A secure tenant can only exercise the RTB if he has fulfilled a qualifying period of residence of two years, during which time he must occupy the dwelling as his only or principal home[1]. In the case of a joint tenancy only one of the joint tenants must satisfy the resident requirement[2]. The rules for calculating the residence period are set out in the HA 1985, Sch 4, and also apply for the purposes of calculating the discount to which the tenant is entitled. A period qualifies towards the residence requirement if it is one during which the secure tenant himself, his spouse (if they were living together at the time) or a deceased spouse occupied the dwelling as his or her only or principal home, and was at that time a public sector tenant of the dwelling[3]. If the tenant dies, a child who has occupied the house as his only or principal home may also qualify for the RTB, provided that he has also occupied it as his only or principal home after reaching the age of 16[4].

1 Ibid, s 119 and Sch 4.
2 Ibid, s 119(2).
3 Ibid, Sch 4, paras 2 and 6.
4 Ibid, Sch 4, para 4.

Cases where the RTB does not arise

[10.77] The tenant will not have the RTB, in any event, in a number of cases specified in the HA 1985, Sch 5. Some of the exclusions are explicable because of the special nature of the premises themselves, some by reason of the insufficiency of the landlord's reversion on the dwelling, and others on policy grounds – principally the consideration that only property acquired or built with public funds should be subject to the RTB.

[10.78] The RTB does *not* arise in the following cases:

(1) The landlord is a charitable housing association or housing trust[1]. This exclusion explains why most tenants of registered social landlords fail to enjoy the RTB under the HA 1985. Following the HA 1996, however, many tenants of charitable housing associations have the right to acquire under that legislation. The RTB also does not arise if the landlord is a cooperative housing association or is a housing association which has not at any time received publicly funded grants; eg under the Housing Associations Act 1985 or the HA 1996[2]. Neither does the RTB arise where the landlord holds a tenancy from the Crown – unless the landlord is entitled to grant a long lease without the concurrence of the appropriate authorities (eg the Crown Estate Commissioners) or that consent has been given to the granting of the long lease by way of exercise of the RTB[3].

(2) The landlord does not own the freehold, or (if it holds a leasehold interest itself) it does not have an interest sufficient to grant a long lease under the RTB for (in the case of a dwelling house) a term of at least 21 years or (in the case of a flat) a term of not less than 50 years[4].

(3) The RTB does not apply if the dwelling was let to the tenant (or his predecessor) in consequence of his being employed by the landlord, and forms part of or is within the curtilage of a building used mainly for non-housing purposes. The landlord by whom the tenant was employed must be either a local authority, a new town corporation, a housing action trust, the Development Board for Rural Wales, an urban development corporation or the governors of a grant-aided school[5]. For the RTB to be excluded the dwelling must be within the 'curtilage' of the building ie an area around the building and attached to it in some way. In *Dyer v Dorset CC*[6] a cottage was let to a lecturer but, although within the perimeter of the college, it was fenced off from the rest of the college grounds. It was held not to be within the curtilage of the college building and the RTB therefore applied. Similarly in *Barwich v Kent CC*[7] the RTB applied where a fireman's house (one of a specially built row) was built near a fire station but outside its perimeter away from the garages and other buildings that were within its clearly defined curtilage.

(4) The RTB does not apply to dwellings specially adapted for the disabled, or to houses that are part of a group particularly suitable for the elderly[8]. In the case

of sheltered housing for the disabled, the RTB is only excluded if the dwelling has features which are substantially different from those of ordinary dwelling houses and which are designed to make it suitable for occupation by the physically disabled. This means it must have special features not normally found in ordinary dwellings, and intended to render it suitable for disabled occupants; eg the presence of widened doorways and access ramps, and not simply additional ground floor toilet facilities[9].

1 Ibid, Sch 5, para 1.
2 Ibid, Sch 5, paras 2 and 3.
3 Ibid, Sch 5, para 12.
4 Ibid, Sch 5, para 4.
5 Ibid, Sch 5, para 5.
6 [1989] QB 346.
7 (1992) 24 HLR 341, CA.
8 Ibid, Sch 5, paras 7–12.
9 *Freeman v Wansbeck DC* (1984) 2 All ER 746.

EXERCISING THE RTB

[10.79] There are four stages in exercising the RTB. The first is the service by the tenant of his notice claiming to exercise the RTB. The second and third stages are the establishment of the right and the agreement (or in default of agreement the determination) of the terms of the grant. The fourth and final stage is the grant of the relevant interest – the freehold if the property is a house and the landlord owns the freehold, or a long lease if the landlord is not the freeholder or if the property is a flat. The RTB can be lost at any of these four stages if the procedures in the HA 1985 are not followed[1]. Similarly, the RTB will be lost if the tenant ceases to be a 'secure' tenant at any stage during the completion of the RTB procedures. The HA 1985, s 138 places the landlord under a duty to convey his interest in the dwelling where a *secure tenant* has exercised his RTB and that right has been established, and this has been interpreted to mean that the tenancy must remain secure until the grant pursuant to the RTB has been made[2].

1 See *Muir Group Housing Association Ltd v Thornley* (1992) 25 HLR 89, CA.
2 *Jennings v Epping Forest DC* (1992) 25 HLR 241, CA (tenant sublet whole of dwelling before a completion date had been agreed, thereby ceasing to occupy as his principal residence and ceasing to be a secure tenant – RTB lost).

Notice exercising the RTB

[10.80] The tenant exercises the RTB by serving a written notice in prescribed form on the landlord[1]. The tenant can include up to three members of his family even if they are not secure tenants, provided they occupy the house as their principal home[2]. To be validly joined in the application a family member must either be the spouse of the tenant or must have resided in the dwelling with the tenant for a period of 12 months immediately prior to the giving of the notice exercising the RTB. If neither of these conditions is met, they can be validly joined in the application only if the landlord consents[3]. Family members joined in the application for the RTB are treated as if they were joint tenants of the dwelling. If, therefore, the secure tenant dies before the purchase is completed, the remaining family members can complete the purchase under the RTB even if they would be ineligible to succeed to the tenancy on the death of the former tenant[4]. Where there is a change in the identity of the tenant after the notice exercising the RTB is served, but before a contract of sale is concluded, the new secure tenant is treated as if he served the notice[5]. The new tenant is entitled to claim the same discount as the original secure tenant would have been entitled to, even if the discount attributable to him personally would have been less if separately calculated[6]. Similarly, where the identity of the landlord changes after the initial notice is given, but before contract, the parties are in the same position as if the new landlord had been in situ from the outset, and had taken all the steps the original landlord undertook[7]. The RTB will cease to be exercisable, however, if the new landlord is an exempt body, such as a charitable housing trust or cooperative housing association. In this event, both landlord and tenant must take steps to ensure that the parties are restored to the position that would have obtained if the change in landlord had occurred before the claim for RTB had been initiated[8].

1 HA 1985, s 122. For the prescribed forms see Housing (Right to Buy) (Prescribed Forms) Regulations 1986, SI 1986/2194 as amended.
2 Ibid, s 123.
3 Ibid, s 123(2).
4 *Harrow LBC v Tonge* (1992) 25 HLR 99, CA.
5 Ibid, s 136.
6 *McIntyre v Merthyr Tydfil BC* (1989) 21 HLR 320.
7 Ibid, s 137(1).
8 Ibid, s 137)(2).

Subsequent procedures

[10.81] Where a notice claiming to exercise the RTB has been served by the tenant, the landlord must serve written notice either admitting the tenant's right, or denying it and stating the reasons why, in his opinion, the tenant does not have the RTB. The landlord's notice admitting or denying the RTB must be served within four weeks, unless part of the tenant's qualifying period of residence was with another landlord, in which case the period for the landlord's notice is extended to eight weeks[1].

1 HA 1985, s 124.

[10.82] Where the landlord admits the RTB, or it is otherwise established (eg in legal proceedings) the landlord must follow up his first notice with a second – the landlord's notice of purchase price and other matters. This must be served within eight weeks if the right is to the freehold and within 12 weeks where it is to a long lease[1]. This notice must describe the dwelling house, state the price which the tenant must pay for the freehold conveyance or long lease (as the case may be) and must give details of how the price was arrived at, the value at the relevant time, and any discounts made for the tenant's improvements and the amount of the discount to which the tenant is entitled. The notice must also include a statement of all other terms to be included in the conveyance. Where the RTB is to acquire a leasehold interest, the landlord's notice must include details of all service charges and charges for improvements that would be recoverable for the tenant under the proposed long lease[2]. The landlord's second notice must also inform the tenant of the subsequent RTB procedures and the effect of failure on his part to comply with any default notice served by the landlord[3].

1 Ibid, s 125(1).
2 Ibid, s 125(4). See also s 125A and B for the detailed requirements as to estimates of service charge contributions and improvement charges that must be included in the s 125 notice.
3 See further s 125(5).

[10.83] Following service of the second of the landlord's notices – the notice of purchase price – the tenant must serve a written notice of intent stating either that he intends to pursue his claim to exercise the RTB or withdraw it[1]. The tenant's notice of intent must be served within the period of 12 weeks beginning either with the date of service of the landlord's notice of purchase price or (if the calculation of the price has been referred to the district valuer) of service of the valuer's determination, whichever is later[2]. If the tenant fails to give his notice of intention within the time allowed, the HA 1985 entitles the landlord to serve a written default notice. This will require the tenant to duly serve his notice of intent within 28 days, failing which the tenants notice claiming to exercise the RTB is deemed to have been withdrawn[3].

1 Ibid, s 125D.
2 Ibid, s 125D(2).
3 Ibid, s 125E. The landlords default notice must inform the tenant of the consequences of failure to comply with its terms.

Purchase price

[10.84] The purchase price to be paid by the tenant is governed by the HA 1985. This requires the calculation of the dwelling's value in accordance with criteria set out in the HA 1985, s 127, and then the application of the relevant discount to arrive at the purchase price.

Open market valuation

[10.85] The value of the dwelling house is the price which it would realise if sold on the open market by a willing vendor, disregarding any of the tenant's improvements and any failure by the tenant to keep the dwelling in good internal repair. The relevant valuation date is the date on which the tenant serves his notice claiming the RTB, and any subsequent increase or decrease in value is left out of account[1]. Certain statutory assumptions must be made when valuing the dwelling for these purposes. Where the RTB leads to a freehold conveyance, the principal assumptions are that the vendor is selling for an estate in fee simple with vacant possession, and that neither the tenant nor a member of his family residing with him wanted to buy. For the grant of a long lease the assumptions are that the landlord is granting a lease with vacant possession for the appropriate term (in most cases 125 years[2]) at a ground rent not exceeding £10 per annum, and that neither the tenant nor any member of his family residing with him wanted to take the lease[3]. Disputes as to the applicable purchase price are determinable by the district valuer[4].

1 Ibid, s 127(1).
2 See Sch 6, para 12 ibid. Where the landlord's interest is greater than a lease for 125 years the tenant is entitled to a leasehold estate for 125 years. In other cases, the tenant is entitled to a lease for the residue unexpired of the landlord's lease, minus five days.
3 Ibid, s 127(3).
4 See s 128 ibid.

Discount

[10.86] By virtue of s 129, the discount to be applied is a percentage calculated by reference to the qualifying period of residence for RTB. In the case of a house, the basic discount is 32 per cent plus 1 per cent for each complete year by which the qualifying residence exceeds two years up to a maximum of 60 per cent. In the case of a flat the basic discount is 44 per cent plus 2 per cent for each complete year by which the qualifying residence exceeds two years, up to maximum of 70 per cent[1].

1 Ibid, s 129(2). The secretary of state has power to increase the applicable discounts by order made with the consent of the Treasury – s 129(2A),(2B) ibid.

Landlord's duty to complete

[10.87] Once the tenant's RTB has been admitted or established, and all matters relating to the grant have been agreed or determined, the landlord is placed under a statutory duty to convey the freehold title or, if the landlord does not own the freehold or the dwelling is a flat, to grant a long lease in accordance with the terms of the HA 1985[1]. The landlord's duty to complete is enforceable by injunction[2]. The duty is, however, suspended if the tenant is in arrears of rent for a period of four weeks or more. Although the duty to complete is, on the face of the HA 1985 itself, apparently unqualified, there are several situations where problems may arise and the landlord may refuse to complete. If the tenant ceases to be a secure tenant prior to completion the duty to complete ceases to apply[3]. However, if the tenant dies before the RTB is completed, a successor entitled to succeed under the HA 1985 is entitled to continue with the RTB application[4]. If, however, the tenant is survived by a non-qualifying family member or was himself a successor (no second succession being possible) the 'successor' can only continue the RTB application if he or she was included in the tenant's initial RTB claim notice[5]. Where a change of tenant occurs in some other way after the RTB has been exercised, but before completion, the new tenant is entitled to continue with the application but cannot add members of his own family to the application. The exception is where there is a change of tenant following a tenancy exchange effected by an assignment of the tenancy under the HA 1985, s 93, where the new tenant is not entitled to continue the RTB application[6]. A new tenant proposing to continue with a RTB application initiated by his predecessor must serve notice under s 125D indicating that he intends either to continue the RTB application or to exercise a right to purchase on rent to mortgage terms. This must be done whether or not the previous tenant had served a s 125D notice, and must be done within 12 weeks of his becoming the secure tenant[7].

1 Ibid, s 138(1).
2 Ibid, s 138(3).
3 *Muir Group Housing Ltd v Thornley* (1992) 25 HLR 89.
4 See s 136 ibid.
5 *Harrow LBC v Tonge* (1992) 5 HLR 99 (above para 10.80). Cf *Bradford CC v McMahon* (1993) 25 HLR 534 where the right to buy was lost following the secure tenant's death, as none of the surviving family members had been included in the notice of claim.
6 Ibid, s 136(1).
7 Or, where relevant, within 12 weeks of the district valuer's determination of the price payable: s 136(2) ibid.

[10.88] The principles on which the jurisdiction to award an injunction to enforce completion operates were examined by the House of Lords in *Bristol CC v Lovell*[1]. It was there held, reversing previous decisions to the contrary[2], that the tenant does not acquire any equitable or proprietary interest under the RTB once the claim has been established, until the grant of the freehold is actually made. He is not, therefore, entitled to an injunction under s 138(3) by virtue of any equitable title. The courts' discretionary power to adjourn proceedings under CCR Order 13 remains unaffected. The net effect here was that the court refused to grant an injunction to enforce completion, and stayed the proceedings pending the hearing of possession proceedings against the tenant under Sch 2, Ground 2 alleging nuisance and anti-social behaviour.

1 (1999) L&TR 66, HL.
2 Notably *Dance v Welwyn Hatfield DC* [1990] 3 All ER 572, cf *Taylor v Newham LBC* [1993] 2 All ER 649, which is also no longer sound authority.

Sanctions for delay

[10.89] The HA 1985 makes provision for the service of a first and second notice to complete by the landlord, where the terms of the transfer have been agreed or determined and the tenant delays completion. The first notice to complete can only be served if not less than 12 months have elapsed since the landlord's notice of purchase price etc was served[1]. It must give the tenant a period of at least 56 days to complete the transaction. If the tenant fails to comply with the first notice to complete, the landlord can serve a second[2], again giving a minimum of 56 days in which to complete the transaction. If the tenant fails to comply with the second notice to complete, the tenant's notice claiming the RTB is deemed to be withdrawn at the end of the period allowed in the second notice to complete[3]. Likewise, the tenant can serve a 'notice of delay' if the landlord fails to serve the notices required under ss 124 and 125 (purchase price etc) or fails to complete as required by the HA 1985. The tenants notice must give the landlord a period of at least one month in which to respond, failing which a second notice (referred to in the HA 1985 as an 'operative notice') can be served, If the landlord fails to comply with the operative notice of delay, then any subsequent rent payments made by the tenant are attributed to payments towards the purchase price payable under the RTB.

1 Ibid, s 140(2).
2 Ibid, s 141.
3 Ibid, s 141(4).

Terms of conveyance or lease

[10.90] The terms on which the dwelling must be conveyed to the tenant are set out in the HA 1985, Sch 6. The aim is to ensure the tenant enjoys the full advantages of the grant of title. For example, the conveyance must be expressed to be made by the landlord with full title guarantee[1], and cannot exclude the effect of the Law of Property Act 1925, s 62. The tenant will therefore have the benefit of the appropriate implied covenants for title[2] and of all rights and privileges being exercised by him at the time of conveyance[3]. The tenant is also entitled to all rights of support for the building, rights of access of light and air, rights of passage of water and piped fuel (eg gas and electricity) and to maintenance of cables and installations for the supply of electricity and telephone etc as are necessary to secure him the same rights he previously enjoyed as a secure tenant of the dwelling[4]. The landlord must, so far as it is able, grant any rights of way necessary for the reasonable enjoyment of the property conveyed[5].

1 Ibid, Sch 6, para 4A.
2 That is, those specified in the Law of Property (Miscellaneous Provisions) Act 1994, Pt 1.

3 These will become easements accruing to the benefit of the property under s 62 of the Law of Property Act 1925. Freehold conveyances commonly exclude the effect of s 62 ibid.
4 Ibid, Sch 6, para 2.
5 Ibid, Sch 6, para 3.

[10.91] The landlord is entitled to take a covenant providing indemnity against breaches of any restrictive covenants affecting the dwelling and restricting the uses to which it or the land can be put[1]. The landlord's ability to take other covenants is restricted by the HA 1985, which provides that other covenants or conditions can only be included in the conveyance if they are 'reasonable in all the circumstances'[2]. This would enable the landlord to take covenants restricting the use of the premises in a manner causing a nuisance or noise. The assumption remains, however that the conveyance under the RTB is an arm's length transaction conveying the fee simple with vacant possession. The landlord cannot, therefore, take a covenant the effect of which would reserve to him the right to enjoy the profits from any future development value that may accrue to the property conveyed. Thus, in *R v Braintree DC ex parte Halls*[3] a covenant by a RTB purchaser to use the property solely for the purposes of a single dwelling house had to be released where the buyer later obtained planning permission for another dwelling to be built on the land conveyed. The effect of the covenant in these circumstances was to reserve development value to the erstwhile landlord. *Query*, however, the taking of a covenant to restrict subsequent use to residential purposes would be reasonable on the facts in many cases; eg to prevent the conversion of the premises to a business use in an otherwise predominantly residential area. This type of covenant is commonly taken from purchasers in private residential developments, and would appear unobjectionable in this context, notwithstanding the *Braintree* decision.

1 Ibid, Sch 6, para 4.
2 Ibid, Sch 6, para 5.
3 (2000) 32 HLR 770.

[10.92] Where the right is to the grant of a long lease, the terms of the lease are regulated by the HA 1985, Sch 6, Pt III. This is intended to maximise the benefit to the tenant. The term granted must be a minimum of 125 years, unless the landlord's interest is itself a lease for less than this period, in which case the lease must be for the residue unexpired of the landlord's term minus five days. Rights enjoyed in common with other tenants are to be included in the lease and enjoyed to the same extent as under the former secure tenancy. The landlord has an implied obligation to repair the structure and exterior of the dwelling house and the building in which it is situated and to make good any defect affecting the structure, to keep common parts in repair in so far as he is able, and to ensure that services provided by the landlord are maintained at a reasonable level and installations connected, with their supply maintained. The tenant has an implied obligation to keep the house in good repair and the interior in good decorative repair. The landlord is entitled to include provision for variable service charges to enable him to recover a 'reasonable' proportion of the costs incurred in complying with his repairing rebuilding and insurance obligations. Variable service charges are controlled under the HA 1985 in much the same way as those applicable in private sector leases[1]. The service charge payments cannot exceed those specified in the landlord s 125D notice, but the controls in the HA 1985 can be side-stepped by the application of a service charge which is initially fixed, subject to indexation to protect the landlord against escalating building costs[2].

1 See Sch 6, para 16A ibid. For private sector provision see Landlord and Tenant Act 1985, s 18 et seq and Chapter 13 below.
2 See *Coventry CC v Cole* [1994] 1 All ER 997.

[10.93] The freehold title, or (if granted) title to the long lease, must be registered even if the title to the land at the time was not[1]. Once the conveyance or lease has been made under the HA 1985, Pt V, the former secure tenancy comes to an end[2].

1 Ibid, s 154.
2 Ibid, s 139(2).

Repayment of discount

[10.94] Because of the generous nature of the discounts given, the HA 1985 contains provisions to enforce a 'claw back' of discount should the tenant sell or lease the premises shortly after exercising the RTB. These are intended to prevent abuse of the scheme for private gain. Any conveyance of the freehold under the RTB, or grant of a long lease, must contain a covenant binding on the secure tenant and his successors in title to repay the discount if a relevant disposal occurs within three years of completion of the RTB[1]. The amount of discount to be repaid reduces by one third for each full year that has elapsed after the conveyance or grant, and before the disposal. Relevant disposals which will trigger the claw back include the further conveyance of the freehold or (if a long lease was granted under RTB) an assignment of the lease, or the grant of a lease for more than 21 years otherwise than at a rack rent[2]. The liability to repay the discount is a charge on the dwelling house, taking effect as if it had been created by deed expressed to be by way of legal mortgage[3].

1 Ibid, s 155.
2 Ibid, s 159(1).
3 Ibid, s 156.

RENT TO MORTGAGE SCHEME

[10.95] A number of attempts have been made since 1980 to extend the right to buy scheme to tenants unable to afford to buy from their own resources. The HA 1980 gave the tenant the right to a mortgage, and in a further innovation shared-ownership leases were introduced under the Housing and Building Control Act 1984. These were replaced by a rent to mortgage scheme, introduced by the Leasehold Reform, Housing and Urban Development Act 1993.The provisions governing the right to acquire on rent to mortgage terms are now set out in the HA 1985, s 143 et seq, as amended.

[10.96] Under the rent to mortgage scheme, a secure tenant exercising the RTB can instead choose rent to mortgage. This gives him the option of paying an initial sum financed by mortgage payments equivalent to his current rent payments. The initial payment is calculated by reference to the tenant's weekly rent multiplied by a multiplier set by the Secretary of State, in order to arrive at the minimum payment that could be financed by a 25-year repayment mortgage where the repayments are at the same level as the tenant's existing rent[1]. The purchase price is discounted in accordance with the applicant's RTB discount (discussed above) and the remainder of the purchase price is treated as an interest free loan made by the landlord. The loan is secured by a mortgage over the dwelling house. This can be paid off at any time, and the mortgage is automatically redeemed if the house is sold or the tenant dies. As with the RTB, the right to rent to mortgage belongs to joint tenants equally. The right can only be exercised if the tenant has not been in receipt of housing benefit for the past 12 months[2].

1 See s 143B ibid.
2 HA 1985, s 143A.

[10.97] The procedures to exercise the RTB on rent to mortgage terms closely follow the RTB procedures outlined above. The tenant must have served notice of intent to exercise the RTB, and his notice of intention to exercise it must remain in force[1]. The tenant can claim the right to acquire on rent to mortgage terms by serving notice to that effect under the HA 1985, s 144. Where he does so any prior notices to complete the RTB served by the landlord are deemed withdrawn. The landlord must then serve notice admitting or denying the right to acquire under rent to mortgage terms. This must state the amount of the initial minimum payment, the multipliers currently in force and used to deduce that sum, the proportion that the initial payment bears to the total price payable, and the discount applied. The tenant then has 12 weeks from service of the landlords reply in which to signify his intention to proceed by giving written notice that he intends to pursue his claim to acquire on rent to mortgage terms. If the tenant fails to give notice of intent, the HA 1985 gives the landlord power to serve a default notice, requiring him to comply within 28 days with the requirement to give his notice of intent, or lose the right. Where the procedure is followed, the tenant (as is the case with the RTB) acquires the right to a conveyance of the house or a long lease (if the dwelling is a flat) on similar terms to those outlined above in relation to the RTB[2].

1 Ibid, s 143(1).
2 Ibid, s 150.

REGISTERED SOCIAL LANDLORDS: THE RIGHT TO ACQUIRE

[10.98] It was noted above that secure tenants whose landlords are charities do not enjoy the RTB. As most registered social landlords have charitable status this excludes from RTB the majority of tenants in the independent rented sector. The only secure tenants of registered social landlords to enjoy the RTB were the minority whose landlords did not have charitable status. Moreover, where the home of a secure tenant of a local authority or non-charitable social landlord is transferred into the private sector, he ceases to be a secure tenant. In this event he will become an assured tenant. Assured tenants in this category retain their right to buy post-transfer under the so-called 'preserved right to buy' set out in the HA 1985, s 171A–171H.

[10.99] The HA 1996, Pt 1 sought to address these anomalies by granting to all tenants of registered social landlords the right to acquire their homes, whether they are assured or secure tenants, provided the property was built or acquired with public funds after the commencement of the HA 1996. The HA 1996, s 16 lays down three qualifying conditions for the exercise of the right to acquire:

(1) The tenant must be a tenant under an assured tenancy (other than an assured shorthold tenancy or a long tenancy) or under a secure tenancy.

(2) The dwelling must have been provided with public money and must have remained in the social rented sector. It must, in other words, have remained in the ownership of a social landlord registered with the Housing Corporation under the HA 1996, or of a local authority or other public sector landlord[1].
(3) The tenant must satisfy any further qualifying conditions applicable to the RTB under the HA 1985, Pt V (above), in so far as they apply. The qualifying conditions for the RTB apply subject to variation by statutory instrument made by the secretary of state under powers in the HA 1996, s 17[2].

1 See HA 1996, s 15(2).
2 Ibid, s 17(2).

[10.100] The policy of the HA 1996 is to extend the right to acquire only to dwellings built with public funding, and to exclude those acquired or built with private finance. For this purpose only a building built or acquired with public money on or after 1 April 1997 can be bought under the HA 1996 provisions. A dwelling will be regarded as provided with public money if it was acquired wholly or partly by means of a social housing grant from the Housing Corporation, where it was acquired or built wholly or partly out of funds kept by a registered social landlord in a disposal proceeds fund, or if it was acquired by a registered social landlord after 1 April 1997 following disposal by a public sector landlord at a time when it was capable of being let as a separate dwelling.

[10.101] The HA 1996 does not set out the detailed procedures to be applied to exercise the right to acquire. These are contained in three statutory instruments made under the powers conferred in the HA 1996[1]. The combined effect of the applicable regulations and the HA 1996, s 17 is to apply the procedures for the RTB under the HA 1985 (discussed above) with a number of substantive and procedural variations. For example, the preserved right to buy does not apply and neither does the right to buy on rent to mortgage terms – this is limited to the RTB in the public sector. The exceptions to the RTB set out in the HA 1985, Sch 5 are also modified in their application to the right to acquire under the HA 1996. The right applies to charities and dwellings for the elderly, but excludes the right to acquire for dwellings in designated rural areas, for persons with special needs, and for dwellings that are charged with debts greater than the discounted purchase price that would be recouped from the tenant on the exercise of the right to acquire. Where the right to acquire applies, the procedural steps for its exercise mirror those for exercise of the RTB in the public sector, as described above.

1 That is, the Housing (Right to Acquire) Regulations 1997 SI 1997/619, the Housing (Right to Acquire)(Discount) Order 1997 SI 1997/626 and the Housing (Right to Acquire)(Discount)(Wales) Order 1997 SI 1997/569.

CHAPTER 11

Long residential tenancies

A Introduction

[11.1] Long leaseholders occupying residential property at a low rent originally enjoyed no security of tenure beyond the end of the contractual tenancy, and could be faced with losing their homes when it expired. Because the rent payable under long tenancies is usually too low, this type of tenancy falls outside the Rent Acts. Long leaseholders were first given security of tenure on the termination of their lease by the Landlord and Tenant Act 1954 (LTA 1954), Pt I. This conferred Rent Act-style security of tenure on long leaseholders by providing that, at the end of the contractual term, the tenancy would statutorily continue unless/until the landlord offered a statutory tenancy under LTA 1954. The latter could be terminated by the landlord only by making out one of the grounds provided for in LTA 1954, Sch 3 – these were similar in most respects to the Rent Act grounds for possession[1].

1 Discussed above in Chapter 6, para 6.106 ff.

[11.2] The LTA 1954 conferred protection on long residential tenants occupying both houses and long leasehold flats. The position as regards single dwelling houses was, however, significantly improved in the tenant's favour by the Leasehold Reform Act 1967(LRA 1967)[1]. This gave tenants of houses[2] with a long lease (ie of at least 21 years) at a low rent, the right to enfranchise and purchase the landlord's freehold interest or to obtain a 50-year extension of the tenancy[3]. The Leasehold Reform, Housing and Urban Development Act 1993 (LRHUDA 1993) complemented these provisions by extending a right of collective enfranchisement to long leaseholders of residential flats.

1 See further Hill and Redman *Law of Landlord and Tenant* (18th edn) E 52 ff; Evans and Smith *Law of Landlord and Tenant* (5th edn) p 422 ff.
2 See LRA 1967, s 2.
3 LRHUDA 1993, ss 8 and 14.

[11.3] Protection on termination based on the LTA 1954, Pt I has now been replaced by the Local Government and Housing Act 1989 (LGHA 1989), Sch 10. The latter substituted for the former Rent Act scheme a form of protection on termination based on the assured tenancy model introduced for private sector tenancies by the Housing Act 1988 (HA 1988). The assured tenancy scheme was phased in over a ten-year period from 1989, and now applies on the termination of all long leases after 15 January 1999, whether or not the lease was initially granted before that date[1]. This reflects official policy to phase out Rent Act-style protection as speedily as possible, and replace it with a single tenancy model, based upon the assured tenancy, for all types of residential tenancy.

1 See para 11.7 below.

[11.4] Most long leaseholders will, therefore, not only have security of tenure at the end of their lease, but also be entitled to extend their lease, or to enfranchise and buy the freehold in their home. The tenant's right to security of tenure under the LGHA 1989, Sch 10 retains considerable significance, however, notwithstanding the enfranchisement provisions in the LRA 1967 and the LRHUDA 1993. It will give residential security where a long leaseholder cannot enfranchise under the LRA 1967 or the LRHUDA 1993 (whichever applies), for example in the case of a block of flats because the requisite majority of tenants to exercise enfranchisement rights under the LRHUDA 1993 cannot be achieved. The LGHA 1989 will also remain significant if for some reason, such as financial exigency, the tenant does not wish to enfranchise. Similarly, it will also remain important if the tenant fails to exercise his right to an extension of his lease under either the LRA 1967 or the LRHUDA 1993 (whichever applies).

B Security of tenure

SCOPE OF STATUTORY PROTECTION

[11.5] Prior to the introduction of the LTA 1954, Pt I, the tenant enjoyed no security following the termination of a long residential tenancy at a low rent, and would have to quit. The protection introduced by the LTA 1954, Pt I was based on the Rent Act model. Following expiry of a long residential tenancy, the tenancy was statutorily continued by the LTA 1954 on the same terms, and at the same rent, until terminated by the landlord in the manner prescribed by the Act. The landlord could either offer a statutory tenancy, or seek possession on one of a number of grounds set out in the LTA 1954, Sch 3. These are based largely on the Rent Act grounds to be found in the Rent Act 1977 (RA 1977), Sch 15[1].

1 See Chapter 6, para 6.106 ff.

[11.6] Following the introduction of assured tenancies in the HA 1988, provision was made to replace the LTA 1954 regime with protection based instead on the assured tenancy model. The LGHA 1989, Sch 10 makes provision for protection based on an assured tenancy arising post-expiry, and introduces a modified assured tenancy scheme for long residential tenancies. The introduction of protection based on the assured tenancy model was phased in, applying initially only to tenancies entered into on or after 1 April 1990. Since 15 January 1999 it has applied on the termination of all long tenancies at a low rent, whenever granted.

[11.7] By virtue of the LGHA 1989, s 186, protection based on Sch 10 applies to three categories of tenancy of a dwelling house:

(a) a long tenancy at a low rent which is entered into on or after 1 April 1990, otherwise than in pursuance of a contract made before that date; *and*
(b) to a tenancy which was in existence on 15 January 1999 and which, immediately before that date, was a long tenancy at a low rent for the purposes of the LTA 1954, Pt I. In this case, on and after 15 January 1999, the LTA 1954, Pt I ceased to apply to the tenancy. LGHA 1989, Sch 10 (ie the assured tenancy regime) now applies on its termination instead unless the landlord had served a notice under the LTA 1954 specifying a date of termination of the tenancy which was earlier than 15 January 1999[1].

(c) to a long tenancy of a house where the lease has been extended under the LRA 1967. The 1967 Act gives the tenant the right to an extension of 50 years on his lease, if he so chooses, instead of full enfranchisement. Where the tenant chose to extend the lease, rather than buy the freehold, however, he enjoyed no security of tenure on the later expiry of the extended lease. This was remedied by the Commonhold and Leasehold Reform Act 2002 (CLRA 2002), which deleted the provision in the LRA 1967 preventing long leaseholders who have extended their leases from remaining in possession under an assured tenancy when the extended lease later expires. This reform brings the position of long leaseholders who have extended their leases into line with the rights accruing to those who do not extend the original lease or purchase the freehold, but chose to remain in possession under an assured tenancy[2].

1 That is under LTA 1954, s 4. See LGHA 1989, s 186(2) and (3).
2 See Commonhold and Leasehold Reform Act 2002, Sch 14 repealing LRA 1967, s 16(1)(a). See also *Commonhold and Leasehold Reform: Draft Bill and Consultation Paper* (Cm 4843 2000) p 160.

ASSURED TENANCY ON TERMINATION

[11.8] LGHA 1989, Sch 10 provides for an assured tenancy to arise on termination of a long lease at a low rent, on the terms below.

Qualifying for protection

[11.9] LGHA 1989, Sch 10 applies to a long tenancy of a dwelling house at a low rent as respects which, for the time being, the circumstances are such that, if the tenancy were not at a low rent, it would at that time be an assured tenancy within the meaning of the HA 1988, Pt 1[1]. For the purpose of the qualifying condition:

(i) 'long tenancy' means a tenancy granted for a term of years certain exceeding 21 years, whether or not subsequently extended by act of the parties or by any enactment, but excluding any tenancy which may become terminable before the end of the term by notice given to the tenant (ie by exercise of a 'break' clause in the tenancy)[2];

(ii) a tenancy is at a 'low rent' if under the tenancy *either* (a) no rent is payable, *or* (b) where the tenancy is entered into on or after 1 April 1990 the maximum rent payable at any time is payable at a rate of £1,000 or less per annum if the dwelling house is in Greater London or £250 or less per annum if the dwelling house is elsewhere *or* (c) where the tenancy was entered into before 1 April 1990, *or* (where the dwelling house had a rateable value on 31 March 1990) it is entered into on or after 1 April 1990 in pursuance of a contract made before that date, and the maximum rent payable at any time under the tenancy is less than two-thirds of the rateable value of the dwelling house on 31 March 1990[3].

1 LGHA 1989, Sch 10, para 1(1). For the qualifying conditions for protection under Pt I of the 1988 Act see Ch 3 para 3.12 ff above. For the purposes of LGHA 1989, Sch 10, the qualifying conditions in HA 1988, Sch 1, take effect with the omission of HA 1988, Sch 1, para 1 – LGHA 1989, Sch 10, para 1(2). Special rules are provided for ascertaining the rateable value of dwellings let on or after 1 April 1990 for this purpose – see LGHA 1989, Sch 10, para 1(2A).
2 Ibid, Sch 10, para 2(3).
3 Ibid, Sch 10, para 2(4).

Continuation of tenancy

[11.10] Where a tenancy to which LGHA 1989, Sch 10 applies expires the landlord can allow the tenant to continue in possession under the terms of the original tenancy. By virtue of LGHA 1989, Sch 10, para 3, a tenancy which, immediately before its term date, is a long residential tenancy, shall not come to an end on expiry unless terminated under the provisions of Sch 10. If not so terminated, the tenancy shall statutorily continue until terminated in accordance with the provisions in LGHA 1989, Sch 10 and, while continuing, is deemed to be a long residential tenancy, notwithstanding any change in circumstances. Where a tenancy is statutorily continued after the term date, the tenancy continues with the same rent and in other respects with the same terms as before the term date[1]. Provision is made for the landlord to apply for an interim rent to be awarded. This facility, however, is available only if he has served notice under LGHA 1989, Sch 10 proposing an assured tenancy. To take advantage of this facility the landlord must serve notice on the tenant in prescribed form[2], proposing an interim monthly rent to take effect from a date specified in the notice – this must not be earlier than the date from which the tenancy has been terminated[3]. The tenant can ask the Rent Assessment Committee for a determination within the period of two months following service of the landlord's notice of interim rent. In this event the committee shall determine the monthly rent at which they consider the premises might reasonably be expected to be let on the open market by a willing landlord under a monthly periodic tenancy, making the following assumptions:

(i) that the tenancy begins on the day following the specified date of termination;
(ii) that the tenancy is one under which the terms are the same as those of the existing tenancy at the date on which was given the landlord's notice proposing a short tenancy; and
(iii) that the tenancy affords the tenant security of tenure equivalent to that afforded to assured tenancies under the HA 1988, Sch 1, Pt 1. The assured tenancy is to be assumed to be one in respect of which possession may not be recovered under any of Grounds 1–5 in the HA 1988, Sch 2[4].

1 LGHA 1989, Sch 10, para 3(1) and (3).
2 See the Long Residential Tenancies (Principal Forms) Regulations 1997, SI 1997/3008.
3 Ibid, Sch 10, para 6(1).
4 Ibid, Sch 10, para 6(3). For Sch 2 and the grounds for possession see Chapter 4 above.

TERMINATION OF TENANCY BY THE LANDLORD

[11.11] On expiry of a long residential tenancy, the landlord has two choices if he wishes to terminate the tenancy:

(i) he can give notice to terminate the tenancy and seek possession; or
(ii) he can give notice proposing an assured tenancy of the dwelling house. The tenancy proposed must be an assured monthly periodic tenancy and the rent proposed by the landlord must be such that the tenancy would *not* be a tenancy at a low rent. The notice must propose that the other terms of the tenancy should be the same as those of the long residential tenancy immediately before it was terminated (these are referred to as 'the implied terms' of the assured tenancy)[1].

1 LGHA 1989, Sch 10, para 4(5).

[11.12] Whichever course the landlord chooses, he must serve a notice terminating the tenancy which complies with the requirements of LGHA 1989, Sch 10, para 4. The landlord's notice of termination must be in prescribed form[1] and must specify the date at which the tenancy is to come to an end, being either the term date of the tenancy or a later date, and the notice must be served on the tenant not more than 12 nor less than six months before the termination date specified[2].

1 See the Long Residential Tenancies (Principal Forms) Regulations 1997, SI 1997/3008, Form 1.
2 LGHA 1989, Sch 10, para 4(1). Compare with the service of notices under LTA 1954, ss 25, 26 (business tenancies). For the 'corresponding date' rule applied under the LTA 1954 for calculating the period for service see *Dodds v Walker* [1981] 2 All ER 609, HL; *EJ Riley Investments Ltd v Eurostile Holdings Ltd* [1985] 1 WLR 1139, CA.

[11.13] If the landlord's notice proposes an assured tenancy, he may propose terms of the tenancy different from the terms otherwise implied[1] by LGHA 1989, Sch 10 (ie the terms of the long residential tenancy immediately prior to termination)[2]. In this event, however, the tenant can refer to the Rent Assessment Committee for a determination of the terms of the tenancy (see below, para 11.25 ff).

1 That is those implied by LGHA 1989, Sch 10, para 4(5)(a).
2 Ibid, Sch 10, para 4(6).

[11.14] The landlord's notice must invite the tenant, within the period of two months beginning on the date on which the notice was served, to notify the landlord in writing whether, if the landlord's notice proposes an assured tenancy, the tenant wishes to remain in possession, or if the landlord's notice seeks to resume possession, whether the tenant is willing to give up possession as demanded[1].

1 LGHA 1989, Sch 10, para 4(7).

RECOVERING POSSESSION

[11.15] Where the landlord has served notice under LGHA 1989, Sch 10, para 4 to resume possession[1], he may apply to the court for an order for possession. The landlord may make an application to the court if, following service of notice to resume possession, there is an election by the tenant to retain possession, or if at the end of the period of two months following the date of service of the notice, the qualifying condition is fulfilled as respects the tenancy, viz it is a long tenancy at a low rent within the meaning of LGHA 1989, Sch 10, para 1.

1 See SI 1997/3008, Form 2 for the prescribed form of notice.

[11.16] The landlord's application to the court must be made within the following time limits:

(i) it must be made within the period of two months beginning on the date of the election by the tenant to retain possession; or
(ii) if there is no election by the tenant to retain possession, then the landlord's application must be made within the period of four months beginning on the date of service of the landlord's notice to resume possession.

[11.17] In proceedings under the LGHA 1989, Sch 10 the landlord may seek to recover possession on a number of grounds specified in the LGHA 1989,

Sch 10, para 5. The grounds to be relied upon must be specified in the landlord's notice to resume possession. These are modelled on the assured tenancy grounds found in the HA 1988, Sch 2, but modified to take account of the special circumstances appropriate to the termination of a long residential tenancy. The grounds available to the landlord in proceedings under the LGHA 1989, Sch 10 are the following[1]:

(i) Ground 6 (Redevelopment) in the HA 1988, Sch 2 and the discretionary grounds in HA 1988, Sch 2, Pt II, other than Ground 16 (termination of employment). Ground 6 (the redevelopment ground) may not be specified in a landlord's notice to resume possession if the tenancy is a former LTA 1954 tenancy, eg if it was granted prior to 15 January 1999 but terminated after the phasing in of the assured tenancy regime on 15 January 1999. In addition, LGHA 1989, Sch 10, para 5(1) specifies two grounds which are additional to the assured tenancy grounds in Sch 2 to the 1988 Act; viz
(ii) the ground that, for the purposes of redevelopment after the termination of the tenancy, the landlord proposes to demolish or reconstruct the whole or a substantial part of the premises; and
(iii) the premises or part of them are reasonably required by the landlord for occupation as a resident for himself or any son or daughter of his over 18 years of age, or his or his spouse's father or mother and, if the landlord is not the immediate landlord, that he will be at the specified date of termination[2].

1 See LGHA 1989, Sch 10, para 5(1). The assured tenancy grounds are considered in detail in Chapter 4, above.
2 Ibid, Sch 10, para 5(1)(c).

[11.18] Note that ground (ii) above (the demolition/reconstruction ground) cannot be specified unless the landlord is a body to which LRA 1967, s 28 applies, and the premises are required for relevant 'development' within the meaning of that provision[1]. This limits the application of this ground to situations where the landlord is a local authority, the Commission for New Towns, or certain other of specified public bodies, eg a university or regional health authority[2].

1 LGHA 1989, Sch 10, para 5(4) ibid.
2 See LRA 1967, s 28(5).

[11.19] The ground mentioned in (iii) above (requirement for own or family residence) cannot be specified by the landlord, if his interest was purchased or created after 18 February 1966[1].

1 LGHA 1989, Sch 10, para 5(5).

[11.20] Detailed provision is made in the LGHA 1989, Sch 10, paras 13 and 14, for the amended application of the assured tenancy grounds for possession to long residential tenancies[1]. Where the landlord's application is successful, the tenancy will terminate on the termination date specified in the landlord's notice to resume possession, although the court has power under the LGHA 1989, Sch 10, para 14 to award a postponed date of termination if the ground specified is the redevelopment ground in para (ii) above (ie where the landlord is a public body wishing to demolish/reconstruct the premises)[2].

1 See LGHA 1989, Sch 10, paras 13(3)–(7) and para 14.
2 Ibid, Sch 10, para 14(1) and (2).

[11.21] If no application is made by the landlord in the time allowed then his notice to resume possession shall cease to have effect. It will, similarly, cease to have effect if an application to the court has been made, but the result of that application is that no order is made. In this situation, also, the landlord's notice to resume possession shall cease to have effect[1].

1 LGHA 1989, Sch 10, para 15(2) and (3).

THE ASSURED PERIODIC TENANCY

Creation and commencement

[11.22] Where the tenancy is terminated by a landlord's notice which proposes an assured tenancy, the tenant is entitled to remain in possession of the dwelling house and his right to possession shall depend upon an assured periodic tenancy arising under the LGHA 1989, Sch 10, para 9. The assured period tenancy which arises in this way is one which[1]:

(i) takes effect in possession on the day following the date of termination specified in the landlord's notice;
(ii) is deemed to have been granted by the person who was the landlord under the former tenancy on the date of termination to the person who was then the former tenant under that tenancy;
(iii) under which the premises let are the dwelling house; and
(iv) under which the periods of the tenancy, and the intervals at which rent is to be paid, are monthly beginning on the day following the date of termination.

1 LGHA 1989, Sch 10, para 9(2).

[11.23] The tenant is not entitled to remain in possession under an assured periodic tenancy if, at the end of the period of two months beginning on the date of service of the landlord's notice, the qualifying condition was not fulfilled as respects the tenancy, ie it was not at that date a long tenancy at a low rent within the meaning of the provisions outlined above[1].

1 LGHA 1989, Sch 10, para 9(3).

[11.24] Where the landlord has served a notice proposing an assured tenancy, the tenant has two months, beginning on the date of service of the landlord's notice, in which to serve notice in prescribed form[1] on the landlord proposing a rent different from that proposed in the landlord's notice of termination and/or terms of the tenancy different from those so specified[2]. If the tenant does not serve notice proposing terms different from those set out in the landlord's notice of termination, then the rent and other terms specified in the landlord's notice take effect as terms of the tenancy. If the tenant serves notice challenging the rent and/or other terms specified, then the landlord can (within a further period of two months beginning on the date of service of the tenant's notice) make application to the Rent Assessment Committee for a determination[3].

1 See SI 1997/3008, Form 4.
2 LGHA 1989, Sch 10, para 10(1).
3 Ibid, Sch 10, para 10(2).

[11.25] Where a tenant's notice as to terms is referred to the Rent Assessment Committee, the Committee's first duty is to determine whether there is any dispute as to the terms (other than those relating to the rent) of the assured periodic tenancy, and if so what the disputed terms are, and whether there is any dispute as to rent under the tenancy. In determining whether there is a dispute as to the terms or rent, the Committee must have regard only to the contents of the landlord's and tenant's notices served under the LGHA 1989, Sch 10, para 10 (above). Where the Committee decide that there are disputed terms, they are obliged to give a ruling on the terms of the tenancy (other than those as to rent) in the first instance, before considering the rent appropriate under the assured periodic tenancy.

Disputed terms (other than as to rent)

[11.26] If the Rent Assessment Committee decide that there are disputed terms, then they must determine whether the terms in the landlord's notice, the terms in the tenant's notice, or some other terms dealing with the same subject matter as the terms in dispute, are such as, in the committee's opinion, might reasonably be expected to be found in an assured monthly periodic tenancy of the dwelling house (not being an assured shorthold tenancy)[1]. The notional assured periodic tenancy is to be assumed to be one which begins on the day following the date of termination, which is granted by a willing landlord on terms which (except in so far as they relate to the subject matter of the disputed terms) are the undisputed terms, and which must be assumed to be one in respect of which possession cannot be recovered under any of Grounds 1–5 of the HA 1988, Sch 2. The Committee shall, if they consider it appropriate, specify an adjustment of the undisputed terms to take effect on the terms as determined and can, if they consider it appropriate, specify an adjustment of the rent to take account of the terms so determined and adjusted. The Committee must disregard any effect on the terms, or the amount of the rent, which is attributable to the granting of a tenancy to a sitting tenant[2].

1 LGHA 1989, Sch 10, para 11(3).
2 Ibid, Sch 10, para 11(4).

Dispute as to rent

[11.27] If the Committee decide that there is a dispute as to the rent under the assured periodic tenancy, then they must determine the monthly rent at which they consider that the dwelling house might reasonably be expected to be let on the open market by a willing landlord under an assured tenancy (not being an assured shorthold tenancy). The following assumptions must be made as to the notional assured tenancy used as a yardstick for valuing the rent:

(i) it must be assumed to be a monthly periodic tenancy;
(ii) the notional tenancy must be assumed to begin on the day following the date of termination;
(iii) it is assumed to be one in respect of which possession may not be recovered under any of Grounds 1–5 in the HA 1988, Sch 2; and (further)
(iv) the terms of the assured tenancy (other than those relating to the amount of the rent) are to be assumed to be the same as the undisputed terms in the tenancy under consideration, or if there has been a determination as to disputed terms other than the rent, the terms determined by the committee under the LGHA 1989, Sch 10[1].

The valuation provisions in the HA 1988, s 14 (rent under assured tenancies) are applied with modifications appropriate to a determination of rents under long residential tenancies[2].

1 LGHA 1989, Sch 10, para 11(5).
2 See ibid, Sch 10, para 11(7). For s 14 see Ch 3 para 3.116 ff. above. For instance tenants' improvements are discounted if effected during the long residential tenancy, but not if effected during the 21 years prior to termination.

TERMINATION BY TENANT

[11.28] A long residential tenancy can be brought to an end at its contractual term date if the tenant gives to his immediate landlord not less than one month's notice of termination in writing. If the tenancy has been statutorily continued after expiry, the tenancy can be terminated at any time by the giving of not less than one month's written notice, whether the notice is given before or after the term date of the tenancy. The fact that the landlord has served notice of termination, or that there has been an election by the tenant to retain possession, shall not prevent the tenant from giving notice of termination terminating the tenancy at an earlier date than that specified in the landlord's notice[1].

1 LGHA 1989, Sch 10, para 8.

CHAPTER 12

Leasehold enfranchisement

[12.1] The Leasehold Reform Act 1967 (LRA 1967) gives the tenant of a leasehold house, who has a long residential tenancy at a low rent, the right to 'enfranchisement', ie to purchase the landlord's freehold interest on fair terms, or (alternatively) to acquire an extended lease. Tenants of leasehold flats were given the right to enfranchise by the Leasehold Reform, Housing and Urban Development Act 1993 (LRHUDA 1993). The Commonhold and Leasehold Reform Act 2002 (CLRA 2002) substantially extended the enfranchisement rights of both groups of tenants, and made a number of important amendments to both the LRA 1967 and the LRHUDA 1993.

A Leasehold houses: the Leasehold Reform Act 1967

THE RIGHT TO ENFRANCHISE

Scope of enfranchisement rights

[12.2] The Leasehold Reform Act 1967 (LRA 1967), s 1[1] confers a right to acquire the freehold or an extended lease on a tenant of a leasehold house where certain qualifying conditions are satisfied.

1 The LRA 1967 has generated a not inconsiderable legal literature, and a substantial volume of case law over the past 30 years. The account given here focuses on the extension of LRA 1967 and enfranchisement rights under the LRHUDA 1993 effected by the CLRA 2002. For more detailed discussion of the LRA 1967 per se, see inter alia *Hill and Redman's Law of Landlord and Tenant* (18th edn). E 52–E 157; *Evans and Smith Law of Landlord and Tenant* (5th edn) p 422 ff.

Qualifying long tenancies

[12.3] The tenancy must be a long tenancy granted for a term of years exceeding 21 years. Originally, different rules applied for enfranchisement of a long tenancy for 21 years or more at a low rent and to long tenancies that are not at a low rent. The LRA 1967 originally only applied to long tenancies at a low rent. The rules were relaxed by the LRHUDA 1993, and the Housing Act 1996 (HA 1996)[1] extended enfranchisement to especially long tenancies of 35 years or more, in which case the low rent test did not apply. The requirement for the lease to be 35 years or more in length was removed by the CLRA 2002, with the result that, after the coming into force of the CLRA 2002, all long leases (whether or not they are granted at a low rent) can be enfranchised, provided the term granted is at least 21 years[2]. Although enfranchisement can be claimed in this case even though the rent payable exceeds the low rent test (below) the cost of enfranchisement is likely to be high.

1 HA 1996, Sch 9, inserting a new s 1AA to LRA 1967.
2 CLRA 2002, s 141, amending LRA 1967, s 1AA.

[12.4] Another category of tenancy were long leases for 21 years or more granted at a low rent, but which were excluded from the right to enfranchise because the rateable value of the premises exceeded the threshold set in LRA 1967, s 1. Before the LRHUDA 1993, the right to enfranchise was limited to houses below fixed rateable value limits. The LRHUDA 1993[1] brought these tenancies within the enfranchisement provisions, and LRA 1967, Pt I, now applies to them as if the value limit was not exceeded. In this type of case, however, the valuation rules will make enfranchisement more expensive for this category of occupier.

1 LRHUDA 1993, s 63, inserting a new s 1A to LRA 1967.

Abolition of residence test

[12.5] At the relevant time (ie when he gives notice to acquire the freehold or an extended lease) the claimant must have been the tenant of the house under a long tenancy for a period of two years[1]. The LRA 1967 originally imposed an additional residence test, requiring the tenant to have been occupying the dwelling as his residence for the last three years, or for periods amounting to three years in the last ten years[2].

1 The qualifying period as tenant was reduced from three years (or three out of the previous ten years) to two years by the CLRA 2002, s 139, amending LRA 1967, s 1(1)(b).
2 LRA 1967, s 1(1)(b).

[12.6] The residence requirement was abolished by the CLRA 2002[1]. Following the commencement of the CLRA 2002, therefore, a tenant can enfranchise whether or not he is actually living in the house, provided a period of two years has elapsed since he acquired the lease of the property. This will facilitate enfranchisement by, for example, those purchasing property with the intention of renting it out under 'buy to let' arrangements, as well as by resident tenants. A particular concern to which the abolition of the residence test gave rise during the parliamentary debates on the CLRA 2002 was the possibility of windfall profits being made by a non-resident head lessee who sublets flats in a building to resident tenants on long leases. An amendment to the CLRA 2002 was moved in the final stages of its parliamentary scrutiny to provide that when part of a house is sublet to a person who qualifies for collective enfranchisement under the LRHUDA 1993, the house itself cannot be enfranchised under the LRA 1967 unless the head lessee has occupied the house, or part of it, for two years or for periods totalling two years in the past ten[2]. This is intended to prevent a non-resident head lessee enfranchising the house and making windfall gains from subsequent enfranchisement and/or lease renewal by the subtenants of flats in the building. The CLRA 2002 retains the existing right for resident head lessees to enfranchise in these circumstances. For the purposes of establishing 'residence', occupation must be personal, and cannot be satisfied by a company of which the tenant has a controlling interest, or by a corporation sole or other entity with artificial legal personality[3]. Whether the tenant is 'residing' in the required sense is a question of fact, and physical occupation of part of the demised premises may suffice, eg, if the remainder is sublet by the long lessee[4].

1 CLRA 2002, s 138.
2 LRA 1967, s 1(1ZB), inserted by s 138 of the CLRA 2002. See Hansard (House of Lords Debates) 15 April 2002 Col 699 (Lords consideration of Commons Amendments).
3 Ibid, s 37(5).
4 *Baron v Phillips* (1978) 38 P & CR 91; *Harris v Swick Securities Ltd* [1969] 3 All ER 1131, CA.

Excluded categories of tenancy

[12.7] Enfranchisement rights under the LRA 1967 do not arise if the house is let to and occupied by the tenant with other land or premises to which it is ancillary, or if it is comprised in an agricultural holding[1].

1 LRA 1967, s 1(3). For definition of an agricultural holding and the protected status of a dwelling let ancillary to parcels of land, see Rodgers *Agricultural Law* (2nd ed 1998) p 111ff, Muir Watt *Agricultural Holdings* (14th edn) paras 8.16 et seq. And see above para 3.81 et seq, for protection under HA 1988 in similar circumstances (if the rateable value limits for protection are met).

[12.8] Neither does the LRA 1967 confer any enfranchisement rights on the tenant of a house which is let as a business tenancy to which LTA 1954, Pt II applies – unless the tenant has been occupying the house or part of it as his main residence for the last two years or for periods amounting to two years in the last ten[1]. Furthermore, where a long tenancy is of business premises to which the LTA 1954 applies, the right to enfranchise only arises in limited circumstances[2]. The tenancy must either be granted for a term of years exceeding 35 years; or be a lease which takes effect for a fixed term of 90 years by operation of law[3]; or be a tenancy initially granted for less than 35 years but which is renewed without payment of a premium, and which has been so renewed so as to bring the total period of tenancy to more than 35 years.

1 LRA 1967, s 1(1B), inserted by CLRA 2002, s 139(2).
2 Ibid, s 1(1ZC). inserted by CLRA 2002, s 140.
3 That is to say it must be a perpetually renewable lease (Law of Property Act 1922, s 122) or a lease determinable on death or marriage (Law of Property Act 1925, s 149(6))

[12.9] Special rules apply to houses in designated rural areas. Although the low rent test was abolished by the Housing Act 1996 (HA 1996) for houses let for more than 35 years, it was retained for houses in rural areas designated by the Secretary of State. The rationale for this exception was to exclude rack rented properties let on long leases by rural estates, for example where a house or farm was surplus to estate purposes. Most of these properties would not have been let on long leases had the estate owner realised that they may be enfranchiseable later. The CLRA 2002 therefore extends the right to enfranchise to long leaseholders of dwellings in designated rural areas in two situations[1].

(i) where the lease commenced on or after 31 March 1997, but before the coming into force of the CLRA 2002, and the original term was over 35 years; and
(ii) where the lease commenced after the commencement of the CLRA 2002, and the term was a fixed term for 21 years or more.

Houses let in rural areas before these dates will continue to be subject to the low rent test if the freehold was owned together with land used for non-residential purposes.

1 CLRA 2002, s 141, amending LRA 1967, s 1AA(3).

The rateable value test

[12.10] The LRA 1967 originally only applied to properties below a certain rateable value. Although the qualifying condition was removed by the LRHUDA 1993, the rateable value test (like the low rent test) continues to have relevance for valuation purposes. If the tenancy was entered into before 1 April 1990, or pursuant to a contract made before that date[1], the rateable value of the premises on the appropriate day must not have been more than £200, or (in Greater London) £400[2]. If the tenancy was entered into on or after 1 April 1990 the value of the premises is calculated using a formula based on the premium paid on grant, the term of years granted, and a multiplier, as provided for in the References to Rating (Housing) Regulations 1990[3]. The value of the premises, thus calculated, must not exceed £25,000 on the date the contract for the grant of the tenancy was concluded, or (if none) the date of grant itself.

1 Provided the house had a rateable value at 30 March 1990.

2 The appropriate day means 23 March 1965 or such later date as would be such for the purposes of RA 1977, s 25(3), (Rent Act rateable value limits) (LRA 1967, s 1(4)). And see LRA 1967, s 1(5) and (6) for variations in the limits for tenancies granted (i) on or before 18 February 1966 and rated separately before 1 April 1973 (£750 or £1,500 (London)) *and* (ii) after 18 February 1966 but rated only after 1 April 1973 (£500 or £1,000 (London)).

3 SI 1990/434, reg 2, Schedule. The formula is:

$$R = \frac{P \times I}{1 - (1 + I) - T}$$

where P is the premium paid on grant, T is the term of years and I is 0.06.

The low rent test

[12.11] It has already been noted that the CLRA 2002 has abolished the low rent test as a qualifying condition for enfranchisement. The test still has relevance, however, as one of the factors to be taken into account in valuing the price to be paid when purchasing the freehold. Since the LRHUDA 1993, there have been two alternative low rent tests; one in the LRA 1967, s 4 which apples to both the acquisition of the freehold and the extension of a lease under the Act, and an alternative low rent test under section 1A(2). The latter was a new provision introduced by the LRHUDA 1993 and dealt with the problem where the house was outside the LRA 1967 solely because the rent reserved was not a 'low rent' within the meaning of the LRA 1967, and applied a more liberal test in order to extend the enfranchisement regime. The more liberal test only applies to purchase of the freehold, however, and not to lease extensions.

(i) By virtue of the LRA 1967, s 4, the tenancy will be at a 'low rent' at any time when the yearly rent payable is less than two-thirds of the rateable value of the house on the appropriate day[1] *or*, if the tenancy was entered into on or after 1 April 1990, not more than £1,000 (Greater London) or £250 (elsewhere). Special rules apply to long tenancies granted between the end of August 1938 and the beginning of April 1963, requiring the rent to be not more than two-thirds of the 'letting value' of the premises at the commencement of the tenancy[2]. For these purposes the 'low rent' test has to be satisfied at the time of giving notice to enfranchise[3].

(ii) The alternative test in LRA 1967, s 4A, provides that a tenancy is to be treated as a tenancy at a low rent if during *the initial year* of the tenancy the rent payable did not exceed a certain amount. The rent limit during the first year depends on which of three categories the tenancy falls into. These are[4]:

(1) *Tenancies entered into before 1 April 1963*; two-thirds of the letting value[5] of the property on commencement of the tenancy.
(2) *Tenancies entered into on or after 1 April 1963 and before 1 April 1990*[6]; two-thirds of the rateable value (RV) on commencement of the tenancy, or (if there was no RV on commencement) on the date at which it first had a RV.
(3) *Other tenancies*; £1,000 if the property is in Greater London, or £250 if it is elsewhere. This category covers, for example, tenancies granted on or after 1 April 1990.

1 LRA 1967, s 4(1), amended References to Rating (Housing) Regulations 1990, reg 2 and Schedule. For the 'appropriate day' see RA 1977, s 25(3), above Chapter 7 p 177 ff.
2 This prevents tenancies granted during this period from accruing enfranchisement rights under the LRA 1967 simply by virtue of the rating revaluation effected in 1965.
3 LRA 1967, s 1(1)(b).
4 Ibid, s 4A(1)(a)–(c), as inserted by LRHUDA 1993, s 65.
5 'Letting value' has the same meaning as under LRA 1967, s 4 (see n 2 above), on which see: *Manson v Duke of Westminster* [1981] QB 323, CA; *Johnston v Duke of Westminster* [1986] AC 839, HL; *Hembry v Henry Smith's Charity Trustees* [1987] 2 EGLR 109, CA.
6 This category includes tenancies entered into after 1 April 1990 pursuant to a contract made before that date.

Right to enfranchise during an extended lease

[12.12] The LRA 1967 gives most leaseholders the right to acquire an extension on their leases of 50 years, as an alternative to full enfranchisement (see below para 12.39 ff). Under the original legislation this right carried several disadvantages, most notably the fact that the right to enfranchise and purchase the freehold did not apply during the lease extension. The CLRA 2002 removed this restriction, thus enabling a tenant with an extended tenancy to acquire the freehold under the LRA 1967[1]. The CLRA 2002 also removed the provision in the LRA 1967 which prevented enfranchisement by a subtenant where an intermediate landlord has been given a lease extension and the extension has commenced[2]. Where a long leaseholder enfranchises after the expiry of the original long lease, however, the purchase price will reflect the open market value including any relevant element of marriage value[3]. The valuation of the price is discussed further below (para 12.31 ff).

1 See CLRA 2002, s 142, amending LRA 1967, s 16.
2 See LRA 1967, s 16(4), as amended by CLRA 2002, s 143(1)(b).
3 See LRA 1967, s 9(1AA), as inserted by CLRA 2002, s 143(4).

Right of personal representatives to enfranchise

[12.13] The LRA 1967 gave members of a deceased tenant's family the right to succeed to the tenancy of a house and then qualify for enfranchisement or lease extension provided they were resident in the house as their only or main residence at the time of the tenant's death[1]. As we have seen, the CLRA 2002 abolished the residence requirement for enfranchisement, and replaced it with an ownership requirement stipulating that the long leaseholder own the lease for two years prior to enfranchising. The CLRA 2002 therefore now provides that, where a tenant who has died had (immediately before his death) the right to acquire the freehold or an extended lease, then that right is exercisable by his personal representatives while the tenancy is vested in them. The latter can, however, only exercise their right to enfranchise or acquire a lease extension within two years after the grant of probate or letters of administration[2].

1 LRA 1967, s 7.
2 LRA 1967, s 6A, as inserted by CLRA 2002, s 142. The two-year 'window' during which this right can be exercised by the personal representatives is more generous than that originally proposed in the draft Commonhold Bill, which limited it to a six month period following the tenant's death: see Commonhold and Leasehold Reform: Draft Bill and Consultation Paper (Cm4843, DETR 2001), p 190.

QUALIFYING CRITERIA FOR ENFRANCHISEMENT

[12.14] The right to enfranchisement applies only where there is a 'tenancy' of a 'house' which is a 'long' tenancy within the meaning of the LRA 1967. Further, the right to enfranchise gives the tenant the right to acquire the freehold to not only the house itself, but to the 'house and premises' occupied by him under the long tenancy. These concepts all require careful definition.

'House'

[12.15] For the purposes of the LRA 1967 a 'house' includes any building designed or adapted for living in and 'reasonably so called' – notwithstanding that the building is not structurally detached, or was or is not solely designed or adapted for living in, or is divided horizontally into flats or maisonettes[1]. There must be a building designed or adapted for living in, and which might reasonably be regarded as a 'house' in the broadest sense. This would include mixed-use premises that can reasonably be called a house, eg a building with a flat above a shop[2]. Special rules apply to subdivided buildings[3]:

(i) if a building is divided horizontally, the flats or units into which it is so divided are not separate 'houses' – though the building as a whole may be[4]. Separate flats are excluded from the LRA 1967 altogether, and are now separately provided for in the LRHUDA 1993 (below, para 12.43 ff);
(ii) if a building is divided vertically, then the building as a whole is not a 'house', though any of the units into which it is divided may be. This provision excludes, eg, a row of terraced houses or a pair of semi-detached houses from enfranchisement under the LRA 1967 – though individual houses within a terrace can qualify if the criteria for enfranchisement are satisfied in relation thereto.

1 LRA 1967, s 2(1).
2 See *Tandon v Trustees of Spurgeon's Homes* [1982] AC 755, HL ('if the building is designed or adapted for living in . . . only exceptional circumstances would justify a judge in holding that it could not reasonably be called a house. They would have to be such that nobody could reasonably call the building a house'; ibid at 767, per Lord Roskill).
3 See LRA 1967, s 2(1)(a) and (b).
4 See, eg *Sharpe v Duke Street Securities NV* [1987] 2 EGLR 106, CA (building divided into two connecting flats a 'house') and *Malpas v St Ermin's Property Co Ltd* [1992] 1 EGLR 109, CA.

[12.16] It is further provided that the LRA 1967 does not apply to a house which is not structurally detached and of which a material part lies above or below a part of the structure *not* comprised in the house[1], eg a house over an archway giving access to mews at the rear of the property. Where however, the archway *is* comprised in the house and let with it, this exclusion will not apply[2].

1 LRA 1967, s 2(2).
2 *Cresswell v Duke of Westminster* [1985] 2 EGLR 151, CA. See also *Parsons v Viscount Gage* [1974] 1 All ER 1162, HL.

'House and premises'

[12.17] Where the qualifying conditions are met, the LRA 1967 gives the tenant the right to claim the freehold or an extended lease of the house 'and premises' let[1]. The 'premises' in relation to which a claim may be made include any garage, outhouse, garden, yard and appurtenances which at the relevant time (ie when the notice is served) are let to the tenant with the house and are occupied with, and used for the purposes of, the house or any part of it by him or by another occupant[2]. Land let with the house can be an appurtenance, and thus part of the premises, but only if let with and used in connection with the house. This is a question of fact[3]. If premises have been let to the tenant with the house, but are not occupied by him at the relevant time, then the landlord has a right to have them included in the freehold conveyance of the house if the court considers it unreasonable for him to retain them without the house and other premises let[4]. On the other hand, the landlord can object to the inclusion in the house and premises conveyed of any part of them which lies above or below other premises retained by the landlord. In this case, if the tenant objects to the exclusion proposed, the court must assess whether any hardship to the tenant caused by the premises' exclusion is outweighed by the hardship, inconvenience and/or difficulties occasioned by further severance of the premises to those retaining an interest in them[5].

1 LRA 1967, s 1(1).
2 Ibid, s 2(3).
3 See *Gaidowski v Gonville and Caius College, Cambridge* [1975] 2 All ER 952, CA.
4 LRA 1967, s 2(4). The landlord must exercise this right by notice in writing within two months after the relevant time.
5 Ibid, s 2(5). The landlord's objection here must, similarly, be exercised by notice within two months of the relevant time.

[12.18] Enfranchisement does not extend to underlying minerals comprised in the tenancy if the landlord objects to their inclusion, provided proper provision is made for the support of the house and premises concerned[1].

1 LRA 1967, s 2(6).

'Tenant'

[12.19] It is 'the tenant' who must give notice of intention to enfranchise, and who must occupy the dwelling as his residence for three years prior to doing so in order to qualify under the LRA 1967. Once the tenant has exercised his right under the Act to acquire the freehold or an extended lease, by giving notice, he can assign his right to enfranchise together with the tenancy. It will remain enforceable in the hands of the assignee, even though the latter has not satisfied the ownership condition[1]. The right, similarly, remains enforceable by his administrator or executors if the tenant dies after giving notice to enfranchise. If the tenancy of the house is vested in trustees but it is occupied by a beneficiary, then the trustees will enjoy the same rights under the Act as if the tenancy had been vested in the beneficiary who has been occupying the house by reason of his interest, and who has satisfied the occupancy condition for enfranchisement[2]. Further, the widow and certain other close relatives of the tenant who succeed to the tenancy following his death will be treated as having been the tenant (and having occupied the house) during any period when the successor was resident in the house as his/her only or main residence at the same time as the tenant[3]. For this purpose a successor is a member of the deceased tenant's family if he/she is the other's wife or husband, a son or daughter of the tenant, his son-in-law or daughter-in-law, stepchild, father or mother, or parent-in-law. The definition includes illegitimate, adopted and stepchildren[4].

1 LRA 1967, s 5(1).
2 Ibid, s 6(1) and (3). A similar rule applies where the house is occupied by the tenant for life under a strict settlement: ibid, s 6(2).
3 Ibid, s 7(1).
4 See ibid, s 7(7) for the categories of relative qualifying under this provision.

[12.20] 'Tenancy' is defined in LRA 1967, s 37 to mean a tenancy in law or in equity. It does not, however, include a tenancy at will, a mortgage term nor an interest created by way of trust under a settlement[1], and occupiers in these categories will not enjoy rights under the LRA 1967.

1 LRA 1967, s 37(1)(f).

'Long' tenancy

[12.21] This is defined by the LRA 1967, s 3(1) as a tenancy granted for a term of years certain[1] exceeding 21 years. A lease for more than 21 years is a 'long' tenancy (and therefore within the Act) whether or not the tenancy is (or may become) terminable[2] before the end of its term by notice given by or to the tenant or by re-entry, forfeiture or otherwise. The extension of the definition[3] to include all leases terminable by notice following a death or marriage has already been considered[4]. The LRA 1967 also applies where, following expiry of a long tenancy, the tenant takes another tenancy of the whole or part of the premises[5], and where a tenancy for less than 21 years, which contains a covenant or obligation for renewal without payment of a premium, is renewed for periods which in total exceed 21 years[6]. A tenancy continues to be a 'long' tenancy within the LRA 1967 provisions at any time when it is being statutorily continued under of the LTA 1954, Pt I or the Local Government and Housing Act 1989 (LGHA 1989), Sch 10[7] – but it ceases to be such when a statutory or assured tenancy arises under the provisions of either the LTA 1954 or LGHA 1989 (whichever applies)[8]. Shared ownership leases are statutorily excluded from enfranchisement under the LRA 1967, until the shared owner has acquired 100 per cent of the equity in the premises[9].

1 As to which see *Roberts v Church Comrs for England* [1972] 1 QB 278, CA.
2 For consideration of the meaning of 'terminable' in this context, see *Eton College v Bard* [1983] Ch 321, CA.
3 By the Leasehold Reform, Housing and Urban Development Act 1993, s 64(1).
4 See p 347 above.
5 The later tenancy is deemed to be a 'long' tenancy if for less than 21 years: s 3(3), LRA 1967.
6 LRA 1967, s 3(4).
7 Ibid, s 3(5).
8 For which see para 11.5 ff above.
9 See HA 1985, s 173, and LRA 1967, s 33A.

[12.22] Before 1980 it was not uncommon for clauses to be inserted in long tenancies making them terminable by notice following a death or marriage, eg after the death of the last survivor of a named member of the royal family[1]. The effect was to prevent the tenancy qualifying as a 'long' tenancy under the LRA 1967[2], and thus to prevent enfranchisement rights arising. The Housing Act 1980[3] amended the legislation to nullify the effect of such clauses in leases granted on or after 18 April

1980. During the passage of the Leasehold Reform, Housing and Urban Development Act 1993 it was accepted that enfranchisement should be extended to all long leases with 'royal lives' clauses aimed solely at excluding the legislation on technical grounds, including those granted before the HA 1980 came into force. The LRHUDA 1993, s 64 therefore introduced a new s 1B to the LRA 1967 retrospectively nullifying the effect of this type of device. This provides that where a tenancy granted so as to become terminable by notice after a death or marriage is (apart from s 1B) a long tenancy in accordance with the LRA 1967, but was granted before 18 April 1980[4], then the tenancy shall be a long tenancy for the purposes of the 1967 Act – but only so far as it has effect to confer on the tenant a right to acquire the freehold of the house and premises. The LRA 1967 has also been amended to include within the definition of a long tenancy a lease for life, which takes effect under the Law of Property Act 1925 as a fixed term of 90 years[5]. A lease terminable by notice on death or marriage will now only fall outside the legislation if it comes within the new proviso to the definition of a 'long' tenancy inserted by the LRHUDA 1993, s 64(2). This provides that a lease terminable by notice following a death or marriage is not a long lease only if the notice of termination can be given at any time after the death or marriage, is of not more than three months in duration, and if the terms of the tenancy preclude both assignment and subletting[6].

1 The construction of the provisions applicable to 'royal lives' clauses of this sort is somewhat technical. See further Hill and Redman *Law of Landlord and Tenant* (18th edn), E 512 ff.
2 See LRA 1967, s 3.
3 See HA 1980, s 141 and Housing (Consequential Provisions) Act 1985, s 4, Sch 2, para 12.
4 Or pursuant to contract made before 1 April 1980. This is the date when the amendment in HA 1980, s 141 came into effect.
5 See LPA 1925, s 149(6). See also LRHUDA 1993, s 64(2)(a) amending LRA 1967, s 3(1) to this effect.
6 See LRHUDA 1993, s 64(2), inserting a new provision to LRA 1967, s 3(1). Assignment by exchange under HA 1985, s 42 can be permitted without infringing the proviso.

Exceptions to enfranchisement rights

[12.23] A claim to acquire the freehold or an extended lease cannot be made after the tenant has given notice to terminate his tenancy[1]. Once a notice of claim has been made under the LRA 1967, however, any notice purporting to terminate the tenancy is of no effect[2]. A notice of claim will, however, be invalid if made more than two months after a landlord's notice of termination has been served under the LTA 1954 or the LGHA 1989, ie following expiry and statutory continuance of a long tenancy[3]. Where a claim for enfranchisement has been made, proceedings for forfeiture or re-entry cannot be brought without the leave of the court[4].

1 See LRA 1967, Sch 3, para 1. This includes a notice under the LTA 1954, s 26 (business tenancies).
2 Ibid, Sch 3, para 1(2).
3 Ibid, Sch 3, para 2(i).
4 Ibid, Sch 3, para 4.

[12.24] Certain categories of property are excluded altogether from enfranchisement under the LRA 1967. Property owned by the National Trust is excluded, and special rules apply to Crown land[1]. Two further exclusions were added by the LRHUDA 1993, s 67. These are discussed below.

1 See LRA 1967, ss 32 and 33.

Charitable housing trusts

[12.25] Tenants of charitable housing trusts with long tenancies granted before the commencement of the LRHUDA 1993 will enjoy enfranchisement rights under the LRA 1967. The latter will not now apply, however, to confer enfranchisement rights on long tenancies granted after commencement of the LRHUDA 1993[1]. A special rule applies, further, to tenancies brought within the LRA 1967 by the extension of enfranchisement rights effected by the LRHUDA 1993[2]. Where the tenancy is within sections 1A or 1B then, if the landlord is a charitable housing trust, enfranchisement rights are excluded whether the tenancy was granted before or after commencement of the LRHUDA 1993[3].

1 LRA 1967, s 1(3A)(a) (inserted by LRHUDA 1993, s 67(3)).
2 Above para 12.3 ff.
3 LRA 1967, s 1(3A)(b) (added by LRHUDA 1993, s 67(3)). See generally Matthews and Millichap *Guide to the Leasehold Reform, Housing and Urban Development Act 1993*, paras 5.13, 5.14.

Property transferred for public benefit

[12.26] Where property has been designated by the Treasury as of outstanding historic, scenic or architectural interest, and the transferee undertakes to allow public access, he may be granted an exemption from Inheritance Tax by the Inland Revenue[1]. If enfranchisement were subsequently to take place, the landlord could find himself with a substantial tax liability if the tenant failed to adhere to the undertakings given to acquire the tax exemption. The LRHUDA 1993, s 68 therefore introduced a new restriction[2] excluding from the LRA 1967 any property which is subject to a Treasury designation under the Inheritance Tax Act 1984, s 31, or where a designation has been applied for[3]. A notice of intention to acquire the freehold will, further, be rendered ineffective if the property becomes subject to a designation, or an application for Treasury designation is made[4]. Like the exemption for charitable trusts (above), the exemption applies to all long tenancies brought within the LRA 1967 by s 1A and 1B – whenever granted. In all other cases, it applies only to long tenancies granted after commencement of the LRHUDA 1993[5].

1 Inheritance Tax Act 1984 ('IHTA 1984'), ss 30 and 31.
2 In the form of a new s 32A to LRA 1967.
3 IHTA 1984, s 32A(2).
4 IHTA 1984, s 32A(4).
5 IHTA 1984, s 32A(1).

CONTRACT AND CONVEYANCE

[12.27] Where the qualifying conditions are met the tenant may serve notice of his desire to acquire the freehold[1]. This may be served at any time, including during the period after expiry of the contractual tenancy when it is being statutorily continued under, eg the LTA 1954. Where notice has been given, the landlord shall be bound to make to the tenant, and the tenant to accept (at the price statutorily provided for), a grant of the house and premises[2] for an estate in fee simple, free from encumbrances other than tenant's encumbrances[3]. The tenant's notice is registrable as an estate contract (Class C(iv)) under the Land Charges Act 1972, or as a notice or caution under the Land Registration Act 1925 where the freehold title is registered[4].

1 In prescribed form: Leasehold Reform (Notices) Regulations 1967 (SI 1967/1768).
2 See above p 349 ff for definition of 'premises'.
3 LRA 1967, s 8(1).
4 LRA 1967, s 5(5).

[12.28] The freehold conveyance to the tenant must be free of encumbrances (such as mortgages or rent charges) created by the landlord, but subject to 'tenant's encumbrances', ie subleases, mortgages, etc, created out of his leasehold interest by the tenant. The conveyance will have overreaching effect under the LPA 1925, sweeping off the title any equitable interests attaching to the freehold arising from a trust for sale or settlement[1]. Third-party interests binding the land in the hands of the landlord – such as easements or covenants – will bind the land in the hands of the transferee, however, unless defeated under the provisions of the general law, eg for want of registration. By virtue of the LRA 1967, s 10 the tenant is entitled to the benefits of the rights implied into the conveyance by the LPA 1925, ss 62 and 63. Similarly, the landlord must – in so far as he is able to – grant to the tenant the same rights and easements over other property as he formerly enjoyed under the tenancy with regard to the following:

(i) rights of support,
(ii) rights to access of light and air,
(iii) rights to the passage of water, gas or other fuel; drainage or disposal of water, sewage, smoke or fumes; or to the use of installations for such passage, drainage or disposal, and
(iv) rights to the use and maintenance of cables and installations for the use of telephones, electricity, etc[2].

1 LRA 1967, s 8(4).
2 Ibid, s 10(2).

[12.29] The land can also be made subject to such rights in these categories as may need to be imposed on the tenant for the benefit of other land[1]. The conveyance must also include provision, so far as the landlord is able to give it, for securing rights of way over other land necessary to the reasonable enjoyment of the property[2].

1 LRA 1967, s 10(2)(b).
2 Ibid, s 10(3).

[12.30] The right of assignees and successors to enforce the terms of the tenant's notice to acquire the freehold have already been considered[1].

1 See para 12.19 ff above.

THE PRICE PAYABLE

[12.31] The price payable for the freehold under the LRA 1967 depends upon the rateable value of the house at the time of service of the tenant's notice.

Premises with rateable values below £1,000 (London) or £500 (elsewhere)

[12.32] The general principles for establishing the price payable are set out in LRA 1967, s 9(1). This stipulates that the price payable shall be the amount which, at the relevant time[1], the house and premises might be expected to realise if sold on the open market by a willing seller, with the tenant and members of his family who reside in the house not seeking to buy. Certain statutory assumptions must be made when establishing the free market value[2]:

(i) it must be assumed that the vendor is selling for an estate in fee simple, subject to the tenancy. It must be assumed that no right to acquire the freehold under the LRA 1967 exists, but that the lease has been extended by 50 years pursuant to the statutory right of extension in LRA 1967, s 14 (below, para 12.39 ff)[3];
(ii) it must be assumed that the property is being sold subject to the same annual rent charge (if any) as the conveyance to the tenant is to be subject to; and
(iii) it must be assumed that the vendor is selling subject to all the same rights and burdens subject to which the conveyance to the tenant is to be made (including extended rights and burdens created to give effect to the requirements of LRA 1967, s 10 (above)).

1 That is the date of service of the tenant's notice under LRA 1967, s 8 to acquire the freehold.
2 See LRA 1967, s 9(1)(a)–(c). The valuation provisions are complex. For the detailed provisions see further, inter alia, Hill and Redman *Law of Landlord and Tenant* (18th edn), E 582–589.
3 But, subject to the landlord's right to repossess under LRA 1967, s 17 for redevelopment purposes in such circumstances.

[12.33] The price will therefore be the hypothetical free market value of the landlord's reversion on the tenancy, which is deemed to have been extended by 50 years. The length remaining unexpired, the ground rent for the site and the current rent will all influence the valuation of the hypothetical reversion. 'Marriage value' (ie the greater value the sitting tenant would pay to acquire the freehold than a third party) is not, however, to be taken into account[1].

1 This was made explicit by amendments to LRA 1967, s 9(1) made by HA 1996, s 82.

Premises with rateable values above £1,000 (London) or £500 (elsewhere)

[12.34] A different test applies to high value properties, properties where the low rent test is not satisfied, and to enfranchisement during a leasehold extension if one is obtained under the LRA 1967[1]. This basis of valuation will apply to leases brought within enfranchisement by the abolition of the low rent test by the CLRA 2002, and to enfranchisement during an extension of the original lease (another situation brought within enfranchisement by the CLRA 2002). A controversial, and very important, part of the valuation of the price for these properties is the 'marriage value' attaching to the freehold by virtue of the fact that the sitting tenant will be willing to bid more highly than a third party for the property.

1 See LRA 1967, s 9(1C) (as amended). As to lease extensions and enfranchisement during the extended term see CLRA 2002, s 147, amending LRA 1967, s 9(1C). If the right to enfranchise is exercised before the original term has expired, the basis of valuation may, in the alternative, be that in s 9 (above), provided the tenancy was originally a tenancy at a low rent satisfying the requirements of s 9.

[12.35] The valuation formula is set out in LRA 1967, s 9(1A)[1]. The starting point remains the amount which the landlord's reversion might be expected to realise if sold on the open market[2]. The assumptions to be made when valuing the reversion differ in material respects, however, to those applicable under LRA 1967, s 9(1). There is no assumption that the lease has been statutorily extended by 50 years, and if it has been extended under the LRA 1967, it must be assumed that the tenancy will terminate on the original term date. It must also be assumed that the tenant has the right to remain in possession at the end of the tenancy as an assured tenant under LGHA 1989, Sch 10, but that there is no right to acquire the freehold or an extended lease under the LRA 1967. In addition, it is to be assumed that the tenant has no liability to carry out any maintenance, repairs or redecorations to the house, and the price must be diminished by the extent to which the house's value has been increased by any improvement carried out by the tenant or his predecessors in title at their own expense. The other basic assumptions are the same as those applicable under LRA 1967, s 9(1).

1 As amended by the References to Rating (Housing) Regulations 1990, SI 1990/434, reg 2 and Schedule. The formula in LRA 1967, s 9(1A) applies not only to properties with a RV above £1,000 (Greater London) or £500 (elsewhere) on 31 March 1990, but also (where a property had no RV on 31 March 1990) to properties with a value exceeding £16,353 calculated under the formula in s 6(1)(a).

2 LRA 1967, s 9(1A) has been extensively amended by the Housing Act 1980, the Housing and Planning Act 1986, and the LGHA 1989. It is given in its full (amended) present form in the LRHUDA 1993, Sch 14. See also Hill and Redman *Law of Landlord and Tenant* (18th edn), E 584, 585.

[12.36] Note in particular that 'marriage value' accruing because of the willingness of the sitting tenant to pay a higher price than third parties to acquire the freehold is to be taken into account under LRA 1967, s 9(1A)[1]; cf s 9(1) (above) where it is discounted. Prior to reform in the CLRA 2002, the legislation provided that, where marriage value fell to be accounted, the tenant's share of it should not exceed one half. The marriage value had to be apportioned, with the freeholder being guaranteed 50 per cent of it. In practice many cases were referred to the Leasehold Valuation Tribunal (LVT) for adjudication, and in this event (and given the lack of guiding criteria in the legislation) the Tribunal invariably split the marriage value in equal proportions between landlord and tenant. The formula was amended by the CLRA 2002 to provide that in all cases where, in future, marriage value falls to be taken into account, the tenant shall be entitled to one half of the marriage value[2]. In other words, it will be split 50/50 between landlord and tenant in all cases. This will not only prevent costly references to the LVT, but also bring the provisions for enfranchising houses into line with the reformed law governing enfranchisement for leasehold flats (below paras 12.91 and 12.92), where the same rule is applied by the CLRA 2002 to value the freehold reversion. In the case of very long leases, where 80 years of the term remains unexpired at the relevant time, the marriage value is to be taken as nil, and none will be payable to the landlord on enfranchisement[3]

1 See LRA 1967, s 9(1C); *Norfolk v Masters, Fellows and Scholars of Trinity College, Cambridge* (1976) 32 P & CR 147.

2 CLRA 2002, s 145, inserting a new s 9(1D) to the LRA 1967.

3 CLRA 2002, s 146, inserting a new s 9(1E) to the LRA 1967.

Landlord's compensation

[12.37] Where the tenant's right to enfranchise arises under LRA 1967, s 1(1A) or 1(1AA), he may be liable to pay compensation to the landlord for any loss or damage the latter suffers as a consequence. This applies to cases where the property has a high rateable value (see para **[12.34]** above) or where the tenancy is not at a low rent (LRA 1967, s 1(1AA)). Tenancies brought within the enfranchisement regime by the abolition of the low rent test by the CLRA 2002 will, if the rent exceeds the low rent threshold at the relevant time, fall within the compensation provisions. Similarly, compensation will be payable (where relevant) if the tenant enfranchises during an extension of the original lease obtained under the LRA 1967[1]. LRA 1967, s 9A, provides that the landlord can claim compensation for any diminution in the value of any interest the landlord has in other property which arises from the tenant's acquisition of the freehold in the subject dwelling, and any other loss or damage resulting therefrom to the extent that it is referable to the landlord's ownership of any interest in other property. The tenant will have to compensate him, therefore, for loss occasioned by severance of the house enfranchised from other properties retained by the landlord, including loss of development value[2].

1 CLRA 2002, s 147, amending LRA 1967, s 9A(1).
2 LRA 1967, s 9A(3).

Dispute resolution

[12.38] In default of agreement the Leasehold Valuation Tribunal has jurisdiction to determine the price payable, and the terms of the conveyance to the tenant[1].

1 LRA 1967, s 21.

RIGHT TO AN EXTENSION OF LEASE

[12.39] As an alternative to full enfranchisement, the LRA 1967 gives a qualifying tenant the right to an extended lease. By virtue of LRA 1967, s 14 the extended lease is for a term of 50 years from the term date of the original tenancy. Before reforms introduced by the CLRA 2002, this was not a very attractive option for the tenant. He would lose his right to enfranchise under the LRA 1967 during the extended term, and the LTA 1954 did not apply to confer Rent Act protection on termination of the extended term[1]. Neither was the extended lease a protected tenancy under the Rent Act 1977 or an assured tenancy within the Housing Act 1988[2]. The CLRA 2002 introduced a number of reforms to improve the position of tenants extending their lease, with a view to putting them on the same basis as tenants of flats under the new regime. The restriction on tenants enfranchising and purchasing the freehold during a lease extension were removed by the CLRA 2002[3]. Furthermore, the LGHA 1989, Sch 10 will now apply to any tenancy extended under the LRA 1967, so as to confer the security of tenure of an assured tenancy on expiry of the term[4]. The reform gives the tenant the option to extend the lease, which otherwise represents a wasting asset as it nears expiry, and to then enfranchise at a later time if so wished.

1 LRA 1967, s 16(1).
2 Ibid, s 16(1A) and (1B).
3 CLRA 2002, s 143(1) (above para 12.12).
4 CLRA 2002, s 143(2), adding a new section 16(1B) to the LRA 1967. See Ch11 para 11.5 ff for the protection conferred under the Local Government and Housing Act 1989 on expiry of long leases.

[12.40] The tenant can give notice to enfranchise at any time up to the termination date of the original term – even after he has requested an extension of the lease under LRA 1967, s 14. But, thereafter, he loses his rights under the LRA 1967 once an extended lease has been granted. The tenant must pay the landlord's costs in investigating title, valuing the property, and executing a lease to grant the new tenancy[1].

1 LRA 1967, s 14(2). The landlord is not obliged to execute the new lease until his costs have been met and all rent owing paid: LRA 1967, s 14(3).

[12.41] The terms of the tenancy granted by way of extension are governed by the LRA 1967, s 15. The terms will be the same as those of the old tenancy, with modifications to take account of the omission (for example) of property comprised in the original tenancy, or alternations.

[12.42] The rent payable is to be a ground rent representing the letting value of the site (excluding buildings), if let for the purposes to which the house and premises have been put since the commencement of the existing tenancy[1]. The letting value thus assessed must be the letting value of the site at the date from which the new rent is to take effect, ie its current rental site value at the time of the extension taking effect. The landlord can, if he wishes, have a rent review clause inserted in the new tenancy providing for a review of the site rent once 25 years of the extended leasehold term has expired.

1 See LRA 1967, s 15(2) for the detailed formula encompassing this proposition. And see further Hill and Redman *Law of Landlord and Tenant* (18th edn) E 645–653.

B Leasehold flats: collective enfranchisement

INTRODUCTION

[12.43] Enfranchisement under the LRA 1967 was limited to dwelling houses. Tenants of leasehold flats did not have rights to enfranchise and acquire the freehold of their block until the Leasehold Reform, Housing and Urban Development Act 1993 came into force on 1 November 1993. The LRHUDA 1993 was the subject of much controversy during its passage through Parliament[1]. It provides for a collective right for long lessees to acquire the freehold of the premises in which their flat is situated at a market value to be determined in accordance with the provisions of the Act, and also gives long lessees a separate right to purchase a lease extension. Much of the procedural detail which gives effect to the provisions of this part of the Act is contained in the Leasehold Reform (Collective Enfranchisement and Lease Renewal) Regulations 1993[2] and the Rent Assessment Committee (England and Wales) (Leasehold Valuation Tribunal) Regulations 1993[3]. The detailed provisions in the LRHUDA 1993 are largely modelled on the LRA 1967, and on the Landlord and Tenant Act 1987, Pt I (LTA 1987) which grants the tenants a collective right of first refusal if the landlord sells his reversion (this is considered in Chapter 13 below para 13.12 ff). They are unduly complex, and have been subjected since 1993 to extensive criticism, much of it not dissimilar to criticism frequently made of the LRA 1967 and LTA 1987. For example, the procedure and time limits that need to be adhered to in order to take advantage of the enfranchisement rights place a heavy logistic burden on those seeking to organise a collective purchase. It has proved relatively easy for landlords to use the complex procedures to frustrate collective enfranchisement[4].

1 Some members of the House of Lords were fiercely opposed to the Bill. The Duke of Westminster went so far as to resign from the Conservative Party in protest.
2 SI 1993/2407.
3 SI 1993/2408.
4 See *Commonhold and Leasehold Reform: Draft Bill and Consultation Paper* (Cm4843, DETR 2000), p 137.

[12.44] After an extensive consultation, the CLRA 2002 substantially reformed the collective enfranchisement provisions. The principal aims of the CLRA 2002[1] were to simplify and relax the qualifying criteria for exercising the right, to reduce the scope for costly disputes about the purchase price of the freehold, to allow all qualifying tenants to participate in a purchase if they so wish, and to provide a standardised company structure for the exercise of the right to enfranchise. This is modeled on the company structure for commonhold tenure, and (where tenants opt to continue renting) for the exercise of the right to manage in relation to leasehold premises[2]. The reforms introduced in the CLRA 2002 are intended to provide a single model of company structure for exercising all three of the new rights, so that tenants can progress easily from the right to manage to enfranchisement, and then to establish commonhold tenure of the block if they so wish, using a single company as the legal vehicle to do so. The principal changes to the qualifying rules made by the CLRA 2002 were the abolition of the low rent test and residence qualification, and the extension of the right to enfranchise to premises where up to 25 per cent of the building is used for non residential purposes (previously the limit was 10 per cent). This will enable tenants to enfranchise in blocks of four storeys or more where the ground floor is currently a shop or business offices, whereas previously only tenants in properties of ten or more storeys had this right.

1 *Commonhold and Leasehold Reform: Draft Bill and Consultation Paper* (Cm4843 DETR 2000), p 139.
2 'Right to manage' (RTM) is considered in Chapter 13 para 13.46 ff below.

THE RIGHT TO COLLECTIVELY ENFRANCHISE

[12.45] The LRHUDA 1993, s 1(1) confers the right of collective enfranchisement on qualifying tenants of flats and entitles them to have the freehold of the premises acquired on their behalf by a company (hereafter referred to as the 'RTE company') formed for that purpose, at a price to be determined in accordance with the provisions of the Act. In order to take advantage of the collective right of enfranchisement, there must be a requisite majority of 'qualifying tenants' of flats situated in premises which conform to the requirements of the Act, who are able and willing to purchase the freehold at the price provided for. In large blocks of flats, the logistics of accurately ascertaining whether this is the case may well be far from simple, even allowing for the relaxation in the qualifying rules made by the CLRA 2002.

Qualifying tenants

[12.46] LRHUDA 1993, s 5(1) defines a qualifying tenant as a 'tenant of a flat under a long lease'. The additional requirement that the lease must be at a low rent was removed by the CLRA 2002[1]. A long lease is principally one where the original term exceeds 21 years whether or not it is terminable before the end of that term[2]. LRHUDA 1993, s 5(3) provides that there can be only one qualifying tenant per flat, and joint tenants therefore constitute only one qualifying tenant for these purposes. Where the flat is let under more than one long lease, the qualifying tenant will be the most 'inferior' underlessee whose tenancy meets the requirements. In this case the underlessee will have the right to acquire the superior lessees' interest(s) at the same time as acquiring the freehold[3].

1 CLRA 2002, s 117
2 See LRHUDA 1993, s 7(1)(a). The remainder of LRHUDA 1993, s 7 includes within the term 'long lease' a lease for a term fixed by law under a grant with a covenant or obligation for perpetual renewal, or a lease terminable by death or marriage taking effect under LPA 1925, s 149(6), other than those requiring less than three months' notice at any time after the death or marriage and which also preclude both

assignment and the subletting of the whole of the premises. Leases and shared ownership leases granted pursuant to the right to buy or rent or to mortgage provisions of HA 1985, Pt V are also specifically included within the definition

3 See LRHUDA 1993, s 5(4).

[12.47] Enfranchisement is intended to be limited to tenants with residential leases, and certain types of lease are therefore excluded. By virtue of LRHUDA 1993, s 5(2) tenants with business leases[1], leases of flats where the immediate landlord is a charitable housing trust and the flat is let in accordance with the trust's charitable housing objectives, and under leases granted in breach of the terms of a superior lease (not being a long lease at a low rent) where the breach has not been waived, cannot qualify. Similarly, a lessee who would be the qualifying tenant of two or more flats in a building is specifically excluded, even where the flats are held under a single lease[2]. Flats in this category will normally therefore have no qualifying tenant. This provision is aimed at preventing speculators from dominating the collective enfranchisement process

1 Note that this may exclude flats used for business purposes as in *Cheryl Investments Ltd v Saldanha* [1978] 1 WLR 1329, where the Court of Appeal held that a tenancy of a flat occupied as a residence by a company director but also used for business was a business lease.

2 See LRHUDA 1993, s 5(5).

Premises to which the right applies

[12.48] The right extends only to flats in either a self-contained building or part of a building[1] where the same person owns the freehold of the whole building or that part of it. In addition, there must be at least two flats held by qualifying tenants in the building. This rule can cause anomalies. For example, where one or more occupiers own their flat in a building and accordingly cannot be 'qualifying tenants', then if this has the effect of reducing the number of qualifying tenants to fewer than two, that tenant is effectively disenfranchised[2]. Such a situation is likely to arise chiefly in smaller buildings.

1 See LRHUDA 1993, s 3(2). A building is defined as self-contained if it is structurally detached. Part of a building will be self-contained within the meaning of the Act if it is a vertical division and could be redeveloped independently of the remainder of the building, and the relevant services for occupiers of that part are either already provided for independently of those of the remainder of the building or could be so provided 'without involving the carrying out of any works likely to result in a significant interruption of the provision of any such services for occupiers of the remainder of the building'. It seems likely that where a freeholder of part of a building is reluctant to accede to the collective right of enfranchisement, the interpretation of this section is likely to be problematic. See also *Willingale v Globalgrange Ltd* [2000] L&TR 549, CA.

2 In practice, as discussed below, a tenant in this position will only be entitled to an extension of his lease.

[12.49] By virtue of the LRHUDA 1993, s 4, certain types of premises are specifically excluded from the collective enfranchisement provisions.

Non-residential use of part

[12.50] Premises are excluded where more than 25 per cent of the internal floor space of the premises taken as a whole, excluding the common parts, is occupied for non-residential purposes[1]. Parts of the premises which are used (or intended to be used) in conjunction with the dwelling, such as a garage, parking space or storage area, are taken to be occupied for residential purposes and will not affect the calculation[2]. The exclusion will operate chiefly to exempt blocks where the ground floor is used as a shop or office, and this takes up more than 25 per cent of the total internal floor space of the building.

1 LRHUDA 1993, s 4(1), amended by CLRA 2002, s 115
2 LRHUDA 1993, s 4(2).

Premises with resident landlord

[12.51] Premises are also excluded from enfranchisement where the building is not a purpose-built block of flats, contains four or fewer units and has a resident landlord. For these purposes a building is a purpose built block if, as constructed, it contained two or more flats[1]. The definition of a resident landlord is found in LRHUDA 1993, s 10 and is broader than that contained in either the RA 1977 or the LTA 1987. The condition is met where either the freeholder or an adult member of the freeholder's family occupies a flat in the premises as his only or principal home and has occupied it for a period of not less than 12 months. An adult member of the family includes a spouse; son, son-in-law, daughter or daughter-in-law if over the age of 18; and a parent and parent-in-law. Adult stepchildren also qualify, but the terms do not appear to extend to similar relationships within 'unmarried families'. The 12-month period can be waived if the freehold of the building is acquired by a freeholder who takes up residence of a flat in the building as his principal home within 28 days of acquiring it from a freeholder who was a resident landlord within the meaning of the Act and that residence continues[2]. The CLRA 2002 tightened the resident landlord exception by adding a further requirement that the landlord or a member of his/her family must have owned the freehold since before the time at which the property was converted into flats[3]. This will prevent landlords benefiting fortuitously where they have acquired a block whose previous owner was a resident landlord[4].

1 LRHUDA 1993, s 10(6).
2 Ibid, s 10(2)(b).
3 Ibid, s 10(1)(b), inserted by CLRA 2002, s 118.
4 *Commonhold and Leasehold Reform: Draft Bill and Consultation Paper* (Cm4843, DETR 2000), p 141.

Special Categories of Property

[12.52] Other excluded premises include certain properties in cathedral precincts[1], certain heritage properties designated under the Inheritance Tax Act 1984[2], properties where the Crown is currently the landlord[3], premises where the freehold includes the track of an operational railway[4] and properties where an interest in it is vested inalienably in the National Trust[5].

1 See LRHUDA 1993, s 96.
2 See ibid, s 31.
3 See ibid, s 94.
4 See ibid, s 4(5), added by CLRA 2002, s 116.
5 See ibid, s 95.

The qualifying group of leaseholders

[12.53] The qualifying tenants must hold the leases of at least half of the total number of flats in the building[1]. The rules applicable before the coming into force of the CLRA 2002 were more stringent, and required at least two thirds of the qualifying tenants in a block to participate in the enfranchisement. This proved very difficult to achieve in many cases, especially in blocks with a high turnover of tenants. Moreover, it facilitated the use of artificial devices by landlords to avoid the legislation. Many landlords, for example, insisted that leases be assigned to limited companies, and not the intended occupier, as a company could not qualify for enfranchisement under the residence test in the LRHUDA 1993. The abolition of the residence test by the CLRA 2002[2], together with the relaxation of the rules for the size of the qualifying group of leaseholders, is intended to ensure that landlords cannot prevent enfranchisement taking place for speculative investment purposes[3]. The abolition of the residence test means that a limited company could now be a qualifying tenant for these purposes, and if half of the flats in the building are held by qualifying tenants (including corporate tenants) then the qualifying rules will have been met, irrespective of whether the tenants are occupying them or not. The reformed rules are much simpler, and should prevent the adoption of artificial avoidance schemes to frustrate enfranchisement.

1 LRHUDA 1993, s 13(2)(b), as amended by the CLRA 2002, s 119.
2 CLRA 2002, s 120, amending LRHUDA 1993, s 13(2).
3 *Commonhold and Leasehold Reform: Draft Bill and Consultation Paper* (Cm4843, DETR 2000) p 141.

The RTE company

[12.54] Under the original collective enfranchisement provisions in the LRHUDA 1993, the tenants could select a 'nominated purchaser' to take the freehold on their behalf. Usually, the tenants would form a company for this purpose, but the Act did not formally regulate the form and constitution of the nominee purchaser, and a variety of alternative acquisition modes could be employed. In small blocks, for example, the tenants may acquire the freehold directly and hold it in their own names. The CLRA 2002 replaces this liberal arrangement with a prescribed corporate structure for enfranchisement. Collective enfranchisement can only be exercised by a company limited by guarantee (the 'RTE Company') that has articles and memorandum of association that comply with the requirements laid down in the legislation[1]. Detailed provision is to be made about the form and content of the articles and memorandum of association by regulations made by the Secretary of State[2].

1 LRHUDA 1993, ss 13(2ZA) and 4A, inserted respectively by CLRA 2002 ss 121 and 122. The company's memorandum of association must state that its object (or one of them) is the exercise of the right of collective enfranchisement with respect to the premises.
2 LRHUDA 1993, s 4C, inserted by CLRA 2002, s 122.

[12.55] This change in approach is linked to the introduction of commonhold tenure in the CLRA 2002. By prescribing a corporate structure for the RTE company, which is identical to that for a commonhold association, the CLRA 2002 is intended to enable leaseholders to enfranchise and convert to commonhold at the same time[1]. Alternatively they can enfranchise, and convert to commonhold later if they so wish, again using the RTE company as the vehicle to do so. The RTE company is also identical in all relevant respect to the RTM company which tenants must adopt to exercise the right to manage, if they wish to take control of management functions without enfranchising[2]. In principle, therefore, tenants could move seamlessly from exercising the right to manage, through to enfranchisement, and then (ultimately) to the formation of a commonhold association to holds the block under the new commonhold tenure – using the same corporate vehicle for each of the three stages in the process.

1 *Commonhold and Leasehold Reform: Draft Bill and Consultation Paper* (Cm4843, DETR 2000) p 142.
2 As to which see Ch 13 para 13.46 ff below.

Membership of the RTE company

[12.56] The CLRA 2002 seeks to achieve the widest possible participation in enfranchisement by encouraging all tenants to join the RTE company. All qualifying tenants are entitled to become members of the RTE company, and if it is also an RTM company where the tenants have previously exercised their right to manage the premises, then the landlord is also entitled to become a member. Because the enfranchisement price to be paid[1] is calculated by reference to the number of participating tenants in the RTE company, however, the CLRA 2002 applies a cut off point, after which tenants cannot join the company – if tenants were to be admitted to membership after the price has been determined the company would otherwise obtain the freehold on advantageous terms. For this reason, only tenants who are 'participating members' of the company can benefit from enfranchisement, and any member who is not a participating member when the conveyance to the RTE company takes place ceases at that point to be a member of the company[2]. To become a participating member, a tenant must either give a participation notice before the RTE company serves it's initial notice claiming the right to enfranchise, or within the 'participation period'. This extends for six months after the giving of the initial enfranchisement notice by the company, or until the company and landlord exchange contracts of sale if earlier[3]. Six months was chosen as the relevant participation period because in practice it is unlikely that the purchase price will have been agreed before then[4]. However, the CLRA 2002 gives the Secretary of State power to vary the period by statutory instrument if experience of the operation of the rules later dictates that the period be reduced or extended[5]. The landlord cannot be a participating member of the RTE company[6]. This means that, where the company has already been formed by the tenants to manage the premises under the CLRA 2002, the landlord will be entitled to participate in the RTM company but his participation will cease if they later initiate an enfranchisement. He will cease to be a member of the company upon the conveyance to the RTE company taking place – a logical consequence, as he will at that point cease to have an interest in the building.

1 See below para 12.88 ff.
2 LRHUDA 1993, s 4B(3), as inserted by CLRA 2002, s 122.
3 See LRHUDA 1993, s 4B (5),(7),(8) and (9).
4 *Commonhold and Leasehold Reform: Draft Bill and Consultation Paper* (Cm4843, DETR 2000) p 148.
5 LRHUDA 1993, s 4B(9)(a).
6 See ibid s 4B(4) and 4B(1)(a), read together.

THE REVERSIONARY INTEREST ACQUIRED

[12.57] The tenants have the right to have the freehold of the premises that contains their flats purchased by the RTE company[1]. In addition to this they are also entitled, but not obliged to, have the company acquire the freehold of appurtenant property[2] which is not part of the freehold of the building, such as a garage, garden, yard or outhouse belonging to or usually enjoyed with the flat of a qualifying tenant, providing it is demised by lease and owned by the same freeholder[3]. Further, the tenants may also acquire the freehold of other property owned by the same freeholder, and which any qualifying tenant is entitled under the terms of their lease to use in common with occupiers of other premises, eg a driveway or parking area. However, this can be satisfied instead by the freeholder granting permanent rights to ensure as nearly as possible the same rights enjoyed by the qualifying tenant over the property under the lease will be enjoyed by the occupier in future[4].

1 LRHUDA 1993, s 1(1).
2 As defined in LRHUDA 1993, s 1(7).
3 See LRHUDA 1993, s1(2)–(4).
4 See ibid, s 1(4).

[12.58] The right to collective enfranchisement does not have to be exercised in respect of the entirety of the premises to which it applies, providing the part of the premises seeking to be acquired can meet the requirements for collective enfranchisement alone[1]. The Act also provides that any underlying minerals which form part of the freehold or an intermediate interest will not automatically be subject to the right of collective enfranchisement. If the owner of the interest requires them to be excepted from the right then they will be, providing proper provision is made for the support of the property[2]. The tenants have the right to acquire intervening leasehold interests where the collective right to enfranchisement is exercised[3]. This constitutes a very significant improvement upon the tenants right of first refusal conferred by the Landlord and Tenant Act 1987[4], which extends only to the immediately superior interest. Where collective enfranchisement is exercised, then subject to some exceptions, any intervening interests will be purchased at the same time by the RTE company, thus ensuring that they will merge with the freehold. Intermediate leases relating to appurtenant property or common parts will be acquired only if the acquisition of that interest is 'reasonably necessary for the proper management or maintenance' of those common parts or property on behalf of those exercising the collective right to enfranchisement. Intermediate leases which cannot be acquired include those relating to premises which are occupied by someone other than a qualifying tenant and which do not fall into the category of common parts or appurtenant property[5]. An example of this would be where an intermediate lessee who cannot be a qualifying tenant has granted a tenancy of a flat other than on a long tenancy at a low rent or some other right to occupy (such as a service license to a resident caretaker) out of the intermediate lease. This could make the interest purchased by the RTE company rather untidy in the sense that the freehold interest will still be subject to the intermediate lessee's interest.

1 LRHUDA 1993, s 1(5).
2 Ibid, s 1(6).
3 Ibid, s 2.
4 As to which see Chapter 13 below, para 13.12 ff.
5 LRHUDA 1993, s 2(4).

[12.59] An important exception to the general right to acquire intermediate leasehold interests applies where there is a public sector landlord who is the qualifying tenant of a flat which has been let on a secure tenancy. Generally, public sector landlords are, as freeholders, subject to the right of collective enfranchisement. However, LRHUDA 1993, s 2(5) and (6) aims to protect existing secure tenants. Providing the public sector landlord who is a qualifying tenant is the immediate landlord under the secure tenancy or there is an unbroken chain of public sector landlords between the qualifying tenant and the secure tenant, then the interest of a secure tenant of a public sector landlord, who is also a qualifying tenant for enfranchisement purposes, cannot be acquired by the collective right to enfranchisement.

1 See the right of first refusal under the LTA 1987 from which they are exempt.

ACQUISITION PROCEDURES

Invitation to participate

[12.60] The first stage in exercising the right to enfranchise requires the RTE company to serve a notice on all qualifying tenants of flats in the premises. This is referred to as a 'notice of invitation to participate'[1]. Notice must be served on all those tenants who have not agreed to become participating members, and must give details of the names of the participating members of the RTE company, the price at which it is proposed to acquire the freehold, an estimate of associated costs and the rights and obligations of the members of the company. The notice must invite those on whom it is served to become participating members of the company. It must either be accompanied by copies of the company's memorandum and articles of association, or include a statement specifying where they can be inspected or what provision is being made for copies to be provided at cost[2].

1 LRHUDA 1993, s 12A(1) and (2), as inserted by CLRA 2002, s 123.
2 LRHUDA 1993, s 12A(3) and (4).

Tenants' discovery notice and preliminary action

[12.61] In some cases the tenants may need to be able to discover the identity of the freeholder and details of intermediate leases. LRHUDA 1993, s 11 gives any qualifying tenant of a flat the right to serve a notice on the immediate landlord or any other person (such as a managing agent who receives rent on the landlord's behalf) requiring them to give, so far as is known to them, the names and addresses of the freeholder of the premises in which the flat is situated and of any other persons having a superior leasehold interest in it. In addition, details of the freeholder of any other property demised by or used in common under the terms of the qualifying tenant's lease can be required. The tenant can also serve on the freeholder a notice requiring additional information in relation to any tenant of the whole of the premises, any tenant or licensee of separate sets of premises within them or of common parts whether contained in the premises or not[1]. A further notice may be served on any person having such an interest requiring them to give details of their interest and any interest derived out of it. The information notice can be served by any individual qualifying tenant, and does not have to be served by the RTE company.

1 See LRHUDA 1993, s 11(3).

[12.62] In this way an individual qualifying tenant should be able to obtain details of all the relevant superior interests as well as information about other qualifying tenants and those with non-qualifying interests in the premises. It should be noted that the information which must be disclosed is limited to that which is known to the recipient of the notice and does not require them to take any steps to find information additional to that already in their possession. In addition to providing relevant names and addresses, if asked to do so by the qualifying tenant, the recipient of the notice must also list all relevant documents, and upon payment of a reasonable fee provide copies or permit inspection of them. The documents deemed to be relevant are those under the control of the recipient which are reasonably required to be seen by the qualifying tenant in connection with the claim for collective enfranchisement[1].

1 LRHUDA 1993, s 11(5) and (6).

[12.63] The request should be complied with within 28 days, although there is no direct sanction for non-compliance[1]. LRHUDA 1993, s 92 does, however, permit the tenant to enforce compliance by applying to the county court on 14 days' notice for an order for discovery of documents in the usual way. Clearly, there is scope for delaying tactics by the landlord at this initial stage, and the onus is on the tenant's advisers to be both comprehensive and specific in relation to the information required by their s 11 notice. Where the freehold of the block is registered land, it may be advisable to make a search of the land register to obtain as much of the information as possible and thus limit the potential for delay.

1 LRHUDA 1993, s 11(7).

[12.64] Strict duties are imposed on any landlord receiving a notice under LRHUDA 1993, s 11, although the absence of any direct sanction for non-compliance is a weakness in the process. LRHUDA 1993, s 12 obliges the recipient to disclose whether any notices claiming to exercise the right to collective enfranchisement have been served in relation to the premises containing the qualifying tenant's flat. Where, within six months of service of the qualifying tenant's notice, an application for collective enfranchisement is made by other qualifying tenants, the landlord is obliged to notify the tenant of the fact within 28 days, giving details of the date and the RTE company, and subsequently inform them whether the application is granted, refused or withdrawn, provided this is known within six months of service of the s 11 notice[1].

1 LRHUDA 1993, s 12.

[12.65] Generally, all notices under the Act must be in writing and service may be effected by post (s 99(1)). Where the discovery notice fails to reveal the identity of the landlord and all the intermediate interests, the collective right to enfranchisement or lease renewal will not necessarily be thwarted as the court may be able to make a vesting order permitting transfer of the necessary interests as discussed below[1]. Once enough information is available, both tenant and landlord can ascertain whether the collective right is potentially exercisable. In essence, the first stage is to establish the number of the total flats in the building held by qualifying tenants, the proportion of the internal space which is occupied for non-residential purposes, and the details of the freeholder and intermediate lessors of all the premises affected whose interests will be purchased. The tenant must next ascertain whether the necessary majority of qualifying tenants are willing collectively to exercise the right of enfranchisement. In practical terms, particularly where there are large numbers of tenants involved, this could be time-consuming and not necessarily straightforward. For example, it is necessary to confirm the identity of the qualifying tenants and ensure that they occupy at least half of the flats in the premises. In the absence of a well-organised residents' association, some form of representative body will need to be established if it does not already exist.

1 LRHUDA 1993, ss 26(1) and 27(1).

[12.66] Once the tenants are confident that they have the necessary majority of qualifying tenants, they will need to instruct a surveyor to carry out a valuation of the interests to be purchased, and then form an RTE company to effect the transaction. Once the valuation has been obtained, the tenants will need to meet to discuss the proposed price and, in appropriate cases, whether the whole or just part of the freehold interest should be purchased. Both of these factors, as shall be seen, need to be included in the subsequent purchase notice and the tenants need to agree the method of financing the purchase. At this stage, the tenants could consider entering into direct negotiations with the landlord in order to avoid the procedures in the Act. However, this could be exploited by the landlord to delay the whole process and, until contracts are exchanged, there is no means of preventing the landlord from withdrawing from the sale. If the negotiation has been lengthy and time consuming it may no longer be possible to obtain the necessary majority of qualifying tenants to use the compulsory enfranchisement provisions in the LRHUDA 1993, eg in a large block with a high turnover where some tenants may have subsequently moved. Using the statutory collective enfranchisement provisions from the outset offers a better bargaining stance and underpins the tenant's position more effectively.

Tenants' purchase notice

[12.67] The formal acquisition procedure is commenced by the RTE company serving a Purchase Notice under the LRHUDA 1993, s 13. The notice must be served on behalf of participating tenants who, on the date the notice is given, occupy at least one-half of the total number of flats contained in the premises[1]. The purchase notice cannot be served until at least 14 days has elapsed following service of the notice inviting participation on all qualifying tenants who are entitled to participate in the RTE company[2]. This is intended to ensure that enfranchisement cannot be manipulated by a small group of tenants, and to give all qualifying tenants time to consider taking part in the process. A copy of the notice must be given to all qualifying tenants of flats in the premises covered by the purchase notice[3].

1 LRHUDA 1993, s 13(1) and (2).
2 Ibid, s 13(2ZB), as inserted by CLRA 2002, s 123(2).
3 Ibid, s 13(5A), as inserted by CLRA 2002, Sch 8. para 6.

[12.68] The information which the notice must contain is specified in the LRHUDA 1993, s 13(3). It must be accompanied by a plan, specify the freehold premises and any appurtenant property to be acquired or over which it is proposed rights should be granted and contain a statement as to why the right extends to the premises. All superior leasehold interests or other units such as shops to be acquired and any other premises where leasebacks are required must be specified[1], as must the proposed purchase price for each of the freehold and superior leasehold interests to be acquired. The full names and addresses of all the flats of all the participating tenants together with short particulars of their leases and ground rent must be included. In addition, the notice must declare that the tenants have obtained a valuation from a qualified surveyor[2] whose name and address must be supplied (although the details of the valuation do not have to be disclosed), and a date not less than two months after the serving of the initial notice must be specified as the date by which the landlord must respond by counter notice. The notice must also give details of the RTE company which will purchase the freehold on the tenant's behalf.

1 Situations where leasebacks will arise are contained in LRHUDA 1993, Sch 9, Pt II, an example being where a flat is let on a secure tenancy, which entitles the freeholder to a leaseback of the flat concerned.
2 LRHUDA 1993, s 13(7) defines qualified surveyor as one who is a fellow or professional associate of the RICS or ICVA and is reasonably believed by the tenants to have ability and experience in relation to valuation of property in the area. Valuations have to be in the form prescribed by LRHUDA 1993, Sch 6.

[12.69] The landlord upon whom the notice is served has a duty to pass it on to the owners of other superior interests in the building. The immediate landlord (termed in the Act the 'reversioner') will be deemed to act on behalf of the owners of all the superior interests unless they object[1]. The initial notice is registrable as a caution where the land is registered or as a land charge under the Land Charges Act 1925, which should ensure that the tenants' position is protected as against other prospective purchasers until contracts are exchanged[2]. Once a purchase notice has been served, it remains in force until contracts are exchanged or a vesting order has been made by the court, or until the notice is withdrawn or deemed to be withdrawn by the RTE company. It also has the effect of rendering ineffective any subsequent notice served on a tenant and forfeiture proceedings can be continued only with leave of the court.

1 LRHUDA 1993, s 9 and Sch 1. LRHUDA 1993, Sch 1, para 7 sets out the procedure when other relevant landlords wish to deal directly with the purchaser. They may also apply to the court for someone other than the freeholder to act as the reversioner where incapacity, absence or other circumstances make this appropriate. LRHUDA 1993, Sch 2 deals with certain special categories of landlords such as where the interests are owned under the terms of a trust or settlement or where there is a university or college landlord or an ecclesiastical landlord. Most importantly, where there is a mortgagee in possession, they must be treated as the reversioner under the Act.
2 See LRHUDA 1993, s 97.

[12.70] If a participating tenant assigns his lease once the process has been commenced, the assignee must give the RTE company a participation notice within 28 days indicating whether he wishes to participate[1]. Similarly, where a participating tenant dies, his personal representative must give a participation notice informing the company whether indicating whether the tenant's successors wish to participate[2].

1 LRHUDA 1993, s 4B (5), as inserted by CLRA 2002, s 122.
2 Ibid, s 4B(6). The notice is not in this case time limited: the personal representative can give a participation notice at any time, and on giving it is entitled to become a participating member of the RTE company.

[12.71] All the relevant landlords have a right of access to the premises in order to carry out valuations, and for any other reasonable purpose connected with the tenants exercise of the right to collectively enfranchise[1]. The right of access is exercisable at any reasonable time and on giving not less than 10 days' notice[2]. The landlord may, within 21 days of service of the purchase notice, also request evidence of the participating tenants' title from the RTE company, by virtue of which it is claimed he has the right to participate in enfranchisement[3]. If the company does not provide the evidence requested within 21 days, and the purchase notice could not have been served without the participation of the tenants in respect of whom the evidence is sought, then the initial notice is deemed to have been withdrawn. This will result in the tenants becoming responsible for the landlord's costs, and they will be unable to make a further application for 12 months. It follows that the RTE company will be well advised to have evidence of the eligibility of all the participating tenants ready and waiting, as otherwise the landlord could frustrate the enfranchisement procedure simply by requesting evidence of the titles of all the participating tenants.

1 LRHUDA 1993, s 17(1), as amended by CLRA 2002, s 125.
2 Ibid, s 17(3).
3 Ibid, s 20.

[12.72] The service of the initial purchase notice has far-reaching effects. Once the purchase notice has been registered, the reversioner or other relevant landlord cannot sever their interest nor grant a lease that would have been liable to acquisition by the tenants if in existence at the time of the initial notice. Any transaction attempting to do this is void[1]. Any other disposition of the freehold or other superior interest will take effect subject to the purchaser being treated as if they were the relevant landlord and had been served with the purchase notice under LRHUDA 1993, s 13[2]. Where contracts had been exchanged but not completed in relation to the sale of any of the relevant landlords' interests before the service of the tenant's purchase notice, the sale is suspended for as long as the notice remains in force[3].

1 LRHUDA 1993, s 19(1).
2 Ibid, s 19(2) and (3).
3 See ibid, s 19(4)–(6).

[12.73] The right to collective enfranchisement is supposed to benefit only participating tenants, and not others, and as we shall see[1] the number of participating tenants affects the calculation of the purchase price. The LRHUDA 1993 therefore provides[2] that the RTE company must disclose any agreements made with any non-participating tenants (other than those relating to security for a loan) and any shareholding by a non-participating tenant must also be disclosed to the reversioner before the valuation date. The sanction for non-compliance is the joint and several liability of the RTE company and the participating tenants for any difference in the purchase price arising from the non-disclosure of relevant interests.

1 See below para 12.88 ff.
2 LRHUDA 1993, s 18.

Reversioner's counter notice

[12.74] The procedure relating to the landlord's counter notice is contained in LRHUDA 1993, s 21. The reversioner must respond to the tenants purchase notice by serving a counter notice by the date specified in the tenants' notice. This must be a date at least two months from the date on which the purchase notice was itself served and the latter must give an address for service in England and Wales[1]. The reversioner has three options. The counter notice can indicate that he either:

(i) admits the qualifying tenants' claim to the right to enfranchisement and agrees to or rejects some or all the terms specified in the notice;
(ii) disputes the claim; or
(iii) whether or not he admits the claim, indicate that the landlord intends to redevelop the whole or a substantial part of the premises, and that a court order is to be sought under s 23(1). The latter provision enables the court to make a declaration that the right to collective enfranchisement is not exercisable on the grounds that the landlord has established to the courts satisfaction an intention to redevelop the premises.

1 LRHUDA 1993, s 13(3)(g).

[12.75] Time is of the essence as failure to respond by the due date entitles the RTE company to apply to the court within six months of the date by which the counter notice should have been served for an order determining the terms on which it may purchase the reversioner's interest 'in accordance with the proposals contained in the initial notice'[1]. This seems to entitle, although not require, the court to order the sale only on the terms specified in the notice (subject to any appropriate leaseback provisions) providing it is satisfied that the tenants were entitled to exercise the collective right to enfranchisement and that they have complied with all the procedural requirements relating to giving copies of the initial notice to all relevant landlords[2].

1 See LRHUDA 1993, s 25.
2 See ibid, Sch 3, Pt II.

Admitting the claim

[12.76] If the reversioner admits the tenants' claim, the counter notice must state this and also state which of the proposals are accepted and which are not. In the case of the latter, the notice must specify the reversioner's counterproposals, for example a different purchase price, and the details of any additional leaseback proposals, other than those already prescribed[1]. The reversioner can also require the RTE company to acquire any other of his interests or those of another relevant landlord in any property which would for all practical purposes cease to be of benefit to them or could not be reasonably managed or maintained by the landlord following the collective enfranchisement[2]. In this situation, the reversioner must state these interests in the counter notice[3]. Where this occurs, the RTE company is then given a right of access to the specified property for valuation purposes[4].

1 LRHUDA 1993, Sch 9 prescribes the term of the leaseback as 999 years at a peppercorn rent.
2 See LRHUDA 1993, s 21(4).
3 Ibid, s 21(3)(c).
4 Ibid, s 21(5).

[12.77] Where the collective right is admitted but the 'terms of acquisition'[1] are in dispute and the parties cannot resolve their differences within two months of the service of the counter notice, either the RTE company or the reversioner may apply to the Leasehold Valuation Tribunal to resolve the dispute[2]. Such an application must be made within six months of the service of the counter notice. If neither party makes the application, then the initial notice is deemed to be withdrawn under LRHUDA 1993, s 29. This will render the participating tenants liable to pay the reversioner's costs up to the date of withdrawal.

1 These are defined in LRHUDA 1993, s 24(8) and include the interests to be acquired, the extent of the property to which those interests relate or the rights to be granted over any property, the purchase price, the apportionment or other matters relating to severance of the reversionary interest and any provision to be included in the conveyance.
2 See LRHUDA 1993, s 24.

Denying the claim

[12.78] Where the counter notice denies the participating tenants' claim to the right to collective enfranchisement, it must specify the reasons why[1]. The RTE company then has two months from receipt of the landlord's counter notice to apply to the court for a declaration[2] that the participating tenants were, on the date when the initial notice was served, entitled to exercise the collective right in relation to the premises. The issue here does not appear to be whether there are any technical defects in the initial notice itself, but only the question of the participating tenants' eligibility to exercise the collective right. Thus it seems a declaration must be made by the court where the participating tenants are considered eligible, even if other aspects of the procedure potentially render the initial notice invalid. Any other such defects would form the basis of a separate application to the county court but would not of themselves prevent a declaration of eligibility being made under the 1993 Act.

1 LRHUDA 1993, s 21(2)(b).
2 See ibid, s 22(1).

[12.79] Where a declaration is made, the court will normally declare the reversioner's counter notice invalid and order them to serve a further counter notice by a given date[1]. Where the court concludes that the participating tenants were not eligible to exercise the collective right, they will dismiss the application and the tenants purchase notice will cease to have effect when the order becomes final[2].

1 LRHUDA 1993, s 22(3) and (5).
2 This occurs in relation to all orders made under Pt I of the Act when all possibility of appeal has been removed. See LRHUDA 1993, s 101(9).

Reversioner's intention to redevelop

[12.80] This 'defence' to the collective right to enfranchise applies only in cases where the leases are nearing the end of the original term, but is exercisable whether or not the landlord admits the participating tenants' claim[1]. In the counter notice, the reversioner must, in addition to admitting or denying the claim, state his intention to apply to the court for an order preventing the exercise of the collective right on this ground. Either the reversioner (or one or more of any of the other relevant landlords acting either alone or together) may make the application within two months of the counter notice being served. However, in cases where the collective right is denied by the reversioner, the application cannot proceed until after any order made pursuant to LRHUDA 1993, s 22 (see above) has become final.

1 See generally LRHUDA 1993, s 23.

[12.81] In order to resist the collective right in this way, two-thirds of the flats in the specified premises must be held on long leases due to expire within five years of the date of the tenant's initial purchase notice. The reversioner must intend, after the expiry of the leases, to demolish, reconstruct or carry out substantial building work on all or a substantial part of the premises, and be unable to do so without obtaining possession of the flats in question. Where the court is satisfied on all three counts, they may declare that the collective right of enfranchisement is not exercisable in relation to the premises. The court has a discretion, however, and is not obliged to do so. If the reversioner's application is not granted, then the counter notice will be of no effect and they will be required to serve another by a date specified by the court[1].

1 See LRHUDA 1993, s 23(5). If the landlord's application is withdrawn the counter notice must be given within a further 2 months: LRHUDA 1993, s 23(6).

Where the reversioner or other relevant landlord cannot be found

[12.82] If the reversioner can be found but one of the other relevant landlords cannot, then the court has power to dispense with service on that particular landlord[1]. If the reversioner is 'missing' but another relevant landlord has been identified then they may be appointed to act in place of the reversioner by the court[2]. Where all the relevant landlords are missing, then the RTE company may apply to the court for the reversionary interest to be vested in it by the court[3]. In this situation, the terms of the acquisition are determined by the Leasehold Valuation Tribunal (LVT) and the purchase price is paid into court. Although the RTE company will not have served a purchase notice on the tenants behalf under LRHUDA 1993, s 13, the reversionary interest will be conveyed to it in accordance with the order of the court. Before making the vesting order the court may require the RTE company to take steps to try to trace the reversioner and other relevant landlords. Should the reversioner or other relevant landlord be found the parties are deemed to be in the same position as if a purchase notice under s 13 had been served[4]. Before making a vesting order, the court must be satisfied[5]; first, that the identity of the reversioner or other relevant landlord cannot be ascertained or they cannot be found; second, that the premises were, on the date of the application, premises to which the collective right of enfranchisement applied; and last, that on that date there was nothing in the Act to prevent the applicant giving a valid purchase notice under the LRHUDA 1993.

1 LRHUDA 1993, s 26(2).
2 Ibid, s 26(3).
3 Ibid, ss 26 and 27, as amended by CLRA 2002, Sch 8, paras 15 and 16.
4 Paradoxically, however, there is no duty upon the tenants to inform the court that the missing reversioners or other relevant landlords have been traced after the application has been made.
5 LRHUDA 1993, s 26(5)(a).

Withdrawal and deemed withdrawal from acquisition

[12.83] The RTE company can withdraw at any time before entering into a binding contract of sale, by giving notice[1] that they wish to withdraw their purchase notice[2]. The withdrawal notice must be served upon the reversioner and all other landlords who are believed not to be acting through the reversioner. All must be named as recipients on the notice. It is for the RTE company to copy the notice to any other relevant landlords dealing independently who have not received the notice direct.

1 Pursuant to LRHUDA 1993, s 28.
2 Ie the purchase notice served under LRHUDA 1993, s 13 (above, para 12.67 ff).

[12.84] As noted above, deemed withdrawal occurs where the enfranchisement process is begun and:

(i) the reversioner denies the claim, but the RTE company fails to apply to the court for a declaration of entitlement within two months of the landlord's counter notice (LRHUDA 1993, s 29 (1)); or
(ii) where the claim is admitted but there is a dispute as to the terms and neither party applied to the Leasehold Valuation Tribunal within six months of the counter notice (LRHUDA 1993, s 29(2)(a)) and also
(iii) where the RTE company does not comply with the reversioner's request for proof of any of the participating tenants' title (LRHUDA 1993, s 29(5)(c)).

[12.85] In addition, withdrawal is deemed where no counter notice is served and the RTE company purchaser does not apply to the court within six months to determine the terms (LRHUDA 1993, s 29(3));

(i) where the terms are agreed but no binding contract is *entered into* within two months of the end of the appropriate period (LRHUDA 1993, s 29(2)(b)); and finally
(ii) where the court orders that there be a deemed withdrawal pursuant to LRHUDA 1993, s 24(4)(c) or s 25(6)(c) for failure to enter into a binding contract.

[12.86] Generally, withdrawal or deemed withdrawal leads to the RTE company and the participation tenants being jointly and severally liable for such of the reversioner's costs and those of any other relevant landlord up to the date of the withdrawal for which the RTE company would have been responsible had the acquisition been completed[1].

1 See LRHUDA 1993, s 28(4)–(7) and s 29(6) for the details of liability applicable in the different situations.

Entering into a binding contract

[12.87] The Act assumes that the parties will enter into a binding contract once all the disputes are settled, and does not make statutory provision for breach of contract. This is left to the terms agreed by the parties and the general law. However, where the parties fail to enter into a binding contract after the 'appropriate period' has elapsed, the RTE company can apply to the court for an order vesting the landlord's interest in it on the terms agreed. The appropriate period within which the contract should be concluded is either (i) two months from the date on which the terms in dispute were agreed by the parties, or (ii) two months from the date on which the LVT decision became final, in cases where the disputed terms have been referred to the tribunal for resolution[1]. Where delay beyond this period has occurred either the reversioner or the RTE company may apply to the court for an order, provided they do so within a further two months following the end of the appropriate period for conclusion of the contract[2]. In the case of an application by the RTE company a vesting order may be sought on the terms agreed[3]. In the case of an application by the reversioner the court can make an order of deemed withdrawal where the RTE company has failed to enter into the contract by the end of the appropriate period pursuant to LRHUDA 1993, s 24(3) and (4).

1 See LRHUDA 1993, s 24(3) and (6).
2 See ibid, s 24(5).
3 LRHUDA 1993, s 24(4) does, however, permit appropriate modifications to be made by the LVT due to any change of circumstances which has occurred since the terms in question were agreed.

THE PURCHASE PRICE

[12.88] The purchase price to be paid by the RTE company for the freehold is determined in accordance with the formula set out in LRHUDA 1993, Sch 6. The valuation provisions were amended by the HA 1996[1], and again by the CLRA 2002[2]. The CLRA 2002 amended LRHUDA 1993, Sch 6 to provide that the different values to be included in the price paid by the RTE company shall be determined at the date of service of the initial purchase notice, and not (as formerly) the date on which all the terms of the acquisition have been agreed or decided by the LVT[3]. This brings the collective enfranchisement provisions into line with the LRA 1967, where the price of the freehold for houses is calculated at the date of service of the initial claim. It also removes the incentive for landlords to delay the enfranchisement process in a rising housing market, in order to maximise the price eventually paid by the tenants[4].

1 See HA 1996, ss 109 and 110.
2 CLRA 2002, ss 126–128.
3 See CLRA 2002, s 126. The valuation date is the 'relevant date' under the new provision, which in most cases will be the date of the initial section 13 'purchase notice' served by the RTE company. Previously the freehold was valued at the 'valuation date' – a later date following agreement or determination of all the relevant terms of the disposal.
4 See *Commonhold and Leasehold Reform: Draft Bill and Consultation Paper* (Cm4843, DETR 2000), p 150.

[12.89] The principles set out in the LRHUDA 1993, Sch 6 require participating tenants to pay a price for the freehold which is the aggregate of:

(i) the open market value of the freeholder's interest;
(ii) the freeholder's share of the 'marriage value' arising on merger of the freehold and leasehold interests; and
(iii) any compensation payable for the losses suffered by the freeholder as a consequence of the enfranchisement, eg loss of development value .

[12.90] The *open market value* is that which would be expected to be paid to a willing seller for the freehold interest on certain assumptions[1]. It must be assumed that the freeholder is selling the fee simple in the property subject to the tenants' leases and any intervening leasehold interests; that the leases carry no right to enfranchise nor to lease extension; that tenants' improvements are disregarded; and that the landlord is selling subject to all rights and burdens which affect the property.

1 LRHUDA 1993, Sch 6, para 3.

[12.91] The *marriage value* is the increase in the total value which will result from the merging of the freehold or other superior leasehold interest with the participating tenants' interest[1]. This is a controversial concept, the valuation of which is often disputed before the LVT. It is used in relation to acquisitions under the LRA 1967, but in the context of the collective enfranchisement of blocks of flats is somewhat artificial, in that in this case the freehold and leasehold interests never in fact merge as the freehold will vest in the RTE company, which cannot also be the owner of all the leasehold interests within a block[2]. Despite calls for its abolition, the CLRA 2002 retained the principle that this additional element of value should, where it exists, be payable to the landlord on the compulsory purchase of his interest[3]. LRHUDA 1993, Sch 6 defines marriage value as the increase in the aggregate value of the freehold which is attributable to the participating tenants' ability through the RTE company to grant themselves new leases without the payment of a premium and for any length of term without restriction[4]. It is calculated by subtracting the aggregate value of all the superior interests including the freehold in the premises in their former owners' hands before collective enfranchisement from the aggregate value of the same interests under the control of the participating tenants through the RTE company.

1 Note that the calculation is not based on the value of all the tenants' flats but only the participating tenants, hence the duty to disclose any agreements with other tenants contained in LRHUDA 1993, s 18, as this affects the calculation of the price.

2 For a discussion of this point see Daiches 'Marriage Values and Flats' [1993] 43 EG, p 104 (30 October 1993).
3 See *Commonhold and Leasehold Reform: Draft Bill and Consultation Paper* (Cm4843, DETR 2000) pp 138–139 and 150–151.
4 See LRHUDA 1993, Sch 6, para 4(2).

[12.92] Where marriage value exists, the LRHUDA 1993 originally provided that the freeholder's share be decided by agreement between the parties or by a LVT, subject to a guarantee that the freeholder receive at least 50 per cent of the marriage value. In practice LVTs usually apportion marriage equally between landlord and tenant in disputed cases. The CLRA 2002 therefore amended the valuation provisions to provide that, where marriage value is found to exist, it must be apportioned 50/50 ie the freeholder is entitled to a fixed 50 per cent proportion of the relevant marriage value[1]. The CLRA 2002 also provided that marriage value must be disregarded where the unexpired term of any of the leases held by participating tenants are very long. Where the unexpired term of any of the leases held by participating tenants exceeds 80 years, the marriage value shall therefore be taken to be nil[2]. These changes mirror those made by the CLRA 2002 to the valuation provisions for enfranchisement of houses under the LRA 1967 (above para 12.36 ff)

1 LRHUDA 1993, Sch 6, para 4(1), as amended by CLRA 2002, s 127.
2 CLRA 2002, s 128, inserting a new para 4(2A) to LRHUDA 1993, Sch 6.

[12.93] Compensation for other losses is the final element of the price and is payable in respect of diminution in value or loss or damage to other property interests including development value consequent upon the sale of the freehold[1].

1 LRHUDA 1993, Sch 6, para 5.

[12.94] Where enfranchisement takes place, the RTE company will, of course, acquire any intermediate leasehold interests that exist in the block. The holders of these interests must, however, be compensated. Intermediate leasehold interests must be separately valued and will be added to the price payable by the RTE company. The price here constitutes the value of the interest plus any appropriate compensation for loss on its acquisition[1]. In most cases the calculation will be the same as that used in relation to the freeholder's interest, although the proportion of the marriage value attributable to the nominal merger of the superior leasehold interest is payable by the freeholder and is not calculated as a separate element of the price to be paid by the RTE company.

1 See generally LRHUDA 1993, Sch 6, Pt III. Note that a formula is applied to value minor intermediate leases where there is an expectation of possession for no longer than a month. This capitalises a profit rent which does not exceed £5: see LRHUDA 1993, Sch 6, para 7(3) and (7). This might apply where the intermediate leaseholder has sublet to tenants qualifying for enfranchisement for his whole term less a few days.

[12.95] It may be that there are other interests which are to be acquired, eg where property which is to be purchased is used in common with others. As is the case on acquisition of the freehold and intermediate leases, the price to be paid constitutes the value of the interests plus any compensation and a share of the marriage value where the interest to be acquired is freehold[1]. The method of calculation is the same as that used to value the directly superior interests to be acquired. Where the superior interest has a negative value, then no price is payable by the RTE company. Generally, the RTE company is liable for the reversioner's reasonable costs and those of any other relevant landlord in respect of specified matters in connection with the acquisition. These include investigations reasonably undertaken pursuant to matters arising out of the purchase notice served under LRHUDA 1993, s 13, the valuation of all the relevant premises, deducing title to the landlords' interests, the costs of providing abstracts and copies for the RTE company and the conveyance[2]. However, costs incurred in connection with applications to the LVT are not recoverable.

1 See LRHUDA 1993, Sch 6, Pt IV, paras 11–13.
2 LRHUDA 1993, s 33.

COMPLETION OF THE PURCHASE

[12.96] LRHUDA 1993, s 34 and Sch 7 deal with the requirements of the Act in this regard. The interest granted must be a fee simple absolute and the conveyance of the freehold must conform with Sch 7. Existing mortgages will be discharged[1] even though the sum payable is insufficient. Where there is to be a leaseback which arises where for example there is a secure tenant of one or more of the flats, the terms of the lease are set out in LRHUDA 1993, Sch 9, Pt IV.

1 LRHUDA 1993, s 35.

RIGHT TO ACQUIRE A NEW LEASE

[12.97] The collective enfranchisement provisions are complemented by LRHUDA 1993, Pt I, Ch II, which gives long leaseholders the right to acquire a new lease, thereby adding 90 years to the term remaining on the original tenancy. This is an individual right enjoyed by each qualifying tenant, and is not contingent upon collective co-operation. It is particularly useful where a qualifying tenant cannot apply for the collective right of enfranchisement, for example where the flat is above commercial premises, where there is a resident landlord, and where the sufficient majority for enfranchisement cannot be obtained or where they do not wish or cannot afford to enfranchise. Many of the provisions determining whether and how this right is exercisable are the same as those which relate to the collective right. The CLRA 2002 relaxed the qualifying rules for lease extension in order to reflect the more liberal rules which it introduced for collective enfranchisement.

Qualifying for lease extension

[12.98] To be entitled to a lease extension, the tenant must be a qualifying tenant of the flat, and must have held the long lease of the flat for a period of at least two years[1]. The lease does not have to be at a low rent[2]. In addition to tenants who qualify for the purposes of the collective right discussed above, tenants of more than one flat in the building are not excluded from being qualifying tenants in relation to the individual right[3]. The LRHUDA 1993 originally imposed a three-year residence requirement before the right to a lease extension accrued, but this was removed by the CLRA 2002. It follows that people who sublet residential flats will be able to claim an extension on the lease, as will those who occupy flats as second homes. Being unable to obtain a lease extension, these categories of occupier were previously faced with a wasting asset.

1 LRHUDA 1993, s 39(1) and (2), as amended by CLRA 2002, s 130.
2 Ibid, s 39(3), as amended by CLRA 2002, s 131.
3 Ibid, s 39(4).

Procedure for obtaining new lease

[12.99] The right is exercisable against the 'competent landlord', ie the person who is the owner of the first superior interest in relation to the qualifying tenant's lease out of which it is possible to grant a new 90-year term from the date of expiry of the tenant's lease[1]. This may or may not be the tenant's immediate landlord or the freeholder. In order to discover the identity of the competent landlord and obtain other appropriate information, LRHUDA 1993, s 41 enables a tenant to serve either the landlord, or an agent who is in receipt of rent, with a discovery notice requiring details of the names and addresses of the landlord, the duration of the landlord's lease and details of any superior interest. The recipient must respond within 28 days and must declare any purchase notices exercising collective enfranchisement which have been received and provide details of the date received and of the RTE company seeking to acquire the freehold.

1 LRHUDA 1993, s 40.

[12.100] LRHUDA 1993, s 42 provides for the service of a notice of claim by the tenant, claiming the right to acquire a new lease. The tenant's notice of claim must contain principally the same information as a section 13 notice (ie a purchase notice exercising collective enfranchisement, above) but must also specify the terms proposed by the tenant to be included in the new lease. It differs from a section 13 notice in that does not have to name a nominee purchaser, but it must name any persons acting in connection with the claim and give an address for service. It must give details of the tenant, the flat, the lease and the qualifying period of ownership of the lease, as well as the proposed premium. It must be served upon the competent landlord and any third party with an interest in the lease. It must also specify a date for the landlord's counter notice, and this must be at least two months from service of the tenants claim notice. The tenants claim notice remains in force until it is withdrawn or is deemed to be withdrawn or the new lease is granted. No further notices in relation to the flat may be served within 12 months of withdrawal. Note that where there is a collective enfranchisement in progress, following the service of a s 13 purchase notice either prior to or after the tenants notice claiming a lease extension, the latter notice will be suspended whilst the collective enfranchisement notice is current, but will be reactivated if it ceases to be current[1]. LRHUDA 1993, Sch 12, Pt I deals with the effect of the notice on other proceedings. No notice can be given by either the landlord or the tenant terminating the lease and any right of re-entry can be enforced only with leave of the court. This will be granted only if the court is satisfied that the main reason for serving the s 42 notice was precisely to avoid such consequences[2].

1 See LRHUDA 1993, s 54 for the interaction between the collective and individual rights to enfranchisement under the 1993 Act.
2 LRHUDA 1993, Sch 12, para 6.

[12.101] The landlord's counter notice[1] must be given by the date specified in the tenants claim notice and must state whether the landlord admits or denies the tenant's claim, giving reasons if it is disputed. Where the claim is admitted the landlord may set out counterproposals. The provisions mirror those on enfranchisement. So, for example, where the lease is due to expire within five years of the claim notice, the landlord can resist the claim upon the grounds that the he intends to demolish or reconstruct the premises or carry out substantial works which cannot reasonably be done without obtaining possession of the flat[2]. However, s 57(7)(b) provides that the terms of the new lease include a redevelopment break option exercisable by the landlord in the last year of the existing term and/or within five years of the date of expiry of the additional 90-year term[3]. If the court grants an order for possession on these grounds the tenant will be entitled to compensation[4].

1 See generally LRHUDA 1993, s 45.
2 See ibid, s 47.
3 Where the landlord exercises the right to terminate the new lease he must comply with the requirements of LRHUDA 1993, s 61.
4 As to which see LRHUDA 1993, Sch 14.

[12.102] Either party may apply to the court or the LVT, the situations in which they can do so being similar to those that apply in relation to the collective right to enfranchise, eg where the landlord cannot be found, or the terms cannot be agreed[1], and the court and tribunal again have powers to resolve the dispute or make vesting orders granting a new lease. The tenant is responsible for the landlord's reasonable costs in connection with the new lease[2] and where there is a withdrawal or deemed withdrawal by the tenant he is liable to pay the landlord's costs up to that time[3].

1 See LRHUDA 1993, ss 46, 48, 49 and 50.
2 Ibid, s 60.
3 See ibid, ss 52 and 53.

Granting the new lease

[12.103] If the renewal procedures have been completed satisfactorily, the landlord is bound to grant and the tenant bound to accept the new lease on payment of the appropriate premium[1]. The premium payable on grant is calculated in accordance with the LRHUDA 1993, Sch 13. The new lease will be for the unexpired period of the original lease plus a further 90 years at a peppercorn rent, and all rent arrears under the old lease must be paid. LRHUDA 1993, s 57 provides that the terms of the new lease must be the same as those of the original lease with certain modifications. Once a new lease has been granted, the tenant will lose the security of tenure granted by the LGHA 1989 on expiry of the term[2], although there is a right to a further renewal of the new lease on its expiry[3]. Where the landlord's interest is mortgaged, then if the existing lease was granted after the mortgage was created, even if the lease was not authorised by the mortgagee, a new lease granted under the Act will be deemed to authorised by the mortgagee and will be binding on it[4]. The new lease will not bind the mortagee however, if the existing lease was granted after the commencement of the LRHUDA 1993 and without the authority of the mortgagee[5].

1 LRHUDA 1993, s 56.
2 As to which see Ch 11 above
3 LRHUDA 1993, s 59.
4 Ibid, s 58(1).
5 Ibid, s 58(2).

[12.104] The valuation of the premium payable to the competent and other relevant landlords is governed by the LRHUDA 1993, Sch 13. The provisions were amended by the CLRA 2002 to bring them into line with the amended provisions applicable on collective enfranchisement. Consequently, the relevant date for valuing the premium is that on which the tenant's claim notice was given[1]. The premium is made up of three elements which are to be calculated and then aggregated. These are:

(i) the diminution in the value of the landlord's interest in the flat, which will be the difference in the value of the landlord's interest in the flat before and after the lease renewal, and

(ii) the landlord's share of the marriage value, which in this case is the difference between the aggregate values of all of the landlord's interests before the grant of the new lease and the aggregate of the values of those same interests after the grant. The landlord's share of marriage value is fixed at 50 per cent[2]. In the case of very long leases where the unexpired term of the lease exceeds 80 years at the time the notice is served, marriage value is to be disregarded altogether[3]: and

(iii) compensation payable in respect of consequential losses in relation to other property.

1 LRHUDA 1993, Sch 13 as amended by CLRA 2002, s 134.
2 Ibid, Sch 13, para 4(1) as amended by CLRA 2002, s 135.
3 Ibid, Sch 13, para 4(2A), as inserted by CLRA 2002, s 136.

CHAPTER 13

Residential flats

[13.1] Tenants of residential flats have, since 1993, had a collective right to acquire the freehold reversion on their properties, and (by exercising their right to enfranchise) to assume control of the management of the blocks in which they live. As we have seen (above Ch 12) these rights were extended by the Commonhold and Leasehold Reform Act 2002 (CLRA 2002). The enfranchisement provisions leave intact, however, the existing legislation governing repair and maintenance of leasehold flats, and this will continue to apply where the freehold remains with a private landlord. The relevant provisions are chiefly to be found in the Landlord and Tenant Act 1985 (LTA 1985) and the Landlord and Tenant Act 1987 (LTA 1987). These were extensively amended by the CLRA 2002.

A Introduction

LONG LEASEHOLD FLATS – REPAIR AND MAINTENANCE PROBLEMS IDENTIFIED

[13.2] Private blocks of residential flats present considerable problems in ensuring efficient management, and in providing a comprehensive legal framework within which the reciprocal maintenance and repairing obligations of landlord and tenant can be enforced. Problems in enforcing satisfactory standards of repair and maintenance will commonly be most severe where blocks contain flats of mixed tenure – some held on long leases and others on rack-rented tenancies. Some problems will be present whatever the form of tenure The James Committee (set up under the auspices of the Royal Institution of Chartered Surveyors) reported in 1982 that the most persistent complaints by tenants focused on their difficulty in identifying their landlords, lack of consultation relating to the insurance arrangements of their properties, and the level of service charges and their administration by landlord-appointed managing agents[1]. They recommended, inter alia, the introduction of legislation to improve tenants' rights to details of their landlord's identity and address, increased standardisation of leases, and an extension of legal controls on service charges to cover control of the cost of services levied on tenants[2]. Some measure of control of the latter was introduced by the LTA 1985 (below).

1 See the Report of the Working Party on the Management of Blocks of Flats (Chairman J James) (RICS 1982) (hereafter referred to as the James Report). The James Report was published as Annex 1 to the Report of the Committee of Inquiry on the Management of Privately-Owned Blocks of Flats (DoE 1985) (the Nugee Report).

2 James Report (ibid) para 14.6.

[13.3] A thorough survey of long leasehold tenure was subsequently presented by the Report of the Committee of Inquiry on the Management of Privately-Owned Blocks of Flats (the Nugee Report) in 1985[1]. The Nugee Report singled out five recurring problems for particular criticism. The majority of tenants complained of excessive delay by landlords in acting on requests to carry out maintenance or repairs, and in acting on requests to provide information. A large proportion of tenants complained of excessive service charges, and of the poor quality of services provided, and only a third of the tenants questioned had a sinking fund into which regular service charge payments could be paid[2]. The worst problems were found to exist in ageing mixed tenure blocks, and especially in those with foreign landlords or owned by property companies – a fact already noted by the James Committee[3].

1 Report of the Committee of Inquiry on the Management of Privately-Owned Blocks of Flats (1985) paras 5 and 6, Table A. See generally (1986) Conv 12 (A J Hawkins).
2 Ibid, para 5.13.
3 Ibid, para 5.8. See also James Report, para 1.6. The Nugee Report, Ch 3, Table 1 gives a detailed breakdown of ownership, region by region.

LANDLORD AND TENANT ACT 1987

[13.4] The Nugee Committee made specific proposals, aimed chiefly at improving communication and promoting a better understanding of the legal regime governing the relations of landlord and tenant. If a landlord failed to carry out his obligations as to repair and maintenance of a block comprising leasehold flats, then the tenants should have the right to remove him and seek the appointment of a manager by the court. Monies collected by managing agents should be set aside in a trust fund and used solely for the purpose for which they were collected, and there should be a legal mechanism for varying deficient leases, eg those that failed to deal with repairing obligations. Perhaps most controversially of all, they suggested that a landlord, when selling his reversion in a block of flats, should be legally obliged to give his tenants the right of first refusal[1].

1 Report of the Committee of Inquiry on the Management of Privately-Owned Blocks of Flats (1985), para 6.3 and 6.25. More radical solutions, such as the adoption of strata titles on the Australian model, were beyond the committee's remit.

[13.5] Most, but not all, of the Nugee Report's suggestions were incorporated in the LTA 1987. Although the LTA 1987 in some respects goes further than the Nugee proposals (for instance by providing for compulsory acquisition by tenants of the landlord's interest in cases of persistently bad management), it is essentially a conservative measure[1]. Its provisions are aimed chiefly at improving communication, and on the control of repair issues within the landlord-and-tenant relationship, rather than providing for compulsory expropriation of the landlord's interest in leasehold property. The tenants' right of first refusal on the sale of a block (introduced by the LTA 1987, Pt I), and the powers of compulsory acquisition conferred by LTA 1987, Pt III, have in practice proved of limited utility. Indeed, a comprehensive survey undertaken for the Department of the Environment subsequently concluded that there was a marked lack of awareness (especially among tenants) of the provisions and implications of the LTA 1987[2].

1 See generally Percival (1988) 51 MLR 97, Rodgers (1988) Conv 122 and Smith (1992) 12 LS 42.
2 *The Landlord and Tenant Act 1987: Awareness, Experience and Impact* (DoE 1991) p 32.

COMMONHOLD AND LEASEHOLD REFORM ACT 2002

[13.6] The lengthy consultation process preceding the introduction of the Commonhold and Leasehold Reform Bill identified a number of continuing problems linked to the management of long leasehold properties. Its most radical solution to these was the introduction of the 'Right to Manage' in CLRA, Pt 2, Ch 1. This gives leaseholders the right to collectively assume responsibility for the management of the building in which their flats are situate, using a 'Right to Manage' (RTM) company as the medium for doing so. The CLRA 2002 lays down a model for the RTM company, a company limited by guarantee with prescribed memoranda and articles of association, in similar terms to that prescribed for the establishment of commonhold tenure and for collective enfranchisement. The intention is to enable tenants who have taken the RTM to later use the management company as a vehicle for assuming ownership of the block under either the commonhold tenure regime established by CLRA 2002, Pt 1 or the provisions for collective enfranchisement. The RTM is exercisable irrespective of proof of fault or mismanagement on the part of the landlord. The existing rights under the LTA 1987 to apply to the court for the appointment of a manager are unaffected, and remain exercisable by tenants who have not taken the RTM where mismanagement by the landlord or his managing agent is established.

[13.7] The CLRA 2002 also strengthened the regime governing leasehold management in cases where this remains in the hands of the landlord. The regulation of service charge payments was initially restricted to charges payable for services, repairs, maintenance, insurance and the landlord's costs of management. In practice, however, landlords frequently make charges in respect of matters falling outside the definition of 'service charges' in the LTA 1985, eg for improvements to the property made by the landlord during the lease. These were not covered by the LTA 1985, and long leaseholders were not able to challenge the reasonableness of charges for improvements imposed by landlords[1]. This was a particular problem for tenants acquiring long leases from local authorities under the right to buy[2]. Similarly, charges payable under a lease for the processing of applications for landlords' consent did not come within the regime for service charges. Leases commonly provide for the granting of landlords' written consent before structural works can be carried out or (for example) minor additions/alterations are made to property, such as the installation of satellite dishes or other electronic equipment. Excessive charges made for the granting of consent would not be subject to challenge under the service charge regime in the LTA 1985. Further problems were identified in the operation of the consultation requirements before the landlord initiates major works. The consultation thresholds laid down in the LTA 1985 (expenditure by the landlord of £1,000 or more, or £50 multiplied by the number of service charge payers, whichever was the greater) operated in an arbitrary fashion, and no consultation at all was imposed where the landlord proposed to enter into a contract for the long-term provision of services (as opposed to 'works') such as ongoing maintenance, cleaning and gardening.

1 See *Sutton (Hastoe) Housing Association v Williams* (1988) 20 HLR 321, CA.
2 See *Commonhold and Leasehold Reform: Draft Bill and Consultation Paper* (Cm 4843, DETR 2000), Ch 5, p 162.

[13.8] The CLRA 2002 implemented a number of changes to the service charge regime, premised upon the overall policy objective that existing rights to consultation and to challenge unreasonable charges should apply to all variable charges which are required to be paid as a condition of a lease. The CLRA 2002 extended the meaning of 'service charges' to include charges for improvements, and made the levying of administration charges for landlords' approvals subject to challenge if unreasonable. A new requirement has been introduced requiring landlords to consult long leaseholders before entering into any contract to provide ongoing services for a period of 12 months or more, and in future consultation over major works will be required in any case where the amount payable by any individual leaseholder exceeds a fixed sum to be prescribed by regulations made under the CLRA 2002. The latter also strengthened the requirements for the management of service charge funds by the landlord. All service charge monies must in future be held in individual designated client accounts for each separate group of leaseholders, and annual service charge statements must be provided for each leaseholder.

[13.9] Despite the amendments made by the CLRA 2002, many of the tenants' rights remain hedged around with procedural difficulties and notice requirements which, arguably, impair their effectiveness. The drafting of the legislation is also, in some instances, obscure and gives rise to uncertainty[1].

1 This was commented upon in the 1991 DoE survey (see *Commonhold and Leasehold Reform: Draft Bill and Consultation Paper* (Cm 4843, DETR 2000) pp 63–64). Successive amendments since then in the HA 1996 and the CLRA 2002 have, if anything, made the interpretation and application of some aspects of the legislation even more complex.

CURRENT FRAMEWORK OF LEGAL REGULATION

[13.10] The statutory framework within which issues of repair and management are currently dealt with is somewhat complex. It may, therefore, be apposite to outline the chief measures by way of background to their detailed exposition.

[13.11] When considering problems of repair and management of flats held on long leases, the terms of the lease itself remain the starting point in ascertaining the reciprocal obligations of landlord and tenant. Freedom of contract is preserved by the CLRA 2002, and the parties are free to make such contractual provision for these matters as they choose. Problems may arise where the landlord later fails to carry out repairs, or where not all tenants in a block are willing to contribute to the cost of repair, or (most commonly) where the tenants consider the costs levied for repair to be excessive. Recovery of the costs of repair will be levied by the landlord in the form of a variable service charge. The various statutory provisions deal with these problems in the following manner:

(i) *The LTA 1985 (ss 1–3)*: requires the landlord to disclose his identity and any assignment of his interest.
(ii) *The LTA 1987 (ss 47 and 48)*: requires rent or other charge demands to state the landlord's name and address in England or Wales where notices can be served.
(iii) *Amount of service charges*: LTA 1985, ss 18–20, and 29–30B, as amended by the LTA 1987 and CLRA 2002, limit any recoverable service charges over a prescribed amount per leaseholder to costs reasonably incurred. These provisions also require the obtaining of estimates, and prior consultation with tenants and (where applicable) tenants associations. (See para 13.83 ff below.)

(iv) *Service charge monies*: Must be held in a separate client account, in a sinking fund for each group of leaseholders (LTA 1987, s 42, as amended by CLRA 2002).
(v) *Appointment of manager by Leasehold Valuation Tribunal (LVT)*: LTA 1987, Pt II, gives a tenant the right to apply to the LVT for the appointment of a manager to carry out works which the landlord has failed to do.
(vi) *Right of compulsory acquisition*: LTA 1987, Pt III, enables a majority of long leaseholders in a block to apply to the court for an acquisition order to acquire the freeholder's interest. This right is circumscribed, however, in that it applies only if the freeholder is in breach of the terms of the lease, if his breach of obligation is likely to continue, and if the appointment of a manager would not provide a sufficient remedy (LTA 1987, s 29 and see para 13.105 ff below).
(vii) *Variation of leases*: LTA 1987, Pt IV, enables a party to a *long* lease which has no (or unsatisfactory) provision for repair, maintenance and insurance to apply to the LVT for variation of the lease terms.
(viii) *First refusal*: LTA 1987, Pt I, gives a majority of qualifying tenants (which may include both long leaseholders and other tenants) the right to acquire the freehold reversion should the landlord propose to sell to a third party.
(ix) *Right to manage*: CLRA 2002, Pt 2, Ch 1, gives a qualifying majority of tenants (those holding two thirds of the flats in the property) the right to serve notice on the landlord assuming the right to manage the property themselves through a RTM company, in which all participating leaseholders will have shares. If they do so, management will be assumed collectively, using the RTM company as the medium for doing so, subject to the legal requirements as to management otherwise applicable to the landlord, eg as to levying of service charges etc.

B Tenant's right of first refusal

SCOPE AND APPLICATION OF PRE-EMPTION RIGHTS

[13.12] The Nugee Report was specifically asked to consider the *management* of blocks only, and not wider issues of tenure. Nevertheless the Nugee Report recommended the introduction of rights of pre-emption for tenants in blocks of flats, enabling them to collectively exercise an option to purchase whenever their landlord proposed to sell his interest to a third party[1]. Nugee's detailed proposals were enacted in the LTA 1987, Pt I. The tenants' right of first refusal subsequently proved relatively easy for landlords to avoid. The right was commonly avoided by the simple device of the landlord transferring his interest to an associated company, and then transferring ownership of the block by selling the company's shares to the new purchaser[2]. Additionally, the right of first refusal only applied to transfers of the immediate landlord's interest – it could be readily avoided by creating an intermediate lease with residential subleases, and then transferring the superior landlord's interest (to which the LTA 1987 did not apply). A further weakness in the LTA 1987 was the lack of a direct sanction against a defaulting landlord. If the landlord sold his interest without giving tenants the right of first refusal, they could force the purchaser to transfer the freehold to them at the price at which it was sold in breach of the Act. There was, however, no direct remedy against the defaulting landlord.

1 Nugee Report paras 7.9.14 ff.
2 See the first edition of this work, *Private Sector Housing law* (1995) p 387; *Butterworths Residential Landlord and Tenant Guide* (1997) p 315 (Driscoll).

[13.13] To remedy some of its perceived defects, and to strengthen tenants' rights, the HA 1996 made substantial changes to the LTA 1987, Pt I. It extended the scope of 'relevant disposals' triggering the right of first refusal, in an attempt to prevent avoidance by landlords, and made it a criminal offence not to afford tenants the right of first refusal. The right was also extended to contracts of sale, and the assignment of contracts to buy blocks of flats[1]. The HA 1996 also made a number of changes aimed at simplifying the procedures to be followed where tenants accept the landlord's offer of first refusal[2].

1 The Court of Appeal had held, in *Mainwaring v Henry Smith's Charity Trustees* [1998] QB 1, [1996] 2 All ER 220, that the right of first refusal did not apply to an exchange of contracts, which was not a relevant disposal under the LTA 1987 as originally drawn. This decision was reversed by the amendments made in the HA 1996.

2 HA 1986, ss 89–95 amended LTA 1987, s 4, redefining relevant disposals caught by the right of pre emption and imposing criminal sanctions for disregarding it. HA 1996, Sch 6 replaced the remainder of LTA 1987, Pt I (s 5 et seq) in their entirety, with redrafted provisions amending the statutory procedures to be followed when exercising the right.

RELEVANT DISPOSALS TRIGGERING RIGHT OF FIRST REFUSAL

[13.14] A landlord may not make a 'relevant disposal' affecting a block of flats unless he has first served an offer notice on his tenants informing them of the principal terms of the proposed sale, and the price at which his interest is to be sold[1]. If the qualifying tenants accept the landlord's offer to sell or otherwise dispose of his interest, he must then follow the statutory procedures in LTA 1987, Pt I when completing the transaction.

1 LTA 1987, ss 1 and 5.

Premises to which right applicable

[13.15] Pre-emption rights apply whenever premises consist of the whole or part of a building containing two or more flats held by qualifying tenants, and the number of flats held by the latter exceeds 50 per cent of the total number of flats contained in the premises[1]. The LTA 1987 does not apply if part of the premises is to be used for non-residential purposes (eg business use) but only if the internal floor area of that part(s) exceeds 50 per cent of the total internal floor area of the property[2]. Similarly, the Act does not apply if there is an exempt or resident landlord[3]. Pre-emption rights are not restricted to tenants with long leases, and will, for example, also accrue to protected and statutory tenants under the RA 1977. However 'assured' tenants with tenancies within the HA 1988, Pt I, *are* excluded from the definition of 'qualifying' tenants[4], and will not enjoy pre-emption rights. The rationale for the different treatment of regulated and assured tenants is not immediately apparent. Tenants holding under protected shorthold tenancies, business tenancies within the LTA 1954, Pt II, and service tenancies are, likewise, specifically excluded[5]. In order to prevent landlords manipulating occupancies, LTA 1987, s 3(2)[6] provides that a person does not qualify if he is the tenant of a flat under a tenancy comprising that flat *and* at least two other flats contained in the premises. This provision is intended to exclude those who are in reality merely intermediary landlords but would, it seems, also disqualify a genuine tenant with multiple tenancies. Subtenants are likewise excluded, but only if their immediate landlord is himself a qualifying tenant enjoying the right of first refusal[7].

1 LTA 1987, s 1(2). *Query* the presence of one or more *empty* flats may, it seems, take the premises outside the 50 per cent occupation condition in s 1.
2 Ibid, s 1(3).
3 Ibid, s 1(4). Resident landlords are defined by LTA 1987, s 58(2) in similar terms to the RA 1977, s 12.
4 HA 1988, Sch 13 para 2(1), adding a new s 3(1)(d) to the LTA 1987.
5 LTA 1987, s 3(1).
6 As amended by HA 1988, Sch 13, para 2(2). The amendment ensures that a tenant whose tenancy agreement includes common parts of the building, in addition to his flat, still enjoys pre-emption rights under the LTA 1987.
7 LTA 1987, s 3(4).

Relevant 'disposal'

[13.16] The LTA 1987 applies whenever a landlord makes a 'disposal' of any legal or equitable estate or interest in the premises, other than the grant of a tenancy of a single flat[1]. There are, however, a number of important exceptions to this broad principle. Where the freehold is held by a corporate body (typically a holding company), the Act does not apply to a disposal to an associated company, provided it has been an associated company of that body for two years[2]. The subsequent transfer of ownership by a transfer of shares in the associated company will not be caught by the LTA 1987, thus avoiding the right of first refusal. The imposition of a two-year 'qualifying' period during which the two companies must be associated was introduced by the HA 1996 in an attempt to prevent too ready an avoidance of the tenants' pre-emption right using this device. Pre-emption rights do not accrue upon the disposal of the interest of a beneficiary of a settlement, of an interest under a mortgage or an incorporeal hereditament, to disposals by a trustee in bankruptcy or liquidator, to disposals pursuant to property adjustment orders in matrimonial proceedings, or to disposals under the Inheritance (Provision for Family and Dependants) Act 1975. Disposals pursuant to compulsory purchase orders and disposals by charities are likewise exempt. A disposal by way of gift to a member of the landlord's family (or to a charity) will not attract pre-emption rights. Neither will a disposal pursuant to an option or right of pre-emption which is binding on the landlord, irrespective of whether it was granted before or after the commencement of the Act[3]. The grant of an option to purchase will not therefore trigger the pre-emption provisions provided the transaction is not demonstrably a sham aimed solely at avoiding the Act. However, if the option to purchase is exercised within four months of being granted, that is treated as 'disposal' and the pre-emption rights will apply[4]. Pre-emption rights under Pt I *will* apply, however, where a disposal is made by a mortgagee in exercise of a power of sale or leasing[5]. However, the *creation* of an interest or estate by way of security for a loan will not trigger the pre-emption provisions.

1 LTA 1987, s 4(1). The exceptions discussed below are contained in LTA 1987, s 4(2), as amended by the HA 1996 ss 89 and 90.
2 Ibid, s 4(2)(l), as inserted by HA 1996, s 90. 'Associated company' is defined by section 20 (1) ibid to mean a body's holding company, a subsidiary of that company or another subsidiary of that holding company. These terms are, in turn, defined by reference to the companies legislation (Companies Act 1985, s 736).
3 Ibid, s 4(2)(i). This could, arguably, lead to increased use of option contracts as a means of disposing of this type of property. This must be read with s 8D ibid (n 4 below).
4 See s 8D ibid. This is intended to catch the artificial use of option contracts to sidestep the tenants pre-emption rights. *Query*, however, if there is more than a four-month time lapse between the grant and exercise of the option, the latter will not be caught by the 1987 Act.
5 Ibid, s 4(1A), added by HA 1988, Sch 13 para 3. This closed a loophole in the LTA 1987 as originally drafted (see Adams (1988) 43 EG 64).

[13.17] Special rules apply where the immediate landlord is himself a tenant under a superior lease, and not the freehold owner. If the landlord's interest is a term of more than seven years, then pre-emption rights apply to that interest only, and not the freehold. This may cause problems where the head lease is extended, necessitating an offer to the tenants under LTA 1987, Pt I, before the decision to extend it can be made. If the landlord holds under a lease for less than seven years, or (significantly) under a tenancy for a longer period but which is terminable within the first seven years at the option of the superior landlord, then the statutory pre-emption rights apply to the freehold also[1]. In this event, extending the head lease could necessitate offering the freehold to qualifying tenants under LTA 1987, Pt I. Head leases with break clauses exercisable within the first seven years will also be vulnerable under the new provisions, although, it is suggested, the mere presence of a proviso for re-entry in the usual form will not activate the pre-emption provisions[2].

1 LTA 1987, s 2(2).
2 LTA 1987, s 2(2)(b) is more restrictively drafted than the analogous provisions in the HA 1980, s 52(1) (protected shorthold tenancies). Note in the latter context, it is now clear that a forfeiture clause in the usual form will *not* take a tenancy outside the short hold provisions even though (strictly) there is no 'obligation' on a tenant not (for instance) to go bankrupt: *Patterson v Aggio* [1987] 2 EGLR 127, CA. By analogy, as LTA 1987, s 2(2) requires the tenancy to contain an *option* to terminate at the landlord's behest, it is unlikely a forfeiture clause in standard form would meet this requirement.

Application to contracts

[13.18] Under LTA 1987, s 4[1], the right of first refusal now applies to a contract to create or transfer an estate or interest in land, in the same manner as it applies to a 'disposal' which consists of the creation or transfer of such an interest or estate. The right applies whether the contract is conditional or unconditional and whether or not it is enforceable by specific performance. If the landlord enters into a contract to sell the freehold, therefore, this will be a disposal triggering the application of the tenants' right of first refusal. A landlord who exchanges contracts to sell the freehold or the residue of an intermediary lease, without first observing the procedures in LTA 1987, Pt 1, therefore commits a criminal offence.

1 Inserted by HA 1996, s 89.

[13.19] Although LTA 1987, s 4A expressly applies whether the contract is conditional or unconditional, it may be necessary to distinguish contracts subject to a condition precedent to performance from those subject to a condition precedent to contract. Where the landlord enters into a contract to sell the freehold subject to a condition precedent to performance of the contract (eg the contract is conditional upon the landlord obtaining planning permission for alterations), the contract will clearly be a 'disposal' triggering the right of first refusal. On the other hand, it is suggested that merely entering into an agreement subject to a condition precedent to contract will not be caught by the LTA 1987 (as amended), as a contract will not come into existence (and thus trigger the application of s 4A) until the condition is satisfied. This might be the case, for example, where the landlord himself holds an intermediary lease, and contracts to sell the residue unexpired, conditional upon his first obtaining a renewal of the lease from the superior landlord. Upon the condition becoming satisfied a contract will arise and it will at this point, it is suggested, be caught by LTA 1987, s 4A. An assignment of one's rights under a contract to sell is also a disposal to which the right of first refusal applies.

PROCEDURE ON SALE AND ACQUISITION

[13.20] The detailed provisions in the LTA 1987 for notification of impending sale, offers and counter offers were simplified and replaced by new procedural rules set out in the HA 1996, Sch 6[1].

1 HA 1996, Sch 6 substituted a new ss 5–18A in the LTA 1987, replacing in their entirety the original provisions. References hereafter to the LTA 1987, Pt I, are to the sections substituted into the 1987 Act by HA 1996, Sch 6.

Offer notice

[13.21] Whenever a landlord 'proposes' to dispose of his interest, or to enter into a contract to do so, he must first serve an offer notice on the tenants of the flats affected informing them of the estate or interest to be sold and the price at which he proposes to sell[1]. This must be expressed as an offer to dispose of his interest on those terms if accepted by the 'requisite majority' of the tenants. The requisite majority of tenants to exercise the right of first refusal are those qualifying tenants of flats who have (between them) more than 50 per cent of the available votes. For this purpose each qualifying tenant has one vote, and the total number of available votes is equal to the number of constituent flats let to qualifying tenants at the date when the period for accepting the offer expires[2]. Where there has been a disposition in breach of Pt I, however, and the tenants subsequently seek to purchase the freehold from the new owner, the requisite majority of qualifying votes is 51 per cent (or more) of the total number of constituent flats let to qualifying tenants on the date they serve notice exercising their right to purchase[3].

1 LTA 1987, s 5(1).
2 Ibid, s 18A(1).
3 Ibid, s 18A(2).

[13.22] The *form* that the offer notice must take depends upon the nature of the proposed transaction. If the conveyance is to be preceded by a contract of sale (the commonest scenario) the landlord must serve on all qualifying tenants an offer notice complying with LTA 1987, s 5A. The notice must contain particulars of the principal terms of the disposal, including the property to be sold, the estate or interest to which the contract relates, the price at which it is to be sold and the other principal terms of the contract. The notice must state that it constitutes an offer by the landlord to enter into a contract on those terms that must be accepted by the requisite majority of qualifying tenants in the constituent flats. The notice must give the tenants at least *two months* within which to accept the offer, and must also specify a further period of not less than two months within which a purchaser can be nominated to take the conveyance on their behalf. Having decided to buy the freehold, the tenants may, for example, wish to acquire a company to effect the transaction. The nomination period commences at the end of the initial offer period. The notification requirements are relaxed where there are a large number of tenants (ie more than ten), and will be satisfied provided notice is served on 90 per cent of qualifying tenants[1]. This is understandable, as difficulties in effecting service may otherwise be faced by the landlord of a large block with a constantly changing occupancy. The LTA 1987 also relaxes the requirement for small properties, however, by providing that where there are fewer than ten qualifying tenants the landlord must notify all but one of the tenants[2]. It might be noted that there is no requirement for the landlord to prove he has *tried* to serve notice on *all* tenants; actual service on the stipulated majority suffices.

1 LTA 1987, s 5(5)(a).
2 Ibid, s 5(5)(b). There is less justification for this exclusion, as a landlord with fewer than ten tenants in a block of flats should be able to ascertain their identity and whereabouts with little difficulty. *Query* where there are only two tenants service on one will apparently suffice.

[13.23] These requirements are modified for sales by auction, transactions involving the grant of options or pre-emption rights, transactions where there is no contract of sale preceding the conveyance, and sales with a non-monetary consideration[1]. In the case of a sale by auction, for example, the offer notice must specify not only the terms of the proposed sale (as above) but also that it constitutes an offer to sell to the qualifying tenants at whatever price the property reaches in the subsequent auction[2]. In other words, the contract finalised at auction will take effect as if made with the qualifying tenants (or their nominated purchaser), and not the successful bidder. The notice must give the tenants two months in which to accept and a further period of 28 days (if they do so) in which to nominate a purchaser to take the conveyance on their behalf. The offer notice must be served not less than four and not more than six months before the date of the auction[3]. The landlord must also specify the time and place of the auction, and the name of the auctioneer, and must either do so in the offer notice or in a separate notice served at least 28 days before the auction[4]. Clearly, this is a procedure fraught with difficulties for the qualifying tenants involved, who will (effectively) have to commit themselves to purchase the block at a price which remains unknown until after the auction has taken place.

1 The detailed requirements are set out in LTA 1987, s 5B–5E, inserted by HA 1996, s 92 and Sch 6, Pt I.
2 LTA 1987, s 5B.
3 Ibid, s 5B(7).
4 Ibid, s 5B(8).

[13.24] Where the landlord proposes to grant an option or right of pre-emption over a block of flats he must first serve an offer notice complying with LTA 1987, s 5C. This must specify the principal terms of the proposed disposal, including the price to be paid for the option or pre-emption right, and offer to grant the right on those terms to the qualifying tenants. The offer notice must specify the terms subject to which the option or pre-emption right would be exercisable, eg if an option to purchase is to be granted which is exercisable for a fixed period from grant (say ten years) this must be stated. The offer notice must give a period of two months for acceptance by the tenants, and a further period of two months for the nomination of the purchaser to take the conveyance on the tenants' behalf. Where there is to be a conveyance which is not preceded by a contract of sale, an offer notice must first be served giving the tenants two months to accept and a further two months to nominate a purchaser, and the principal terms of the conveyance must be specified as required by LTA 1987, s 5D. Similar requirements apply to disposals wholly or partly for a non-monetary consideration under LTA 1987, s 5E.

Acceptance of landlord's offer

[13.25] Where the landlord has served an offer notice, he cannot sell until the expiry of the period given in the notice for its acceptance by the tenants (a minimum of two months)[1]. Where the requisite majority accept the landlord's terms, a statutory bar on disposals comes into play, preventing the landlord from disposing of his interest to anyone other than the tenant's nominee. The bar on disposals lasts until the end of the two-month nomination period (or such longer period as may be given in the offer notice)[2]. If a purchaser is nominated by the tenants, the landlord must not dispose of his interest except to the nominate purchaser[3]. The Act requires the acceptance notice to be given by the 'requisite majority' of qualifying tenants ie qualifying tenants of constituent flats with more than 50 per cent of the available votes[4]. For the purposes of calculating the requisite majority, there is one vote for each flat occupied by a qualifying tenant.

1 LTA 1987, s 6(1).
2 Ibid, s 6(4).
3 Ibid, s 8(2).
4 Ibid, s 6(3) and s 18A for the definition of 'requisite majority'. See above para 13.21.

Failure to accept offer or nominate

[13.26] If no acceptance notice is served, or (having accepted the offer) no purchaser is nominated by the tenants within the period allowed, the landlord is free to sell to a third party. He may only do so subject to restrictions laid down in the LTA 1987, s 7. He must dispose of the interest concerned within 12 months of the end of the notification period, the price he accepts must be not less than that offered to the tenants, and the other terms of the disposition must correspond to those in the offer notice served on the tenants[1]. Where the offer notice was given under the LTA 1987, s 5B (sale by auction), the landlord is restricted to selling at public auction on terms that correspond to those in the offer notice.

1 LTA 1987, s 7(2).

Procedure following tenants' acceptance

[13.27] Where the tenants have served an acceptance notice, and followed this up by nominating a purchaser to take the property on their behalf, the landlord is precluded from disposing of his interest to anyone except the tenants' nominated purchaser[1]. The landlord has one month following service of the tenants nomination notice in which to withdraw from the transaction[2]. If he fails to elect to withdraw, then he must comply with the procedures laid down in LTA 1987, ss 8A–10A for completing the sale of his interest to the tenants. These are based on the principle of 'advance or withdraw' ie if either landlord or tenant fails to complete each stage within the period prescribed he is assumed to have withdrawn from the transaction.

1 LTA 1987, s 8(2).
2 LTA 1987, s 8(3).

[13.28] *Step 1*] Within one month of being notified that someone has been nominated to take the conveyance, the landlord must send the nominated person a contract[1]. If the landlord fails to do so he is deemed to have withdrawn from the transaction.

1 LTA 1987, s 8A(2).

[13.29] *Step 2*] The nominated purchaser must, within two months of receiving the contract, offer to exchange contracts by signing it and sending it to the landlord together with a deposit[1]. Alternatively he must notify the landlord that he no longer intends to proceed. If he does so, or fails to deliver a contract to schedule, he is deemed to have withdrawn from the transaction. The withdrawal is effective from service of the notice of withdrawal or (if no notice of withdrawal or contract is served) at the end of the two-month period.

1 LTA 1987, s 8A(4). The deposit will either be 10% of the consideration, or a sum calculated by reference to the contract (if a different deposit is contractually provided for).

[13.30] *Step 3*] If the tenant offers to exchange contracts, the landlord must complete an exchange of contracts within 7 days of receiving the tenant's signed part of the contract and the deposit[1].

1 LTA 1987, s 8A(6).

[13.31] These procedures are modified in the case of auction sales. Where the tenants have nominated a purchaser to take the conveyance following the auction, they must give the landlord at least 28 days' notice before the auction that they wish to consider buying on the terms at which the landlord's interest is sold at auction. If the property is then sold at auction, the landlord has 7 days in which to send the nominated purchaser a contract. Having received the contract, the nominated purchaser then has 28 days in which to notify the landlord that he accepts the terms of the contract and to fulfill any conditions to be met by the purchaser on entering into the contract (eg payment of a deposit or provision of credit references). If he does so, the contract takes effect as if the nominated person, and not the purchaser, had entered into the contract[1].

1 LTA 1987, s 8B. If the nominated person fails to give notice, he is assumed to have withdrawn.

[13.32] The nominated purchaser can give notice of withdrawal at any stage, indicating that he no longer intends to proceed with the transaction, provided he does so before a binding contract of sale comes into being between himself and the landlord. The LTA 1987 provides that he *must* give notice of withdrawal if he becomes aware that the number of qualifying tenants wishing to proceed with the purchase has fallen below the requisite majority for exercising the right of first refusal[1]. There are costs implications in withdrawing from the transaction part way through the statutory timetable. If the tenants withdraw before the end of the first four weeks of the nomination period specified in the landlord's offer notice, then neither they nor the nominated person are liable for any of the landlord's costs incurred in connection with the disposal[2]. If a withdrawal notice is served after the end of this four-week period, the landlord may recover any costs reasonably incurred by him in connection with the disposal between the end of that four-week period and the time when the notice of withdrawal was served on him[3]. If the tenants withdraw, the landlord is free to dispose if his interest during the ensuing 12-month period, provided he does so on the same terms as those offered to the tenants, and at a price which is at least as high as that offered to them[4]. Similarly, the landlord is entitled to withdraw during the statutory procedure, but if he does so he is not entitled to dispose of his interest for 12 months beginning with the date of service of his notice of withdrawal[5]. His exposure to costs is the same as that applicable where the tenants withdraw. He is protected from liability for the tenants' costs provided he withdraws before the end of the four-week nomination period, but is liable if he withdraws thereafter until the date of withdrawal.

1 For the requisite majority see LTA 1987, s 18A and above para 13.21.
2 Ibid, s 9A(6).

3 Ibid, s 9A(7).
4 Ibid, s 9A(4) and (5).
5 Ibid, s 9B(2).

Criminal liability[1]

[13.33] The landlord commits an offence if, without reasonable excuse, he makes a disposal to which the LTA 1987 applies without having served an offer notice on qualifying tenants of flats in the premises, or if he later disposes of the interest concerned in contravention of a restriction imposed by the Act, eg where the tenants withdraw from the purchase and he then disposes of the interest to a third party for less than the price offered to the tenants. Where the landlord is a body corporate, and the offence has been committed with the consent or connivance of a director, manager, secretary or other officer of the company, or is due to the neglect of such an officer, then the individual concerned as well as the company will be guilty of the offence and liable to be proceeded against. Proceedings under the LTA 1987 can be brought by a local housing authority.

1 LTA 1987, s 10A. The offence under this section is punishable on summary conviction by a fine not exceeding level 5 on the standard scale.

ENFORCING THE RIGHT OF FIRST REFUSAL

Right to adopt transaction

[13.34] If the landlord disposes of his interest in the block, the new owner is obligated to inform the tenants of the assignment[1]. Moreover, if the transaction was one to which LTA 1987, Pt I applied, he must give the tenants prescribed information, including information about their right to acquire the reversion under the LTA 1987[2]. This notice must be served by the new landlord before the date on which the next payment of rent is due, or if that is within two months of the transfer, by the end of that two-month period. Failure to serve the change of landlord notice is an offence[3].

1 LTA 1985, s 3.
2 LTA 1985, s 3A, inserted by HA 1996, s 93.
3 Ibid, s 3(3).

[13.35] Where the landlord sells a block in breach of LTA 1987, Pt I, the requisite majority of the qualifying tenants can, by notice, require the purchaser to provide details of the terms on which the disposal was made, and if it consisted of entering into a contract to provide a copy of the contract[1]. To avoid continuing uncertainty attaching to the purchaser's title this must be done within four months after the tenants have received written notice of the assignment from the purchaser (above). If the tenants discover the transfer in some other way (for instance by receiving service charge demands from the new owner), then the four-month time limit runs from the date on which the requisite majority of tenants received documents alerting them to the transfer and the existence of their rights under the LTA 1987. The purchaser has one month in which to comply with the tenants' request.

1 LTA 1987, s 11A.

[13.36] Where the landlord has disposed of his interest contrary to the requirements of the LTA 1987, s 12 gives the requisite majority of qualifying tenants the right to adopt the transaction and compel a sale to them (or their nominated purchaser) instead. If the landlord has entered into a contract to sell, the tenants have six months in which to adopt the benefit of the contract by serving notice on the landlord under LTA 1987, s 12A. If, on the other hand, the transaction has been completed before the tenants become aware of it, they can compel the purchaser to sell his interest to their nominee by serving a 'purchase notice' under LTA 1987, s 12B. This requires the purchaser to sell the block to them at the price paid for the original disposal[1]. The purchase notice must be served within six months of the landlord complying with a request for information under LTA 1987, s 11A or of notice of change of landlord being given under LTA 1985, s 3A (above). In some cases the landlord may himself only have a leasehold interest, and in this case the disposal triggering the application of the right of first refusal may be his surrendering his head lease to the superior landlord. In such cases LTA 1987, s 12C gives the tenants the right to compel the superior landlord to grant a new head lease on the same terms as that which was surrendered.

1 LTA 1987, s 12B.

[13.37] The Leasehold Valuation Tribunal (LVT) has jurisdiction to determine disputes arising out of purchase notices, including (for instance) the consideration payable where the original disposal also included property other than that affected by the LTA 1987[1]. If the tenants have served a purchase notice on the new owner, or have adopted a contract entered into by their landlord, they have three months in which to enter into a binding contract or to make an application to the LVT. If the notice is not acted upon within the three-month deadline the purchaser can serve a notice stating that the purchase notice and anything done under it is of no effect[2]. The right to compel a resale also ceases to apply if at any time the premises cease to be subject to the Act, irrespective of the position at the time of the original disposal – the one statutory concession made to the assignee[3].

1 LTA 1987, s 13.
2 Ibid, s 17(3).
3 Ibid, s 17(1).

Prospective purchasers – precautionary notice

[13.38] Clearly, a prospective purchaser of a block of flats may be deterred if he thinks that sitting tenants may enjoy the right of first refusal, and can unravel the sale transaction before it is completed. To safeguard his position, LTA 1987, s 18 empowers the prospective purchaser of a block to serve notice of the proposed sale on qualifying tenants. He can request the latter to inform him whether the landlord has himself served an offer notice as required by the Act, and whether they would wish to take advantage of their statutory pre-emption rights. If the purchaser serves notice on at least 80 per cent of the qualifying tenants and *either* not more than 50 per cent reply in writing within two months *or* over 50 per cent reply to the effect that they do not regard themselves as enjoying pre-emption rights or would not exercise them in any event, then the statutory pre-emption rights cease to apply[1]. There is no statutorily prescribed form for the purchaser's 'clearance notice', which will commonly therefore adopt the rather dense legal terminology of LTA 1987, s 18. The time limit for the tenants' response (two months) is generally perceived to be unrealistically short to enable the latter collectively to decide whether to exercise their rights under Pt 1. Not surprisingly, therefore, the 'clearance notice' procedure continues to offer prospective purchasers a legitimate (and relatively straightforward) way of freeing themselves of the pre-emption provisions of the LTA 1987[2].

1 LTA 1987, s 18(3). Note that the relevant criterion (LTA 1987, s 18(3)(b)(i)) is whether the tenants *think* they enjoy statutory rights, not whether they in fact do. If a majority of tenants, ignorant of their rights, reply that they do not think they enjoy pre-emption rights then the latter will apparently cease to apply – a novel proposition, it is suggested.

2 There was evidence of abuse of this procedure soon after the LTA 1987 came into force; see for example *Landlord and Tenant Act 1987: Awareness, Experience and Impact* (DoE 1991) para 5.3, p 71 (notice served over Christmas period to avoid likely response).

Enforcement against subsequent purchasers

[13.39] Complex problems will arise if the purchaser of the reversion, having acquired it in breach of the LTA 1987, sells on to a new landlord, *viz* where there is a chain of disposals. Clearly, it may prove difficult for tenants wishing to invoke their pre-emption rights to ascertain the identity of the 'landlord' for the time being, upon whom an information notice (under s 11) or purchase notice (under s 12) can be served. To assist in this regard, LTA 1987, s 16 contains 'passing on' provisions which apply where a new landlord is served with an information and/or purchase notice at a time 'when he no longer holds the *estate* or *interest* that was the subject matter of the original disposal' (italics added). Where an information notice has been served, the new landlord must furnish the tenants with the information about the original transaction required and give the name and address of the person to whom he disposed of the reversion, as well as forwarding copies to the latter[1]. In the case of a purchase notice he must forward it to the new owner and give the tenant details of the latter's name and address. If he does so, then the purchase notice applies to the subsequent purchaser (instead of the original purchaser) 'as if he were the transferee under the original disposal'[2]. Provision is also made for apportionment of parts of the reversion among the original and subsequent purchasers[3].

1 LTA 1987, s 16(2).
2 Ibid, s 16(4).
3 Ibid, s 16(5).

[13.40] A potential problem with the 'passing on' provisions is that the duty to forward notices applies only when the original transferee no longer 'holds the estate or interest' purchased. What if he has contracted to sell on the reversion to X (a subsequent purchaser) but receives an information or purchase notice prior to completion? If the contract is specifically enforceable, the equitable estate in the reversion will vest in the next transferee, while the original purchaser retains the legal title pending completion. Arguably, he still retains the estate or interest originally purchased and is (hence) under no duty to pass on notices to X. It would appear, therefore, that no disposal, for the purposes of the Act, can take place until completion of the freehold transfer to the subsequent owner (ie to X), and the original transferee remains the proper recipient of notices until this has occurred[1]. This raises the possibility of tenants' notices being effectively 'lost' where a chain of contracts is entered into for sale of the reversion.

1 See *Wilkins v Horrowitz* [1990] 2 EGLR 217 (a rent assessment committee decision).

[13.41] Where a chain of disposals takes place, LTA 1987, s 17(1) enables the subsequent purchaser or new landlord to give notice disapplying the Act where the premises are ones to which Pt I has ceased to apply. Additionally, LTA 1987, s 17(3) provides that if three months have expired following service of a purchase notice on the new landlord without *either* a binding contract to purchase having been concluded with the tenants' nominee, *or* an application having been made to the LVT, then the landlord can give notice that the purchase notice is to be treated as of no effect. Similarly, if an LVT *has* made a determination and within two months thereafter no binding contract is concluded (and no other application to the tribunal is pending) then the new landlord can give notice that Pt I rights have ceased to apply. These provisions are problematic, in that they require the conclusion of a binding contract within the time allowed, and this will require the signature of both parties[1]. There is no *obligation* on the landlord to sign a contract transferring the freehold to the tenants. The landlord is theoretically free, therefore, to prevaricate until the time limit expires and then serve notice under s 17 disapplying LTA 1987, Pt I – a loophole which does no credit to the legislation, and which the extensive amendments in the HA 1996 failed to close[2].

1 Law of Property (Miscellaneous Provisions) Act 1989, s 2(1).
2 For evidence of this abuse see for example *Landlord and Tenant Act 1987: Awareness, Experience and Impact* (DoE 1991) p 73.

DISPUTE RESOLUTION

[13.42] The county court has jurisdiction to determine any question arising under LTA 1987, Pt I[1]. More specifically, section 19 of the latter gives the count court jurisdiction to determine whether one of the parties is in default in complying with any duty imposed by the Act. Before making an application to the court, the applicant must have served a notice on the defaulting party requiring him to comply and make good his default, and 14 days must have elapsed without his having done so[2]. The court's powers include the power to make injunctions. This jurisdiction might be useful to compel compliance, for example, if the landlord attempted to sell to another purchaser after serving an offer notice on his tenants, or did so after receiving an acceptance notice from them agreeing to purchase the block on the terms offered.

1 LTA 1987, s 52.
2 Ibid, s 19(2).

[13.43] The LVT's jurisdiction under the LTA 1987, Pt I is more circumscribed[1]. It has a limited jurisdiction to determine any matters specified in the purchase notice served by the tenants under whichever of s 12A, 12B or 12C applies in the case concerned. The tenants' purchase notice can only require the landlord (or, where the block has been sold in breach of the LTA 1987, the purchaser) to dispose of his interest in so far as it relates to premises to which LTA 1987, Pt I applies. The landlord's ownership may encompass not only the block but other adjacent properties sold with it, including gardens, garages, outhouses etc (the block may, for example, be part of a larger property). The tenants' purchase notice can require the landlord to convey not only the buildings comprising the premises let, but also any appurtenances of that building, ie property over which the tenants enjoy rights by virtue of their lease of the flat concerned, such as gardens[2]. The LVT has jurisdiction to determine the extent of the property to which the purchase notice applies in these circumstances. In general, however, its jurisdiction is limited to adjudicating on the contents of the tenants' purchase notice. This includes the price payable for the freehold and the terms of the disposal, but the LVT does not have power to reopen the terms on which the original disposal was made. Neither does it have jurisdiction to decide on the validity of a purchase notice served under s 12[3].

1 See LTA 1987, ss 12A(5), 12B(4) and 13(1).
2 See *Denetower Ltd v Toop* [1991] 3 All ER 661, CA (gardens validly included in purchase notice, but not garages over which tenants had no rights under their leases).
3 This is a matter for the court: *Denetower v Toop* ibid. *Saga Properties v Palmeira Square Nos 2-6 Ltd* [1995] 1 EGLR 199.

[13.44] Where the price and other relevant terms are not specified in the tenants purchase notice, the notice can expressly refer them to the LVT[1] for determination. In *Cousins v Metropolitan Guarantee Ltd*[2], however, it was established that these provisions do not give the committee jurisdiction to determine afresh a value for the premises. They do not in general have power to revalue the premises sold, but may do so where they have subsequently become affected by an incumbrance[3] or have increased in value[4]. The tenants are not, therefore, able to challenge the price at which the landlord proposes to sell or (if a sale has taken place in breach of the LTA 1987) to renegotiate the price at which the original landlord sold the property. Neither do they have power to decide whether rent and service charges are payable to the original landlord or the purchasers, as these are not matters directly relevant to the tenants' purchase notice served under LTA 1987, s 12[5]. They do, however, have power to omit terms in the purchase notice and the original disposal, eg where the sale granted the landlord an option to repurchase the block which, if perpetuated on the disposal to the tenants under the LTA 1987, would have had the effect of nullifying their statutory right to purchase the freehold[6].

1 See LTA 1987, ss 12A(5), 12B(4) and 13(1).
2 [1989] 2 EGLR 223.
3 See LTA 1987, s12B(5). This can include leases lawfully granted by the new landlord, eg leases of roof space (see *Englefield Court Tenants v Skeels* [1990] 2 EGLR 230). The new landlord therefore retains some freedom of action, and the retransfer of the freehold to the tenants under the enforcement provisions in the LTA 1987 will be subject to any leases so granted.
4 LTA 1987, s 12B(7).
5 *Venus v Khan* [1990] 2 EGLR 237, *Davis v Stone* [1992] 2 EGLR 222.
6 *Newman v Kay* [1991] 2 EGLR 237. The tribunal here omitted an option to repurchase at any time for £10,000 and a bar on disposals by the new landlord for five years. The consideration paid (£8,000) was adjusted to £10,000 to reflect the removal of these restrictions in the conveyance under the LTA 1987, Pt I, to the tenants.

C Leasehold management – rights and remedies

[13.45] The LTA 1987 introduced new provisions aimed at improving communication between landlord and tenant, as well as new rights for tenants suffering mismanagement. Many of these rights were expanded by the CLRA 2002. The CLRA 2002 also introduced the 'Right to Manage' (hereafter 'RTM') enabling tenants to collectively assume management responsibility for the property in which their flats are situate, irrespective of default or mismanagement by the landlord or his managing agents.

THE RIGHT TO MANAGE ('RTM')

[13.46] Under the general law, control of the management, repair and insurance of the property vests in the landlord, even though most leases will require tenants to pay the full cost of services supplied by the landlord. Prior to the introduction of RTM in the CLRA 2002, the tenants could assume control of management in one of two ways: either by exercising their right to collective enfranchisement and assuming ownership of the building, or by applying to the Leasehold Valuation Tribunal (LVT) for the appointment of a manager (under rights conferred in LTA 1987, Pt II, considered below). The latter is an adversarial procedure requiring the proof of fault on the part of the landlord or his managing agent, and this is often difficult to substantiate, especially against a well-resourced landlord with professional advice. And the consultation prior to the introduction of the 2002 Act revealed that leaseholders rarely wish to assume freehold ownership of the property – the quality of management and services, not ownership, is usually the issue[1]. The CLRA 2002 therefore removes the landlord's monopoly on the supply of management services by giving qualifying tenants the right to assume management themselves, without having to prove fault on the part of the landlord or to pay compensation. For consistency, RTM can be exercised where tenants have the right to collective enfranchisement, and must be exercised by a limited RTM company on the same model as that used for exercising enfranchisement rights or for establishing commonhold ownership. The exercise of RTM does not affect the ownership of property interests in the building – the leases of participant tenants remain agreements between landlord and tenant on the same terms, but with many of the landlord's functions under the agreement transferred and carried out by the managing RTM body. Once RTM has been exercised, however, the leaseholders will lose the right to compulsorily acquire the landlord's freehold interest under the LTA 1987, Pt III[2].

1 See *Commonhold and Leasehold Reform: Draft Bill and Consultation Paper* (Cm 4843, DETR 2000) p 115.
2 The compulsory acquisition power is viewed primarily as a remedy against poor management by the landlord, and it was considered inappropriate for it to be available where the leaseholders themselves have assumed management responsibility: *Commonhold and Leasehold Reform: Draft Bill and Consultation Paper* (Cm 4843, DETR 2000) pp 134–135.

Premises qualifying for RTM

[13.47] RTM applies to premises containing two or more flats held by qualifying tenants[1]. The building containing the flats must be self contained (that is, structurally detached), or it must be a self-contained part of a building[2]. For RTM to be exercisable the following criteria must be met at the time the right is exercised[3]:

(i) the number of flats held by qualifying tenants must be not less that two thirds of the total number of flats in the premises, and
(ii) the tenants exercising the RTM must hold the leases of at least half of the flats in the building. Where there are only two qualifying tenants of flats contained in the premises *both* must be members of the RTM company exercising the right.

There can only be one qualifying tenant per flat, so that where more than one person holds the lease of a flat they will jointly count as a single qualifying tenant. If the flat has been sublet on another long lease, the sub-lessee (and not the superior lessee) counts as the qualifying tenant.

1 CLRA 2002, s 72(1).
2 A part of a building is self contained for these purposes if it constitutes a vertical division of a building, services are proved separately for that part of the building and the structure of the building is such that it could be redeveloped separately: see CLRA 2002, s 72(3)(4).
3 See CLRA 2002, ss 72(1)(c), 79 (4) and 79(5).

[13.48] Several types of property are excluded from the RTM. The most important is property in mixed residential and business use (for example a building with a shop on the ground floor) where the internal floor area of the non-residential parts exceeds 25 per cent of the total internal floor area of the premises taken as a whole[1]. This is the same rule as that applicable to collective enfranchisement, where the proportion of business uses required to take a property out of the statutory regime was increased from 10 to 25 per cent by the CLRA 2002. For the purposes of the necessary calculation of the floor area devoted to non-residential use, common parts of the building do not count and neither do specific areas (such as garages or storages rooms) which are intended for use in conjunction with a particular dwelling in the building[2]. Premises with a resident landlord will also be outside the RTM, but only if the building contains no more than four flats and the freeholder (or a member of his family) has lived there for the last 12 months[3]. The RTM does not apply to properties owned by a local authority (in respect of which a separate management code applies)[4]. The CLRA 2002 also prevents the RTM being exercised where the RTM company (for whatever reason) loses control of the block. In this case, new leaseholders cannot exercise the RTM for the following four-year period, unless they apply to the Leasehold Valuation Tribunal for permission to do so[5].

1 CLRA 2002, Sch 6, para 1.
2 Ibid, Sch 6, para 1(2)(3).
3 Ibid, Sch 6, para 3. The building must not be a purpose-built block of flats, and the premises must be the landlord's principal home.
4 Ibid, Sch 6, para 4.
5 Ibid, Sch 6, para 5. The four-year period was chosen as representative of the normal period for a turnover of new tenants in many buildings.

Qualifying tenants

[13.49] A qualifying tenant is one who has a lease originally granted for a period of 21 years or more (ie a long lease)[1]. A long lease qualifies irrespective of whether it can be terminated before the expiry of 21 years by a break notice or by re-entry or forfeiture, and special provision is made for perpetually-renewable leases and leases terminable on death or marriage which are statutorily converted into long fixed terms under LPA 1925[2]. A long lease granted by a local authority under the right to buy legislation is a qualifying lease for these purposes, as is a shared ownership lease – but only in the latter case where the tenants share in the lease is 100 per cent. The legislation is restricted to residential tenancies, and if the tenancy is a business tenancy within LTA 1954, Pt II it does not qualify[3].

1 CLRA 2002, ss 75(2) and 76(2)(a).
2 Ibid, s 76(2). These are converted into terms of 90 years terminable by notice (LPA 1925, s 149). Additional rules are applied by CLRA 2002, s 77.
3 Ibid, s 75(3).

The RTM company

[13.50] The policy adopted in the CLRA 2002 is to require RTM to be exercised through a company limited by guarantee, with a defined corporate structure and prescribed memorandum and articles of association[1]. This is consistent with the rules for the exercise of collective enfranchisement, where leaseholders acquiring the freehold must use a corporate structure on the same model as the vehicle for doing so, and with converting to commonhold tenure. Ultimately, having exercised

RTM, those leaseholders who wish to take the further step of acquiring the freehold will be able to use the existing RTM company as the medium for the right to acquire under the enfranchisement legislation. To this extent, therefore, where tenants so choose, RTM can be the first step to the full acquisition of both management and ownership.

1 CLRA 2002, s 73.

[13.51] The membership and regulation of the internal affairs of the RTM company are set out in the CLRA 2002 and regulations to be made thereunder. The Act specifies that all qualifying tenants of the premises in relation to which the company is established are entitled to be members, as is the landlord of the premises[1]. This will include all tenants exercising the RTM when the company is established, but other qualifying tenants will be entitled to become members at any time afterwards if they so wish. The landlord will retain an important interest in the property and the way it is managed, and this is reflected in the voting arrangements for the conduct of the company. Each landlord will have a voting entitlement on equal terms with the leaseholders. The CLRA 2002 envisages a weighting to be given to the landlord's voting rights, adjusted according to the number of landlords who have an interest in the building. The rights of superior landlords will be correspondingly less than those of the immediate landlord of the premises let on long leases. The voting arrangements ensure that landlords will not retain control of the decision making process, but retain a say (and vote) on important decisions affecting the property and its management. As long as the company adheres to the weighting arrangements in regulations made under the CLRA 2002, it can allocate votes to members as it wishes, provided it is on a non-discriminatory basis. Any provision in the articles or memorandum of association which is inconsistent with the regulations is, however, void to the extent that it is inconsistent[2].

1 CLRA 2002, s 74.
2 Ibid, s 74(5).

Exercising the RTM

[13.52] Where the management of a block is to be assumed by the tenants using RTM, it is clearly desirable that as many tenants as possible are given the opportunity to participate in management through the RTM company, and that its affairs are conducted as democratically as possible. The first step is for those tenants considering exercising their right to manage to form a RTM company. The CLRA 2002 then requires the RTM company to serve a notice of invitation to participate on all qualifying tenants who have not already agreed to become members of the RTM company[1]. *Query* the formation of a RTM company does not require the participation of a qualifying majority of the tenants, and the necessary quorum can be achieved at a later stage. In this case the notice inviting participation can be used to canvass support and bring together sufficient qualifying tenants in the company to enable them to serve a notice of claim, ie the qualifying tenants of not less than half the total number of flats in the building[2].

1 CLRA 2002, s 78.
2 Ibid, s 79(5).

[13.53] The second stage in the process begins with the RTM company serving a 'claim notice' on all landlords with an interest in the building, informing them of its intention to exercise the RTM[1]. After serving the initial notice inviting participation on long leaseholders, the RTM company must wait at least two weeks before it can serve a claim notice on the landlord[2]. The claim notice must demonstrate that the qualifying conditions for RTM have been fully met, and to this end the CLRA 2002 lays down in some detail the information which must be included in it[3]. The notice must give the name and registered office of the RTM company, specify the premises and the grounds on which it is claimed they are covered by the RTM, give the full name of each qualifying tenant who is a member of the RTM company, and details of their leases. It must also specify two dates which are key to the procedure for acquiring the RTM:

(i) **date for landlord's counter notice.** The claim notice must give a date by which the landlord (or each of them) must respond by giving a counter notice under the Act. This must be a date not less than one month after the relevant date when the initial claim notice was served[4].
(ii) **date of intended acquisition of RTM.** This must be a date at least a further three months after that specified for the landlord's counter notice[5].

1 CLRA 2002, s 79(1).
2 Ibid. s 79(2).
3 Ibid, s 80.
4 Ibid, s 80(6).
5 Ibid, s 80(7).

[13.54] The form of the claim notice will be prescribed by regulations made under the CLRA 2002. As well as serving it on the landlords, the company is also required to serve it on all qualifying tenants (not just those participating in the RTM process). This will ensure that all leaseholders in the block are aware that RTM is being exercised, and they will have the opportunity to consider becoming members at this stage.

[13.55] The landlord has a minimum of one month (or a longer period if one is specified in the claim notice) in which to respond by serving his counter notice. The landlord can either admit the claim, in which event the RTM vests in the company on the date specified in the tenants' notice of claim, or he can dispute that the RTM applies[1]. In this case, however, the grounds of challenge are limited to alleging that the qualifying criteria have not been met. The landlord can allege that the company's constitution does not comply with the prescribed requirements, that insufficient qualifying tenants are members of the RTM company at the relevant date, or that more than 25 per cent of the ground floor area of the building is in business use. The landlord cannot contest the RTM on wider issues, eg by making general allegations that the tenants (acting through the RTM company) have insufficient experience to manage the block[2]. Where there are multiple landlords with interests in the building, the tenant may receive a number of counter notices, some of which accept RTM and some which contest it. The CLRA 2002 provides for dispute resolution through the LVT. If the RTM company has been given one or more counter notices alleging that the company is not entitled to exercise the RTM, it can apply to the Tribunal for a determination as to its eligibility. The application to the Tribunal must be made not later than two months beginning on the day when the counter notice (or where there are more than one, the last of the counter notices) was given[3]. If the company fails to do so, then the claim notice is deemed to be withdrawn[4].

1 CLRA 2002, s 84(2).

2 See further *Commonhold and Leasehold Reform: Draft Bill and Consultation Paper* (Cm 4843, DETR 2000) p124.
3 CLRA 2002, s 84(4).
4 Ibid, s 87(1).

[13.56] If the LVT decides that the company is eligible for RTM, it can then assume management responsibility. On the other hand, if it decides that the company is not eligible, then the notice is treated as withdrawn. The landlord can recover costs if the Tribunal dismisses an application by the company for a determination that it is eligible for RTM[1].

1 CLRA 2002, s 88(3).

[13.57] The acquisition date from which the company can exercise the RTM depends upon whether a counter notice was given or not. If no counter notices have been given by landlords contesting the RTM, then the company assumes management responsibility from the date specified in its claim notice. If there is a dispute, the RTM is acquired and becomes exercisable three months after the Tribunal's determination becomes final[1].

1 CLRA 2002, s 90(4).

Management functions of the RTM company

[13.58] Once RTM has been exercised, all management functions in relation to the company pass to, and become exercisable by, the RTM company[1]. The 'management functions' transferred to the company are widely defined by CLRA 2002, s 96(5) to include all functions with respect to services, repairs, maintenance, improvements, insurance and management. In order to facilitate the handover of management responsibility to the company, the landlord (or his managing agent if there is one) must hand over all relevant documents and information within 28 days of being required by the company to do so after it has assumed responsibility for management of the property[2]. All service charge monies which relate to the premises in question, and which are being held by the landlord on trust to discharge management functions, must be handed to the RTM company on the acquisition date 'or as soon after that date as is reasonable practicable'[3]. These must be held in a nominated client account on trust for contributing leaseholders, in the same manner as applies to monies held by the landlord or his managing agent[4]. Where the landlord currently holds service charge monies for a group of properties, and the tenants of one of them exercise RTM, an apportionment will be required. In default of agreement the LVT has jurisdiction to determine the amount of payments to be transferred[5].

1 CLRA 2002, s 96(2).
2 Ibid, s 93. Provision is made in ibid, ss 91 and 92 for the landlord to notify parties to existing management contracts of the assumption of control by the RTM.
3 Ibid, s 94(4).
4 See below para 13.91 ff.
5 CLRA 2002, s 94(2) and (3).

[13.59] After RTM has been established, all management functions relating to the premises vest exclusively in the company to the exclusion of the landlord, any managing agent formerly employed by him or any other party to the lease who is not landlord or tenant (eg a guarantor or surety)[1]. The RTM company has the same right as the landlord to apply for variation of a lease under the LTA 1987, and may choose to do so where defects in the leases are preventing it from managing the building properly[2]. The RTM company has a duty to monitor the performance of the obligations placed upon tenants by the terms of their leases, and must report all breaches of covenant to the landlord within three months of their coming to its attention[3]. The reporting and monitoring role applies in principle to all breaches of covenant, however minor. However, the CLRA 2002 makes provision for the landlord and tenant to agree their own reporting and monitoring regime by agreeing the description of covenant to which the statutory obligation is to attach[4]. Clearly, the landlord will want to be informed of any breach of important terms of the lease, such as subletting without consent or the carrying out of unauthorised improvements. He may not wish to require reports on all minor or technical breaches of covenant (eg minor delays in the payment of service charges).

1 CLRA 2002, s 97(2) prevents any person other than the RTM from exercising management functions post transfer, other than by agreement with the latter.
2 See para 13.74 ff for discussion of variation of leases.
3 CLRA 2002, s 101(2) and (3).
4 Ibid, s 101(4).

[13.60] All service charge payments which relate to services or work undertaken after RTM has commenced must be paid to the company, not the landlord, and all other leasehold obligations which relate to the management functions of the company are henceforth owed to the company[1]. To protect the landlord's financial interest in the premises, however, the CLRA 2002 places the RTM company under the same obligations to the landlord to carry out its functions as it owes to the leaseholders, and either can take court action to enforce compliance with the company's statutory management duties[2]. The company's management functions only relate to long leases of flats held by qualifying tenants in the block. The landlord retains responsibility for management functions in relation to all other leases in the premises, eg short-term leases and other non long leasehold units[3].

1 CLRA 2002, s 97(4).
2 Ibid, s 97(1).
2 Ibid, s 96(6).

[13.61] Two aspects of the company's managerial role merit particular consideration.

Exercise of landlord's consent functions

[13.62] The lease will commonly require the leaseholder to obtain the landlord's written consent before assigning or subletting the flat, before carrying out improvements or alterations, or undertaking other activities. The policy underlying RTM is for the leaseholders to assume day-to-day management responsibility for the premises, and the CLRA 2002 therefore vests the responsibility for the grant of all relevant consents in the RTM company[1]. Some consents required under a lease will relate more directly to the landlords interest in the building than others, eg where the tenant has requested consent to assign or sublet the premises, in which case the landlord will wish to take references from the proposed assignee and satisfy himself he is secured for future payment of rent. Before granting an approval relating to assignment, subletting, sharing or parting with possession, or to the making of improvements or alterations of use, the company must give 30 days' notice to the landlord. In relation to all other consents 14 days' notice must be given[2]. If the landlord objects to the grant of consent, the RTM company can only grant it with the landlord's written agreement (eg following a negotiation of the terms on which it is to be given), or in accordance with a determination by the LVT. The same rules apply for assessing the validity or otherwise of the landlord's objection as would apply if the consent function were exercisable by the landlord himself[3]. So, for example, where the landlord objects to a proposed grant of consent to assign or sublet the premises, the principles established at common law must be applied to determine whether or not it would be reasonable to grant consent[4]. Similarly, a covenant requiring the landlord's consent to the carrying out of improvements or alterations imports a condition that consent not be unreasonably withheld[5], and the established principles for assessing reasonableness will be relevant in this context[6].

1 See generally CLRA 2002, s 98. There was initially a question whether this function should extend to the grant of consent for assignment and subletting, but in the event the draft Bill transferred all consent functions to the leaseholders: see *Commonhold and Leasehold Reform: Draft Bill and Consultation Paper* (Cm 4843, DETR 2000) pp 130–131.
2 See CLRA 2002, s 98(4).
3 Ibid, s 99(2) and (3).
4 In the case of a qualified covenant against assignment or subletting, the LTA 1927, s 19(1) implies a condition that consent must not be unreasonably withheld. For the principles as to reasonableness in this context see *International Drilling Fluids Ltd v Louisville Investments (Uxbridge) Ltd* [1986] Ch 513 and the extensive case law on LTA 1927, s 19(1).
5 LTA 1927, s 19(2).
6 See for example *Lambert v FW Woolworth & Co Ltd (No 2)* [1938] Ch 883, CA, *Duke of Westminster v Swinton* [1948] 1 KB 524.

Enforcing leasehold covenants

[13.63] The RTM company has power to enforce the payment of service charges, and to pursue other breaches of the lease which are detrimental to the management of the property. The company does not, however, have functions relating to re-entry or forfeiture, and cannot initiate forfeiture proceedings to enforce performance of the tenants' covenants. Forfeiture and re-entry remains the sole prerogative of the landlord, acting in accordance with the terms of the lease. The RTM company has the same powers as the landlord, short of forfeiture, to enforce compliance with leasehold obligations. The company also has power to enforce 'untransferred' tenants' covenants where necessary, short of taking forfeiture proceedings[1].

1 See CLRA 2002, s 100.

Failure of management by RTM company

[13.64] Where the company is failing to carry out its management obligations satisfactorily, the landlord's primary remedy would be to apply for the appointment of a replacement manager. The existing grounds under the LTA 1987, Pt II, permit leaseholders to apply to the Leasehold Valuation Tribunal where the landlords managing agent is in default. The CLRA 2002 extends the grounds for an application to include the situation where an RTM company is failing to manage in accordance with its statutory obligations, and makes provision for the landlord or freeholder to make an application for replacement where necessary. Additionally, a landlord who is required to pay towards management costs has the same remedies against the company as long leaseholders who pay a service charge. This includes the power to challenge the reasonableness of charges, to be consulted on proposed major works and to inspect and challenge insurance policies effected by the company. These provisions are discussed further below (see para 13.83 ff).

Withdrawal of RTM company from management

[13.65] The RTM company can voluntarily withdraw from management if it so wishes – for example if there has been a substantial turnover of tenants and those now occupying the premises no longer wish to manage it themselves. A voluntary withdrawal can be effected by agreement between the RTM company and each person who is landlord under a lease of the whole or part of the premises[1]. The effect will be to revoke the RTM and the management of the block will return to the landlord under the normal operation of the lease. Additionally, the RTM ceases to be exercisable if a winding up or administration order is made against the RTM company, if a receiver or manager is appointed to conduct its affairs, or if a voluntary arrangement is proposed and approved under of the Insolvency Act 1986, Pt 1[2].

1 CLRA 2002, s 105(2).
2 Ibid, s 105(3). It will also cease it the company is struck off the companies register maintained under the Companies Act 1985, s 652.

[13.66] Where an RTM company loses the right to manage, for whatever reason, then RTM cannot be exercised again in relation to the premises within four years of the company losing the right[1].

1 CLRA 2002, Sch 6, para 5(1).

APPOINTMENT OF MANAGER BY LEASEHOLD VALUATION TRIBUNAL

[13.67] The Nugee Committee recommended that tenants be given power to apply to the court for a manager's removal and a fresh appointment. This would, it was felt, maintain the clear responsibility of managers to the landlord for mismanagement, while giving residents a sanction to compel efficient management[1]. These proposals were enacted the LTA 1987, Pt 2. The expense and uncertainty of court action to compel an appointment initially made this an unattractive remedy, prompting the transfer of the jurisdiction to the LVT for all applications after the HA 1996 came into force[2]. In many cases the lease will place management responsibility not on the landlord, but on a third-party manager – for example a management company. The CLRA 2002 therefore extended the scope of the LTA 1987, Pt 2 provisions to give leaseholders the same rights of redress against a third-party manager as they would have against the landlord himself[3].

1 Report of the Committee of Inquiry on the Management of Privately-Owned Blocks of Flats (1985) (the Nugee Report) para 7.2.6 ff, and especially para 7.2.11.
2 HA 1996, s 86(1)(2)(4) – the court's jurisdiction remains only for applications where notice under LTA 1987, s 22 was served before 1 September 1997.
3 CLRA 2002, s 160, amending LTA 1987, s 22 (1).

[13.68] LTA 1987, s 21 enables two or more tenants of flats to which the Act applies to apply for an order appointing a manager to act in relation to those premises. Tenants must first serve notice[1] specifying the matters to be relied upon, and if they are capable of remedy give the landlord a reasonable period within which to take steps to remedy the breaches of obligation complained of[2]. No application can be made until this period has elapsed without remedial steps being taken by the landlord. The HA 1996 extended the grounds on which the Tribunal can appoint a manager. It removed the need for the tenants to prove that the breach complained of is likely to continue, and added a new ground for excessive service charge demands. The onus remains on the tenants, however, to make out a case of mis-management. By virtue of LTA 1987, s 24 the LVT can appoint a receiver or manager only if satisfied[3]:

(a) that the landlord (or any other person by whom management obligations are owed to the tenant under the lease) is in breach of an obligation owed by him to the tenant under his tenancy and relating to the *management* of the premises, ie relating to the repair, maintenance, improvement, or insurance of the premises[4]; or
(b) the Tribunal is satisfied that unreasonable service charge demands have been made (or are proposed or are likely to be made)[5]. For these purposes a service demand is unreasonable if the amount is unreasonable having regard to the items for which is it payable, if the items for which it is payable are of an unnecessarily high standard, or if the items are of such an insufficient standard that additional charges may have to be incurred[6]; or
(c) the Tribunal is satisfied that the landlord has failed to comply with a code of practice approved by the Secretary of State under the LRHUDA 1993[7]; and
(d) that it is just and convenient to make an order in all the circumstances of the case.

1 This must be served either on the landlord or (if there is one) on the manager having responsibility under the lease for the landlord's management obligations eg a management company. See the definition of 'relevant person' in LTA 1987, s 24 (2ZA), inserted by the CLRA 2002, s 160.
2 LTA 1987, s 22. The court can dispense with the requirement to serve notice where satisfied that it would not be reasonably practicable to do so; LTA 1987, s 22(3).
3 See ibid, s 24(2) as amended.
4 See ibid, s 24(11). The reference to improvements was added by the CLRA 2002, Sch 9, para 8, giving tenants ground to apply for the appointment of a manager where the landlord is failing in his obligations to carry out improvements to the property.
5 Ibid, s 24(2)(ab) ibid.
6 Ibid, s 24(2A), inserted by HA 1996, s 86.
7 See the Approval of Codes of Management Practice (Residential Property) Order 1996, SI 1996/2839 (Approval of codes of practice prepared by the RICS for this purpose).

[13.69] An appointment order can make provision for such matters relating to the exercise of managerial functions and such incidental matters as the court thinks fit. It can specifically provide for the transfer of contractual rights and liabilities to the appointee and for him to pursue contractual or tortious causes of action accruing before or after his appointment, and for his remuneration to be paid either by the landlord or the tenants of the premises affected. The appointment can be for a fixed or unlimited period. On receiving notice of an application the landlord must serve notice on mortgagees. The court has power to suspend the appointment on terms, and the tenants' right to protect their position by registering a land charge or caution against the landlord's title is unaffected[1].

1 LTA 1987, s 24(8).

[13.70] *Exempt premises* An application for the appointment of a manager cannot be made where the landlord is either a resident landlord or an 'exempt landlord', ie a local authority or registered housing association, or other public sector landlord. The resident landlord exception was restricted by amendments in the CLRA 2002, and no longer applies where a majority interest in the property is held by long leaseholders. As a result, where more than half the flats in a building are held by long leaseholders, any tenant will be able to apply for the appointment of a manager[1].

1 LTA 1987, s 21(3A), inserted by CLRA 2002, s 161.

[13.71] In relation to premises to which the LTA 1987 (as amended) applies, the power of appointment supersedes and excludes other remedies. The general jurisdiction to appoint a receiver or manager, conferred by the Supreme Court Act 1981, s 37 and not infrequently used before the introduction of the LTA 1987[1], is therefore excluded. It will continue to apply, however, in cases where the premises are outside the ambit of the LTA 1987; for instance where there is a resident landlord, where the landlord is exempt, or where the premises do not contain two or more flats.

1 See *Hart v Emelkirk Ltd* [1983] 1 WLR 1289; *Parker v Camden London Borough Council* (1985) 17 HLR 380, CA; *Daiches v Bluelake Investments Ltd* [1985] 2 EGLR 67; *Clayhope Properties Ltd v Evans* [1986] 2 EGLR 34, CA; *Evans v Clayhope Properties Ltd* [1987] 1 EGLR 67.

COMMUNICATION AND INFORMATION

[13.72] The LTA 1987, Pt IV, enacted the Nugee Committee's recommendation for improving tenants' rights to information[1].

1 See Nugee Report para 7.1.5 for their detailed proposals.

[13.73] By virtue of LTA 1987, s 46, any demand for rent or other sums (eg service charges) served on private sector residential tenants must state the name and address of the landlord. In the case of foreign landlords an address in England and Wales must be given at which notices can be served. If the required information is not given, then any service charge demanded shall not be treated as due until the required information has been supplied. Rent, however, will remain payable[1]. Additionally, LTA 1987, s 48 requires the landlord to notify tenants of an address in England and Wales at which notices can be served, in default of which both rent and service charge demands will be inoperative[2]. Where a sale of the reversionary interest takes place, LTA 1985, s 3[3] imposes an obligation on the original landlord to inform tenants of the assignment and of the new landlord's name and address (a duty which previously fell to the new landlord alone). He will remain liable, jointly and severally with the new landlord, for any breach of tenancy occurring after assignment, and until such notice is given. The original landlord's liability ceases, however, upon notice being served either by himself *or by the new landlord*[4]. Although there would seem little point in imposing an affirmative duty to notify on the original landlord if the assignee has already done so, it follows that the former may not always know when his liability under the lease actually ceases. The Land Registration Act 1925, s 112 was also amended by the LTA 1987 to allow tenants to inspect the register to ascertain the name and address of their landlord. This right extends to 'any part of any register' kept by the land registry, and is presumably not restricted to the proprietorship register[5].

1 See s 47(2) of the 1987 Act. In this respect the Act is narrower than Nugee's recommendations, which were that *all* monies demanded be irrecoverable (see Nugee Report para 7.1.5(i)).

2 Rent due prior to service of notice under LTA 1987, s 48 will become recoverable again following service – it is only treated as not lawfully due during such period when no notice under s 48 has been

given. Once notice is given, rent and service charges become recoverable for periods prior to the date of notice; see *Dallhold Estates (UK) Pt y Ltd v Lindsey Trading Properties Inc* [1992] 1 EGLR 88; revsd [1994] 1 EGLR 93, CA; and *Hussain v Singh* [1993] 2 EGLR 70, CA.
3 As amended by LTA 1987, s 50.
4 LTA 1985, s 3(3B)(b), inserted by LTA 1987, s 50. Compare with Nugee Report para 7.1.5(ii) which recommended the old landlord should remain liable until he had served notice of the assignment on the tenants.
5 See LTA 1987, s 51(2), inserting a new s 112C into the Land Registration Act 1925, and in particular s 112C(1). Compare with Nugee Report para 7.1.5(iii) which recommended that tenants should *not* have rights to inspect the charges register.

VARIATION OF LEASES

[13.74] The management-related aspects of a lease may be defective, ambiguous or poorly worded, making management of the building difficult. Like any other private contract, the parties can vary the lease by agreement. This requires the landlord's consent, however. In order to ensure that an adequate legal framework exists in all cases, LTA 1987, Pt IV introduced a statutory right for the tenant to apply to the county court for the variation of a defective lease which fails to make satisfactory provision for repair, maintenance and other fundamental obligations. This jurisdiction was transferred to the Leasehold Valuation Tribunal by the CLRA 2002[1].

1 CLRA 2002, s 163, amending LTA 1987, ss 35, 36, 39 and 40.

[13.75] LTA 1987, s 35 enables any party to a long lease[1] to apply to the LVT for a variation order if the lease does not make 'satisfactory provision' for one or more of a number of matters specified in s 35(2)[2]. These include the repair, maintenance and insurance of the flat or block as a whole, or the repair and maintenance of installations necessary to ensure a reasonable standard of accommodation, the provision of necessary services, and the computation of service charges payable under the lease. Service charge terms are deemed unsatisfactory if the aggregate of proportional amounts collected from all leaseholders would either exceed or be less than the whole of the landlord's expenditure in providing the stipulated services[3]. The CLRA 2002 extended the grounds so that an application to vary the lease can be made where there is not a single insurance policy for the whole building and where it fails to provide for the payment of interest on overdue service charge payments[4]. Other long lessees – either in the same block or in another block with the same landlord[5] – can apply for corresponding variation of their own leases. Failure to notify affected parties of an application for variation will give other lessees a right to apply for cancellation or modification of the variation order, and to sue for damages for breach of statutory duty[6].

1 Pre-emption rights and the notification provisions apply to all residential lettings, not just long leases.
2 The need for a definition of what constituted satisfactory provision for the relevant matters in a lease was a weakness identified in the consultation preceding the CLRA 2002: *Commonhold and Leasehold Reform: Draft Bill and Consultation Paper* (Cm 4843, DETR 2000) pp181–182.
3 LTA 1987, s 35(4), as amended by LRHURDA 1993, s 86.
4 CLRA 2002, s 162(4), amending LTA 1987, s 35(2)(3A).
5 See LTA 1987, s 36(2)(b).
6 LTA 1987, s 39(3) and (4).

[13.76] Individual variation rights may often suffice, but there may be major defects in the drafting of leases which prevent the block as a whole being maintained in a state of good repair with necessary amenities. The Nugee Committee recommended that compulsory amendment of all leases in a block should be possible at the instigation of a majority of tenants, subject to safeguards to protect minority leaseholders[1]. The LTA 1987, s 37 provides for compulsory variation where 'the object to be achieved by the variation cannot be satisfactorily achieved unless all leases are varied to the same effect'. An application can be made only if:

(a) where there are fewer than nine leases, all or all but one of the lessees consent to it; or
(b) where the application relates to more than eight leases at least 75 per cent of those affected consent and it is not opposed by more than 10 per cent of those concerned[2].

1 Nugee Report, para 7.6.6.
2 LTA 1987, s 37(5).

[13.77] Whichever mode of variation is used, the Act provides safeguards for minority lessees. A variation order cannot be made if the LVT considers it would be likely to substantially prejudice the landlord or any lessee not a party to the application, and that an award of compensation would not adequately compensate the latter for any disadvantage or loss arising out of the proposed variation[1]. The LVT also has a wide jurisdiction to refuse a variation if for any other reason it does not consider it to be reasonable in all the circumstances.

1 LTA 1987, s 38(6) and (10). The tribunal can order compensation to be paid by the applicant to the landlord or any affected leaseholder. The Nugee Committee recommended more specific safeguards based on Law Comm No 127 para 20.22–20.27.

[13.78] In the case of residential lettings *other than long leases*, LTA 1987, s 40 provides similar rights to seek variation, but only where leases fail to make adequate provision for any matter connected with insurance of the dwelling.

CONSULTATION IN APPOINTMENT OF MANAGERS

[13.79] The LTA 1987, s 44 conferred on recognised tenants' associations the right to serve a consultation notice requiring their landlord to consult with them on the appointment of managing agents[1]. If a managing agent is not already employed the landlord must serve notice on the association informing them of the name of any proposed appointee, the landlord's obligations he is to discharge, and giving at least one month for observations. If an agent is already employed, the landlord must respond by giving the association notice (within one month) of the obligations the agent performs and a reasonable period within which to make observations on the performance by him of his functions. Once a consultation notice has been served, the landlord must keep the association updated with details of management arrangements at least once every five years. Following a change of landlord a fresh consultation notice has to be served – a requirement which may cause difficulty where (as is common) the assignee of the reversion fails to notify tenants of the change of ownership. Although the LTA 1987 tackled a major source of discontent among long leaseholders, there was ample evidence that dubious practice in the appointment and activities of some managers remained unaffected[2].

1 This was achieved by inserting a new s 30B into the Landlord and Tenant Act 1985.
2 See *Landlord and Tenant Act 1987: Awareness, Experience and Impact* (DoE 1991) pp 51–52.

SERVICE CHARGES AND INSURANCE

[13.80] The levying of excessive service charges, and disputes as to the quality of repair work commissioned and paid for via service charge payments, are a constant source of landlord–tenant disputes. The LTA 1985 contains provisions regulating the service charges for which tenants can be liable. The LTA 1987, HA 1996 and CLRA 2002 have each substantially amended the LTA 1985, and have together introduced a more rigorous statutory framework for the regulation of service charge payments[1].

1 The LTA 1987 substantially implemented the Nugee Committee's recommendations on service charges; see Nugee Report, para 7.3.1 ff.

[13.81] The aim of these provisions is to ensure that money received by the landlord or his managing agent by way of service charges is used only for the purposes for which it was collected, and that it is protected against misappropriation or the landlord's insolvency by being held in a properly administered trust fund. Improved consultation rights and rights to challenge the level of charges were also introduced in the CLRA 2002.

Service charges: Definition

[13.82] The LTA 1985, s 18 defines a 'service charge' to mean an amount payable by a tenant of a dwelling as part of or in addition to the rent that is payable (directly or indirectly) for services, repairs, maintenance, and improvements or insurance or the landlord's costs of management[1]. To come within the regulation imposed by the LTA 1985 the charge must be variable, ie the whole or part of it varies (or may vary) according to the relevant costs. Costs includes overheads, and costs are 'relevant' (and therefore regulated under the LTA 1985) in relation to a service charge whether they are incurred in the period for which the service charge is payable or a later or earlier period[2]. The provisions regulating service charges were extended by the LTA 1987 to leases of all residential property (and not just flats). They do not apply to local authority tenants, however, unless the tenancy is a long tenancy or one for 21 years or more (for example a tenancy granted under the right to buy)[3]. In the case of tenancies under the RA 1977 the service charge provisions only apply if the charge is entered on the rent register as a variable charge[4].

1 LTA 1985, s 18 amended by CLRA 2002, s 150 and Sch 9, para 7 The amendments extend the meaning to include payments for improvements within the regulation of the LTA 1985.
2 LTA 1985, s 18(3).
3 Ibid, s 26.
4 Ibid, s 27.

Variable service charges: Recoverability

Reasonableness of service charge demands

[13.83] LTA 1985, s 19 limits the recovery by the landlord of variable service charges to costs which have been reasonably incurred, and only in respect of works or services which have been carried out to a reasonable standard. For this purpose relevant costs must be taken into account to determine the service charge payable only to the extent that they are reasonably incurred, and (if they are incurred in the provision of services or the carrying out of works) only if the works or services are of a reasonable standard. Many leases require service charge payments to be made in advance. In this case, the amount payable must be reasonable, and the service charge must be adjusted to reflect the reasonableness criteria once the relevant costs have been incurred. This can be done by repayment, or in the reduction or adjustment of subsequent service charges[1]. The parties cannot contract out of the statutory requirements, and the LTA 1985 specifically provides that any agreement by the tenant (other than an arbitration agreement) is void insofar as it purports to provide for the determination of whether costs have been reasonably incurred or whether services or works have been provided to a reasonable standard[2]. Any provision in the lease (or otherwise) which provides that the landlords surveyors certificate is conclusive of these matters is, therefore, void and unenforceable. The Leasehold Valuation Tribunal has jurisdiction to assess the reasonableness or otherwise of the standard and cost of works or services.

1 LTA 1985, s 19(2).
2 Ibid, s 19(3).

[13.84] Additional restrictions on service charges are imposed by LTA 1985, s 20B, which provides that costs incurred more than 18 months before a demand for payment are irrecoverable. Tenants can also challenge any proportion of a service charge demand that reflects legal costs incurred by the landlord in previous legal proceedings. The passing on of legal costs in this way is an abuse frequently complained of by tenants, and will now be possible only where the LVT considers it just and equitable in the circumstances[1]. LTA 1985, s 21 (as amended) requires the landlord to supply additional information to tenants' and residents' associations of costs incurred in the previous year (or last accounting period) which are likely to be reflected in subsequent demands for service charges. These are discussed below in the context of the new accounting requirements[2].

1 LTA 1985, s 20, substituted by CLRA 2002, s 151.
2 LTA 1985, s 21, substituted by CLRA 2002, s 152.

Consultation with leaseholders

[13.85] LTA 1985, s 20[1] requires the landlord to consult tenants before undertaking works, or entering into a contract for works or services in two situations:

(i) Where relevant costs will be incurred under a *long-term agreement* for a term of 12 months or more, entered into by the landlord or a superior landlord[2]. This would encompass contracts for the provision of services such as cleaning or gardening, as well as long-term maintenance contracts. The extension of the consultation requirements to this type of arrangement was introduced by the CLRA 2002.
(ii) Where *major works* are proposed, and the amount any individual tenant may be required to contribute by way or service charge exceeds a fixed amount prescribed by regulations made under the LTA 1985 (as amended).

1 LTA 1985, s 20, substituted by the CLRA 2002, s 151.
2 Ibid, s 20 (1), (2).

[13.86] If a long-term contract is awarded without consultation, the whole of the relevant costs incurred under it will be irrecoverable as service charges, which are limited accordingly. In the case of major works, unless prior consultation is undertaken, the excess cost per leaseholder over and above the prescribed consultation threshold cannot be taken into account in determining the amount of any service charge[1]. The Leasehold Valuation Tribunal has jurisdiction to determine applications by either party to dispense with the consultation requirements, and can make a determination if satisfied that the landlord has acted reasonably[2]. Clearly, where the landlord proposes to enter into a long-term contract it may be appropriate to make a protective application to dispense with the consultation requirement, before concluding the agreement.

1 LTA 1985, s 20(1), (4).
2 Ibid, s 20ZA(1), inserted by CLRA 2002, s 151.

[13.87] The changes introduced by the CLRA 2002 replace the consultation regime originally introduced under the LTA 1985 in its entirety. The latter had been amended by the LTA 1987, and required both consultations *and* the obtaining of two estimates for work above a threshold cost of £50 multiplied by the number of flats in a building or £1,000, whichever were the greater[1]. The retention of a low threshold cost encouraged evasion by landlords dividing proposed maintenance work up into smaller items costing less than £50 per flat. It was also arbitrary. In a building with just two flats, there would be no consultation requirement before carrying out works costing each leaseholder £499, whereas in a larger block with a hundred or more flats, of which 90 were let to long leaseholders, consultation would be required for works costing each as little as £10[2]. The CLRA 2002 therefore replaced the existing thresholds with a requirement to consult whenever work will cost each individual leaseholder more that a fixed amount prescribed by regulations. Consultation on long-term contracts was also an innovation introduced by the CLRA 2002. Long-term maintenance contracts may have substantial cost implications for long leaseholders, even though individual items to be provided do not exceed the prescribed amount triggering the consultation requirement for major works. The requirement to consult before awarding a long-term contract does not, however, remove the obligation to consult on individual items of work carried out under that contract if the cost exceeds the prescribed amount laid down in regulations made under the LTA 1985.

1 LTA 1985, s 20(3), inserted by LTA 1987, Sch 2, para 3; and see Nugee Report, para 7.3.14, James Report, para 10.5.
2 *Commonhold and Leasehold Reform: Draft Bill and Consultation Paper* (Cm 4843, DETR 2000) p163.

Administration charges

[13.88] The CLRA 2002 introduced regulation of administration charges made under long leases. The lease may make provision for charges to be made for a wide variety of administrative matters – for instance for processing applications for consent to make alterations to the dwelling, penalties for late payment of ground rent or for technical breaches of covenant, or for providing information or copies of documents requested by the tenant. The consultation exercise prior to the introduction of the new legislation revealed disquiet at abuse by landlords making excessive charges in some cases, and proposed the introduction of regulation in line with that for service chargers. The new provisions are now contained in CLRA 2002, Sch 11.

[13.89] The scope of the new provisions is wide. Administration charges are very broadly defined, to include any payment made by a tenant of a dwelling as part of or in addition to the rent which is payable (directly or indirectly)[1]:

(i) for or in connection with the grant of approvals under his lease, or applications for such approvals. Leases commonly require the landlord's consent before making additions or alternations to the property (such as the installation of satellite dishes or other fixtures), as well as for assignment of the leasehold to a prospective purchaser;
(ii) for or in connection with the provision of information or documents by or on behalf of the landlord;
(iii) in respect of a failure by the tenant to make a payment by the due date to the landlord or a person which is a party to the lease otherwise than as landlord or tenant (eg a mortgagee or guarantor); or
(iv) in connection with a breach (real or alleged) of a covenant or condition of the lease.

1 CLRA 2002, Sch 11, para 1.

[13.90] The Act differentiates between fixed and variable administration charges. A fixed administration charge is one where the charge payable by the tenant is specified in the lease itself, or is calculated by reference to a formula specified in the lease. All other charges are treated as variable. A variable administration charge is only payable to the extent that the amount of the charge is reasonable[1]. In the case of a fixed administration charge, either party can apply to the Leasehold Valuation Tribunal for an order varying the lease on the grounds that an administration charge specified in it is unreasonable, or that the formula for calculating any charge is unreasonable. The Tribunal has power to vary the lease by order, or to make an order requiring the parties to themselves vary the lease in accordance with its terms[2]. The LVT also has a general jurisdiction to determine whether and by whom an alleged administration charge is payable, the amount payable and the date and manner of payment to be made – unless the matter has been agreed or admitted by the tenant, or referred to post-dispute arbitration or is subject to a determination by the court[3].

1 CLRA 2002, Sch 11, para 2.
2 Ibid, Sch 11, para 3.
3 Ibid, Sch 11, para 5.

Management of service charge accounts

[13.91] The CLRA 2002 introduced a more rigorous regime for the protection of monies paid by long leaseholders into sinking funds and service charge accounts. The existing law gave some limited protection. As far as accounting arrangements for the expenditure of service charge monies was concerned, the LTA 1985 gave the tenant a right to require the production of a summary of relevant costs that had been expended and of service charge accounts[1]. There was no obligation on the landlord, however, to provide these on a regular basis for all leaseholders. The CLRA 2002 strengthens the law by requiring the holding of all service charge monies in separate client accounts for each property, and obliging landlords to make annual statements of account available to all service charge payers.

1 LTA 1985, s 21.

Statements of account

[13.92] The CLRA 2002 introduced a new accounting regime, under which the landlord must supply to each tenant an annual written statement of account which includes the service charges of the tenant and of other tenants of dwellings in the building, the balance of the account at the beginning of the year, relevant costs incurred and income during the year, and the balance of the account at the end of the accounting period[1]. The statement of account must be supplied to each tenant not later than six months from the end of the accounting period, and must be accompanied by an accountants certificate certifying that it is sufficiently supported by accounts and receipts etc as to be accurate[2]. The Secretary of State has power, by regulations made under the LTA 1985, to specify the form and content of the statement of account and accountants certificate accompanying it[3].

1 LTA 1985, s 21(1), substituted by CLRA 2002, s 152. The landlord can choose the date from which the accounting period should run, but it must end not later than 12 months from the relevant date, and must therefore be a 12-monthly (or shorter) period; see ibid, s 21(9).
2 Ibid, s 21(2) and (3).
3 Ibid, s 21(4).

[13.93] If the landlord fails to supply a statement of account, the tenant can withhold service charge payments under new provisions in the LTA 1985, s 21A[1]. The tenant can withhold an amount equal to the aggregate of the service charges he paid during the accounting period for which the statement has not been provided, and so much of the opening balance of the service charge account as stood to his credit[2]. Where the tenant withholds service charge payments in this way, any provisions of the tenancy relating to non-payment or late payment of service charges do not have effect for the period in relation to which he withholds payment. Non-payment will not, therefore, trigger the exercise of a forfeiture clause in the lease, or (for example) a penalty clause for late payment.

1 Introduced by CLRA 2002, s 152.
2 See LTA 1985, s 21A(2).

[13.94] The new accounting regime also gives leaseholders better rights of access to receipts, quotations and invoices relating to service charge payments. The right to see receipts and invoices etc was previously applicable only after the landlord had given a service charge summary in response to a request from the tenant. This meant that tenants might not see receipts etc for well over a year after expenditure had been incurred. The CLRA 2002 now gives tenants the right to see quotations, accounts, receipts or other relevant documents at any time on giving notice to the landlord, who must comply with 21 days[1]. The landlord's obligation, though more onerous than hitherto, is not open ended. The tenants' right to require the disclosure of documents for each accounting period ends six months after the date on which the annual statement of account is to be given[2].

1 LTA 1985, s 22(1), (6), inserted by CLRA 2002, s 154.
2 This principle is encapsulated somewhat clumsily in LTA 1985, s 22(3) as amended by the CLRA 2002, ibid.

Insurance arrangements – right to information

[13.95] The LTA 1985 gives tenants important rights to information as to insurance arrangements[1]. Where insurance arrangements are defective, for example if there is not a single policy for the whole block[2], the tenant can apply for a variation of his lease to make appropriate insurance provision (above para 13.75 ff). Accordingly, a tenant whose service charge includes insurance premiums can compel his landlord to supply a written summary of the amount insured, the name of the insurer, and the risks in respect of which the tenants dwelling and the block containing it are insured. The CLRA 2002 extended this right so that the leaseholder can also require the landlord to make reasonable provision for him to inspect (and make copies), or to provide copies of the insurance policy itself, in addition to or instead of a summary of the building insurance cover[3]. If requested, both the summary and copies of the insurance documents must be provided within 21 days of the landlord receiving notice of the tenant's request[4]. If a recognised tenants' association represents the tenant, this information can be requested by the secretary of the association and supplied to him on behalf of the tenants. If a superior landlord has effected insurance, the statutory provisions enable the tenants' immediate landlord to compel the former to allow access to policies, receipts and other information in like manner. Failure to comply with a written notice for information is a criminal offence.

1 See LTA 1985, s 30A and Schedule, inserted by the LTA 1987, s 43 and Sch 3.
2 LTA 1987, s 35(2)(b), as amended by the CLRA 2002, s 162(2).
3 LTA 1985, Schedule, para 3, amended by the CLRA 2002, Sch 10, para 9.
4 LTA 1985, Schedule, para 3(4), as amended by the CLRA 2002.

Holding of service charge funds

[13.96] LTA 1987, s 42 requires that service charges be held by the landlord (or his manager) in a trust fund maintained for that purpose[1], with the contributing tenants to be treated as entitled to such share in the residue of the fund as reflects their individual liability to pay service charges. Although this was, at the time, considered a beneficial reform, considerable uncertainty has surrounded the operation of trust funds under s 42. There was, for example, no legal duty to account to tenants for interest on trust monies and (indeed) to invest funds in interest-bearing accounts. Neither was a specific penalty imposed on landlords for failing to comply with its requirements. In practice, therefore, this safeguard merely ensured that if the landlord went bankrupt or (in the case of a limited company) was liquidated, the leaseholders' funds would be protected from the landlord's creditors[2].

1 LTA 1987, s 42(2) and (3).
2 See *Commonhold and Leasehold Reform: Draft Bill and Consultation Paper* (Cm 4843, DETR 2000) p 169.

[13.97] The CLRA 2002 introduced new provisions requiring service charge monies to be held in a separate designated account meeting criteria to be laid down in regulations made by the Secretary of State[1]. Previously, many landlords kept all service charges monies relating to different properties in one bank or building society account, making it difficult to clearly identify and account for expenditure and income for specific properties. Another potential problem was the seizure of monies in the account by the bank or building society to offset personal liabilities of the account holder. This could easily occur if the bank had not been told the monies in the account are client monies, and as such unavailable to meet the account holder's personal liabilities. Although tenants would be able to retrieve trust funds misused in this way, it could prove time consuming and inconvenient. The new law seeks to avoid these problems by requiring all service charge funds to be held in a properly designated client account for each group of leaseholders[2]. Contributing tenants can require the account holder[3] to give them reasonable facilities for inspecting the accounts and associated documents, and for taking copies or extracts of relevant documents[4]. An account holder served with written notice exercising this right must comply within 21 days, and cannot charge for providing the information concerned[5].

1 LTA 1987, s 42A, inserted by the CLRA 2002, s 156.
2 That is to say '... the tenants of two or more dwellings [who] may be required under the terms of their leases to contribute to the same costs by the payment of service charges; (LTA 1987, s 42(1)).
3 Usually the landlord or his managing agent.
4 LTA 1987, s 42A(3).
5 See ibid, s 42A(6) and (7). The landlord or other payee can, however, treat the costs of providing the information as part of its management costs for administering the account: LTA 1987, s 42A(7).

[13.98] These arrangements are enforced by several sanctions. If a contributing tenant has reasonable grounds for believing that the recipient of service charge monies (eg the landlord's managing agent) has not complied with the duty to hold the funds in a designated client account, he may withhold advance payment of future service charges[1]. Any provisions in the lease which relate to the non-payment or late payments of service charge contributions[2] have no effect while payments are being withheld in this way. More generally, non-compliance with *any* of the duties imposed by LTA 1987, s 42A is a criminal offence punishable on summary conviction with a fine not exceeding level 4 on the standard scale[3]. This applies both to the principal duty to hold monies in a client account etc, and also the duty to provide account details when requested.

1 LTA 1987, s 42A(9).
2 For example a proviso for re entry or forfeiture, or a clause imposing a penalty for late payment.
3 LTA 1987, s 42B(1) and (2), inserted by CLRA 2002, s 156.

Leasehold Valuation Tribunals: Jurisdiction

[13.99] Before 1 September 1997, the county court had sole jurisdiction to hear applications by landlord or tenant for a declaration whether service charge costs had been reasonably incurred, or whether service charge payments were reasonable. The HA 1996 conferred jurisdiction on the Leasehold Valuation Tribunal (LVT) to make determinations as to the reasonableness of service charges[1]. This provides a less costly and time consuming procedure for determine landlord and tenant disputes, and has the advantage (from the tenants perspective) that no costs are awarded in proceedings before the LVT, nor can they be recovered under a court order[2]. The court's jurisdiction remains intact, but if Tribunal proceedings are commenced any application before the county court will normally be transferred to the LVT for determination. The jurisdiction of the LVT has been further extended and clarified by the CLRA 2002, and now applies to the following.

1 HA 1996, s 83, inserting a new s 19(2A) and (2B), and new s 31A–C to LTA 1985.
2 LTA 1985, s 31A(4).

Liability to pay service charges

[13.100] The LVT has jurisdiction to hear applications to determine whether an amount alleged to be payable by way of service charge is so payable. If the tribunal upholds a liability to pay service charges, it can also be asked to determine by whom and to whom it is payable, the amount payable, the date by which it must be paid and the manner of payment[1]. Similarly, an application can be made to determine if any costs incurred for services, improvements etc would be recoverable as a service charge (and if so by whom and in what amount)[2]. This might be useful in enabling the landlord to make a protective application before commencing projected works, if he needs to clarify the tenant's legal responsibilities to contribute by way of service charge payments. Likewise, it would enable tenants to challenge works they consider outside the scope of their service charge obligations, without having to wait for the landlord to demand payment before doing so.

1 LTA 1985, s 27A, inserted by CLRA 2002, s 155. An application can be made to determine liability whether or not any payment has actually been made: LTA 1985, s 27A(2).
2 Ibid, s 27A(3).

Reasonableness of charge or costs incurred

[13.101] Either party to the lease can make an application to the LVT to determine what amount payable (before costs are incurred) would be reasonable, whether if costs were incurred for services, maintenance improvements etc they would be reasonable, or whether the works or services actually provided have been of a reasonable standard[1]. This limb of the jurisdiction will apply where there is a clear liability to pay service charges, but the tenants consider the work undertaken to be unreasonably expensive or performed to a poor standard. Similarly, it would enable the landlord who is proposing expensive major works to go to the Tribunal for a declaration as to reasonableness. This will guarantee his ability to recover the full cost by way of service charges if the LVT certifies the reasonableness of the costs to be incurred prior to the project's commencement.

1 LTA 1985, s 19(2B).

Consultation requirements

[13.102] The CLRA 2002 transferred jurisdiction for determining whether or not the landlord's consultation requirements have been met from the county court to the LVT. This will in future enable disputes as to both failure to consult and the reasonableness of charges to be determined at the same time. Either party can apply for a determination to dispense with all or any of the requirements of the landlord to consult tenants before commencing major works[1]. The LVT can make a determination dispensing with any or all of the consultation requirements if satisfied that it is reasonable to dispense with them[2]. A counsel of caution would suggest that the landlord should make a pre-emptive application before commencing a major project to be funded from service charge contributions. The application can, however, be made after work had been commenced (or even completed). The LVT can make a determination to dispense with the consultation requirements if it is satisfied that the landlord has acted reasonably.

1 LTA 1985, s 20(1) and 20ZA, inserted by CLRA 2002, s 151.
2 Ibid, s 20ZA(1).

Accounting requirements

[13.103] As we have seen, (above para 13.93), if the landlord fails to produce annual accounts, or supporting documents on request, the tenant now has a right to withhold future service charge payments. The landlord can apply to the LVT for a determination that he has a reasonable excuse for his failure to comply with the accounting requirements. If the Tribunal agrees and makes a determination, the tenant cannot withhold service charge payments after the determination has been made[1].

1 LTA 1985, s 21A(4).

Administration charges

[13.104] The LVT has jurisdiction to hear application to vary the terms of a lease concerning fixed administration charges levied by the landlord, and to determine any question concerning liability to pay variable administration charges[1]. This has already been considered (above paras 13.88–13.90).

1 CLRA 2002, Sch 11, paras 3–5.

COMPULSORY ACQUISITION OF LANDLORD'S INTEREST

[13.105] The LTA 1987, Pt III introduced measures to enable tenants to compulsorily acquire their landlord's interest. This went further than the Nugee Committee recommendations[1], and at the time represented a radical departure from the prevalent managerial approach to leasehold problems. The compulsory acquisition provisions were (and remain) a measure of last resort enforceable only where there has been persistent bad management or where a receiver has been in situ for a lengthy period. The conditions for the obtaining of an acquisition order make this an unattractive remedy, and one little used in practice.

1 The Nugee Committee were divided on the question of compulsory powers of acquisition, but drew back from making detailed recommendations on the basis that their introduction would not provide solutions to management problems, and would involve expropriation of property interests – see Nugee Report paras 7.9.20–7.9.22.

[13.106] The introduction of the Right to Manage in the CRLA 2002 – a remedy which is not fault based – make the compulsory acquisition procedure an even more unattractive option for tenants seeking to take control of their homes and remedy poor property management. It may be an appropriate mechanism, however, where tenants wish to take ownership of the block, but cannot meet the more stringent qualifying conditions for collective enfranchisement (Chapter 12, above). If successful, the tenants will also be able to seek an order that the landlord pay their costs.

Acquisition procedure

[13.107] A majority of qualifying tenants of a building which comprises two or more flats can apply to the court for an 'acquisition order' vesting the landlord's interest in their nominated purchaser[1]. This right applies (unlike, for example, statutory pre-emption rights) only where all (or virtually all) of the flats concerned are held on *long leases*[2]. Further, the right applies only to premises which contain two or more flats held by qualifying tenants of the landlord, and the total number of flats held by such tenants is not less than two-thirds of the total number of flats contained in the premises[3].

1 LTA 1987, ss 25(1) 27(4).

2 For the definition of 'qualifying tenants' see LTA 1987, s 26. Where the premises contain less than 4 flats, *all* must be held on long leases; where more than three but less than eleven flats all but one must be so held; and in all other cases 90 per cent of flats must be held on long leases: LTA 1987, s 25(3).
3 LTA 1987, s 25(2)(c), added by LRHUDA 1993, s 85(2).

[13.108] Compulsory acquisition rights are excluded where the premises are partly used for non-residential purposes and the internal floor area of the part so used exceeds 50 per cent of the internal floor area of the building. This is more generous than the position for collective enfranchisement, where the proportion of a building used for business purposes must not exceed 25 per cent if the right to enfranchise is to apply[1]. Accordingly, where managerial fault on the part of the landlord can be established, the tenants of a block which falls outside the enfranchisement regime because more than 25 per cent of its internal floor area is devoted to business use may be able to assume freehold ownership using the alternative acquisition procedure in the LTA 1987 – provided, of course, that the ground area devoted to non residential use does not exceed 50 per cent. Property let by resident landlords and charities is also excluded. Tenants with multiple lettings, and subtenants, are not qualifying tenants within the Act[2]. The latter exclusion may suggest another avenue of avoidance.

1 LRHUDA 1993, s 4(1), as amended by CLRA 2002, s 115.
2 LTA 1987, s 26(2) and (3).

[13.109] The procedure for applying for an acquisition order is very similar to that for the appointment of a manager under LTA 1987, Pt 2, save that the application is made to the county court (not the LVT) and the notice to be served by the tenants must state that they intend to apply for a compulsory acquisition order under Pt 3[1]. If remediable breaches of tenancy are alleged the landlord must be given a reasonable period in which to take steps to remedy them. An application to the court (under LTA 1987, s 28) cannot subsequently be made unless the period allowed has elapsed without remedial action being taken by the landlord. By virtue of LTA 1987, s 28(5) an application is registrable as a pending land action.

1 See LTA 1987, s 27. A requisite majority for the purpose of instituting acquisition proceedings is not less than two-thirds of qualifying tenants: LTA 1987, s 27(4) as amended by LRHUDA 1993, s 85(3).

Acquisition orders

[13.110] An acquisition order can be made if one of two conditions is satisfied[1]:

(a) the landlord is in breach of his maintenance obligations. This was widened by the CLRA 2002 and refers to his obligations as to the maintenance, repair, improvement or insurance of the premises[2]. The circumstances must be such that the breach is likely to continue; or
(b) for the period of two years preceding the application there has been in force a court order appointing a manager to carry out the landlord's management functions[3].

1 LTA 1987, s 29(2) and (3).
2 CLRA 2002, Sch 9, para 9, amending LTA 1987, s 29.
3 LTA 1987, s 29(3), as amended by HA 1996, s.88. The previous qualifying period was 3 years, applicable to cases where notice exercising the right had been given before 1 October 1996 or where an application to the court for an order dispensing with notice had been made before this date (see the Housing Act 1996 (Commencement No 2) Order 1996, SI 1996/2212, Schedule, para 1).

[13.111] Prior to amendments made by the LRHUDA 1993[1], where mismanagement ((a) above) was argued an acquisition order could be made only if the appointment of a manager would not be an adequate remedy. This is no longer a necessary prerequisite. In both situations the court has discretion to make such order as it considers appropriate in the circumstances. It is suggested, therefore, that the presence of a court-appointed manager for the requisite period ((b) above) will not of itself necessarily justify an acquisition order, especially if management arrangements are working adequately. Here too it is likely that the inadequacy of the continuance of the manager's appointment will be a necessary prerequisite to an acquisition order, even though this is not expressly required by the Act. In default of agreement, the LVT are by s 31 given jurisdiction to determine the terms of the acquisition. The price to be paid is to be fixed as that for which the premises might be expected to be sold on the open market by a willing seller, on the assumption that none of the sitting tenants was seeking to buy the property[2]. The bids of tenants are, it seems, to be ignored in the valuation process. Section 32 and Sch 1 to the Act lay down detailed rules for the discharge of existing mortgages, following acquisition by the tenants.

1 LRHUDA 1993, s 85(4).
2 See *139 Finborough Road Management Ltd v Mansoor* [1990] 2 EGLR 225.

MANAGEMENT AUDITS

Introduction

[13.112] A major obstacle to enforcing many of the provisions discussed above – for instance the controls on excessive service charges – lies in the difficulty of obtaining sufficient relevant information from landlords and managing agents. The LRHUDA 1993 sought to remedy this by introducing rights for tenants with long leases of residential flats to require a management audit, with the objective of assessing whether the premises are being managed in an efficient and effective manner. These provisions are contained in the LRHUDA 1993, ss 76–84.

Right to management audit

[13.113] LRHUDA 1993, s 76 confers on two or more qualifying tenants of dwellings, held on leases from the same landlord, the right to have an audit carried out on their behalf relating to the management of the relevant premises (and any appurtenant property) by the landlord, or by agents acting on his behalf. The audit is carried out by an independent surveyor appointed by the tenants.

Dwellings in respect of which exercisable

[13.114] The right to an audit is exercisable in two situations:

(i) *Residential flats*: where the relevant premises consist of or include two dwellings let to qualifying tenants of the same landlord, the right can be exercised by *either* or *both* of those tenants. Where the premises consist of three or more dwellings so let, the right can be exercised by not less than two-thirds of the qualifying tenants[1]. The 'relevant premises' to which this right attaches are defined to be so much of the buildings containing the dwellings let (together with any other building/s), as constitute premises in relation to which (a) management functions are discharged *and* (b) in respect of the cost of which *common service charge* contributions are payable under the leases of the qualifying tenants[2]. The audit applies also to 'appurtenant' property, ie so much of property not contained in the leases, but in relation to which any such management functions are discharged[3].

(ii) *Single dwellings*: although primarily concerned with flats, the LRHUDA 1993 also has effect to confer audit rights on a single qualifying tenant of a dwelling. This right applies where the relevant premises contain no other dwelling let to a qualifying tenant apart from that let to him[4]. For this purpose 'relevant' premises means so much of the building containing the dwelling let to him, and any other building/s, as constitute premises in relation to which a service charge is payable under his lease for management functions (whether paid as a common service charge with others or not)[5].

1 LRHUDA 1993, s 76(2).
2 Ibid, s 76(3)(a).
3 Ibid, s 76(1) and (for definition) s 76(3)(b).
4 Ibid, s 76(4).
5 Ibid, s 76(6).

Qualifying tenants

[13.115] A tenant is a qualifying tenant if he occupies the dwelling under a long lease (other than a business lease), and any service charge is payable under the lease. A lease is a 'long lease' for this purpose if it is[1]:

(i) a lease granted for a term certain exceeding 21 years, whether or not it may be terminated by notice by either landlord or tenant before the expiry of the term, or by re-entry or forfeiture or otherwise; *or*

(ii) a lease for life or terminable on marriage, taking effect under the LPA 1925, s 149(6) as a term of 90 years, or a perpetually renewable lease taking effect as a term for 2,000 years under the LPA 1922, s 145; *or*

(iii) a lease granted under the 'right to buy' provisions of HA 1985, Pt V, or on rent to mortgage terms under the 1985 Act; *or*

(iv) if it is a shared ownership lease, whether granted under the HA 1985 or otherwise, and whatever the share of the tenant under it. Note that the tenant under a shared ownership lease must have a 100 per cent share for enfranchisement rights under LRHUDA 1993, Pt I to apply.

Audit rights do not accrue to periodic tenants, or to tenants with Rent Act protected or statutory tenancies, or to assured tenancies under the HA 1988.

1 LRHUDA 1993, s 77(1) and (2). 'Long lease' is defined by reference to LRHUDA 1993, s 7.

[13.116] No one dwelling can have more than one qualifying tenant at any one time. So, where there is a mesne tenancy it will be disregarded, and joint tenants will count, for the purposes of the LRHUDA 1993, as one qualifying tenant[1]. This has implications for, eg the calculation of the requisite majority of tenants wishing to exercise the right to an audit. Where joint tenants collectively constitute a single 'qualifying' tenant for these purposes, any one joint tenant can sign notices exercising audit rights on behalf of both or all of them[2]. A person can, however, be a qualifying tenant of each of two or more dwellings at the same time, whether he is tenant of those premises under one lease, or two or more leases at the same time[3].

1 LRHUDA 1993, s 77(3) and (4).
2 Ibid, s 77(6).
3 Ibid, s 77(5).

The management audit

Objectives

[13.117] The audit must be carried out by a person who is appointed by the qualifying tenants, or two-thirds of them (if more than two), and who is qualified for appointment. By virtue of LRHUDA 1993, s 78(4) a person is qualified to act as an auditor if he is a qualified accountant[1] or a qualified surveyor, he is not disqualified from acting and he is not the tenant of any premises covered by the audit. A person is a 'qualified' surveyor for these purposes if he is a fellow or professional associate of the Royal Institution of Chartered Surveyors or of the Incorporated Society of Valuers and Auctioneers, or if he satisfies requirements to be introduced by regulations made by the Secretary of State[2].

1 As to which see LTA 1985, s 28(1).
2 LRHUDA 1993, s 78(5).

[13.118] The auditor's remit is defined by the LRHUDA 1993, s 78(1). The latter specifies that an audit is to have two objectives, *viz*:

(a) to ascertain the extent to which the obligations of the landlord involved in discharging management functions in relation to the relevant premises are being discharged *in an efficient and effective manner*. For these purposes the landlords management functions include functions with respect to the provision of services for repair, maintenance, improvement or insurance of the property[1]; and
(b) to ascertain the extent to which sums payable by the qualifying tenants as service charges are being *applied in an efficient and effective manner*.

For the purpose of determining whether management functions are being exercised, and service charges spent, in an 'efficient and effective manner' the auditor is obliged to have regard to the provisions of the code of practice for the time being approved by the Secretary of State under LRHUDA 1993, s 87.

1 LRHUDA 1993, s 84, as amended by CLRA 2002, Sch 9, para 10.

Utility of audit process

[13.119] The LRHUDA 1993 provides no mechanism for the enforcement of the auditor's findings, eg where the landlord is not found to be applying service charge moneys in an effective and efficient manner. The audit process will prove useful, however, in enforcing a number of important rights already discussed, for example:

(i) in ascertaining whether costs have been reasonably incurred by the landlord, for the purpose of the rules limiting recoverable service charge payments in the LTA 1985, ss 18–21;
(ii) in ascertaining whether the landlord is in breach of his obligations as to repair, and whether his default is likely to continue, for the purpose of enforcing the tenants' rights under the LTA 1987, ss 24 and 29 to have a manager appointed by the court, or compulsorily to acquire the landlord's interest.

Rights exercisable by auditor

[13.120] When carrying out an audit under these provisions, the auditor has the following rights[1]:

(i) he can require the landlord to supply him with a summary of relevant costs in connection with any service charges payable by the qualifying tenants[2];
(ii) he can require the landlord to afford him reasonable facilities for inspecting (or taking copies of) the accounts, receipts and other documents supporting the summary of costs (above);
(iii) he has a right to require the landlord to afford him reasonable facilities for inspecting any other documents reasonably required by him for the purposes of conducting the audit, and a right to make copies of any such documentation;
(iv) he can, on giving notice, carry out an inspection of any common parts comprised in the relevant premises or appurtenant property.

The auditor must exercise these rights when giving written notice of the audit to the landlord in accordance with LRHUDA 1993, s 80 (below).

1 See LRHUDA 1993, s 79(2).
2 As to which see LTA 1985, s 21(1). The contents of the summary to be provided are defined by LTA 1985, s 21(5).

[13.121] The landlord is obliged to make inspection facilities available to the auditor free of charge, but is entitled to make a reasonable charge for the cost of supplying, or making available facilities for the making of, copies or extracts of documents[1].

1 LRHUDA 1993, s 79(5).

Procedure on management audit

[13.122] The tenants' right to have a management audit conducted must be exercised in accordance with the procedure set out in LRHUDA 1993, ss 80 and 81. The procedure is set out below.

Notice of audit

[13.123] The tenants' right to have a management audit carried out on their behalf must be exercised in the first instance by the giving of a written notice of audit under LRHUDA 1993, s 80. The notice must be given to the landlord by the auditor, and must be signed by each of the tenants on whose behalf it is given[1]. The notice of audit must state the name and address of each tenant, and the address of the dwelling of which he is a qualifying tenant for audit purposes, the name and address of the auditor, and any documents of which copies or inspection facilities are required. If the auditor wishes to carry out an inspection of common parts of the premises, he must give a date on which he proposes to do so. The date proposed must be not less than one, and not more than two, months after the date of service of the s 80 notice. Service on an agent receiving rent on behalf of the landlord suffices for the purposes of LRHUDA 1993, s 80[2].

1 LRHUDA 1993, s 80(2).
2 Ibid, s 80(5).

Notification of objections

[13.124] Following service of the notice of audit (above), the landlord has one month in which to supply documents requested by the auditor, and to furnish facilities for the inspection and copying of documentation (if required). If he objects to giving the auditor access to any documents then he must, within the one month allowed, give the latter notice of his objection and the reasons for it. If he objects to the date suggested by the auditor for his inspection of the common parts of the premises, he must give notice suggesting an alternative date, which latter must be not later than two months after service of the s 80 notice[1].

1 LRHUDA 1993, s 81(2).

Managing agents

[13.125] If a managing agent is given notice requiring him to give access to documents or facilities for inspection/copying, he must do so within one month, or give notice within that time of his objection to doing so and the reasons for it[1].

1 LRHUDA 1993, s 81(3). For the definition of 'relevant person', see LRHUDA 1993, s 79(7).

Enforcement provisions

[13.126] If, by the end of the period of two months following service of notice of audit, the landlord has failed to comply with the auditor's requirements, the auditor can apply to the court for an enforcement order. By virtue of LRHUDA 1993, s 81(4), the court has power to make an order requiring the landlord, or (as the case may be) a managing agent, to comply with the requirements set out in the notice of audit. The court must be satisfied that the documents requested by the auditor are ones to which he has a right of access under the LRHUDA 1993. If an inspection of the common parts of the premises has not been carried out within two months of the notice of audit, the court can fix a date for an inspection to be carried out.

[13.127] The enforcement provisions also apply where a managing agent has failed to comply, within two months, with a notice under LRHUDA 1993, s 79 requesting information or documentation.

[13.128] The application to the court must be made within the period of four months, beginning with the date of service of the notice of audit under LRHUDA 1993, s 80, or (in the case of a notice served on a managing agent under s 79) within four months of the giving of that notice to the agent concerned[1].

1 LRHUDA 1993, s 81(7).

Transfer of reversion, etc

[13.129] Special provision is made for the continuance of obligations under a notice of audit where the landlord's reversion is transferred before he has fully complied with its terms[1]. Where any relevant information requested by the auditor is in the possession of a superior landlord, the LRHUDA 1993 makes special provision for the service of a written request by the immediate landlord for the information required, and the application of the enforcement provisions if the superior landlord fails to comply[2].

1 See LRHUDA 1993, s 83(1). The transferor landlord remains liable to supply information required under the LRHUDA 1993 if he 'is . . . still in a position to discharge those obligations to the extent referred to in [s 83](1)'. But otherwise the responsibility passes to the transferee to the exclusion of the landlord – LRHUDA 1993, s 83(2).
2 See generally provisions contained in ibid, s 82.

RIGHT TO APPOINT A SURVEYOR TO ADVISE ON SERVICE CHARGES

[13.130] The right to have a management audit conducted will be useful in ascertaining whether service charge funds are being spent efficiently and economically. However, a speedier and less costly remedy may be provide by appointing a qualified surveyor to advise on the manner in which service charge funds are being spent. The right to appoint a surveyor to advise on matters relating to service charges is conferred by the HA 1996, s 84. It is only exercisable, however, where there is a recognised tenants association[1], and in many cases tenants may not have established one. The right is exercised by the tenants association serving notice on the landlord (or on a managing agent if the latter receives rent on behalf of the landlord) giving the name and address of the surveyor, the duration of his appointment and the matters in respect of which he is appointed[2]. The surveyor has a number of statutory rights to assist him in carrying out his advisory functions. These are set out in the HA 1996, Sch 4, and include the right to inspect any documents he may reasonably require to see to give advice (eg invoices, contracts, work schedules), the right to take copies of relevant documents and the right to appoint assistants to assist him in carrying out his functions. Copies must be made available free of charge, but the landlord can treat any costs incurred by him in response to the surveyors requests as a management cost incurred in connection with making that facility available. Provided they are reasonable, these management costs can be recouped through service charges. The surveyor also has a right to inspect the premises, and reasonable access must be provided free of charge. The surveyor's rights are exercised by giving written notice of the documents etc, or access required, to the landlord or his managing agent[3]. If the landlord fails to respond to a notice from the appointed surveyor exercising rights under these provisions, the latter may apply to the county court for an order directing his cooperation. The landlord has one month in which to comply with a surveyor's notice requesting access to documents or copies, and must comply within a 'reasonable period' with a request for access to the premises[4]. If the landlord disposes of his interest in the block, the new landlord is under a duty to carry out the obligations under any notices requiring information of access which have already been given if 'he is in a position to discharge any of those obligations to any extent'[5]. The meaning is unclear, but presumably this means that the new landlord must make any documents available which have passed into his possession, and must allow access to the premises after he has assumed ownership. Otherwise the original landlord remains liable to carry out the duties imposed by the HA 1996.

1 As to which see LTA 1985, s 29.
2 HA 1996, s 84(3) and (5).
3 Ibid, Sch 4, para 3.
4 Ibid, Sch 4, para 5.
5 Ibid, Sch 4, para 7.

DEMAND FOR GROUND RENT

[13.131] The CLRA 2002 introduced a new requirement for the landlord to notify long leaseholders when ground rent payments are due. The consultation preceding the CLRA 2002 revealed concern at abuses where landlords often charge high administration charges for sending out reminder letters and processing late payments, and with charges which often bear no relation to the administration costs involved[1]. To prevent this kind of abuse, the CLRA 2002 now provides that[2] a tenant under a long lease of a dwelling is not liable to make a payment of ground rent unless the landlord has given him a written notice relating to the payment, and the date on which he is liable to make due payment is that specified in the notice. The notice must specify the amount of the payment, the date on which the tenant is liable to make it and (if different from the date from which payment is demanded) the date on which he would have been liable to pay it under the lease . The date on which the tenant is liable to make payment must be not less than 30 days nor more than 60 days after the date on which the notice is given, or before the date on which he would have been liable to make it under the terms of the lease[3]. The practical effect is to prevent the landlord from making any additional charge in respect of collection of the rent if the rent is paid either within 30 days of when it is due under the lease or within 30 days of it being demanded (whichever is the later of the two dates). The landlord's written demand must be in prescribed form, and the Secretary of State has power (by statutory instrument) to specify additional information to be included in the notice. The requirement for a written demand only applies to ground rent payments: it does not apply to service charge or administration charge payments[4].

1 See *Commonhold and Leasehold Reform: Draft Bill and Consultation Paper* (Cm 4843, DETR 2000) p 193. Administration charges typically of £110 or £200 were found to be charged for sending out reminder letters to tenants who had missed payment dates.
2 CLRA 2002, s 166.
3 Ibid, s 166(3).
4 Ibid, s 166(7).

RESTRICTION ON RE-ENTRY OR FORFEITURE

[13.132] A long residential lease will usually have a covenant allowing the landlord to re-enter and to forfeit the lease in the event of the tenant failing to pay rent or service charges, or on some other breach of the terms of the lease occurring. Forfeiture rarely occurs, and the tenant is protected by a range of measures, including the Protection from Eviction Act 1977, under which a landlord cannot re-enter a dwelling without a court order[1]. Where the landlord alleges there are breaches other than non-payment of rent, he must first serve a notice under the LPA 1925, s 146, signifying his intention to take forfeiture proceedings, specifying the breaches concerned and giving the leaseholder a reasonable period in which to remedy them. The HA 1996 further strengthened the tenant's protection by preventing the landlord from exercising a right of re-entry or forfeiture for failure to pay service charges unless the charge has either been admitted or agreed by the leaseholder, or determined by a court or by arbitration[2]. This restriction did not affect forfeiture for other breaches of the terms of the lease, nor did it prevent the landlord from serving a s 146 notice, provided the notice drew the tenants attention to the restrictions on his commencing forfeiture proceedings in reliance upon it[3].

1 Protection from Eviction Act 1977, s 2, above ch 2.
2 See HA 1996, s 81.
3 See ibid, s 82(1).

[13.133] Although the tenant can challenge the reasonableness of service charge and other payments before the LVT, this would not prevent an unscrupulous landlord from securing unreasonable charges by exploiting the tenants fear of legal proceedings and additional costs by serving s 146 notices alleging minor breaches of other terms of the lease, eg failures to obtain landlord's consent before carrying out alternations. In some cases, the landlord may even institute forfeiture proceedings in parallel with the proceedings before the LVT to determine the reasonableness of the charges demanded[1]. In order to prevent this type of abuse of the relevant legal procedures, the CLRA 2002 extended to all alleged breaches of covenant the principle that the landlord should be prevented from issuing s 146 notices until the facts have been determined by the LVT. The underlying approach is to separate proceedings leading to forfeiture (which will be dealt with by the courts) from proceedings to determine facts (which will be dealt with by the LVT). All factual disputes as to whether an alleged breach of the lease has occurred are assigned to the tribunal[2], and no legal proceedings for forfeiture (including the service of preliminary s 146 notices) can be taken until the tribunal has finally determined the facts or they have been admitted by the leaseholder.

1 For a discussion of some of the issues see *Commonhold and Leasehold Reform: Draft Bill and Consultation Paper* (Cm 4843, DETR 2000) pp 195–196.
2 See CLRA 2002, s 168. Note that CLRA 2002, s 169 prevents contracting out of the tribunals fact finding jurisdiction in this regard.

[13.134] By virtue of CLRA 2002, s 168, the landlord under a long lease of a dwelling house cannot service a s 146 notice of intended forfeiture proceedings unless either:

(i) the LVT has finally determined, on an application made to it by the landlord, that the breach alleged has occurred, or
(ii) the tenant has admitted the breach, or
(iii) a court, or an arbitral tribunal in proceedings pursuant to a post-dispute arbitration agreement, has finally determined that the breach has occurred.

The provisions concerning forfeiture for non-payment of service charges were amended by the CLRA 2002 to make similar provision for reference of factual disputes to the LVT[1].

1 CLRA 2002, s 170, amending HA 1996, s 81.

[13.135] Once the LVT has determined that the breach has occurred, or the tenant has agreed his liability, the tenant has a 14-day period in which to pay the charges outstanding, in which event he will be liable to no further costs other than the landlords application fee to the LVT and his costs before the LVT (if the tribunal has exercised its discretion to award costs). Once the period for making an appeal has expired following the final determination of liability by the LVT, the landlord is free to issue a s 146 notice informing the tenant of his intention to take forfeiture action[1]. The tenant will become potentially liable for the landlords costs from this point.

1 CLRA 2002, s 169 (2) and (3).

Appendix

ASSURED TENANCIES AND AGRICULTURAL OCCUPANCIES (FORMS) REGULATIONS 1997

SI 1997 No 194

1 Citation and commencement

These Regulations may be cited as the Assured Tenancies and Agricultural Occupancies (Forms) Regulations 1997 and shall come into force on 28th February 1997.

2 Interpretation

In these Regulations any reference to a section or Schedule is a reference to a section of, or Schedule to, the Housing Act 1988 and any reference to a numbered form is a reference to the form bearing that number in the Schedule to these Regulations, or to a form substantially to the same effect.

3 Prescribed forms

The forms prescribed for the purposes of Part I (rented accommodation) of the Housing Act 1988 are—

(a) for a notice under section 6(2) proposing terms of a statutory periodic tenancy different from the implied terms, Form No 1;

(b) for an application under section 6(3) referring a notice under section 6(2) to a rent assessment committee, Form No 2;

(c) for a notice under section 8 informing a tenant or licensee that the landlord intends to begin proceedings for possession of a dwelling-house let on an assured tenancy or an assured agricultural occupancy, Form No 3;

(d) for a notice under section 13(2) proposing a new rent for an assured tenancy or an assured agricultural occupancy, Form No 4 [or 4A]:

(e) for an application under section 13(4) referring to a rent assessment committee a notice under section 13(2) relating to an assured tenancy or an assured agricultural occupancy, Form No 5;

(f) for an application under section 22(1) to a rent assessment committee for a determination of rent under an assured shorthold tenancy, Form No 6;

(g) for a notice under section 41(2) requiring a landlord or tenant to give information to a rent assessment committee, Form No 7;

(h) for a notice under paragraph 7 of Schedule 2A, by the tenant to the landlord proposing that an assured tenancy be replaced by an assured shorthold tenancy, Form No 8;

(i) for a notice under paragraph 9 of Schedule 2A, by the landlord to the prospective tenant, proposing an assured shorthold tenancy where the tenancy meets the conditions for an assured agricultural occupancy, Form No 9.

Annotations

In para (d) words 'or 4A' in square brackets inserted by SI 2002/337, reg 3(1), (2).

4 Revocations and savings

(1) The Assured Tenancies and Agricultural Occupancies (Forms) Regulations 1988 ("the 1988 Regulations"), the Assured Tenancies and Agricultural Occupancies (Forms) (Amendment) Regulations 1989, the Assured Tenancies and Agricultural Occupancies (Forms) (Amendment) Regulations 1990 and the Assured Tenancies and Agricultural Occupancies (Forms) (Amendment) Regulations 1993 are hereby revoked.

(2) Nothing in paragraph (1) affects the validity of a notice served before the coming into force of these Regulations if, at the date of service of the notice, the notice was in the form then prescribed by the 1988 Regulations.

SCHEDULE
FORMS PRESCRIBED FOR THE PURPOSES OF PART I OF THE HOUSING ACT 1988

Regulation 3

Form No 1

Housing Act 1988 section 6(2)

Notice proposing different terms for a Statutory Periodic Tenancy

- Please write clearly in black ink.
- Please tick boxes where appropriate and cross out text marked with an asterisk (*) that does not apply.
- This form can be used by either a landlord or a tenant to propose changes to the terms of a statutory periodic tenancy, which arises when a fixed term of an assured tenancy, an assured shorthold tenancy or an assured agricultural occupancy ends.
- This notice must be served on the landlord or tenant no later than the first anniversary of the day on which the former fixed term tenancy or occupancy ended.
- Do not use this notice if you are a landlord proposing only an increase in rent. Instead, you should use the form headed *Landlord's Notice proposing a new rent under an Assured Periodic Tenancy or Agricultural Occupancy*, which is available from a rent assessment panel or law stationers.

1 To:...

*Name(s) of landlord(s)/tenant(s)**

Address of premises to which the tenancy relates:...
....
....
....

2 This is to give notice that I/we* propose different terms for the statutory periodic tenancy from those of the fixed term assured tenancy which has now ended and that they should take effect from:...

Insert date which must be at least three months after the date on which this notice is served.

3 Changes to the terms

(a) The existing provisions of the tenancy to be changed are:.................................
....
....
....

Please attach relevant sections of the tenancy agreement if available

(b) The proposed changes are: ....
....
....
....

Continue on a separate sheet if necessary

4 Changes to the rent (if applicable). Go to section 5 if this does not apply.

- You should not propose a change to the rent on this form unless it is to take account of the proposed new terms at section 3. A change may be made if either the landlord or the tenant considers it appropriate.

(a)	The existing rent is	£..........per............... *(e g week, month, year)*
(b)	Does the rent include council tax?	Yes/No
(c)	If yes, the amount that is included for council tax is:	£..........per............... *(e g week, month, year)*
(d)	Does the rent include water charges?	Yes/No *(e g week, month, year)*
(e)	If yes, the amount that is included for water charges is:	£..........per............... *(e g week, month, year)*
(f)	The new rent which takes into account the proposed changes in the terms of the tenancy will be:	£..........per............... *(e g week, month, year)*
(g)	Will the new rent include council tax?	Yes/No
(h)	If yes, the amount that will be included for council tax is:	£..........per............... *(e g week, month, year)*
(i)	Will the new rent include water charges?	Yes/No
(j)	If yes, the amount that will be included for water charges is:	£..........per............... *(e g week, month, year)*

5 Name and address of landlord or tenant proposing the changes

To be signed and dated by the landlord or his agent (someone acting for him) or the tenant or his agent. If there are joint landlords or joint tenants each landlord/tenant or the agent must sign unless one signs on behalf of the rest with their agreement.

Signed.................................... Date...

Please specify whether: landlord/landlord's agent/tenant/tenant's agent

Name(s) (Block Capitals) ....

Address

....
....
....
....

Telephone—Daytime .... Evening ....

What to do if this notice is served on you

- If you agree with the new terms and rent proposed, do nothing. They will become the terms of the tenancy agreement on the date specified in section 2.
- If you don't agree with the proposed terms and any adjustment of the rent (see section 4), and you are unable to reach agreement with your landlord/tenant, or you do not wish to discuss it with him, you may refer the matter directly to your local rent assessment committee, before the date specified in section 2, using the form headed *Application referring a Notice proposing different terms for a Statutory Periodic Tenancy to a Rent Assessment*

Committee which you can obtain from a rent assessment panel or a law stationer.
- The rent assessment committee will decide what, if any, changes should be made to the terms of the tenancy and, if applicable, the amount of the new rent.
- If you need help or advice about this notice and what you should do about it, take it immediately to a citizens advice bureau, a housing advice centre, a law centre or a solicitor.

Form No 2

Housing Act 1988 section 6(3)

Application referring a Notice proposing different terms for a Statutory Periodic Tenancy to a Rent Assessment Committee

- Please write clearly in black ink.
- Please tick boxes where appropriate and cross out text marked with an asterisk (*) that does not apply.
- This form should be used by a landlord or a tenant who has been served with a notice under section 6(2) of the Housing Act 1988, varying the terms of a statutory periodic tenancy which arises when a fixed term of an assured tenancy, an assured shorthold tenancy or an assured agricultural occupancy ends.
- When you have completed the form, please send it to your local rent assessment panel with a copy of the notice served on you proposing the new terms of the statutory periodic tenancy.

1 Name(s) of tenant(s): ....
....
....
....

2 Address of premises to which the tenancy relates: ....
....
....
....

3 Name(s) of landlord(s)/agent*: ....
....
....
....

Address of landlord(s)/agent*: ....
....
....
....

4 Details of premises.

(a) What type of accommodation is rented?

Room(s)	Flat	Terraced House
Semi-Detached House	Fully Detached House	Other *(Please specify)*

(b) If it is a flat or room(s) what floor(s) is it on?

Ground First Second Other *(Please specify)*

(c) Give the number and type of rooms, e g living room, bathroom etc ....
....
....

(d) Does the tenancy include any other facilities, e g garden, garage or other separate building or land?

Yes/No

(e) If yes, please give details: ....
....
....
....

(f) Is any of the accommodation shared with:

(i) the landlord? Yes/No
(ii) another tenant or tenants? Yes/No
(g) If yes, please give details: ....
....
....
....

5 When did the statutory periodic tenancy begin? ....
....

6 Services

(a) Are any services provided under the tenancy (e g cleaning, lighting, heating, hot water or gardening etc)? Yes/No
(b) If yes, please give details:
....

(c) Is a separate charge made for services, maintenance, repairs, landlords' costs of management or any other item? Yes/No
(d) If yes, what charge is payable? £..........per............ *(e g week, month, year)*
(e) Does the charge vary according to the relevant costs? Yes/No
(f) If yes, please give details:
....

7

(a) Is any furniture provided under the tenancy?
Yes/No
(b) If yes, please give details. Continue on a separate sheet if necessary or provide a copy of the inventory. ....
....
....
....

8 What repairs are the responsibility of:

(a) the landlord? Continue on a separate sheet if necessary. ....
....
....
....
....

(b) the tenant? Continue on a separate sheet if necessary. ....
....
....
....

9 Give details (if known) of the other terms of the tenancy, e g can you assign the tenancy (pass it on to someone else) and if so is a premium (a payment which is in addition to rent and equivalent to more than two months rent) payable on an assignment? Continue on a separate sheet if necessary. ....
....

....
....

10

(a) Is there a written tenancy agreement? Yes/No
(b) If yes, please attach the tenancy agreement (with a note of any variations). It will be returned to you as soon as possible.

11

(a) I/We* attach a copy of the notice proposing changes to the statutory periodic tenancy and, if applicable, an adjustment of the amount of rent and apply for it to be considered by the rent assessment committee.

Signed .... *Date*.......................................

....

....

To be signed and dated by the landlord or his agent (someone acting for him) or the tenant or his agent if there are joint landlords or joint tenants each landlord/tenant or the agent must sign unless one signs on behalf of the rest with their agreement.

Please specify whether: landlord/landlord's agent/tenant/tenant's agent

(b) Name and address of landlord or tenant referring to the rent assessment committee.

Name(s) (Block Capitals) ....
....
....

Address ....
....
....
....

Telephone—Daytime ....

Form No 3

Housing Act 1988 section 8 as amended by section 151 of the Housing Act 1996

Notice seeking possession of a property let on an Assured Tenancy or an Assured Agricultural Occupancy

- Please write clearly in black ink.
- Please tick boxes where appropriate and cross out text marked with an asterisk (*) that does not apply.
- This form should be used where possession of accommodation let under an assured tenancy, an assured agricultural occupancy or an assured shorthold tenancy is sought on one of the grounds in Schedule 2 to the Housing Act 1988.
- Do not use this form if possession is sought on the "shorthold" ground under section 21 of the Housing Act 1988 from an assured shorthold tenant where the fixed term has come to an end or, for assured shorthold tenancies with no fixed term which started on or after 28th February 1997, after six months has elapsed. There is no prescribed form for these cases, but you must give notice in writing.

1 To:...

*Name(s) of tenant(s)/licensee(s)**

2 Your landlord/licensor* intends to apply to the court for an order requiring you to give up possession of: ....
....
....
....

Address of premises

3 Your landlord/licensor* intends to seek possession on ground(s) .... in Schedule 2 to the Housing Act 1988, as amended by the Housing Act 1996, which read(s):
....
....
....

Give the full text (as set out in the Housing Act 1988 as amended by the Housing Act 1996) of each ground which is being relied on. Continue on a separate sheet if necessary.

4 Give a full explanation of why each ground is being relied on: ....
....
....
....

Continue on a separate sheet if necessary.

Notes on the grounds for possession

- If the court is satisfied that any of grounds 1 to 8 is established, it must make an order (but see below in respect of fixed term tenancies).
- Before the court will grant an order on any of grounds 9 to 17, it must be satisfied that it is reasonable to require you to leave. This means that, if one of these grounds is set out in section 3, you will be able to suggest to the court that it is not reasonable that you should have to leave, even if you accept that the ground applies.
- The court will not make an order under grounds 1, 3 to 7, 9 or 16, to take effect during the fixed term of the tenancy (if there is one) and it will only make an order during the fixed term on grounds 2, 8, 10 to 15 or 17 if the terms of the tenancy make provision for it to be brought to an end on any of these grounds.
- Where the court makes an order for possession solely on ground 6 or 9, the landlord must pay your reasonable removal expenses.

5 The court proceedings will not begin until after: ....
....

Give the earliest date on which court proceedings can be brought

- Where the landlord is seeking possession on grounds 1, 2, 5 to 7, 9 or 16, court proceedings cannot begin earlier than 2 months from the date this notice is served on you (even where one of grounds 3, 4, 8, 10 to 13, 14A, 15 or 17 is specified) and not before the date on which the tenancy (had it not been assured) could have been brought to an end by a notice to quit served at the same time as this notice.
- Where the landlord is seeking possession on grounds 3, 4, 8, 10 to 13, 14A, 15 or 17, court proceedings cannot begin earlier than 2 weeks from the date this notice is served (unless one of 1, 2, 5 to 7, 9 or 16 grounds is also specified in which case they cannot begin earlier than two months from the date this notice is served).
- Where the landlord is seeking possession on ground 14 (with or without other grounds), court proceedings cannot begin before the date this notice is served.
- Where the landlord is seeking possession on ground 14A, court proceedings cannot begin unless the landlord has served, or has taken all reasonable steps to serve, a copy of this notice on the partner who has left the property.
- After the date shown in section 5, court proceedings may be begun at once but not later than 12 months from the date on which this notice is served. After this time the notice will lapse and a new notice must be served before possession can be sought.

6 Name and address of landlord/licensor*.

To be signed and dated by the landlord or licensor or his agent (someone acting for him) . If there are joint landlords each landlord or the agent must sign unless one signs on behalf of the rest with their agreement.

Signed .... *Date*..

Please specify whether: landlord/licensor/joint landlords/landlord's agent

Name(s) (Block Capitals) ....

....

Address ....

....

....

Telephone—Daytime .... *Evening* ....

What to do if this notice is served on you

- This notice is the first step requiring you to give up possession of your home. You should read it very carefully.
- Your landlord cannot make you leave your home without an order for possession issued by a court. By issuing this notice your landlord is informing you that he intends to seek such an order. If you are willing to give up possession without a court order, you should tell the person who signed this notice as soon as possible and say when you are prepared to leave.
- Whichever grounds are set out in section 3 of this form, the court may allow any of the other grounds to be added at a later date. If this is done, you will be told about it so you can discuss the additional grounds at the court hearing as well as the grounds set out in section 3.
- If you need advice about this notice, and what you should do about it, take it immediately to a citizens' advice bureau, a housing advice centre, a law centre or a solicitor.

Form No 4

Annotations

Revoked, with savings, by SI 2002/337, reg 4.

Housing Act 1988 section 13(2)

Landlord's Notice proposing a new rent under an Assured Periodic Tenancy or Agricultural Occupancy

- *Please write clearly in black ink.*
- *Please tick boxes where appropriate.*
- *This form should be used to propose a new rent under an assured periodic tenancy, including an assured shorthold periodic tenancy.*
- *This form may also be used to propose a new rent or licence fee for an assured periodic agricultural occupancy. In such cases reference to "landlord"/"tenant" can be read as references to "licensor"/"licensee" etc.*
- *Do not use this form if there is a current rent fixing mechanism in the tenancy.*
- *Do not use this form to propose a rent adjustment for a statutory periodic tenancy solely because of a proposed change of terms under section 6(2) of the Housing Act 1988. You should instead use the form headed Notice proposing different terms for a Statutory Periodic Tenancy which you can obtain from a rent assessment panel or a law stationer.*

1 To:...

Name(s) of tenant(s)

2 Address of premises to which the tenancy relates: ....
....
....
....

3 This is to give notice that as from ....*your landlord proposes to charge a new rent.*

- *The new rent must take effect at the beginning of a new period of the tenancy and not earlier than any of the following:*

(a) *the minimum period after this notice was served,*
(The minimum period is:
—in the case of a yearly tenancy, six months;
—in the case of a tenancy where the period is less than a month, one month;
—in any other case, a period equal to the period of the tenancy;)

(b) *the first anniversary of the start of the first period of the tenancy except in the case of:*
—a statutory periodic tenancy, which arises when a fixed term assured tenancy ends, or;
—an assured tenancy which arose on the death of a tenant under a regulated tenancy;

(c) *if the rent under the tenancy has previously been increased by a notice under section 13 or a determination under section 14 of the Housing Act 1988, the first anniversary of the date on which the increased rent took effect.*

4

(a)	*The existing rent is:*	*£..........per...............* *(e g week, month, year)*
(b)	*Does the rent include council tax?*	Yes/No
(c)	*If yes, the amount that is included for council tax is:*	*£..........per...............* *(e g week, month, year)*
(d)	*Does the rent include water charges?*	Yes/No
(e)	*If yes the amount that is included for water charges is:*	*£..........per...............* *(e g week, month, year)*

5

(a)	The proposed new rent will be:	£..........per.............. *(e g week, month, year)*
(b)	Will the new rent include council tax?	Yes/No
(c)	If yes, the amount that will be included for council tax will be:	£..........per.............. *(e g week, month, year)*
(d)	Will the new rent include water charges?	Yes/No
(e)	If yes the amount that will be included for water charges will be:	£..........per.............. *(e g week, month, year)*

6 Name and address of landlord.

To be signed and dated by the landlord or his agent (someone acting for him). If there are joint landlords each landlord or the agent must sign unless one signs on behalf of the rest with their agreement.

Signed...................................... *Date* ....

Please specify whether: landlord/joint landlords/landlord's agent

Name(s) (Block Capitals)..
....

Address ....
....
....
....

Telephone—Daytime .... *Evening* ....

What to do if this notice is served on you

- *You should read this notice carefully. Your landlord is proposing a new rent.*
- *If you agree with the new rent proposed, do nothing. If you do not agree and you are unable to reach agreement with your landlord or do not want to discuss it directly with him, you may refer this notice to your local rent assessment committee prior to the date specified in section 3, using the form headed Application referring a Notice proposing a new rent under an Assured Periodic Tenancy or Agricultural Occupancy to a Rent Assessment Committee. You can obtain this form from a rent assessment panel or a law stationer.*
- *The rent assessment committee will consider your application and will decide what the rent for the premises will be. The committee may set a rent that is higher, lower or the same as the landlord has proposed in section 5.*
- *If you are required to include payments for council tax and water charges in your rent, the rent the committee determines will be inclusive of council tax and water charges.*
- *If you need help or advice please take this notice immediately to a citizens advice bureau, a housing advice centre, a law centre or a solicitor.*

Annotations

Revoked, with savings, by SI 2002/337, reg 4.

[Form No 4A]

Annotations

Inserted by SI 2002/337, reg 3(1), (3), Schedule.

[Housing Act 1988 Section 13(2)—Landlord's Notice proposing a new rent under an Assured [Periodic] Tenancy] [Agricultural Occupancy]*

delete as appropriate

The notes over the page give guidance to both landlords and tenants about this notice.

To:...................... [*Tenant(s)*]
of:....................... [*Address of the premises subject to the tenancy*]
....
....
....
From: [*Landlord(s)] [Landlord's Agent]* delete as appropriate*
.... [*Address for correspondence*]
....
....
.... [*Contact telephone number*]

1 **This notice affects the amount of rent you pay.** Please read it carefully.

2 The landlord is proposing a new rent of **£............. per [week] [month] [year]***, in place of the existing one of £ .... per [week] [month] [year]*

**delete as appropriate*

3 The starting date for the new rent will be .... (see notes 12–16 over the page).

4 Certain charges may be included and separately identified in your rent. The amounts of the charges (if any) are: (see note 10 over the page)

Charges Amount included and separately identified *(enter "nil" if appropriate)*

	In the existing rent	In the proposed new rent
Council tax	£	£
Water charges	£	£
Fixed service charges	£	£

5 If you accept the proposed new rent, you should make arrangements to pay it. If you do not accept it, there are steps you should take before the starting date in section 3 above. Please see the notes over the page for what to do next.

Signed: .... [Landlord(s)] [Landlord's Agent]* (see note 11 over the page)
**delete as appropriate*

Date: ....

Please read these notes carefully.

Guidance notes for [tenants] [agricultural occupants]*

**delete as appropriate*

What you must do now

1 This notice proposes that you should pay a new rent from the date in section 3. **If you are in any doubt or need advice about any aspect of this notice, you should immediately either discuss it with your landlord or take it to a citizens' advice bureau, a housing advice centre, a law centre or a solicitor.**

2 If you accept the proposed new rent, please make arrangements to pay it. If you pay by standing order through your bank, you should inform them that the amount has changed. You should also notify your Housing Benefit office, if you are claiming benefit. If you are worried that you might not be able to pay your rent, you should seek advice from a citizens' advice bureau or housing advice centre.

3 If you do not accept the proposed new rent, and do not wish to discuss it with your landlord, you can refer this notice to your local rent assessment committee. **You must do this before the starting date of the proposed new rent in section 3 of the notice.** You should notify your landlord that you are doing so, otherwise he or she may assume that you have agreed to pay the proposed new rent.

4 To refer this notice to the local rent assessment committee, you must use the form *Application referring a notice proposing a new rent under an Assured Periodic Tenancy or Agricultural Occupancy to a Rent Assessment Committee*. You can obtain this from a rent assessment panel, housing advice centre or legal stationer (details can be found in the telephone directory).

5 The rent assessment committee will consider your application and decide what the maximum rent for your home should be. In setting a rent, the committee must decide what rent the landlord could reasonably expect for the property if it were let on the open market under a new tenancy on the same terms. The committee may therefore set a rent that is higher, lower or the same as the proposed new rent.

Guidance notes for landlords on how to complete the notice

6 This notice can either be completed in ink or printed.

7 This notice should be used when proposing:

— a new rent under an assured periodic tenancy (including an assured shorthold periodic tenancy); or

— a new rent or licence fee for an assured agricultural occupancy. In such cases, reference to "landlord" and "tenant" can be read as references to "licensor" and "licensee".

8 Do not use this notice if the tenancy agreement contains a term allowing rent increases, or there is some other basis such as a separate agreement with the tenant for raising the rent. Any provision you rely on needs to be binding on the tenant. Legal advice should be sought if there is any doubt on this score.

9 You need to use a different form to propose a rent increase for a statutory periodic tenancy (the first case mentioned in note 15) if you are seeking to adjust rent solely because of a proposed change of terms under section 6(2) of the Housing Act 1988. Seek legal advice if you think this may apply to you. You can obtain the form headed *Notice proposing different terms for a Statutory Periodic Tenancy* from a rent assessment panel or a legal stationer.

10 In every notice each of the boxes in the table in section 4 should be completed, by either entering "Nil" or the amount of the existing or proposed charge in the second and third columns. Do **not** include in the table any **variable** service charges as referred to in section 18–30 of the Landlord and Tenant Act 1985.

11 You or your agent (someone acting on your behalf) must sign and date this notice. If there are joint landlords, each landlord must sign unless one signs on behalf of the rest with their agreement. The signature does not have to be hand-written if, for instance, the form is being printed or if you wish to use a laser or autosignature.

When the proposed new rent can start

12 The date in section 3 of the notice must comply with the following three rules.

13 **First,** a minimum period of notice must be given before the proposed new rent can take effect. That period is:

— one month for a tenancy which is monthly or for a lesser period, for instance weekly or fortnightly;
— six months for a yearly tenancy;
— in all other cases, a period equal to the length of the period of the tenancy—for example, three months in the case of a quarterly tenancy.

14 **Secondly,** the starting date for the proposed new rent must not be earlier than the first anniversary of the date on which the rent was last increased using this statutory notice procedure or, if the tenancy is new, the date on which it started.

15 This rule does not apply in two cases where a statutory tenancy has followed on from an earlier tenancy. In these cases the landlord can propose a new rent at once, but the first and third rules must still be followed. These cases are:

— where the tenancy was originally for a fixed term (for instance, 6 months), but continues on a periodic (for instance a monthly) basis after the term ends; and
— where the tenancy came into existence on the death of the previous tenant who had a regulated tenancy under the Rent Act 1977.

16 **Thirdly,** the proposed new rent must start at the beginning of a period of the tenancy. For instance, if the tenancy is monthly, and started on the 20th of the month, rent will be payable on that day of the month, and a new rent must begin then, not on any other day of the month. If the tenancy is weekly, and started, for instance, on a Monday, the new rent must begin on a Monday.]

Annotations

Inserted by SI 2002/337, reg 3(1), (3), Schedule.

Form No 5

Housing Act 1988 section 13(4)

Application referring a Notice proposing a new rent under an Assured Periodic Tenancy or Agricultural Occupancy to a Rent Assessment Committee

- Please write clearly in black ink.
- Please tick boxes where appropriate and cross out text marked with an asterisk (*) that does not apply.
- This form should be used when your landlord has served notice on you proposing a new rent under an assured periodic tenancy, including an assured shorthold periodic tenancy.
- This form may also be used to refer a notice proposing a new rent or licence fee for an assured periodic agricultural occupancy. In such a case references to "landlord"/"tenant" can be read as references to "licensor"/"licensee" etc.
- This form must be completed and sent to your local rent assessment panel—with a copy of the notice served on you proposing the new rent—before the date it is proposed that the new rent will take effect.

1 Address of premises: ....
....
....
....

2 Name(s) of landlord(s)/agent*: ....
....
....

Address of landlord(s)/agent*: ....
....
....
....

3 Details of premises.

(a) What type of accommodation do you rent?

Room(s)	Flat	Terraced House
Semi-Detached House	Fully Detached House	Other *(Please specify)*

(b) If it is a flat or room(s) what floor(s) is it on?

Ground First Second Other *(Please specify)*

(c) Give the number and type of rooms, e g living room, bathroom etc

....
....
....

(d) Does the tenancy include any other facilities, e g garden, garage or other separate building or land?

Yes/No

(e) If yes, please give details: ....
....
....

(f) Do you share any accommodation with

(i) the landlord? Yes/No
(ii) another tenant or tenants? Yes/No

(g) If yes to either of the above, please give details: ....
....
....

4 When did the present tenancy begin?

....

5

(a) Did you pay a premium?

Yes/No

- a premium is a payment which is additional to rent and is equivalent to more than two months rent. It may give you the right to assign the tenancy (pass it on to someone else) unless the tenancy agreement states or implies otherwise.

(b) If yes, please give details: ....
....
....
....

6 Services

(a) Are any services provided under the tenancy (e g cleaning, lighting, heating, hot water or gardening)?

Yes/No

(b) If yes, please give details: ....
....
....
....

(c) If yes, is a separate charge made for services, maintenance, repairs, landlord's costs of management or any other item?

Yes/No

(d) What charge is payable? £.......... per .... *(e g week, month, year)*

(e) Does the charge vary according to the relevant costs?

Yes/No

(f) If yes, please give details: ....
....
....
....

7

(a) Is any furniture provided under the tenancy?
Yes/No
(b) If yes, please give details. Continue on a separate sheet if necessary or attach a copy of the inventory: ....
....
....

8 Improvements

(a) Have you, or any former tenant(s) carried out improvements or replaced fixtures, fittings or furniture for which you or they were not responsible under the terms of the tenancy?
Yes/No

(b) If yes, please give details. Continue on a separate sheet if necessary: ....

9 What repairs are the responsibility of:

(a) the landlord? ....

(b) the tenant? ....

10

(a) Is there a written tenancy agreement?
Yes/No

(b) If yes, please attach the tenancy agreement (with a note of any variations). It will be returned to you as soon as possible.

11 Do you have an assured agricultural occupancy?

Yes/No

12

(a) I/we* attach a copy of the notice proposing a new rent under the assured periodic tenancy and I/we* apply for it to be considered by the rent assessment committee.

Signed .... *Date* ....

To be signed and dated by the tenant or his agent. If there are joint tenants each tenant or the agent must sign unless one signs on behalf of the rest with their agreement.

Please specify whether: tenant/joint tenants/tenant's agent

(b) Name and address of tenant(s) referring to the rent assessment committee.

Name(s) (Block Capitals) ....

Address ....

Telephone—Daytime ....

Form No 6

Housing Act 1988 section 22(1) as amended by section 100 of the Housing Act 1996

Application to a Rent Assessment Committee for a determination of a rent under an Assured Shorthold Tenancy

- Please write clearly in black ink.
- Please tick boxes where appropriate and cross out text marked with an asterisk (*) that does not apply.

- This form should be used by a tenant with an assured shorthold tenancy which began (or for which a contract had been made) before 28th February 1997, to apply to the local rent assessment committee, during the fixed term of the original tenancy, to have the rent reduced.
- This form should also be used by a tenant with an assured shorthold tenancy which began on or after 28th February 1997 (unless a contract had been made before that date), to apply to the rent assessment committee within six months of the beginning of the original tenancy, to have the rent reduced.
- This form cannot be used in the cases specified at the end of this form.
- When you have completed the form please send it to your local rent assessment panel.

1 Address of premises: ....
....
....
....

2 Name(s) of landlord(s)/agent*

....
......

Address of landlord(s)/agent*

....
....
....
....

3 Details of premises.

(a) What type of accommodation do you rent?

Room(s) Flat Terraced House
Semi-Detached House Fully Detached House Other *(Please specify)*

(b) If it is a flat or room(s) what floor(s) is it on?

Ground First Second Other *(Please specify)*

(c) Give the number and type of rooms, e g living room, bathroom etc. ....
....

(d) Does the tenancy include any other facilities, e g garden, garage or other separate building or land?

Yes/No

(e) If yes, please give details: ....
....
....
....

(f) Do you share any accommodation with:

(i) the landlord? Yes/No
(ii) another tenant or tenants? Yes/No

(g) If yes to either of the above, please give details: ....
....
....
....

4

(a) What is the current rent? £..........per.............
(e g week, month, year)

(b) Does the rent include council tax? Yes/No

(c) If yes, the amount that is included for council tax is: £..........per.............
(e g week, month, year)

(d) Does the rent include water charges? Yes/No

(e) If yes, the amount that is included for water charges is: £..........per.............
(e g week, month, year)

5

(a) When did the present tenancy begin?

....

(b) When does the present tenancy end?

....

(c) Does the tenancy replace an original tenancy? Yes/No

If yes, when did the original tenancy begin? ....

6

(a) If the tenancy began before 28th February 1997, please confirm by ticking the box that you received a notice saying that the tenancy was to be an assured shorthold tenancy before the agreement was entered into.

(b) Attach a copy of the notice, if available. It will be returned to you as soon as possible.

7

(a) Did you pay a premium?
Yes/No

- a premium is a payment which is additional to rent and is equivalent to more than two months rent. It may give you the right to assign the tenancy (pass it on to someone else) unless the tenancy agreement states or implies otherwise.

(b) If yes, please give details: ....
....
....
....

8 Services.

(a) Are any services provided under the tenancy (e g cleaning, lighting, heating, hot water or gardening etc)? Yes/No

(b) If yes, please give details:

....

(c) Is a separate charge made for services, maintenance, repairs, landlords' costs of management or any other item? Yes/No

(d) If yes, what charge is payable? £..........per.............
(e g week, month, year)

(e) Does the charge vary according to the relevant costs? Yes/No

(f) If yes, please give details:

....

9

(a) Is any furniture provided under the tenancy?
Yes/No

(b) If yes, please give details. Continue on a separate sheet if necessary or provide a copy of the inventory. ....
....
....

....

10 What repairs are the responsibility of:

(a) the landlord. Continue on a separate sheet if necessary: ....
....
....
....
....

(b) the tenant. Continue on a separate sheet if necessary: ....
....
....
....
....

11

(a) Give details (if known) of the other terms of the tenancy, e.g. whether the tenancy is assignable and whether a premium may be charged on an assignment. (Continue on a separate sheet if necessary). ....
....
....
....

(b) Is there a written tenancy agreement? Yes/No

(c) If yes, please attach the tenancy agreement (with a note of any variations). It will be returned to you as soon as possible.

12

(a) I/We* apply to the rent assessment committee to determine a rent for the above mentioned premises.

Signed.................................... Date ....

To be signed and dated by the tenant or his agent. If there are joint tenants each tenant or the agent must sign unless one signs on behalf of the rest with their agreement.

Please specify whether: tenant/joint tenants/tenant's agent

(b) Name and address of tenant(s) referring to the rent assessment committee.

Name(s) (Block Capitals) ....
....
....

Address ....
....
....
....

Telephone—Daytime...

Cases where this form should not be used

- An application cannot be made if—

(a) the rent payable under the tenancy is a rent previously determined by a rent assessment committee; or

(b) the tenancy is a replacement tenancy and more than six months have elapsed since the beginning of the original tenancy. A replacement tenancy is an assured shorthold tenancy that came into being on the ending of a tenancy which had been an assured shorthold of the same, or substantially the same, property and the landlord and tenant under each tenancy were the same at that time.

- The rent assessment committee cannot make a determination unless it considers—

(a) that there is a sufficient number of similar properties in the locality let on assured tenancies (whether shorthold or not) for comparison; and

(b) that the rent payable under the shorthold tenancy in question is significantly higher than the rent which the landlord might reasonably be expected to get in comparison with other rents for similar properties let on assured tenancies (whether shorthold or not) in the locality.

Form No 7

Housing Act 1988 section 41(2)

Notice by Rent Assessment Committee requiring further information

1 To: ....
landlord(s)/tenant(s) of: ....
....
....
....

Address of premises

2 An application has been made to the rent assessment committee for consideration of:

the terms of a statutory periodic assured tenancy
an increase in rent under an assured periodic tenancy
the rent under an assured shorthold tenancy
an increase in rent under an assured agricultural occupancy
of the above property. The committee needs more information from you to consider the application.

3 The information needed is: ....
....
....
....
....
....
....
....
....
....

4 Please send it to: ....
....
....
....
....
.... no later than. ....

5 If you fail to comply with this notice without reasonable cause you will be committing a criminal offence and may be liable to a fine.

6 Signed on behalf of the rent assessment committee.

Signed .... *Date* ....

Name (Block Capitals) ....
....

Address ....

....
....
....

Telephone ....

Form No 8

Housing Act 1988 Schedule 2A, paragraph 7(2) as inserted by Schedule 7 to the Housing Act 1996

Tenant's notice proposing that an Assured Tenancy be replaced by an Assured Shorthold Tenancy

- Please write clearly in black ink.
- Please cross out text marked with an asterisk (*) that does not apply.
- This notice should only be used by an assured tenant. You should only use this notice to notify your landlord that you wish your assured tenancy to be replaced by an assured shorthold tenancy.
- This notice must be served by a tenant on a landlord before an assured tenancy can be replaced by an assured shorthold tenancy.
- **You should be aware that by serving this notice, you will be giving up your right to stay in the property after the first six months of the assured shorthold tenancy or, if you agree a fixed term with your landlord, after the end of the fixed term.**
- **You do not have to complete this form even if your landlord has asked you to do so. Your existing security of tenure as an assured tenant will be unaffected if you do not complete it.**
- **If you are in any doubt about whether to complete this form, take it immediately to a citizens' advice bureau, housing advice centre, a law centre or a solicitor.**
- Once you are clear that you wish to issue this notice, complete the form and send it to your landlord.

1 To: ....
Name(s) of landlord(s)

2 I/We*, the tenant(s) of: ....
....
....
....

Address of premises

give notice that I/we* propose that the assured tenancy to which this notice relates should be replaced by a shorthold tenancy.

3 I/We* propose that the new shorthold tenancy should commence on:

......../......../...... (day/month/year)

- The new shorthold tenancy cannot commence until after the date this notice is served on the landlord.

4

(a) I/We* understand that under my/our* existing tenancy, I/we* can only be required to give up possession in accordance with the grounds set out in Schedule 2 to the Housing Act 1988, whereas under the new shorthold tenancy, the landlord(s) will be able to recover possession of the premises without being required to prove a ground for possession, after the first six months of the assured shorthold tenancy, or, if there is a fixed term for longer than 6 months, at the end of that fixed term, subject to two months' notice.

Signed .... *Date*.......................................

To be signed and dated by the tenant. If there are joint tenants each tenant must sign.

(b) Name and address of tenant.

Name(s) (Block Capitals) ....
....
....

Address ....
....
....
....

Telephone—Daytime.................................... Evening.............................

Form No 9

Housing Act 1988 Schedule 2A, paragraph 9, as inserted by Schedule 7 to the Housing Act 1996

Landlord's notice proposing an Assured Shorthold Tenancy where the tenancy meets the conditions for an Assured Agricultural Occupancy

- Please write clearly in black ink.
- Please tick boxes where appropriate.
- If the agricultural worker condition in Schedule 3 to the Housing Act 1988 is met with respect to the property to which the proposed assured tenancy relates, and the landlord wishes that tenancy to be an assured shorthold tenancy, he must serve this notice on the tenant before the tenancy is entered into.
- This notice cannot be used where the landlord has already granted to the prospective tenant (or, in the case of joint tenants, to at least one of them) a tenancy or licence under section 24 of the Housing Act 1988 (an assured agricultural occupancy).
- This notice does not commit the tenant to taking the tenancy.

1 To: ....
....
....
....

Name of the proposed tenant. If a joint tenancy is being offered, enter the names of the joint tenants.

2 You are proposing to take a tenancy at the following address: ....
....
....
....

commencing on ..../......./ ...... (day/month/year)

3 This notice is to tell you that your tenancy is to be an assured shorthold tenancy.

- Provided you keep to the terms of the tenancy, you are entitled to remain in the property for at least six months after the start of the tenancy. Depending on the terms of the tenancy, once the first six months have elapsed, the landlord may have the right to seek possession at any time, subject to two months' notice.
- As an assured shorthold tenant, you have the right to apply to a rent assessment committee for the determination of a reasonable rent for the tenancy. An application to your local rent assessment committee must be made on the form headed *Application to a Rent*

Assessment Committee for a determination of a rent under an Assured Shorthold Tenancy within six months of the beginning of the tenancy. You can obtain the form from a rent assessment panel or a law stationer.
- If you need help or advice about this notice, and what you should do about it, take it immediately to a citizens' advice bureau, a housing advice centre, a law centre or a solicitor.

4 Name and address of landlord.

To be signed and dated by the landlord or his agent (someone acting for him). If there are joint landlords each landlord or the agent must sign unless one signs on behalf of the rest with their agreement.

Signed .... *Date*..................................

....

Please specify whether: landlord/joint landlords/agent

Name(s) (Block Capitals) ....

....

Address: ....

....

....

....

Telephone—Daytime ....Evening ....

Index